HISPANIC FOUNDATION PUBLICATIONS, 2

A series issued under a co-operative agreement between The Johns Hopkins University and the Library of Congress to include works prepared and published on private funds, especially those furnished to the Library by the Ford Foundation for expansion of Hispanic Foundation activities.

LATIN AMERICA IN SOVIET WRITINGS

A Bibliography
Volume II: 1959-1964

Compiled by Leo Okinshevich
Edited by Robert G. Carlton

Published for the Library of Congress
by The Johns Hopkins Press, Baltimore

TABLE OF CONTENTS

ﻉ

INTRODUCTION

ě

The bibliographic evidence presented in the following volume mirrors developments which merit serious attention.

Marked interest in Latin America has become lately a significant feature of the Soviet state and party activities. A special section on Latin America was added in the early 1960's to the organizational structure of the Ministry of Foreign Affairs in Moscow. After many setbacks, the Soviet Union is engaged at present in active diplomatic, trade, and cultural relations with a number of Central and South American countries. In 1961 a Soviet diplomatic handbook, edited by the Soviet Minister of Foreign Affairs, Andrei Gromyko, and others, discounted the Monroe Doctrine and declared it no longer effective; as if to press the point, one year later in 1962, large contingents of Soviet military personnel appeared on Cuban soil, and recently a Soviet official legal publication told its readers that "the Soviet Union continues to be watchful with regard to the security of Cuba, and the United States of America will have to live in peaceful coexistence with a neighboring socialist-type state." Of the delegations of eighteen Communist parties of the world which participated in the ill-fated conclave in Moscow in March of 1965, three came from Latin American countries—Argentina, Brazil, and Cuba. Indeed, in the Soviet interpretation, events taking place in this part of the world augur well for the Soviet cause. An article in *Pravda* of April 12, 1965, offered a whole catalog of phenomena demonstrating the growth of the revolutionary movement in Latin America. Specifically cited were the increase in the number of strikes and in the membership of the Communist parties, the spreading of guerrilla warfare, the growing *rapprochement* between the peasantry and the labor class, the broadening of the anti-imperialist struggle, greater participation of the national bourgeoisie in the fight for social reform, and, last but not least, the favorable record of the Soviet diplomatic effort in Latin America.

As to the field of scholarly research, here also the amount of effort, time, money, and other resources allocated to the survey and study of the various facets of life in Latin America is a clear indication of the active interest Soviet officialdom takes in what is for them a remote region. It is of interest that the USSR Academy of Sciences, in response to the obvious desires of Soviet leadership, established in April, 1962, a new research institute devoted exclusively to Latin American affairs. The announcement of the type of investigations to be pursued by the members of this body reveals the character and intent of the undertaking. It stresses the study of the agrarian question and the history of peasant movements, of the history of labor and Communism, of the part played by the Latin American Socialist parties, of the role of the national bourgeoisie, of U.S. economic and political activities, and of the influence changes in Cuba had on revolutionary movements in Latin America.

No adequate, up-to-date assessment of the magnitude of Soviet publication activities centered on Latin America was, however, possible because of lack of precise information. Bibliographies released in the Soviet Union in this area failed to show the total picture. The number of references listed in a special bibliography on Cuba issued in Leningrad in 1963 and covering the preceding four years does not exceed 295. And even the comprehensive bibliographic record of Russian monographs and periodical articles on Latin American politics, history, economics, and culture—a 1964 publication of the Latin American Institute of the Academy prepared by no fewer than five editors and sixteen assistants—consists only of 1,928 titles which appeared between 1946 and 1962.

The painstaking work of the compiler of the present volume, carried out with the help of an industrious assistant, has now unearthed nearly 5,000 titles of Soviet publications of the years 1959 through 1964 dealing with Latin America. The year-by-year count of the output reveals a remarkable twenty-fold increase within the last twenty years, reaching a peak of 898 pertinent titles in 1961. One may note further that nearly three-quarters of the materials listed in the volume fall into the following seven broad categories: Politics and Government, Languages and Literatures, Foreign Relations, Travel, Society and Social Conditions, International Economic Relations, and Economic Conditions and Policies. Finally, an impression of the nature of Soviet documentation can be derived from the fact that some of the entries on the Alliance for Progress appearing in the present volume read as follows: Alliance for Regress, Alliance for Poverty, Alliance for Plundering, and Alliance against Progress.

SERGIUS YAKOBSON

September, 1965

EDITORIAL NOTES—VOLUME TWO

Scope

The bibliographical coverage of this two-volume work embraces the geographical and cultural area known as Latin America, including the non-Hispanic Caribbean, the Guianas, and the possessions of some of the Latin American countries (for example, Easter Island and the Galápagos Islands).

This is fundamentally a compilation of writings in the Russian language. Books and articles in other languages of the Soviet Union (e.g., Ukrainian, Belorussian, and others) were also included when bibliographical identification could be established. Periodical articles in languages not indigenous to the Soviet Union are not recorded. The only exception is that material from the English language journals *World Student News* and *World Youth* for 1963-64 was used due to the temporary unavailability of their Russian equivalents for that period.

Also recorded are Soviet translations of works by Latin American authors, including in this category writings produced by writers such as B. Traven and Rafael Alberti during their residence in Latin America.

Arrangement

The basic chapter arrangement is topical. Some chapters (e.g., History, International Cultural Relations) are subdivided directly according to geographical criteria into writings dealing with the area as a whole or with three or more countries, and writings on individual countries. Other chapters covering broader subjects (e.g., Politics and Government, Society and Social Conditions) are arranged topically into major categories which in turn are subdivided geographically. Material treating the same subject in two countries is recorded under the country of major emphasis, with a reference provided from the country of secondary emphasis. Similarly, writings dealing with more than one topic are listed under the subject of primary stress, with references given from the secondary subject or subjects. Within the same topical or geographical subsection, monographs are listed first, and are separated from articles by a hairline.

Geographical Designations

Conventional geographical terminology is used with the following exceptions: the term "West Indies" excludes Cuba, the Dominican Republic, Haiti, Jamaica, Puerto Rico, and Trinidad and Tobago, which constitute separate categories; and the term "The Guianas" includes the British, Dutch, and French areas, with the specific focus indicated in the annotation when the bibliographical entry is not self-explanatory.

Bibliographical Form

The bibliographical data in the entries are as complete as could be established through use of the materials and sources available in the Library of Congress. Correct identification of authors' names was sometimes hindered by the differences between Latin American and Russian usage and by inconsistencies in transliteration.

Call numbers are provided for books that have been cataloged by the Library of Congress. The symbol "DLC" indicates that a book is in the Library's collections, but has not been fully cataloged. The symbol "DLC-LL" is used for books which form part of the Library's separate collections of legal materials.

Generally, standard bibliographical practices were followed in the composition of the entries. A few departures are noted below:

a. Titles and names in Russian, Ukrainian, and Belorussian are rendered in transliterated form on the basis of the Library of Congress system, with the exception that diacritical marks and ligatures have been omitted. Because of the manner in which material is recorded in Soviet bibliographies, non-Russian titles were sometimes available only in a Russian language version. In such cases the title is given in transliterated Russian, and the actual language of the publication is indicated in the annotation. Titles are followed by English translations in brackets.

b. Full names are provided in author entries wherever possible.

c. A few items contain a question mark in parentheses following the title. This indicates that the original title could not be established directly, and that the version of it given in the entry is a re-translation of the available English title.

d. Names of some publishing houses are abbreviated, in keeping with Soviet practice. Appendix I shows the expanded forms of these abbreviations.

e. Titles of periodicals are normally abbreviated in the entries and annotations. Appendix II gives the expansions of the abbreviations and other available bibliographical information.

f. The annotations are intended to be descriptive and not evaluative. The language from which a translation was made is noted only if such information could be established directly. In many cases, it was not possible to determine with certainty whether translations were made from the original or from another translation.

g. As a general rule, a book published in the Soviet Union in more than one language is recorded only for the most widely used language—in the majority of cases, Russian. However, the annotations for such books provide data on publication in other languages. All writings published in periodicals are recorded as separate entries, regardless of language, with the exception that reviews of books that are listed as individual items in this volume are cited in the annotations to those entries.

Indexes

The name index lists names of authors, editors, compilers, and translators. An effort was made to consolidate all material relating to the same person under a single entry, usually the most complete possible form of the name. In many cases, however, separate entries were retained for two similar names when there was no firm basis for combining them.

The subject index provides both topical references with geographical subdivisions, and geographical references with topical subdivisions.

L. O.
R. G. C.

LATIN AMERICA IN SOVIET WRITINGS

A Bibliography
Volume II: 1959-1964

I

GENERAL WORKS, BIBLIOGRAPHIES, AND REFERENCE AIDS

❦

A. WRITINGS DEALING WITH THREE OR MORE COUNTRIES

1. Akhmedov, B. Latinskaia Amerika [Latin America] Tashkent, Gosizdat UzSSR, 1963. 112 p.
   In Uzbek.
   General information.

2. Akimova, N. A., *and others.* Strany Latinskoi Ameriki; rekomendatel'nyi ukazatel' literatury [The Latin American countries; a recommended list of literature] Moscow, Gos. biblioteka SSSR im. V. I. Lenina, 1962. 117 p.   Z1601.M6

3. Holovko, M. K., *and* R. M. Mikhn'ov. Krainy Latyns'koi Ameryky; korotkyi dovidnyk [Latin American countries; a brief handbook] Kiev, Derzhpolitvydav URSR, 1962. 234 p.

4. Latinskaia Amerika segodnia; spravochnik [Latin America today; a reference book] Moscow, Znanie, 1962. 127 p.

5. Latinskaia Amerika v sovetskoi pechati; bibliografiia knig i zhurnal'nykh statei na russkom iazyke o sovremennom politicheskom polozhenii, istorii, ekonomike i kul'ture stran Latinskoi Ameriki, 1946—1962 [Latin America in the Soviet press; a bibliography of books and articles in Russian on the present-day political situation, history, economic conditions, and culture of the Latin American countries, 1946-1962] Moscow, Izd-vo Akad. nauk SSSR, 1964. 132 p.   DLC

6. Shur, Leonid Avel'evich. Khudozhestvennaia literatura Latinskoi Ameriki v russkoi pechati; annotirovannaia biblio-grafiia russkikh perevodov i kriticheskoi literatury na russkom iazyke, 1765–1959 [Russian publications of Latin American fiction; annotated bibliography of translations and criticism in the Russian language, 1765–1959] Moscow, Izd-vo Vses. knizhn. palaty, 1960. 290 p. Z1609.T7M6
   Reviewed by I. Terterian in *Kul't. i zhizn'*, v. 4, no. 8, 1960: 62; by L. Ospovat in *Vop. lit.*, v. 4, no. 9, Sept. 1960: 236–239; by I. R. Grigulevich in *Vest. ist. mir. kul't.*, no. 5, Sept.-Oct. 1960: 140–141 [in French]; by V.IAsnyi in *Inostr. lit.*, no. 12, Dec. 1960: 248.

7. Vasil'kov, I., *and others.* Kuba, Gaiti, IAmaika, Dominikanskaia Respublika, Puerto Riko [Cuba, Haiti, Jamaica, the Dominican Republic, Puerto Rico] Vilnius, Gospolitnauchizdat, 1959. 26 p.
   In Lithuanian. Translated from the Russian.
   Also published in Latvian.
   General information.

8. Volkov, Aleksandr Vasil'evich, *and* A. A. Dolinin. Argentina, Fol'klendskie Ostrova, Peru i Chili [Argentina, the Falkland Islands, Peru, and Chile] Frunze, Kirgizgosizdat, 1959. 32 p.
   In Kirghiz.
   General information.

9. ———. Boliviia, Paragvai, Urugvai [Bolivia, Paraguay, and Uruguay] Vilnius, Gospolitnauchizdat, 1959. 19 p.
   In Lithuanian. Translated from the Russian.

———

10. Bobrik, N. Knigi o stranakh Latinskoi Ameriki [Books on Latin American countries] Nov. knigi, v. 9, no. 27, July 1964: 57–59.

11. Guterman, E. Chto chitat' o stranakh Latinskoi Ameriki [Recommended literature on the countries of Latin America] Bibliotekar', no. 8, Aug. 1960: 50–54.

12. Latinskaia Amerika [Latin America] *In* Moscow. Vsesoiuznaia gosudarstvennaia biblioteka inostrannoi literatury. Osnovnye proizvedeniia inostrannoi khudozhestvennoi literatury; literaturno-bibliograficheskii spravochnik. Moscow, Izd-vo Vses. knizhn. palaty, 1960. p. 261–295.

    Z6511.M68
    An annotated bibliography of Latin American literary works.

13. Latinskaia Amerika [Latin America] Za rubezhom, no. 1, Jan. 1961: 21.
    General information.

14. Pukhovskaia, N., *and* V. Kerov. V stranakh Latinskoi Ameriki [In the Latin American countries] Chto chitat', v. 3, no. 12, Dec. 1960: 6–7.
    A bibliography.

15. Strany mira; kratkii politiko-ekonomicheskii spravochnik [The countries of the world; a brief reference book of politics and economics] Moscow, Gospolitizdat, 1962.   D10.S75
    Partial contents. —Argentina, p. 305–307. —Bahama Islands, p. 307–308. —Bermuda, p. 308. —Bolivia, p. 308–310.—Brazil, p. 310–312. —British Guiana, p. 322–323. —British Honduras, p. 325. —Chile, p. 359–360. —Colombia, p. 329–331. —Costa Rica, p. 331–332. —Cuba, p. 332–336. —Dominican Republic, p. 326–327. —Dutch Guiana, p. 323. —Dutch West Indies, p. 314–315. —Ecuador, p. 360–362. —El Salvador, p. 347–348. —Falkland Islands, p. 358–359. French Guiana, p. 323. —Guadeloupe, p. 319–320. —Guatemala, p. 320–321. —Guiana, p. 321–322. —Haiti, p. 318–319. —Honduras, p. 323–325. —Latin America, p. 297–305. —Martinique, p. 336–337. —Mexico, p. 337–338. —Nicaragua, p. 339–340. —Panama, p. 340–342. —Paraguay, p. 342–344. —Peru, p. 344–345. —Puerto Rico, p. 345–347. —Uruguay, p. 357–358. —Venezuela, p. 312–314. —Virgin Islands, p. 317. —West Indies, p. 315–317.

16. Zarubezhnye gosudarstva, nesamoupravliaiushchiesia territorii i kolonii [Foreign countries, non-self-governing territories, and colonies] *In* Bol'shaia sovetskaia entsiklopediia. Ezhegodnik, 1959. Moscow, Sovetskaia entsiklopediia, 1959. p. 191–405.

    Partial contents. —Argentina, p. 200–203. —Bolivia, p. 213–214. —Brazil, p. 215–218. —British Guiana, p. 238. —Chile, p. 387–389. —Colombia, p. 291–292. —Costa Rica, p. 298. —Cuba, p. 298–299. —Dominican Republic, p. 250–251. —Dutch Guiana, p. 239. —Ecuador, p. 395. —El Salvador, p. 342. —French Guiana, p. 238. —Guatemala, p. 237–238. —Haiti, p. 235. —Honduras, p. 244–245. —Mexico, p. 310–312. —Nicaragua, p. 319–320. —Panama, p. 330–331. —Paraguay, p. 331–332. —Peru, p. 332–333. —Puerto Rico, p. 339. —Uruguay, p. 363–364. —Venezuela, p. 228–229. —West Indies, p. 229–231.

17. Zarubezhnye gosudarstva, nesamoupravliaiushchiesia territorii i kolonii [Foreign countries, non-self-governing territories, and colonies] *In* Bol'shaia sovetskaia entsiklopediia. Ezhegodnik, 1960. Moscow, Sovetskaia entsiklopediia, 1960. p. 184–400.

    Partial contents. —Argentina, p. 194–196. —Bolivia, p. 207–208. —Brazil, p. 209–212. —British Guiana, p. 230. —Chile, p. 382–383. —Colombia, p. 282–283. —Costa Rica, p. 288–289. —Cuba, p. 289–291. —Dominican Republic, p. 243–244. —Dutch Guiana, p. 231. —Ecuador, p. 389–390. —El Salvador, p. 334–335. —French Guiana, p. 231. —Guatemala, p. 230. —Haiti, p. 228. —Honduras, p. 237. —Mexico, p. 302–304. —Nicaragua, p. 312. —Panama, p. 324. —Paraguay, p. 324–325. —Peru, p. 325–326. —Puerto Rico, p. 332. —Uruguay, p. 356–357. —Venezuela, p. 221–222. —West Indies, p. 223–224.

18. Zarubezhnye gosudarstva, nesamoupravliaiushchiesia territorii i kolonii [Foreign countries, non-self-governing territories, and colonies] *In* Bol'shaia sovetskaia entsiklopediia. Ezhegodnik, 1961. Moscow, Sovetskaia entsiklopediia, 1961. p. 168–381.

    Partial contents. —Argentina, p. 177–179. —Bolivia, p. 188–189. —Brazil, p. 190–193. —British Guiana, p. 211. —Chile, p. 365–366. —Colombia, p. 261–262. —Costa Rica, p. 271. —Cuba, p. 271–274. —Dominican Republic, p. 223–224. —Dutch Guiana, p. 211. —Ecuador, p. 371. —El Salvador, p. 319. —French Guiana, p. 211. —Guatemala, p. 210–211. —Haiti, p. 208. —Honduras, p. 217. —Mexico, p. 287–289. —Nicaragua, p. 297–298. —Panama, p. 307–308. —Paraguay, p. 308–309. —Peru, p. 309. —Puerto Rico, p. 314–315. —Uruguay, p. 342–343. —Venezuela, p. 201–202. —West Indies, p. 203–204.

19. Zarubezhnye gosudarstva, nesamoupravliaiushchiesia territorii i kolonii [Foreign countries, non-self-governing territories, and colonies] *In* Bol'shaia sovetskaia entsiklopediia. Ezhegodnik, 1962. Moscow, Sovetskaia entsiklopediia, 1962. p. 190–415.

Partial contents. —Argentina, p. 201–203. —Bolivia, p. 212–213. —Brazil, p. 214–217. —British Guiana, p. 236–237. —Chile, p. 396–397. —Colombia, p. 285–286. —Costa Rica, p. 293. —Cuba, p. 294–296.—Dominican Republic, p. 250–251. —Dutch Guiana, p. 237. —Ecuador, p. 403–404. — El Salvador, p. 343. —French Guiana, p. 237. —Guatemala, p. 236. —Haiti, p. 233. —Honduras, p. 243–244. —Mexico, p. 310–312. —Nicaragua, p. 321–322. —Panama, p. 331–332. —Paraguay, p. 332–333. —Peru, p. 333–334. —Puerto Rico, p. 339.—Uruguay, p. 368–370. —Venezuela, p. 226–228. —West Indies, p. 229–230.

20. Zarubezhnye gosudarstva, nesamoupravliaiushchiesia territorii i kolonii [Foreign countries, non-self-governing territories, and colonies] *In* Bol'shaia sovetskaia entsiklopediia. Ezhegodnik, 1963. Moscow, Sovetskaia entsiklopediia, 1963. p. 188–408.

Partial contents. —Argentina, p. 197–200. —Bolivia, p. 210–211. —Brazil, p. 212–214. —British Guiana, p. 233–234. —British Honduras, p. 241. —Chile, p. 389–390. —Colombia, p. 282–283. —Costa Rica, p. 288–289. —Cuba, p. 289–291. —Dominican Republic, p. 248. —Dutch Guiana, p. 234. —Ecuador, p. 396. —El Salvador, p. 337–338. —French Guiana, p. 234. —Guatemala, p. 233. —Haiti, p. 230. —Honduras, p. 240–241. —Mexico, p. 305–306. —Nicaragua, p. 315–316. —Panama, p. 325. —Paraguay, p. 326. —Peru, p. 326–327. —Puerto Rico, p. 333–334. —Uruguay, p. 363–364. —Venezuela, p. 224–225.

21. Zarubezhnye gosudarstva, nesamoupravliaiushchiesia territorii i kolonii [Foreign countries, non-self-governing territories, and colonies] *In* Bol'shaia sovetskaia entsiklopediia. Ezhegodnik, 1964. Moscow, Sovetskaia entsiklopediia, 1964. p. 193–409.

Partial contents. —Argentina, p. 203–206. —Bolivia, p. 215–216. —Brazil, p. 216–220. —British Guiana, p. 239. —British Honduras, p. 245. —Chile, p. 391–392. —Colombia, p. 287–289. —Costa Rica, p. 294. —Cuba, p. 294–297. —Dominican Republic, p. 250.

—Dutch Guiana, p. 239. —Ecuador, p. 398. —El Salvador, p. 346. —French Guiana, p. 240. —Guadeloupe, p. 237–238. —Guatemala, p. 238. —Haiti, p. 235–236. —Honduras, p. 244–245. —Jamaica, p. 404–405. —Martinique, p. 311–312. —Mexico, p. 312–313. —Nicaragua, p. 322–323. —Panama, p. 332. —Paraguay, p. 332–333. —Peru, p. 333–334. —Puerto Rico, p. 339–340. —Trinidad and Tobago, p. 365. —Uruguay, p. 369. —Venezuela, p. 230–231.

B. INDIVIDUAL COUNTRIES

1. Argentina

22. Cherkasov, M. F. Argentina; spravka [Argentina; an information note] Mezhdunar. polit.-ekon. ezhegodnik, 1959: 298–303.

23. Romanova, Z. I., *and* K. S. Tarasov. Argentina; spravka [Argentina; an information note] Mezhdunar. ezhegodnik; politika i ekonomika, 1961: 65–70.

2. Bolivia

24. Boliviia; kratkaia spravka [Bolivia; a brief information note] Za rubezhom, no. 26, Dec. 1960: 28.

3. Brazil

25. Bulatov, B. Braziliia [Brazil] Moscow, Znanie, 1963. 47 p.   DLC
General information.

26. Aglin, G. N. Braziliia; spravka [Brazil; an information note] Mezhdunar. ezhegodnik; politika i ekonomika, 1962: 121–128.

27. Braziliia; kratkaia spravka [Brazil; a brief information note] Za rubezhom, no. 24, Nov. 1960: 14–15.

28. Dymov, V. Braziliia [Brazil] Mezhdunar. zhizn', v. 11, no. 8, Aug. 1964: 150–151.
General information.

29. Glinkin, A. N. Braziliia; spravka [Brazil; an information note] Mezhdunar. ezhegodnik; politika i ekonomika, 1961: 92–98.

30. Klesmet, O. G. Braziliia; spravka [Brazil; an information note] Mezhdunar. polit.-ekon. ezhegodnik, 1959: 320–327.

4. Chile

31. Kudachkin, M. F.   Chili [Chile] Moscow, Znanie, 1961. 31 p.
General information.

32. Lymar, IUrii Vasyl'ovych.   Chili [Chile] Kiev, Derzhpolitvydav URSR, 1961. 37 p.   F3099.L9
General information.

33. Mokhnachev, M. I.   Chili; spravka [Chile; an information notc] Mczhdunar. polit.-ekon. ezhegodnik, 1960: 327–331.

5. Colombia

34. Lukashova, Evgeniia Nikolaevna, *and* Dmitrii Nikolaevich Lialikov. Kolumbiia [Colombia] Moscow, Geografgiz, 1959. 48 p.   HC197.L8
General information.

6. Cuba

35. Aseeva, N. V.   Afrika—probudivshiisia kontinent. Kuba idet vpered; rekomendatel'nye spiski literatury [Africa, an awakened continent. Cuba marches forward; lists of recommended literature] Leningrad, Gos. publichnaia biblioteka im. Saltykova-Shchedrina, 1962. 35 p.

36. Bogomolova, P., *and* E. Viner, *comps.* Revoliutsionnaia Kuba; kul'turnoe stroitel'stvo, fol'klor, khudozhestvennaia literatura, iskusstvo, Kuba v khudozhestvennoi literature i iskusstve. Vyborochnyi spisok literatury [Revolutionary Cuba; cultural development, folklore, fiction, art, Cuba in literature and art. An index of selected publications] Leningrad, Gos. publichnaia biblioteka im. Saltykova-Shchedrina, 1963. 23 p.

37. Braginskaia, E. V., *and* L. A. Shur, *comps.* Kuba v sovetskoi pechati; bibliografiia knig i zhurnal'nykh statei o sovremennom politicheskom polozhenii, istorii, ekonomike, kul'ture, literature i iskusstve Kuby [Cuba in the Soviet press; a bibliography of books and articles on the present-day political and economic situation, history, culture, literature, and art of Cuba] Moscow, Vses. biblioteka inostr. lit., 1963. 75 p.   Z1511.M6
Introductory article by E. V. Anan'eva.

38. Levina, O. I.   Ostrov svobody; pamiatka chitateliu [The island of freedom; a reference book for readers] Moscow, Gos. biblioteka SSSR im. Lenina, 1962. 15 p.

39. Ostrov svobody Kuba; pamiatka uchashchikhsia VII kl. [Cuba, the island of freedom; an information pamphlet for seventh-grade students] Petrozavodsk, Karel. kn. izd-vo, 1964. 2 p.

40. Kalinin, A. I.   Kuba; spravka [Cuba; an information note] Mezhdunar. polit.-ekon. ezhegodnik, 1960: 215–223.

41. ———.   Kuba; spravka [Cuba; an information note] Mezhdunar. ezhegodnik; politika i ekonomika, 1961: 190–198.

42. ———.   Respublika Kuba; spravka [The Republic of Cuba; an information note] Mezhdunar. ezhegodnik; politika i ekonomika, 1962: 211–219.

43. Kremnev, M.   Kuba; spravka [Cuba; an information note] Nov. vrem., v. 17, no. 3, Jan. 1959: 18–19.

44. Kuba [Cuba] Blok. agit. [Ukr.] no. 18, June 1960: 61–63.
General information.

45. Respublika Kuba [The Republic of Cuba] Kal. znam. i pam. dat, v. 6, no. 7, July 1961: 30–35.
A bibliography.

46. Respublika Kuba [The Republic of Cuba] Kal. znam. i pam. dat, v. 7, no. 1, Jan. 1962: 10–14.
A bibliography.

47. Respublika Kuba [The Republic of Cuba] Kal. znam. i pam. dat, v. 8, no. 1, Jan. 1963: 16–20.
A bibliography.

48. Respublika Kuba [The Republic of Cuba] Kal. znam. i pam. dat, v. 8, no. 7, July 1963: 28–32.
A bibliography.

49. Respublika Kuba [The Republic of Cuba] Kal. znam. i pam. dat, v. 8, no. 12, Dec. 1963: 48–52.
A bibliography.

50. Respublika Kuba [The Republic of Cuba] Kal. znam. i pam. dat, v. 9, no. 6, July 1964: 25–28.
A bibliography.

7. Ecuador

51. Ekvador; spravka [Ecuador; an information note] Mezhdunar. zhizn', v. 8, no. 12, Dec. 1961: 149–150.

8. The Guianas

52. Leshchiner, Roal'd Efimovich. Gviana [Guiana] Moscow, Geografgiz, 1960. 76 p.   F2351.L4
General information.

53. Slepneva, G. Britanskaia Gviana; spravka [British Guiana; an information note] Mezhdunar. zhizn', v. 6, no. 7, July 1959: 139–141.

9. Mexico

54. Kalinin, A. I. Meksika; spravka [Mexico; an information note] Mezhdunar. polit.-ekon. ezhegodnik, 1959: 367–374.

55. Tarasov, K. S. Meksika; spravka [Mexico; an information note] Mezhdunar. ezhegodnik; politika i ekonomika, 1962: 230–236.

10. Paraguay

56. Gvozdarev, Boris Ivanovich. Paragvai [Paraguay] Moscow, Gosiurizdat, 1962. 79 p.
General information.

11. Peru

57. Peru; spravka [Peru; an information note] Za rubezhom, no. 16, Apr. 1961: 22.

12. Venezuela

58. Nitoburg, E. L. Venesuela [Venezuela] Moscow, Geografgiz, 1959. 79 p.
HC237.N57
General information.

59. Shul'govskii, A. F. Venesuela; spravka [Venezuela; an information note] Mezhdunar. polit.-ekon. ezhegodnik, 1960: 132–137.

60. Strana "chernogo zolota"; kratkaia spravka [The country of "black gold"; a brief information note] Za rubezhom, no. 27, Dec. 1960: 17.

13. West Indies

61. Slepneva, G. Vest-indskaia federatsiia; spravka [The West Indian Federation; an information note] Mezhdunar. zhizn'. v. 6, no. 10, Oct. 1959: 144–145.

II

GEOGRAPHY AND GEOLOGY

❦

A. GENERAL WORKS

1. Writings Dealing With Three or More Countries

62. Argentina, Paragvai, Urugvai, Chili; 1:5,000,000 [Maps ofArgentina,Paraguay, Uruguay, Chile; 1:5,000,000] Moscow, Geografgiz, 1961.
    —— [Text] 1961. 36 p.

63. Bakirov, A. A. Nefte-gazonosnye oblasti Severnoi i IUzhnoi Ameriki; geologicheskie usloviia regional'nogo neftegazonakopleniia [Oil and gas bearing areas in North and South America; geological conditions governing regional oil and gas accumulations] Moscow, Gosgeoltekhizdat, 1959. 295 p.
    TN872.A2B3

64. Gerth, Heinrich. Geologiia And; stroenie iuzhno-amerikanskikh Kordil'er [Geology of the Andes; geological structure of the South American Cordilleras] Moscow, Izd-vo inostr. lit., 1959. 291 p.
    Translated by S. M. Sheinmann from the German *Die Kordilleren von Südamerika*.

65. Humboldt, Alexander. Kartiny prirody [Aspects of nature] Moscow, Geografgiz, 1959. 269 p.
    Physical geography of South America.
    Translated from the German *Anischten der Natur*.
    Reviewed by IU. Saushkin in *Geog. v shkole*, v. 22, no. 5, Sept.-Oct. 1959: 74–75.

66. International Geological Congress. *20th, Mexico, 1956.* Materialy po geologii nefti. t. 3. Severnaia i IUzhnaia Amerika [Materials on the geology of petroleum. v. 3. North and South America] Moscow, Gostoptekhizdat, 1959. 586 p.
    TN870.5.I5 1956

67. Jenks, William Furness, *ed.* Ocherki po geologii IUzhnoi Ameriki; sbornik statei [Notes on South American geology; collected articles] Moscow, Izd-vo inostr. lit., 1959. 341 p.
    QE230.J417
    Translated by F. R. Al'tsin and N. A. Titova from the English *Handbook of South American Geology.*

68. Orlova, Elena Vladimirovna. Osobennosti geologicheskoi obstanovki vulkanogennoosadochnykh mestorozhdenii bora na primere boronosnykh provintsii Severnoi i IUzhnoi Ameriki [Geological characteristics of the volcanic sedimentary deposits of boron based on the example of boron-bearing areas in North and South America] Moscow, Vses. nauch.-issl. in-t miner. syr'ia, 1961. 30 p.
    TN4.M663, vyp. 13

69. Rosliakova, A. F. Klimaty Severnoi i TSentral'noi Ameriki [The climates of North and Central America] Moscow, Mosk. zaochn. ped. institut, 1960. 49 p.

70. Shebalin, N. V., *ed.* Seismologicheskie missii IUNESKO v strany IUzhnoi Ameriki, raiona Sredizemnogo moria i Srednego Vostoka [Unesco's seismological missions to South America, the Mediterranean area, and the Middle East] Moscow, Nauka, 1964. 110 p.
    Translated from the English.

71. TSentral'naia Amerika i Vest-Indiia; 1:5,000,000 [Map of Central America and the West Indies; 1:5,000,000] Moscow, Geografgiz, 1959.
    G4390 1959.R8
    —— [Text] by V. Gokhman. 1959. 41 p.

72. Usik, L. E. Fiziko-geograficheskie oblasti IUzhnoi Ameriki [Physical-geo-

graphical regions of South America] Orenburg, Pedagogich. in-t im. V. P. Chkalova, 1960. 33 p.

73. Vol'skii, Viktor Votslavovich, *and* R. E. Leshchiner. Venesuela, Kolumbiia, Ekvador, Gviana [Venezuela, Colombia, Ecuador, and Guiana] Vilnius, Gospolitnauchizdat, 1960. 36 p.
   In Lithuanian. Translated from the Russian.

74. Wisser, E. H. Rudonosnye raiony Kordil'er i ikh sviaz' s regional'nymi strukturami [Cordilleran ore deposits and regional structure] Moscow, Otd. nauchn.tekhn. informatsii VIMS, 1960. 18 p.
   Translated from the English original which appeared in *The Canadian Mining and Metallurgical Bulletin*, v. 52, 1959.

75. Borisov, O. M., *and* L. N. Lordkipanidze. Rudno-petrograficheskie provintsii IUzhnoi Ameriki [Ore-bearing petrographic areas in South America] Uzb. geol. zhur., v. 6, no. 5, 1962: 65–78.

76. Brodetskii, V. I. U dal'nikh beregov; Peruanskoe techenie [At the faraway seashores; the Peru Current] Priroda, v. 53, no. 7, 1964: 92–94.

77. Egorova, A. IU. Vlagosoderzhanie atmosfery nad TSentral'noi Amerikoi i ego sviaz' s osadkami [Moisture content of the atmosphere over Central America and its connection with precipitation] Trudy GGO, no. 142, 1963: 13–21.

78. Fomichev, A. V. K kharakteristike struktury vodnykh mass Peruanskogo techeniia [Structural characteristics of the water masses of the Peru Current] Trudy Inst. okean., v. 40, 1960: 83–92.

79. Kol'man, O. V. Okeanograficheskie konferentsii v Latinskoi Amerike [Oceanographic conferences in Latin America] Okeanologiia, v. 3, no. 1, 1963: 184–185.

80. Kunin, V. N. Latino-Amerikanskaia konferentsiia dlia izucheniia aridnykh raionov [A Latin American conference on the study of arid regions] Izv. AN SSSR. Ser. geog., no. 5, Aug.-Sept. 1964: 106–111.

81. Kuznetsov, A. S., *and* K. M. Sevost'ianov. Neftegazonosnye basseiny IUzhnoi Ameriki [The oil and gas bearing basins of South America] Razved. i okhr. nedr, v. 30, no. 5, May 1964: 58–63.

82. Maksimovich, G. A. Karst IUzhnoi Ameriki [The karst of South America] Uch. zap. Perm. gos. un., v. 24, no. 3, 1962: 172–176.

83. Mashbits, IA. G. O latinoamerikanskoi geograficheskoi literature [Latin American geographical literature] Vop. geog., no. 44, 1959: 240–249.

84. Murzaev, E. M., *and* A. M. Riabchikov. Review. Izv. AN SSSR. Ser. geog., no. 4, July-Aug. 1959: 146–147.
   A review of Evgeniia Nikolaevna Lukashova's *IUzhnaia Amerika; fizicheskaia geografiia* (Moscow, Uchpedgiz, 1958. 466 p.).

2. Individual Countries

a. Argentina

85. Whiting, F. B. Strukturnye poiasa i mestorozhdeniia poleznykh iskopaemykh Severo-Zapadnoi Argentiny [Structural zones and mineral deposits of northwestern Argentina] Moscow, Otd. nauch.-tekhn. informatsii VIMS, 1960. 12 p.
   Translated from the English original which appeared in *Economic Geology*, no. 5, 1959.

86. Geodezicheskie raboty kapitalisticheskikh stran; iz natsional'nykh otchetov, predstavlennykh na XII general'nyi s"ezd Mezhdunarodnogo geodezicheskogo i geofizicheskogo soiuza, Khel'sinki, 1960 g. [Argentina] [Geodetic operations in capitalistic countries; from national reports presented at the 12th General Assembly of the International Union of Geodesy and Geophysics in Helsinki, 1960 (Argentina)] Geod. i kart., no. 2, Feb. 1962: 63–69.

87. Markov, K. K. Paleogeografiia Ognennoi Zemli i Patagonii v sviazi s obshchimi problemami paleogeografii antropogena [Paleogeography of Tierra del Fuego and Patagonia as related to the general paleogeographical problems of the Tertiary era] Vest. Mosk. un. Ser. 5: Geog., v. 15, no. 5, Sept.-Oct, 1960: 3–13.

88. Zemlia vohnianykh strumiv [The land of flaming streams] Vsesvit, v. 6, no. 5, May 1963: 136–137.
    Tierra del Fuego.

b. Bolivia

89. Na ozeri tysiachi legend [On a lake of a thousand legends] Vsesvit, v. 4, no. 11, Nov. 1961: 90–91.

90. Smirnov, F. L. Mestorozhdeniia Bolivii, soderzhashchie argirodit i kanfil'dit [Bolivian deposits containing argyrodite and canfieldite] *In* Moscow. Vsesoiuznyi nauchno-issledovatel'skii institut mineral'nogo syr'ia. Mineraly germaniia i ikh mestorozhdeniia. Moscow, Gosgeoltekhizdat, 1959. p. 74–77. (Geologiia mestorozhdenii redkikh elementov, no. 5)
    TN490.A2M646

    See also entry no. 2398

c. Brazil

91. Braziliia i Gviana; 1:5,000,000 [Maps of Brazil and Guiana; 1:5,000,000] Moscow, Geografgiz, 1962.
    ——— [Text] 1962. 51 p.

92. Link, W. K. Perspektivy obnaruzheniia nefti v osadochnykh basseinakh Brazilii [Prospects for finding oil in the sedimentary basins of Brazil] Moscow, Gos. nauch.-issled. in-t nauch. i tekhn. informatsii, 1960. 15 p.
    Translated from the English original which appeared in *Oil and Gas International*, v. 57, no. 47.

93. Fawcett, Percy Harrison. Zateriannye rudniki Muribeki [Muribeca's forgotten mines] Vokrug sveta, no. 9, Sept. 1960: 25–29.
    A ghost town.
    Translated from the English.

94. Ginsburg, I. I., *and others.* Sovremennoe i drevnee lateritnoe vyvetrivanie bazal'tov Brazilii i Russkoi platformy [Recent and ancient laterite weathering of basalts in Brazil and the Russian Platform] Kora vyvetr., no. 4, 1962: 3–95.

95. Men'shikov, V. Bich Brazillii [The scourge of Brazil] Vokrug sveta, no. 7, July 1959: 48–49.
    Droughts.

96. Review. Geog. v shkole, v. 22, no. 1, Jan.-Feb. 1959: 92–93.
    A review of *Liudi i landshafty Brazilii* (Moscow, Izd-vo inostr. lit., 1958. 290 p.).

97. Shprintsin, N. G., *and* M. A. Kogan. Review. Izv. Vses. geog. ob-va, v. 91, no. 1, Jan.-Feb. 1959: 101–103.
    A review of Arkady Fiedler's *Wyspa Robinsona* (Warsaw, Iskry, 1955. 254 p.); his *Orinoko* (Warsaw, Iskry, 1957. 419 p.) and his *Taina Rio de Oro* (Moscow, Geografgiz, 1958. 128 p.).
    Description of Brazil in Polish works.

98. Vernov, S. N., *and others.* Geograficheskoe raspredelenie intensivnosti radiatsii v raione Brazil'skoi magnitnoi anomalii na vysote okolo 300 km. [Geographic distribution of radiation intensity in the region of the Brazilian magnetic anomaly at an altitude of about 300 km.] Kosm. issl., v. 2, no. 3, May-June 1964: 485–491.

99. ———. Issledovanie radiatsionnykh poiasov Zemli v raione Brazil'skoi magnitnoi anomalii na vysotakh 235–345 km. [Study of the earth's radiation belts in the region of the Brazilian magnetic anomaly at altitudes between 235 and 345 km.] Kosm. issl., v. 2, no. 3, May-June 1964: 492–497.

d. Chile

100. Howell, Fred H., *and* John S. Molley. Geologicheskoe stroenie mestorozhdeniia medno-porfirovykh rud Braden v Chili [Geology of the Braden porphyry copper orebody in Chile] Moscow, Vses. nauch.-issl. in-t miner. syr'ia, 1961. 15 p.
    Translated from the English original which appeared in *Economic Geology*, v. 55, no. 8, 1960: 863–905.

101. Popov, G. I. TSunami u beregov Chili i usloviia ikh obrazovaniia [Conditions governing the formation of tsunamis near the coast of Chile] Okeanologiia, v. 4, no. 1, 1964: 74–80.

e. Cuba

102. Kuba; 1:1,500,000 [Map of Cuba; 1:1,500,000] Moscow, Geografgiz, 1962.
    DLC
    ——— [Text] by IA. G. Mashbits. 1962. 16 p.

103. Núñez Jiménez, Antonio. Geografiia Kuby [Geography of Cuba] Moscow, Izd-vo inostr. lit., 1960. 607 p.
Translated from the Spanish *Geografía de Cuba.*
Reviewed by V. Chichkov in *Vokrug sveta,* no. 5, May 1960: 61; by A. Dridzo in *Izv. Vses. geog. ob-va,* v. 93, no, 2, Mar.-Apr. 1961: 179–181.

104. Rusin, N. P. Ot Gavany do Ostrova sokrovishch [From Havana to "Treasure Island"] Leningrad, Gidrometeoizdat, 1964. 163 p.
Geography and climate of Cuba.

105. Adamovich, A. F., *and* V. D. Chekhovich. K voprosu ob usloviiakh obrazovaniia kory vyvetrivaniia v geosinklinal'nykh oblastiakh; na primere Vostochnoi Kuby [Conditions governing the formation of weathering surface in geosyncline areas as revealed by a study made in eastern Cuba] Izv. AN SSSR. Ser. geol., v. 29, no. 9, Sept. 1964: 84–93.

106. ———. Osnovnye cherty geologicheskogo stroeniia Vostochnoi Kuby [Basic features of the geological structure of eastern Cuba] Biul. MOIP, Otd. geol., v. 38, no. 5, Sept.-Oct. 1963: 126; v. 39, no. 1, Jan.-Feb. 1964: 10–21.

107. Burdiugov, I. S. Mineral'nye bogatstva Kuby [Cuban mineral resources] Razved. i okh. nedr, v. 26, no. 11, Nov. 1960: 57–61.

108. Dridzo, A. D. Review. Izv. Vses. geog. ob-va, v. 95, no. 4, July-Aug. 1963: 378–380.
A review of José Alvarez Conde's *Historia de la geografía de Cuba* (Havana, Junta Nacional de Arqueología y Etnología, 1961. 574 p.).

109. Geologiia vostochnoi Kuby [The geology of eastern Cuba] Priroda, v. 53, no. 3, 1964: 111.

110. Grigor'eva. V. M. Novye dannye o mineral'nykh formakh nakhozhdeniia nikelia v vyvetrelykh serpentininakh Kuby [New data on the mineral bedding of nickel in the weathered serpentine of Cuba] Kora vyvetr., no. 6, 1963: 55–57.

111. Mashbits, IA. G. Istoriia i sovremennoe sostoianie issledovanii po geografii Kuby [History and present-day status of research on the geography of Cuba] Izv. AN SSSR. Ser. geog., no. 3, May-June 1962: 113–117.

112. ———. Poseshchenie Instituta geografii AN SSSR kubinskim geografom professorom Antonio Nun'es Khimenesom [A visit of the Cuban geographer, Professor Antonio Núñez Jiménez, to the Institute of Geography of the USSR Academy of Sciences] Izv. AN SSSR. Ser. geog., no. 5, Sept.-Oct. 1960: 159–160.

113. ———. Vozrozhdenie "zelonogo raia"; prirodnye bogatstva Kuby sluzhat narodu [The regeneration of a "green paradise"; Cuba's natural resources in the people's service] Priroda, v. 50, no. 10, Oct. 1961: 101–112.

114. Nesteruk, E. IA. Vodnye resursy svobodnoi Kuby [The water resources of free Cuba] Rech. transp., v. 21, no. 8, Aug. 1962: 50–52.

115. Olenin, A. S. Torfianye resursy Kuby [Cuba's peat resources] Torf. prom., v. 38, no. 4, 1961: 36–37.

116. Olenin, A. S., *and* I. V. Sedov. Torf na Kube [Peat in Cuba] Priroda, v. 52, no. 2, Feb. 1963: 88–90.

117. Rautenshtein, IA. I. Pervaia Natsional'naia konferentsiia pochvovedov Kuby [The First Conference of Cuban Soil Scientists] Vest. AN SSSR, v. 34, no. 7, July 1964: 99–100.

118. ———. Pervaia Natsional'naia pochvennaia konferentsiia Kuby [The First Cuban Conference on Soil Conservation] Izv. AN SSSR. Ser. biol., no. 5, Sept.-Oct. 1964: 804–806.

119. Semevskii, B. N. Geografiia v Gavanskom universitete [Geographical studies in Havana University] Izv. Vses. geog. ob-va, v. 95, no. 4, July-Aug. 1963: 351–353.

120. ———. Nauchnye geograficheskie konferentsii v Gavane [Geographical conferences in Havana] Izv. AN SSSR. Ser. geog., no. 2, Mar.-Apr. 1964: 168–169.

121. Sheinbaum, L. Review. Sov. etn., no. 2, Mar.-Apr. 1964: 161–163.
Speleology.
A review of *20 años explorando a Cuba* (Havana, 1961. 382 p.).

See also entries no. 2505 and 2506.

f. Ecuador

122. Eibl-Eibesfeldt, Irenäus. Galapagosy—zapovednik ili pustynia? [The Galápagos Islands—a preserve or a desert?] Vokrug sveta, no. 7, July 1959: 26–28.
Wildlife conservation.
Translated from the German.

g. The Guianas

See entry no. 91.

h. Mexico

123. Litvin, I. P. Geograficheskie nazvaniia Meksiki [Geographical names of Mexico] Vop. geog., no. 58, 1962: 139–150.

124. Osipova, A. I. Tipy mestoobitanii i naselenie Ferganskogo zaliva paleogeo-novogo moria i ikh sovremennye analogii; poberezh'e Meksikanskogo zaliva [Habitat types and population of the Fergana Bay of the Paleogene Sea and their modern analogues; the coastal area of the Gulf of Mexico] Buil. MOIP. Otd. geol., v. 35, no. 3, May-June 1960: 171–172.

125. Turkin, V., *and* I. Turkin. Rozhdennyi okeanom [Born of the ocean] Vokrug sveta, no. 2, Feb. 1960: 6–8.
Cyclones.

See also entries no. 2550 and 2556.

i. Paraguay

See entry no. 2560.

j. Peru

126. Kravchenko, D. V. Sovetskaia geo-graficheskaia nauka na stranitsakh peru-anskogo geograficheskogo zhurnala [Soviet geography on the pages of a Peruvian geographical journal] Izv. AN SSSR. Ser. geog., no. 5, Sept.-Oct. 1960: 147.

See also entry no. 89.

k. Puerto Rico

See entry no. 2568.

l. Trinidad and Tobago

127. Presto, U. Asfal'tnoe ozero [An asphalt lake] Znan.-sila, v. 37, no. 3, Mar. 1962: 41.

128. Trinidad i Tobago [Trinidad and Tobago] Agitator, no. 18, Sept. 1962: 22.

m. Venezuela

129. Machado, Eduardo. Neft' v Venesuele [Petroleum in Venezuela] Moscow, Izd-vo inostr. lit., 1960. 84 p.
Translated by G. R. Sergeev from the Spanish *Petróleo en Venezuela*.
Reviewed by A. Smol'nikov in *Agitator*, no. 11, 1962: 60.

B. GEOGRAPHICAL EXPEDITIONS

1. Writings Dealing With Three or More Countries

130. Fawcett, Percy Harrison. Neokon-chennoe puteshestvie [An unfinished journey] Moscow, Mysl', 1964. 415 p.
Translated from the English *Exploration Fawcett*. Introductory article by L. A. Fainberg.

131. Humboldt, Alexander. Puteshestvie v ravnodenstvennye oblasti Novogo Sveta v 1799–1804 godakh. t.1. Ostrov Tenerife i Vostochnaia Venesuela [A voyage to the equinoctial regions of the New World in 1799–1804. v.1. Tenerife Island and eastern Venezuela] Moscow, Geografgiz, 1963. 502 p.
Translated from the French *Voyage aux régions équinoxiales du nouveau continent*.

132. ———. Puteshestvie v ravnodenstvennye oblasti Novogo Sveta v 1799–1804 godakh. t.2. Plavanie po Orinoko [A voyage to the equinoctial regions of the New World in 1799–1804. v.2. A trip up the Orinoco River] Moscow, Mysl', 1964. 655 p.
Translated from the French *Voyage aux régions équinoxiales du nouveau continent*.

133. Poeppig, Eduard Friederik. Cherez Andy k Amazonke [Across the Andes to the Amazon] Moscow, Geografgiz, 1960. 222 p.

Translated from the German *Über die Anden zum Amazon.*

134. Svet, IA. M., *ed.* Otkrytie velikoi reki Amazonok; khroniki i dokumenty XVI veka o puteshestviiakh Frantsisko de Orel'iany [Discovery of the great Amazon River; chronicles and documentary materials of the 16th century, which describe Francisco de Orellana's journeys] Moscow, Geografgiz, 1963. 203 p.

135. Von Hagen, Victor Wolfgang. Ikh prizvala IUzhnaia Amerika [South America called them] Moscow, Geografgiz, 1961. 383 p.
 Translated from the English.
 Reviewed in *Priroda*, v. 5, no. 10, Oct. 1961: 58.

136. Lukin, B. V. K 50-letiiu russkoi nauchnoi ekspeditsii v Latinskuiu Ameriku [The 50th anniversary of a Russian scientific expedition to Latin America] Vest. AN SSSR, v. 34, no. 6, June 1964: 107–109.

137. Lukin, B. V., *and* A. M. Chernikov. Proekt sovetskoi akademicheskoi ekspeditsii v IUzhnuiu Ameriku; k istorii sovetsko-latinoamerikanskikh nauchnykh sviazei [A plan to send a Soviet scientific expedition to South America; from the history of Soviet scientific contacts with Latin America] Vest. AN SSSR, v. 33, no. 7, July 1963: 101–103.

See also entries no. 4561 and 4568.

2. Individual Countries

a. Brazil

138. Lange, Algot. V dzhungliakh Amazonki [In the Amazon jungle] Yerevan, Aipetrat, 1959. 130 p.
 In Armenian. Translated from the English.

139. Molnár, Gábor. U kraini iaguariv [In the land of the jaguars] Kiev, Molod', 1963. 202 p.
 Translated by K. A. Bibikov from the Hungarian *Jaguárországban.*
 Reviewed by V. Shykan in *Vsesvit*, v. 7, no. 5, May 1964: 159–160.

140. Chernega, M. Review. Geog. v shkole, v. 22, no. 2, Mar.-Apr. 1959: 92–93.

A review of Arkady Fiedler's *Taina Rio de Oro* (Moscow, Geografgiz, 1958. 128 p.).

141. Gerasimov, Innokentii Petrovich. Brazil'skie dnevniki—1956 god [My Brazilian diaries, 1956] *In his* Moi zarubezhnye puteshestviia. Moscow, Geografgiz, 1959. p. 93–142. G464.G45

142. Komissarov, B. N. Braziliia pervoi chetverti XIX veka v opisaniiakh russkikh moreplavatelei [Brazil in the first quarter of the 19th century as described by Russian seafarers] Vest. LGU, v. 16, no. 14, 1961: 43–54.
 Summary in English.

143. Novospasskii, V. V gostiakh u kannibalov [Visiting the cannibals] Vokrug sveta, no. 9, Sept. 1959: 62.
 A review of Algot Lange's *V dzhungliakh Amazonki* (Moscow, Geografgiz, 1958. 96 p.).

144. Pokhvalin, V. Russkie uchenye v Brazilii [Russian scientists in Brazil] Nauka i zhizn', v. 30, no. 11, Nov. 1963: 65–68.
 A Russian geographical expedition.

145. Raush, V. Review. Geog. v shkole, v. 22, no. 1, Jan.-Feb. 1959: 93.
 A review of Algot Lange's *V dzhungliakh Amazonki* (Moscow, Geografgiz, 1958. 96 p.).

146. Vasilevskii, L. Taina ekspeditsii Fosetta [Mystery of the Fawcett expedition] Vokrug sveta, no. 2, Feb. 1962: 47–49.

b. Chile (*including Easter Island*)

147. Heyerdahl, Thor. The Kon-Tiki expedition. 2d ed. Moscow, Vyssh. shkola, 1964. 135 p.
 In English.

148. ———. Puteshestvie na "Kon-Tiki"; na plotu ot Peru do Polinezii [The Kon-Tiki expedition; by raft across the South Seas] Tiflis, Nakduli, 1963. 305 p.
 In Georgian. Translated from the English. Introductory article by S. Obruchev.

149. Butinov, N., *and others.* Review. Sov. etn., no. 1, Jan.-Feb. 1959: 144–153.
 A review of Thor Heyerdahl's *Aku-Aku; påskeøyas hemmelighet* (Oslo, Gyldendal norsk forlag, 1957. 359 p.).

150. Solov'eva, I. Liudi dlia liudei [People live for people] Nov. mir, v. 35, no. 3, Mar. 1959: 187–197.

A review of Thor Heyerdahl's *Puteshestvie na "Kon-Tiki"* (Moscow, Mol. gvardiia, 1957).

c. Cuba

151. Suziumov, E. M. Sovetsko-kubinskaia okeanologicheskaia ekspeditsiia [A joint expedition of Soviet and Cuban oceanographers] Vest. AN SSSR, v. 34, no. 8, Aug. 1964: 89–94.

d. The Guianas

152. Guppy, Nicholas. V strane Vai-Vai; cherez lesa k severu ot Amazonki [Wai-Wai; through the forests north of the Amazon] Moscow, Geografgiz, 1961. 344 p.

Translated from the English. Introductory article by L. E. Rodin and L. A. Fainberg.

Reviewed by A. Turkov in *Vokrug sveta*, no. 1, Jan. 1963: 62–63.

e. Mexico

153. Pashaeva, N. M. Dokumenty meksikanskogo arkhiva o russkikh geograficheskikh otkrytiiakh [Documentary materials of the Mexican Archives relating to Russian geographical discoveries] Vop. ist., v. 39, no. 11, Nov. 1964: 205–206.

f. Peru

154. Fiedler, Arkady. Ryby poiut v Ukaiali [Ucayali, the river of singing fish] Moscow, Geografgiz, 1963. 239 p.

Translated from the Polish *Ryby śpiewają w Ukajali*.

Reviewed by IU. Monchenko in *V mire knig*, v. 4, no. 7, 1964: 19; by A. Zaitsev in *Nov. mir*, v. 40, no. 6, June 1964: 284.

g. Venezuela

155. Fiasson, Raymond. Navstrechu nevedomomu [Toward the unknown] Vokrug sveta, no. 2, Feb. 1963; 24–27, 55; no. 3, Mar. 1963: 48–52; no. 4, Apr. 1963: 47–50.

A geographical expedition.

Excerpts from the book *Des Indiens et des mouches* (Tournai, Caserman, 1960. 211 p.).

156. Saint-Blancat, Henri de. Poslednie iz "zateriannykh mirov" [The last of the "lost worlds"] Vokrug sveta, no. 2, Feb. 1960: 44–46.

An expedition to the remote parts of Venezuela.

Translated from the French.

C. FLORA AND FAUNA

1. Writings Dealing With Three or More Countries

157. Durrell, Gerald Malcolm. Pod pologom p'ianogo lesa [The drunken forest] Moscow, Geografgiz, 1963. 184 p.

Translated from the English.

Reviewed by G. Zelenko in *Znan.-sila*, v. 39, no. 7, July 1964: 43; by IU. Skrylev in *Sem'ia i shkola*, v. 19, no. 7, July 1964: 34–35.

158. ———. Pod pologom p'ianogo lesa [The drunken forest] 2d ed. Moscow, Mysl', 1964. 188 p.

Translated from the English.

159. Ivanov, IU. Karibskii suvenir [A Caribbean souvenir] Moscow, Det. lit., 1964. 239 p.

A Russian ichthyological expedition to the Caribbean region.

160. Klingel, Gilbert C. Ostrov v okeane [The Ocean Island] Moscow, Geografgiz, 1963. 344 p.

Reptiles.

Translated from the English. Introductory article by I. I. Akimushkin.

161. Richards, Paul Westmacott. Tropicheskii dozhdevoi les [The tropical rain forest] Moscow, Izd-vo inostr. lit., 1961. 448 p.

Translated by T. P. Komov and T. I. Podol'skaia from the English. Introductory article by An. A. Fedorov.

Reviewed by B. V. Gorzdov in *Les. khoz.*, v. 17, no. 10, Oct. 1964: 90.

162. Vavilov, Nikolai Ivanovich. Piat' kontinentov; povest' o puteshestviiakh v poiskakh novykh rastenii [Five continents; a story of travels in search of new plants] Moscow, Geografgiz, 1962. 253 p.

G464.V35 1962

Includes travels to South America.

———

163. Akimushkin, I. I. Obez"iana iz S'erra Periia [The ape from the Sierra de

Perija] Nauka i zhizn', v. 27, no. 12, Dec. 1960: 49–52.

164. Boiko, Elena. Biufeo—veselyi del'fin ["Bufeo," the merry dolphin] Vokrug sveta, no. 5, May 1959: 60.
Dolphins.

165. Durrell, Gerald Malcolm. Pod pologom p'ianogo lesa; otryvok iz knigi [The drunken forest; excerpt from a book] Vokrug sveta, no. 1, Jan. 1963: 55–57.
Flora and fauna.
Translated from the English.

166. Linnik, E. Zelenaia iguana [The green iguana] IUn. nat., no. 1, Jan. 1963: 25.

167. Poznakom'tes': mata-mata [Let us tell you about the matamata] Priroda, v. 52, no. 6, June 1963: 120–121.
Turtles.

168. Pro lamu, guanako i drugikh . . . [On llamas, guanacos and others . . .] IUn. nat., no. 12, Dec. 1960: 35–39.
Animals.

169. Sosnovskii, I. P. Ochkovyi medved' [The spectacled bear] Priroda, v. 49, no. 1, Jan. 1960: 114–115.

170. Zhukovskii, P. M. Po tsentram proiskhozhdeniia kul'turnykh rastenii Latinskoi Ameriki; ocherk ekspeditsii 1958 goda [Through the centers of origin of cultivated plants in Latin America; an account of the Expedition of 1958] Bot. zhur., v. 44, no. 2, Feb. 1959: 262–272.

171. ———. Po tsentram proiskhozhdeniia kul'turnykh rastenii Latinskoi Ameriki; resursy kul'turnykh rastenii [Through the centers of origin of cultivated plants in Latin America; the resources of cultivated plants] Bot. zhur., v. 44, no. 5, May 1959: 722–737.

2. Individual Countries

a. Argentina

172. Darrell, John. More starykh ofitsiantov [The sea of old waiters] Vokrug sveta, no. 10, Oct. 1963: 60–61.
Penguins.

b. Brazil

173. Ivanauskas, Tadas. Tri mesiatsa v Brazilii [Three months in Brazil] Vilnius, Goslitizdat, 1960. 269 p.
Animals and birds.
In Lithuanian.

174. Bazunov, B. IAd spasaet ot smerti [Poison saves from death] Vokrug sveta, no. 3, Mar. 1962: 11–12.
Poisonous snakes.

175. Kukharenko, S. Okhotniki na zhakare [Jacaré hunters] Vokrug sveta, no. 9, Sept. 1960: 64–[65].
Caimans.

176. Opasnyi "sport" [Dangerous "sport"] Vokrug sveta, no. 1, Jan. 1959: 56.
Crocodiles.

177. Wolniewicz, Janusz. Zmii v probirtsi [Snakes in test tubes] Vsesvit, v. 4, no. 3, Mar. 1961: 89.
The venom of snakes.
Translated from the Polish.

c. Cuba

178. Cardoso, Onelio Jorge. Ob otvazhnykh okhotnikakh, tugikh lasso i krovozhadnykh obitateliakh kasimb [On courageous hunters, tight lassos, and the bloodthirsty population of the swamps] Vokrug sveta, no. 10, Oct. 1962: 59–60.
Alligators.
Abbreviated translation from the Spanish.

179. Dudar', IU. A. Botanicheskii sad Atkinsa na Kube [The Atkins Botanical Garden in Cuba] Bot. zhur., v. 49, no. 8, Aug. 1964: 1227–1229.

180. Mukin, A. F. Lesa ostrova svobody [The forests of the island of freedom] Les. khoz., v. 17, no. 2, Feb. 1964: 84–90.

181. Ostrovskaia, L. N. O lesakh Kuby [Forests in Cuba] Les. khoz., v. 16, no. 2, Feb. 1963: 89–90.

d. Ecuador

182. Blomberg, Rolf. IAguar [The jaguar] Vokrug sveta, no. 2, Feb. 1963: 32.

See also entry no. 122.

e. Mexico

183. Suárez, Luis.   Belye cherepakhi Kintana Roo [White turtles from Quintana Roo] Vokrug sveta, no. 9, Sept. 1960: 37.
     Translated from the Spanish.

184. Zaikonnikova, T. I.   Meksikanskie vidy roda Deutzia Thunb. [Mexican species of the genus Deutzia Thunb.] Bot. mat. Gerb., v. 22, 1963: 155–161.

f. Venezuela

185. Dokalski, Gabriel. Venesuel'skaia krasavitsa [Venezuelan beauty] Priroda, v. 52, no. 9, Sept. 1963: 102–103.
     Orchids.

g. West Indies

186. Lopatin, IU.   Bich Martiniki [The scourge of Martinique] Ogonek, v. 38, no. 18, May 1960: 32.
     Snakes.

D. EARTHQUAKES, HURRICANES, AND FLOODS

1. Writings Dealing With Three or More Countries

187. Batiaeva, T., *and* L. Minina. Tam, gde proshla "Flora" [Where "Flora" passed] Ogonek, v. 41, no. 43, Oct. 1963: 31.
     Hurricanes.

2. Individual Countries

a. Brazil

188. Navodnenie v Brazilii [The flood in Brazil] Vokrug sveta, no. 12, Dec. 1960: 45.

b. Chile

189. Mikhaleva, D. N.   Chiliiskie zemletriaseniia 1960 goda [The 1960 earthquakes in Chile] Izv. Vses. geog. ob-va, v. 94, no. 4, July-Aug. 1962: 349–351.

190. Savarenskii, E. F.   Chiliiskie zemletriaseniia [Chilean earthquakes] Priroda, v. 49, no. 9, Sept. 1960: 78–86.

191. ———. Katastrofa v Chili [Disaster in Chile] Nov. vrem., v. 18, no. 23, June 1960: 28–29.
     Earthquakes.

192. Savarenskii, E. F., *and others*. Nabliudeniia dlinnoperiodnykh voln chiliiskogo zemletriaseniia 1960 g. [Studying the long-period waves of the Chilean earthquake of 1960] Izv. AN SSSR. Ser. geofiz., no. 8, Aug. 1961: 1132–1140.

193. Stikhiinoe bedstvie v Chili [A disastrous earthquake in Chile] Za rubezhom, no. 1, June 1960: 30.

194. Studenty pomogaiut postradvshim [Students help disaster victims] Vsem. stud. nov., v. 14, no. 8, Aug. 1960: 21–24.
     Earthquakes.

195. Sushkina, N. N. Chiliiskaia katastrofa [The Chilean catastrophe] IUn. nat., no. 10, Oct. 1960: 26–28.
     Earthquakes.

196. Zemletriasenie v Chili [Earthquake in Chile] Ogonek, v. 38, no. 23, June 1960: 31.

III

ANTHROPOLOGY

❦

A. GENERAL WORKS

1. Writings Dealing With Three or More Countries

197. Kinzhalov, R. V., *and others.* Amerika; kratkii putevoditel' po ekspozitsii Muzeia antropologii i etnografii im. Petra Velikogo, Leningrad [America; a brief guidebook to an exhibition in the Peter the Great Museum of Anthropology and Ethnography in Leningrad] Moscow, Nauka, 1964. 35 p.

2. Individual Countries

a. Brazil

198. Komissarov, B. N. Novyi russkii istochnik po istorii i etnografii Brazilii 20kh godov XIX veka [A new Russian source on the history and ethnography of Brazil in the 1820's] Sov. etn., no. 3, May-June 1963: 172–176.

b. Chile (*including Easter Island*)

199. Rozina, L. G. Novye kollektsii otdela Avstralii i Okeanii Muzeia antropologii i etnografii Akademii nauk SSSR [The new collections of the Department of Australia and Oceania of the Museum of Anthropology and Ethnography of the Academy of Sciences of the USSR] Krat. soob. Inst. etn., no. 36, 1962: 69–74.
    Antiquities of Easter Island.

c. Cuba

200. Grigulevich, I. R. Etnograficheskaia i antropologicheskaia nauka na Kube posle revoliutsii [Postrevolutionary ethnographical and anthropological studies in Cuba] Sov. etn., no. 6, Nov.-Dec. 1963: 124–137.

d. Venezuela

201. Grigulevich, I. Review. Sov. etn., no. 3, May-June 1961: 128–129.
    A review of the periodical *Revista venezolana de sociología y antropología* (Caracas, 1960).

B. ARCHAEOLOGY

1. Writings Dealing With Three or More Countries

202. Kinzhalov, Rostislav Vasil'evich. Iskusstvo drevnei Ameriki [The art of ancient America] Moscow, Iskusstvo, 1962. 237 p.
    E59.A7K49
    Reviewed by I. Karetnikova in *Iskusstvo*, v. 26, no. 9, 1963: 72–73.

203. ———. Osnovnye problemy v izuchenii drevneamerikanskogo iskusstva [Basic problems concerning the study of ancient American art] Moscow, Nauka, 1964. 11 p.

204. Knorozov, IU. V. Panteon drevnikh maiia [The pantheon of the ancient Mayas] Moscow, Nauka, 1964. 9 p.

205. ———. Pis'mennost' indeitsev Maiia [Writings of the Maya Indians] Moscow, Izd-vo Akad. nauk SSSR, 1963. 663 p.
    DLC
    Reviewed by A. B. Dolgopol'skii in *Vest. AN SSSR*, v. 33, Nov. 1963: 141–144.

206. Zhukov, Dmitrii Anatol'evich. Zagadochnye pis'mena [Enigmatic writings] Moscow, Znanie, 1962. 79 p.
    PG3962.Z5
    Maya writing.

207. Castedo, Leopoldo. Maski Latinskoi Ameriki [Latin American masks] Teatr, v. 30, no. 4, Apr. 1959: 184–185.

208. Guliaev, A. Golos drevnego Tikalia [The voice of ancient Tikal] Vokrug sveta, no. 3, Mar. 1964: 6–7, 44–45.
Mayan antiquities.

209. Guliaev, V. V glubinakh sviashchennogo senota [In the depths of a holy well] Nauka i zhizn', v. 30, no. 6, June 1963: 94–99.
Maya antiquities.

210. Its, Rudol'f. Freska Bonampaka [The fresco of Bonampak] Vokrug sveta, no. 12, Dec. 1963: 24–27.
The frescos of Maya Indians.

211. Novikova, L. V gostiakh u drevnikh maiev [Visiting the ancient Mayas] Nauka i zhizn', v. 29, no. 12, Dec. 1962: 45–49.

212. Novoe v izuchenii rukopisei Maiia [New methods in the study of Mayan manuscripts] Vest. AN SSSR, v. 31, no. 4, Apr. 1961: 64–67.

213. Prokof'ev, O. Vnov' otkrytye pamiatniki kul'tury drevnei Ameriki [Recent discoveries of the ancient monuments of American culture] Iskusstvo, v. 26, no. 12, 1963: 74–76.

2. Individual Countries

a. Argentina

214. Bashilov, V. Zagadka El' Toro [The secret of El Toro] Nauka i zhizn', v. 30, no. 8, Aug. 1964: 156–157.
Ancient burial grounds.

b. Brazil

215. Delrío, Alberto. Tainy Amazonii [Secrets of the Amazon Valley] Nauka i zhizn', v. 29, no. 1, Jan. 1962: 106–108.
Antiquities.

c. Chile (including Easter Island)

216. Heyerdahl, Thor. Aku-Aku, taina ostrova Paskhi; ob ekspeditsii po issledovaniiu pamiatnikov material'noi kul'tury [Aku-Aku, the secrets of Easter Island; an expedition for studying the monuments of material culture] Moscow, Mol. gvardiia, 1959. 383 p.
Translated from the Norwegian. Also published in Armenian and Lithuanian.
Reviewed by A. Semenov in Znan. sila, no.

7, July 1959: 23; by I. Shishkin in Sem'ia i shkola, no. 3, Mar. 1960: 28–29.

217. ———. Aku-Aku, taina ostrova Paskhi [Aku-Aku, the secrets of Easter Island] Kiev, Molod', 1959. 328 p.
Antiquities.
In Ukrainian. Translated from the Norwegian.

218. ———. Puteshestvie na "Kon-Tiki." Aku-Aku [The Kon-Tiki expedition. Aku-Aku] Alma-Ata, Kazuchpedgiz, 1960. 579 p.
Translated from the English and the Norwegian.

219. Butinov, N. A. Ieroglificheskie teksty ostrova Paskhi; Rapa-Nui [Hieroglyphic writings of Easter Island; the Rapanui writing] Vest. ist. mir. kul't., no. 3, May-June 1959: 69–80.
Summary in English.

220. ———. Novaia monografiia o pis'mennosti ostrova Paskhi [A new study of the writings of Easter Island] Vest. ist. mir. kul't., no. 3, May-June 1959: 174–176.
A review of Thomas Barthel's Grundlagen zur Entzifferung der Osterinselschrift (Hamburg, Cram, de Gruyter, 1958. 346 p.).

221. Fedorova, I. Review. Sov. etn., no. 4, July-Aug. 1962: 221–223.
A review of Jordi Fuentes' Diccionario y gramática de la lengua de la Isla de Pascua (Santiago de Chile, Editorial Andrés Bello, 1960. 1082 p.).

222. Fedorova, I. K. K voprosu o kharaktere iazyka tekstov ostrova Paskhi [Linguistic characteristics of Easter Island texts] Sov. etn., no. 2, Mar.-Apr. 1963: 85–92.
Summary in English.

223. La Faye, Howard. Mandrivka na ostriv Paskhy [A trip to Easter Island] Vsesvit, v. 5, no. 9, Sept. 1962: 47–52.

224. Zhivago, A. V. Na ostrove Paskhi [On Easter Island] Nauka i zhizn', v. 27, no. 7, July 1960: 44–49.

d. Cuba

225. Grigulevich, I. Review. Sov. etn., no. 2, Mar.-Apr. 1961: 152.
Indian antiquities.
A review of Antonio Núñez Jiménez' Facatativá, santuario de la rana (Havana,

Universidad Central de Las Villas, 1959. 96 p.).

226. Núñez Jiménez, Antonio. Peshchera solntsa [Cave of the sun] Vokrug sveta, no. 1, Jan. 1962: 60–62.
Antiquities.
Translated from the Spanish.

e. Ecuador

227. Heyerdahl, Thor. Arkheologi na Galapagosskikh ostrovakh [Archaeologists on the Galápagos Islands] Priroda, v. 53, no. 10, 1964: 81–88.

f. Jamaica

228. Link, Marion Clayton. Podvodnyi Port-Roial' [Submerged Port Royal] Vokrug sveta, no. 6, June 1961: 25–28.
Underwater archaeology.
Abbreviated translation from the English.

229. Nakhodka na IAmaike [Finds in Jamaica] Vokrug sveta, no. 11, Nov. 1960: 31.
Underwater archaeology.

g. Mexico

230. Golomshtok, I., *ed.* Iskusstvo drevnei Meksiki; al'bom [Art of ancient Mexico; an album] Moscow, Izogiz, 1962. 16 p.

231. Karetnikova, I. Traditsii drevneishego iskusstva [Traditions of an ancient art] Ogonek, v. 39, no. 23, June 1961: 24.
Indian antiquities.

232. Kinzhalov, R. V. Atstekskoe zolotoe nagrudnoe ukrashenie [A golden Aztec breast ornament] Sbor. Muz. ant. i etn., v. 19, 1960: 206–220.
Indian antiquities.

233. ———. Drevniaia meksikanskaia alebastrovaia maska (?) [An ancient Mexican alabaster mask] Sbor. Muz. ant. i etn., v. 22, 1964: 248–253.

234. ———. Iskusstvo plemen nakhua na Meksikanskom ploskogor'e v XIV–XVI vv. [Art of the Nahua tribes on the Mexican plateau in the 14th to 16th centuries] Sbor. Muz. ant. i etn., v. 21, 1963: 185–251.

235. ———. Tol'tekskaia maska [A Toltec mask] Soob. Gos. Erm., no. 15, 1959: 54–56.
Indian antiquities.

236. Lebedev, IU. Skul'ptura drevnei Meksiki [Sculpture of ancient Mexico] Iskusstvo, v. 23, no. 6, 1960: 60–67.

237. Pamiatniki drevnei kul'tury pod ugrozoi [A peril to the monuments of Mexican culture] Inostr. lit., no. 9, Sept. 1961: 281.
Ancient frescoes.

238. Sorokin, S. Sokrovishcha meksikanskogo iskusstva v zalakh Gosudarstvennogo Ermitazha [Treasures of Mexican art in the exhibition halls of the Hermitage] Soob. Gos. Erm., no. 22, 1962: 60–64.

239. Varshavskii, S. Nakhodka v Kaliksauake [A find in Calixlauca] Vokrug sveta, no. 12, Dec. 1961: 21.
Antiquities.

240. Zhdanova, L. Iskusstvo drevnei Meksiki [The art of ancient Mexico] Dekorat. isk. SSSR, no. 1, Jan. 1961: 21–26.

h. Peru

241. Uvarova, I. Iskusstvo naskov [The art of the Nazcas] Iskusstvo, v. 27, no. 5, 1964: 54–57.
Indian art.

C. ETHNOLOGY

1. Writings Dealing With Three or More Countries

242. Efimov, Aleksei Vladimirovich, *and* Sergei Aleksandrovich Tokarev, *eds.* Narody Ameriki. t. 2. TSentral'naia i IUzhnaia Amerika [The peoples of America. v. 2. Central and South America] Moscow, Izd-vo Akad. nauk SSSR, 1959. 670 p.   E18.A38
Reviewed by B. N. Semevskii and A. A. Dolinin in *Izv. Vses. geog. ob-va*, v. 96, no. 2, Mar.-Apr. 1964: 145–147; by M. S. Al'perovich in *Sov. etn.*, no. 3, May-June 1960: 199–206; by B. I. Bruk in *Vest. ist. mir. kul't.*, no. 1, Jan.-Feb. 1960: 136–142 [in English].

243. Fainberg, L. A. O formakh sotsial'noi organizatsii indeitsev severo-zapadnoi

chasti basseina Amazonki v kontse XIX-nachale XX v. [Forms of social organization of the Indians of the north-western part of the Amazon Basin at the end of the 19th century and in the beginning of the 20th century] Trudy Inst. etn., v. 58, 1960: 127–155.

244. Zibert, E. V.   Kollektsii cheshskogo issledovatelia A. V. Fricha v sobraniiakh MAE [Collections of the Czech explorer A. V. Frič in the Museum of Anthropology and Ethnography] Sbor. Muz. ant. i etn., v. 20, 1961: 125–143.
Indians of South America.

245. Zubov, A. Review. Vop. antr., no. 12, 1962: 157–158.
A review of Juan Comas' *Relaciones inter-raciales en América Latina; 1940–1960* (Mexico City, Universidad Nacional Autó-noma de México, 1961. 77 p.).
Ethnology.

2. Individual Countries

a. *Argentina*

246. Zubov, A. Liudi Ognennoi Zemli [The people of Tierra del Fuego] Moscow, Geografgiz, 1961. 40 p.
Indians.

b. *Bolivia*

247. Camacho Ruiz, Rubén. Narod, kotoryi zhivet v proshlom [A people who live in the past] Nauka i zhizn', v. 29, no. 6, June 1962: 86–87.
Indians.
Translated from the Spanish.

c. *Brazil*

248. Loukotka,   Čestmir.   Material'naia kul'tura   maloizvestnogo   indeiskogo plemeni shtata Parana, Braziliia [Material culture of a little-known Indian tribe in the Brazilian state of Paraná] Sov. etn., no. 3, May-June 1964: 134–138.

See also entries no. 3227, 3229, 3232, and 3233.

d. *Chile (including Easter Island)*

249. Butinov, N. A.   Korotkoukhie i dlin-noukhie na ostrove Paskhi ["The short-eared" and "the long-eared" on Easter Island] Sov. etn., no. 1, Jan.-Feb. 1960: 72–82.
Ethnology.

250. Nechistaia sila khodit sleva [The evil spirit comes from the left] Nauka i rel., v. 4, no. 3, Mar. 1963: 78.
Superstition on Easter Island.

e. *Cuba*

251. Dridzo, A. D.   Naselenie Kuby [The population of Cuba] Sov. etn., no. 2, Mar.-Apr. 1960: 123–135.
Ethnology.

f. *Ecuador*

252. Molchanov, V. Znakomstvo s aukami prodolzhaetsia [They continue their friendly contacts with the Aucas] Vokrug sveta, no. 4, Apr. 1959: 24–25.
Indians.

See also entries no. 411 and 3237.

g. *The Guianas*

See entry no. 3239.

h. *Jamaica*

253. Dridzo, A. D.   Naselenie IAmaiki [The population of Jamaica] Sov. etn., no. 5, Sept.-Oct. 1962: 100–110.
Ethnology.

i. *Mexico*

254. Chichkov, V. Masateki zhivut v dzhun-gliakh [Mazatecs live in the jungle] Vokrug sveta, no. 5, May 1964: 46–48.
Mazatec Indians.

255. Gamboa, Fernando. Prazdniki meksi-kanskogo naroda [Holidays of the Mexican people] Dekorat. isk. SSSR, no. 1, Jan. 1961: 27–31.
Decorative folk art.

256. Maldonado, Sandra. "Kalaveras," sta-rinnye meksikanskie obychai [The "Cala-veras," old Mexican customs] Zhen. mira, no. 10, 1962: 23–26.

See also entries no. 3240 and 3242.

j. Paraguay

257. Vikhotskii, G. Sokrovishcha Karai Puku [The treasures of Karai Puku] Vokrug sveta, no. 9, Sept. 1959: 62.
Ethnography.
A review of Alberto Vojtěch Frič's *Prikliucheniia okhotnika v Gran-Chako* (Moscow, Geografgiz, 1958. 141 p.).

k. Trinidad and Tobago

258. Dridzo, A. D. Indiitsy ostrova Trinidad [The East Indians of Trinidad Island] Strany i nar. Vost., no. 2, 1961: 89–102.

259. Fainberg, L. A. Naselenie Trinidada i Tobago [The population of Trinidad and Tobago] Sov. etn., no. 6, Nov.-Dec. 1962: 14–16.
Ethnology.

l. Venezuela

260. Kak i piat' vekov nazad zhivut indeitsy v Venesuele [The Indians of Venezuela are living as they did five centuries ago] Zhen. mira, no. 3, 1962: 23–26.

261. Kinzhalov, R. V. Drama kiche "Rabinal'-achi" ["Rabinal-Achi," a Quiché drama] Vest. ist. mir. kul't., no. 5, Sept.-Oct. 1961: 92–96.
Literature of Guatemalan Indians.

D. ETHNOHISTORY

1. Writings Dealing With Three or More Countries

262. Efimov, Aleksei Vladimirovich, *and* I. A. Zolotarevskaia, *eds.* Kul'tura indeitsev; vklad korennogo naseleniia Ameriki v mirovuiu kul'turu [The culture of the Indians; the contribution of the aboriginal population of America to world culture] Moscow, Izd-vo Akad. nauk SSSR, 1963. 326 p.   E58.A45
Reviewed by S. Vorob'ev in *Nov. mir*, v. 40, no. 3, Mar. 1964: 278–279; by IA. G. Mashbits in *Vop. ist.*, no. 8, Aug. 1964: 156–157; by Sh. Bogina in *Sov. etn.*, no. 5, Sept.-Oct. 1964: 180–183.

263. Danysz, Pernette. Zhili li liudi v Amerike za 30.000 let do nashei ery? [Did man live in America 30,000 years before our era?] V zashch. mira, no. 12, Dec. 1960: 82–90.
Remnants of prehistoric man.

264. Echevarria, Carmen. Dvadtsat' vekov tsivilizatsii Maiia [The twenty-centuries old civilization of the Maya] Zhen. mira, no. 6, 1962: 23–26.

265. Gorbovskii, A. Zagadki drevnei istorii [Puzzles of ancient history] Baikal, v. 8, no. 4, July-Aug. 1962: 50–60, 63–84.
The origin of the American Indians.

266. Guliaev, V. Amerika i Staryi Svet v dokolumbovu epokhu [America and the Old World before Columbus] Nauka i zhizn', v. 30, no. 7, July 1964: 97–102; v. 31, no. 9, Sept. 1964: 126–134.

267. Kinzhalov, R. Novye raboty po kul'ture drevnei Ameriki [New studies on the ancient culture of America] Sov. etn., no. 1, Jan.-Feb. 1963: 163–166.
A review of *Essays in Pre-Columbian Art and Archaeology* by Samuel K. Lothrop and others (Cambridge, Harvard University Press, 1961. 507 p.).

268. ———. Review. Sov. arkheol., v. 4, no. 3, 1960: 353.
A review of Herbert Joseph Spinden's *Maya Art and Civilization* (Indian Hills, Colo., Falcon's Wing Press, 1957. 432 p.).

269. Materialy Instituta marksizma-leninizma pri TsK KPSS; iz neopublikovannykh rukopisei Karla Marksa [Materials of the Institute of Marxism-Leninism of the Central Committee of the CPSU; unpublished manuscripts of Karl Marx] Nar. Azii i Afr., no. 2, 1962: 3–17.
Land tenure in the pre-Columbian period.

270. Varshavskii, A. Tainy maiia; po sledam drevnikh tsivilizatsii [Secrets of the Mayas; tracing the history of ancient civilizations] Znan.-sila, no. 12, Dec. 1963: 45–48.

271. Viernes, A. Indeitsy i ikh kul'tura [Indians and their culture] V zashch. mira, no. 102, Nov. 1959: 79–85.
Maya Indians.

272. Zubov, A. A. Review. Vop. antr., no. 9, 1962: 145–146.
Pygmies.

A review of Juan Comas' ¿ *Pigmeos en América?* (Mexico City, Universidad Nacional Autónoma de México, 1960. 54 p.).

See also entry no. 287.

2. Individual Countries

a. Chile (*including Easter Island*)

273. Butinov, N. A. O "teorii beloi rasy" i o plavaniiakh s zapada na vostok v Tikhom Okeane [The "white race theory" and the voyages from west to east in the Pacific] Sov. etn., no. 4, July-Aug. 1963: 154–156.
Origin of the population of Easter Island.

274. Heyerdahl, Thor. Otvet "Sovetskoi etnografii" [My answer to "Sovetskaia etnografiia"] Sov. etn., no. 4, July-Aug. 1963: 120–139.
Origin of the population of Easter Island.

275. ———. Razgadka tain ostrova Paskhi [How we solved the secrets of Easter Island] Nauka i zhizn', v. 30, no. 12, Dec. 1963: 33–38.

276. ———. Statui ostrova Paskhi; problemy i itogi [Statues of Easter Island; problems and conclusions] Nov. mir, v. 38, no. 9, Sept. 1962: 216–229.
Translated from the Norwegian.

277. ———. Tainy ostrova Paskhi raskryty [How we solved the secrets of Easter Island] Nauka i chelovechestvo, 1963: 142–161.

278. Kinzhalov, R. V. O stat'e T. Kheierdala "Otvet 'Sovetskoi etnografii' " [On T. Heyerdahl's article "My answer to 'Sovetskaia etnografiia' "] Sov. etn., no. 4, July-Aug. 1963: 140–142.
Origin of the population of Easter Island.

279. Knorozov, IU. V. Legendy o zaselenii ostrova Paskhi [Legends on the settlement of population on Easter Island] Sov. etn., no. 4, July-Aug. 1963: 143–153.

280. Kondratov, A. "Kokhau rongo-rongo khraniat tainu" [The rongorongo wooden tablets retain their secrets] Zvezda, no. 6, June 1964: 152–161.
Inscriptions on Easter Island.

281. Zhdanov, L. S zapada ili s vostoka? [From the west or from the east?] Vokrug sveta, no. 5, May 1962: 49–51, 59.
Origin of the population of Easter Island.

b. Mexico

282. Al'perovich, M. S. K voprosu o chislennosti indeiskogo naseleniia Meksiki v kolonial'nyi period [On the question of the numerical strength of the Indian population in Mexico during the colonial period] Sov. etn., no. 3, May-June 1962: 71–80.

283. ———. Sotsial'nyi stroi drevnikh atstekov [The social system of the ancient Aztecs] Vop. ist., v. 39, no. 4, Apr. 1964: 198–199.

284. V zashchitu indeitsev Taraumara [In defense of the Tarahumara Indians] Inostr. lit., no. 9, Sept. 1961: 281.
A review of Fernando Benítez' *Viaje a la Tarahumara* (Mexico City, Ediciones Era, 1960. 86 p.).

c. Paraguay

285. Mozheiko, I. Plemia, kotorogo net [A tribe which is no longer here] Vokrug sveta, no. 11, Nov. 1964: 34–37.
Indians.

d. Peru

286. Heyerdahl, Thor. Na plotakh—protiv vetra [Against the wind on rafts] Nauka i zhizn', v. 30, no. 2, Feb. 1963: 70–73.
The voyages of ancient Indians.
Translated from the Norwegian.

IV

HISTORY

❦

A. WRITINGS DEALING WITH THREE OR MORE COUNTRIES

287. Efimov, Aleksei Vladimirovich, *and others*, *eds*. Natsii Latinskoi Ameriki; formirovanie, razvitie [The formation and development of the Latin American nations] Moscow, Nauka, 1964. 442 p.

F1410.N3

Reviewed by E. L. Rovinskaia in *Nov. i noveish. ist.*, no. 6, 1964: 129–131.

288. Gonionskii, Semen Aleksandrovich. Ocherki noveishei istorii stran Latinskoi Ameriki [Studies on the recent history of Latin American countries] Moscow, Prosveshchenie, 1964. 384 p.   DLC

289. Lavretskii, Iosif Romual'dovich. Bolivar. Moscow, Mol. gvardiia, 1960. 285 p.

F2235.3.L387

Reviewed by IU. Zubritskii in *Ogonek*, v. 38, no. 40, Oct. 1960: 18; by M. Okuneva in *Mol. gvard.*, no. 4, Apr. 1961: 225–226; by V. Kuteishchikova in *Kul't. i zhizn'*, v. 4, no. 8, 1960: 60.

290. Lavrov, N. M., *ed*. Voina za nezavisimost' v Latinskoi Amerike, 1810–1826 [The War for Independence in Latin America, 1810–1826] Moscow, Nauka, 1964. 316 p.

291. Popol vuh. Rodoslovnaia vladyk Totonikapana [Genealogy of the rulers of Totonicopán] Moscow, Izd-vo Akad. nauk SSSR, 1959. 251 p.

F1465.P8387

Translated from the Quiche language under the supervision of R. V. Kinzhalov.

Reviewed by I. Lavretskii in *Inostr. lit.*, no. 12, Dec. 1960: 249; by D. Sergeev in *Vest. ist. mir. kul't.*, no. 3, May-June 1961: 154–155 [In English].

292. Revunenkov, Vladimir Georgievich. Istoriia stran Latinskoi Ameriki v noveishee vremia [Recent history of the countries of Latin America] Moscow, Vyssh. shkola, 1963. 457 p.

F1414.R46

Reviewed by V. K. Furaev in *Vest. LGU*, v. 19, no. 14, 1964: 146–148.

293. Slezkin, Lev IUr'evich. Rossiia i voina za nezavisimost' v Ispanskoi Amerike [Russia and the War for Independence in Spanish America] Moscow, Nauka, 1964. 381 p.   F1412.S55

294. Thomas, Alfred Barnaby. Istoriia Latinskoi Ameriki [Latin America; a history] Moscow, Izd-vo inostr. lit., 1960. 647 p.

Translated by I. Z. Romanov from the English. Introductory article by M. S. Al'perovich and L. IU. Slezkin.

Reviewed by E. S. Dabagian in *Vest. ist. mir. kul't.*, no. 5, Sept.-Oct. 1961: 119–125.

295. Vol'skii, Viktor Votslavovich, *and others*, *eds*. Latinskaia Amerika v proshlom i nastoiashchem; sbornik statei po ekonomike, istorii i kul'ture stran Latinskoi Ameriki [Latin America in the past and present; collected articles on the economy, history, and culture of the Latin American countries] Moscow, Sotsekgiz, 1960. 464 p.   HC165.L35

Reviewed by B. Kostritsyn in *Kul't. i zhizn'*, v. 4, no. 8, 1960: 61–62; by A. Glinkin in *Mir. ekon. i mezhdunar. otn.*, no. 5, May 1961: 145–149; by B. I. Koval' in *Nov. i noveish. ist.*, no. 4, 1960: 151–153; by M. A. Okuneva in *Vest. ist. mir. kul't.*, no. 3, May-June 1961: 149–154.

296. Al'perovich, Moisei Samoilovich. Izuchenie istorii stran Latinskoi Ameriki [Studying the history of Latin American

countries] *In* Akademiia nauk SSSR. Institut istorii. Sovetskaia istoricheskaia nauka ot XX k XXII s"ezdu KPSS; istoriia Zapadnoi Evropy i Ameriki. Sbornik statei. Moscow, Izd-vo Akad. nauk SSSR, 1963. p. 151–170.

D13.A52

297. ———. Novye raboty ob osvoboditel'noi voine 1810–1826 gg. v Ispanskoi Amerike [New works on the liberation war of 1810–1826 in Spanish America] Nov. i noveish. ist., no. 4, 1964: 151–154.

298. Beseda sovetskikh istorikov s Uil'iamom Z. Fosterom [Soviet historians' talk with William Z. Foster] Nov. i noveish. ist., no. 3, 1959: 162–163.
Some problems of Latin American history.

299. Bolkhovitinov, N. N. Otnoshenie Rossii k nachalu voiny Latinskoi Ameriki za nezavisimost' [Position of the Russian Government in the early stage of the Latin American Wars of Independence] Ist. arkh., v. 8, no. 3, May-June, 1962: 120–131.

300. Ermolaev, V. I. Nekotorye voprosy osvoboditel'noi bor'by amerikanskikh kolonii Ispanii i Portugalii [Some problems concerning the liberation struggle of Spanish and Portuguese colonies in America] Nov. i noveish. ist., no. 3, 1960: 23–37.

301. ———. Pod"em revoliutsionnogo dvizheniia v Latinskoi Amerike, 1918–1923 gg. [The intensification of the revolutionary movement in Latin America, 1918–1923] *In* Akademiia nauk SSSR. Otdelenie istoricheskikh nauk. Mezhdunarodnoe znachenie Velikoi Oktiabr'skoi sotsialisticheskoi revoliutsii. Moscow, Sotsekgiz, [1959]. p. 495–541.

DK265.9. I5A6

302. ———. Vozniknovenie pervykh rabochikh organizatsii i marksistskikh kruzhkov v stranakh Latinskoi Ameriki, 1870–1900 gg. [The rise of the first workers' organizations and Marxist groups in Latin American countries, 1870–1900] Vop. ist., no. 1, Jan. 1959: 81–97.

303. Foster, William Z. Revoliutsiia 1810–1826 godov v Latinskoi Amerike [The Latin American Revolution of 1810–1826] Vop. ist., no. 5, May 1961: 48–50.
Translated from the English original which appeared in *Political Affairs*, Nov. 1960.

304. Ganelin, R. Sh. Popytki razvitiia ekonomicheskikh sviazei mezhdu Rossiei i stranami Latinskoi Ameriki v kontse XIX-nachale XX v. [Attempts to develop economic relations between Russia and the countries of Latin America at the end of the 19th and the beginning of the 20th century] Trudy LOII AN SSSR, no. 4, 1962: 315–358.

305. Glushko, I. F. Iz istorii latinoamerikanskikh stran v kontse XVIII-nachale XIX v. [From the history of Latin American countries in the late 18th and the early 19th century] Nov. i noveish. ist., no. 6, 1959: 162–163.
A review of the periodical *Revista de historia de América* (Mexico City, 1960–1961).

306. Grigor'ev, IA. G. Burzhuazno-reformistskaia kontseptsiia natsional'no-osvoboditel'nogo dvizheniia v Latinskoi Amerike [A bourgeois and reformist conception of the national liberation movement in Latin America] Vop. ist., v. 39, no. 11, Nov. 1964: 201–202.

307. Grigor'ian, IU. M. Evropeiskii torgovyi kapital v Latinskoi Amerike v XVI veke [European merchant capital in 16th-century Latin America] Vop. ist., no. 11, Nov. 1962: 199–200.

308. ———. Iz istorii kolonial'nogo proniknoveniia Germanii v IUzhnuiu Ameriku v XV–XVI vekakh [From the history of German colonial penetration into Latin America in the 15th and 16th centuries] Vop. ist., no. 9, Sept. 1961: 187–188.

309. ———. Latinskaia Amerika v bor'be za nezavisimost'; nauchnaia konferentsiia v Institute Latinskoi Ameriki AN SSSR [Latin America's struggle for independence; a conference in the Institute of Latin America of the Academy of Sciences of the USSR] Nov. i noveish. ist., no. 4, 1964: 192–193.

310. Guber, A. A., *and* N. M. Lavrov. K 150-letiiu voiny za nezavisimost' Latinskoi Ameriki [The 150th anniversary of

the Latin American War for Independence] Nov. i noveish. ist., no. 4, 1960: 11–18.

311. Kedrov, A. I. Politika SShA v Latinskoi Amerike v gody vtoroi mirovoi voiny v traktovke amerikanskikh burzhuaznykh istorikov [How American bourgeois historians present U.S. policy in Latin America during the Second World War] Vop. ist., no. 11, Nov. 1961: 172–182.

312. Khronika [Brief notes] Nov. i noveish. ist., no. 4, 1960: 189.
A paper on the War of Independence, 1806–1830.

313. Kolybin, B. I. K 150-letiiu voiny za nezavisimost' v Latinskoi Amerike [The 150th anniversary of the War of Independence in Latin America] Vop. ist., no. 8, Aug. 1960: 172–174.

314. Komissarov, B. N. Ob otnoshenii Rossii k voine Ispanskoi Ameriki za nezavisimost'; po materialam arkhiva V. M. Miroshevskogo [Russia's attitude to the war of Spanish America for its independence; a study based on materials from the V. M. Miroshevskii archives] Vest. LGU, v. 19, no. 8, 1964: 60–71.
Summary in English.

315. ———. Zametki o Latinskoi Amerike v "Zhurnale" F. F. Matiushkina, 1817–1818 gg. [Notes on Latin America in F. F. Matiushkin's "Journal," 1817–1818] Vest. LGU, v. 17, no. 2, 1962: 165–166.
Summary in English.

316. Koval', B. I. Politika Anglii v TSentral'noi Amerike, 1823–1850 gg. [English policy in Central America, 1823–1850] Vop. ist., no. 3, Mar. 1961: 214.

317. Lavretskii, I. Bolivar perekhodit Andy; otryvok iz knigi [Bolivar crosses the Andes; excerpt from a book] Vokrug sveta, no. 5, May 1960: 21–23.

318. ———. Katolicheskaia tserkov' i voina za nezavisimost' Ispanskoi Ameriki [The Catholic Church and the Wars of Independence in Spanish America] Nov. i noveish. ist., no. 3, 1961: 70–84.
Summary in English, p. 173.

319. ———. Konferentsiia, posviashchennaia istorii osvoboditel'nogo dvizheniia v Latinskoi Amerike [A conference devoted to the history of the Latin American liberation movement] Vop. ist., no. 1, Jan. 1961: 207–210.

320. ———. Review. Vop. ist., no. 12, Dec. 1959: 94–107.
A review of the periodical The Hispanic-American Historical Review (Baltimore, 1956–1958).

321. ———. Izuchenie istorii Latinskoi Ameriki [Studies of the history of Latin America] Vest. AN SSSR, v. 32, no. 8, Aug. 1962: 128–129.

322. ———. 150-letie nachala voiny za nezavisimost' [Sesquicentennial of the beginning of the War of Independence] Kul't. i zhizn', v. 4, no. 8, 1960: 10–13.

323. Lavrov, N. M., and A. M. Zorina. Strany Latinskoi Ameriki v 1918–1939 gg. [The Latin American countries in the years 1918–1939] In Akademiia nauk SSSR. Institut istorii. Noveishaia istoriia stran Zapadnoi Evropy i Ameriki, 1918–1939. v. 1. Moscow, Sotsekgiz, 1959. p. 649–709.   D443.A37

324. Literatura po novoi i noveishei istorii stran Latinskoi Ameriki, opublikovannaia v SSSR v 1945–1960 godakh [Soviet studies on the modern and recent history of Latin America published in 1945–1960] Nov. i noveish. ist., no. 4, 1960: 175–178.

325. Markov, W., and M. Kossok. O popytkakh reaktsionnoi istoriografii reabilitirovat' ispanskii kolonializm v Amerike [Attempts of reactionary historiography to exonerate Spanish colonialism in America] Nov. i noveish. ist., no. 4, 1960: 130–141.

326. Mashbits, IA. G. Marksistskaia kritika idealisticheskikh kontseptsii kolonizatsii Latinskoi Ameriki [Marxist criticism of the idealist conception of the colonization of Latin America] Vop. ist., v. 39, no. 10, Oct. 1964: 205–206.

327. Matveeva, N. R. Braziliia i strany La Platy posle Paragvaiskoi voiny, 1864–1870 [Brazil and the countries of the Río

de la Plata Valley after the Paraguayan War, 1864–1870] Uch. zap. Kalininsk. ped. inst., v. 35, 1963: 246–282.

328. Mel'nikova, G. A., *and* L. V. Pegusheva. 150-letie voiny za nezavisimost' stran Latinskoi Ameriki i SSSR [The USSR and the 150th anniversary of the Latin American War of Independence] Vest. ist. mir. kul't., no. 5, Sept.-Oct. 1961: 151–158.

329. Neruda, Pablo. Pobeda, oderzhannaia narodom [The triumph of the people] Kul't. i zhizn', v. 4, no. 8, 1960: 7–8.
    Wars of Independence.

330. Pechuro, E. A. Lzhefilosofiia burzhuaznogo sotsiologa [The pseudophilosophy of a bourgeois sociologist] Vop. ist., no. 3, Mar. 1962: 195–196.

331. Pintos, Francisco R., *and* L. Sala. O nekotorykh predposylkakh i protivorechiiakh osvoboditel'noi revoliutsii na Rio-de-la-Plate [Some premises and contradictions of the liberation movement in the Río de la Plata Valley] Nov. i noveish. ist., no. 4, 1961: 18–30.
    Summary in English, p. 198.

332. Ponomarev, N. Iz istorii postroiki Kolumbom vodianykh mel'nits v zapadnom polusharii [From the history of the construction of water mills by Columbus in the Western Hemisphere] Muk.-elev. prom., v. 29, no. 6, June 1963: 31.

333. Shtrakhov, A. I. Osvoboditel'naia bor'ba naroda La-Platy v 1810–1816 godakh [The liberation struggle of the people of the La Plata Valley, 1810–1816] Nov. i noveish. ist., no. 4, 1960: 19–35.

334. Slezkin, L. IU. O solidarnosti peredovoi russkoi obshchestvennosti s patriotami Latinskoi Ameriki, 1810–1826 gg. [Solidarity of the progressive elements of Russian society with the patriots of Latin America, 1810–1826] Nov. i noveish. ist., no. 4, 1960: 71–80.

335. ———. Pozitsiia Rossii v otnoshenii Ispanskoi Ameriki na rubezhe 18–19 vekov [Russia's attitude toward Spanish America in the late 18th and the early 19th century] Vop. ist., v. 38, no. 6, June 1963: 47–59.
    Summary in English, p. 219.

336. 150[Stopiatidesiati]-letie bor'by Latinskoi Ameriki za nezavisimost' [The one hundred and fiftieth anniversary of the Latin American struggle for independence] Vest. AN SSSR, v. 30, no. 7, July 1960: 113–114.

337. Strany Latinskoi Ameriki [The countries of Latin America] *In* Revunenkov, Vladimir Georgievich, *and others.* Noveishaia istoriia; malye strany Zapadnoi Evropy, strany Latinskoi Ameriki, Kanada. Moscow, Uchpedgiz, 1960. p. 85–197.   HC54.R4
    Reviewed by M. IA. Domnich and others in *Nov. i noveish. ist.,* no. 4, 1960: 101–114.

338. Tarasov, V. B. Burzhuaznye istoriki SShA o problemakh Latinskoi Ameriki [U. S. bourgeois historians discuss the problems of Latin America] Nov. i noveish. ist., no. 5, 1963: 171–172.

339. Zorina, A. M. Izuchenie istorii Latinskoi Ameriki v GDR [Studies on the history of Latin America in the German Democratic Republic] Nov. i noveish. ist., no. 2, 1963: 165–166.
    A review of *Lateinamerika zwischen Emanzipation und Imperialismus, 1810–1960* (Berlin, Akademie-Verlag, 1961. 297 p.).

See also entries no. 1715 and 4545.

B. INDIVIDUAL COUNTRIES

1. Argentina

340. Ermolaev, Vasilii Ivanovich, *and others.* Ocherki istorii Argentiny [Studies on the history of Argentina] Moscow, Sotsekgiz, 1961. 571 p.   F2831.E7
    Reviewed by A. N. Glinkin in *Nov. i noveish. ist.,* no. 3, 1962: 142–145.

341. Demushkina, E. V. Unitarii i federalisty v Argentine [Unitarians and federalists in Argentina] Nov. i noveish. ist., no. 6, 1964: 155–156.

342. Domingo Faustino Sarm'iento, 1811–1888 [Domingo Faustino Sarmiento, 1811–1888] Vsesvit, v. 4, no. 4, Apr. 1961: 64.
    Domingo Faustino Sarmiento, the Argentine writer and statesman.

343. García, L. M., *and* I. F. Glushko. Problemy istorii Argentiny [Problems of

Argentine history] Nov. i noveish. ist., no. 1, 1959: 187–188.

A review of the periodical *Cuadernos de cultura* (Buenos Aires, 1960).

344. Ivannikov, A. E. Kratkaia istoriia Argentiny [Brief history of Argentina] Nov. i noveish. ist., no. 1, 1959: 201–202.

A review of Alvaro Yunque's *Breve historia de los argentinos* (Buenos Aires, Editorial Futuro, 1957. 373 p.).

345. Oliver, María Rosa. Domingo Faustino Sarmiento, 15 fevralia 1811—11 sentiabria 1888 [Domingo Faustino Sarmiento, February 15, 1811—September 11, 1888] V zashch. mira, no. 7/8, July-Aug. 1961: 131–139.

346. ———. Zaria nad Rio-de-la-Plata [Dawn over the Río de la Plata] Ogonek, v. 38, no. 22, May 1960: 11.

Translated from the Spanish.

347. Sarmiento, Domingo Faustino. Gaucho v XIX veke [Gauchos in the 19th century] V zashch. mira, no. 7/8, July–Aug. 1961: 141–143.

2. Bolivia

348. Ruiz González, Raúl. Boliviia—Prometei And [Bolivia, the Prometheus of the Andes] Moscow, Izd-vo inostr. lit., 1963. 336 p.

Translated by D. A. D'iakonov and M. I. Poliakov from the Spanish *Bolivia, el prometeo de los Andes*. Introductory article by I. Ershov.

See also entry no. 3100.

3. Brazil

349. Ermolaev, Vasilii Ivanovich, *ed.* Ocherki istorii Brazilii [Studies on the history of Brazil] Moscow, Sotsekgiz, 1962. 567 p.

Reviewed by V. B. Tarasov and Z. M. Khazanov in *Nov. i noveish. ist.*, no. 4, 1963: 157–160; by IU. A. Antonov and others in *Vop. ist.*, v. 39, no. 5, May 1964: 143–147.

350. Faco, Rui. Braziliia XX stoletiia [Brazil in the 20th century] Moscow, Izd-vo inostr. lit., 1962. 303 p.

Translated by D. D'iakonov and V. Stoliarov from the Portuguese *Brasil, século XX*. Introductory article by A. Shul'govskii.

351. Glinkin, Anatolii Nikolaevich. Noveishaia istoriia Brazilii, 1939–1959 [Recent history of Brazil, 1939–1959] Moscow, Izd-vo IMO, 1961. 403 p. DLC

Reviewed by I. Lavretskii in *Nov. i noveish. ist.*, no. 2, 1962: 151–154; by S. Mikhailov in *Mezhdunar. zhizn'*, v. 9, no. 5, May 1962: 132–136; by B. I. Kolybin and I. E. Rybalkin in *Vop. ist.*, v. 38, no. 1, Jan. 1963: 139–141; by S. Vorob'ev in *Nov. mir*, v. 38, no. 6, June 1962: 281.

352. Rocha Pombo, José Francisco da. Istoriia Brazilii [History of Brazil] Moscow, Izd-vo inostr. lit., 1962. 439 p.

Translated by IU. V. Dashkevich and V. I. Pokhvalin from the Portuguese *Historia do Brasil*. Introductory article by A. M. Khazanov.

Reviewed by A. M. Filippov in *Nov. i noveish. ist.*, no. 6, 1962: 165–166.

353. Faco, Rui. Krest'ianskaia voina v Kanudose [The peasant war in the Canudos region] Nov. i noveish. ist., no. 1, 1959: 105–123.

Translated from the Portuguese.

354. Kolybin, B. I. Istoriografiia Brazilii, 1808–1889 [Historiography of Brazil, 1808–1889] Vop. ist., no. 1, Jan. 1961: 199–201.

355. Koval', B. I. Iz istorii revoliutsionnykh boev 1935 goda v Brazilii [History of the revolutionary struggle of 1935 in Brazil] Nov. i noveish. ist., no. 2, 1962: 15–28.

Summary in English, p. 181.

356. ———. K voprosu o sotsial'no-ekonomicheskom razvitii Brazilii v seredine XIX veka [The socioeconomic development of Brazil in the mid-19th century] Vop. ist., v. 38, no. 2, Feb. 1963: 112–121.

Summary in English, p. 222.

357. ———. O roli plantatsionnogo rabstva v koloniiakh dlia pervonachal'nogo nakopleniia kapitalov v Zapadnoi Evrope; na materialakh istorii Brazilii [Role of slave labor on colonial plantations in the primary accumulation of capital in Western Europe; based on the materials of Brazilian history] Sred. veka, no. 23, 1963: 198–215.

358. ———. O sotsial'no-politicheskom razvitii Brazilii v kontse XIX–XX veke

[Social and political development of Brazil in the late 19th and the 20th century] Vop. ist., no. 9, Sept. 1962: 188–189.

359. ———. Review. Nov. i noveish. ist., no. 5, 1961: 184–186.

Review of Rui Faco's *Brasil, Século XX* (Rio de Janeiro, Vitória, 1960. 261 p.).

360. Mashbits, IA. G. Khoziaistvo Meksiki i Brazilii v kolonial'nyi period [The national economy of Mexico and Brazil in the colonial period] Vop. ist., no. 11, Nov. 1961: 195–196.

361. Mel'nikova, G. Obsuzhdenie maketa "Ocherkov istorii Brazilii" [Discussing the plan of "Studies on the history of Brazil"] Nov. i noveish. ist., no. 4, 1959: 182–183.

See also entries no. 198, 327, 428, and 1440.

4. Chile

362. Kapskii, E. V. Review. Nov. i noveish. ist., no. 1, 1960: 151–153.

A review of Hernán Ramírez Necochea's *Balmaceda y la contrarrevolución de 1891* (Santiago de Chile, Editorial Universitaria, 1958. 243 p.).

363. Neruda, Pablo. Rukopis' bortsa za svobodu [Manuscript of a fighter for freedom] Ogonek, v. 38, no. 24, June 1960: 14.

See also entries no. 2744 and 3156.

5. Colombia

364. Grigulevich, I. R. Review. Nov. i noveish. ist., no. 2, 1960: 182–185.

A review of Anteo Quimbaya's *Cuestiones colombianas; ensayos de interpretación y crítica* (Bogotá, Ediciones Suramérica, 1958. 338 p.).

365. Il'ina, N. G. Narodnoe vosstanie v Bogote 9 aprelia 1948 goda [The popular uprising in Bogota on April 9, 1948] Nov. i noveish. ist., no. 6, 1964: 87–95.

Summary in English, p. 182.

6. Costa Rica

366. Rybalkin, I. E. Grazhdanskaia voina 1948 goda v Kosta-Rike [The civil war of 1948 in Costa Rica] Nov. i noveish. ist. no. 4, 1959: 55–71.

7. Cuba

367. Efimov, Aleksei Vladimirovich, *and* I. R. Grigulevich, eds. Kuba; istoriko-etnograficheskie ocherki [Cuba; historical and ethnographical studies] Moscow, Izd-vo Akad. nauk SSSR, 1961. 559 p.

368. ———. Kuba; istoriko-etnograficheskie ocherki [Cuba; historical and ethnographical studies] 2d enl. ed. Moscow, Izd-vo Akad. nauk SSSR, 1961. 598 p.

F1788.K8

Reviewed by V. Afanas'ev in *Sov. etn.*, no. 6, Nov.-Dec. 1961: 143–148; by L. A. Gaidukova in *Izv. AN SSSR. Ser. geog.*, no. 1, Jan.-Feb. 1962: 158–159; by E. S. Dabagian in *Vop. ist.*, no. 12, Dec. 1962: 136–138; by S. D. Skazkin in *Vest. AN SSSR*, v. 32, no. 2, Feb. 1962: 116–118; by Sergei L'vov in *Nov. mir*, v. 38, no. 3, Mar. 1963: 276–278; by E. Litavrina in *Prep. ist. v shkole*, v. 17, no. 4, July-Aug. 1962: 105–106; by IA. Mashbits in *Vop. ekon.*, no. 9, Sept. 1963: 120–123; by E. Surenian in *Nov. i noveish. ist.*, no. 6, 1961: 149–150.

369. Foner, Philip Sheldon. Istoriia Kuby i ee otnoshenii s SShA [A history of Cuba and its relations with the United States] v. 1. 1492–1845. Moscow, Izd-vo inostr. lit., 1963. 303 p.

Translated by V. L. Kon from the English. Introductory article by A. M. Zorina.

Reviewed by L. I. Zubok in *Nov. i noveish. ist.*, no. 1, Jan. 1963: 170–171; by S. Gonionskii in *Nov. vrem.*, v. 21, no. 31, Aug. 1963: 29–31.

370. ———. Istoriia Kuby i ee otnoshenii s SShA. t. 2. Ot ery anneksionizma do nachala vtoroi voiny za nezavisimost' (1845–1895 gg.) [A history of Cuba and its relations with the United States. v. 2. From the era of annexationism to the beginning of the second war for independence (1845–1895)] Moscow, Progress, 1964. 472 p.

Translated by A. O. Zelenina and N. F. Paisov from the English. Introductory article by A. M. Zorina.

371. Grinevich, Emiliia Andreevna. Stranitsy istorii Kuby, 1939–1952 gg. [Pages of Cuban history, 1939–1952] Moscow, Mezhdunarodnye otnosheniia, 1964. 184 p.

DLC

372. Núñez Jiménez, Antonio. Respublika Kuba; istoricheskii ocherk [The Republic

of Cuba; a historical study] Moscow, Sotsekgiz, 1963. 134 p.

Translated by A. A. Kartsev and S. A. Pakin from the Spanish. Introductory article by S. S. Mikhailov. Also published in Lithuanian.

373. Shustov, K. S. Kuba v planakh imperializma SShA do i posle amerikano-ispanskoi voiny, 1895–1902 gg. [Cuba in the plans of U. S. imperialism before and after the Spanish-American War, 1895–1902] Alma-Ata, Kazakh. gos. un-t im. S. M. Kirova, 1963. 27 p.

Author's abstract of a dissertation for the degree of Candidate in Historical Sciences.

374. Vartanov, Grigorii Akopovich. Revoliutsionnaia Kuba [Revolutionary Cuba] Leningrad, O-vo po raspr. polit. i nauchn. znanii RSFSR, 1963. 71 p.   F1788.V36

375. Zorina, A. M. Iz geroicheskogo proshlogo kubinskogo naroda [From the heroic past of the Cuban people] Moscow, Izd-vo Akad. nauk SSSR, 1961. 302 p.   DLC

Reviewed by M. I. Mokhnachev in *Nov. i noveish. ist.*, no. 1, 1962: 153–155.

376. Al'perovich, M. S. Ob istoriografii kubinskogo osvoboditel'nogo dvizheniia kontsa XIX veka [Historiography of the Cuban liberation movement in the late 19th century] Vop. ist., v. 39, no. 7, July 1964: 194–195.

377. ———. Poezdka sovetskikh istorikov na Kubu i v Meksiku [A trip of Soviet historians to Cuba and Mexico] Nov. i noveish. ist., no. 3, 1962: 187–188.

Historical research.

378. ———. Staraia pesnia kolonizatorov [Colonialists tell us the same old story] Vop. ist., no. 11, Nov. 1961: 191–192.

History of Cuban relations with the United States.

379. ———. Zadachi kubinskoi istoricheskoi nauki [The tasks of Cuban historiography] Nov. i noveish. ist., no. 3, 1963: 712–173.

380. Bazhova, A. P. U kubinskikh istorikov [A conference of Cuban historians] Vop. ist., v. 38, no. 5, May 1963: 202.

381. Dzagurova, IU. P., *and others.* Dva dokumenta o kubinskom osvoboditel'nom dvizhenii, 1934–1935 [Two documents concerning the liberation movement in Cuba, 1934–1935] Ist. arkh., v. 6, no. 5, Sept.-Oct. 1960: 208–210.

382. Fernández Retamar, Roberto. Istoriia Kuby [The history of Cuba] Kuba, no. 3, Nov. 1964: 5–17.

383. Grigor'ian, IU. M. Iz istorii agressii SShA protiv Kuby [History of U.S. aggression against Cuba] Vop. ist., v. 38, no. 1, Jan. 1963: 172.

A review of an article by L. Montfort in *Wissenschaftliche Zeitschrift der Karl Marx Universität* (Leipzig), no. 1, 1962: 1–22.

384. Grigulevich, I. R. Istochniki i literatura po istorii natsional'noi kul'tury i kul'turnoi revoliutsii na Kube [Sources and literature concerning the history of national culture and the cultural revolution in Cuba] Nov. i noveish. ist., no. 2, 1964: 121–131.

385. Grinevich, E. A. Demokraticheskoe dvizhenie i vnutripoliticheskoe polozhenie na Kube v gody vtoroi mirovoi voiny [The democratic movement and internal political situation in Cuba during the Second World War] Uch. zap. IMO, no. 13, 1963: 192–205.

386. Guber, A. A., *and others, comps.* Agressiia SShA na Kube, 1898–1912 gg. [U.S. aggression in Cuba, 1898–1912] Ist. arkh., v. 7, no. 3, May-June, 1961: 33–54.

387. Istoricheskaia nauka revoliutsionnoi Kuby [The historiography of revolutionary Cuba] Vop. ist., v. 39, no. 6, June 1964: 170–173.

388. Iz geroicheskogo proshlogo kubinskogo naroda [From the heroic past of the Cuban people] Mezhdunar. zhizn', v. 11, no. 3, Mar. 1964: 150–160.

389. Kirik, O. I. Natsional'nyi arkhiv Kuby [The National Archives of Cuba] Ist. arkh., v. 7, no. 1, Jan.-Feb. 1961: 166–169.

390. Lara, Tunon de. Vzryv kreisera "Men," ili kak Soedinennye Shtaty "osvobodili" Kubu [Explosion of the battleship "Maine," or how the United States "liberated" Cuba] V zashch. mira, no. 3, Mar. 1961: 28–34.

391. Lavretskii, I. R. Kubinskii istorik Roig de Leuchsenring [Emilio Roig de Leuchsenring, a Cuban historian] Vop. ist., no. 5, May 1962: 195–197.

392. Le Riverend, Julio. Blizhaishie plany istorikov Kuby [The immediate plans of Cuban historians] Vop. ist., v. 39, no. 4, Apr. 1964: 204–206.

393. ———. Pervye otkliki kubinskogo naroda na Velikuiu Oktiabr'skuiu sotsialisticheskuiu revoliutsiiu [First reactions of the Cuban people to the Great October Socialist Revolution] Nov. i noveish. ist., no. 5, 1964: 22–25.
   Summary in English, p. 188.

394. Merin, B. M. Noveishie amerikanskie raboty o kubinskoi revoliutsii [Recent American works on the Cuban Revolution] Vop. ist., v. 38, no. 5, May 1963: 159–165.

395. Nibaut, G. D. Kuba; staroe i novoe [Cuba; the old and the new] V zashch. mira, no. 94, Mar. 1959: 40–45.

396. Nitoburg, E. L. K voprosu ob interventsii SShA na Kube v 1933 godu [The U.S. intervention in Cuba in 1933] Nov. i noveish. ist., no. 2, 1963: 108–117.
   Summary in English, p. 189.

397. Núñez Jiménez, Antonio. Krakh tiranii Machado [The collapse of the Machado tyranny] Nov. i noveish. ist., no. 6, 1962: 53–57.
   Summary in English, p. 189.

398. Petrash, V. Istoriia obviniaet SShA [History accuses the United States] Ogonek, v. 38, no. 44, Oct. 1960: 3.
   Cuban relations with the United States during the Spanish-American War.

399. Rabinovich, V. Fedor Karzhavin—pervyi russkii na Kube [Fedor Karzhavin, the first Russian visitor in Cuba] Tekh. mol., v. 32, no. 8, 1964: 35.

400. Shur, L. A. Ob uchastii russkikh dobrovol'tsev v natsional'no-osvoboditel'noi voine kubinskogo naroda 1895–1898 godov [Participation of Russian volunteers in the national liberation war of the Cuban people, 1895–1898] Vop. ist., v. 38, no. 1, Jan. 1963: 200–207.

401. Shustov, K. S. Iz istorii bor'by kubinskogo naroda protiv ispanskogo kolonial'nogo gospodstva, 1895–1898 gg. [From the history of the struggle of the Cuban people against Spanish colonial rule, 1895–1898] Vest. AN Kazakh. SSSR, v. 20, no. 1, Jan. 1964: 39–46.

402. Ternovoi, O. S. Natsional'nyi geroi Kuby Khose Marti—borets protiv imperializma SShA [José Martí, the Cuban national hero who struggled against U.S. imperialism] Nov. i noveish. ist., no. 1, 1962: 46–54.
   Summary in English, p. 197.

403. Vinogradov, V., *and* V. Koldobskii. Russkie na Kube [Russians in Cuba] Smena, v. 38, no. 16, Aug. 1961: 30.
   History of Russian participation in the Cuban uprisings against Spain.

404. Vladimirov, A. Letopisets geroicheskoi bor'by kubintsev; zabytye stat'i zabytogo publitsista [An annalist of the heroic struggle of the Cubans; forgotten sociopolitical articles of a forgotten writer] Druzh. nar., no. 8, Aug. 1964: 253–258.

405. Vladimirov, V. "Prevoskhodnaia malen'kaia voina" ["A beautiful little war"] Ogonek, v. 40, no. 6, Feb. 1962: 18–19.
   The war of 1898.

406. Zerchaninov, IUrii. V tu noch' posle Montesuelo; istoriia kotoraia nachalas' na Kube 66 let nazad [On the night after the Battle of Montezuelo; a story which began in Cuba 66 years ago] IUnost', v. 8, no. 3, 1962: 96–106.
   Russian participation in the Cuban liberation movement.

407. Zorina, A. M. Review. Nov. i noveish. ist., no. 4, 1964: 165–168.
   A review of Philip Sheldon Foner's *A History of Cuba and Its Relations with the United States*, v. 2, *1845-1895* (New York, International Publishers, 1963. 381 p.).

408. ———. Vstrecha s Khulio Le Riverendom [A meeting with Julio Le Riverend] Vop. ist., v. 38, no. 9, Sept. 1963: 134–135.
   Historical research.

409. Zubok, L. I. Istoricheskie istoki kubinskoi revoliutsii [The historical origins of the Cuban Revolution] Nov. i noveish. ist., no. 1, 1963: 170–171.

A review of Philip Sheldon Foner's *A History of Cuba and Its Relations with the United States*, v. 1, *1492–1845* (New York, International Publishers, 1962. 255 p.).

See also entries no. 1478, 3235, 3528, and 3530.

8. Dominican Republic

410. Nikolaev, P. Istoriia odnoi diktatury [History of a dictatorship] Nov. vrem., v. 19, no. 36, Sept. 1961: 8–11.

9. Ecuador

411. Efimov, Aleksei Vladimirovich, *and others, eds.* Ekvador; istoriko-etnograficheskie ocherki [Ecuador; historical and etnographical sketches] Moscow, Izd-vo Akad. nauk SSSR, 1963. 221 p.
HN313.5.A65
Reviewed by E. V. Rubtsova in *Nov. i noveish. ist.*, no.1,1964: 159–160; by V. Putsko in *Nov. mir*, v. 40, no. 2, Feb. 1964: 286; by S. Fedorova in *Sov. etn.*, no. 1, Jan.-Feb. 1964: 187–190.

10. Guatemala

412. Díaz Rozzotto, Jaime. Kharakter gvatemal'skoi revoliutsii; zakat traditsionnoi burzhuazno-demokraticheskoi revoliutsii [The nature of the Guatemalan revolution; the decline of the traditional bourgeois-democratic revolution] Moscow Izd-vo inostr. lit., 1962. 350 p.
Translated from the Spanish *El carácter de la revolución guatemalteca; ocaso de la revolución democrático-burguesa corriente.*

413. Aleksandrovskii, B. Iz istorii i zhizni Gvatemaly [From the history and life of Guatemala] Nov. vrem., v. 17, no. 30, July 1959: 16–17.

11. The Guianas

414. Svet, IA. Lotsman kolonizatorov [The pilot of the colonizers] Vokrug sveta, no. 11, Nov. 1963: 47–49.

12. Mexico

415. Al'perovich, Moisei Samoilovich. Voina za nezavisimost' Meksiki, 1810–1824 [The Mexican War for Independence, 1810–1824] Moscow, Nauka, 1964. 476 p
F1232.A36
Summary in Spanish.

416. Al'perovich, Moisei Samoilovich, *and* Nikolai Matveevich Lavrov, *eds.* Ocherki novoi i noveishei istorii Meksiki, 1810–1945 [Studies on modern and recent Mexican history, 1810–1945] Moscow, Sotsekgiz, 1960. 509 p. F1231.5.A57
Reviewed by A. F. Shul'govskii in *Vop. ist.*, no. 3, Mar. 1961: 161–164; by B. I. Kolibin in *Vest. ist. mir. kul't.*, no. 2, Mar.-Apr. 1961: 145–147 [in English] ; by A. A. Guber and V. N. Kuteishchikova in *Nov. i noveish. ist.*, no. 1, 1961: 143–145.

417. Belen'kii, Aleksandr Borisovich. Razgrom meksikanskim narodom inostrannoi interventsii, 1861–1867 [How the Mexican people defeated the foreign intervention, 1861–1867] Moscow, Izd-vo Akad. nauk SSSR, 1959. 155 p.
F1233.B42
Reviewed by V. L. Afanas'ev in *Nov. i noveish. ist.*, no. 4, 1960: 169–170.

418. Kinzhalov, R., *and* A. Belov. Padenie Tenochtitlana [The fall of Tenochitlán] Kiev, Ditvydav, 1959. 275 p.
In Ukrainian. Translated from the Russian. Also published in Latvian.
Reviewed by E. Kucherov in *Prep. ist v shkole*, no. 3, May-June 1959: 118–120.

419. Lavretskii, Iosif Romual'dovich. Pancho Vil'ia, 1878–1923 [Pancho Villa, 1878–1923] Moscow, Mol. gvardiia, 1962. 256 p. F1234.V687

420. Potokova, Nina Vasil'evna. Agressia SShA protiv Meksiki, 1846–1848 [U.S. aggression against Mexico, 1846–1848] Moscow, Sotsekgiz, 1962. 139 p.
E404.P86

421. Reed, John. Vosstavshaia Meksika; rasskazy i ocherki [Insurgent Mexico; stories and sketches] Moscow, Goslitizdat, 1959. 503 p.
Translated by I. I. Anisimova from the English.
Reviewed by I. Kramov in *Nov. mir*, v. 36, no. 10, Oct. 1960: 258–262; by Konst. Simonov in *Ogonek*, v. 38, no. 40, Oct. 1960: 18.

422. Al'perovich, M. S. Istoricheskaia nauka v Meksike [Historical studies in Mexico] Vop. ist., no. 8, Aug. 1962: 198–202.

423. ———. Istoriografiia Meksiki posle voiny za nezavisimost' [Mexican historiography of the period after the Wars of Independence] Vop. ist., no. 3, Mar. 1961: 212–214.

424. ———. Iz istorii voiny meksikanskogo naroda za nezavisimost' [From the history of the Mexican War for Independence] Nov. i noveish. ist., no. 1, 1962: 180–181.

425. ———. Review. Vop. ist., no. 2, Feb. 1962: 178–187.
A review of the periodical *Historia mexicana* (Mexico City, 1958–61).

426. ———. Rol' narodnykh mass v voine za nezavisimost' Meksiki [The role of the masses in the Mexican War of Independence] Nov. i noveish. ist., no. 5, 1960: 52–63.

427. ———. Sovremennaia meksikanskaia istoriografiia voiny za nezavisimost' [Present-day Mexican historiography of the War of Independence] Vop. ist., no. 2, Feb. 1961: 166–176.

428. Ganelin, R. Sh. Iz istorii ekonomicheskikh sviazei Rossii s Meksikoi i Braziliei v seredine XIX veka [History of Russia's economic contacts with Mexico and Brazil in the mid-19th century] Nov. i noveish. ist., no. 6, 1963: 59–64.
Summary in English, p. 169.

429. Gortari, Eli de. Nauka v istorii Meksiki [Science in Mexican history] Vest. ist. mir. kul't., no. 6, Nov.-Dec. 1959: 17–28.

430. Ivanov, G. I. Enkom'enda v Meksike i vosstaniia indeitsev v XVI veke [The "encomienda" in Mexico and the Indian uprisings in the 16th century] Uch. zap. Ivan. gos. ped. inst., v. 35, 1964: 99–157.

431. ———. Narodnye vosstaniia v Meksike vo vtoroi polovine XVII veka [Uprisings of the Mexican people in the second half of the 17th century] Nov. i noveish. ist., no. 1, 1964: 57–72.
Summary in English, p. 204.

432. ———. Repartim'ento v Meksike v XVI–XVIII vv.; iz istorii feodal'no-kolonial'noi ekspluatatsii indeiskogo naseleniia [The "repartimiento"in Mexico in the 16th–18th century; from the history of the feudal and colonialist exploitation of the Indian population] Uch. zap. Ivan. gos. ped. inst., v. 35, 1964: 158–195.

433. Lapshev, E. G. Meksikanskaia revoliutsiia i SShA [The Mexican Revolution and the U.S.A.] Nov. i noveish. ist., no. 5, May 1962: 155–156.
A review of Alfonso Taracena's *Madero, víctima del imperialismo yanqui* (Mexico City, Classica Selecta-Editora Librera, 1960. 270 p.).

434. Lavrov, N. M. Review. Nov. i noveish. ist., no. 5, 1959: 174–176.
A review of *Meksikanskaia revoliutsiia 1910-1917 gg. i politika SShA* by M. S. Al'perovich and B. T. Rudenko (Moscow, Sotsekgiz, 1958. 328 p.).

435. Pechuro, E. E. Novye materialy o krest'ianskom vosstanii pod rukovodstvom Emiliano Sapaty [New materials on the peasant movement led by Emiliano Zapata] Vop. ist., no. 10, 1961: 187–189.

436. Potokova, N. V. Iz istorii amerikanskoi ekspansii [From the history of American expansion] Nov. i noveish. ist., no. 1, 1962: 167–169.
A review of Otis A. Singletary's *The Mexican War* (Chicago, University of Chicago Press, 1960. 181 p.).

437. Revoliutsionnyi prazdnik Meksiki [Mexico's independence day] Nov. vrem., v. 18, no. 38, Sept. 1960: 10–11.

438. Rubtsova, E. V. Review. Vop. ist., no. 1, Jan. 1960: 190–193.
A review of *Meksikanskaia revoliutsiia 1910–1917 gg. i politika SSHA* by M. S. Al'perovich and B. T. Rudenko (Moscow, Sotsekgiz, 1958. 328 p.).

See also entries no. 377, 1730, 1731, and 3139.

13. Nicaragua

439. Gonionskii, S. A. Novye knigi o legendarnom generale Sandino [New books on the legendary General Sandino] Nov. i noveish. ist., no. 4, 1963: 168–170.

440. ———. "Polkovodets svobodnykh liudei" [Commander of free peoples] Nov. vrem., v. 17, no. 19, May 1959: 28–29.
A review of Gregorio Selser's *El pequeño ejército loco* (Buenos Aires, Editorial Triángulo, 1958. 399 p.).

441. Larin, N. S. Iz istorii osvoboditel'noi bor'by naroda Nikaragua protiv vooruzhennoi interventsii SShA v 1927–1933 godakh [History of the liberation struggle of the Nicaraguan people against the armed intervention of the United States, from 1927 to 1933] Vop. ist., no. 8, Aug. 1961: 86–96.
Summary in English, p. 221–222.

14. Paraguay

442. Juárez, Claudio. Strana, o kotoroi govoriat: Paragvai [Paraguay, a country in the news] V zashch. mira, no. 3, Mar. 1960: 30–37.

15. Peru

443. Mariátegui, José Carlos. Sem' ocherkov istolkovaniia peruanskoi deistvitel'nosti [Interpretation of present-day Peruvian conditions in seven sketches] Moscow, Izd-vo inostr. lit., 1963. 423 p.
Translated from the Spanish Siete ensayos de interpretación de la realidad peruana. Introductory article by Jorge del Prado.
Reviewed by V. Kuteishchikova in Vop. lit., v. 7, no. 11, Nov. 1963: 218–222.

444. Komissarov, B. N. Peru na poroge nezavisimosti; zapiski russkikh moreplavatelei o Peru, 1817–1818 (?) [Peru on the eve of independence; Russian seafarers' notes on Peru, 1817–1818.] Sbor. stud. nauch. rab. LGU, no. 4, 1963: 147–157.

445. Nefedova, L. D. Iz istorii razvitiia marksizma v Peru [From the history of the development of Marxist ideas in Peru] Vop. ist., v. 39, no. 11, Nov. 1964: 199–200.

16. Uruguay

446. Pintos, Francisco R. Batl'e i protsess istoricheskogo razvitiia Urugvaia [Batlle and the historical development of Uruguay] Moscow, Izd-vo inostr. lit., 1962. 159 p.
Translated by G. P. Paporova and IU. V. Dashkevich from the Spanish Batlle y el proceso histórico del Uruguay.

447. ———. Khose Artigas, 1764–1850 [José Artigas, 1764–1850] Moscow, Progress, 1964. 114 p.
Translated by IU. V. Dashkevich from the Spanish. Introductory article by V. G. Korionov.

448. 200 [Dvukhsot]-letie so dnia rozhdeniia Kh. Artigasa [The 200th anniversary of José Gervasio Artigas' birth] Vest. AN SSSR, v. 34, no. 9, Sept. 1964: 145–146.

449. Mikhailov, S. Dva issledovaniia o Batl'izme [Two studies on the José Batlle movement] Nov. i noveish. ist., no. 1, 1964: 152–157.
A review of Göran G. Lindahl's Uruguay's New Path; a Study in Politics during the First Collegiado, 1919-1933 (Stockholm, Library and Institute of Ibero-American Studies, 1962. 369 p.), and R. M. Gés' El Uruguay batllista (Montevideo, Ediciones de la Banda Oriental, 1962. 74 p.).

450. ———. Khose Artigas—borets za svobodu Urugvaia [José Artigas, a fighter for the freedom of Uruguay] Nov. vrem., v. 21, no. 25, June 1964: 27–29.

17. Venezuela

451. Al'perovich, M. S. Venesuel'skii istorik o problemakh voiny za nezavisimost', 1810–1826 godov [A Venezuelan historian's views on the problems of the War of Independence, 1810–1926] Vop. ist., v. 39, no. 9, Sept. 1964: 207–208.

452. Demushkina, E. V. Istoricheskaia nauka v Venesuele [Historical studies in Venezuela] Vop. ist., v. 38, no. 7, July 1963: 200–202.

453. ———. Review. Vop. ist., v. 39, no. 2, Feb. 1964: 186–189.
A review of the periodical Revista de historia (Caracas, 1960–1962).

454. Lavretskii, I. R. Novye issledovaniia po istorii Venesuely [New studies on the history of Venezuela] Vop. ist., no. 8, Aug. 1961: 175–178.

455. ———. Venesuel'skie istoriki obsuzhdaiut zadachi svoei raboty [Venezuelan historians discuss the objectives of their work] Vop. ist., no. 7, July 1960: 221–222.

V

LAW

❧

A. WRITINGS DEALING WITH THREE OR MORE COUNTRIES

456. Gonionskii, Semen Aleksandrovich, *ed.* Mezhdunarodnoe pravo i Latinskaia Amerika; sbornik materialov [International law and Latin America; collected documentary materials] Moscow, Izd-vo IMO, 1962. 270 p.

457. Barsegov, IU. G. Iz praktiki razresheniia territorial'nykh konfliktov mezhdu gosudarstvami Amerikanskogo kontinenta [How the American states settle their territorial conflicts] Uch. zap. Kaf. mezhdunar. prava IMO, no. 3, 1960: 88–95.

458. Blishchenko, I. P. Diplomaticheskoe i konsul'skoe pravo v praktike stran Latinskoi Ameriki [Diplomatic and consular laws governing the foreign relations of Latin American countries] Vop. mezhdunar. prava, no. 4, 1962: 148–174.

B. INDIVIDUAL COUNTRIES

1. Argentina

459. Razumovich, N. Antidemokraticheskoe zakonodatel'stvo Argentiny [Antidemocratic laws in Argentina] Sov. iust., no. 16, Aug. 1963: 18–20.

2. Chile

460. Mezger, Edmund, *ed.* Sovremennoe zarubezhnoe ugolovnoe pravo. t. 3. Chili, Angliia, Gretsiia, Avstriia [Present-day criminal law of foreign countries. v. 3. Chile, England, Greece, and Austria] Moscow, Izd-vo inostr. lit., 1961. 759 p.
DLC-LL

Translated by S. L. Liberman from the German. Introductory article by A. A. Piontkovskii.

461. Korovin, E. A., *and* M. I. Lazarev. Voina narodov i sovremennoe mezhdunarodnoe pravo v knige chiliiskogo iurista-mezhdunarodnika Alekhandro Al'varesa [The war of the peoples and present-day international law in the book of Alejandro Alvarez, a Chilean student of international law] Vop. mezhdunar. prava, no. 4, 1962: 175–186.

A review of Alejandro Alvarez' *Le droit international nouveau dans ses rapports avec la vie actuelle des peuples* (Paris, Librairie Pédone, 1959. 636 p.).

462. Neruda, Pablo. Kazn' peona [The execution of a peon] Ogonek, v. 41, no. 30, July 1963: 6–7.

Administration of criminal justice.

3. Cuba

463. Razumovich, Nikolai Nikanorovich, *ed.* Osnovnye zakonodatel'nye akty Kubinskoi Respubliki [Basic legislative enactments of the Republic of Cuba] Moscow, Gosiurizdat, 1962. 389 p.
DLC-LL

464. Kolodkin, A. L. Morskaia blokada i sovremennoe mezhdunarodnoe pravo [The naval blockade and present-day international law] Sov. gos. i pravo, v. 33, no. 4, Apr. 1963: 92–103.

465. Lazarev, M. I. Voennaia baza SShA v Guantanamo i sovremennoe mezhdunarodnoe pravo [The U.S. military base at Guantánamo and present-day international law] Vop. mezhdunar. prava, no. 4, 1962: 117–147.

466. Olteanu, O. Arbitrazhyne komissii v revoliutsionnoi Kube [Arbitration commissions in revolutionary Cuba] Sov. iust., no. 15, Aug. 1963: 26–27.

467. ———. Trudovoe zakonodatel'stvo revoliutsionnoi Kuby [Labor legislation of revolutionary Cuba] Vest. Mosk. un. Ser. 10: Pravo, v. 16, no. 1, Jan.-Mar. 1961: 61–70.

468. Schick, F. B. Kuba i mezhdunarodnoe pravo [Cuba and international law] Mezhdunar. zhizn', v. 10, no. 9, Sept. 1963: 85–94.

    Translated from the English.

See also entries no. 1996, 2219, 2993, and 4516.

4. Mexico

See entry no. 3205.

5. Panama; the Panama Canal

469. Khlestov, O. Mezhdunarodnoe pravo—na storone Panamy [International law sides with Panama] Mezhdunar. zhizn', v. 11, no. 4, Apr. 1964: 118–120.

470. Spirin, V. G., *and* L. M. Romanov. K voprosu o suverenitete Panamy nad zonoi Panamskogo kanala [The problem of Panamanian sovereignty over the Panama Canal Zone] Sov. gos. i pravo, v. 32, no. 7, July 1962: 122–127.

6. Uruguay

471. Durdenevskii, V. N., *and* G. A. Osnitskaia. Monografiia o mezhduplanetnoi navigatsii [A monograph on interplanetary navigation] Sov. gos. i pravo, no. 12, Dec. 1959: 143–144.

    A review of Alvaro Bauzá Araújo's *Hacia un derecho astronáutico* (Montevideo, 1957. 223 p.).

7. Venezuela

472. Tridtsat' piat' tysiach prestuplenii [35,000 criminal offenses] Nov. vrem., v. 22, no. 40, Oct. 1964: 22.

    Crime.

See also entry no. 3381

VI

POLITICS AND GOVERNMENT

❦

A. GENERAL WORKS

1. Writings Dealing With Three or More Countries

473. Arismendi, Rodney. Problemy latino-amerikanskoi revoliutsii [Problems of the Latin American revolution] Moscow, Progress, 1964. 691 p.
Translated from the Spanish.

474. Avarin, Vladimir IAkovlevich, *and* M. V. Danilevich, *eds.* Natsional'no-osvo-boditel'noe dvizhenie v Latinskoi Amerike na sovremennom etape; materialy rasshirennoi sessii Uchenogo soveta Instituta mirovoi ekonomiki i mezhdunarodnykh otnoshenii AN SSSR, posviashchennoi 150-letiiu voiny za nezavisimost' narodov Latinskoi Ameriki [The present-day national liberation movement in Latin America; materials of the enlarged session of the Scientific Council of the Institute of World Economics and International Relations, devoted to the 150th anniversary of the War for Independence of the Latin American nations] Moscow, Sotsekgiz, 1961. 298 p.   F1414.A43

475. Bezrodnyi, IE. F. Latyns'ka Ameryka boret'sia [Latin America fights] Kiev, Radians'ka Ukraina, 1963. 56 p.

476. Carnero Checa, Genaro. Ocherki o stranakh Latinskoi Ameriki [Sketches of the countries of Latin America] Moscow, Izd-vo inostr. lit., 1960. 555 p.
                F1413.C317
Translated by M. N. Deev and B. V. Kostritsyn from the Spanish *Ensayos latino-americanos.* Introductory article by A. F. Shul'govskii.
Reviewed in *Nov. vrem.*, v. 19, no. 2, Jan. 1961: 31.

477. Danilevich, I. V. Problemy natsional'no-demokraticheskoi revoliutsii v teorii i praktike sotsialistov Latinskoi Ameriki, 1956–1963 [Problems of the national and democratic revolution in the theory and practice of Latin American socialists, 1956–1963] Moscow, 1963. 19 p. (Institut mirovoi ekonomiki i mezhdunarodnykh otnoshenii Akademii nauk SSSR)
Author's abstract of a dissertation for the degree of Candidate in Historical Sciences.

478. Ge, V. N. Novaia stranitsa istorii; na putiakh k gosudarstvu natsional'noi demo-kratii [A new page of history; the road toward the national democratic state] Moscow, Znanie, 1962. 48 p.   DLC

479. Guber, A. A., *ed.* Bor'ba za edinyi rabo-chii i antiimperialisticheskii front v stranakh Latinskoi Ameriki; sbornik statei [The struggle for a united labor and anti-imperialist front in the countries of Latin America; collected articles] Moscow, Izd-vo VPSh i AON, 1963. 306 p.

480. Gurvich, Georgii Semenovich, *ed.* Kon-stitutsii gosudarstv Amerikanskogo kontinenta [Constitutions of the states of the American continent] v. 2 and 3. Moscow, Izd-vo inostr. lit., 1959.
                DLC-LL
v. 2. Kanada, Kolumbiia, Kosta-Rika, Kuba, Meksika, Nikaragua [Canada, Colombia, Costa Rica, Cuba, Mexico, and Nicaragua] Compiled by N. N. Razumovich. 525 p.
v. 3. Panama, Paragvai, Peru, Sal'vador, Soedinennye Shtaty Ameriki, Urugvai, Chili, Ekvador [Panama, Paraguay, Peru, El Salvador, the United States of America, Uruguay, Chile, and Ecuador] Compiled by N. N. Razumovich. 470 p.

481. Kalinin, A. I., *and* M. A. Manasov. Front aktivnoi bor'by; Latinskaia Amerika

[The front of active struggle; Latin America] Moscow, Znanie, 1962. 46 p.

DLC

482. Kim, G. F. The national democratic state; the national liberation movement in Asia, Africa, and Latin America. Moscow, Izd-vo vost. lit., 1963. 40 p.

In English. Also published in French, Arabic, and Spanish.

483. Mikhailov, Sergei Sergeevich, *ed.* Osvoboditel'noe dvizhenie v Latinskoi Amerike [The liberation movement in Latin America] Moscow, Nauka, 1964. 426 p.

F1408.A54

484. Vartanov, Grigorii Akopovich. Natsional'no-osvoboditel'noe dvizhenie v stranakh Latinskoi Ameriki [The national liberation movement in the countries of Latin America] Leningrad, Ob-vo po rasprostr. polit. i nauchn. znanii, 1960. 56 p.

F1414.V36

485. Al'perovich, M. S. Pod"em natsional'no-osvoboditel'nogo i demokraticheskogo dvizheniia v Latinskoi Amerike posle vtoroi mirovoi voiny [Rapid development of the national liberation and democratic movement in Latin America after World War II] Prep. ist. v shkole, v. 14, no. 4, July-Aug. 1959: 20–32.

486. Al'tman, I. Znamia kubinskoi revoliutsii reet nad Latinskoi Amerikoi [The banner of the Cuban Revolution waves over Latin America] Kommunist (Vilnius) no. 1, 1961: 60–63.

487. Andrianov, V. Svobodu ne zadushit' [They cannot suppress freedom] Agitator, no. 14, July 1959: 33–34.

488. Arismendi, Rodney. K voprosu o roli natsional'noi burzhuazii v antiimperialisticheskoi bor'be; v poriadke issledovaniia problem osvoboditel'nogo dvizheniia v Latinskoi Amerike [The role of the national bourgeoisie in the antiimperialist struggle; studying the problems of the liberation movement in Latin America] Probl. mira i sots., v. 2, no. 5, May 1959: 32–42; v. 2, no. 6, June 1959: 28–35.

489. ———. Nekotorye aktual'nye aspekty revoliutsionnogo protsessa v Latinskoi Amerike [Some aspects of the present-day revolutionary process in Latin America] Probl. mira i sots., v. 7, no. 10, Nov. 1964: 9–18.

490. ———. Programma kommunizma i natsional'no-osvoboditel'noe dvizhenie [The program of communism and the national liberation movement] Probl. mira i sots., v. 4, no. 11, Nov. 1961: 17–25.

491. ———. V vek kommunizma [In the age of communism] Agitator, no. 9, May 1959: 14–17.

Translated from the Spanish.

492. Bako, G. Chto proizoshlo na bortu "Santa Marii" [What happened aboard the "Santa María"] Nov. vrem., v. 19, no. 8, Feb. 1961: 14–15.

Political activities of Portuguese refugees in Latin America.

493. Bělič, Oldřich, *and* Rubens Iscaro. Novyi rubezh bor'by narodov Latinskoi Ameriki [New phase in the struggle of the Latin American peoples] Probl. mira i sots., v. 4, no. 5, May 1961: 48–51.

494. Bel'skaia, A. Latinskaia Amerika burlit [Latin America is seething] Rabotnitsa, v. 40, no. 1, Jan. 1962: 20.

495. Bezrodnyi, IE. Natsional'no vyzvol'nyi rykh u Latyns'kii Amerytsi pislia druhoi svitovoi viiny [The national liberation movement in Latin America after the Second World War] Rad. shk., v. 42, no. 7, July 1963: 102–106.

496. Bochkarev, IU. Nad volnami moria Karibskogo [Over the waves of the Caribbean Sea] Nov. vrem., v. 17, no. 33, Aug. 1959: 7–9.

497. ———. Snova voennye khunty [Military juntas again] Nov. vrem., v. 21, no. 41, Oct. 1963: 10–11.

498. Bor'ba stala ostree [Intensification of the political struggle] Za rubezhom, no. 15, Apr. 1962: 3.

499. Campos, Miguel. "Novaia" politika i starye soiuzniki [The "new" policy and the old allies] Probl. mira i sots., v. 5, no. 6, June 1962: 64–65.

500. Cherkasov, Boris. "Santa Mariia"— vestnik svobody [The "Santa María" is a

herald of freedom] Smena, v. 38, no. 6, Mar. 1961: 22–23.
Political activities of Portuguese refugees in Latin America.

501. Danilevich, I. V. Sdvigi v politike sotsialisticheskikh partii Latinskoi Ameriki [Shifts in the policy of the socialist parties of Latin America] Mir. ekon. i mezhdunar. otn., no. 8, Aug. 1960: 104–106.

502. Delgado, Emilio. Svoboda—dcviz kontinenta [Freedom—the slogan of a continent] Za rubezhom, no. 2, Jan. 1961: 9.

503. Edinstvo—zalog uspekha [Unity is a guarantee of success] Sov. profsoiuzy, v. 17, no. 11, June 1961: 30–32.

504. Ermashev, I. "Kaudil'o" v Latinskoi Amerike [Latin American "caudillos"] Mezhdunar. zhizn', v. 11, no. 1, Jan. 1964: 46–55.

505. Ermolaev, V., and S. Mikhailov. Boriushchiisia kontinent [A struggling continent] Kommunist, v. 39, no. 17, Nov. 1962: 124–126.
A review of Rodney Arismendi's Problemas de una revolución continental (Montevideo, Ediciones Pueblos Unidos, 1962. 556 p.).

506. Fedorov, M. Na novom etape [At a new stage] Mir. ekon. i mezhdunar. otn., no. 5, 1963: 122–129.
Socialist parties.

507. Ferreira, Pinto. Odisseia "Santa Marii" [The odyssey of the "Santa María"] Inostr. lit., no. 5, May 1961: 244–250.
Political activies of Portuguese refugees in Latin America.

508. Ghioldi, Rodolfo. Za natsional'nuiu nezavisimost', protiv gneta monopolii [For national independence and against oppression by monopolies] Agitator, no. 9, May 1960: 36–39.

509. Grigor'ev, IA. G. Rol' armii v politicheskoi zhizni Latinskoi Ameriki [The role of the army in the political life of Latin America] Vop. ist., no. 8, 1964: 198.

510. Gugushkin, V. "Gorilly" i svastika ["Gorillas" and the swastika] Smena, v. 40, no. 11, June 1963: 30–31.
Fascism.

511. Gvozdev, IU. Kuba—rassvet Ameriki [Cuba is the dawn of America] Ogonek, v. 41, no. 17, Apr. 1963: 1.

512. Ibarburu, Rita. Pervaia stranitsa epokhi [The first page of an epoch] Sov. zhen., v. 20, no. 11, 1964: 13.

513. IU. B. Pazhul reaktsii na amerykans'komu kontynenti [Intensificaiion of reactionary persecutions on the American continent] Rad. pravo, no. 1, Jan.-Feb. 1962: 145 146.

514. Jiménez, Liliam. Mne khotelos' by otvetit' g-zhe Sinkler! [Let me reply to Mrs. Sinclair!] Zhen. mira, no. 2, 1962: 6.

515. Kak podgotovit' lektsiiu na temu: "Natsional'no-osvoboditel'noe dvizhenie v Latinskoi Amerike" [How to prepare a lecture on the topic "National liberation movement in Latin America"] Mezhdunar. zhizn', v. 10, no. 6, June 1963: 146–148.

516. Kamynin, Leonid. Vskipaiushchii vulkan [A seething volcano] Za rubezhom, no. 44, Oct. 1964: 7.

517. Kartsev, A. Partizany v Latinskoi Amerike [Guerrillas in Latin America] Mezhdunar. zhizn', v. 9, no. 7, July 1962: 124–125.

518. Kontinent so 180-millionnym naseleniem podnialsia na bor'bu [A continent with a population of one hundred and eighty million has risen in struggle] Vsem. prof. dvizh., no. 8/9, Aug.-Sept. 1960: 4–5.

519. Kremnev, M. Na poberezh'e Karibskogo moria [On the shores of the Caribbean Sea] Nov. vrem., v. 18, no.50, Dec. 1960: 6–8.

520. Kuba i Latinskaia Amerika [Cuba and Latin America] Mir. ekon. i mezhdunar. otn., no. 7, July 1961: 26–30.

521. Kudachkin, M., and N. Mostovets. Osvoboditel'noe divzhenie v Latinskoi Amerike [The liberation movement in Latin America] Kommunist, v. 41, no. 11, July 1964: 121–130.

522. Latinoamerikanskaia konferentsiia za natsional'nyi suverenitet, ekonomicheskuiu nezavisimost' i za mir [(Declaration of) the Latin American Conference for

National Sovereignty, Economic Independence, and Peace] Vop. mezhdunar. prava, no. 4, 1962: 228–268.

523. Letopis' rabochego i osvoboditel'nogo dvizheniia za 1959–1960 gody; Latinskaia Amerika [Chronology of the labor and liberation movement in 1959 and 1960; Latin America] *In* Akademiia nauk SSSR. Institut mirovoi ekonomiki i mezhdunarodnykh otnoshenii. Rabochee dvizhenie v kapitalisticheskikh stranakh, 1959–1961 g. Moscow, Gospolitizdat, 1961: p. 530–543.   HD4854.A43

524. Levin, V. Bor'ba za zhiznennye interesy narodov Latinskoi Ameriki [Struggle for the vital interests of the Latin American nations] Polit. samoobr. v. 4, no. 3, Mar. 1960: 44–53.

525. ———. Latinskaia Amerika boretsia za svobodu [Latin American struggles for freedom] Agitator, no. 22, Nov. 1960: 45–49; no. 24, Dec. 1960; 33–38; no.1, Jan. 1961: 33–36; no. 2, Jan. 1961: 33–36.

526. ———. Latinskaia Amerika prishla v dvizhenie [Latin America is on the march] Mezhdunar. zhizn', v. 6, no. 10, Oct. 1959: 94–102.

527. Lima, Pedro Motta. Zlokliucheniia antikommunizma [The failure of anticommunism] Probl. mira i sots., v. 5, no. 9, Sept. 1962: 74–76.

528. Loziuk, M. Pod"em osvoboditel'nogo dvizheniia v Latinskoi Amerike [Progressive development of the liberation movement in Latin America] Komm. Ukr., v. 34, no. 3, Mar. 1959: 76–86.

529. Lytovchenko, IAkiv. Pid dzvin rozirvanykh kaidaniv [To the clinking of broken shackles] Ukraina, no. 10, May 1960: 20–21.

530. M. S. K voprosu o kharaktere osvoboditel'noi bor'by v Latinskoi Amerike [Special features of the liberation struggle in Latin America] Nov. i noveish. ist., no. 2, 1961: 196.

531. Mazur, Janusz, *and* Tomasz Mieczyk. Ostannii rezervat [The last reservation] Vsesvit, v. 2, no. 4, Apr. 1959: 12–14.
Translated from the Polish.

532. Nalet'ko, V. Narody latinoamerikanskikh stran boriutsia za svoiu nezavisimost' [The nations of Latin America struggle for their independence] Komm. Bel., v. 34, no. 7, 1960: 68–71.

533. Ordynskii, B. Problemy novogo etapa natsional'no-osvoboditel'nogo i rabochego dvizheniia v Latinskoi Amerike; nauchnaia konferentsiia v Institute Latinskoi Ameriki AN SSSR [Problems of the new phase in the national-liberation and labor movements of Latin America; a conference in the Institute of Latin America of the Academy of Sciences of the USSR] Mir. ekon. i mezhdunar. otn., no. 3, 1963: 151–153.

534. Ortega, Luis. Krepnet edinstvo narodov Latinskoi Ameriki [The growing unity among the peoples of Latin America] Mol. mira, no. 6, 1960: 16.

535. Peña, Alcira dc la, *and others*. Narody Latinskoi Ameriki zashchishchaiut svoi prava [The peoples of Latin America defend their rights] Probl. mira i sots., v. 7, no. 1, Jan. 1964: 32–39.

536. Poblete, Olga. Zhivoi primer [An instructive example] Sov. zhen., v. 20, no. 11, 1964: 11.

537. Pod"em antiimperialisticheskoi bor'by mass v Latinskoi Amerike [The intensification of the mass struggle against imperialism in Latin America] Mir. ekon. i mezhdunar. otn., no. 7, July 1962: 89–105.

538. Probuzhdenie [Awakening] Za rubezhom, no. 25, Dec. 1960: 2–3.

539. Provokatsii v Karibskom more [Provocations in the Caribbean] Nov. vrem., v. 17, no. 29, July 1959: 25–26.

540. Revoliutsiia na Kube i Latinskaia Amerika [The revolution in Cuba and Latin America] Mir. ekon. i mezhdunar. otn., no. 1, Jan. 1961: 21–26.

541. Reyes, Pedro. Nekotorye problemy osvoboditel'nogo dvizheniia v Latinskoi Amerike [Some problems facing the liberation movement in Latin America] Probl. mira i sots., v. 2, no. 1, Jan. 1959: 36–42.

542. Rivero, Adolfo. Natsional'no-osvoboditel'naia bor'ba i razoruzhenie [The national liberation struggle and disarmament] Mol. mira, no. 3, 1960: 19.

543. Rodríguez, E. Pod"em krest'ianskogo dvizheniia v stranakh Latinskoi Ameriki [The upsurge of the peasant movement in the Latin American countries] Mir. ekon. i mezhdunar. otn., no. 10, 1963: 41–54.

544. Rodríguez, Enrique. Kuba i revoliutsiia v Latinskoi Amerike [Cuba and the revolution in Latin America] Kommunist, v. 40, no. 16, Nov. 1963: 100–106.

545. Samsonova, N. Natsional'no-osvoboditel'naia bor'ba narodov TSentral'noi Ameriki [The national liberation struggle of the peoples of Central America] Mir. ekon. i mezhdunar. otn., no. 10, Oct. 1960: 89–92.

546. "Santa Mariia" [The "Santa María"] Nov. vrem., v. 19, no. 6, Feb. 1961: 2–3.
　　Political activities of Portuguese refugees.

547. Semenov, S. Novyi kurs latinoamerikanskikh sotsialistov [The new course of the Latin American Socialists] Probl. mira i sots., v. 4, no. 12, Dec. 1961: 65–68.
　　A review of Vivian Trías' El plan Kennedy y la revolución latinoamericana (Montevideo, Ediciones "El Sol," 1961. 221 p.).

548. Sivolobov, A. Nekotorye voprosy osvoboditel'noi bor'by v Latinskoi Amerike [Some problems of the liberation struggle in Latin America] Polit. samoobr., v. 8, no. 12, Dec. 1964: 33–40.

549. Slavnye traditsii [Glorious traditions] Nov. vrem., v. 18, no. 22, May 1960: 2–3.

550. Solidarnost' narodov Latinskoi Ameriki so svoimi ispanskimi i portugal'skimi brat'iami [Solidarity of Latin American nations with their Spanish and Portuguese brothers] Vsem. prof. dvizh., no. 3, Mar. 1960: 41.
　　Political activities of Spanish and Portuguese political refugees.

551. Strelin, A. Eshche odin souiz radi agressii [A new aggressive alliance] Mezhdunar. zhizn', v. 9, no. 4, Apr. 1962: 118–119.

552. Tarasov, K. Gavanskaia deklaratsiia—prizyv k bor'be protiv imperializma [The Havana Declaration is an appeal for the struggle against imperialism] Kommunist, v. 38, no. 4, Mar. 1962: 80–89.

553. V. B. Bditel'nyi polkovnik Nun'es [Vigilant Colonel Nunes] Nov. vrem., v. 17, no. 5, Jan. 1959: 19.
　　Alleged subversive activities of the USSR.

554. Varnavinskii, A. M. Pod"em natsional'no-osvoboditel'nogo dvizheniia v stranakh Latinskoi Ameriki [Intensification of the national liberation movement in the countries of Latin America] Biul. Ob-va po rasprostr. polit. i nauchn. znanii RSFSR, no. 1, 1959: 37–47.

555. Vishnevetskii, K. "Santa Mariia"—korabl' svobody [The "Santa María," a ship of freedom] Za rubezhom, no. 5, Feb. 1961: 28–29.
　　Political activities of Portuguese refugees.

See also entries no. 301, 306, 1871, 2329, 2338, 2351, 2359, 2360, 2364–2366, 2369, 2370, 2652, 3033, 3082, 4525, 4528, and 4530.

2. Individual Countries

a. Argentina

556. Alberdi, Juan Bautista. Prestuplenie voiny [The crime of war] Moscow, Izd-vo inostr. lit., 1960. 256 p.
　　Social and political writings.
　　Translated by IU. V. Dashkevich from the Spanish El crimen de la guerra. Introductory article by S. A. Gonionskii.
　　Reviewed by I. Lavretskii in Inostr. lit., no. 9, Sept. 1960: 263.

557. Razumovich, Nikolai Nikanorovich. Gosudarstvennyi stroi Argentiny [The governmental system of Argentina] Moscow, Gosiurizdat, 1959. 99 p.
　　　　JL2015 1959.R39

558. A. P. Rozbyta "vitryna" zakhidnoi demokratii [A shattered "showcase" of western democracy] Rad. pravo, no. 6, Nov.-Dec. 1963: 122–123.

559. Arturo Il'ia; biograficheskaia spravka [Arturo Illía; a biographical note] Nov. vrem., v. 21, no. 36, Aug. 1963: 31.

560. Ataka i kontrataka [An attack and a counterattack] Za rubezhom, no. 22, May 1964: 3.

561. Castro, José. Makkartizm v Argentine [McCarthyism in Argentina] Probl. mira i sots., v. 3, no. 12, Dec. 1960: 95–96.

562. Chto takoe "Takuara"? [What is the "Tacuara"?] Nov. vrem., v. 21, no. 11, Mar. 1964: 22–23.
Rightist organizations.

563. Codovilla, Victorio. Krepnet edinstvo narodnykh sil Argentiny [The unity of Argentine national forces is growing stronger] Probl. mira i sots., v. 5, no. 12, Dec. 1962: 24–30.

564. ———. Velichestvennye perspektivy stroitel'stva kommunizma i ukrepleniia mira [Great prospects for the building of communism and preserving peace] Probl. mira i sots., v. 2, no. 1, Jan. 1959: 16–18.

565. Ferrari, Alberto. Kommunisty Argentiny ob opasnosti reaktsionnogo perevorota [The Argentine Communists warn against the menace of a reactionary coup] Probl. mira i sots., v. 7, no. 9, Sept. 1964: 45–47.

566. Ghioldi, Rodolfo. Argentinskaia voenshchina na sluzhbe reaktsii [The Argentine military are in the service of reaction] Probl. mira i sots., v. 6, no. 3, Mar. 1963: 10–16.

567. Giudici, Ernesto. Antikommunizm—vrag chelovechestva [Anticommunism is the enemy of mankind] Probl. mira i sots., v. 5, no. 10, Oct. 1962: 76–78.

568. González Alberdi, Paulino. Klassy i osvoboditel'naia bor'ba v Argentine [Social classes and the struggle for liberation in Argentina] Probl. mira i sots., v. 2, no. 9, Sept. 1959: 69–70.

569. Gutiérrez, Osvaldo. Razbitaia "vitrina" zapadnoi demokratii [A shattered "showcase" of western democracy] Probl. mira i sots., v. 6, no. 9, Sept. 1963: 94–95.

570. Husseini, Mazen. Bor'ba s tsenzorami [Struggle with censors] Vsem. stud. nov., v. 16, no. 4, Apr. 1962: 1.

571. IAroshevskii, B. Boi v Buenos-Airese [Battles in Buenos Aires] Za rubezhom, no. 39, Sept. 1962: 28–29.

572. ———. Tri generala za chetyre dnia; reportazh o sobytiiakh v Argentine [Three generals in four days; a news story about political events in Argentina] Za rubezhom, no. 33, Aug. 1962: 28.

573. Iscaro, Rubens. Argentina [Argentina] Vsem. prof. dvizh., no. 8/9, Aug.-Sept. 1960: 5–6.

574. Marini, Salvador. Dve nedeli posle vyborov [Two weeks after the elections] Za rubezhom, no. 13, Mar. 1962: 15.

575. Neradostnyi prazdnik [A sad holiday] Za rubezhom, no. 21, May 1962: 2.

576. "Okhota za ved'mami" ["Witch hunting"] Inostr. lit., no. 10, Oct. 1963: 277.

577. "Operatsiia vozvrashchenie" [Operation "Homecoming"] Za rubezhom, no. 47, Nov. 1964: 2–3.
The Peronista movement.

578. P. G. A. Chemu uchat vybory v Argentine [What the lessons of the Argentine elections are] Probl. mira i sots., v. 3, no. 6, June 1960: 77–80.

579. Pedronsini, Alberto. Otmenit' antinarodnye dekrety! [The reactionary decrees must be repealed!] Probl. mira i sots., v. 7, no. 1, Jan. 1964: 88–90.

580. Peña, Alcira de la. Protiv voennoi diktatury, za pravitel'stvo demokraticheskoi koalitsii [Against military dictatorship, for a government of democratic coalition] Part. zhizn', no. 14, July 1962: 65–71.

581. Pérez, Silvia. Aresty i pytki ne zaglushat gnev argentinskogo naroda [Arrests and tortures will not cool the wrath of the Argentine people] Probl. mira i sots., v. 5, no. 8, Aug. 1962: 93.

582. Pervyi shag [The first step] Nov. vrem., v. 22, no. 48, Nov. 1964: 24.

583. Po komande generalov [By order of the generals] Za rubezhom, no. 14, Apr. 1962: 2.

584. Poliakovskii, V. Burnye sobytiia v Argentine [Stormy events in Argentina] Za rubezhom, no. 17, Apr. 1962: 13.

585. Polozhenie po-prezhnemu ostroe [The situation is still stormy] Za rubezhom, no. 18, May 1962: 2.

586. "Preliudiia" voenshchiny [A prelude to the action of military groups] Za rubezhom, no. 13, Mar. 1963: 4.

587. Russkikh, G.   Sobytiia v Argentine [Events in Argentina] Nov. vrem., v. 20, no. 15, Apr. 1962: 12–13.

588. Review. Mir. ekon. i mezhdunar. otn., no. 4, 1963: 156.
     German fascists.
     A review of Michael Frank's *Die letzte Bastion Nazis in Argentinien* (Hamburg, Ruetten und Loening, 1962. 158 p.).

589. Review. Probl. mira i sots., v. 2, no. 8, Aug. 1959: 93–94.
     Political science.
     A review of J. Marinello's *Ocho notas sobre Aníbal Ponce* (Buenos Aires, Cuadernos de Cultura, 1958. 72 p.).

590. Sinai, Rubén. Sorvat' zamysly reaktsii v Argentine [Let us thwart the reactionary intrigues in Argentina] Probl. mira i sots., v. 5, no. 11, Nov. 1962: 94–95.

591. Strelin, A. K sobytiiam v Argentine [On events in Argentina] Mezhdunar. zhizn', v. 9, no. 5, May 1962: 108–110.

592. Tarasov, K.   Sobytiia v Argentine [Events in Argentina] *In* K voprosam sovremennykh mezhdunarodnykh otnoshenii. no. 2. Moscow, Ob-vo po rasprostr. polit. i nauchn. znanii, 1959: 16–25.

593. Vybory s ogovorkami [Elections with reservations] Za rubezhom, no. 28, July 1963: 4.

594. Vybory v Argentine [Elections in Argentina] Za rubezhom, no. 12, Mar. 1962: 2.

595. Zatiazhnoi krizis [A lingering crisis] Za rubezhom, no. 20, May 1962: 3.

See also entries no. 460, 2391, and 2396.

b. Bolivia

596. Livantsev, Konstantin Evgen'evich, *and* Sh. I. Vidgop. Boliviia; ocherk konstitutsionnogo razvitiia, obshchestvennogo i gosudarstvennogo stroia [Bolivia; a study of its constitutional history and its social and governmental system] Leningrad, Izd-vo Leningr. un-ta, 1963. 89 p.
     F3321.L5

597. Chto i pochemu proizoshlo v Bolivii, Ekvadore [What happened and why it happened in Bolivia and Ecuador] Smena, v. 37, no. 14, July 1960: 15.

598. Ershov, I.   Boliviia: dve tendentsii v natsional'no-osvoboditel'nom dvizhenii [Two different trends in the Bolivian national liberation movement] Mir. ekon. i mezhdunar. otn., no. 7, July 1964: 54–63.

599. Ignat'ev, O. Chto proizoshlo v Bolivii [What happened in Bolivia] Nov. vrem., v. 22, no. 47, Nov. 1964: 21–22.

600. Levin, V. Vybory v Bolivii i Ekvadore [Elections in Bolivia and Ecuador] Za rubezhom, no. 1, June 1960: 11.

601. Narod pred"iavliaet schet [The people make their demands] Za rubezhom, no. 45, Nov. 1964: 10–11.

602. Neobychnye vybory [Strange elections] Za rubezhom, no. 23, June 1964: 3.

603. "Operatsiia zagovor" [Operation "Conspiracy"] Za rubezhom, no. 40, Oct. 1964: 2.

604. Pas Estensoro; biograficheskaia spravka [Paz Estenssoro; a biographical note] Nov. vrem., v. 18, no. 34, Aug. 1960: 21.

605. Ruben Khulio Kastro; biograficheskaia spravka [Rubén Julio Castro; a biographical note] Nov. vrem., v. 19, no. 21, May 1961: 15.

See also entries no. 2399 and 2400.

c. Brazil

606. Razumovich, Nikolai Nikanorovich. Gosudarstvennyi stroi Brazilii [The governmental system of Brazil] Moscow, Gosiurizdat, 1959. 87 p.
     JL2415 1959.R3

607. Afonso Arinos; biograficheskaia spravka [Afonso Arinos; a biographical note] Nov. vrem., v. 19, no. 7, Feb. 1961: 31.

608. Aliab'ev, M.   Mesiats spustia [One month later] Za rubezhom, no. 18, May 1964: 26.

609. Almeida, Josué. Oni edut v Moskvu [They go to Moscow] Za rubezhom, no. 27, July 1962: 8.
The peace movement.

610. Arauzho Kastro; biograficheskaia spravka [De Araujo Castro; a biographical note] Nov. vrem., no. 38, Sept. 1963: 15.

611. Arismendi, Rodney. Bitva ne konchilas' [The battle isn't over] Za rubezhom, no. 15, Apr. 1964: 9.

612. Bazarian, Zh. Review. Nov. vrem., v. 19, no. 44, Oct. 1961: 30–31.
A review of Rui Faco's Brasil, século XX (Rio de Janeiro, Vitória, 1960. 261 p.).

613. Bonavides, Anibal. Vdokhnovliaiushchii primer [An inspiring example] Agitator, no. 21, Nov. 1963: 11–12.

614. Borisov, V. Brazil'tsy vybiraiut; reportazh [Brazilians elect their parliament; a news story] Za rubezhom, no. 41, Oct. 1962: 19.

615. Brandão, Octavio, and Oleg Ignat'ev. Zhiv chernyi admiral [The black admiral is still alive] Ogonek, v. 41, no. 26, June 1963: 20–21.
A mutiny of Brazilian sailors.

616. Braziliia; mesiats posle krizisa [Brazil; a month after the crisis] Za rubezhom, no. 40, Oct. 1961: 9.

617. Broshado da Rosha; biograficheskaia spravka [Brochado da Rocha; a biographical note] Nov. vrem., v. 20, no. 32, Aug. 1962: 27.

618. Chto proiskhodit v Brazilii [Current events in Brazil] Za rubezhom, no. 35, Sept. 1961: 2–3.

619. Dias, Giocondo. Nekotorye problemy klassovoi bor'by v Brazilii [Some problems concerning the class struggle in Brazil] Probl. mira i sots., v. 7, no. 1, Jan. 1964: 21–25.

620. Dutra, Eloy. IBAD—brazil'skie berchisty; otryvok iz knigi [IBAD, the Brazilian Birch Society; excerpt from a book] Za rubezhom, no. 17, Apr. 1964: 12–13.

621. Eliutin, IU. Sverzhenie pod vidom "otstavki" [An overthrow under the pretense of "resignation"] Mezhdunar. zhizn', v. 8, no. 10, Oct. 1961: 115–117.

622. Ermes Lima [Hermes Lima] Nov. vrem., v. 20, no. 11, Mar. 1963: 23.

623. Frantsisko Klementino de Sant'iago Dantas; biograficheskaia spravka [Francisco Clementino de San Thiago Dantas; a biographical note] Nov. vrem., v. 19, no. 49, Dec. 1961: 29.

624. Front naroda [A popular front] Za rubezhom, no. 44, Nov. 1961: 4.

625. Front natsional'nogo osvobozhdeniia Brazilii [The National Liberation Front in Brazil] Mezhdunar. zhizn', v. 10, no. 2, Feb. 1963: 147–148.

626. Golubev, D. K polozheniiu v Brazilii [Political situation in Brazil] Agitator, no. 12, June 1964: 56–58.

627. Gramatov, A. Aktivizatsiia patrioticheskikh sil [The activation of patriotic groups] Mezhdunar. zhizn', v. 10, no. 3, Mar. 1963: 117–118.

628. ———. Luchshii put' razvitiia [The best path of development] Mezhdunar. zhizn', v. 9, no. 10, Oct. 1962: 130–131.
A review of Franklin de Oliveira's Revolução e contra-revolução no Brasil (Rio de Janeiro, Editôra Civilização Brasileira, 1962. 139 p.).

629. Juárez, Claudio. Zhanio—da, Laserda—net! [Janio—yes, Lacerda—no!] V zashch. mira, no. 11, Nov. 1961: 23–31.

630. Kakim budet avgust? [What will happen in August?] Za rubezhom, no. 29, July 1963: 4.

631. Kamynin, L. Novye gorizonty Brazilii [Brazil's new horizons] Nov. vrem., v. 20, no. 10, Mar. 1963: 19–20.

632. Koval', B. I. Iz istorii rasprostraneniia marksizma v Brazilii [History of the dissemination of Marxist ideas in Brazil] Vop. ist., v. 38, no. 3, Mar. 1963: 191.
A review of an article by A. Pereira in Estudos sociais (Rio de Janeiro) no. 12, 1962: 404–419.

633. Kraminov, D. Braziliia burlit [Seething Brazil] Za rubezhom, no. 41, Oct. 1963: 7–9.

634. Ne sgushchaia krasok [It isn't an exaggeration] Za rubezhom, no. 43, Oct. 1964: 2.

635. Ordem contra progresso. World student news, v. 18, no. 4, 1964: 5–8.

636. Plebistsit nadezhdy [A plebescite of hope] Za rubezhom, no. 1, Jan. 1963: 4.

637. Podskazka-provokatsiia [A provocative suggestion] Za rubezhom, no. 5, Feb. 1963: 4–5.
    False interpretation of the Brazilian political situation in the U.S. press claimed.

638. Poliakovskii, V. Braziliia zhdet peremen [Brazil awaits a change] Za rubezhom, no. 36, Sept. 1963: 18.

639. ———. Burnyi mart v Brazilii [Stormy March in Brazil] Za rubezhom, no. 12, Mar. 1964: 9.

640. ———. God spustia [One year later] Za rubezhom, no. 36, Sept. 1962: 14–15.

641. ———. Povzroslevshii za den' Rio [A day which brought maturity to Rio] Za rubezhom, no. 33, Aug. 1963: 5.

642. ———. Rozhdenstvenskoe leto v Rio [The Christmas summer in Rio] Za rubezhom, no. 1, Jan. 1964: 14–15.

643. Posle krizisa: kakim kursom? [What course will they choose after the crisis?] Za rubezhom, no. 37, Sept. 1961: 3.

644. Prestes, Luis Carlos. O politicheskom polozhenii v Brazilii [The political situation in Brazil] Nov. vrem., v. 19, no. 50, Dec. 1961: 12–13.

645. Putchisty poluchili otpor [The putschists have suffered a repulse] Za rubezhom, no. 36, Sept. 1961: 2–3.

646. Reshat' budet narod [The decision rests with the people] Za rubezhom, no. 28, July 1962: 12–13.

647. Review. Probl. mira i sots., v. 2, no. 11, Nov. 1959: 95.
    A review of Luis Carlos Prestes' *A situação política e a luta por um governo nacionalista e democrático* (Rio de Janeiro, Editorial Vitória, 1959. 74 p.).

648. Rubio, C. Nastuplenie reaktsii v Brazilii [An offensive by reaction in Brazil] Probl. mira i sots., v. 7, no. 5, May 1964: 89–90.

649. Silva, José. Brazil'skaia tragediia [Brazilian tragedy] Za rubezhom, no. 21, May 1964: 21–22.

650. Skhvatka s kongressom [A brush with the Congress] Za rubezhom, no. 38, Sept. 1962: 3.

651. Tankredo Neves; biograficheskaia spravka [Tancredo Neves; a biographical note] Nov. vrem., v. 19, no. 49, Dec. 1961: 29.

652. Tavares de Sá, J. B. Peregruppirovka demokraticheskikh sil v Brazilii [A realignment of democratic forces in Brazil] Probl. mira i sots., v. 7, no. 12, Dec. 1964: 85–87.

653. Tuchnin, R. Zhoao Gulart; biograficheskaia spravka [João Goulart; a biographical note] Mir. ekon. i mezhdunar. otn., no. 8, 1963: 136–137.

654. V ozhidanii peremen [Waiting for changes] Za rubezhom, no. 5, Feb. 1961: 2–3.

655. Vladimirov, V. Chernyi admiral [The black admiral] Ogonek, v. 40, no. 50, Dec. 1962: 30–31.
    A mutiny in the Brazilian Navy.

656. Za mesiats do plebistsita [A month before the plebiscite] Za rubezhom, no. 49, Dec. 1962: 4.

657. Zakulisnaia storona gosudarstvennogo perevorota [Behind the scenes of a coup d'état] Vsem. prof. dvizh., no. 6, June 1964: 13–15.

658. Zhanio Kuadros; biograficheskaia spravka [Janio Quadros; a biographical note] Nov. vrem., v. 18, no. 47, Nov. 1960: 27.

659. Zharkaia zima [A hot winter] Za rubezhom, no. 27, July 1962: 2–3.

660. Zhoao Gulart; biograficheskaia spravka [João Goulart; a biographical note] Nov. vrem., v. 19, no. 1, 1961: 31.

See also entries no. 2401, 2404, 2418, 2419, 2424 and 3036.

d. Chile

661. Gvozdarev, Boris Ivanovich. Gosu-darstvennyi stroi Chili [The governmental system of Chile] Moscow, Gosiurizdat, 1960. 68 p.   JL2615 1960.G8

662. Allende, Salvador. IA otvechaiu senatoru Freiu [My answer to Senator Frei] Za rubezhom, no. 36, Sept. 1964: 18.

663. Artiushenkov, M. Uspekh demokraticheskikh sil Chili [A success of democratic forces in Chile] Mezhdunar. zhizn', v. 8, no. 4, Apr. 1961: 123–124.

664. Bol'shaia pobeda [A great victory] Za rubezhom, no. 11, Mar. 1961: 5.

665. Borovskii, V. "Pravye" smotriat vlevo ["Right-wingers" look toward the left] Za rubezhom, no. 37, Sept. 1964: 18.

666. Corvalán, Luis. Bor'ba za sozdanie narodnogo pravitel'stva v Chile [Efforts to establish a people's government in Chile] Probl. mira i sots., v. 5, no. 12, Dec. 1962: 17–23.

667. ———. Za sozdanie narodnogo pravitel'stva [For the establishment of a people's government] Kommunist, v. 39, no. 6, Apr. 1962: 93–102.

668. Eduardo Frei Montal'va; biograficheskaia spravka [Eduardo Frei Montalva; a biographical note] Nov. vrem., v. 22, no. 39, Sept. 1964: 27.

669. Federiko Garcia Lorka o sobytiiakh v Chili [Federico García Lorca on events in Chile] Inostr. lit., no. 12, Dec. 1960: 257.
Political events of 1931 in Chile.

670. Gladkii, V. Viva Al'ende! Progressivnaia pechat' Chili v dni prezidentskikh vyborov [Viva Allende! How the progressive press of Chile covered the presidential election] Sov. pech., no. 8, Aug. 1964: 56–57.

671. Gornov, M. Chto pokazali vybory v Chili [What the results of Chilean elections show us] Nov. vrem., v. 22, no. 38, Sept. 1964: 7–8.

672. ———. Kto budet prezidentom Chili? [Who will be the next president of Chile?]

Nov. vrem., v. 21, no. 24, June 1964: 16–18.

673. Kamynin, L. Chili—predvybornyi vulkan [A pre-election volcano in Chile] Mezhdunar. zhizn', v. 11, no. 8, Aug. 1964: 60–65.

674. Kudachkin, M. F. Bor'ba za demokratiiu i sotsial'nyi progress v Chili [The struggle for democracy and social progress in Chile] Nov. i noveish. ist., no. 4, 1964: 18–28.
Summary in English, p. 196.

675. ———. Novaia pobeda [New victory] Part. zhizn', no. 7, Apr. 1961: 65–66.

676. Millás, Orlando. Antiimperialisticheskoe edinstvo—zalog pobed naroda Chili [Anti-imperialist unity ensures the victory of the Chilean people] Probl. mira i sots., v. 4, no. 7, July 1961: 27–32.

677. Pavlenko, A. Narodnyi front na pod"eme [The popular front moves ahead] Mezhdunar. zhizn', v. 11, no. 5, May 1964: 117–118.

678. Pobeda v Kuriko [The victory in Curicó] Za rubezhom, no. 13, Mar. 1964: 3.

679. Tuchnin, R. Chili nakanune vyborov [Chile on the eve of elections] Mir. ekon. i mezhdunar. otn., no. 8, 1964: 96–99.

See also entries no. 2435, 2438, 3046, 3047, 3106, 3109, and 3110.

e. Colombia

680. Molochkova, R. A. Bor'ba trudiashchikhsia mass i Kommunisticheskoi partii Kolumbii za natsional'nuiu nezavisimost' strany, 1948–1958 gg. [The struggle of the Colombian toiling masses and the Communist Party for national independence, 1948–1958] Moscow, Mysl', 1964. 18 p.
Author's abstract of a dissertation for the degree of Candidate in Historical Sciences.

681. Avad, José Elías. Den' pridet . . . [The day will come . . .] Zhen. mira, no. 10, 1964: 24–25.
Guerrilla movement.

682. Cardona Hoyos, José. Kolumbiiskaia voenshchina terpit porazhenie [The

Colombian military suffer a defeat] Probl. mira i sots., v. 7, no. 11, Nov. 1964: 93–95.
Guerrilla movement.

683. ———. Snova grazhdanskaia voina v Kolumbii? [A civil war in Colombia again?] Probl. mira i sots., v. 7, no. 7, July 1964: 94–95.

684. ———. Usilenie terrora v Kolumbii [Intensification of political terrorism in Colombia] Probl. mira i sots., v. 6, no. 12, Dec. 1963: 77 79.

685. ———. V usloviiakh antinarodnogo rezhima [Under a reactionary regime] Probl. mira i sots., v. 6, no. 10, Oct. 1963: 84–85.

686. Gil'ermo Leon Valensia; biograficheskaia spravka [Guillermo León Valencia; a biographical note] Nov. vrem., v. 20, no. 21, July 1962: 24.

687. IArov, L. Soldaty v gorakh [Soldiers in the mountains] Za rubezhom, no. 17, Apr. 1964: 24.
Guerrilla movement.

688. Istoriia Vioty [The history of Viotá] Zhen. mira, no. 10, 1964: 26.
Guerrilla movement.

689. Jiménez, Rafael. Krov' na nivakh Kolumbii [Blood on the fields of Colombia] Mol. komm., no. 1, Jan. 1963: 114–117.

690. Khose Ansizan Lopes; biograficheskaia spravka [José Ancizan López; a biographical note] Nov. vrem., v. 21, no. 35, Aug. 1963: 13.

691. Kniazev, R. K polozheniiu v Kolumbii [The situation in Colombia] Mezhdunar. zhizn', v. 9, no. 2, Feb. 1962: 123–124.

692. Kobysh, Vitalii. Violencia—smert' iz-za ugla [Violencia, murder by ambush] Ogonek, v. 42, no. 50, Dec. 1964: 26–27.

693. "Krasnye raiony" Kolumbii [The "red regions" of Colombia] Smena, v. 41, no. 17, Sept. 1964: 11.
Guerrilla movement.

694. Leonidov, B. Tam, za gorami, Marketaliia [Marquetalia is behind the hills] Mol. komm., no. 11, Nov. 1964:105–109.
Guerrilla movement.

695. Listov, V. Urok Kolumbii [The lesson of Colombia] Nov. vrem., v. 22, no. 44, Oct. 1964: 16–18.
Guerrilla movement.

696. ———. "Operatsiia Marketalia" ["Operation Marquetalia"] Nov. vrem., v. 21, no. 28, July 1964: 27–28.
Guerrilla movement.

697. Moreno Díaz, Joaquín. Griaznye ruki antikommunizma [The dirty hand of anticommunism] Probl. mira i sots., v. 5, no. 9, Sept. 1962: 77–78.

698. Nizskii, V. Tam, za kholmami,—Marketaliia [Marquetalia is behind the hills] Za rubezhom, no. 38, Sept. 1964: 25–26.
Guerrilla movement.

699. Osobniak v kvartale Chapinero [A mansion in the Chapinero residential area] Za rubezhom, no. 33, Aug. 1963: 4.

700. Piedrait, J. Respublika Marketaliia [The Republic of Marquetalia] Za rubezhom, no. 22, May 1964: 17.
Guerrilla movement.

701. Rozhdenie novykh sil v Kolumbii [The birth of new forces in Colombia] Vsem. prof. dvizh., no. 5, May 1960: 47–48.

702. Vieira, Gilberto. Politicheskoe polozhenie v Kolumbii [Political situation in Colombia] Nov. vrem., v. 21, no. 28, July 1963: 11–14.

See also entries no. 2444, 2445, 3049 and 3112.

f. Costa Rica

703. Gamboa, Francisco. Burliashchii kotel [A boiling kettle] Za rubezhom, no. 30, July 1962: 25.

704. Gutiérrez, Joaquín. Kosta-Rika: vozmushchennaia tishina [Indignant calm in Costa Rica] Za rubezhom, no. 12, Sept. 1960: 21.

705. Jiménez, Jorge. Khunty sodeistviia progressu v Kosta-Rike [Juntas for the promotion of progress in Costa Rica] Probl. mira i sots., v. 2, no. 5, May 1959: 74–75.

706. Zamyshliaiut nedobroe [Evil intentions] Nov. vrem., v. 21, no. 10, Mar. 1964: 22.

See also entry no. 2446.

g. Cuba

707. Al'tman, I. I. Kuba boretsa za svobodu [Cuba fights for freedom] Vilnius, Gospolitnauchizdat, 1960. 39 p.
In Lithuanian.

708. Andrianov, Vasilii Vasil'evich. Svobodnaia Kuba [Free Cuba] Moscow, Sotsekgiz, 1960. 84 p.   F1788.A76
Reviewed in *Moskva*, v. 5, no. 1, 1961: 212; in *V mire knig*, v. 1, no. 2, Feb. 1961: 10.

709. Avetisian, G. S. Kuba nesgibaema [Inflexible Cuba] Yerevan, Aipetrat, 1961. 57 p.
In Armenian.

710. Borovik, Genrikh. Kak eto bylo na Kube; glavy iz dokumental'noi povesti [How it happened in Cuba; chapters from a documentary tale] Moscow, Pravda, 1961. 63 p.

711. Borovskii, V. N. Znamia revoliutsii nad Kuboi [The banner of revolution over Cuba] Moscow, Gospolitizdat, 1964. 78 p.   F1788.B63

712. Calderío, Francisco (Blas Roca, *pseud.*) Kuba—svobodnaia territoriia Ameriki; doklad na VIII Natsional'noi Assamblee Narodno-Sotsialisticheskoi Partii Kuby [Cuba—the free territory of America; report to the Eighth National Assembly of the Popular Socialist Party of Cuba] Moscow, Izd-vo inostr. lit., 1961. 151 p.
Translated by A. B. Zykova and R. Martínez from the Spanish.

713. Castro, Fidel. Rech' na XV sessii General'noi Assamblei OON 26 sentiabria 1960 goda [Speech at the 15th session of the General Assembly of the United Nations, September 26, 1960] Moscow, Izd-vo inostr. lit., 1960. 63 p.
Translated from the Spanish.
Reviewed by IU. Pavlov in *Nov. mir*, v. 36, no. 12, Dec. 1960: 267–270.

714. ———. Rechi i vystupleniia [Speeches and addresses] Moscow, Izd-vo inostr. lit., 1960. 575 p.   F1788.C2717
Translated from the Spanish.
Reviewed by V. Vagin in *Agitator*, no. 9,

May 1961: 61–63; by M. Kremnev in *Nov. vrem.*, v. 18, no. 52, Dec. 1960: 30–31; by V. Mozhaiskii in *V mire knig*, v. 1, no. 4, Apr. 1961: 8.

715. ———. Rechi i vystupleniia, 1961–1963 gg. [Speeches and addresses, 1961–1963] Moscow, Izd-vo inostr. lit., 1963. 815 p.
                F1788.C2717 1963
Translated from the Spanish.
Reviewed by B. Gorbachev and A. Kalinin in *Kommunist*, v. 40, no. 11, June 1963: 110–113; by O. Vasil'ev in *Za rubezhom*, no. 21, May 1963: 6.

716. Chichkov, Vasilii Mikhailovich. Zaria nad Kuboi; zapiski zhurnalista [Dawn over Cuba; notes of a journalist] Moscow, Izd-vo IMO, 1960. 124 p.
                F1788.C46

717. ———. Zaria nad Kuboi; zapiski zhurnalista [Dawn over Cuba; notes of a journalist] 2d ed. Moscow, Izd-vo IMO, 1961. 144 p.   F1788.C46 1961

718. Efimov, Aleksei Vladimirovich, *and others, eds.* Piat' let Kubinskoi revoliutsii [Five years of the Cuban Revolution] Moscow, Izd-vo Akad. nauk SSSR, 1963. 292 p.   HC157.C9A55
Reviewed by L. Lerer in *Nov. mir*, v. 40, no. 3, Mar. 1964: 276–277; by V.V. Andrianov in *Nov. i noveish. ist.*, no. 2, 1964: 140–143; by M. Ionesian in *Sov. etn.*, no. 5, Sept.-Oct. 1964: 183–186; by N. Bobrik in *Nov. knigi*, v. 9, no. 1, Jan. 1964: 55–57.

719. Espín de Castro, Vilma. Kuba borctsia—Kuba pobedit [Cuba is struggling and she will win] Moscow, Sotsekgiz, 1960. 61 p.
                F1788.E785
Translated by V. Kuteishchikova and E. Rovinskaia from the Spanish *Cuba lucha—Cuba vencerá*.
Reviewed by M. A. Okuneva in *Nov. i noveish. ist.*, no. 4, 1960: 166–167.

720. Gaidaenko, Ivan. Zvezda svobody [The star of freedom] Kiev, Gospolitizdat, 1963. 59 p.   DLC
Reviewed by IA. Gorenko in *Raduga*, no. 10, Oct. 1963: 181–184.

721. Guevara, Ernesto. Partizanskaia voina [Guerrilla warfare] Moscow, Izd-vo inostr. lit., 1961. 136 p.
Translated from the Spanish *La guerra de guerrillas*.
Reviewed by N. Mil'gram in *Voen.-ist.*

zhur., v. 3, no. 7, July 1961: 103–106; by S. Vorob'ev in *Nov. mir*, v. 37, no. 9, Sept. 1961: 274–276.

722. Kamynin, Leonid Ivanovich. Zdravstvui, Kuba! [Hello, Cuba!] Moscow, Izvestiia, 1960. 78 p.   F1765.K3

723. Kuba—da; sbornik [Cuba—yes; collected articles] Moscow, Pravda, 1962. 77 p.   F1765.K8
Reviewed by P. Portnov in *Sov. pech.*, no. 2, Feb. 1962: 48.

724. Lapova, R. A. Obshchestvennyi i gosudarstvennyi stroi Kubinskoi Respubliki [The social and political system of the Cuban Republic] Saratov, Izd-vo Sarat. un-ta, 1963. 44 p.

725. Lisniak, V. A. Heroichna Kuba [Heroic Cuba] Kiev, Derzhpolitvydav, 1961. 61 p.

726. Nitoburg, E. L. Kuba v bor'be za nezavisimost' [Cuba in the struggle for independence] Moscow, Znanie, 1960. 40 p.   AS262.V833, ser. 7, 1960, no. 10

727. North, Joseph. Kuba—nadezhda kontinenta [Cuba: the hope of a hemisphere] Moscow, Izd-vo inostr. lit., 1961. 103 p.
Translated by I. Gurova from the English.

728. ———. Kubinskaia revoliutsiia; ia videl pobedu naroda [Cuba's Revolution; I saw the people's victory] Moscow, Izd-vo inostr. lit., 1960. 42 p.
F1788.N617
Translated by V. E. Repin from the English. Introductory article by K. M. Obyden.

729. Obyden, Konstantin Mikhailovich. Kuba v bor'be za svobodu i nezavisimost' [Cuba struggling for her freedom and independence] Moscow, Gospolitizdat, 1959. 93 p.   F1788.O2
Also published in Latvian.

730. Osheverov, G. Fidel' Kastro [Fidel Castro] Moscow, Gospolitizdat, 1961. 29 p.   F1788.C307
Also published in Lithuanian, Kirgiz, Altai, and Tajik.

731. ———. Shchedroe serdtse Fidelia [Fidel's generous heart] Moscow, Izvestiia, 1961. 87 p.

732. Osheverov, G., *and others*. Kuba—da! [Cuba—yes!] Moscow, Mol. gvardiia, 1961. 91 p.

733. Pardo Llada, José. V gorakh S'erra-Maestra; zapiski zhurnalista [In the Sierra Maestra mountains; notes of a journalist] Moscow, Izd-vo inostr. lit., 1960. 118 p.   F1788.P317
Translated by IU. N. Paporov from the Spanish *Memorias de la Sierra Maestra*.
Reviewed by Genrikh Borovik in *Inostr. lit.*, no. 12, Dec. 1960: 243–244.

734. Partido Socialista Popular (Cuba). Materialy 8-go Natsional'nogo s"ezda Narodno-sotsialisticheskoi partii Kuby, Gavana, 16–21 avgusta 1960 g. [Materials of the Eighth National Congress of the Popular Socialist Party of Cuba, Havana, August 16–21, 1960] Moscow, Gospolitizdat, 1961. 288 p.
Translated from the Spanish.

735. Razumovich, Nikolai Nikanorovich. Gosudarstvennye preobrazovaniia revoliutsionnoi Kuby [Governmental reforms in Revolutionary Cuba] Moscow, Mezhdunarodnye otnosheniia, 1964. 105 p.
F1788.R34

736. Rubinshtein, Lev. Malen'kii kubinets [Little boy from Cuba] Moscow, Detskii mir, 1962. 20 p.   DLC

737. Saari, E., *ed.* Kuba; sbornik statei [Cuba; collected articles] Tallinn, Estgosizdat, 1963. 87 p.
In Estonian.

738. Shervashidze, IU. L. Revoliutsionnaia Kuba [Revolutionary Cuba] Irkutsk, Obl. otd. O-va po rasprostr. polit. i nauch. znanii, 1961. 38 p.

739. Talovov, V. P. Kubinskii reportazh [News stories from Cuba] Leningrad, Lenizdat, 1964. 87 p.

740. Tikhmenev, Vladimir Evgen'evich. Kuba—da! [Cuba—yes!] Moscow, Gospolitizdat, 1961. 174 p. F1788.T5

741. Varela, Alfredo. Kuba revoliutsionnaia [Revolutionary Cuba] Moscow, Sotsekgiz, 1962. 318 p.
Translated from the Spanish. Introductory article by S. A. Gonionskii.

742. Velasco Gil, Carlos M. Kuba—da! IAnki—net! [Cuba—yes! Yankees—no!] Moscow, Izd-vo inostr. lit., 1961. 282 p.
F1788.V437
Translated by V. N. Kuteishchikova from

the Spanish *Cuba si! Yanquis no!* Introductory article by S. A. Gonionskii.

743. Wasilewska, Wanda. Arkhipelag svobody [An archipelago of freedom] Moscow, Pravda, 1961. 94 p.   F1788.W3
Translated from the Polish. Also published in Chuvash.

744. ———. Fidel' Kastro [Fidel Castro] Moscow, Znanie, 1962. 110 p.
Translated from the Polish.

745. Zavriev, D. S. Gosudarstvo natsional'noi demokratii [The national democratic state] Tiflis, Sabchota Sakartvelo, 1964. 197 p.
In Georgian.

746. Aguirre, Severo. Bor'ba prodolzhaetsia [The struggle continues] Mol. kolkh., v. 26, no. 4, Apr. 1959: 8.
Translated from the Spanish.

747. ———. Revoliutsiia na Kube [The revolution in Cuba] Mir. ekon. i mezhdunar. otn., no. 5, May 1959: 22–27.

748. Akulai, V. E. Revoliutsionnye organizatsii Kuby vo glave bor'by za sozdanie natsional'noi assotsiatsii melkikh zemledel'tsev, dekabr' 1960-mai 1961 g. [Cuban revolutionary organizations in the vanguard of the struggle for the establishment of an association of small farmers, December 1960–May 1961] Uch. zap. Kishinevskogo un., v. 73, 1964: 143–159.

749. Alleg, Henri. Velikii patriot; otryvki iz knigi [The great patriot; excerpts from a book] Za rubezhom, no. 3, Jan. 1964: 7.
Fidel Castro.
Translated from the French.

750. Al'perovich, M. S. Kubinskaia revoliutsiia i poiski amerikanskim zhurnalom "retsepta" protiv revoliutsii [The Cuban Revolution and an American periodical's efforts to establish a "remedy" against revolutions] Vop. ist., no. 12, Dec. 1960: 198–199.
A review of the periodical *Current History* (Philadelphia, March 1960).

751. Andrianov, V. "Gusanos" i ikh pokroviteli ["Los gusanos" and their protectors] Mezhdunar. zhizn', v. 11, no. 7, July 1964: 109–110.

752. Arcocha, Juan. Kuba: tri goda revoliutsii [Three years of revolution in Cuba] Mezhdunar. zhizn', v. 9, no. 1, Jan. 1962: 117–119.

753. Armando Khart Davalos; biograficheskaia spravka [Armando Hart Dávalos; a biographical note] Nov. vrem., v. 19, no. 22, May 1961: 17 .

754. Bako, G. Gnezdo sterviatnikov [A nest of vultures] Nov. vrem., v. 19, no. 17, Apr. 1961: 26–28.
Political activity of Cuban refugees in the United States.

755. Baliño, Félix. Kuba prazdnuet pervuiu godovshchinu svoei nezavisimosti [Cuba celebrates the first anniversary of her independence] Mol. mira, no. 1, 1960: 18–20.

756. Blas Roka; biograficheskaia spravka [Blas Roca; a biographical note] Nov. vrem., v. 19, no. 41, Oct. 1961: 13.

757. Blok, A. Rodina ili smert'! [Fatherland or death!] Uzbekiston, v. 22, no. 7, July 1963: 26.

758. Bobrovskii, A. Svetleet nebo nad Kuboi [The sky grows brighter in Cuba] Ogonek, v. 37, no. 3, Jan. 1959: 26–27.

759. Borovik, Genrikh. Kak eto bylo na Kube [How it happened in Cuba] Ogonek, v. 38, no. 27, July 1960: 22–25; v. 38, no. 28, July 1960: 25–28; v. 38, no. 29, July 1960: 28–31; v. 38, no. 30, July 1960: 26–30.

760. ———. Kak eto bylo na Kube [How it happened in Cuba] Znamia, v. 32, no. 2, Feb. 1962: 77–93; v. 32, no. 3, Mar. 1962: 88–102.

761. ———. Kolybel' [Cradle] Starsh.-serzh., no. 2, Feb. 1961: 16.

762. ———. Kuba vstrechaet rassvet [Cuba is welcoming the dawn] Vokrug sveta, no. 9, Sept. 1960: 30–33.

763. Borovskii, V. Shturm Monkada; kak nachinalas' Kubinskaia revoliutsiia [The attack on Moncada; how the Cuban Revolution began] Nov. vrem., v. 21, no. 30, July 1963: 4–7.

764. Borrero, Félix. "Tam, gde zvezdy goriat tak blizko . . ." ["Where the stars are burning so closely . . ."] Mol. mira, no. 9, 1960: 20–21.

765. Burguete A., R. Stranitsy, smotriashchie v budushchee [Pages which look into the future] Vop. filos., v. 15, no. 6, 1961: 169–173.
A review of Blas Roca's *Cuba, territorio libre de América* (Bogotá, 1960. 152 p.) and his *Los fundamentos del socialismo en Cuba* (Havana, Edicioncs Popularcs, 1960. 219 p.).

766. Burlak, A. Svetoch svobody v Zapadnom polusharii [A beacon light of freedom in the Western Hemisphere] Mezhdunar. zhizn', v. 8, no. 7, July 1961: 161–163.
A review of Fernando Benítez' *La batalla de Cuba* (Mexico City, Ediciones Era, 1960. 185 p.).

767. Burlak, O. Grazhdanskaia voina na Kube [Civil war in Cuba] Mezhdunar. zhizn', v. 6, no. 1, Jan. 1959: 161–162.

768. Calderío, Francisco (Blas Roca, *pseud.*) Kubinskii narod v bor'be za svobodu i nezavisimost' [The Cuban people are striving for freedom and independence] Kommunist, v. 37, no. 7, May 1960: 77–89.
An abbreviated translation from the Spanish.

769. ——. Kak slozhilos' edinstvo revoliutsionnykh sil Kuby [How the unity of the revolutionary forces of Cuba was achieved] Polit. samoobr., v. 5, no. 12, Dec. 1961: 55–60.

770. ——. Narodnaia revoliutsiia na Kube i perspektivy ee dal'neishego razvitiia [The national revolution in Cuba and prospects for its development] Part. zhizn', no. 6, Mar. 1959: 68–73.

771. Carbonell Orroitiner, Héctor, *and others.* Vdokhnovliaiushchii primer [An inspiring example] Sov. profsoiuzy, v. 16, no. 21, Nov. 1960: 58–59.

772. Castro, Fidel. Edinstvenno zakonnaia garantiia kreposti nashei vlasti [The only legal guarantee of the stability of our government] Mezhdunar. zhizn', v. 9, no. 2, Feb. 1962: 87–95.

773. ——. Moe prizvanie—delat' revoliutsiiu [My vocation is to make the revolution] Za rubezhom, no. 29, July 1961: 6–7.
Cuba and the revolutionary movement in Latin America.

774. ——. Narod za nas [The people support us] Za rubezhom, no. 29, July 1963: 14.

775. ——. O Kube, ee nastoiashchem i budushchem [On Cuba's present and future] Nov. vrem., v. 20, no. 18, May 1963: 10–12.

776. ——. Revoliutsiia idet vpered [The revolution marches forward] Za rubezhom, no. 16, Apr. 1963: 11–12.

777. ——. Soldat revoliutsii [Soldier of the revolution] Za rubezhom, no. 18, May 1963: 6.

778. Castro, Raúl. Oni boiatsia primera Kuby [They are frightened by the example of Cuba] Za rubezhom, no. 23, June 1964: 23.
Counterrevolutionary activities.

779. Česnulis, V. Narod Kuby nepobedim [The Cuban people are invincible] Kommunist (Vilnius), no. 8, 1960: 65–68.

780. Chernov, L. Reshimost' kubinskogo naroda [Courage of the Cuban people] Agitator, no. 3, Feb. 1960: 58–60.

781. Chichkov, V. Prazdnik svobodnoi Kuby [The festival of free Cuba] Ogonek, v. 38, no. 1, Jan. 1960: 22–24.

782. ——. Svezhii veter nad Kuboi [A fresh wind over Cuba] Oktiabr', v. 37, no. 2, Feb. 1960: 185–198.

783. Chudesa, sovershennye revoliutsiei [Marvelous accomplishments of the revolution] Inostr. lit., no. 4, Apr. 1962: 278.

784. Demokratychni peretvorennia na Kubi [Democratic reforms in Cuba] Blok. agit. [Ukr.] no. 14, May 1960: 62–64.

785. Eliutin, IU. Gavanskaia deklaratsiia [The Havana declaration] Mezhdunar. zhizn', v. 7, no. 10, Oct. 1960: 119–121.

786. Eremeev, T. Na kubinskoi zemle [In Cuba] Sov. profsoiuzy, v. 7, no. 14, July 1959: 56–59.

787. Ernesto Gevara; biograficheskaia spravka [Ernesto Guevara; a biographical note] Nov. vrem., v. 18, no. 45, Nov. 1960: 13.

788. Escalante, Aníbal. Zashchishchat' i razvivat' dal'she revoliutsiiu [Defend and develop the revolution] Part. zhizn', no. 2, Jan. 1961: 64–69.

789. Fedotov, A. Mal'chishka s bananami [Boy with bananas] IUn. nat., no. 9, Sept. 1961: 32.

790. Gavrikov, IU. P. Izbrannye proizvedeniia Raulia Roa [Raúl Roa's selected works] Nov. i noveish. ist., no. 4, 1964: 177–178.
   A review of Raúl Roa's *Retorno a la alborada* (Las Villas, Universidad, 1964. 2 v.).

791. Gershberg, A. "Kubinskaia revoliutsiia v fotografiiakh" ["The Cuban revolution in photographs"] Sov. foto, v. 23, no. 2, Feb. 1963: 5.

792. Glazami druga [Through the eyes of a friend] Inostr. lit., no. 4, Apr. 1962: 277.
   A review of Jorge Zalamea's *Antecedentes históricos de la Revolución Cubana* (Bogotá, Ediciones Suramérica, 1961. 172 p.).

793. Glushko, I. F. Kniga o kubinskoi revoliutsii [A book on the Cuban Revolution] Nov. i noveish. ist., no. 2, 1961: 174–175.
   A review of Armando Gimenez' *Sierra Maestra; a revolução de Fidel Castro* (São Paulo, Ediçoes Zumbi, 1959. 252 p.).

794. Gómez, José Jorge (Baltazar Enero, *pseud.*) Narod okhraniaet zavoevaniia revoliutsii [The people guard the achievements of the revolution] Kuba, no. 4, Dec. 1964: 28–31.

795. Gorbachev, B., *and* A. Kalinin. Maiak sotsializma na amerikanskom kontinente [A beacon light of socialism on the American continent] Kommunist, v. 40, no. 18, Dec. 1963: 96–105.

796. ———. Zhivaia istoriia Kubinskoi revoliutsii [The living history of the Cuban Revolution] Kommunist, v. 40, no. 11, July 1963: 110–113.

797. Grant, IU. Chto proizoshlo na Kube [What happened in Cuba] Komm. Sov. Latvii, v. 16, no. 5, May 1961: 73–74.

798. Gvozdev, IU. Sem' millionov Kolumbov [Seven million Columbuses] Mezhdunar. zhizn', v. 10, no. 6, June 1963: 103–104.

799. Horda Kuba ide vpered [Proud Cuba is marching forward] Ukraina, no. 4, Feb. 1961: 10–11.

800. Huberman, Leo, *and* Paul Marlor Sweezy. IAk tse bylo [It happened this way] Ukraina, no. 4, Feb. 1961: 11.
   Translated from the English.

801. ———. S'erra-Maestra—Gavana; otryvki iz knigi [From the Sierra Maestra to Havana; excerpts from a book] Za rubezhom, no. 21, Nov. 1960: 16–18.
   Translated from the English.

802. ———. Velikolepnyi primer Kuby; otryvki iz knigi [The impressive example of Cuba; excerpts from a book] Za rubezhom, no. 22, Nov. 1960: 3, 26–27.
   Translated from the English.

803. IAkhontova, M. Ostrov geroev [The island of heroes] Neva, no. 9, 1960: 174–180.

804. Interv'iu "VSN" s Raulem Kastro [An interview of the "World Student News" with Raúl Castro] Vsem. stud. nov., v. 14, no. 9, Sept. 1960: 3–5.

805. Ivanov, G. Na pylaiushchem ostrove; pis'ma s Kuby [An island in flame; letters from Cuba] Stavropol'e, no. 3, 1962: 34–38.

806. Iz-za ugla [Underhanded activities] Nov. vrem., v. 17, no. 34, Aug. 1959: 21.
   Political activities of the "counterrevolutionaries."

807. Kalinin, A. I. Kuba—demokraticheskoe revoliutsionnoe gosudarstvo [Cuba is a democratic revolutionary state] Sov. gos. i pravo, no. 9, Sept. 1960: 54–61.

808. Kamynin, L. V revoliutsionnoi Kube [In revolutionary Cuba] Sov. voin, v. 43, no. 4, Feb. 1961: 42–43.

809. Kashkaev, R. Chestnaia kniga o Kube [A fair book about Cuba] Nov. vrem., v. 18, no. 39, Sept. 1960: 28–30.
   A review of *Cuba; Anatomy of a Revolution* by Leo Huberman and Paul M. Sweezy (New York, Monthly Review Press, 1960. 176 p.).

810. Kerner, S. Pro Fidelia Kastro [Let me tell you about Fidel Castro] Vsesvit, v. 4, no. 10, Oct. 1960: 145–147.
Translated from the Polish.

811. Khuan Marinel'o; biograficheskaia spravka [Juan Marinello; a biographical note] Nov. vrem., v. 17, no. 9, Feb. 1959: 30.

812. Khusainov, M. Ostrov svobody beret novye rubezhi [New achievements of the island of freedom] Sov. profsoiuzy, v. 19, no. 3, Feb. 1963: 24–25.

813. Kniga byla sozhzhena [A book was burned] Inostr. lit., no. 7, July 1959: 282–283.
The burning of Antonio Núñez Jiménez' book by the Batista Government.

814. Kniga o bor'be patriotov [A book on the struggle of patriots] Inostr. lit., no. 1, Jan. 1959: 279.
A review of Jorge Ricardo Masatti's *Los que luchan y los que lloran* (Buenos Aires, Editorial Freeland, 1958. 142 p.).

815. Kolobkova, Emiliia. Dvanadtsiat' vynohradyn [Twelve grapes] Ukraina, no. 24, Dec. 1962: 16.
Experiences of a Cuban student during the Revolution.

816. Kozni protiv Kuby [Machinations against Cuba] Za rubezhom, no. 19, Oct. 1960: 8.
Counterrevolutionary activity of Cuban refugees.

817. Kremnev, M. Na Kube [In Cuba] Nov. vrem., v. 17, no. 22, May 1959: 13–15.

818. ———. Vosstanie na Kube [Revolt in Cuba] Nov. vrem., v. 17, no. 1, Jan. 1959: 23–24.

819. Kuba boretsia i pobedit! [Cuba is fighting and she will win!] Komm. Bel., v. 36, no. 11, Nov. 1962: 12–15.

820. Kuba nacheku! [Cuba on the alert] Nov. vrem., v. 17, no. 4, Jan. 1959: 22.

821. Leante, César. Razom z narodnoiu militsiieiu [With the people's militia] Vitchyzna, v. 31, no. 8, Aug. 1963: 109–130; v. 31, no. 9, Sept. 1963: 116–133.
Translated from the Spanish.

822. ———. Tak rozhdalas' pobeda [Victory

was born that way] Sov. voin, v. 45, no. 14, July 1963: 36–37.

823. Levin, V. Kuba bditel'na i edina [Cuba is alert and united] Blok. agit. [Bel.] no. 34, Dec. 1959: 46–48.

824. ———. Kuba—da, ianki—net! [Cuba—yes, Yankee—no!] Mol. komm., no. 9, Sept. 1960: 90–94.

825. ———. Kuba segodnia [Cuba today] Mezhdunar. zhizn', v. 6, no. 4, Apr. 1959: 127–128.

826. Listov, Vadim. Kamilo S'enfuegos, geroi Kuby [Camilo Cienfuegos, the hero of Cuba] Nov. vrem., v. 21, no. 47, Nov. 1963: 22–24.

827. Maidanik, K. L. Issledovanie frantsuzskogo istorika-marksista o kubinskoi revoliutsii [A Marxist study of the Cuban Revolution by a French historian] Vop. ist., v. 38, no. 10, Oct. 1963: 162–171.
A review of Jacques Arnault's *Cuba et le marxisme* (Paris, Editions sociales, 1962. 214 p.).

828. Mal'kov, A. Svobodnuiu Kubu ne slomat'! [They won't subdue free Cuba] Blok. agit. Sov. Armii, v. 19, no. 13, May 1961: 29–32.

829. Manuel' Urrutia; biograficheskaia spravka [Manuel Urrutia; a biographical note] Nov. vrem., v. 17, no. 3, Jan. 1959: 31.

830. Marcos, Armando. Mir ne bez druzei [The world is wide but not alien] Vsem. stud. nov., v. 13, no. 11, Nov. 1959: 19–20.

831. Marinello, Juan. Chto proizoshlo na Kube [What happened in Cuba] Ogonek, v. 37, no. 13, Mar. 1959: 13–17.

832. Marksistskaia literatura na Kube [Marxist publications in Cuba] Probl. mira i sots., v. 6, no. 12, Dec. 1963: 95.

833. Martínez Sánchez, August. Pobeda kubinskoi revoliutsii—pobeda trudovogo naroda [The victory of the Cuban Revolution is a victory of the working people] Sots. trud., v. 6, no. 9, Sept. 1961: 21–24.

834. Más Martín, Luis. Eto byl ne "sherman" no oni ego vzorvali [It wasn't a "Sherman" but they blew it up anyway] Mol. mira, no. 5, 1959: 11.

835. ———. Pervaia stranitsa [The first page] Mol. gvard., no. 6, June 1960: 198–213. Translated from the Spanish.

836. Mashkin, V., *and* I. Khuzemi. Gavana maiskaia [Havana in May] Ogonek, v. 41, no. 20, May 1963: 2–3.

837. Mdivani, Georgii. Maiak svobody [The beacon light of freedom] Teatr. zhizn', no. 10, May 1962: 7–8.

838. Merin, B. M. Rost natsional'no-osvoboditel'nogo dvizheniia narodov Latinskoi Ameriki; pobeda narodnoi revoliutsii na Kube [Growth of the national liberation movement of the peoples of Latin America; triumph of the people's revolution in Cuba] Prep. ist. v shkole, v. 18, no. 2, Mar.-Apr. 1963: 77–84.

839. Mikhailov, A., *and* A. Grekov. Kubinskii narod v bor'be za svobodu i nezavisimost' [The Cuban people are struggling for freedom and independence] Voen.-ist. zhur., v. 5, no. 7, July 1963: 33–48.

840. Mikoian, S. Narodnaia revoliutsiia na Kube [People's revolution in Cuba] Polit. samoobr., v. 5, no. 3, Mar. 1961: 21–31.

841. My s toboi, Kuba! [We are with you, Cuba!] Sov. Soiuz, no. 5, 1961: 4.

842. Na drugom polusharii [In another hemisphere] Voen. znan., v. 37, no. 11, Nov. 1961: 7–8.

843. Narodnaia kubinskaia revoliutsiia [The people's revolution in Cuba] Rev.-ist. kalendar'-spravochnik, 1963: 196–200.

844. Ne zakryt' solntsa! [They can't darken the sun!] Ogonek, v. 39, no. 3, Jan. 1961: 2. Cuban refugees in the United States.

845. Neispravimye [The incorrigible] Nov. vrem., v. 17, no. 51, Dec. 1959: 24. Counterrevolutionary activities of Cuban refugees.

846. Nikto ne ostanovit temp razvitiia Kubinskoi Revoliutsii [Nobody can slow down the development of the Cuban Revolution] Inostr. lit., no. 3, Mar. 1962: 279.

847. Obyden, K. Pobeda kubinskogo naroda [Victory of the Cuban people] Agitator, no. 2, Jan. 1959: 48–49.

848. Olteanu, O. Slom starogo i sozdanie novogo gosudarstvennogo apparata na Kube [The destruction of the old state apparatus and the establishment of the new governmental organization in Cuba] Izv. vys. ucheb. zav.; prav., v. 6, no. 1, 1962: 127–134.

849. Osval'do Dortikos Torrado; biograficheskaia spravka [Osvaldo Dorticós Torrado; a biographical note] Nov. vrem., v. 17, no. 31, July 1959: 17.

850. Osval'do Dortikos Torrado; biograficheskaia spravka [Osvaldo Dorticós Torrado; a biographical note] Nov. vrem., v. 19, no. 38, Sept. 1961: 29.

851. Osvobozhdenie Kuby [The liberation of Cuba] Nov. vrem., v. 17, no. 2, Jan. 1959: 2.

852. Otvet Kuby [Cuba's answer] Nov. vrem., v. 20, no. 7, Feb. 1962: 1–2.

853. Pakin, S. Kuba—nadezhda Ameriki [Cuba is the hope of America] Mezhdunar. zhizn', v. 9, no. 5, May 1962: 127–129.
A review of Ramón Ramírez Gómez' *Cuba, despertar de América; ensayo económico-social* (Mexico City, Escuela Nacional de Economía, 1961. 267 p.).

854. Pardo Llada, José. Vospominaniia o S'erra-Maestre [Recollections of the Sierra Maestra] Vsem. stud. nov., v. 15, no. 1, Jan. 1961: 7–8, 17.

855. Pavlenko, A. Vragi svobody ne unimaiutsia [The enemies of freedom are still at work] Mezhdunar. zhizn', v. 11, no. 9, Sept. 1964: 122. Counterrevolutionary activity of Cuban refugees.

856. Pavlov, IU. Viva Kuba! [Viva Cuba!] Nov. mir, v. 36, no. 12, Dec. 1960: 267–270.
A review of Enrique González Pedrero's *La revolución cubana* (México, Escuela Nacional de Ciencias Políticas y Sociales, 1959. 156 p.).

857. Peña, Alcira de la. Kuba i marksizm [Cuba and Marxism] Probl. mira i sots., v. 6, no. 6, June 1963: 78–81.

A review of Jacques Arnault's *Cuba et le marxisme* (Paris, Editions sociales, 1962. 214 p.).

858. Peremoha kubyns'koho narodu [Victory of the Cuban people] Blok. agit. [Ukr.] no. 3, Jan. 1959: 44.

859. Pimenov, P. Ruki proch' ot Kuby! [Hands off Cuba!] Sov. profsoiuzy, v. 16, no. 23, Dec. 1960: 50–51.

860. Pineda Barnet, Enrique. My znaem: Kuba ne odinoka [We know Cuba is not alone] Ogonek, v. 40, no. 9, Feb. 1962: 2.

861. Poliakovskii, V. Kubu ne zapugat' [They cannot intimidate Cuba] Za rubezhom, no. 1, Jan. 1961: 3.

862. ———. Kuba: vintovka, kniga, trud [Cuba: a rifle, a book, and work] Za rubezhom, no. 3, Jan. 1961: 5.

863. Portuondo, José Antonio. Revoliutsiia na Kube i intelligentsiia [The revolution in Cuba and the intelligentsia] Nov. vrem., v. 22, no. 35, Aug. 1964: 18–21. Translated from the Spanish.

864. Pravoe delo naroda Kuby; khronika sobytii [The just cause of the Cuban people; a chronicle of events] Agitator, no. 15, Aug. 1960: 42–43.

865. "Primer, dostoinyi podrazhaniia" ["An example which deserves imitation"] Inostr. lit., no. 8, Aug. 1962: 281.

866. Provokatsii protiv mira [Provocations against peace] Za rubezhom, no. 44, Nov. 1963: 9–10. Counterrevolutionary activities of Cuban refugees.

867. Provokatsiia v Maiami [Provocation in Miami] Za rubezhom, no. 1, Jan. 1963: 2. Counterrevolutionary activity of Cuban refugees.

868. Raul' Kastro; biograficheskaia spravka [Raúl Castro; a biographical note] Nov. vrem., v. 18, no. 30, July 1960: 19.

869. Raul' Roa Garsia; biograficheskaia spravka [Raúl Roa García; a biographical note] Nov. vrem., v. 19, no. 41, Oct. 1961: 20.

870. Razumovich, N. N. Kubinskaia revoliutsiia i novoe nezavisimoe gosudarstvo [The Cuban Revolution and the new independent state] Sov. gos. i pravo, v. 31, no. 7, July 1961: 80–90.

871. Revoliutsiia pobedila—revoliutsiia prodolzhaetsia [The revolution has triumphed and the revolution goes on] Smena, v. 37, no. 17, Sept. 1960: 16–17.

872. Rísquet Valdés, Jorge. Kube neobkhodim mir [Cuba needs peace] Mol. mira, no. 8/9, 1961: 27–29.

873. Rukovoditeli svobodnoi Kuby [Leaders of free Cuba] Mezhdunar. zhizn', v. 8, no. 6, June 1961: 153–154.

874. Ruky het' vid Kuby! [Keep away from Cuba!] Ukraina, no. 21, Nov. 1962: 4–5.

875. Sánchez Olivares, Carlos. Ostrov svobody [The island of freedom] Agitator, no. 3, Feb. 1963: 27–30.

876. Snova gremiat barabany [They are beating the drums again] Za rubezhom, no. 42, Oct. 1961: 10. Counterrevolutionary activities of Cuban refugees.

877. Sovremennik. Na perevale [At the turning point] Nov. vrem., v. 20, no. 1, Jan. 1963: 5–6.

878. Stoliarov, A. Tovarishch Kuba [Comrade Cuba] Komm. Sov. Latvii, v. 18, no. 7, July 1963: 83–85.

879. Surpin, L. Vekhi Kubinskoi revoliutsii [Principal stages of the Cuban Revolution] Mezhdunar. zhizn', v. 7, no. 5, May 1960: 148–149. A review of Fidel Castro's *Pensamiento político, económico y social* (Havana, Editorial Lex, 1959. 138 p.).

880. TSepulin, G. Machete ne dozhdalis' khoziaev [They didn't return their machetes] Mol. komm., no. 1, Jan. 1964: 104–111.

881. Turov, A. Pobeda kubinskogo naroda [Victory of the Cuban people] Sov. voin, v. 40, no. 5, Mar. 1959: 19.

882. Turover, G. Piat' glavnykh zadach Kubinskoi revoliutsii (?) [Five principal objectives of the Cuban Revolution] Blok. agit. [Bel.] no. 3, Jan. 1964: 47ff.

883. Utegenov, Sh. Kuba na puti ukrepleniia svoei nezavisimosti [Cuba's efforts to consilidate her independence] Part. zhizn' Kazakh., v. 30, no. 5, May 1960: 58–61.

884. V fil'me i v zhizni [On the motion-picture screen and in real life] Nov. vrem., v. 22, no. 49, Dec. 1964: 22.
Counterrevolutionary activities of Cuban refugees.

885. Valdés Vivó, Raúl. Oktiabr'skaia reka [The river of the October Revolution] Za rubezhom, no. 45, Nov. 1961: 9.
The inspiring example of the Russian Revolution.

886. Vargas, Otto César. Dukh svobody tsarit na Kube [The spirit of liberty reigns on Cuba] Mol. mira, no. 5, 1959: 10–11.

887. Vásquez, Heradio. Strana solntsa, pal'm i pesen [The country of sun, palm trees, and songs] Vsem. stud. nov., v. 15, no. 3/4, Mar.-Apr. 1961: 17.

888. Vladimirov, S. Narod Kuby nepobedim [The Cuban people are invincible] Agitator, no. 8, Apr. 1961: 38–42.

889. Vorob'ev, S. Rassvet nad Kuboi [Dawn over Cuba] Prop. i agit., v. 41, no. 15, Aug. 1960: 19–23.

890. Zaria nad Kuboi [Dawn over Cuba] Nov. vrem., v. 19, no. 1, Jan. 1961: 3–4.

891. Zlokliucheniia Khuana Nadalia [Juan Nadal's misadventures] Nov. vrem., v. 22, no. 45, Nov. 1964: 23.
Uruguayan embassy as a sanctuary for "counterrevolutionaries."

See also entries no. 2449, 2452, 2456, 2458, 2462, 2463, 2465–2469, 2483, 2484, 2488, 2490, 2497, 2499, 2501–2504, 2507, 2508, 2510, 2514, 2517, 2518, 2525, 2526, 2528, 2529, 2533, 2536, 2538, 3052, 3114, 3396, 3397, 4649, 4653, 4661, 4691, 4717, 4719, 4721, and 4741.

h. Dominican Republic

892. Artiushenkov, M. Rezhim Trukhil'o bez Trukhil'o [A Trujillo regime without Trujillo] Mezhdunar. zhizn', v. 8, no. 7, July 1961: 148–149.

893. Bochkarev, IU. V svete dominikanskogo krizisa [In the light of the Dominican crisis] Nov. vrem., v. 20, no. 2, Jan. 1962: 11–13.

894. Borisov, IA. Dominikanskaia drama [Dramatic events in the Dominican Republic] Za rubezhom, no. 49, Dec. 1961: 30.

895. Dominikanskie mistifikatsii [Dominican hoaxes] Nov. vrem., v. 18, no. 33, Aug. 1960: 19.

896. Egorova, N. Razbitaia "vitrina" [The smashed "show-case"] Mezhdunar. zhizn', v. 10, no. 11, Nov. 1963: 115.

897. Flot ushel, opasnost' ostalas' [The fleet is gone, but the situation is still dangerous] Za rubezhom, no. 50, Dec. 1961: 2–3.

898. J. D. Trukhil'o beschinstvuet [Trujillo's outrageous acts] Probl. mira i sots., v. 4, no. 1, Jan. 1961: 95.

899. Juárez, Claudio. Dominikanskaia Respublika [The Dominican Republic] V zashch. mira, no. 4, Apr. 1960: 25–35.

900. Kak pri Trukhil'o [The same way as it was during the rule of Trujillo] Nov. vrem., v. 21, no. 11, Mar. 1964: 23.

901. Kamynin, L. Vybory ili fars? [Elections or a farce?] Mezhdunar. zhizn', v. 10, no. 2, Feb. 1963: 121.

902. Khuan Bosh [Juan Bosch] Nov. vrem., v. 20, no. 7, Feb. 1963: 13.

903. Koly padaiut' tyrany [When the tyrants are overthrown] Vsesvit, v. 5, no. 3, Mar. 1962: 10–12.

904. Konets diktatora [A dictator's end] Nov. vrem., v. 19, no. 24, June 1961: 24–25.

905. Konets eksperimenta [The end of an experiment] Za rubezhom, no. 40, Oct. 1963: 4.

906. Krest'ianskie volneniia v Dominikanskoi Respublike i v Peru [Peasant unrest in the Dominican Republic and Peru] Za rubezhom, no. 2, Jan. 1963: 24.

907. Levin, V. Diktatura Trukhil'o daet treshchiny [The dictatorship of Trujillo is

breaking down] Mir. ekon. i mezhdunar. otn., no. 6, June 1959: 103–104.

908. Liubimets Vashingtona [Washington's darling] Nov. vrem., v. 18, no. 16, Apr. 1960: 22.

909. Lockwart, Antonio. Liberty from a tyrant, not from tyranny. World student news, v. 17, no. 5, 1963: 10–11.

910. Mashbits, IA. G. Novyi etap natsional'no-osvoboditel'noi bor'by naroda Dominikanskoi respubliki [A new phase in the national liberation struggle of the people of the Dominican Republic] Vop. ist., no. 8, Aug. 1962: 191–192.

911. Nikolaev, P. Oshibka prezidenta Bosha [A mistake of President Bosch] Nov. vrem., v. 21, no. 43, Oct. 1963: 20–21.

912. ———. V chem beda Dominikanskoi Respubliki [The root of the troubles in the Dominican Republic] Nov. vrem., v. 20, no. 50, Dec. 1962: 12–13.

913. Novyi vid rabotorgovli v Karibskom more [A new form of slave trade in the Carribean Sea region] Mol. mira, no. 9, 1960: 17.

914. Ob urokakh vooruzhennoi bor'by v Dominikanskoi Respublike [The lessons of the armed struggle in the Dominican Republic] Probl. mira i sots., v. 7, no. 6, June 1964: 51–53.

915. Po ukazke diktatora Trukhil'o [On dictator Trujillo's orders] Inostr. lit., no. 12, Dec. 1960: 257.
Political murders.

916. Pokroviteli tiranov [The protectors of tyrants] Nov. vrem., v. 19, no. 31, July 1961: 23.

917. Poliakovskii, V. Generalissimus—denshchik [An orderly has become a generalissimo] Za rubezhom, no. 3, July 1960: 26.

918. Prizyv k solidarnosti [A call to solidarity] Probl. mira i sots., v. 7, no. 3, Mar. 1964: 87.

919. Protiv proizvola reaktsionnykh sil [Against the arbitrary violence of reactionary forces] Probl. mira i sots., v. 4, no. 9, Sept. 1961: 51–52.

920. Rano obradovalis' [Premature rejoicing] Nov. vrem., v. 19, no. 40, Sept. 1961: 21–22.

921. Samoilov, R. Manolo-neistovyi [Manolo, the Furious] Smena, v. 41, no. 15, Aug. 1964: 21.
Revolutionary activities of leftist groups.

922. Trukhil'izm bez Trukhil'o ["Trujillism" without Trujillo] Za rubezhom, no. 40, Oct. 1961: 3.

923. Trukhil'o i konets "Bozh'ei ery" [Trujillo and the end of the "era of God"] Vsem. stud. nov., v. 13, no. 12, Dec. 1959: 22.

i. Ecuador

924. Kalinin, Arnol'd Ivanovich. Gosudarstvennyi stroi Ekvadora [The governmental system of Ecuador] Moscow, Gosiurizdat, 1959. 60 p.

JL3015 1959.K3

925. Borisov, V. Vulkan deistvuet [An active volcano] Mezhdunar. zhizn', v. 9, no. 10, Oct. 1962: 113–114.

926. Campaign of murder and torture in Ecuador. World student news, v. 18, no. 1, 1964: 17.

927. Dva diktatora—odin khoziain [Two dictators have the same master] Za rubezhom, no. 41, Oct. 1964: 2–3.

928. Ekvadors'kyi vulkan [The Ecuadorian volcano] Vsesvit, v. 5, no. 2, Feb. 1962: 67–70.

929. Gómez, Joaquín. Pis'mo iz Ekvadora [A letter from Ecuador] Nov. vrem., v. 19, no. 49, Dec. 1961: 14–15.

930. Hernández, Rubén. Tragediia Ekvadora; pis'mo iz Kito [The tragedy of Ecuador; a letter from Quito] Nov. vrem., v. 21, no. 46, Nov. 1963: 16–17.

931. IAroshevskii, B. Porazhenie rezhima oligarkhii v Ekvadore [The defeat of the oligarchic system in Ecuador] Mir. ekon. i mezhdunar. otn., no. 1, Jan. 1962: 111–113.

932. Karlos Khulio Arosemena; biograficheskaia spravka [Carlos Julio Arose-

mena; a biographical note] Nov. vrem., v. 19, no. 31, July 1961: 31.

933. Khose Maria Velasko Ibarra; biograficheskaia spravka [José María Velasco Ibarra; a biographical note] Nov. vrem., v. 18, no. 48, Nov. 1960: 7.

934. Lorenzo, Ventura. Prestupleniia "zashchitnikov demokratii" v Ekvadore [Criminal acts committed by the "defenders of democracy" in Ecuador] Probl. mira i sots., v. 6, no. 11, Nov. 1963: 90–92.

935. Patruli v Guaiakile [Patrols in Guayaquil] Za rubezhom, no. 27, July 1963: 4.

936. Politseiskii proizvol [Arbitrary acts of the Ecuadorian police] Inostr. lit., no. 4, 1963: 287.

937. Ríos, Demetrio. Logika bor'by trebuet edinstva; pis'mo iz Ekvadora [The logic of struggle calls for unity; a letter from Ecuador] Probl. mira i sots., v. 7, no. 6, June 1964: 89–90.

938. Stavka—voenshchina [Counting on the military] Za rubezhom, no. 29, July 1963: 4.

939. Vulkan deistvuet [An active volcano] Za rubezhom, no. 46, Nov. 1961: 4.

See also entries no. 597, 600, 3136, and 4757.

j. El Salvador

940. Katorga—za ubezhdeniia [Imprisoned because of political convictions] Nov. vrem., v. 20, no. 42, Oct. 1962: 22.

941. Latinskaia Amerika segodnia; Sal'vador [Latin America today; El Salvador] Mezhdunar. zhizn', v. 10, no. 1, Jan. 1963: 176–177.

942. Luk'ianov, IU. Bol'shie sobytiia v maloi strane [Important events in a small country] Mezhdunar. zhizn', v. 8, no. 3, Mar. 1961: 135–137.

943. Rodríguez, José. S vostoka svet [The light comes from the East] Za rubezhom, no. 45, Nov. 1961: 9.

944. Rosales, Manuel. V strane "zolotykh zeren" [In the country of "golden grains"] Za rubezhom, no. 14, Apr. 1961: 22.

945. Rushatsia bastiony [The bastions are falling] Nov. vrem., v. 18, no. 45, Nov. 1960: 23–24.

k. Guatemala

946. Baglai, Marat Viktorovich. Gosudarstvennyi stroi Gvatemaly [The governmental system of Guatemala] Moscow, Gosiurizdat, 1959. 63 p.

JL1483 1959.B3

947. Asturias, Miguel Angel. Uik-end v Gvatemale [Weekend in Guatemala] Zhen. mira., no. 7, 1962: 32–34.

948. Barrios Klee, Hugo. Problemy revoliutsionnoi situatsii i osvoboditel'naia bor'ba naroda Gvatemaly [Problems arising from the revolutionary situation and the liberation struggle of the Guatemalan people] Probl. mira i sots., v. 7, no. 3, Mar. 1964: 16–24.

949. ———. V Gvatemale nazrevaiut peremeny [Changes are in the making in Guatemala] Probl. mira i sots., v. 5, no. 11, Nov. 1962: 26–31.

950. Borisov, IA. Eshche odin dvortsovyi perevorot [One more palace revolution] Za rubezhom, no. 14, Apr. 1963: 24.

951. Del Campo, C. Gvatemal'skaia revoliutsiia; opyt i uroki [Experience and lessons of the Guatemalan Revolution] Probl. mira i sots., v. 3, no. 6, June 1960: 31–37.

952. Demokratiia polkovnika Asurdia [The democracy of Colonel Azurdía] Nov. vrem., v. 21, no. 6, Mar. 1964: 22.

953. Gómez, Benjamín. Na styke dvukh Amerik [Where the two Americas meet] Za rubezhom, no. 1, Jan. 1962: 12–13.

954. Guerra Borges, Alfredo. Opyt Gvatemaly i nekotorye problemy sovremennoi revoliutsionnoi bor'by [The experience of Guatemala and some problems of present-day revolutionary struggle] Probl. mira i sots., v. 7, no. 6, June 1964: 11–17.

955. Gvozdarev, B. Ketsal' raspravliaet kryl'ia [The quetzal spreads its wings]

Mezhdunar. zhizn', v. 8, no. 1, Jan. 1961: 152–153.

956. Izbityi priem [Habitual tricks] Nov. vrem., v. 19, no. 15, Apr. 1961: 22.

957. Ketsal' ne mozhet zhit' v nevole [The quetzal cannot live in captivity] Za rubezhom, no. 7, July 1960: 25.

958. Ketsal' raspravliaet kryl'ia [The quetzal spreads its wings] Nov. vrem., v. 20, no. 13, Mar. 1962: 22.

959. Kniazev, R. Polozhenie v Gvatemale [The situation in Guatemala] Mezhdunar. zhizn', v. 9, no. 6, June 1962: 103–105.

960. Levin, V. Ocherednoi fars [One more farce] Mezhdunar. zhizn', v. 11, no. 7, July 1964: 113.

961. Listov, V. Eshche odna gvatemal'skaia avantiura [One more Guatemalan adventure] Nov. vrem., v. 20, no. 15, Apr. 1963: 20–21.

962. López, Carlos. Antikommunizm—vrag chelovechestva [Anticommunism is the enemy of mankind] Probl. mira i sots., v. 5, no. 10, Oct. 1962: 79–80.

963. Milla, José. Nekotorye problemy sozdaniia edinogo demokraticheskogo fronta [Some problems concerning the establishment of a united democratic front] Probl. mira i sots., v. 7, no. 12, Dec. 1964: 52–54.

964. Morales, Eduardo. Desiat' let spustia [Ten years later] Za rubezhom, no. 10, Mar. 1964: 15.

965. Narody ne zabyli etogo [The peoples have not forgotten it] Ogonek, v. 38, no. 41, Oct. 1960: 29.

966. Ovando Sánchez, Antonio. Shirokaia podderzhka nashei bor'by [Broad support for our struggle] Probl. mira i sots., v. 7, no. 3, Mar. 1964: 86–87.

967. Rodríguez, José. Terroristicheskii rezhim v Gvatemale [The terrorist regime in Guatemala] Probl. mira i sots., v. 4, no. 9, Sept. 1961: 92–93.

968. Samayoa, Rubén, and José Ortiz. Nadezhda Gvatemaly [The hope of Guatemala] Agitator, no. 9, May 1963: 49–51.

969. Tzul, C. Gvatemal'skie demokraty dob'iutsia prava svobodno zhit' u sebia na rodine [Guatemalan democrats will win the right to live freely in their country] Probl. mira i sots., v. 6, no. 4, Apr. 1963: 94.

970. ———. Obostrenie politicheskoi obstanovki; pis'mo iz Gvatemaly [The aggravation of the political situation; a letter from Guatemala] Probl. mira i sots., v. 6, no. 8, Aug. 1963: 79–80.

971. ———. Razgul reaktsii v Gvatemale [An intensification of reactionary persecutions in Guatemala] Probl. mira i sots., v. 7, no. 9, Sept. 1964: 91–92.

972. ———. Sila bratskoi solidarnosti [The power of fraternal solidarity] Probl. mira i sots., v. 6, no. 10, Oct. 1963: 95.

973. ———. Svobodu Karlosu Al'varado Kheresu! [Freedom to Carlos Alvarado Jerez!] Probl. mira i sots., v. 7, no. 2, Feb. 1964: 94.

974. Villatoro, Efraín. Kanun grozy [On the eve of a thunderstorm] Nov. vrem., v. 20, no. 23, June 1962: 31.

975. Zaiavlenie Luisa Kardosy-i-Aragona [A statement by Luis Cardoza y Aragón] Inostr. lit., no. 9, Sept. 1962: 276.

976. Zhizn' na vulkane [Living on a volcano] Nov. vrem., v. 18, no. 31, July 1960: 23.

See also entries no. 2544, 2545, 2822, and 3138.

l. The Guianas

977. Aizman, IU. Vybory v Britanskoi Gviane [Elections in British Guiana] Nov. vrem., v. 22, no. 51, Dec. 1964: 18–20.

978. Behind the headlines. World student news, v. 17, no. 8, 1963: 4–5.
British Guiana.

979. Britanskaia Gviana na puti k nezavisimosti [British Guiana on the road to its independence] Mezhdunar. zhizn', v. 8, no. 10, Oct. 1961: 155–156.

980. Cheddi Dzhagan; biograficheskaia spravka [Cheddi Jagan; a biographical note] Mir. ekon. i mezhdunar. otn., no. 8, Aug. 1962: 128–129.

981. Cheddi Dzhagan; biograficheskaia spravka [Cheddi Jagan; a biographical note] Nov. vrem., v. 19, no. 36, Sept. 1961: 26.

982. Cox, Idris. Intrigi imperialistov v Britanskoi Gviane [Imperialist intrigues in British Guiana] Mezhdunar. zhizn', v. 10, no. 10, Oct. 1963: 94–99.

983. Drugie vremena [Changing times] Nov. vrem., v. 20, no. 9, Feb. 1962: 27.
British Guiana.

984. Dzhanet Dzhagan [Janet Jagan] Smena, v. 39, no. 20, Oct. 1962: 16–17.

985. Dzhanet Dzhagan; biograficheskaia spravka [Janet Jagan; a biographical note] Nov. vrem., v. 20, no. 38, Sept. 1962: 21.

986. "Fidel' Gviany" ["The Fidel of British Guiana"] Vsesvit, v. 7, no. 3, Mar. 1964: 81–82.
Cheddi B. Jagan.

987. Flag po-prezhnemu angliiskii [The flag is still English] Za rubezhom, no. 46, Nov. 1962: 2–3.
British Guiana.

988. Gurnov, B. 10 let bor'by [The ten-year struggle] Za rubezhom, no. 49, Dec. 1964: 21.
British Guiana.

989. IAroshevskii, B. Gviana uzhe ne britanskaia [Guiana isn't British anymore] Za rubezhom, no. 34, Aug. 1961: 24.

990. Jagan, Cheddi B. Litsemerie kolonizatorov [Hypocrisy of the colonizers] Nov. vrem., v. 20, no. 4, Jan. 1963: 15–17.

991. ———. Moia pozitsiia [My position] Za rubezhom, no. 49, Dec. 1961: 21.
Translated from the English.

992. Jagan, Janet. Britanskoi Gviane—nezavisimost' v 1962 godu [British Guiana will achieve independence in 1962] Vsem. stud. nov., v. 16, no. 3, Mar. 1962: 12–13.

993. Kogda Britanskaia Gviana poluchit nezavisimost'? [When will British Guiana be given her independence?] Mezhdunar. zhizn', v. 10, no. 2, Feb. 1963: 152–154.

994. Kovarstvo kolonizatorov [The perfidy of colonizers] Za rubezhom, no. 25, July 1964: 10.
British Guiana.

995. Kulibin, N. I Surinam tozhe [The same with Surinam] Nov. vrem., v. 19, no. 34, Aug. 1961: 14–15.

996. Levin, V. Chto proiskhodit v Britanskoi Gviane [Political events in British Guiana] Nov. vrem., v. 21, no. 26, July 1964: 18–19.

997. Na ocheredi—Surinam [It's Surinam's turn now] Nov. vrem., v. 19, no. 17, Apr. 1961: 21.

998. Oppozitsiia i ee opekuny [The opposition and its protectors] Za rubezhom, no. 25, July 1963: 8.
British Guiana.

999. P. H. Novye pregrady na puti k nezavisimosti [New obstacles on the road to independence] Probl. mira i sots., v. 5, no. 7, July 1962: 91–97.
British Guiana.

1000. Po shablonu [Stereotyped method] Nov. vrem., v. 18, no. 15, Apr. 1960: 21–22.
British Guiana.

1001. Po staromu retseptu [Using a tried method] Za rubezhom, no. 51, Dec. 1964: 2–3.
British Guiana.

1002. Porot' ili ne porot' [To flog or not to flog] Nov. vrem., v. 22, no. 31, July 1964: 23.
British Guiana.

1003. Prokop'ev, V. Angliiskie kolonizatory bez maski [The real face of English colonizers] Mezhdunar. zhizn', v. 9, no. 4, Apr. 1962: 122–123.
British Guiana.

1004. Provokatsiia v Dzhordzhtaune [A provocation in Georgetown] Za rubezhom, no. 8, Feb. 1962: 3.
British Guiana.

1005. Rasskaz ochevidtsa o sobytiiakh v Britanskoi Gviane [An eyewitness account of events in British Guiana] Nov. vrem., v. 20, no. 18, Apr. 1962: 13–16.

1006. Spektakl' povtorilsia [A repeat performance] Za rubezhom, no. 46, Nov. 1963: 4.
British Guiana.

1007. Vol'skii, D. Zagovor protiv Gviany [A plot against Guiana] Nov. vrem., v. 21, no. 41, Oct. 1963: 11–12.
British Guiana.

1008. Wright, Wilson. Makhinatsii kolonizatorov v Britanskoi Gviane [Colonialist machinations in British Guaina] Nov. vrem., v. 19, no. 20, May 1961: 14–15.

m. Haiti

1009. Gauthier, René. Narod Gaiti boretsia za svobodu [The Haitian people fight for their freedom] Probl. mira i sots., v. 5, no. 6, June 1962: 94–95.

1010. Jean-Jacques, Manuel. Terror na Gaiti [Terror in Haiti] Probl. mira i sots., v. 7, no. 4, Apr. 1964: 90–91.

1011. Kamynin, L. Diktator na vulkane [A dictator on a volcano] Za rubezhom, no. 34, Aug. 1963: 24.

1012. Monferet, Pierre. Partiia narodnogo edineniia Gaiti v bor'be [The struggle of the People's Unity Party in Haiti] Part. zhizn', no. 8, Apr. 1963: 72–74.

1013. Novaia operatsiia TsRU [A new operation of the CIA] Za rubezhom, no. 19, May 1963: 4.

1014. O sovmestimom i nesovmestimom [On compatible and incompatible principles] Nov. vrem., v. 20, no. 8, Feb. 1962: 23.

1015. Sekret Diuval'e [Duvalier's secret] Nov. vrem., v. 19, no. 21, May 1961: 20.

1016. V kol'tse nenavisti [In the ring of hatred] Nov. vrem., v. 22, no. 35, Aug. 1964: 25.

n. Honduras

1017. Castro, Isidoro. Nastuplenie reaktsii v Gondurase [Reactionary offensive in Honduras] Nov. vrem., v. 19, no. 20, May 1961: 31.

1018. Fuentes, Celedonio. Chto proizkhodit v Gondurase? Pis'mo iz Tegusigal'py [What is going on in Honduras? A letter

from Tegucigalpa] Probl. mira i sots., v. 3, no. 9, Sept. 1960: 93–95.

1019. Gvozdev, IU. V strane "semidesiati protsentov" [In a "70-per cent" country] Mezhdunar, zhizn', v. 11, no. 5, May 1964: 96–98.

1020. Muñoz, Alonso. Narod Gondurasa v bor'be protiv reaktsii i imperializma [The Honduran people struggle against reaction and imperialism] Probl. mira i sots., v. 7, no. 6, June 1964: 24–29.

1021. Paz, Hernán Midence. Makkartizm v Gondurase; pismo iz Tegusigal'py [McCarthyism in Honduras; a letter from Tegucigalpa] Probl. mira i sots., v. 6, no. 8, Aug. 1963: 92–93.

1022. Sánchez, Pedro. Perevorot v Gondurase sprovotsirovan ianki [The Honduran coup d'état was provoked by the Yankees] Probl. mira i sots., v. 7, no. 1, Jan. 1964: 78–81.

1023. Trust the devil. World student news, v. 18, no. 1, 1964: 16–17.

1024. Zavala, Felix J. Kogda u vlasti "gorilly" [When a country is ruled by "gorillas"] Probl. mira i sots., v. 7, no. 11, Nov. 1964: 92–93.

See also entry no. 2547.

o. Jamaica

1025. IAmaika [Jamaica] Agitator, no. 17, Sept. 1962: 21.

1026. IAmaika; spravka [Jamaica; an information note] Mezhdunar. zhizn', v. 9, no. 10, Oct. 1962: 145–146.

1027. Novaia era IAmaiki [New era in Jamaica] Nov. vrem., v. 20, no. 33, Aug. 1962: 3.

See also entry no. 2549.

p. Mexico

1028. Grigor'ev, IA. G. O nekotorykh politicheskikh tendentsiiakh v Meksike [Some political trends in Mexico] Vop. ist., v. 38, no. 5, May 1963: 183–184.
A review of an article by David L. Graham in *The Yale Review*, v. 52, no. 1, Oct. 1962: 102–111.

1029. Gustavo Dias Ordas; biograficheskaia spravka [Gustavo Díaz Ordaz; a biographical note] Nov. vrem., v. 22, no. 51, Dec. 1964: 27.

1030. Lapshev, E. Meksika—arena klassovykh bitv [Mexico as an arena of class struggle] Mezhdunar. zhizn', v. 11, no. 2, Feb. 1964: 139–141.

1031. Lara, H. Meksika [Mexico] Probl. mira i sots., v. 3, no. 3, Mar. 1960: 91–92.
Alleged political persecutions.

1032. Otpor antidemokraticheskim silam [A rebuff to antidemocratic forces] Probl. mira i sots., v. 2, no. 8, Aug. 1959: 55–57.

1033. Pavlenko, A. V poiskakh uteriannykh pisem [In search of lost letters] Nov. vrem., v. 22, no. 47, Nov. 1964: 26–28.
V. I. Lenin's correspondence with Mexican politicians.

1034. ———. Vybory v Meksike [Elections in Mexico] Za rubezhom, no. 27, July 1964: 23.

1035. Perez Gaytán, José Encarnación. Svobodu politicheskim zakliuchennym! Pis'mo iz meksikanskoi tiur'my [Freedom for political prisoners! A letter from a Mexican prison] Probl. mira i sots., no. 4, Apr. 1964: 89–90.

1036. Rivera Urbina, Ulises. Kak oruduet antikommunizm v nashei strane [How anticommunism operates in our country] Probl. mira i sots., v. 5, no. 9, Sept. 1962: 76–77.

1037. Ten' Makkarti nad Meksikoi [McCarthy's shadow over Mexico] Probl. mira i sots., v. 5, no. 7, July 1962: 94.

1038. Vbyvstvo v Ksokhikal'ko [A murder in Xochicalco] Vsesvit, v. 6, no. 1, Jan. 1963: 56–57.

See also entries no. 2559, 4224, 4252, 4254, 4256, 4263, 4264, and 4266–4268.

q. Nicaragua

1039. Chichkov, Vas. Nikaragua vzlamyvaet tiuremnuiu reshetku [Nicaragua is breaking the prison bars] Ogonek, v. 37, no. 34, Aug. 1959: 22–23.

1040. Protiv diktatury [Against the dictatorship] Vsem. stud. nov., v. 13, no. 9/10, Sept.-Oct. 1959: 31.

1041. Pruzhina raspriamliaetsia [The spring recoils] Nov. vrem., v. 17, no. 24, June 1959: 3.

1042. Sukiny vnuki [The grandsons of a bitch] Nov. vrem., v. 18, no. 33, Aug. 1960: 20.

r. Panama

1043. Marko Aurelio Robles; biograficheskaia spravka [Marco Aurelio Robles; a biographical note] Nov. vrem., v. 22, no. 44, Oct. 1964: 31.

s. Paraguay

1044. Gvozdarev, Boris Ivanovich, *and* Viktor Anatol'evich Kropotov. Gosudarstvennyi stroi Paragvaia [The governmental system of Paraguay] Moscow, Gosiurizdat, 1962. 80 p.   JL3215 1962.G85

1045. Da zdravstvuet svobodnyi Paragvai! [Long live free Paraguay!] Vsem. stud. nov., v. 14, no. 3/4, Mar.-Apr. 1960: 30.

1046. IUr'ev, E. Terror v Paragvae [Terror in Paraguay] Mezhdunar. zhizn', v. 8, no. 5, May 1961: 129–130.

1047. Kharitonov, V. Paragvai: bor'ba protiv diktatury [The struggle against the dictatorship in Paraguay] Mir. ekon. i mezhdunar. otn., no. 12, 1964: 99–103.

1048. Lemi, M. V zashchitu patriotov Paragvaiia [In defense of Paraguayan patriots] Probl. mira i sots., v. 6, no. 7, July 1963: 90–91.

1049. Lemus, Germán. Vody, okrashennye krov'iu [Bloody waters] Vsem. stud. nov., v. 15, no. 8/9, Aug.-Sept. 1961: 31–33.

1050. Nemchinskii, IA. Vosstanie v Paragvae [A rebellion in Paraguay] Sov. voin, v. 41, no. 4, Feb. 1960: 30.

1051. Poiarkova, N. Byvaiut i takie "vybory" [There are "elections" of this kind too] Mezhdunar. zhizn', v. 10, no. 4, Apr. 1963: 114–115.

1052. Poliakovskii, V. Paragvaiskii narod trebuet: "Doloi Stressnera!" ["Down with Stroessner!", the Paraguayans say] Za rubezhom, no. 2, June 1960: 27.

1053. Ramírez, José. Ostanovit' ruku ubiitsy [Let us stay the hand of the murderer!] Probl. mira i sots., v. 4, no. 1, Jan. 1961: 94–95.

1054. ———. Zhizn' politicheskikh zakliuchennykh v opasnosti [The lives of political prisoners are in danger] Probl. mira i sots., v. 3, no. 7, July 1960: 96.

1055. Rodríguez, Miguel. Revoliutsionnyi pod"em narastaet [Revolutionary activity is rising] Agitator, no. 17, Sept. 1962: 22–24.

1056. Stressnera chekaie dolia Batisty [Stroessner will share Batista's fate] Vsesvit, v. 4, no. 1, Jan. 1961: 156–158.

1057. Tuchnin, R. Paragvaiskaia drama [The Paraguayan drama] Nov. vrem., v. 21, no. 10, Mar. 1964: 16–18.

1058. Vásquez, Liborio. Svobodu patriotam Paragvaiia! [Free the patriots of Paraguay!] Probl. mira i sots., v. 5, no. 12, Dec. 1962: 92–93.

See also entries no. 442, 927, 1041, 2562, 3062, and 3063.

t. Peru

1059. Razumovich, Nikolai Nikanorovich. Gosudarstvennyi stroi Peru [The governmental system of Peru] Moscow, Gosiurizdat, 1960. 66 p. JL3415 1960.R3

1060. Cárdenas, Luis. Rise up . . . Tupac Amaru! World student news, v. 17, no. 2/3, 1963: 4–6.

1061. Fajardo, Teodoro. Tainaia voina v Peru [The secret war in Peru] Za rubezhom, no. 16, Apr. 1964: 22.

1062. Fernando Belaunde Terri; biograficheskaia spravka [Fernando Belaúnde Terry: a biographical note] Nov. vrem., v. 21, no. 27, July 1963: 22.

1063. Gómez, Manuel. Politicheskoe polozhenie v Peru [The political situation in Peru] Nov. vrem., v. 21, no. 44, Nov. 1963: 18–19.

1064. Munar, José. Proiski imperialistov v Peru i bor'ba peruanskogo naroda; pis'mo iz Limy [The intrigues of imperialists in Peru and the struggle of the Peruvian people; a letter from Lima] Probl. mira i sots., v. 6, no. 5, May 1963: 84–86.

1064. Munar, José. Proiski imperialistov v Peru i bor'ba peruanskogo naroda; pis'mo iz Limy [The intrigues of imperialists in Peru and the struggle of the Peruvian people; a letter from Lima] Probl. mira i sots., v. 6, no. 5, May 1963: 84–86.

1065. Ovcharki i demokratiia [Sheep dogs and democracy] Nov. vrem., v. 20, no. 3, Jan. 1962: 22.

1066. Pavlenko, A. Porazhenie imperialisticheskikh sil [The defeat of the imperialist forces] Mezhdunar. zhizn', v. 10, no. 8, Aug. 1963: 154–155.

1067. Perevorot v Peru [A coup d'état in Peru] Nov. vrem., v. 20, no. 31, July 1962: 23.

1068. Peruanskii retsidiv [Peruvian relapse] Za rubezhom, no. 30, July 1962: 2–3.

1069. Rosendo, Libertad. Fal'shivki iz Maiami [Fabrications from the city of Miami] Probl. mira i sots., v. 4, no. 5, May 1961: 94–95.

1070. Shtyki ukhodiat v ten'? [Will the bayonets withdraw into the background?] Za rubezhom, no. 23, June 1963: 4.

1071. Zverstva voennoi khunty; dva pis'ma iz Peru [Atrocities committed by the military junta; two letters from Peru] Probl. mira i sots., v. 6, no. 7, July 1963: 94–95.

u. Puerto Rico

1072. Kolonializm v Puerto-Riko [Colonialism in Puerto Rico] Mol. mira, no. 4, 1960: 15.

1073. Konstantinovskaia, E. Bor'ba prodolzhaetsia [The struggle continues] Neva, no. 6, 1960: 217–218.

1074. Martínez, Narciso Rabell. Puerto-Riko—koloniia SShA [Puerto Rico, a U.S. colony] Probl. mira i sots., v. 6, no. 9, Sept. 1963: 89–90.

1075. Pakin, S. "Plebistsit" vmesto nezavisimosti [A "plebiscite" instead of independence] Mezhdunar. zhizn', v. 9, no. 9, Sept. 1962: 127–128.

1076. Poiarkova, N. Puerto-Riko nakanune vyborov [Puerto Rico on the eve of elections] Mir. ekon. i mezhdunar. otn., no. 10, 1964: 116–119.

1077. Rabell, Narciso. Kennedy orders: a plebiscite in Puerto Rico. World student news, v. 16, no. 9/10, 1962: 20.

1078. ———. Tightening the screws in Puerto Rico. World student news, v. 17, no. 4, 1963: 17–19.

1079. Rivera, Juan Santos. Al'bisu Kampos—simvol bor'by za nezavisimost' Puerto-Riko [Albizu Campos, the symbol of Puerto Rico's struggle for independence] Probl. mira i sots., v. 5, no. 1, Jan. 1962: 86–88.

1080. Viscal, Olga. Puerto-Riko; amerikanskaia koloniia [Puerto Rico; a United States colony] Vsem. stud. nov., v. 13, no. 9/10, Sept.-Oct. 1959: 27, 29.

v. Trinidad and Tobago

1081. Erik IUstas Uil'iams; biograficheskaia spravka [Eric Eustace Williams; a biographical note] Nov. vrem., v. 20, no. 39, Sept. 1962: 28.

1082. Gusarov, L. Eshche odnoi koloniei men'she [Another colony less] Nov. vrem., v. 20, no. 36, 1962: 21.

w. Uruguay

1083. Khachaturov, Karen. Urugvai segodnia [Uruguay today] Moscow, Izd-vo IMO, 1962. 174 p.   HN353.5.K5
Reviewed by L. Novikova in *Nov. mir*, v. 39, no. 8, Aug. 1963: 278–280; by L. Luganov in *Vokrug sveta*, no. 9, Sept. 1963: 62.

1084. Kostritsyn, Boris Vladimirovich. Gosudarstvennyi stroi Urugvaia [The governmental system of Uruguay] Moscow, Gosiurizdat, 1959. 59 p.
JL3615 1959.K6

1085. Ibarburu, Rita. Narod zashchishchaet demokratiiu [The people defend democracy] Probl. mira i sots., v. 5, no. 1, Jan. 1962: 90–91.

1086. Khachaturov, K. Chto pokazali vybory [What we can learn from the results of the elections] Mezhdunar. zhizn', v. 10, no. 1, Jan. 1963: 148.

1087. ———. Kak "vybiraiut" v Urugvae [How they "vote" in Uruguay] Sov. deput. trud., no. 1, Jan. 1963: 107–109.

1088. Kremnev, M. Na beregakh La-Platy [On the Río de la Plata] Nov. vrem., v. 17, no. 23, June 1959: 26–28.

1089. Piris, Hernán. Krepnet levyi front [The left front is growing stronger] Za rubezhom, no. 2, Jan. 1963: 20.

1090. Shiblinskii, P. Bor'ba za edinstvo deistvii demokraticheskikh sil Urugvaia [Struggle for the concerted action of Uruguayan democratic forces] Mir. ekon. i mezhdunar. otn., no. 1, Jan 1960: 112–115.

x. Venezuela

1091. IEremenko, V. F. Burliashchii vulkan; Venesuela [Venezuela, a seething volcano] Kiev, Politvydav Ukrainy, 1964. 56 p.
In Ukrainian.

1092. Nitoburg, E. L. Veter svobody v neftianom El'dorado; osvoboditel'noe dvizhenie v Venesuele [The wind of freedom in an oil-rich Eldorado; the liberation movement in Venezuela] Moscow, Sotsekgiz, 1960. 86 p.   F2326.N5

1093. Aliab'ev, M. Proiski reaktsii v Venesuele [Reactionary plots in Venezuela] Mezhdunar. zhizn', v. 7, no. 3, Mar. 1960: 97–98.

1094. Aparnikov, B. Na shtykakh [With the support of bayonets] Za rubezhom, no. 45, Nov. 1962: 25.

1095. Bor'ba prodolzhaetsia [The struggle isn't over] Za rubezhom, no. 48, Nov. 1964: 2–3.

1096. Burlak, A. K polozheniiu v Venesuele [On the situation in Venezuela] Mezhdunar. zhizn', v. 7, no. 12, Dec. 1960: 111–112.

1097. Carrera, Jerónimo. Bor'ba za amnistiiu v Venesuele [The struggle for amnesty for political prisoners in Venezuela] Probl. mira i sots., v. 7, no. 10, Nov. 1964: 81–83.

1098. Chernye biulleteni [Black bulletins] Za rubezhom, no. 49, Dec. 1963: 3.
Presidential elections.

1099. Fernández, Ramón. Venesuela pered vyborami [Venezuela on the eve of elections] Nov. vrem., v. 21, no. 39, Sept. 1963: 19–20.

1100. Gallegos Mancera, Eduardo. Ne slomat' narod Venesuely! [The will of the Venezuelan people cannot be broken!] Probl. mira i sots., v. 5, no. 5, May 1962: 95.

1101. Gangstery v politseiskikh mundirakh [Gangsters in police uniforms] Nov. vrem., v. 22, no. 44, Oct. 1964: 21–22.
Police corruption.

1102. González Muñoz, Eduardo. Venesuela v bor'be [Political struggle in Venezuela] Probl. mira i sots., v. 6, no. 10, Oct. 1963: 80–82.

1103. Gvozdev, IU. Venesuela—o'kei! [Venezuela, okay!] Sov. pech., no. 3, Mar. 1964: 59–60.
Alleged suppression of freedom of the press.

1104. IAroshevskii, B. Fabricio Okheda ukhodit v gory [Fabricio Ojeda goes to the mountains] Za rubezhom, no. 30, July 1962: 25.
Guerrilla movement.

1105. IEremenko, V. Dyktator na vulkani [The dictator is standing on a volcano] Ukraina, v. 23, no. 26, Oct. 1963: 12–13.

1106. J. D. Bor'ba obostriaetsia [The aggravation of political struggle] Probl. mira i sots., v. 4, no. 3, Mar. 1961: 89–91.

1107. Kandidat v diktatory [A candidate for dictator] Za rubezhom, no. 25, July 1963: 8.

1108. Kandidaty i narod [The candidates and the people] Za rubezhom, no. 38, Sept. 1963: 4.

1109. Karlos Sosa Rodriges; biograficheskaia spravka [Carlos Sosa Rodríguez; a biographical note] Nov. vrem., no. 41, Oct. 1963: 9.

1110. Kartsev, A. Politicheskaia obstanovka obostriaetsia [The political situation becomes tense again] Mezhdunar. zhizn', v. 10, no. 11, Nov. 1963: 109.

1111. Korotkov, V. Za vitrinoi "predstavitel'noi demokratii" [Behind the showcase of "representative democracy"] Mezhdunar. zhizn', v. 9, no. 6, June 1962: 100–102.

1112. Lavretskii, I. R. Review. Vop. ist., no. 9, Sept. 1960: 181–183.
A review of Pompeyo Márquez' ¿ Hacia dónde va el 23 de enero? (Caracas, Pensamiento Vivo, 1959. 170 p.).

1113. Listov, V. Partizany v Venesuele [Venezuelan guerrillas] Mezhdunar. zhizn', v. 10, no. 12, Dec. 1963: 86–91.

1114. ———. V Venesuele gremiat vzryvy [Thunderous blasts in Venezuela] Za rubezhom, no. 19, May 1963: 13.

1115. Machado, Gustavo. Antikommunizm—vrag chelovechestva [Anticommunism is the enemy of mankind] Probl. mira i sots., v. 5, no. 10, Oct. 1962: 78–79.

1116. Mancera, E. Chto proiskhodit v Venesuele? [What is going on in Venezuela?] Probl. mira i sots., v. 6, no. 6, June 1963: 53–56.

1117. Mujica, Héctor. Venesuela na rasput'e [Venezuela at the crossroads] Mezhdunar. zhizn', v. 8, no. 12, Dec. 1961: 93–96.

1118. Obeshchaniia sen'ora Leoni [Señor Leoni's promises] Nov. vrem., v. 22, no. 50, Dec. 1964: 29.

1119. Pakin, S. Novyi etap v zhizni Venesuely [A new stage in the life of Venezuela] Mir. ekon. i mezhdunar. otn., no. 4, Apr. 1959: 111–112.

1120. Piris, Hernán. Ot soglashatel'stva k predatel'stvu [From concessions to treachery] Za rubezhom, no. 11, Mar. 1961: 19.

1121. Podvig "Ansoategi" [Heroic story of the "Anzoátegui"] Za rubezhom, no. 8, Feb. 1963: 3.

1122. Poliakovskii, V. Chto proiskhodit v Venesuele [What is happening in Venezuela] Za rubezhom, no. 27, Dec. 1960: 16–17.

1123. Rángel, Díaz. Obostrenie krizisa v Venesuele [Aggravation of the crisis in Venezuela] Nov. vrem., v. 20, no. 12, Mar. 1962: 19–20.

1124. Raul' Leoni; biograficheskaia spravka [Raúl Leoni; a biographical note] Nov. vrem., v. 21, no. 14, Apr. 1964: 17.

1125. Regalado, S. Krovavye zlodeianiia pravitel'stva Venesuely [The bloody crimes of the Venezuelan government] Probl. mira i sots., v. 5, no. 9, Sept. 1962: 95.

1126. Saher, José Manuel. Dear father! World student news, v. 17, no. 4, 1963: 3–4, 7.

1127. Shiblin, P. Venesuel'skii tupik [The Venezuelan blind alley] Nov. vrem., v. 20, no. 9, Feb. 1962: 11–13.

1128. ———. Vnutrenniaia bor'ba v Venesuele [The internal struggle in Venezuela] Nov. vrem., v. 21, no. 47, Nov. 1963: 18–19.

1129. ———. Zachem Betankur ezdil v Soedinennye Shtaty? [Why did Betancourt go to the United States?] Nov. vrem., v. 20, no. 11, Mar. 1963: 26–27.

1130. Sobytiia v Venesuele [Events in Venezuela] Nov. vrem., v. 18, no. 18, May 1960: 19–20.

1131. 44 [Sorok chetyre] chasa vosstaniia [A forty-four-hour rebellion] Za rubezhom, no. 19, May 1962: 4–5.

1132. Tuchnin, R. Romulo Betankur; biograficheskaia spravka [Rómulo Betancourt; a biographical note] Mir. ekon. i mezhdunar. otn., no. 3, 1963: 134–135.

1133. ———. Venezuela: krizis antinarodnogo rezhima [Crisis of the antinational regime in Venezuela] Mir. ekon. i mezhdunar. otn., no. 2, 1963: 100–102.

1134. Villalobos, Héctor. Edinstvo naroda pomoglo svergnut' diktaturu [The unity of the people helped to overthrow the dictatorship] Mol. mira, no. 1, 1960: 20–21.

y. West Indies

1135. Ponce, Maurice. Kolonii pod vyveskoi departamentov: Martinika i Gvadelupa [Martinique and Guadeloupe; colonies under the name of "departments"] Moscow, Gospolitizdat, 1961. 48 p.
Translated from the French.

1136. Ablina, E. "Zamorskie departamenty" Frantsii v bor'be za avtonomiiu [The "overseas departments" of France struggle for autonomy] Mir. ekon. i mezhdunar. otn., no. 8, 1964: 103–106.

1137. Antil'skie ostrova, Gviana; nikakikh kompromissov s kolonizatorami i ikh soiuznikami—natsional'noi burzhuaziei [The Antilles and Guiana; there should be no compromise with colonizers and their allies—the national bourgeoisie] Mol. mira, no. 1/2, 1962: 16–17.

1138. French colonialists reach agreement. World student news, v. 18, no. 7/8, 1964: 22–25.

1139. IUkhin, V. Martinika trebuet svobody [Martinique demands freedom] Nov. vrem., v. 41, no. 6, Feb. 1964: 14–15.

1140. Marquant, Arthur. Martinika boretsia [Martinique continues its struggle] Probl. mira i sots., v. 4, no. 8, Aug. 1961: 95.

1141. Nicolas, Armand. Martinika trebuet avtonomii [Martinique demands autonomy] Probl. mira i sots., v. 6, no. 1, Jan. 1963: 34–39.

1142. ———. Sbrosim tsepi kolonializma! [We shall break the chains of colonialism!] Part. zhizn', no. 24, Dec. 1961: 60–63.
Martinique.

1143. René, Emile. Kolonial'nyi proizvol na Martinike [Arbitrary action of colonizers on Martinique] Nov. vrem., v. 19, no. 49, Dec. 1961: 28–29.

1144. Slepneva, G. Vest-indskaia federatsiia [The West Indian Federation] *In* Otvety na voprosy o sovremennom mezhdunarodnom polozhenii. no. 2. Moscow, 1959. p. 20–25.

1145. Sobytiia na Kiurasao [The events in Curaçao] Nov. vrem., v. 18, no. 9, Feb. 1960: 18.

1146. V. IU. Vbyvstvo z politychnykh motyviv [Assassination of a political adversary] Rad. pravo, no. 2, Mar.-Apr. 1963: 130–131.
Martinique.

1147. Verges, Paul, *and others.* "Demokratiia" frantsuzskikh kolonizatorov [The "democracy" of French colonialists] Probl. mira i sots., v. 6, no. 2, Feb. 1963: 49–52.
French West Indies.

B. POLITICAL ACTIVITY OF COMMUNIST PARTIES

1. Writings Dealing With Three or More Countries

1148. Manasov, M. A. Marksistsko-leninskie partii Latinskoi Ameriki; spravochnyi material [Reference materials on the Marxist-Leninist parties of Latin America] Moscow, Znanie, 1963. 45 p.

1149. Osnovnye problemy kommunisticheskogo i rabochego dvizheniia v stranakh Latinskoi Ameriki; kratkii spisok literatury [Basic problems of the Communist and labor movement in Latin America; brief bibliography] Moscow, Gos. publichnaia biblioteka, 1960. 8 p.

1150. Programnye dokumenty kommunisticheskikh i rabochikh partii stran Ameriki [Documentary materials concerning the programs of the Communist and workers' parties of American countries] Moscow, Gospolitizdat, 1962. 336 p.

1151. Rumiantsev, Aleksei Matveevich, *ed.* Problemy sozdaniia edinogo antiimperialisticheskogo fronta; materialy obmena mneniiami organizovannogo redaktsiei zhurnala "Problemy mira i sotsializma" letom 1962 goda [Problems concerning the establishment of a united anti-imperialist front; materials of a discussion organized by the editors of the periodical "Problemy mira i sotsializma" in the summer of 1962] Prague, Mir i sotsializm, 1963. 129 p.   HX177.R8

1152. Bochkarev, IU. Kommunisty—samye stoikie bortsy za natsional'nuiu nezavisimost' [Communists are the most resolute fighters for national independence] Kommunist, v. 39, no. 5, Mar. 1963: 105–113.

1153. Burliashchii kontinent [A seething continent] Nov. vrem., v. 21, no. 47, Nov. 1963: 1–3.

1154. Chernov, Leonid Nikolaevich. Latinskaia Amerika—novyi front aktivnoi bor'by s imperializmom [Latin America is the new front of the militant struggle against imperialism] *In his* Mezhdunarodnoe kommunisticheskoe i rabochee dvizhenie na sovremennom etape. Moscow, Gospolitizdat, 1961. p. 78–100.
HX44.C48
Political activity of the Communist parties.

1155. Codovilla, Victorio. Utverzhdenie idei marksizma-leninizma v Latinskoi Amerike [The ideas of Marxism-Leninism gain strength in Latin America] Probl. mira i sots., v. 7, no. 8, Aug. 1964: 38–48.

1156. Dabagian, E. S. Literatura po istorii kommunisticheskogo i rabochego dvizheniia v stranakh Latinskoi Ameriki [Literature on the history of the Communist and labor movement in Latin America] Vop. ist. KPSS, v. 6, no. 1, 1962: 164–176.

1157. Deklaratsiia kommunisticheskikh partii stran Latinskoi Ameriki [Declaration of the Communist parties of the Latin American countries] Part. zhizn', no. 1, Jan. 1959: 69–70.

1158. Galin, IU. Gost', kotoryi ne ukhodit [A visitor who won't leave] Mezhdunar. zhizn', v. 8, no. 1, Jan. 1961: 163–164.
A review of Juan José Arévalo's *Anticomunismo en América Latina* (2d ed. Mexico City, América Nueva, 1959. 206 p.).

1159. González Alberdi, Paulino. 30-letie pervoi konferentsii kompartii Latinskoi Ameriki [The 30th anniversary of the First Conference of Latin American Communist Parties] Probl. mira i sots., v. 2, no. 7, July 1959: 59–63.

1160. Khachaturov, K. A. Vo imia sotsial'nogo progressa [In the name of social progress] Vop. ist. KPSS, v. 8, no. 5, May 1964: 114–116.
A review of Rodney Arismendi's *Problemas de una revolución continental* (Montevideo, Ediciones Pueblos Unidos, 1962. 556 p.).

1161. Konferentsiia kommunisticheskikh i rabochikh partii stran TSentral'noi

Ameriki [A conference of the Communist and Workers' parties of Central America] Probl. mira i sots., v. 4, no. 10, Oct. 1961: 56.

1162. Manasov, M. Kommunisticheskie partii Latinskoi Ameriki (?) [Communist parties of Latin America] Otv. na vop. trud., no. 5, May 1961: 29–35.

1163. ———. Kommunisticheskie partii stran Latinskoi Ameriki [Communist parties of the countries of Latin America] Polit. samoobr., v. 7, no. 6, June 1963: 124–131.

1164. Nedelia solidarnosti s Latinskoi Amerikoi [A week of solidarity with Latin America] Nov. vrem., v. 21, no. 17, Apr. 1964: 6.

1165. Priem Predsedatelem Mao TSze-dunom rukovodiashchikh tovarishchei bratskikh partii 12 stran Latinskoi Ameriki [A reception by Chairman Mao Tse-tung for the leaders of fraternal parties in 12 countries of Latin America] Kitai, no. 6, Mar. 1959: 1.

1166. Rumiantsev, A. M., *and others.* Problemy sozdaniia edinogo antiimperialisticheskogo fronta [Problems of the establishment of a united anti-imperialist front] Probl. mira i sots., v. 6, no. 1, Jan. 1963: 69–85.

1167. Sotnikov, I. Simpatii i antipatii Anri Benaze [The likes and dislikes of Henri Benazet] Nov. vrem., v. 17, no. 38, Sept. 1959: 17.

2. Individual Countries

a. Argentina

1168. Dolinin, A. A. Bor'ba kommunisticheskikh partii Chili i Argentiny za edinstvo antiimperialisticheskikh i antifeodal'nykh sil [The struggle of the Communist parties of Chile and Argentina for the unity of anti-imperialist and antifeudal forces] Moscow, Znanie, 1961. 22 p.

1169. Viatkin, A. V. Kommunisticheskaia partiia Argentiny v bor'be za edinstvo rabochego klassa, 1956–1960 gg. [The Communist Party of Argentina in the struggle for the unity of the laboring classes, 1956–1960] [Moscow] 1963. (Aka-

demiia obshchestvennykh nauk pri TsK KPSS)
Abstract of a dissertation for the degree of Candidate in Historical Sciences.

1170. Andreev, Vlad. Viktorio Kodovil'ia; biograficheskaia spravka [Victorio Codovilla; a biographical note] Mir. ekon. i mezhdunar. otn., no. 2, 1964: 136–138.

1171. Bermúdez, José. Iz opyta izdatel'skoi deiatel'nosti; Argentina [From the practice of publishing houses; Argentina] Probl. mira i sots., v. 4, no. 8, Aug. 1961: 71.
Communist publications.

1172. Besrodnik, Felipe. Finansovaia pomoshch' druzei partii [The financial aid of friends of the Party] Probl. mira i sots., v. 7, no. 5, May 1964: 56–57.

1173. Boevoi avangard trudiashchikhsia Argentiny [The militant vangard of Argentine workers] Komm. Bel., v. 36, no. 12, Dec. 1962: 75.

1174. Codovilla, Victorio. Gimn zhizni, trudu, miru i schast'iu narodov [A hymn to life, work, peace and happiness of the peoples] Kommunist, v. 38, no. 16, Nov. 1961: 151–152.
An Argentine Communist on the program of the CPSU.

1175. ———. Sovremennoe polozhenie v Argentine i taktika Kompartii [Present-day situation in Argentina and the tactics of the Communist Party] Probl. mira i sots., v. 3, no. 2, Feb. 1960: 27–34.

1176. ———. Za aktivnye deistviia mass, za edinstvo demokraticheskikh sil [For the vigorous action of the masses and the unity of democratic forces] Kommunist, v. 40, no. 10, July 1963: 96–102.

1177. Dabagian, E. S. V avangarde bor'by za demokratiiu i sotsializm [In the vanguard of the struggle for democracy and socialism] Nov. i noveish. ist., no. 2, 1959: 200–201.
A review of Victorio Codovilla's *Stat'i i rechi; 1926–1956* (Moscow, Izd-vo inostr. lit., 1957. 362 p.).

1178. Ermolaev, V. I. Kompartiia Argentiny —pervaia sektsiia III Internatsionala v Latinskoi Amerike [The Communist

Party of Argentina as the first section of the Third International in Latin America] Nov. i noveish. ist., no. 3, 1959: 49–66.

1179. Ferrari, Alberto, *and* Fernando Nadra. Ideologicheskaia rabota i zhizn' [Ideological work and the facts of life] Probl. mira i sots., v. 7, no. 5, May 1964: 52–55.

1180. Flores, Jorge. Kompartiia Argentiny usilivaet bor'bu [The Communist Party of Argentina intensifies its struggle] Probl. mira i sots., v. 2, no. 7, July 1959: 73–76.

1181. Gazety na predpriiatiiakh [Newspapers at industrial enterprises] Probl. mira i sots., v. 2, no. 3, 1959: 59.
   Communist newspapers.

1182. Gladkii, V. B. Kommunisticheskaia pressa Argentiny v bor'be za novyi, demokraticheskii kurs strany, 1955–1959 [The Communist press of Argentina in the struggle for a new, democratic course for the country, 1955–1959] Vest. Mosk. un. Ser. 7: Filol., zhur., v. 15, no. 6, Nov.-Dec. 1960: 47–57.

1183. Iscaro, N. Kommunisty na predpriiatiiakh Buenos-Airesa [The Communists in the industrial enterprises of Buenos Aires] Probl. mira i sots., v. 5, no. 4, Apr. 1962: 52–54.

1184. Iscaro, Rubens, *and* Vicente Marisci. Kommunisty v profsoiuzakh [The Communists in trade unions] Probl. mira i sots., v. 7, no. 5, May 1964: 49–52.

1185. Kommunisticheskaia partiia Argentiny [The Communist Party of Argentina] Rev.-ist. kalendar'-spravochnik, 1963: 16–20.

1186. Kommunisty Argentiny na boevykh pozitsiiakh [The Communists of Argentina in battle positions] Kommunist, v. 40, no. 2, Jan. 1964: 112–114.

1187. Marksistsko-leninskoe obrazovanie kommunistov [The Marxist-Leninist education of Communists] Probl. mira i sots., v. 2, no. 1, Jan. 1959: 76.

1188. Peña, Alcira de la. Uspekh bor'by v edinstve levykh sil [Unity of left-wing forces will ensure victory] Part. zhizn', no. 14, July 1963: 67–73.

1189. Pérez, Silvia. Kommunisticheskaia partiia Argentiny [The Communist Party of Argentina] Probl. mira i sots., v. 6, no. 6, June 1963: 41–43.

1190. ———. Vo glave mass [At the forefront of the masses] Probl. mira i sots., v. 7, no. 5, May 1964: 47–49.

1191. Rimak, S. Teoreticheskii zhurnal argentinskikh kommunistov [A theoretical periodical of the Argentine Communists] Probl. mira i sots., v. 2, no. 4, Apr. 1959: 85–87.
   A review of the periodical *Nueva era* (Buenos Aires, 1949–59).

1192. S plenumov tsentral'nykh komitetov; Kommunisticheskaia partiia Argentiny [Plenary sessions of the Central Committees; the Communist Party of Argentina] Probl. mira i sots., v. 5, no. 10, Oct. 1962: 45–47.

1193. S plenumov tsentral'nykh komitetov kommunisticheskikh i rabochikh partii; Argentina [Plenary sessions of the central committees of the Communist and Workers' parties; Argentina] Probl. mira i sots., v. 7. no. 2, Feb. 1964: 59–60.

1194. Tadioli, Pedro. V avangarde demokraticheskikh i progressivnykh sil [At the forefront of democratic and progressive forces] Part. zhizn', no. 15/16, Aug. 1961: 146–151.

1195. Viktorio Kodovil'ia; biograficheskaia spravka [Victorio Codovilla; a biographical note] Nov. vrem., v. 21, no. 6, Feb. 1964: 29.

1196. Voskresnye sobraniia [Sunday meetings] Probl. mira i sots., v. 3, no. 9, Sept. 1960: 68.

See also entry no. 1615.

b. Bolivia

1197. González, Ruiz. Programma KPSS pridaet nam novye sily [The program of the CPSU gives us new strength] Kommunist, v. 38, no. 16, Nov. 1961: 153–154.

1198. Monje, Mario. Razvitie boliviiskoi revoliutsii i taktika partii [The development of the Bolivian Revolution and the tactics of the Communist Party] Probl. mira i sots., v. 4, no. 5, May 1961: 59–62.

c. Brazil

1199. Boevoi avangard brazil'skogo naroda; k 40-letiiu Kommunisticheskoi partii Brazilii [The militant vanguard of the Brazilian people; the 40th anniversary of the Communist Party of Brazil] Komm. Bel., v. 36, no. 3, Mar. 1962: 76.

1200. Carvalho, Apolonio de. Sviaz' partiinoi propagandy s zhizn'iu [The relation of party propaganda to life] Probl. mira i sots., v. 5, no. 12, Dec. 1962: 54–55.

1201. Dvizhenie za legalizatsiiu Kompartii [A movement for the legalization of the Communist Party] Probl. mira i sots., v. 2, no. 6, June 1959: 78–79.

1202. Koval', B. I. Pervaia kniga o brazil'skoi kommunisticheskoi partii [The first book on the Brazilian Communist Party] Nov. i noveish. ist., no. 1, 1963: 171–172.
A review of Astrojildo Pereira's *Formação do PGB, 1922/1928* (Rio de Janeiro, Vitória, 1962. 145 p.).

1203. ———. Rabochee i kommunisticheskoe dvizhenie v Brazilii [The labor and Communist movement in Brazil] Vop. ist., no. 4, Apr. 1961: 195–196.

1204. Krasil'nikova, S. Rytsar' nadezhdy [The knight of hope] Prostor, v. 30, no. 7, 1963: 56–62.
Luis Carlos Prestes.

1205. Lima, Pedro Motta. Prizyv brazil'skikh kommunistov [An appeal of the Brazilian Communists] Probl. mira i sots., v. 7, no. 9, Sept. 1964: 44–45.

1206. Luis Karlos Prestes [Luis Carlos Prestes] Nov. vrem., v. 20, no. 10, Mar. 1963: 31.

1207. Luis Karlos Prestes; biograficheskaia spravka [Luis Carlos Prestes; a biographical note] Mir. ekon. i mezhdunar. otn., no. 5, 1963: 130–131.

1208. Marighella, Carlos. Bor'ba za demokraticheskie svobody, za legalizatsiiu Kompartii v Brazilii [The struggle for democratic freedoms and for the legali-zation of the Brazilian Communist Party] Probl. mira i sots., v. 5, no. 5, May 1962: 56–59.

1209. Massovaia kampaniia za legalizatsiiu Brazil'skoi kompartii [A mass campaign for the legalization of the Communist Party of Brazil] Part. zhizn', no. 23, Dec. 1961: 73.

1210. Plenumy tsentral'nykh komitetov kommunisticheskikh i rabochikh partii; Braziliia [Plenary sessions of the central committees of the Communist and Workers' parties; Brazil] Probl. mira i sots., v. 5, no. 2, Feb. 1962: 68.

1211. Prestes, Luis Carlos. O politicheskoi obstanovke v Brazilii [On the political situation in Brazil] Probl. mira i sots., v. 6, no. 5, May 1963: 49–50.

1212. Saad, Fuad. Sovershenstvuem rabotu v massakh [We are improving our work among the masses] Part. zhizn', no. 3, Feb. 1963: 64–67.

1213. Santos, Antonio. Preodolevaia sektantskie oshibki [Trying to overcome sectarian errors] Probl. mira i sots., v. 2, no. 11, Nov. 1959: 58–60.

1214. Vladimirov, V. Legendarnyi pokhod Prestesa [The legendary march of Prestes] Ogonek, v. 40, no. 14, Apr. 1962: 26.

See also entry no. 1621.

d. Chile

1215. Lafertte Gaviño, Elías. Zhizn' kommunista; stranitsy avtobiografii [The life of a Communist; autobiographic pages] Moscow, Gospolitizdat, 1961. 318 p.
Translated from the Spanish *Vida de un comunista; páginas autobiográficas.*
Reviewed by IU. Fedorov in *Vop. ist. KPSS*, v. 6, no. 3, 1962: 190–193.

1216. Materialy 12-go s"ezda Kommunisticheskoi partii Chili, Sant-IAgo, 13–18 marta 1962 goda [Materials of the 12th Congress of the Communist Party of Chile, Santiago, March 13–18, 1962] Moscow, Gospolitizdat, 1963. 183 p.

1217. Miachin, K. V. Bor'ba Kompartii Chili za edinyi natsional'nyi antiimperialisticheskii i antifeodal'nyi front, 1956–1960 gg. [The struggle of the Chilean Com-

munist Party for a united national anti-imperialist and anti-feudal front, 1956–1960] [Moscow] 1963. (Akademiia obshchestvennykh nauk pri TsK KPSS)
Abstract of a dissertation for the degree of Candidate in Historical Sciences.

1218. Arauco, Juan. Patrioticheskaia pozitsiia chiliiskikh kommunistov [The patriotic position of Chilean Communists] Probl. mira i sots., v. 3, no. 8, Aug. 1960: 46–47.

1219. Corvalán, Luis. Bitva za natsional'noe i sotsial'noe osvobozhdenie [The struggle for national and social liberation] Part. zhizn', no. 2, Jan. 1959: 62–68.
Translated from the Spanish.

1220. ———. Kak my boremsia za ukreplenie fronta natsional'nogo osvobozhdeniia; iz opyta Kompartii Chili [How we try to strengthen the front of national liberation; from the experience of the Chilean Communist Party] Probl. mira i sots., v. 2, no. 4, Apr. 1959: 41–47.

1221. ———. Mirnyi put'—forma revoliutsii [The peaceful path is a form of the revolution] Probl. mira i sots., v. 6, no. 12, Dec. 1963: 1–9.
Political activities of the Communist Party.

1222. ———. Osnova nashikh uspekhov—v edinstve deistvii rabochego klassa i trudiashchikhsia mass [The basis of our achievements lies in the concerted action of the working class and the laboring masses] Part. zhizn', no. 16, Aug. 1960: 64–69.

1223. Fedorov, M. Luis Korvalan; biograficheskaia spravka [Luis Corvalán; a biographical note] Mir. ekon. i mezhdunar. otn., no. 4, 1964: 138–139.

1224. Gazeta oblastnogo komiteta [A newspaper published by a province committee] Probl. mira i sots., v. 2, no. 11, Nov. 1959: 63–64.
A Communist newspaper.

1225. Gómez, Pedro. Nashi pozitsii sred studenchestva [Our positions among the university students] Probl. mira i sots., v. 4, no. 9, Sept. 1961: 54–55.

1226. González, José. Chili: uspekh kampanii za rost partii [Successful campaign for an increase in party membership in Chile] Probl. mira i sots., v. 5, no. 5, May 1962: 62–63.

1227. ———. Pouchitel'nyi opyt bor'by narodnykh mass [An instructive experience of the struggle of the masses] Probl. mira i sots., v. 3, no. 5, May 1960: 75–76.

1228. J. C. Plenumy tsentral'nykh komitetov kommunisticheskikh i rabochikh partii; Chili [Plenary sessions of the central committees of the Communist and Workers' parties; Chile] Probl. mira i sots., v. 4, no. 10, Oct. 1961: 58.

1229. Kommunisticheskaia partiia Chili [The Communist Party of Chile] Probl. mira i sots., v. 6, no. 9, Sept. 1963: 84–85.

1230. Korionov, V. Na s"ezde kommunistov Chili [At the Congress of the Chilean Communists] Agitator, no. 9, May 1962: 52–55.

1231. Krepit' edinstvo kommunistov i sotsialistov [Strengthen the cooperation of Communists and Socialists] Part. zhizn', no. 24, Dec. 1959: 57–58.

1232. Kudachkin, M. F. Kompartiia Chili v bor'be za edinstvo natsional'nykh sil [The Communist Party of Chile struggles for the unity of national forces] Vop. ist. KPSS, v. 8, no. 2, Feb. 1964: 54–65.

1233. Luis Korvalan; biograficheskaia spravka [Luis Corvalán; a biographical note] Nov. vrem., v. 20, no. 19, May 1962: 28.

1234. Millás, Orlando. Novye techeniia v katolitsizme i politika chiliiskikh kommunistov [New trends in Catholicism and the policy of the Chilean Communists] Probl. mira i sots., v. 7, no. 3, Mar. 1964: 25–31.

1235. ———. Uspekh nashei bor'by—v edinstve natsional'nykh i demokraticheskikh sil [The success of our struggle depends on the unity of national and democratic forces] Part. zhizn', no. 5, Mar. 1962: 64–70.

1236. XI [Odinnadtsatyi] s"ezd Kommunisticheskoi partii Chili [The 11th Congress of the Communist Party of Chile] Probl. mira i sots., v. 2, no. 1, Jan. 1959: 72–73.

1237. Pamiati Eliasa Lafertte [In memory of Elías Lafertte] Probl. mira i sots., v. 4, no. 4, Apr. 1961: 48.

1238. Predvybornaia agitatsiia [Pre-election propaganda] Probl. mira i sots., v. 4, no. 4, Apr. 1961: 61.

1239. Ramírez Necochea, Hernán. Iz opyta ideologicheskoi raboty [From our experience in ideological work] Probl. mira i sots., v. 4, no. 9, Sept. 1961: 51–53.

1240. Rojas, Rodrigo. Kak rasshiriaiutsia nashi riady [How we enlarge our ranks] Probl. mira i sots., v. 3, no. 1, Jan. 1960: 59–61.

1241. Sovmestnoe zaiavlenie kommunisticheskoi i sotsialisticheskoi partii Chili [A joint statement of the Communist and Socialist parties of Chile] Part. zhizn', no. 14, July 1959: 69.

1242. Teitelboim, V. Iz nashego opyta vzaimootnoshenii s burzhuaziei [From our experience in contacts with the bourgeoisie] Probl. mira i sots., v. 2, no. 8, Aug. 1959: 76–79.

1243. V interesakh naroda [For the people] Part. zhizn', no. 13, July 1960: 72.

See also entries no. 1168, 1627, and 3105.

e. Colombia

1244. Cardona Hoyos, José. Vos'moi s"ezd Kompartii Kolumbii [The Eighth Congress of the Colombian Communist Party] Probl. mira i sots., v. 2, no. 2, Feb. 1959: 60–61.

1245. Delgado, Alvaro. V klassovykh boiakh vykovyvaetsia massovaia partiia Kolumbii [The class struggle helps the Colombian Communist Party to develop into a party of the masses] Probl. mira i sots., v. 6, no. 9, Sept. 1963: 69–71.

1246. Lafond Herrera, Manlio. Kolumbiia; krizis oligarkhicheskoi sistemy i politika Kompartii [Colombia; the crisis of the oligarchic system and the policy of the Communist Party] Probl. mira i sots., v. 4, no. 9, Sept. 1961: 47–49.

1247. Progressivnaia literatura na knizhnoi iarmarke [Progressive literature at a book fair] Inostr. lit., no. 6, June 1959: 280.
Communist publications.

1248. Tridtsatiletie Kommunisticheskoi partii Kolumbii [The 30th anniversary of the Colombian Communist Party] Probl. mira i sots., v. 3, no. 7, July 1960: 62.

1249. V zashchitu melkikh torgovtsev [Protecting the interests of small retail merchants] Probl. mira i sots., v. 2, no. 8, Aug. 1959: 62.

1250. Vega, M. Ocherk po istorii Kompartii Kolumbii [A study on the history of the Communist Party of Colombia] Vop. ist. KPSS, v. 5, no. 4, 1961: 197–200.
A review of *Treinta años de lucha del Partido Comunista de Colombia* (Bogotá, Ediciones Paz y Socialismo, 1960. 167 p.).

1251. Viana, Juan. U kommunistov Kolumbii; iz praktiki raboty oblastnogo komiteta [From the work practice of a province committee of the Colombian Communists] Probl. mira i sots., v. 7, no. 1, Jan. 1964: 48–52.

1252. Vieira, Gilberto. Krest'ianskoe dvizhenie v Kolumbii i Kommunisticheskaia partiia; iz istorii osvoboditel'noi bor'by [The peasant movement and the Communist Party of Colombia; from the history of the liberation struggle] Probl. mira i sots., v. 4, no. 5, May 1961: 33–39.

1253. ———. Nastuplenie reaktsii i taktika Kompartii [An attack by the reactionaries and the tactics of the Communist Party] Part. zhizn', no. 3, Feb. 1964: 61–67.

1254. ———. Rost militarizma v Kolumbii i taktika Kompartii [The growth of militarism in Colombia and the tactics of the Communist Party] Probl. mira i sots., v. 6, no. 4, Apr. 1963: 15–21.

f. Costa Rica

1255. Espinoza, Francisco. Opyt kommunistov Kosta-Riki [Experience of the Costa Rican Communists] Probl. mira i sots., v. 6, no. 7, July 1963: 45–47.

1256. Marin, S. V usloviiakh polulegal'nogo polozheniia partii [Under the conditions of the Party's semilegal position] Probl. mira i sots., v. 5, no. 12, Dec. 1962: 55–56.

1257. Mora, Manuel.   Nekotorye uroki nashego opyta [Some lessons obtained in practice] Part. zhizn', no. 9, May 1964: 65–70.

1258. Mora Valverde, Eduardo, *and* Alvaro Montero Vega.   Slova i dela rukovoditelei KPK [The words and deeds of the leaders of the Chinese Communist Party] Probl. mira i sots., v. 7, no. 6, June 1964: 55–58.
    The Costa Rican Communists reject the position of the Chinese Communist Party.

1259. Plenumy tsentral'nykh komitetov kommunisticheskikh i rabochikh partii; Kosta Rika [Plenary sessions of the central committees of the Communist and Workers' parties; Costa Rica] Probl. mira i sots., v. 4, no. 11, Nov. 1961: 63–64.

1260. Vargas, Oscar.   Aktivno borot'sia protiv opasnosti raskola [We should tirelessly struggle against the possibility of a split] Probl. mira i sots., v. 7, no. 9, Sept. 1964: 11–14.
    Position of the Costa Rican Communists in the Sino-Soviet conflict.

1261. ———.   Rastet partiia, narodnyi avangard Kosta-Riki [The Communist Party, the vanguard of the Costa Rican people, grows] Probl. mira i sots., v. 6, no. 10, Oct. 1963: 63–64.

1262. ———.   So s"ezdov partii; Kosta-Rika [At the congresses of the Communist parties; Costa Rica] Probl. mira i sots., v. 5, no. 8, Aug. 1962: 64–65.

g. *Cuba*

1263. Barrera, Hernán.   Stroitel'stvo Edinoi partii sotsialisticheskoi revoliutsii na Kube; po stranitsam partiinoi pechati Kuby [The construction of the United Party of the Socialist Revolution in Cuba; a review of the Cuban party press] Probl. mira i sots., v. 6, no. 12, Dec. 1963: 60–62.

1264. Calderío, Francisco (Blas Roca, *pseud.*) VIII natsional'nyi s"ezd Narodno-sotsialisticheskoi partii Kuby [The Eighth National Congress of the Popular Socialist Party of Cuba] Probl. mira i sots., v. 3, no. 11, Nov. 1960: 37–43.

1265. ———.   Znamia podlinnogo gumanizma [The banner of true humanism] Kommunist, v. 38, no. 16, Nov. 1961: 141–142.
    The Cuban Communist on the program of the CPSU.

1266. Gvozdev, IU.   Maiak sotsializma v zapadnom polusharii [The beacon of socialism in the Western Hemisphere] Komm. Vooruzh. Sil, v. 4. no. 24, Dec. 1963: 74–77.

1267. Karlos Rafael' Rodriges; biograficheskaia spravka [Carlos Rafael Rodríguez; a biographical note] Nov. vrem., v. 20, no. 13, Mar. 1962: 12.

1268. Kucher, Ivan.   Soldat revoliutsii [A soldier of the revolution] Ukraina, no. 30, July 1964: 9.

1269. Marinello, Juan.   Znamia narodov vsei zemli [A banner of the peoples of the whole world] Inostr. lit., no. 11, Nov. 1961: 195–197.
    Cuba's attitude toward the program of the Communist Party of the USSR.

1270. Marksistsko-leninskoe vospitanie kadrov [The Marxist-Leninist education of Party members] Probl. mira i sots., v. 5, May 1962: 66–67.

1271. Perestroika pervichnykh organizatsii na Kube [The reorganization of local party units in Cuba] Probl. mira i sots., v. 5, no. 8, Aug. 1962: 68–69.

h. *Dominican Republic*

1272. Konferentsiia Narodno-sotsialisticheskoi partii Dominikanskoi respubliki [A conference of the Popular Socialist Party of the Dominican Republic] Probl. mira i sots., v. 3, no. 8, Aug. 1960: 49.

1273. Protiv sektanstva, za ukreplenie sviazei s massami [Against sectarianism and for closer ties with the masses] Probl. mira i sots., v. 6, no. 4, Apr. 1963: 57–58.

1274. Solidarnost' bratskikh partii [Solidarity of fraternal parties] Probl. mira i sots., v. 3, no. 12, Dec. 1960: 54–55.

i. *Ecuador*

1275. Andreev, V.   Pedro-Antonio Saad; biograficheskaia spravka [Pedro Antonio Saad; a biographical note] Mir. ekon. i mezhdunar. otn., no. 3, 1964: 123–124.

1276. Hernández, H. Sokhraniat' vernost' sovmestno vyrabotannoi general'noi linii [We should adhere faithfully to the jointly established general line] Part. zhizn', no. 13, July 1964: 69–72.

1277. K. S. Kommunisty Ekvadora ukrepliaiut sviazi s massami [The Communists of Ecuador strengthen their contacts with the masses] Probl. mira i sots., v. 6, no. 1, Jan. 1963: 63–64.

1278. Kommunisticheskaia partiia Ekvadora [The Communist Party of Ecuador] Rev.-ist. kalendar'-spravochnik, 1963: 315–316.

1279. Pedro Antonio Saad; biograficheskaia spravka [Pedro Antonio Saad; a biographical note] Nov. vrem., v. 20, no. 14, Apr. 1962: 20.

1280. Plenumy tsentral'nykh komitetov; Kompartiia Ekvadora [Plenary sessions of the central committees; the Communist Party of Ecuador] Probl. mira i sots., v. 4, no. 9, Sept. 1961: 59.

1281. Razoblachenie tselei predstoiashchei mezhamerikanskoi konferentsii [The disclosure of the objectives of the forthcoming Inter-American conference] Probl. mira i sots., v. 2, no. 3, 1959: 59.
Political activities of the Communist Party of Ecuador.

j. El Salvador

1282. Castillo, José. Narod i partiia pobediat! [The people and the Party will win!] Probl. mira i sots., v. 6, no. 2, Feb. 1963: 90–91.

1283. Rodríguez, Miguel. Rastut simpatii k kommunistam [Growing support for the Communists] Probl. mira i sots., v. 3, no. 3. Mar. 1960: 74–75.

k. Guatemala

1284. Calderón, Sebastián. Izuchaem marksizm-leninizm [We study Marxism-Leninism] Probl. mira i sots., v. 7, no. 12, Dec. 1964: 54–55.

1285. E. S. Kommunisty Gvatemaly prodolzhaiut bor'bu [The Guatemalan Communists continue their struggle] Probl. mira i sots., v. 2, no. 2, Feb. 1959: 62–64.

1286. Evgen'ev, V. Kommunist Bernardo i ego soratniki [Communist Bernardo and his associates] Agitator, no. 24, Dec. 1963: 33–35.

1287. Fortuni, J. M. Pod znamenem proletarskogo internatsionalizma [Under the banner of proletarian internationalism] Probl. mira i sots., v. 7, no. 12, Dec. 1964: 50–52.

1288. Guerra Borges, Alfredo. V zashchitu edinstva kommunisticheskogo dvizhenia [In defense of the unity of the Communist movement] Part. zhizn', no. 18, Sept. 1964: 66–70.
Guatemalan Communist Party's position in the Sino-Soviet conflict.

1289. Jonama, Mario Silva. Sochetanie legal'nykh i nelegal'nykh metodov bor'by [A combination of legal and illegal methods of struggle] Part. zhizn', no. 9, May 1962: 65–69.

1290. Pechuro, E. E. Glazami amerikanskogo burzhuaznogo istorika [Through the eyes of an American bourgeois historian] Nov. i noveish. ist., no. 1, 1961: 160–161.
A review of Ronald M. Schneider's *Communism in Guatemala, 1944-1954* (New York, Praeger, 1958. 350 p.).

1291. S. Al. S"ezd Gvatemal'skoi partii truda [A congress of the Guatemalan Labor Party] Probl. mira i sots., v. 3, no. 10, Oct. 1960: 77–78.

1292. Sánchez, S. Partiia truda na boevom postu: pis'mo iz Gvatemaly [The Labor Party in battle position; a letter from Guatemala] Probl. mira i sots., v. 4, no. 6, June 1961: 76–78.

1293. Tzul, C. Sbor sredstv—forma ukrepleniia sviazi s massami [The fundraising campaign is a way to develop contacts with the masses] Probl. mira i sots., v. 7, no. 12, 1964: 56–57.

1294. Usilenie pozitsii partii v derevne [Strengthening the positions of the Party in rural areas] Probl. mira i sots., v. 2, no. 10, Oct. 1959: 69–70.

1295. Villatoro, E. Gvatemal'skaia partiia truda ukrepliaet sviazi s massami [The Guatemalan Labor Party strengthens its ties with the masses] Probl. mira i sots., v. 5, no. 5, May 1962: 61.

l. Haiti

1296. Lebon, Jean. Za podlinnuiu nezavisimost' Gaiti [For the real independence of Haiti] Probl. mira i sots., v. 6, no. 4, Apr. 1963: 84–86.

See also entry no. 1274.

m. Honduras

1297. Fuentes, Celedonio. Aktual'nye zadachi kommunistov Gondurasa [Current problems facing the Communists of Honduras] Probl. mira i sots., v. 5, no. 6, June 1962: 69–71.

1298. Muñoz, Alonso. Za natsional'nye interesy Gondurasa [For the national interests of Honduras] Part. zhizn', no. 5, Mar. 1963: 63–66.

1299. Picacho, Fausto. Gonduras; voliu naroda ne slomat' [Honduras; the will of our people cannot be broken!] Probl. mira i sots., v. 5, no. 4, Apr. 1962: 94.
Arrests of Communists.

n. Mexico

1300. Partido Comunista Mexicano. Congreso. Materialy 13-go Natsional'nogo S"ezda Meksikanskoi Kommunisticheskoi Partii, Mekhiko 1960 [Materials of the 13th National Congress of the Mexican Communist Party, Mexico City, 1960] Moscow, Gospolitizdat, 1961. 67 p.
Translated from the Spanish.

————————

1301. Antikommunism—eto ideologicheskaia diktatura [Anticommunism is an ideological dictatorship] Inostr. lit., no. 4, Apr. 1963: 283.

1302. Boevoi otriad trudiashchikhsia Meksiki [A militant vanguard of Mexican workers] Vop. ist. KPSS, v. 8, no. 11, Nov. 1964: 153–156.

1303. Chávez, Camilo. Meksikanskaia Kompartiia nabiraet sily [The Mexican Communist Party gathers its strength] Probl. mira i sots., v. 4, no. 10, Oct. 1961: 49–51.

1304. Díaz Ramírez, Manuel. Beseda s V. I. Leninym v 1921 godu [A talk with V. I. Lenin in 1921] Vop. ist. KPSS, v. 5, no. 1, 1961: 163–166.
History of the Communist Party of Mexico.

1305. Kommunisty zashchishchaiut interesy truzhenikov derevni [Communists protect the interests of rural toilers] Probl. mira i sots., v. 3, no. 3, Mar. 1960: 77–78.

1306. Konstantinov, O. M. 45 let bor'by za interesy trudiashchikhsia Meksiki [Forty-five years of struggle for the interests of Mexican workers] Vop. ist. KPSS, v. 8, no. 9, Sept. 1964: 85–89.

1307. Lara, H. Meksika; antikommunizm—put' k fashizmu [Mexico; anticommunism is a path toward fascism] Probl. mira i sots., v. 3, no. 12, Dec. 1960: 93–94.

1308. Martínez Verdugo, Arnoldo. Bor'ba meksikanskogo naroda i taktika Kompartii [The struggle of the Mexican people and the tactics of the Communist Party] Probl. mira i sots., v. 7, no. 7, July 1964: 20–27.

1309. Meksikanskaia kommunisticheskaia partiia [The Communist Party of Mexico] Probl. mira i sots., v. 6, no. 9, Sept. 1963: 81–82.

1310. Na puti k splocheniiu i edinstvu [On the path to solidarity and unity] Probl. mira i sots., v. 2, no. 12, Dec. 1959: 46–49.

1311. Natsional'nyi s"ezd Meksikanskoi kommunisticheskoi partii [The National Congress of the Mexican Communist Party] Probl. mira i sots., v. 7, no. 3, Mar. 1964: 52–54.

1312. Novyi period v zhizni partii [A new phase in the life of the party] Probl. mira i sots., v. 3, no. 9, Sept. 1960: 54–56.

1313. Plenumy tsentral'nykh komitetov kommunisticheskikh i rabochikh partii; Meksika [Plenary sessions of the central committees of the Communist and Workers' parties; Mexico] Probl. mira i sots., v. 5, no. 2, Feb. 1962: 69.

1314. Sánchez, Baudelio. Golos kommunistov Meksiki [The voice of Mexican Communists] Probl. mira i sots., v. 5, no. 9, Sept. 1962: 89.
A review of the periodical Nueva época (Mexico City, 1962).

1315. Splachivat' massy [We must rally the masses] Part. zhizn', no. 6, Mar. 1964: 71–73.

o. Nicaragua

1316. J. R. Kommunisty Nikaragua boriutsia protiv proimperialisticheskoi diktatury [The Communists of Nicaragua struggle against the proimperialist dictatorship] Probl. mira i sots., v. 4, no. 4, Apr. 1961: 90–92.

1317. Segovia, Pablo. Kommunisty Nikaragua vystupaiut protiv tiranii [The Communists of Nicaragua oppose the tyranny] Probl. mira i sots., v. 6, no. 2, Feb. 1963: 68–69.

p. Panama

1318. Locho, S. Gazeta kommunistov Panamy [A newspaper of the Panamanian Communists] Probl. mira i sots., v. 4, no. 12, Dec. 1961: 53–54.

1319. Tello, Vicente. Patrioticheskaia pozitsiia narodnoi partii Panamy [The patriotic position of the Panamanian People's Party] Probl. mira i sots., v. 5, no. 6, June 1962: 71–72.

q. Paraguay

1320. Khrushcheva, IU. Tovarishch Marta [Comrade Marta] Ogonek, v. 41, no. 25, June 1963: 18–19.

1321. Linores, Pedro. Podnimem golos v zashchitu Antonio Maidany i ego tovarishchei! [Raise your voice in defense of Antonio Maidana and his comrades!] Probl. mira i sots., v. 5, no. 2, Feb. 1962: 93–94.

1322. Vásquez, Liborio. Krovavoe prestuplenie stressnerovskoi kliki [A bloody crime committed by Stroessner's clique] Probl. mira i sots., v. 6, no. 8, Aug. 1963: 90.
Repression of the Communists.

r. Peru

1323. Gutiérrez, Antonio. V obstanovke repressii i terrora [Under conditions of repression and terror] Part. zhizn', no. 9, May 1963: 65–69.

1324. Konferentsiia Peruanskoi kommunisticheskoi partii [A conference of the Peruvian Communist Party] Probl. mira i sots., v. 7, no. 11, Nov. 1964: 88.

1325. Peruanskaia kommunisticheskaia partiia [The Communist Party of Peru] Rev.-ist. kalendar'-spravochnik, 1963: 273–274.

1326. Plata po schetu [Paying the bill] Nov. vrem., v. 19, no. 5, Jan. 1961: 22.

1327. Plenumy tsentral'nykh komitetov kommunisticheskikh i rabochikh partii; Peru [Plenary sessions of the central committees of the Communist and Workers' parties; Peru] Probl. mira i sots., v. 4, no. 12, Dec. 1961: 62.

1328. Prado, Jorge del. Vse—vmeste s massami, nichego—bez nikh; o politicheskom polozhenii v Peru i taktike Kompartii [Always with the masses and never without their support; the political situation in Peru and the tactics of the Communist Party] Probl. mira i sots., v. 7, no. 5, May 1964: 10–17.

1329. Prizyv k edinstvu patrioticheskikh sil [A call to the unity of patriotic forces] Probl. mira i sots., v. 3, no. 11, Nov. 1960: 82–83.

1330. Rodríguez, S. Peruanskaia kommunisticheskaia partiia [The Communist Party of Peru] Probl. mira i sots., v. 6, no. 1, Jan. 1963: 54–56.

1331. Sumar, I. V zashchitu patriotov Peru [In defense of Peruvian patriots] Probl. mira i sots., v. 6, no. 3, Mar. 1963: 92–93.

s. Puerto Rico

1332. Rivera, Juan Santos. Proval antikommunisticheskoi instsenirovki [Fiasco of an anti-Communist frameup] Probl. mira i sots., v. 3, no. 4, Apr. 1960: 69–70.

t. Uruguay

1333. Arismendi, Rodney. Nekotorye voprosy ideologicheskoi bor'by; obshchie polozheniia i natsional'nye osobennosti v programnoi deklaratsii nashei partii [Some problems of ideological struggle; general principles and national characteristics of the proclaimed program of our party] Moscow, Gospolitizdat, 1963. 107 p.
Translated from the Spanish.

1334. Partido Comunista del Uruguay. *Congreso. 17th, Montevideo, 1958.* XVII s"ezd Kommunisticheskoi partii Urugvaia, Montevideo, 15–17 avgusta 1958 goda; dokumenty i materialy s"ezda [Materials of the 17th Congress of the Communist Party of Uruguay, Montevideo, 1958] Moscow, Gospolitizdat, 1959. 230 p.   JL3698.C74 1958
Translated from the Spanish.

1335. Altezor, Alberto.   Rastet i krepnet nasha partiia [Out party is becoming larger and more powerful] Part. zhizn', no. 7, Apr. 1962: 68–70.

1336. Arismendi, Rodney. Pobeda cheloveka [A victory of man] Nov. vrem., v. 19, no. 43, Oct. 1961: 4–5.
The Uruguayan Communist discusses the program of the Communist Party of the Soviet Union.

1337. Flores, Isidro. Teoreticheskii zhurnal urugvaiskikh kommunistov [The theoretical journal of the Uruguayan Communists] Probl. mira i sots., v. 4, no. 4, Apr. 1961: 78–80.
A review of the periodical *Estudios* (Montevideo, 1957–61).

1338. Gravina, Alfredo Dante.   Voskhishchenie i blagodarnost' [Admiration and gratitude] Inostr. lit., no. 11, Nov. 1961: 200–201.
An Uruguayan author writes on the program of the Communist Party of the USSR.

1339. M. K. Pod znakom bor'by za edinstvo; XVIII s"ezd Kompartii Urugvaia [Marked by the struggle for unity; the 18th congress of the Communist Party of Uruguay] Probl. mira i sots., v. 5, no. 9, Sept. 1962: 63–65.

1340. Mostovets, N., *and* V. Tikhmenov. Boevoi avangard urugvaiskogo naroda [The militant vangard of the Uruguayan people] Agitator, no. 23, Dec. 1962: 18–20.

1341. Pérez, Jaime, *and* Félix Díaz. V avangarde klassovykh bitv [In the forefront of class struggle] Agitator, no. 10, May 1964: 15–18.

1342. Pintos, Francisco R. Narod delaet istoriiu; iz vospominanii delegata IV Kongressa Kominterna [The people are the makers of history; reminiscences of a delegate to the Fourth Congress of the Communist International] Inostr. lit., no. 3, Mar. 1959: 219–223.

1343. Plenumy tsentral'nykh komitetov kommunisticheskikh i rabochikh partii; Urugvai [Plenary sessions of the central committees of the Communist and Workers' parties; Uruguay] Probl. mira i sots., v. 4, no. 12, Dec. 1961: 62.

1344. Radioperedachi Kompartii [Radio broadcasts of the Communist Party] Probl. mira i sots., v. 3, no. 7, July 1960: 61.

1345. Rodnei Arismendi; biograficheskaia spravka [Rodney Arismendi; a biographical note] Nov. vrem., v. 20, no. 13, Mar. 1963: 23.

1346. Rodríguez, Enrique. Sila primera [The force of example] Part. zhizn', no. 19, Oct. 1963: 69–72.

1347. Sobraniia na domu [Meetings in residential blocks] Probl. mira i sots., v. 2, no. 4, Apr. 1959: 80.

1348. Suárez, Alberto. Bor'ba Kompartii Urugvaia za usilenie vliianiia v massakh [Efforts of the Communist Party of Uruguay to increase its influence upon the masses] Vop. ist. KPSS, v. 7, no. 5, May 1963: 42–52.

1349. ———. Partiinoe stroitel'stvo—neot"emlemaia chast' revoliutsionnogo protsessa [Party organization is an indispensable part of the revolutionary process] Probl. mira i sots., v. 4, no. 2, Feb. 1961: 9–16.

1350. ———. Sozdadim partiiu mass [We shall organize a party of the masses] Part. zhizn', no. 20, Oct. 1962: 64–70.

1351. Tri pis'ma ob opyte Kompartii Urugvaia [Three letters on the experience of the Communist Party of Uruguay] Probl. mira i sots., v. 4, no. 1. Jan. 1961: 51–55.

1352. TSentr sotsial'nykh issledovanii [A center for social studies] Probl. mira i sots., v. 4, no. 9, Sept. 1961: 54.

1353. Viera, Eduardo. Gazeta i massovye kampanii [The newspaper and mass cam-

paigns] Probl. mira i sots., v. 3, no. 10, Oct. 1960: 82–84.
Communist newspapers.

1354. ———. Kompartiia Urugvaia—vedushchaia sila v bor'be za natsional'nuiu nezavisimost' svoei rodiny [The Communist Party of Uruguay is the leading force in the struggle for Uruguayan national independence] Part. zhizn', no. 17, Sept. 1960: 60–65.

u. Venezuela

1355. Agaiants, N. Pylaiuschchaia Venesuela [Venezuela in flame] Smena, v. 41, no. 8, Aug. 1964: 28–29.

1356. El Velazco. Venesuela; novye usloviia trebuiut novoi taktiki [Venezuela; a new situation calls for new tactics] Probl. mira i sots., v. 4, no. 8, Aug. 1961: 60–63.

1357. Faria, Jesús. Za natsional'noe osvobozhdenie strany [For the national liberation of our country] Part. zhizn', no. 11, June 1961: 55–59.

1358. Faria, Jesús, *and others*. Venesuela budet svobodnoi! [Venezuela will be free!] Za rubezhom, no. 18, May 1964: 17.

1359. Gustavo Machado; biograficheskaia spravka [Gustavo Machado; a biographical note] Nov. vrem., v. 21, no. 26, July 1964: 9.

1360. Kompartiia Venesuely muzhestvenno boretsia protiv nastupleniia reaktsii [The Communist Party of Venezuela bravely struggles against the onslaught of reaction] Probl. mira i sots., v. 5, no. 7, July 1962: 67.

1361. Legendarnyi Gustavo Machado [The legendary Gustavo Machado] Ogonek, v. 41, no. 30, July 1963: 6.

1362. López, Carlos. Kompartiia Venesuely i sovremennoe polozhenie v strane [The Communist Party of Venezuela and the present-day situation in that country] Probl. mira i sots., v. 7, no. 10, Nov. 1964: 19–26.

1363. Prizyv k edinstvu [A call to unity] Probl. mira i sots., v. 3, no. 8, Aug. 1960: 47–49.

1364. Publichnyi otchet o deiatel'nosti v gody podpol'ia [A public account of activity during the period of underground status] Probpls. mira i sots., v. 2, no. 1, 1959: 76–77.

1365. Regalado, S. Iz opyta nelegal'noi raboty Kompartii Venesuely [From the experience of the underground work of the Venezuelan Communist Party] Probl. mira i sots., v. 5, no. 1, Jan. 1962: 57–59.

1366. Sáez Mérida, Simón. Krepnut patrioticheskie sily Venesuely [The patriotic forces of Venezuela grow stronger] Probl. mira i sots., v. 6, no. 3, Mar. 1963: 79–80.

1367. Sozdat' front oppozitsii rezhimu diktatury; zaiavlenie Kompartii Venesuely [Let us establish a front of opposition against the dictatorship; a statement of the Communist Party of Venezuela] Probl. mira i sots., v. 6, no. 6, June 1963: 50–53.

See also entry no. 1702.

v. West Indies

1368. Dufeal, Philibert. Kommunisty Martiniki [The Communists of Martinique] Probl. mira i sots., v. 3, no. 2, Feb. 1960: 69.

1369. Gvadelupskaia kommunisticheskaia partiia [The Communist Party of Guadeloupe] Rev.-ist. kalendar'-spravochnik, 1963: 73.

1370. Ibenet, Egesippe. Svoboda i nezavisimost'—nasha zavetnaia tsel' [Freedom and independence are our most cherished goals] Part. zhizn', no. 12, June 1962: 65–68.
Guadeloupe.

1371. Pierre-Justin, Serge. Programma KPSS vdokhnovliaet bortsov za mir [The program of the CPSU inspires the fighters for peace] Kommunist, v. 38, no. 16, Nov. 161: 158–159.
Guadeloupe.

1372. ———. Za chto boretsia Kompartiia Gvadelupy [What the Communist Party of Guadeloupe is fighting for] Probl. mira i sots., v. 4, no. 4, Apr. 1961: 60–62.

1373. Za splochenie antikolonial'nykh sil; III s"ezd Martinikskoi kompartii [For the unity of anticolonial forces; the Third Congress of the Communist Party of Martinique] Probl. mira i sots., v. 7, no. 4, Apr. 1964: 40–41.

1374. Zaiavlenie kommunisticheskikh partii Frantsii, Gvadelupy, Martiniki i Reiun'ona [A statement of the Communist parties of France, Guadeloupe, Martinique, and Reunion] Probl. mira i sots., v. 4, no. 12, Dec. 1961: 58–59.

C. POLITICAL ACTIVITY OF LABOR AND TRADE UNIONS

1. Writings Dealing With Three or More Countries

1375. Danilevich, M. V. Rabochii klass v osvoboditel'nom dvizhenii narodov Latinskoi Ameriki [The role of workers in the liberation movement of the Latin American peoples] Moscow, Gospolitizdat, 1962. 468 p.   F1414.D3

1376. ———. Rabochii klass v osvoboditel'nom dvizhenii narodov Latinskoi Ameriki [The role of workers in the liberation movement of the Latin American peoples] Moscow, 1960. 39 p. (Institut mirovoi ekonomiki i mezhdunarodynkh otnoshenii Akademii nauk SSSR)
  Abstract of a dissertation for the degree of Doctor of Historical Sciences.

1377. Rozhkov, Aleksandr Filippovich. Polozhenie i bor'ba trudiashchikhsia stran Latinskoi Ameriki [The situation and the struggle of the workers of Latin America] Moscow, Znanie, 1960. 40 p.
      AS262.V833, Ser. 7, 1960, no. 21

1378. Adducci, Jacomo. Pervaia Latinoamerikanskaia konferentsiia metallurgov [The First Latin American Conference of Metalworkers] Vsem. prof. dvizh., no. 12, Dec. 1960: 25–28.

1379. ———. Za edinstvo trudiashchikhsia metallurgicheskoi promyshlennosti Latinskoi Ameriki [For the unity of the metalworkers of Latin America] Vsem. prof. dvizh., no. 9, Sept. 1959: 24–27.

1380. Chleboun, Edvin. Novyi uspekh v bor'be za edinstvo deistvii profsoiuzov [A new success in the struggle for the united action of trade unions] Vsem. prof. dvizh., no. 3, Mar. 1964: 6–8.

1381. Danilevich, I. V. Proletariat Latinskoi Ameriki v natsional'no-osvoboditel'nom dvizhenii [The role of the proletariat in the Latin American national liberation movement] In Akademiia nauk SSSR. Institut mirovoi ekonomiki i mezhdunarodnykh otnoshenii. Rabochee dvizhenie v kapitalisticheskikh stranakh, 1959–1961 gg. Moscow, Gospolitizdat, 1961: p. 227–250.   HD4854.A43

1382. Danilevich, M., and A. Kondrat'eva. Bor'ba za profsoiuznoe edinstvo v Latinskoi Amerike [The struggle for the unity of trade unions in Latin America] Mir. ekon. i mezhdunar. otn., no. 12, 1964: 63–73.

1383. Domnich, M. IA. Kto zhe spaset Latinskuiu Ameriku? [Who then will save Latin America?] Vop. ist., v. 38, no. 10, Oct. 1963: 192–193.
  Catholic trade unions.
  A review of an article by Emilio Maspero in *Informations catholiques internationales*, no. 146, 1961: 1–3.

1384. Figueroa Mazuela, Luis. Slovo za profsoiuznoi konferentsiei trudiashchikhsia Latinskoi Ameriki [The floor belongs to the Trade-Union Conference of Latin American Workers] Vsem. prof. dvizh., no. 7, July 1962: 19–23.

1385. Grigor'ev, IA. G. Rabochii klass—rukovoditel' natsional'no-osvoboditel'nogo dvizheniia v Latinskoi Amerike [Workers lead the national liberation movement in Latin America] Vop. ist., v. 38, no. 7, July 1963: 195.
  A review of an article by José Branderburgo in *Nueva era*, Buenos Aires, no. 6, 1962: 53–60.

1386. Grigor'ian, IU. M. Nauchnaia konferentsiia po istorii rabochego i natsional'no-osvoboditel'nogo dvizheniia v Latinskoi Amerike [A conference on the history of the labor and national liberation movement in Latin America] Vop. ist., v. 38, no. 3, Mar. 1963: 166–167.

1387. Iscaro, Rubens. Latinskaia Amerika na puti k profsoiuznomu edinstvu [Latin America forges ahead in the unification of trade unions] Vsem. prof. dvizh., no. 2, Feb. 1961: 11–13.

1388. Kondrat'eva, A. Bastuiushchii kontinent [A wave of strikes on a continent] Mezhdunar. zhizn', v. 8, no. 3, Mar. 1961: 132–133.

1389. Larin, U. Klassovye boi v Latinskoi Amerike [Class struggles in Latin America] Mir. ekon. i mezhdunar. otn., no. 12, Dec. 1963: 76–84.

1390. Levin, V. Bastuiushchii kontinent [A wave of strikes on a continent] Blok. agit. [Bel.] no. 4, Feb. 1960: 41–48.

1391. ———. Bastuiushchii kontinent [A wave of strikes on a continent] Blok. agit. [Len.] no. 5, Feb. 1960: 44–ff.

1392. Listov, V. Novoe v profsoiuznom dvizhenii Latinskoi Ameriki [New developments in the Latin American trade-union movement] Nov. vrem., v. 20, no. 28, July 1962: 20–23.

1393. Lombardo Toledano, Vicente. Edinstvo i bor'ba v Latinskoi Amerike [Unity and struggle in Latin America] Vsem. prof. dvizh., no. 5, May, 1961: 12–15.

1394. Makukhin, E. Edinstvo vykovyvaetsia v bor'be [Unity is forged in the struggle] Sov. profsoiuzy, v. 20, no. 13, July 1964: 39–40.

1395. Marillier, Jean. Metallisty Latinskoi Ameriki gotoviat svoiu pervuiu konferentsiiu [Latin American metalworkers prepare their first conference] Vsem. prof. dvizh., no. 6, June 1960: 20–21.

1396. Peña, Lázaro. Latinskaia Amerika idet vpered [Latin America on the march] Vsem. prof. dvizh., no. 5, May 1959: 17–20.

1397. ———. Latinskaia Amerika na puti k edinstvu [Latin America on the path to unity] Vsem. prof. dvizh., no. 4, Apr. 1964: 3–5.

1398. Pod znamenem mira i edinstva [Under the banner of peace and unity] Sov. profsoiuzy, v. 17, no. 21, Nov. 1961: 32.

1399. Programma bor'by postoiannogo Kongressa profsoiuznogo edinstva dlia sovmestnykh deistvii trudiashchikhsia Latinskoi Ameriki [The program of struggle of the Permanent Congress for Trade-Union Unity and Common Action of Latin American Workers] Vsem. prof. dvizh., no. 4, Apr. 1964: 5–7.

1400. Rancaño, José María. Repressii protiv latinoamerikanskikh profsoiuzov [Repressions against Latin American trade unions] Vsem. prof. dvizh., no. 3, Mar. 1964: 20–29.

1401. Rodrigo, José. Bor'ba trudiashchikhsia Latinskoi Ameriki [The struggle of Latin American workers] Vsem. prof. dvizh., no. 6, June 1962: 4–10.

1402. ———. Krepnet edinstvo profsoiuzov Latinskoi Ameriki [The unity of Latin American trade unions is growing stronger] Vsem. prof. dvizh., no. 11, Nov. 1962: 7–11.

1403. ———. Mir, edinstvo, natsional'naia nezavisimost'! [Peace, unity, and national independence!] Sov. profsoiuzy, v. 17, no. 19, Oct. 1961: 39–40.

1404. ———. "Sindikalizm" amerikanskikh monopolii v deistvii [The "syndicalism" of American monopolies in action] Vsem. prof. dvizh., no. 11, Nov. 1964: 17–20.

1405. ———. Znachenie V Vsemirnogo kongressa profsoiuzov dlia trudiashchikhsia Latinskoi Ameriki [The significance of the Fifth International Congress of Trade Unions for Latin American workers] Vsem. prof. dvizh., no. 10, Oct. 1961: 26–28.

1406. Samsonova, N. Massovye zabastovki na plantatsiiakh "IUnaited frut kompani" [Mass strikes on the plantations of the "United Fruit Company"] Mir. ekon. i mezhdunar. otn., no. 4, Apr. 1960: 116–118.

1407. Soto Vergara, Domiciano. Po puti edinstva [On the way to unity] Sov. profsoiuzy, v. 7, no. 11, June 1959: 58–60.

1408. Trudiashchiesia Latinskoi Ameriki v bor'be [The workers of Latin America struggle] Vsem. prof. dvizh., no. 2, Feb. 1961: 14–15.

1409. Trudiashchiesia plantatsii proveli pervuiu konferentsiiu [Plantation workers have conducted their first conference] Vsem. prof. dvizh., no. 6, June 1961: 15–17.

1410. Zabastovki v Latinskoi Amerike [Strikes in Latin America] Nov. vrem., v. 18, no. 49, Dec. 1960: 10–11.

1411. Zabastovki zakhlestyvaiut latinoameri-kanskii kontinent [An outburst of strikes on the Latin American continent] Za rubezhom, no. 3, July 1960: 21.

See also entries no. 523, 1149, and 2345.

2. Individual Countries

a. Argentina

1412. Iscaro, Rubens. Vozniknovenie i raz-vitie profsoiuznogo dvizheniia v Argen-tine [The rise and development of the trade-union movement in Argentina] Moscow, Izd-vo inostr. lit., 1962. 306 p. Translated by S. A. Gonionskii from the Spanish Origen y desarrollo del movimiento sindical argentino.

1413. Alvarez, Rodolfo. Dva mira v San-Isidro [Two worlds in San Isidro] Sov. zhen., v. 17, no. 8, 1961: 26–27.

1414. Arnedo Alvarez, Gerónimo. Bor'ba rabochego klassa Argentiny za svoi zhiznennye prava i interesy [Argentine workers struggle for their vital rights and interests] Mir. ekon. i mezhdunar. otn., no. 4, Apr. 1959: 37–40.

1415. Iscaro, Rubens. Argentina; nedelia bor'by protiv reaktsii [Argentina; a week of protest against reaction] Vsem. prof. dvizh., no. 10, Oct. 1963: 4–8.

1416. ———. Bor'ba za edinstvo rabochego dvizheniia Argentiny [The struggle for the unity of the labor movement in Argentina] Vsem. prof. dvizh., no. 9, Sept. 1961: 29–32.

1417. ———. Itogi bor'by argentinskikh profsoiuzov [Some results of the struggle of Argentine trade unions] Vsem. prof. dvizh., no. 3, Mar. 1959: 35–38.

1418. ———. My v lagere bortsov [We are in the fighters' camp] Sov. profsoiuzy, v. 17, no. 17, Sept. 1961: 34–38.

1419. ———. Opyt profsoiuznoi deiatel'-nosti v 1962 godu [Trade-union activities in 1962] Vsem. prof. dvizh., no. 1, Jan. 1963: 10–14.

1420. ———. Protiv Mezhdunarodnogo valiutnogo fonda, za edinstvo deistvii profsoiuzov [Against the International Monetary Fund, and for the united action of trade unions] Vsem. prof. dvizh., no 11, Nov. 1959: 30–33.

1421. ———. S"ezd Vseobschchei konfede-ratsii truda [The Congress of the General Confederation of Labor] Vsem. prof. dvizh., no. 5, May 1963: 16–18.

1422. ———. Uroki bor'by argentinskikh trudiashchikhsia [Lessons of the Argen-tine workers' struggle] Vsem. prof. dvizh., no. 1, Jan. 1964: 35–39.

1423. ———. Vperedi novye bitvy [There are new battles ahead] Sov. profsoiuzy, v. 20, no. 9, May 1964: 38–40.

1424. ———. Znachenie V Vsemirnogo kon-gressa profsoiuzov dlia trudiashchikhsia Argentiny [The significance of the Fifth International Congress of Trade Unions for Argentine workers] Vsem. prof. dvizh., no. 8, Aug. 1961: 12–13.

1425. Levin, V. Nastuplenie argentinskikh rabochikh [The offensive by Argentine workers] Nov. vrem., v. 22, no. 38, Sept. 1964: 14–15.

1426. Listov, V. "Krainie mery" protiv argentinskikh zheleznodorozhnikov ["Ex-treme measures" against Argentine rail-road workers] Nov. vrem., v. 19, no. 48, Nov. 1961: 19–20.

1427. M. K. Po lozhnomu sledu [Along a false path] Nov. vrem., v. 17, no. 34. Aug. 1959: 16.

1428. Marisci, Vicente. Bor'ba rabochego klassa i naroda Argentiny [The struggle of the working class and people of Argen-tina] Vsem. prof. dvizh., no. 6, June 1962: 10–14.

1429. ———. Opyt argentinskogo rabochego klassa v bor'be za edinstvo [Experiences of the Argentine working class in the fight for unity] Vsem. prof. dvizh., no. 2, Feb. 1960: 8–12.

1430. Vasil'ev, M. Pochemu bastuiut argen-tintsy [Why the Argentines are striking] Nov. vrem., v. 17, no. 42, Oct. 1959: 19–20.

1431. Vincelli, Ricardo E. Gimn edinstvu [A hymn to unity] Sov. profsoiuzy, v. 17, no. 23, Dec. 1961: 17–18.

b. Bolivia

1432. Nemira, I. Zabastovka pod oblakami [A strike beneath the clouds] Za rubezhom, no. 35, Aug. 1963: 23.

1433. Pakin, S. Gorniaki prodolzhaiut bor'bu [Miners continue the struggle] Mezhdunar. zhizn', v. 11, no. 2, Feb. 1964: 110–111.

1434. Rodrigo, José. Boevoi dukh trudiashchikhsia [The fighting spirit of the workers] Vsem. prof. dvizh., no. 8/9, Aug.-Sept. 1962: 23–25.

1435. Vel'min, V. Pozhar v Andakh [Fire in the Andes] Sov. shakht., v. 13, no. 3, Mar. 1964: 45–46.

c. Brazil

1436. Rozhkov, A. F. Polozhenie i bor'ba rabochego klassa Brazilii v poslevoennyi period, 1946–1959 gg. [The post-war situation and struggle of Brazilian workers, 1946–1959] Moscow, 1961. 18 p.
Abstract of a dissertation for the degree of Candidate in Economics.

1437. Carvalho, Agostino de. Perspektivy brazil'skogo profsoiuznogo dvizheniia [Prospects for the Brazilian trade union movement] Vsem. prof. dvizh., no. 6, June 1961: 18–20.

1438. Cerqueira, Benedito. Pobeda unitarnoi i progressivnoi politiki [A victory for the policy of unity and progress] Vsem. prof. dvizh., no. 3, Mar. 1962: 32–33.

1439. Gusinskii, N. V gostiakh u brazil'skikh profsoiuzov [Visiting Brazilian trade unions] Sov. profsoiuzy, v. 19, no. 22, Nov. 1963: 42–43.

1440. Koval', B. I. Rabochee dvizhenie v Brazilii v kontse XIX-nachale XX veka [The Brazilian labor movement in the late 19th and early 20th century] Vop. ist., no. 11, Nov. 1960: 82–97.

1441. Lago, Mario. Bor'ba i uspekhi rabotnikov radioveshchaniia i televideniia [The struggle and achievements of radio and television workers] Vsem. prof. dvizh., no. 1, Jan. 1963: 15–17.

1442. Martinelli, Rafael. Edinstvo vykovyvaetsia v bor'be [Unity is forged in the struggle] Vsem. prof. dvizh., no. 8/9, Aug.-Sept. 1962: 26–29.

1443. Pacheco da Silva, Osvaldo. Mnogoobeshchaiushchaia plodotvornaia vstrecha trudiashchikhsia [A workers' conference with great promise] Vsem. prof. dvizh., no. 12, Dec. 1962: 11–16.

1444. Padilla, Luis. Pervaia profsoiuznaia konferentsiia trudiashchikhsia zhenshchin Brazilii [The First Trade Union Conference of Brazilian Women Workers] Vsem. prof. dvizh., no. 7/8, July-Aug. 1963: 12–13.

1445. Pereira, Antonio. O profsoiuzakh Brazilii [Trade unions in Brazil] Nov. vrem., v. 19, no. 23, June 1961: 12–13.

1446. Sily edinstva [The forces of unity] Vsem. prof. dvizh., no. 6, June 1960: 1–2.

1447. Stafford de Silva, Ormildo. Osnovnye zadachi profsoiuznogo dvizheniia Brazilii [The main tasks of the Brazilian trade union movement] Vsem. prof. dvizh., no. 2, Feb. 1964: 25–26.

1448. Ziller, Armando. Profsoiuznoe dvizhenie idet po puti edinstva [The Brazilian trade union movement marches toward unity] Vsem. prof. dvizh., no. 4, Apr. 1960: 36–39.

1449. ———. Znachenie V Vsemirnogo kongressa profsoiuzov dlia trudiashchikhsia Brazilii [The significance of the Fifth International Congress of Trade Unions for Brazilian workers] Vsem. prof. dvizh., no. 8, Aug. 1961: 13–14.

d. Chile

1450. Campos, Juan. Interv'iu vitse-predsedatelia Edinogo proftsentra chiliiskikh trudiashchikhsia [Interview with Juan Campos, vice president of the Unified Center of Chilean workers] Vsem. prof. dvizh., no. 5, May 1961: 15–16.

1451. Cerda, César. O profsoiuzakh Chili [The trade unions of Chile] Nov. vrem., v. 20, no. 17, Apr. 1962: 15–16.

1452. Figueroa Mazuela, Luis. "Edinstvo! Bor'ba!"—zaiavili chiliiskie profsoiuzy

[Chilean trade unions have called for unity and struggle] Vsem. prof. dvizh., no. 11, Nov. 1962: 3–7.

1453. Lara, R.   Tret'ia natsional'naia konferentsiia Edinogo proftsentra chiliiskikh trudiashchikhsia [The Third National Conference of the United Trade-Union Center of Chilean Workers] Vsem. prof. dvizh., no. 6, June 1959: 19–22.

1454. Lara, Roberto.   Znachenie V Vsemirnogo kongressa profsoiuzov dlia trudiashchikhsia Chili [The significance of the Fifth International Congress of Trade Unions for Chilean workers] Vsem. prof. dvizh., no. 11/12, Nov.-Dec. 1961: 17–18.

1455. Nikitin, M.   Cherez edinstvo—k pobede [To victory through unity] Sov. profsoiuzy, v. 19, no. 20, Oct. 1963: 36–37.

1456. Pradenas, Miguel.   Chili [Chile] Vsem. prof. dvizh., no. 8/9, Aug.-Sept. 1960: 8–9.

1457. Ramírez Necochea, Hernán.   Pod"em rabochego dvizheniia v Chili v 1917–1922 godakh [Intensification of the labor movement in Chile in 1917–1922] Nov. i noveish. ist., no. 5, 1960: 38–51.

1458. Rasstrel v Khose-Maria-Karo [A massacre in José María Caro] Za rubezhom, no. 48, Dec. 1962: 3.
Suppression of a strike.

1459. Rodrigo, José.   Ssylka Klotario Blesta [Clotario Blest's deportation] Vsem. prof. dvizh., no. 4, Apr. 1961: 26.

1460. Soto Vergara, Domiciano.   "Nam neobkhodimo edinstvo" ["Unity is indispensable for us"] Nov. vrem., v. 17, no. 20, May 1959: 15–16.

1461. Uspekh rabochikh mednykh rudnikov "El' Ten'ente" [Success of the workers of "El Teniente" copper mines in Chile] Vsem. prof. dvizh., no. 12, Dec. 1959: 47.

1462. Vargas Puebla, Juan.   Massovye vystupleniia gosudarstvennykh sluzhashchikh [Mass actions of government employees] Vsem. prof. dvizh., no. 7/8, July-Aug. 1964: 28–31.

e. Colombia

1463. XI [Odinnadtsatyi] s"ezd Konfederatsii trudiashchikhsia Kolumbii [The 11th Congress of the Confederation of Colombian Workers] Vsem. prof. dvizh., no. 3, Mar. 1959: 51–52.

1464. Puentes Vanegas, Ventura.   Kolumbiia [Colombia] Vsem. prof. dvizh., no. 8/9, Aug.-Sept. 1960: 7–8.

1465. ———.   Na puti k edinstvu profsoiuznogo dvizheniia [On the path toward the unity of the trade union movement] Vsem. prof. dvizh., no. 7/8, July-Aug. 1963: 5–7.

1466. Velásquez Toro, Jaime.   Kolumbiiskii proletariat boretsia [The Colombian proletariat struggles] Sov. profsoiuzy, v. 20, no. 18, Sept. 1964: 38.

1467. Zhestokaia i besposhchadnaia ekspluatatsiia [The cruel and ruthless exploitation of workers] Vsem. prof. dvizh., no. 6, June 1959: 56.

f. Costa Rica

1468. Bananovye koroli [The banana kings] Nov. vrem., v. 18, no. 4, Jan. 1960: 24.

1469. Ferreto, Arnoldo.   Uroki odnoi zabastovki; pis'mo iz San-Khose [The lessons of a strike; a letter from San José] Probl. mira i sots., v. 3, no. 8, Aug. 1960: 93–94.

1470. Sierra Cantillo, Gonzalo.   Vazhnaia pobeda [An important achievement] Vsem. prof. dvizh., no. 5, May 1960: 30–33.

g. Cuba

1471. Profsoiuzy Kuby; sbornik statei, vystuplenii i materialov [Cuban trade unions; collected articles, addresses, and materials] Moscow, Profizdat, 1963. 166 p.   HD8206.5.P7
Translated by V. Vinogradov and A. Shcherba from the Spanish. Introductory article by V. Vinogradov.

1472. Aguilera, José María de la.   Kuba [Cuba] Vsem. prof. dvizh., no. 8/9, Aug.-Sept. 1960: 15–16.

1473. Alvarez de la Campa, Odon. Triumf natsional'nogo edinstva i mezhdunarodnoi solidarnosti [The triumph of national unity and international solidarity] Vsem. prof. dvizh., no. 4, Apr. 1961: 7–9.

1474. Bras, Marcel. Vpechatleniia o Kube [My impressions of Cuba] Vsem. prof. dvizh., no. 5, May, 1961: 7–11.
The role of trade unions.

1475. Kalinin, A. I. Rabochii klass i kubinskaia revoliutsiia [The working class and the Cuban Revolution] In Akademiia nauk SSSR. Institut mirovoi ekonomiki i mezhdunarodnykh otnoshenii. Rabochee dvizhenie v kapitalisticheskikh stranakh, 1959–1961 gg. Moscow, Gospolitizdat, 1961: p. 203–226.   HD4854.A43

1476. Listov, V. Profsoiuzy v Kubinskoi revoliutsii [Trade unions in the Cuban Revolution] Nov. vrem., v. 19, no. 9, Feb. 1961: 19–21.

1477. ———. Rabochee serdtse Gavany [The heart of working-class Havana] Nov. vrem., v. 21, no. 18, May 1954: 22–24.

1478. Nikirov, B. S. Iz istorii rabochego dvizheniia na Kube, 1944–1948 [History of the Cuban labor movement, 1944–1948] Vop. ist., no. 9, Sept. 1961: 103–115.
Summary in English, p. 222.

1479. ORIT protiv Kuby [The Inter-American Regional Organization of Workers is against Cuba] Vsem. prof. dvizh., no. 5, May 1961: 11.

1480. Peña, Lázaro. 10-i s"ezd Konfederatsii trudiashchikhsia Kuby [The Tenth Congress of the Confederation of Cuban Workers] Vsem. prof. dvizh., no. 3, Mar. 1960: 26–28.

1481. Petrova, Z. Profsoiuznoe dvizhenie na Kube [The trade union movement in Cuba] Mir. ekon. i mezhdunar. otn., no. 3, Mar. 1962: 110–111.

1482. Poslanie trudiashchimsia i profsoiuzam Kuby [A message to the workers and trade unions of Cuba] Vsem. prof. dvizh., no. 5, May 1959: 44.

1483. Zhizn' i "deianiia" odnogo "svobodnogo" profsoiuznogo rukovoditelia [The life and "work" of a leader of "free" trade unions] Vsem. prof. dvizh., no. 4, Apr. 1959: 48–49.

See also entry no. 4834.

h. Ecuador

1484. K. M. Repressii protiv trudiashchikhsia Ekvadora [Repressive action against Ecuadorian workers] Vsem. prof. dvizh., no. 12, Dec. 1963: 23–24.

1485. Ramos, Segundo. Polozhenie v Ekvadore [Conditions in Ecuador] Vsem. prof. dvizh., no. 11, Nov. 1959: 37–39.

1486. Zashchitim zhertvy repressii v Ekvadore [Let us defend the victims of persecutions in Ecuador] Vsem. prof. dvizh., no. 11, Nov. 1963: 51–52.

1487. Zúñiga, Víctor Manuel. Zashchita prava na trud i profsoiuznykh svobod v Ekvadore [How the right to work and the freedom of trade union activities are defended in Ecuador] Vsem. prof. dvizh., no. 7/8, July-Aug. 1959: 40–42.

i. Guatemala

1488. Gutiérrez, Víctor Manuel. Profsoiuznoe dvizhenie Gvatemaly segodnia [The present-day trade union movement in Guatemala] Vsem. prof. dvizh., no. 10, Oct. 1959: 38–40.

j. The Guianas

1489. Camp, George. "Zabastovka v Dzhordzhtaune"—lozh'kapitalisticheskoi pechati ["The strike in Georgetown" is a lie of the capitalist press] Vsem. prof. dvizh., no. 10, Oct. 1963: 10–16.

1490. Chetyre mesiatsa zabastovki [A four-month strike] Za rubezhom, no. 21, May 1964: 3.
British Guiana.

1491. Comrade. Zabastovka v dzhungliakh [Strike in the jungles] Vokrug sveta, no. 7, July 1961: 46–47.
A strike in a logging camp in British Guiana.

1492. Evans, Harry. Profsoiuzy Britanskoi Gviany na rasput'e [British Guiana trade unions at the crossroads] Vsem. prof. dvizh., no. 3, Mar. 1962: 17–20.

1493. Pochemu besliudno na plantatsiiakh [Why there are no workers on plantations] Nov. vrem., v. 21, no. 9, Feb. 1964: 25.
British Guiana.

1494. Sprovotsirovannyi konflikt [A provoked conflict] Za rubezhom, no. 22, June 1963: 4.
British Guiana.

k. Haiti

1495. Hilarion, Manuel. Sozdanie profsoiuznogo fronta [The establishment of a trade union front] Vsem. prof. dvizh., no. 7/8, July-Aug. 1964: 32-34.

l. Mexico

1496. Cruikshank García, Jorge, and Vicente Padilla. Znachenie V Vsemirnogo kongressa profsoiuzov dlia trudiashchikhsia Meksiki [The significance of the Fifth International Congress of Trade Unions for Mexican workers] Vsem. prof. dvizh., no. 11/12, Nov.-Dec. 1961: 21.

1497. García Moreno, Antonio. K edinstvu rabochikh i patrioticheskikh sil Meksiki [Toward the unity of workers and patriotic forces in Mexico] Vsem. prof. dvizh., no. 3, Mar. 1960: 29-31.

1498. Kalinin, A. Sdvigi v rabochem dvizhenii Meksiki [New trends in the Mexican labor movement] Mir. ekon. i mezhdunar. otn., no. 9, Sept. 1959: 135-137.

m. Panama

1499. Dixon, Félix. Problemy trudiashchikhsia Panamy [Problems facing the workers of Panama] Nov. vrem., v. 18, no. 29, July 1960: 16-17.

1500. Matamoros, Marta. Znachenie V Vsemirnogo kongressa profsoiuzov dlia trudiashchikhsia Panamy [The significance of the Fifth International Congress of Trade Unions for Panamanian workers] Vsem. prof. dvizh., no. 11/12, Nov.-Dec. 1961: 20-21.

1501. Zhitkov, V. "Bananovaia imperiia" vstrevozhena [The "banana empire" is restless] Za rubezhom, no. 7, Feb. 1961: 26.

A strike on U.S.-owned banana plantations.

n. Paraguay

1502. Peña, Lázaro. Moshchnaia bor'ba proletariata Paragvaia [The vigorous struggle of the Paraguayan proletariat] Vsem. prof. dvizh., no. 2, Feb. 1959: 15-18.

o. Peru

1503. Guevara, Rolando. Peru [Peru] Vsem. prof. dvizh., no. 8/9, Aug-Sept. 1960: 10-11.

p. Uruguay

1504. Pintos, Francisco R. Profsoiuznoe dvizhenie v Urugvae [The trade-union movement in Uruguay] Moscow, Profizdat, 1964. 391 p.
Translated from the Spanish Historia del movimiento obrero del Uruguay. Introductory article by S. A. Gonionskii.
Reviewed by S. Gonionskii in Nov. vrem., v. 21, no. 15, Apr. 1964: 30-31.

1505. Betancourt, Héctor. Avtotransportniki Urugvaia privetstvuiut sovetskikh tovarishchei [Uruguayan highway transport workers greet their Soviet comrades] Avt. transp., v. 38, no. 1, Jan. 1960: 6-7.

1506. Freire Pizzano, Ramón. Znachenie V Vsemirnogo kongressa profsoiuzov dlia trudiashchikhsia Urugvaia [The significance of the Fifth International Congress of Trade Unions for Uruguayan workers] Vsem. prof. dvizh., no. 11/12, Nov.-Dec. 1961: 19.

1507. Grassi, Luigi. Novyi edinyi proftsentr Urugvaia [A new united trade-union center in Uruguay] Vsem. prof. dvizh., no. 7, July 1961: 20-23.

1508. Padilla, Luis. Profsoiuznoe dvizhenie Urugvaia na pod"eme [The trade union movement in Uruguay is on the upsurge] Vsem. prof. dvizh., no. 10, Oct. 1963: 9.

1509. Pastorino, Enrique. Bor'ba za mir i sotsial'nyi progress v Urugvae [The struggle for peace and social progress in Uruguay] Vsem. prof. dvizh., no. 6, June 1959: 16-19.

1510. ———. Rozhdenie edinogo proftsentra [A united trade-union center is born] Vsem. prof. dvizh., no. 4, Apr. 1960: 33–35.

1511. Pintos, Francisco R. Vliianie leninizma na rabochee dvizhenie Urugvaia [The influence of Leninism on the labor movement in Uruguay] Nov. i noveish. ist., no. 2, 1960: 79–93.

q. Venezuela

1512. Carrera, Jerónimo. Edinyi proftsentr trudiashchikhsia Venesuely sluzhit interesam trudiashchikhsia [The United Trade-Union Center of Venezuelan Workers serves the interests of the workers] Vsem. prof. dvizh., no. 6, June 1964: 16–19.

1513. Miranda, Luis. Profsoiuznoe dvizhenie Venesuely [The trade-union movement in Venezuela] Vsem. prof. dvizh., no. 6, June 1962: 15–16.

1514. Prekratit' repressii protiv profsoiuzov v Venesuele [Stop repressions against trade unions in Venezuela] Vsem. prof. dvizh., no. 11, Nov. 1963: 52.

1515. Quintero, Rodolfo. Profsoiuzy Venesuely [Venezuelan trade unions] Nov. vrem., v. 22, no. 50, Dec. 1964: 24–26.

1516. Torrealba, Laureano. Pered III Natsional'nym kongressom trudiashchikhsia Venesuely [Preparing for the Third National Congress of Venezuelan Workers] Vsem. prof. dvizh., no. 11, Nov. 1959: 34–36.

1517. Torres, Eloy. Sila ob"edinennogo dvizheniia [The strength of a unified movement] Probl. mira i sots., v. 3, no. 6, June 1960: 74–77.

1518. ———. Venesuela [Venezuela] Vsem. prof. dvizh., no. 8/9, Aug.-Sept. 1960: 13–15.

1519. Venesuela—da, ianki—net! [Venezuela, yes; Yankees, no!] Mol. mira, no. 7, 1961: 6.

D. POLITICAL ACTIVITY OF WOMEN

1. Writings Dealing With Three or More Countries

1520. Bettinelli, Adela. Zhenshchiny stran Latinskoi Ameriki gotoviat svoi kongress [Women of Latin America are preparing for their congress] Zhen. mira, no. 10, 1959: 10–11.

1521. Cotton, Eugénie. "My khotim idti v nogu s vremenem!" ["We want to be in step with the times!"] Zhen. mira, no. 3, 1960: 8–10.

1522. Fuentes, María. V zashchitu zhizni, truda i kul'tury [In defense of life, work, and culture] Probl. mira i sots., v. 3, no. 3, Mar. 1960: 60–61.
A congress of Latin American women in Chile.

1523. Konferentsiia v Sant-IAgo [A conference in Santiago] Rabotnitsa, v. 38, no. 1, Jan. 1960: 10.

1524. Ponce, Margarita de. Zhenshchin ob"ediniaiut obshchie radosti, obshchie nadezhdy [Common joys and common hopes unite women] Zhen. mira, no. 6, 1962: 4–9.

2. Individual Countries

a. Argentina

1525. Bettinelli, Adela. Desiat' let deiatel'nosti Soiuza zhenshchin Argentiny [Ten years' activity of the Union of Argentine Women] Zhen. mira, no. 8, 1959: 27–29.

1526. Calvo, Susana. Mir i bor'ba [Peace and struggle] Sov. zhen., v. 20, no. 7, 1964: 22.
Women's peace movement.

1527. Domínguez, Susana. Zhenshchiny—aktivnaia sila [Women are a leading force] Probl. mira i sots., v. 7, no. 5, May 1964: 55–56.

1528. Edelman, Fanny. Iz opyta zhenskogo dvizheniia v Argentine [From the experience of the movement of Argentine women] Probl. mira i sots., v. 5, no. 3, Mar. 1962: 44–46.

1529. Marini, Salvador. Babushka Al'sira i ee druz'ia [Grandmother Alcira and her friends] Rabotnitsa, v. 39, no. 4, Apr. 1961: 23.
Women in public life.

1530. Pantaleón, Rosa. Rol' zhenshchiny v sovremennom obshchestve; Argentina

[The role of women in present-day society; Argentina] Probl. mira i sots., v. 5, no. 10, Oct. 1962: 60–61.

1531. Ponce, Margarita de. Ona dostoina narodnoi liubvi [She is worthy of the love of her people] Zhen. mira, no. 5, 1959: 18–21.
Women in public life.

1532. Vozniknovenie i razvitie zhenskogo dvizheniia; Argentina [The rise and development of the women's movement in Argentina] Zhen. mira, no. 4, 1959: 30–31; no. 5, 1959: 29; no. 6, 1959: 30–31; no. 7, 1959: 30–31.

See also entry no. 3166

b. Brazil

1533. Werner, Ruth. Ol'ga Benario; istoriia otvazhnoi zhizni [Olga Benario; story of a brave life] Moscow, Mol. gvardiia, 1964. 384 p.
Translated by V. Slavutskaia from the German Olga Benario; die Geschichte eines tapferen Lebens. Introductory article by E. Guseva and V. TSapanova.
Reviewed by Inna Avramenko in V mire knig, v. 4, no. 11, 1964: 3.

1534. Pereira, Edy Gomes Duarte. Zhizn' dostoinaia i prekrasnaia [A noble and beautiful life] Zhen. mira, no. 4, 1961: 18–19.
Women in public life.

1535. Polevoi, Boris. Mamita [Mamita] Zhen. mira, no. 1, 1960: 48–49.
Indian women in public life.

1536. Soares Ribeiro, Elsa. Braziliia i mirnoe sosushchestvovanie [Brazil and peaceful coexistence] Sov. zhen., v. 19, no. 9, 1963: 35.
Women's peace movement.

1537. ———. Za chto boriutsia zhenshchiny Brazilii [What Brazilian women are fighting for] Sov. profsoiuzy, v. 20, no. 2, Jan. 1964: 40–41.

1538. Tabak, Fanny. Rol' zhenshchiny v sovremennom obshchestve [The role of women in present-day society] Sov. zhen., v. 19, no. 5, 1963: 13.

1539. Werner, Ruth. Ol'ga Benario [Olga Benario] Rabotnitsa, v. 40, no. 3, Mar. 1962: 14–15.
Translated from the German.

c. Chile

1540. Aguirre, Margarita. IA ne oshiblas' [I wasn't wrong] Sov. zhen., v. 16, no. 11, 1960: 32–33.
Women and the peace movement.

1541. Alvarez, Chela. V parlamente Chili tol'ko tri zhenshchiny-deputata [There are only three women members in the Chilean Parliament] Zhen. mira, no. 2, 1959: 23.

1542. Campusano, Julieta. Rol' zhenshchiny v sovremennom obshchestve; Chili [The role of women in present-day society; Chile] Probl. mira i sots., v. 5, no. 8, Aug. 1962: 76–77.

1543. Coen, Leonardo. Bol'shaia dusha [A noble soul] Za rubezhom, no. 24, June 1962: 6.

1544. Duarte, María Cristina. Chto by ty sdelala, esli by imela vlast'? [What would you do if you were in power?] Sov. zhen., v. 19, no. 7, 1963: 8–9.

1545. Kotov, Mikhail. Professor iz Sant-IAgo [A professor from Santiago] Rabotnitsa, v. 40, no. 6, June 1962: 9.
A female scholar.

1546. Romeo de Jacobi, Tommy. Mir podgotovlen k vzaimoponimaniiu [The world is ripe for mutual understanding] Sov. zhen., v. 15, no. 4, 1959: 19.
Women and the peace movement.

1547. Vicentini, María Luisa. Chiliiskaia zhenshchina, mat' i zhena, boretsia vmeste s gorniakami za ikh prava [A Chilean woman, mother and wife, fights together with miners for their rights] Zhen. mira, no. 6, 1959: 27–28.

1548. ———. Ol'ga Poblete, laureat mezhdunarodnoi leninskoi premii mira [Olga Poblete, the International Lenin Peace Prize winner] Zhen. mira, no. 10, 1962: 15–17.

d. Costa Rica

1549. Vásquez, Gabriela. Odnazhdy na rassvete [Once at the break of dawn] Sov. zhen., v. 16, no. 5, 1960: 37.
Women in the labor movement.

e. Cuba

1550. Aguilar, Onelia. Vil'ma Espin; ot S'erra-Maestry k Federatsii kubinskikh zhenshchin [Vilma Espín; from the Sierra Maestra to the Federation of Cuban Women] Zhen. mira, no. 1, 1963: 6–8.

1551. Ana Betankur [Ana Betancourt] Zhen. mira, no. 1, 1960: 39.

1552. Arcocha, Juan. Kto boretsia za svobodu, tot nikogda ne umiraet [Those who fight for freedom will never die] Sov. zhen., v. 19, no. 3, 1963: 15–16.
Revolutionary activity of Cuban women.

1553. Berezhnaia, N. Doch' ostrova svobody [A daughter of the island of freedom] Rabotnitsa, no. 1, Jan. 1963: 8.
Angela Alonso.

1554. ———. Zhenshchiny Kuby [The women of Cuba] Nov. vrem., v. 21, no. 23, June 1963: 6–7.

1555. Berezhnaia, Nataliia. Velikie zhenshchiny malen'koi strany; interv'iu s Violetoi Kasal' i Sesiliei Garsiia [Great women of a small country; interview with Violeta Casal and Cecilia García] Zhen. mira, no. 4, 1960: 15–17.
Women in politics.

1556. Bolaños Cadena, Laura. Prostaia kubinskaia zhenshchina [An ordinary Cuban woman] Zhen. mira, no. 1, 1964: 6–7.

1557. Cabrera, Luis Rolando. Lila, eto prikaz! [Lila, that's an order!] Zhen. mira, no. 2, 1961: 20–21, 25.

1558. Casal, Violeta. Esli ty potrebuesh', Kuba, my umrem za tebia [If you ask us, we shall die for you, Cuba!] Sov. zhen., no. 12, Dec. 1959: 21.

1559. Cedeño, Libia. Itogi goda deiatel'nosti Federatsii kubinskikh zhenshchin [One year's activities of the Federation of Cuban Women] Zhen. mira, no. 5, 1962: 15, 29.

1560. Díaz, Rita. Pritiagatel'naia sila [A magnetic force] Rabotnitsa, v. 39, no. 11, Nov. 1961: 7.
Cuban women at the 22nd Congress of the CPSU.

1561. Espín de Castro, Vilma. Ne otdadim svoego schast'ia [We shan't give up our happiness] Rabotnitsa, v. 40, no. 10, Oct. 1962: 25.

1562. Gutiérrez, Elsa. God agrarnoi reformy i god obrazovaniia [The year of agrarian reform and the year of education] Sov. zhen., v. 17, no. 2, 1961: 32–33.

1563. Marinello, Juan. Geroicheskie zhenshchiny Kuby [The heroic women of Cuba] Sov. zhen., v. 15, no. 8, Aug. 1959: 43.

1564. Móntez, Rosa. Na beregu sverkaiushchei bukhty [On the shores of a shining bay] Sov. zhen., no. 12, Dec. 1959: 21.

1565. Mujica, Héctor. Kto nazval zhenshchin "slabym polom"? [Who called them "the weaker sex"?] Vsem. stud. nov., v. 13, no. 6, June 1959: 7–8.

1566. Navitski, H. Kuba zmahaetstsa [Struggle of the Cuban people] Rab. i sial., v. 37, no. 4, Apr. 1961: 11.
Women in public life.

1567. Patriotki [Patriotic women] Sov. zhen., v. 15, no. 2, 1959: 43.

1568. Petrenko, IE., *and* IU. Tymchenko. Zhyvut' na sviti dvi Ankhely [There are two Angelas now] Ukraina, v. 23, no. 29, Oct. 1963: 11.

1569. Polum'iana Oniriia [Impassionate Oniria] Rad. zhin., v. 14, no. 5, May 1959: 3.
Women in guerrilla units.

1570. Smirnov, S. S. Docheri Kuby [Daughters of Cuba] Sov. zhen., v. 17, no. 8, 1961: 13–15.

1571. Stoianov, M. Leitenant Ol'ga Gevara [Lieutenant Olga Guevara] Sov. zhen., v. 19, no. 9, 1963: 22.

1572. Tamarin, V. Milisiano vnov' na postu [The militia-woman is back at her post] Smena, v. 40, no. 14, July 1963: 18–19.

1573. Vicentini, María Luisa. Po zavetam Khose Marti [According to the precepts of José Martí] Zhen. mira, no. 3, 1959: 20–21.

f. Guatemala

1574. López, Carlos. Rol' zhenshchiny v sovremennom obshchestve; Gvatemala [The role of women in present-day society; Guatemala] Probl. mira i sots., v. 5, no. 7, July 1962: 85–86.

1575. Nas privetstvuiut: d-r Khakobo Arbens, byvshii prezident Respubliki Gvatemala [Greetings from Dr. Jacobo Arbenz Guzmán, the former President of the Republic of Guatemala] Zhen. mira, no. 2, 1964: 2.

g. The Guianas

1576. Jagan, Janet. Oni osypali tsvetami kandidatov partii, boriushcheisia za nezavisimost' [They showered with flowers the candidates who struggle for independence] Zhen. mira, no. 1, 1964: 13.
Political activities of women in British Guiana.

1577. Zhenshchiny Gviany [The women of British Guiana] Zhen. mira, no. 1, 1964: 12.

h. Honduras

1578. Adaya, Amador. Rol' zhenshchiny v sovremennom obshchestve; Gonduras. [The role of women in present-day society; Honduras] Probl. mira i sots., v. 5, no. 10, Oct. 1962: 52–53.

i. Mexico

1579. Blasco, María. 22 goda napriazhennoi bor'by za pravo golosa dlia meksikanskikh zhenshchin [Twenty-two years of Mexican women's ceaseless struggle for the right to vote] Zhen. mira, no. 7, 1960: 20–21.

1580. Bolaños Cadena, Laura. Epifaniia Garsiia Sun'iga— imia vpisannoe krov'iu v istoriiu meksikanskoi zhenshchiny [Epifania García Zúñiga, a name written in blood in the annals of Mexican women] Zhen. mira, no. 8, 1962: 8–10.

j. Paraguay

1581. Barrett, Deolinda de. Muzhestvo i slezy Paragvaia [The bravery and tears of Paraguay] Rabotnitsa, no. 8, Aug. 1963: 23–24.
Women in politics.

k. Uruguay

1582. Arévalo, Julia. Khotim zhizni, a ne smerti! [We want life, not death!] Sov. zhen., v. 19, no. 9, 1963: 34.
Political views of certain Uruguayan women.

l. Venezuela

1583. Marcailloux, Yvonne. "Mezhdu nashimi organizatsiiami vsegda sushchestvovalo edinstvo" ["There has always been unity among our organizations"] Zhen. mira, no. 3, 1960: 22, 32.

1584. Travieso, Carmen Clemente. Vechno zhivaia v serdtse venesuel'skogo naroda Liviia Guverner [Livia Gouverneur will always live in the hearts of the Venezuelan people] Zhen. mira, no. 9, 1962: 26–27.

E. POLITICAL ACTIVITY OF YOUTH

1. Writings Dealing With Three or More Countries

1585. Alvarado, César Alonso. Otkrytoe pis'mo Ispolnitel'nomu komitetu NSS Kolumbii [An open letter to the Executive Committee of the National Union of Colombian Students] Vsem. stud. nov., v. 13, no. 7, July 1959: 24.

1586. ———. Vstrecha v Karakase [A meeting in Caracas] Vsem. stud. nov., v. 13, no. 12, Dec. 1959: 24.
A student congress.

1587. Amorim, Enrique. Sud'by mira v ikh rukakh [In their hands is the fate of the world] Inostr. lit., no. 10, Oct. 1960: 265–266.
Translated from the Spanish.

1588. Babak, Saadati. Konferentsiia v Peru [A conference in Peru] Vsem. stud. nov., v. 13, no. 6, June 1959: 18–20; v. 13, no. 7, July 1959: 14–19.

1589. Barrantes Lingan, Alfonso. Simfoniia bratstva [A symphony of brotherhood] Vsem. stud. nov., v. 13, no. 2, Feb. 1959: 14–15.

1590. Bor'ba obostriaetsia [The struggle intensifies] Vsem. stud. nov., v. 16, no. 5/6, May-June 1962: 3.

1591. Galván, Juan Pablo. Poznakomimsia s molodezh'iu Latinskoi Ameriki [Let's meet the youth of Latin America] Mol. mira, no. 1, 1960: 16–17.

1592. Gavana, iiul': Kongress molodezhi stran Latinskoi Ameriki [In Havana, in July: The Congress of Latin American Youth] Mol. mira, no. 2, 1960: 13.

1593. Govoriat rukovoditeli studencheskikh organizatsii Latinskoi Ameriki [The voice of the leaders of Latin American student organizations] Vsem. stud. nov., v. 14, no. 11/12, Nov.-Dec. 1960: 23.

1594. Guevara, Ernesto. "Razorvany tsepi meshavshie druzhbe" ["The chains which hindered our friendship are broken"] Mol. mira, no. 5, 1959: 11.

1595. Lemus, Germán. "Posmotrim, chto proiskhodit v Latinskoi Amerike" ["Let us see what is happening in Latin America"] Vsem. stud. nov., v. 15, no. 5, May 1961: 4–6.

1596. Leyens, Germán. Plan terrora na tselom kontinente [A terrorist plan for a whole continent] Vsem. stud. nov., v. 16, no. 5/6, May-June 1962: 1–2.

1597. Mokhnachev, M. Molodezhnoe dvizhenie v stranakh Latinskoi Ameriki [The youth movement in Latin America] Mol. komm., no. 3, Mar. 1960: 106–113.

1598. Obshchaia rezoliutsiia Ispolnitel'nogo komiteta Vsemirnoi federatsii demokraticheskoi molodezhi; vyderzhki [Excerpts from the general resolution of the Executive Committee of the World Federation of Democratic Youth] Mol. mira, no. 5, 1961: 20–22.
Political activities of Latin American youth.

1599. The second CLAJ. World student news, v. 18, no. 5, 1964: 9–10.
The Second Congress of Latin American Youth.

1600. Seguía, C. V bor'be za edinstvo [In the struggle for unity] Mol. mira, no. 1/2, 1962: 18–19.

1601. Skoro: Kongress molodezhi stran Latinskoi Ameriki [The opening of the Congress of Latin American Youth is near] Mol. mira, no. 5, 1960: 10.

1602. Solé, Anselmo. Latinoamerikanskaia molodezh' i bor'ba za mir, razoruzhenie i natsional'nyi suverenitet [Latin American youth and the struggle for peace, disarmament, and national sovereignty] Mol. mira, no. 5, 1961: 20–22.

1603. Studencheskaia zhizn' [Student life] Vsem. stud. nov., v. 14, no. 11/12, Nov.-Dec. 1960: 29–31.

1604. Urbina Ortiz, Ivan, and Pedro Francisco Alvarez. I . . . III kongress studentov Latinskoi Ameriki sostoialsia! [And . . . the Third Congress of Latin American Students was held] Vsem. stud. nov., v. 14, no. 1, Jan. 1960: 4–7.

1605. Vanuzzi, Nelson. Pis'mo v redaktsiiu [A letter to the editor] Nov. vrem., v. 19, no. 31, July 1961: 20.
Political activities of university students.

1606. Varela, Alfredo. Primer Kuby vdokhnovliaet [The example of Cuba is inspiring] Inostr. lit., no. 10, Oct. 1960: 273–275.

2. Individual Countries

a. Argentina

1607. Correa, Jorge. Nezabyvaemyi den' [An unforgettable day] Vsem. stud. nov., v. 13, no. 1, Jan. 1959: 17–18.
Political activities of university students.

1608. Federatsiia universitetskikh studentov Argentiny protiv KAFADE [The Federation of Argentine University Students is Against CAFADE] Vsem. stud. nov., v. 14, no. 2, Feb. 1960: 20–21.

1609. Godio, Julio. Argentine students and the struggle for peace. World student news, v. 18, no. 5, 1964: 20.

1610. ———. Programme of Argentinian students. World student news, v. 16, no. 11/12, 1962: 18, 36.

1611. Korovinskii, A. Za mir, demokratiiu i natsional'noe osvobozhdenie [For peace, democracy, and national liberation] Mol. komm., no. 4, Apr. 1961: 101–105.
Political activities of Argentine youth.

1612. M. M. Ob"edinennyi front argentinskoi molodezhi [The united front of Argentine youth] Mol. mira, no. 11/12, 1961: 15–16.

1613. Monetti, Ernesto. V edinstve deistvii —zalog uspekha [The guaranty of success lies in unity of action] Mol. mira, no. 11, 1959: 4–5.

1614. Piñera, Arnoldo. S uchetom interesov razlichnykh grupp molodezhi [Taking into account the interests of different groups of our youth] Probl. mira i sots., v. 2, no. 11, Nov. 1959: 68–71.

1615. Ratzer, J. Kommunisty i molodezh'; Argentina [The Communists and youth; Argentina] Probl. mira i sots., v. 4, no. 10, Oct. 1961: 79–81.

1616. Viera, Enrique. Uroki odnogo porazheniia [The lessons of a failure] Mol. mira, no. 1, 1960: 22.

b. Bolivia

1617. Tanaka, IUzo. V gostiakh u dvukh natsional'nykh soiuzov [On a visit to the national unions of two countries] Vsem. stud. nov., v. 13, no. 6, June 1959: 8–10.
Student societies.

See also entry no. 1619.

c. Brazil

1618. Alvarado, César Alonso. "Dvizhenie" i idei [The "Movement" and ideas] Vsem. stud. nov., v. 14, no. 2, Feb. 1960: 8–9.
College periodicals.

1619. Cavalho Silva, Milton de. Petrobraz, dogovor v Robore i edinstvo studentov stran Latinskoi Ameriki ["Petrobras," the Roboré Agreement and the unity of Latin American students] Vsem. stud. nov., v. 13, no. 6, June 1959: 14–15.
Brazilian and Bolivian students support the nationalization of Brazilian oil fields.

1620. Hernández, Andrés. Chto proizoshlo v Natale? [What happened in Natal?]

Vsem. stud. nov., v. 15, no. 12, Dec. 1961: 12–13.
Political activity of university students.

1621. Lima, Pedro Motta. Kommunisty i molodezh'; Braziliia [The Communists and youth; Brazil] Probl. mira i sots., v. 5, no. 2, Feb. 1962: 78–79.

1622. Morias, Geraldo da Rocha. UNEB, what is it? What does it want? World student news, v. 17, no. 6, 1964: 11–12.

1623. Moris, Clodomir. Festival' v Resife [The festival in Recife] Vsem. stud. nov., v. 13, no. 2, Feb. 1959: 1.
A festival of Brazilian students.

1624. Pylaiushchii dom na Rua Flamengo; iz bloknota zhurnalista [A burning house on Rua Flamengo Street; from a journalist's notebook] Vokrug sveta, no. 9, Sept. 1964: 4–6.
Revolutionary activity of Brazilian students.

1625. V. N. UNEB outlawed, bogus union imposed by force. World student news, v. 18, no. 9/10, 1964: 14–15.

1626. Vanuzzi, Nelson. Front-line report. World student news, v. 18, no. 6, 1964: 6–7, 30–31.

See also entry no. 635.

d. Chile

1627. Campusano, Julieta. Kommunisty i molodezh'; Chili [The Communists and youth; Chile] Probl. mira i sots., v. 5, no. 1, Jan. 1962: 70–72.

1628. Cárdenas, Luis. Vospominaniia o Vene [Reminiscences of Vienna] Vsem. stud. nov., v. 16, no. 4, Apr. 1962: 14.
Chilean youth at the Vienna festival.

1629. Escribano, Rubén. Zhizn' molodezhi Chili [The way of life of Chilean youth] Mol. mira, no. 7, 1959: 15.

1630. Gómez, Manuel. Sovmestnaia bor'ba molodezhi Chili [The joint struggle of Chilean youth] Mol. mira, no. 1, 1960: 23.

1631. Rojo, Emilio. Krepnet edinstvo molodezhi Chili [The unity of Chilean youth gets stronger] Mol. mira, no. 5/6, 1962: 26–27.

1632. Sánchez, Luis. Vsiu molodost' i energiiu—osvobozhdeniiu naroda [We shall devote our youth and vigor to the liberation of our people] Mol. komm., no. 6, June 1964: 81–83.

1633. Valdés, Patricio. Molodezh' Chili ob"ediniaet sily [Chilean youth consolidates its forces] Mol. mira, no. 3, 1961: 20–21.

See also entries no. 1225 and 3201.

e. Colombia

1634. Arenas, Javier. Novaia pobeda Natsional'nogo soiuza studentov Kolumbii [A new victory of the National Union of Colombian Students] Vsem. stud. nov., v. 13, no. 11, Nov. 1959: 23–24.

1635. Cepeda Vargas, M. Kongress Natsional'nogo soiuza kolumbiiskikh studentov (IUNEK) v Kali [The Congress of the National Union of Colombian Students (UNEC) in Cali] Vsem. stud. nov., v. 13, no. 1, Jan. 1959: 14–15.

1636. ———. Studenty shkoly iziashchnykh iskusstv deistvuiut [Political activities of the students of the Fine Arts School] Vsem. stud. nov., v. 14, no. 2, Feb. 1960: 22.

1637. Fashistskie proiski v Kolumbii [Fascist intrigues in Colombia] Mol. mira, no. 7, 1961: 7.

1638. Guzmán Celis, Gilberto. Pobeda molodezhi Kolumbii [The victory of Colombian youth] Mol. mira, no. 8, 1959: 22.

1639. Pardo, Jaime. V Kolumbii usilivaetsia bor'ba studentov [Intensification of the struggle of Colombian university students] Vsem. stud. nov., v. 15, no. 10/11, Oct.-Nov. 1961: 14–15.

1640. VSN beret interv'iu u prezidenta IUNEK [Our interview with the chairman of the National Union of Colombian students] Vsem. stud. nov., v. 13, no. 6, June 1959: 11.

See also entry no. 1921.

f. Cuba

1641. Filiushkina, S. Dva mira—dve iunosti [Young people are different in these two worlds] Voronezh, Obl. kn. izd-vo, 1962. 15 p.

1642. Khuzemi, I. K., *and* V. K. Mashkin. Vstrecha s iunost'iu ostrova muzhestva [A meeting with the young people of the island of courage] Moscow, Mol. gvardiia, 1964. 78 p.

1643. Mashkin, V. K., *and* M. I. Mokhnachev. Kuba—strana iunosti [Cuba, the country of youth] Moscow, Znanie, 1961. 47 p.
DLC

1644. Alvarez, Aldo. The fight for national liberation is a historic necessity. World youth, no. 4, 1964: 40–42.

1645. Assotsiatsiia molodykh povstantsev—edinaia organizatsiia kubinskoi molodezhi [The Association of Young Rebels is a unified organization of Cuban youth] Mol. mira, no. 1/2, 1961: 18–20.

1646. Castro, Fidel. Missiia molodezhi [The mission of youth] IUnost', v. 8, no. 5, 1962: 2–5.

1647. Da zdravstvuet Kuba! Da zdravstvuet revoliutsiia! [Long live Cuba! Long live the revolution!] Mol. mira, no. 12, 1960: 6–7.

1648. Dzhoel' Iglesias; biograficheskaia spravka [Joel Iglesias; a biographical note] Nov. vrem., v. 20, no. 15, Apr. 1962: 17.

1649. F. Kastro blagodarit MSS [Fidel Castro thanks the International Union of Students] Vsem. stud. nov., v. 13, no. 12, Dec. 1959: 23.

1650. Fedotov, A. Malen'kie revoliutsionery [Little revolutionaries] IUn. nat., no. 1, Jan. 1962: 25.
School children.

1651. Fidel' Kastro razgovarivaet s pionerami [Fidel Castro talks with the Pioneers] Vozhatyi, v. 38, no. 12, Dec. 1962: 30–32.

1652. IUnyi geroi [A young hero] Vsem. stud. nov., v. 16, no. 3, Mar. 1962: 11.

1653. Konovalov, B., *and* M. Mokhnachev. Kuba pobedit potomu chto ona prava! [Cuba will triumph because she is in the

right!] Mol. komm., no. 12, Dec. 1960: 108–116.
Youth and the revolution.

1654. López del Amo, Rolando. V edinom stroiu kubinskaia molodezh' boretsia za ukreplenie novoi Respubliki [Cuban youth is united in the struggle for the consolidation of the new republic] Mol. mira, no. 6, 1959: 20.

1655. Martín, Miguel. Novyi etap v deiatel'nosti Soiuza molodykh kommunistov Kuby [New phase in the work of the League of Young Cuban Communists] Mol. komm., no. 12, Dec. 1964: 101–105.

1656. Mashkin, V. Serdtsa, otdannye revoliutsii [Hearts dedicated to the revolution] Smena, v. 37, no. 15, Aug. 1960: 20.
Young people and the revolution.

1657. Molodost' Kuby [The youth of Cuba] Vokrug sveta, no. 4, Apr. 1963: 17.

1658. "My zashchitim revoliutsiiu!"—govorit prezident fedcratsii universitetskikh studentov Kuby ["We shall defend the revolution!" says the president of the Federation of Cuban University Students] Vsem. stud. nov., v. 14, no. 1, Jan. 1960: 23.

1659. Okuneva, Maiia. Fidel' razgovarivaet s det'mi [Fidel talks to the children] Ogonek, v. 40, no. 31, July 1962: 12–13.

1660. Peñalver, F. Kubinskaia respublika; 250 luchshikh [Republic of Cuba; the 250 best] Mol. mira, no. 4, 1962: 7–8.
Youth and the revolution.

1661. Petrova, A. Kuba—strana iunosti [Cuba, the country of youth] Mol. komm., no. 1, Jan. 1962: 112–114.

1662. Samodin, Viktor. Ucheba, trud i vintovka; ocherk [Study, work, and a rifle; a sketch] Stavropol'e, no. 2, 1962: 49–51.

1663. Soto, Lionel. Kubinskaia molodezh'—aktivnaia sila revoliutsii [Cuban youth is the leading force of the revolution] Mol. komm., no. 8, Aug. 1959: 111–115.

1664. Sushchenko, Ivan. Venceremos! Pobedim! [Venceremos! We shall win!] Mol. gvard., no. 2, Feb. 1962: 249–264.

1665. Tarasov, F. Molodezh' osvobozhdennoi strany [Youth of a liberated country] Mol. mira, no. 11/12, 1961: 14–15.

g. Dominican Republic

1666. Students resist coup. World student news, v. 18, no. 1, 1964: 16.

h. Ecuador

1667. Guerrero, Walter E. Studenty Ekvadora v traure; krov' okrashivaet ulitsy [Students of Ecuador are in mourning; blood stains the streets] Vsem. stud. nov., v. 13, no. 11, Nov. 1959: 20–21.

i. El Salvador

1668. Aparicio, Susana. Vanguard Youth of El Salvador. World youth, no. 2, 1963: 43–44.

j. Guatemala

1669. Duarte, J. The struggle of the youth of Guatemala. World youth, no. 3, 1964: 16–19.

1670. Obrashchenie Universitetskoi studencheskoi assotsiatsii k pravitel'stvu [An appeal of the University Students' Association to the Guatemalan Government] Vsem. stud. nov., v. 13, no. 7, July 1959: 21.

1671. A precedent: Guatemala. World student news, v. 18, no. 6, 1964: 20–21.

k. The Guianas

1672. Cristian, C. British Guiana—once a colony, now a state for youth. World youth, no. 2, 1963: 37–38.

1673. Frédéric, Edmond. Vzory studentov Gviany obrashcheny k Latinskoi Amerike [Guianan university students look toward Latin America] Vsem. stud. nov., v. 13, no. 6, June 1959: 16–17.
French Guiana.

1674. Independence now, watchword of British Guiana. World student news, v. 16, no. 11/12, 1962: 16–17.

1675. Shepherd, Desmond. For democracy and peace. World youth, no. 1, 1964: 23, 43.
British Guiana.

l. Haiti

1676. Obrashchenie studentov Gaiti [An appeal by Haitian students] Nov. vrem., v. 20, no. 17, Apr. 1963: 17.

1677. Studenty Gaiti litsom k litsu s diktaturoi [Haitian students stand against the dictatorship] Vsem. stud. nov., v. 15, no. 3/4, Mar.-Apr. 1961: 30–31.

m. Honduras

1678. Falck, Carlos H. Rasskazyvaet student iz Gondurasa [A student from Honduras tells us his story] Vsem. stud. nov., v. 15, no. 3/4, Mar.-Apr. 1961: 34.

1679. Men'she pushek—bol'she shkol! [Fewer guns—more schools!] Vsem. stud. nov., v. 14, no. 3/4, Mar.-Apr. 1960: 8.
Student activities.

n. Mexico

1680. Guerrero Guerrero, J. Stoimost' proezda v Puebla [Bus fares in Puebla] Vsem. stud. nov., v. 14, no. 2, Feb. 1960: 23.
Political activities of students.

1681. Martínez Verdugo, Arnoldo. Molodaia Meksika boretsia [Young Mexico is in the struggle] Mol. kolkh., v. 26, no. 8, Aug. 1959: 27.
Translated from the Spanish.

o. Nicaragua

1682. Pueblo, Solomón. Molodezh' Nikaragua boretsia [Nicaraguan youth struggles] Vsem. stud. nov., v. 15, no. 2, Feb. 1961: 9–10.

1683. Zagovor molchaniia protiv zabastovki studentov [The strike of university students was hushed up] Vsem. stud. nov., v. 14, no. 1, Jan. 1960: 22.

p. Paraguay

1684. "Come, let's raise our voices together to rid ourselves of these bandits!" World student news, v. 17, no. 8, 1963: 16–17.

q. Peru

1685. Espinoza Montesinos, Gustavo. Tasks of the student movement. World student news, v. 18, no. 5, 1964: 11–12.

1686. Repression in Peru. World student news, v. 18, no. 5, 1964: 12.

r. Puerto Rico

1687. Lemus, Germán. Kak Pachencho Mateo iskal ovtsu, a okazalsia sam podstrizhennym . . . [How Pancho Mateo searched for a sheep, and became shorn himself . . .] Vsem. stud. nov., v. 14, no. 8, Aug. 1960: 19–21.
Political activities of university students.

1688. Pietri, Norman. Studenty v bor'be za nezavisimost' [University students struggle for independence] Vsem. stud. nov., v. 14, no. 3/4, Mar.-Apr. 1960: 31.

1689. Poiarkova, N. T. Chto proiskhodit v vysshei shkole Puerto-Riko [What is happening in the institutions of higher education of Puerto Rico] Vest. vys. shkoly, v. 22, no. 12, Dec. 1964: 71–74.

1690. Puerto Rican student delegation tours for support. World student news, v. 18, no. 6, 1964: 19.

1691. Puerto-Riko—koloniia SShA [Puerto Rico, a colony of the United States] Mol. mira, no. 11/12, 1961: 16–17.
Political struggle of Puerto Rican youth.

1692. Silén, Juan Angel. My stoim tverdo [We stand firmly] Vsem. stud. nov., v. 15, no. 8/9, Aug.-Sept. 1961: 13–15.
Political activity of university students.

s. Uruguay

1693. Medina, Virginia. Urugvaiskie studenty [Uruguayan students] Sov. zhen., v. 20, no. 12, 1964: 14.

1694. Pobeda studentov [Students' victory] Vsem. stud. nov., v. 15, no. 1, Jan. 1961: 23–24.
See also entry no. 1617.

t. Venezuela

1695. Alvarado, César Alonso. No pasarán! Vsem. stud. nov., v. 13, no. 1, Jan. 1959: 15.
Political activities of students.

1696. Escaleno, Julio. Venezuela today. World student news, v. 18, no. 9/10, 1964: 21–22.

1697. FUTS prinimaet gostei iz IUZHEMA [The Federation of University Centers receives the visitors from the General Union of Muslim Students of Algeria] Vsem. stud. nov., v. 13, no. 8, Aug. 1959: 23.

1698. Figueroa, Augusto. Caracas in May. World student news, v. 18, no. 7/8, 1964: 18–19.

1699. Freddy Muñoz speaks. World student news, v. 18, no. 5, 1964: 13–14.

1700. L. C. Venezuela today. World student news, v. 17, no. 4, 1963: 5.

1701. "Million bolivarov vo imia svobody dominikantsev!" ["A million bolivars in the name of freedom for the Dominicans!"] Vsem. stud. nov., v. 13, no. 6, June 1959: 22.
  Venezuelan students pledge their support to the liberation movement in the Dominican Republic.

1702. Muñoz, F. Kommunisty i molodezh'; Venesuela [The Communists and youth; Venezuela] Probl. mira i sots., v. 4, no. 10, Oct. 1961: 86–88.

1703. Nonato, Raimundo. What the student guerillas of the "Anzoátegui" have to say. World student news, v. 17, no. 6, 1963: 1–2.

1704. Núñez, Tenorio J. Molodezh, Venesuely boretsia za luchshuiu zhizn' [The youth of Venezuela fights for a better life] Mol. mira, no. 12, 1959: 15.

1705. Studenty—geroi iz Venesuely [Heroic students from Venezuela] Vsem. stud. nov., v. 16, no. 5/6, May-June 1962: 17.

1706. Suinaga, Héctor. Progress i natsional'- naia nezavisimost' [Progress and national independence] Mol. mira, no. 8/9, 1961: 45–46.
  Revolutionary activity of youth.

1707. Venesuela tri goda spustia [Venezuela three years later] Vsem. stud. nov., v. 15, no. 1, Jan. 1961: 16–17.
  Political activity of university students.

1708. Venezuelan student password: study and struggle. World student news, v. 18, no. 1, 1964: 19.

1709. Venezuelan students again! World student news, v. 16, no. 11/12, 1962: 13.

u. West Indies

1710. Dva kongressa—odni i te zhe problemy [Two congresses and the same problems] Vsem. stud. nov., v. 13, no. 8, Aug. 1959: 23.
  Political activity of university students in the French West Indies.

1711. Pierre-Justin, Serge. Boevoi dukh gvadelupskoi molodezhi [The fighting spirit of the youth of Guadeloupe] Probl. mira i sots., v. 6, no. 1, Jan. 1963: 67–68.

1712. Znakomy li vy so studentami Vest- Indii? [Are you acquainted with the students of the West Indies?] Vsem. stud. nov., v. 14, no. 11/12, Nov.-Dec. 1960: 26–27.

F. THE CHURCH; CHURCH AND STATE

1. Writings Dealing With Three or More Countries

1713. Lavretskii, Iosif Ramual'dovich. Kolonizatory ukhodiat—missionery ostaiutsia [The colonizers are leaving but the missionaries are remaining] Moscow, Izd-vo Akad. nauk SSSR, 1963. 162 p.
              DLC

1714. ———. Ten' Vatikana nad Latinskoi Amerikoi [The shadow of the Vatican over Latin America] Moscow, Izd-vo Akad. nauk SSSR, 1961. 206 p.
  Reviewed by I. Dabagian and E. Dabagian in *Nauka i rel.*, no. 8, Aug. 1961: 93–95; by V. L. Afanas'ev in *Ezhegodnik Muzeia istorii religii i ateisma*, v. 6, 1962: 424–429; by E. V. Rubtsova in *Nov. i noveish. ist.*, no. 3, 1962: 158; by V. Afanas'ev in *Sov. etn.*, no. 4, July-Aug. 1962: 217–220; by E. Surenavičins in *Kommunist* (Vilnius), no. 10, 1961: 77–79.

1715. Lavretskii, I. Pozornaia stranitsa istorii tserkvi [An ignominious page of church history] Nauka i rel., v. 2, no. 11, Nov. 1960: 42–45.

1716. Sergeev, K. Vatikan i Latinskaia Amerika [The Vatican and Latin America] Mosk. prop., v. 16, no. 8, Aug. 1959: 60–65.

See also entries no. 318 and 1383.

2. Individual Countries

a. Argentina

1717. Iz Argentinskogo blagochiniia [New developments in the Argentine Diocese] Zhur. Mosk. Patr., no. 8, Aug. 1963: 19–20.
Orthodox Eastern Church.

1718. Vas'ko, A. G. Priezd episkopa Nikodima (Rusnaka) na Argentinskuiu kafedru [Arrival of Bishop Nikodim (Rusnak) at the Argentine Diocese] Zhur. Mosk. Patr., no. 8, 1964: 14–16.
Orthodox Eastern Church.

b. Brazil

1719. Grigulevich, I. Katolitsizm v sovremennoi Brazilii [The Catholic Church in present-day Brazil] Nauka i rel., v. 4, no. 11, Nov. 1962: 46–50.

c. Chile

1720. Grigulevich, I. U vlasti levye katoliki [Left-wing Catholics in power] Nauka i rel., v. 5, no. 12, Dec. 1964: 82–83.

See also entry no. 1234.

d. Colombia

1721. Borisov, S. Ognem i mechom [By fire and sword] Nauka i rel., v. 4, no. 5, May 1962: 48.
Catholic Church.

e. Cuba

1722. Ardatovskii, V. Sviatye ottsy na Kube [The holy fathers in Cuba] Nauka i rel., v. 3, no. 11, Nov. 1961: 47–49.
Catholic Church.

1723. Castro, Fidel. Govorit Fidel' Kastro [Fidel Castro speaks] Nauka i rel., v. 4, no. 6, June 1963: 34–35.
Communism and religion.

1724. Dyversanty v sutanakh [Saboteurs in cassocks] Voiov. ateist, no. 1, Jan. 1961: 62.
Counterrevolutionary activity of the Catholic Church.

1725. Grigulevich, I. Revoliutsionnaia Kuba i tserkov' [Revolutionary Cuba and the Church] Nauka i rel., v. 2, no. 10, Oct. 1960: 75–76.

1726. ———. Ten' kresta nad Kuboi i Kongo [The shadow of the cross over Cuba and the Congo] Kommunist (Vilnius) no. 10, 1960: 67–70.

1727. Kogo proslavliaet "Pailot"? [Whom does the "Pilot" glorify?] Nauka i rel., v. 4, no. 5, May 1963: 42.
American priests.

1728. Listov, V. Bitaia karta imperilizma [The trumped card of imperialism] Nauka i rel., v. 4, no. 6, June 1963: 36–38.
Communism and religion.

f. Ecuador

1729. Grigulevich, I. Ten' nad Ekvadorom [A shadow over Ecuador] Nauka i rel., v. 4, no. 9, Sept. 1963: 36–39.
Catholic Church.

g. Mexico

1730. Leonov, N. S. Bor'ba reaktsionnogo katolicheskogo dukhovenstva s gosudarstvom v Meksike; vosstanie "Kristeros" v 1926–1929 gg. [The struggle of the reactionary Catholic clergy against the Mexican government; the "Cristero" uprising in 1926–1929] [Moscow] 1963. (Institut istorii Akademii nauk SSSR)
Abstract of a dissertation for the degree of Candidate in Historical Sciences.

1731. Larin, N. S. Kontrrevoliutsionnoe vosstanie klerikalov v Meksike, 1926–1929 [The counterrevolutionary revolt of the clericals in Mexico, 1926–1929] Vop. ist. rel. i ateiz., no. 11, 1963: 239–268.

h. Venezuela

1732. Kuznetsov, I. Na strazhe diktatorov Venesuely [The guardians of Venezuelan dictators] Nauka i rel., v. 4, no. 8, Aug. 1963: 37–40.
Catholic Church.

VII

MILITARY AFFAIRS

❦

A. WRITINGS DEALING WITH THREE OR MORE COUNTRIES

1733. Bazy i lageria podgotovki kubinskikh kontrrevoliutsionerov [Military bases and camps for the training of Cuban counter-revolutionaries] Nov. vrem., v. 20, no. 44, Oct. 1962: 9.

1734. Beliaev, V. Narody Latinskoi Ameriki trebuiut razoruzheniia [The peoples of Latin America demand disarmament] Mezhdunar. zhizn', v. 7, no. 2, Feb. 1960: 115–116.

1735. Borisov, V. Pentagon oruduet v Latinskoi Amerike [Activities of the Pentagon in Latin America] Mezhdunar. zhizn', v. 8, no. 9, Sept. 1961: 113–115.

1736. Eliutin, IU. Komu nuzhna "armiia Rubotoma?" [Who needs "Rubottom's army?"] Mezhdunar. zhizn', v. 7, no. 5, May 1960: 123–124.

1737. ———. Podozritel'nye manevry [Suspicious maneuvers] Mezhdunar. zhizn', v. 6, no. 5, May 1959: 135–137.
Maneuvers of the U.S. Navy.

1738. ———. "Shkoly vmesto kazarm"—trebuiut latinoamerikantsy ["Let's turn barracks into schools," the Latin Americans say] Za rubezhom, no. 15, Sept. 1960: 18.

1739. Galin, IU, and V. Kashirin. Latinskaia Amerika v planakh Pentagona [Latin America in the plans of the Pentagon] Komm. Vooruzh. Sil, v. 1, no. 9, May 1961: 85–88.

1740. Gamutilo, V., and V. Selivanov. Vooruzhennye sily stran Latinskoi Ameriki [The armed forces of the Latin American countries] Mezhdunar. zhizn', v. 11, no. 1, Jan. 1964: 145–147.

1741. Gvozdev, IU. Opasnaia syp' [A dangerous rash] Nov. vrem., v. 20, no. 18, May 1963: 19–21.
U.S. military bases.

1742. IUr'ev, E. Opasnye plany SShA [Dangerous plans of the United States] Mezhdunar. zhizn', v. 7, no. 7, July 1960: 125–126.
U.S. military bases.

1743. Kartsev, A. Bazy v Latinskoi Amerike [Military bases in Latin America] Mezhdunar. zhizn', v. 9, no. 12, Dec. 1962: 106–107.

1744. Latinskaia Amerika i razoruzhenie [Latin America and disarmament] Nov. vrem., v. 17, no. 50, Dec. 1959: 2.

1745. Leonidov, A. Nastuplenie na kontinent [Assault on a continent] Nov. vrem., v. 20, no. 38, Sept. 1962: 5–7; v. 20, no. 39, Sept. 1962: 12–15.
U.S. military policy in Latin America.

1746. Listov, V. Militarizm—opora neokolonializma [Militarism is the backbone of neocolonialism] Mezhdunar. zhizn', v. 11, no. 11, Nov. 1964: 31–39.
Military alliance with the United States.

1747. Loveiko, G. Dela Pentagona na "zadnem dvore" [Machinations of the Pentagon in its "back yard"] Mezhdunar. zhizn', v. 8, no. 4, Apr. 1961: 65–73.

1748. Opasnaia igra [Dangerous game] Nov. vrem., v. 18, no. 48, Nov. 1960: 3–4.
Menacing movements of U.S. naval forces.

1749. Paredes, Ricardo A. Imperializm ianki, militarizm i voennye diktatury; pis'mo

96

iz Ekvadora [Yankee imperialism, militarism, and military dictatorships; a letter from Ecuador] Probl. mira i sots., v. 6, no. 6, June 1963: 87–88.
Latin America in the military policy of the United States.

1750. Plan "Maloi NATO" [A "Little NATO" plan] Nov. vrem., v. 20, no. 11, Mar. 1963: 3.

1751. Santos, Aníbal. Razoruzhenie i Latinskaia Amerika [Disarmament and Latin America] Mol. mira, no. 4, 1960: 22.

1752. Voennaia ekspansiia SShA v stranakh Latinskoi Ameriki [U.S. military expansion in the countries of Latin America] Mezhdunar. zhizn', v. 10, no. 10, Oct. 1963: 138–139.

See also entry no. 509.

B. INDIVIDUAL COUNTRIES

1. Argentina

1753. Sumatokha v Patagonii [Turmoil in Patagonia] Nov. vrem., v. 18, no. 9, Feb. 1960: 20.
Alleged presence of Soviet submarines off the coast of Patagonia.

2. Bolivia

1754. Volki iz Pentagona [Wolves from the Pentagon] Nov. vrem., v. 19, no. 43, Oct. 1961: 25.
Military relations with the United States.

3. Brazil

1755. Castro, Josué de. Razoruzhenie i obshchestvennyi progress [Disarmament and social progress] Probl. mira i sots., v. 6, no. 4, Apr. 1963: 49–50.

1756. Zhorzhi Amadu: Volia narodov k miru pobedit [The peoples' wish for peace will prevail, says Jorge Amado] Inostr. lit., no. 7, July 1962: 257.
Brazil's position in the disarmament problem.

4. Cuba

1757. Gavrilin, Viacheslav Mikhailovich. Soldaty ostrova svobody [Soldiers of the island of freedom] Moscow, Voenizdat, 1962. 134 p. F1788.G3

1758. Agressiia protiv Kuby [Aggression against Cuba] Nov. vrem., v. 19, no. 17, Apr. 1961: 11–12.
The invasion of 1961.

1759. Bandy interventov razgromleny! Kuba pobedila! [The gangs of interventionists have been routed! Cuba has won!] Mol. komm., no. 5, May 1961: 20–21.
The invasion of 1961.

1760. Bermejo González, Ernesto. Koliuchaia provoloka mezhdu dvumia mirami [Barbed wire divides the two worlds] Inostr. lit., no. 1, Jan. 1964: 255–259.
American military bases.

1761. Dymov, V., *and* G. Ushakov. Podlinnaia istoriia Plaiia-Khiron; dokumental'naia povest' [The true story of Playa Girón; a documentary sketch] Nov. vrem., v. 20, no. 17, Apr. 1963: 25–28.
The invasion of 1961.

1762. Fuentes, Norberto. Tanki nashego naroda [The tanks of our people] Kuba, no. 4, Dec. 1964: 16–27.

1763. Goriunov, Dmitrii. Kto i vchem proschitalsia [Who miscalculated and the mistakes they made] Za rubezhom, no. 17, Apr. 1961: 4–5.
The invasion of 1961.

1764. IUdanov, N. Nadezhnyi strazh revoliutsionnoi Kuby [Faithful guardians of revolutionary Cuba] Komm. Vooruzh. Sil, v. 1, no. 10, May 1961: 88–92.
Armed forces.

1765. Ivanenko, V. V te dni ia byl na Kube [I was in Cuba at that time] Nov. vrem., v. 19, no. 22, May 1961: 25–27.
The invasion of 1961.

1766. Ivanov, V. Agressory v Guantanamo [The aggressors in Guantánamo] Starsh.-serzh., no. 3, Mar. 1962: 29.

1767. Kirsanov, A. Guantanamo—zemlia kubinskaia [Guantánamo is a part of Cuba] Agitator, no. 18, Sept. 1961: 60–61.

1768. Kto gotovil agressiiu [The ones who prepared this aggression] Za rubezhom, no. 16, Apr. 1961: 9.
The invasion of 1961.

1769. Kuba—da! [Cuba—yes!] Rabotnitsa, v. 39, no. 5, May 1961: 23.
The invasion of 1961.

1770. Leyens, Germán. War and heroes? World student news, v. 17, no. 4, 1963: 23–24.
The invasion of 1961.
A review of *Historia de una agresión* (Havana, Ediciones Venceremos, 1962. 504 p.).

1771. Luk'ianov, IU. Kto bombit Kubu? [Who is bombing Cuba?] Nov. vrem., v. 18, no. 10, Mar. 1960: 14–15.

1772. L'vov, M. Strelki geroicheskoi Kuby [The riflemen of heroic Cuba] Sov. voin, v. 44, no. 1, Jan. 1962: 43.

1773. "Moral'naia baza" dubiny [The "moral foundation" of the "big stick"] Za rubezhom, no. 43, Oct. 1961: 8.
Plans for joint intervention by Latin American countries.

1774. Nemira, I. Vspomnite Plaiia-Khiron! [Remember Playa Girón!] Mezhdunar. zhizn', v. 10, no. 10, Oct. 1963: 109–110.
The invasion of 1961.

1775. Olan, A. Guantanamo—voenno-morskaia baza SShA na Kube [Guantánamo, the U.S. naval base in Cuba] Mezhdunar. zhizn', v. 8, no. 5, May 1961: 112–115.

1776. Opasnaia provokatsiia protiv vseobshchego mira [A provocation that endangers world peace] Sov. iust., no. 9, May 1961: 1.
The invasion of 1961.

1777. Opasnyi plan [A dangerous plan] Nov. vrem., v. 19, no. 2, Jan. 1961: 21–22.
Denial of Soviet rocket installations.

1778. Ossovskii, P., *and* V. Ivanov. Soldaty revoliutsionnoi Kuby [Soldiers of revolutionary Cuba] Sov. voin, v. 43, no. 16, Aug. 1961: 37–40.

1779. Padilla, Heberto. Armii naroda—slava! [Glory to the people's army!] Sov. voin, v. 45, no. 3, Feb. 1963: 39.

1780. Paramonov, V. Narod pobedil. Narod nacheku! [The people won. The people are alert!] Za rubezhom, no. 17. Apr. 1961: 3.
The invasion of 1961.

1781. Plaiia-Khiron [Playa Girón] Nov.vrem., v. 20, no. 16, Apr. 1963: 4.
The invasion of 1961.

1782. Ponizovskii, V. Boitsy ostrova svobody [Fighters of the island of freedom] Sov. voin, v. 45, no. 16, Aug. 1963: 43.

1783. Ponizovskii, V., *and* I. Khuzemi. Boitsy revoliutsii [Soldiers of the revolution] Smena, v. 41, no. 1, Jan. 1964: 14–15.

1784. Pravoe delo Kuby nepobedimo [The just cause of Cuba is invincible] Sov. zhen., v. 17, no. 5, 1961: 15.
The invasion of 1961.

1785. Predosterezhenie agressoram [A warning to aggressors] Nov. vrem., v. 20, no. 38, Sept. 1962: 1–3.
Soviet military assistance.

1786. Provokatsiia v Guantanamo [A provocative act in Guantánamo] Nov. vrem., v. 19, no. 35, Aug. 1961: 23.

1787. Raskrytyi sekret [A disclosed secret] Nov. vrem., v. 19, no. 3, Jan. 1961: 22.
U.S. military bases for the invasion of Cuba in Guatemala.

1788. Razum protiv bezrassudstva [Reason versus recklessness] Nov. vrem., v. 20, no. 45, Nov. 1962: 1–2.
Soviet military assistance.

1789. Rivero, Adolfo. Kaimanera [Caimanera] Mol. mira, no. 6, 1961: 10.
U.S. military bases.

1790. Rodichev, B., *and* G. Evgen'ev. Samorazoblachenie interventov [The interventionists reveal the truth] Kommunist, v. 41, no. 18, Dec. 1964: 124–127.
The invasion of 1961.
A review of Haynes Bonner Johnson's *The Bay of Pigs* (New York, Norton, 1964. 368 p.).

1791. Ruki proch' ot Kuby! [Hands off Cuba!] Ogonek, v. 39, no. 17, Apr. 1961: 30–31.
The invasion of 1961.

1792. Ruki proch' ot Kuby! [Hands off Cuba!] Za rubezhom, no. 16, Apr. 1961: 1.
The invasion of 1961.

1793. "Sdelano v SShA" ["Made in the U.S.A."] Za rubezhom, no. 16, Apr. 1961: 2.
The invasion of 1961.

1794. Shpirt, A. Nikakikh voennykh baz na chuzhikh territoriiakh [There should be no military bases whatsoever in foreign countries] V zashch. mira, no. 3, Mar. 1961: 14–17.

1795. Strannaia svoboda [Strange freedom] v. 17, no. 45, Nov. 1959: 23.
Air raids.

1796. Tak pobezhdaet revoliutsiia [This is the victorious path of a revolution] Inostr. lit., no. 4, Apr. 1962: 217–232.
The invasion of 1961.

1797. TSaryk, H. IA. Holos myru [The voice of peace] Voiov. ateist, no. 5, May 1961: 11.
The invasion of 1961.

1798. TSybul'skii, E. Kubinskii narod stroit novuiu zhizn' [The Cuban people are building a new life] Komm. Vooruzh. Sil, v. 3, no. 1, Jan. 1963: 81–85.
Defenses.

1799. Uzhvii, N. M. Ne zahasyty polum'ia svobody [The flame of freedom is inextinguishable] Voiov. ateist, no. 5, May 1961: 11.
The invasion of 1961.

1800. Vasilevskii, L. Nad Plaiia-Khiron [Above Playa Girón] Av. i kosm., v. 45, no. 10, 1962: 90–91.
The invasion of 1961.

1801. Zagladin, Vadim. Krakh eksporterov kontrrevoliutsii; pervye uroki sobytii na Kube [Crushing defeat of the exporters of counter-revolution; the first lessons of Cuban events] Probl. mira i sots., v. 4, no. 6, June 1961: 54–58.
The invasion of 1961.

See also entries no. 465, 721, 1804, 2020, 2043, and 2046.

5. Guatemala

See entry no. 1787.

6. The Guianas

1802. Podarok generala [A gift from the general] Nov. vrem., v. 21, no. 14, Apr. 1964: 22.
French Guiana as a place for the testing of rockets.

7. Nicaragua

1803. Urok ne vprok [They haven't learned from this lesson] Za rubezhom, no. 31, Aug. 1963: 4.
Military preparations of Cuban refugees.

1804. Zagovorshchiki [Conspirators] Nov. vrem., v. 18, no. 32, Aug. 1960: 21.
Military training of Cuban refugees in Nicaragua.

8. Puerto Rico

1805. Protiv militarizatsii strany [Against the militarization of the country] Probl. mira i sots., v. 2, no. 2, Feb. 1959: 69.
U.S. military bases.

1806. Vasil'ev, V. Zhertva "blagodeianii" [A victim of "welfare"] Mezhdunar. zhizn', v. 7, no. 7, July 1960: 128.
American military bases.

9. Trinidad and Tobago

1807. Lewis, Christina. Preventivnye mery— luchshaia garantiia protiv radioaktivnykh osadkov [Preventive measures are the best guarantee against radioactive fallout] Zhen. mira, no. 8, 1959: 10.
U.S. military bases.

10. Venezuela

1808. Sekretnaia sdelka [A secret agreement] Nov. vrem., v. 22, no. 52, Dec. 1964: 20.
U.S. military assistance.

VIII

FOREIGN RELATIONS

❦

A. WRITINGS DEALING WITH THREE OR MORE COUNTRIES

1809. Bolkhovitinov, Nikolai Nikolaevich. Doktrina Monro; proiskhozhdenie i kharakter [The origin and nature of the Monroe Doctrine] Moscow, Izd-vo IMO, 1959. 334 p.   JX1425.B74
  Reviewed by V. Kropotov in *Vest. ist. mir. kul't.*, no. 4, July-Aug. 1961: 150–152; by L. IU. Slezkin in *Vop. ist.*, no. 7, July 1960: 164–165.

1810. ———. Proiskhozhdenie i kharakter doktriny Monro, 1823 [The origin and nature of the Monroe Doctrine, 1823] Moscow, 1959. 20 p. (Pedagogicheskii institut imeni V. P. Potemkina)
  Abstract of a dissertation for the degree of Candidate in Historical Sciences.

1811. Egorov, Valerii Nikolaevich. Mezhdunarodnye otnosheniia; bibliograficheskii spravochnik, 1945–1960 gg. [International relations; a bibliographical reference book, 1945–1960] Moscow, Izd-vo IMO, 1961. 405 p.   Z6204.E4
  Partial contents. —Argentina, p. 165. —Brazil, p. 167, 316. —Chile, p. 229. —Colombia, p. 190, 326. —Ecuador, p. 230. —Guatemala, p. 169. —Guiana, p. 169. —Mexico, p. 193, 327. —Panama, p. 197. —Peru, p. 197. —Uruguay, p. 221. —Venezuela, p. 167.

1812. Eliutin, IU. P. Rol' stran Latinskoi Ameriki v sovremennykh mezhdunarodnykh otnosheniiakh [The role of the Latin American countries in present-day international relations] Moscow, Znanie, 1961. 48 p.   DLC

1813. Gonionskii, Semen Aleksandrovich. Latinskaia Amerika i SShA; ocherki istorii diplomaticheskikh otnoshenii, 1939–1959 [Latin America and the U.S.A.; studies on the history of diplomatic relations, 1939–1959] Moscow, Izd-vo IMO, 1960. 541 p.   F1418.G36
  Reviewed by V. IA. Masiukevich in *Vop. ist.*, no. 2, Feb. 1961: 151–154; by N. Razumovich in *Kommunist*, v. 38, no. 6, Apr. 1961: 123–125; by V. Kropotov in *Vest. ist. mir. kul't.*, no. 4, July-Aug. 1961: 154–155.

1814. Isaev, N. S., *and others, comps.* Dokumenty proletarskoi solidarnosti; sbornik dokumentov o sodruzhestve trudiashchikhsia Sovetskogo Soiuza s trudiashchimisia stran Azii, Afriki i Latinskoi Ameriki v 1918–1961 gg. [Documents of proletarian solidarity; collected documentary materials on friendly cooperation between Soviet workers and the toilers of Asia, Africa, and Latin America, 1918–1961] Moscow, Profizdat, 1962. 208 p.   HX544.D585

1815. Korolev, N. V. Strany Latinskoi Ameriki v mezhdunarodnykh otnosheniiakh, 1898–1962 gg. [The countries of Latin America in international relations, 1898–1962] Kishinev, Kartia moldoveniaske, 1962. 305 p.   DLC
  Reviewed by A. Mirkind in *Komm. Mold.*, v. 8, no. 3, Mar. 1963: 68–70: by IU. A. Antonov in *Nov. i noveish. ist.*, no. 4, 1963: 179–180.

1816. Poliakov, M. I. TSentral'naia Amerika; o nekotorykh problemakh mezhdunarodnykh otnoshenii v basseine Karibskogo moria [Central America; some problems relating to international contacts in the Caribbean area] Moscow, Znanie, 1964. 32 p.

1817. Shur, Leonid Avel'evich. Rossiia i Latinskaia Amerika; ocherki politicheskikh, ekonomicheskikh i kul'turnykh otnoshenii [Russia and Latin America; studies on their political, economic, and cultural contacts] Moscow, Mysl', 1964. 158 p.

1818. Sizonenko, A. I. Sovetskii Soiuz i Latinskaia Amerika [The Soviet Union and Latin America] Moscow, Znanie, 1964. 30 p.

1819. Stepanenko, V. A. Imperializm SShA— vrag narodov Latinskoi Ameriki [U.S. imperialism is the enemy of the Latin American nations] Kiev, O-vo po raspr. polit. i nauch. znanii, 1962. 40 p.

1820. Andrianov, V. Burliashchii kontinent [A seething continent] Agitator, no. 1, Jan. 1962: 50–51.
Struggle against the United States.

1821. Arcocha, Juan. Zhandarm i iabluko Adama [The gendarme and the Adam's apple] Vsesvit, v. 5, no. 2, Feb. 1962: 19–21.
United States and Latin America.

1822. Bagramov, L. Politika knuta i prianika [The policy of the carrot and the stick] Mir. ekon. i mezhdunar. otn., no. 9, Sept. 1960: 101–103.
Relations with the United States.

1823. Barrera, Hernán. Imperialisticheskaia politika SShA v Latinskoi Amerike [The imperialist policy of the U.S.A. in Latin America] Probl. mira i sots., v. 6, no. 10, Oct. 1963: 78–80.

1824. ———. Zagovor imperialistov i soli- darnost' narodov [A plot of imperialists and the solidarity of the peoples] Probl. mira i sots., v. 6, no. 5, May 1963: 54–56.
Relations with Cuba.

1825. Barrera, Hernán, *and* C. Medina. Ot "novykh rubezhei"—k "zhestkomu kursu"; krizis burzhuaznogo reformizma v Latinskoi Amerike [From the "new frontier" to a "tough line"; the crisis of bourgeois reformism in Latin America] Probl. mira i sots., v. 7, no. 6, June 1964: 59–64.
Relations with the United States.

1826. Besslavnyi voiazh "persony non grata" [An ignominious trip of a "persona non

grata"] Za rubezhom, no. 25, June 1961: 2.
Adlai Stevenson's trip to Latin America.

1827. Bolkhovitinov, N. Doktrina Monro; legendy i deistvitel'nost' [The Monroe Doctrine; legends and reality] Mir. ekon. i mezhdunar. otn., no. 9, Sept. 1960: 14–26.

1828. ———. Provozglashenie Soedinennymi Shtatami doktriny Monro v 1823 g. [The proclamation of the Monroe Doc- trine by the United States in 1823] Uch. zap. Mosk. gos. ped. inst., v. 93, 1959: 279–340.

1829. Borisov, V. Za shirmoi antikom- munizma [Under the cloak of anti- communism] Mezhdunar. zhizn', v. 7, no. 1, Jan. 1960: 126–128.
Relations with the United States.

1830. Borovskii, V. Rubezhi v tupike [Fron- tiers in a blind alley] Za rubezhom, no. 33, Aug. 1964: 12.
Relations with the United States.

1831. De Goll' peresekaet okean [De Gaulle crosses the ocean] Nov. vrem., v. 21, no. 13, Mar. 1964: 3.
General de Gaulle's visit.

1832. Druz'ia i nedrugi Latinskoi Ameriki [Friends and foes of Latin America] Nov. vrem., v. 20, no. 14, Apr. 1963: 1–2.
Relations with the United States.

1833. Ekhat' ili ne ekhat'? [To go or not to go?] Nov. vrem. v. 17, no. 23, June 1959: 19–20.
Dr. Milton Eisenhower's visit to Central America.

1834. Eliutin, IU. P. Nadezhdy Latinskoi Ameriki [The hopes of Latin America] Mezhdunar. zhizn', v. 6, no. 12, Dec. 1959: 111–112.
Foreign relations.

1835. Eliutin, IU., *and* A. Matlina. Skvoz' prizmu "kholodnoi voiny" [In the light of the "cold war"] Mezhdunar. zhizn', v. 10, no. 6, June 1963: 126–128.
A review of Salvador de Madariaga's *Latin America between the Eagle and the Bear* (New York, Praeger, 1962. 192 p.).

1836. Gonionskii, S. A. Agressivnaia politika SShA v Latinskoi Amerike [The aggressive policy of the U.S.A. in Latin America] Vop. mezhdunar. prava, no. 4, 1962: 3–31.

1837. ———. Naprasnye poiski [A futile search] Mezhdunar. zhizn', v. 6, no. 7, July 1959: 151–154.
Relations with the United States.
A review of T. W. Palmer's *Search for a Latin American Policy* (Gainesville, University of Florida Press, 1957. 217 p.).

1838. ———. Nepogrebennyi trup "doktriny Monro" [The unburied corpse of the "Monroe Doctrine"] Mezhdunar. zhizn', v. 7, no. 10, Oct. 1960: 82–90.

1839. ———. Politika Soedinennykh Shtatov v Latinskoi Amerike posle Kennedi [U.S. policy in Latin America after Kennedy] Nov. vrem., v. 21, no. 25, June 1964: 8–11.

1840. Grigor'ev, IA. G. Revoliutsiia v Latinskoi Amerike i politika SShA [The revolution in Latin America and the policy of the U.S.A.] Vop. ist., no. 12, Dec. 1962: 178–179.

1841. Gritsanov, A. "Korpus" kolonizatorov [A "corps" of colonizers] Komm. Bel., v. 37, no. 2, 1963: 72–75.
The United States Peace Corps.

1842. Gvozdarev, B. Novye neudachi diplomatii SShA [New failures of U.S. diplomacy] Mezhdunar. zhizn', v. 7, no. 10, Oct. 1960: 117–119.
Relations with the United States.

1843. Hernández Segura, Francisco. Latinskaia Amerika razocharovana [Latin America is disappointed] Za rubezhom, no. 9, Mar. 1961: 11.
Relations with the United States.

1844. IAroshevskii, B. Karibskii blok [The Caribbean bloc] Za rubezhom, no. 51, Dec. 1962: 18.
Coordination of the policy of Central American countries.

1845. Interventsiia SShA v Latinskoi Amerike [U.S. intervention in Latin America] Mol. mira, no. 1, 1960: 21.

1846. IU. B. Seti v Karibskom more; k itogam soveshchaniia ministrov inostrannykh del Zapadnogo polushariia v Sant-IAgo [Nets in the Caribbean Sea; on the results of the conference of foreign ministers of the Western Hemisphere in Santiago] Nov. vrem., v. 17, no. 34, Aug. 1959: 5.

1847. IUr'ev, E. Diplomatiia zhestov [A diplomacy of gestures] Mezhdunar. zhizn', v. 7, no. 4, Apr. 1960: 109–110.
President Eisenhower's trip to Latin America.

1848. ———. Interventsiia kolonizatorskikh "idei" v Latinskoi Amerike [The intrusion of colonialist "ideas" in Latin America] Mezhdunar. zhizn', v. 10, no. 11, Nov. 1963: 80–86.
Relations with the United States.

1849. Kamynin, L. Proval "novogo kursa" [The failure of the "new course"] Za rubezhom, no. 42, Oct. 1963: 1–2.
Relations with the United States.

1850. Karanjia, Rustom Khurshedji, *and* Ramesh Sanghvi. Shtorm nad Latinskoi Amerikoi; otryvki iz knigi [Storm over Latin America; excerpts from a book] Za rubezhom, no. 4, Jan. 1962: 6–7.
Relations with the United States.
Translated from the English.

1851. Khachaturian, Aram. Poltora veka [A century and a half] Ogonek, v. 38, no. 40, Oct. 1960: 8.
Relations with Russia.

1852. Khachaturov, Karen. Samoobol'shchenie Vashingtona [Self-deception of the Washington government] Za rubezhom, no. 31, Aug. 1964: 5.
Relations with the United States.

1853. Kontrasty kholma Tiskapa [The contrasts of Tiscapa Hill] Za rubezhom, no. 15, Apr. 1963: 4.
A conference of the states of Central America.

1854. Lapitskii, I. Druzhba mistera Dollara [The friendship of Mr. Dollar] Nov. vrem., v. 18, no. 12, Mar. 1960: 9–10.
President Eisenhower's visit.

1855. Lednev, Val. V bor'be za mir i svobodu narodov [In the struggle for peace and national freedom] Agitator, no. 4, Feb. 1962: 32–35.
Struggle against the United States.

1856. Leont'ev, L. Diplomaticheskoe nastuplenie [A diplomatic offensive] Mezhdunar. zhizn', v. 11, no. 11, Nov. 1964: 106–107.
Relations with France (de Gaulle's visit).

1857. Levin, V. V poiskakh novoi politiki [In search of a new policy] Nov. vrem., v. 17, no. 41, Oct. 1959: 16–18.

1858. Lieuwen, Edwin. Soiuz s tiranami [An alliance with tyrants] Mezhdunar. zhizn', v. 10, no. 2, Feb. 1963: 126–133.
Relations with the United States.
Excerpts from the book *Arms and Politics in Latin America* (New York, Praeger, 1960. 296 p.).

1859. Listov, V. Diplomaty so svastikoi [Diplomats with a swastika] Nov. vrem., v. 21, no. 31, Aug. 1963: 17–18.
German diplomats.

1860. Martillo, Trinidad. Bankrotstvo latinoamerikanskoi politiki SShA [The bankruptcy of U.S. Latin American policy] Mezhdunar. zhizn', v. 8, no. 6, June 1961: 20–28.

1861. ———. Pirog v nebesakh [Pie in the sky] Mezhdunar. zhizn', v. 7, no. 11, Nov. 1960: 29–39.
Relations with the United States.

1862. ———. Politika SShA v Latinskoi Amerike, 1959–1961 [U.S policy in Latin America, 1959–1961] Mir. ekon. i mezhdunar. otn., no. 3, Mar. 1962: 50–64; no. 4, Apr. 1962: 37–52.

1863. Mezhdunarodnyi zhandarm [The international policeman] Mezhdunar. zhizn', v. 8, no. 6, June 1961: 151–153.
Relations with the United States.

1864. Mishin, S. Treshchina v "bol'shoi dubinke" [A crack in the "big stick"] Mezhdunar. zhizn', v. 9, no. 8, Aug. 1962: 69–76.
Relations with the United States.

1865. Mondragon, Tancredo. Bezumie v Punta-del'-Este [Foolish decisions in Punta del Este] Mezhdunar. zhizn', v. 9, no. 4, Apr. 1962: 22–29.
Foreign policy.

1866. N. V. Prezident Tito v Amerike [President Tito in America] Nov. vrem., v. 21, no. 43, Oct. 1963: 14–15.

1867. Neudavshaiasia missiia [A mission that failed] Nov. vrem., v. 19, no. 26, June 1961: 26.
A. Stevenson's trip to Latin America.

1868. Nikolaev, V. Pod gradom kamnei, pod dozhdem plevkov [Under a hail of stones and a shower of spittle] Ogonek, v. 40, no. 36, Sept. 1962: 29.
Richard Nixon's visit to Latin America.

1869. O poezdke Eizenkhauera v Latinskuiu Ameriku [Eisenhower's visit to Latin America] Probl. mira i sots., v. 3, no. 4, Apr. 1960: 74.

1870. Okuneva, M. A. Proiskhozhdenie i kharakter latinoamerikanskoi doktriny Teodora Ruzvel'ta [The origin and nature of Theodore Roosevelt's policy toward Latin America] Nov. i noveish. ist., no. 5, 1961: 52–64.
Summary in English, p. 213.

1871. Pack of hounds follows the leader. World student news, v. 18, no. 7/8, 1964: 20–21.
Latin American countries and Cuba.

1872. Paramonov, Vladimir. Doktrina dollara [The "dollar doctrine"] Za rubezhom, no. 16, Apr. 1964: 7.
Political influence of the United States.

1873. Pered soveshchaniem v Punta-del'-Este [Before the conference in Punta del Este] Nov. vrem., v. 20, no. 2, Jan. 1962: 2–3.
Relations with the United States.

1874. Petrov, S. Pochemu oni smotriat na iug? [Why are they looking southward?] Mezhdunar. zhizn', v. 8, no. 2, Feb. 1961: 131–133.
Relations with the United States.
A review of Edward Tomlinson's *Look Southward, Uncle* (New York, Devin-Adair Co., 1959. 369 p.).

1875. Pirrova pobeda [Pyrrhic victory] Nov. vrem., v. 18, no. 36, Sept. 1960: 2.
Relations with Cuba.

1876. Pis'mo iz Kosta-Riki [A letter from Costa Rica] Probl. mira i sots., v. 6, no. 6, June 1963: 88.
Relations with Cuba.

1877. Poliakovskii, V. Besslavnyi konets [The shameful end] Za rubezhom, no. 18, May 1961: 12–13.
Relations with the United States.

1878. Posly-zagovorshchiki   [Ambassadors and their plots] Nov. vrem., v. 20, no. 12, Mar. 1962: 22–23.
U.S. "plots" in Latin America.

1879. Proryv v zapovednik [Penetrating a forbidden land] Za rubezhom, no. 13, Mar. 1964: 2.
General de Gaulle's visit to Latin America.

1880. Romanov, L. M. "Doktrina Monro"—orudie interventsionistskoi politiki SShA v Latinskoi Amerike [The "Monroe Doctrine" is a weapon of U.S. interventionist policy in Latin America] Vop. mezhdunar. prava, no. 4, 1962: 32–58.

1881. Shakhov, G.   Doktrina agressii [A doctrine of aggression] Mezhdunar. zhizn', v. 9, no. 2, Feb. 1962: 127–128.
Relations with the United States.

1882. Shul'govskii, A.   V poiskakh ideologicheskogo kompasa [In search of an ideological compass] Mezhdunar. zhizn', v. 10, no. 7, July 1963; 16–25; v. 10, no. 8, Aug. 1963: 107–113.
Relations with the United States.

1883. Shur, L. A.   Iz istorii ustanovleniia diplomaticheskikh otnoshenii Rossii so stranami Latinskoi Ameriki [From the history of the establishment of diplomatic relations between Russia and the countries of Latin America] Vop. ist., no. 8, Aug. 1964: 211–215.

1884. Shvetsov, V.   Parlamentskie sviazi ukrepliaiut druzhbu [Parliamentary contacts strengthen friendship] Kul't. i zhizn', v. 4, no. 8, 1960: 48–50.
Relations with the USSR.

1885. Sivachev, N. N.   Review.   Nov. i noveish. ist., no. 5, 1964: 159–161.
A review of Milton Stover Eisenhower's The Wine is Bitter; the United States and Latin America (New York, Doubleday, 1963. 342 p.).

1886. Sobiraias' v tiazhkii put' [Preparing for a trying trip] Za rubezhom, no. 22, June 1961: 2–3.
Adlai Stevenson's visit to Latin America.

1887. Sosed s dubinoi; iz istorii otnoshenii SShA so stranami Latinskoi Ameriki [A neighbor with a club; from the history of U.S. relations with the countries of Latin

America] Ogonek, v. 38, no. 40, Oct. 1960: 13.

1888. Spirin, V. "Vino gor'koe." Dlia kogo? [To whom is the wine bitter?] Mezhdunar. zhizn', v. 11, no. 11, Nov. 1964: 113–116.
A review of Milton Stover Eisenhower's The Wine is Bitter; the United States and Latin America (New York, Doubleday, 1963. 342 p.).

1889. Sychev, M.   Doktrina Monro—orudie kolonizatorov [The Monroe Doctrine is a weapon of colonialists] Agitator, no. 19, Oct. 1960: 58–59.

1890. Tarasov, V.   Diplomatiia biznesa v tupike [Business diplomacy in a blind alley] Mir. ekon. i mezhdunar. otn., no. 3, 1964: 137–140.
A review of Adolf August Berle's Latin America; Diplomacy and Reality (New York, Harper and Row, 1962. 144 p.).

1891. Tarasov, V. B.   Latinskaia Amerika protiv amerikanskogo imperializma [Latin America against American imperialism] Nov. i noveish. ist., no. 6, 1963: 149–150.
A review of Alfredo Lorenzo Palacios' Nuestra América y el imperialismo (Buenos Aires, Editorial Palestra, 1961. 441 p.).

1892. Vainshtok, V., and L. Rubinshtein. Doktrina Monro? [Is it really the Monroe Doctrine?] Ogonek, v. 38, no. 30, July 1960: 6–7.

1893. Valentinov, V.   Makhinatsii TsRU v Latinskoi Amerike [Machinations of the CIA in Latin America] Mezhdunar. zhizn', v. 11, no. 6, June 1964: 77–84.

1894. Voiazh s dalekim pritselom [A trip with wide-ranging objectives] Za rubezhom, no. 38, Sept. 1964: 3.
Relations with France.

1895. Zhdut prikaza [They wait for the order] Za rubezhom, no. 2, Jan. 1962: 29.
The conference of American states in Punta del Este.

1896. Zykov, S.   De Goll' v Latinskoi Amerike [De Gaulle in Latin America] Nov. vrem., v. 22, no. 40, Oct. 1964: 8–9.

See also entries no. 311, 458, 1153, 1956, 2125, and 4529.

B. INDIVIDUAL COUNTRIES

1. Argentina

1897. Alekhandro Lastra; biograficheskaia spravka [Alejandro Lastra; a biographical note] Nov. vrem., v. 22, no. 32, Aug. 1964: 21.

1898. Bezzakoniia v Buenos-Airese [Lawlessness in Buenos Aires] Nov. vrem., v. 19, no. 24, June 1961: 23.
Demonstrations against the USSR.

1899. Kamynin, L. Shag k novomu kursu [A step toward a new policy] Mezhdunar. zhizn', v. 10, no. 12, Dec. 1963: 105–106.

1900. Review. Probl. mira i sots., v. 2, no. 6, June 1959: 89–90.
Relations with the United States.
A review of Rodolfo Ghioldi's *Acerca de la entrega* (Buenos Aires, Editorial Anteo, 1959. 63 p.).

See also entry no. 1957.

2. Bolivia

1901. Boliviia zhdet avgusta [Bolivia is waiting for August] Za rubezhom, no. 6, July 1960: 9.
The problem of diplomatic relations with the USSR.

1902. Galin, IU. V serdtse IUzhnoi Ameriki [In the heart of South America] Za rubezhom, no. 6, Feb. 1961: 18.
A visit of a Soviet parliamentary delegation.

1903. Leigue Peredo, Antonio. Bor'ba prodolzhaetsia [The struggle continues] Za rubezhom, no. 26, Dec. 1960: 28.
Relations with the United States.

1904. Zloveshchaia "shutka" [A sinister "joke"] Nov. vrem., v. 17, no. 12, Mar. 1959: 20.
Anti-American demonstrations.

3. Brazil

1905. Amado, Jorge. Razgovor s Buanga Fele, izvestnym takzhe pod imenem Mario de Andrade, vozhdem boriushcheisia Angoly [My talk with Buanga Fele, alias Mario de Andrade, a revolutionary leader of Angola] Inostr. lit., no. 6, June 1963: 236–238.

1906. Borisov, B. Vneshniaia politika Brazilii [Brazil's foreign policy] Mezhdunar. zhizn', v. 11, no. 4, Apr. 1964: 142–144.
A review of Francisco Clementino de San Thiago Dantas' *Política externa independente* (Rio de Janeiro, Editora Civilização Brasileira, 1962. 258 p.).

1907. Borisov, V. Monopolii nedovol'ny Braziliei [The monopolies are dissatisfied with Brazil] Mezhdunar. zhizn', v. 8, no. 5, May 1961: 123.
Foreign policy.

1908. Braziliia narushaet tabu [Brazil violates a taboo] Za rubezhom, no. 12, Mar. 1961: 4.

1909. Brizola, Leonel. Kliuch k "brazil'skoi zagadke" [The key to the "Brazilian riddle"] Za rubezhom, no. 37, Sept. 1961: 20.
Relations with the United States.

1910. Kurs Brazilii [The course of Brazil] Nov. vrem., v. 19, no. 12, Mar. 1961: 2.

1911. Neudachnyi shantazh [Unsuccessful blackmail] Za rubezhom, no. 12, Mar. 1963: 2–3.
Relations with the United States.

1912. Posol, poimannyi s polichnym [An ambassador was caught red-handed] Za rubezhom, no. 28, July 1961: 3.
Alleged U.S. efforts to influence Brazilian foreign policy.

1913. Skvernaia privychka [A bad habit] Nov. vrem., v. 17, no. 34, Aug. 1959: 21–22.
Alleged interference of U.S. diplomats into Brazilian internal affairs.

1914. Sovremennik. Vashington i Kuadros [Washington and Quadros] Nov. vrem., v. 19, no. 36, Sept. 1961: 7–8.

1915. Ustarelyi metod [Outmoded methods] Nov. vrem., v. 18, no. 43, Oct. 1960: 23.
Activities of U.S. diplomats.

1916. V dukhe vremeni [In the spirit of the times] Nov. vrem., v. 19, no. 49, Dec. 1961: 3.
Relations with the USSR.

1917. Vasko Leitao da Kun'ia; biograficheskaia spravka [Vasco Leitão da Cunha; a biographical note] Nov. vrem., v. 20, no. 20, May 1962: 29.

4. Chile

1918. Sovetskii Soiuz i Chili [The Soviet Union and Chili] Nov. vrem., v. 22, no. 49, Dec. 1964: 5–6.

1919. Valdés, Gabriel. Otnosheniia vosstanovleny [Restoration of diplomatic relations] Za rubezhom, no. 48, Nov. 1964: 7.
Relations with the USSR.

5. Colombia

1920. Ruiz, Alberto. Kontakty s SSSR neobkhodimy [Contacts with the USSR are indispensable] Za rubezhom, no. 44, Nov. 1963: 11.

1921. Solidarnost' s Kuboi [Solidarity with Cuba] Vsem. stud. nov., v. 14, no. 10, Oct. 1960: 21.

See also entries no. 2208, 2209, and 2211.

6. Costa Rica

1922. Prichitaniia "liberala" [Lamentations of a "liberal"] Za rubezhom, no. 28, July 1964: 3.
Relations with the United States.

7. Cuba

a. Foreign Relations and Foreign Policy in General

1923. Druzhba naviky! [Eternal friendship!] Kiev, Molod', 1962. 45 p.   DLC

1924. Kachanov, M. N. Kuba i mirnoe sosushchestvovanie [Cuba and peaceful coexistence] Vilnius, Mintis, 1964. 39 p.
In Lithuanian.

1925. Khrushchev, Nikita Sergeevich. Druzhba—naveki; rech' na mitinge sovetskoi i kubinskoi molodezhi v Kremle 2 iiunia 1962 goda [Eternal friendship; speech at a meeting of Soviet and Cuban youth in the Kremlin, June 1, 1962] Moscow, Gospolitizdat, 1962. 19 p.
F1776.3.R9K5
Relations with the USSR.

1926. ———. Sovremennoe mezhdunarodnoe polozhenie i vneshniaia politika Sovetskogo Soiuza; doklad na sessii Verkhovnogo Soveta SSSR 12 dekabria 1962 goda [The present-day international situation and the foreign policy of the Soviet Union; a report to the session of the Supreme Soviet on 12 December 1962] Moscow, Gospolitizdat, 1962. 63 p.
DLC

1927. Lukovets, Aleksei Illarionovich, *ed.* Narody SSSR i Kuby naveki vmeste; dokumenty sovetsko-kubinskoi druzhby [The peoples of the USSR and Cuba forever together; documents of Soviet-Cuban friendship] Moscow, Pravda, 1963. 446 p.   F1776.3.R9P7
Also published in Spanish.
Reviewed by S. L'vov in *Nov. mir*, v. 39, no. 8, Aug. 1963: 273–275; in *V mire knig*, v. 3, no. 8, Aug. 1963: 5.

1928. Ostroverkhyi, I. I. Krepnut' nashei druzhbe [Our friendly ties will grow stronger] Kiev, Znannia URSR, 1964. 48 p.
In Ukrainian.

1929. Abdurazakov, B. Kuba ne odinoka [Cuba is not alone] Komm. Uz., v. 34, no. 10, Oct. 1962: 85–92.

1930. Aleksandrov, A. Novyi povorot . . . kuda zhe? [A new turn . . . where to?] Mezhdunar. zhizn', v. 11, no. 2, Feb. 1964: 116–117.
Relations with Latin America.

1931. Andrianov, V. Nash drug Kuba [Cuba, our friend] Agitator, no. 10, May 1963: 7–9.
Relations with the USSR.

1932. Bitva v Punta-del'-Este [Battle in Punta del Este] Nov. vrem., v. 20, no. 5, Jan. 1962: 3.
Relations with Latin American countries.

1933. Blasco Cobo, Juan. Narody ne poddaiutsia nazhimu [The peoples resist this pressure] Mezhdunar. zhizn', v. 11, no. 10, Oct. 1964: 110.
Relations with Latin American countries.

1934. Borovik, Genrikh. Kuba-SSSR—druzhba! [Friendship between the USSR and Cuba!] Ogonek, v. 38, no. 8, Feb. 1960: 5.
Relations with the USSR.

1935. Bratstvo narodov SSSR i Kuby [Fraternal contacts between the peoples of the USSR and Cuba] Kuba, no. 3, Nov. 1964: 2–3.
Relations with the USSR.

1936. Burlak, A. Novyi pokhod protiv Kuby [A new campaign against Cuba] Mezhdunar. zhizn', v. 9, no. 3, Mar. 1962: 107–108.

1937. The Caribbean "Suez." World youth, no. 1, 1963: 58–60.
A critical evaluation of British policy in the Cuban problem.
Reprinted from *Challenge*, an English periodical.

1938. Drobot, G. Gavana, vas vyzyvaet Moskva! [Havana, Moscow is calling!] Radio, no. 12, Dec. 1960: 3.
Relations with the USSR.

1939. Druzhba i edinstvo [Friendship and unity] Nov. vrem., v. 21, no. 5, Feb. 1964: 1–2.
Relations with the USSR.

1940. Druzhba naveki [Everlasting friendship] Mol. mira, no. 5/6, 1962: 14–15.
Relations with the USSR.

1941. Eshche odin proval [One more failure] Nov. vrem., v. 21, no. 28, July 1963: 1–4.
Relations with the countries of Latin America.

1942. Faure Chomon Mediavil'ia; biograficheskaia spravka [Faure Chomón Mediavilla; a biographical note] Nov. vrem., v. 18, no. 39, Sept. 1960: 8.

1943. Gavana i Moskva [Havana and Moscow] Nov. vrem., v. 20, no. 19, May 1963: 1–3.
Relations with the USSR.

1944. Gavana i Moskva [Havana and Moscow] Nov. vrem., v. 21, no. 4, Jan. 1964: 1–2.
Relations with the USSR.

1945. Goriunov, D., *and* V. Kondrashov. Plamennyi golos Kuby [The fiery voice of Cuba] Ogonek, v. 38, no. 41, Oct. 1960: 26–27.
Fidel Castro at the session of the United Nations.

1946. IAroshevskii, B. Khartiia svobodnoi Ameriki [The charter of free America] Za rubezhom, no. 6, Feb. 1962: 5, 25.
The Second Havana Declaration.

1947. Joint action with Cuba envisaged, says Ben Bella. World student news, v. 16, no. 11/12, 1962: 2, 4.
Relations with Algeria.

1948. Kamynin, L. Solntse druzhby [The sun of friendship] Mezhdunar. zhizn', v. 11, no. 2, Feb. 1964: 106.
Relations with the USSR.

1949. Karlos Olivares Sanches; biograficheskaia spravka [Carlos Olivares Sánchez; a biographical note] Nov. vrem., v. 20, no. 30, July 1962: 19.

1950. Kartsev, A. Neudavshiisia "krestovyi pokhod" [Failure of a "crusade"] Mezhdunar. zhizn', v. 11, no. 9, Sept. 1964: 125–126.
Relations with Latin American countries.

1951. Levin, V. Napriazhennoe polozhenie v Karibskom basseine [Tension in the Caribbean region] Mir. ekon. i mezhdunar. otn., no. 10, Oct. 1959: 98–99.
Relations with the countries of Latin America.

1952. Listov, Vadim. Izmyshleniia generala Keibella [The fabrications of General Cabell] Nov. vrem., v. 17, no. 45, Nov. 1959: 31.
Political role of Russian advisers.

1953. L'vov, Sergei. Fidel' Kastro v Moskve [Fidel Castro in Moscow] Nov. vrem., v. 20, no. 19, May 1963: 8–9.
Relations with the USSR.

1954. Maiak ne pogasit' [They cannot extinguish this beacon light] Za rubezhom, no. 3, Jan. 1962: 1–2.
Relations with Latin American countries.

1955. Marini, Salvador. Zagovor protiv Kuby [A plot against Cuba] Za rubezhom, no. 3, Jan. 1962: 4–5.
Relations with Latin American countries.

1956. Mikhailov, S. Kubinskaia revoliutsiia i Latinskaia Amerika [The Cuban Revolution and Latin America] Mezhdunar. zhizn', v. 10, no. 12, Dec. 1963: 62–69.

1957. Mimo tseli [Wide of the mark] Nov. vrem., v. 19, no. 41, Oct. 1961: 23.
Relations with Argentina.

1958. Narody SSSR i Kuby—brat'ia naveki! [The peoples of the USSR and Cuba are brothers forever!] Sov. voin, v. 45, no. 10, May 1963: 1.

1959. Nesostoiatel'nye obvineniia [Groundless accusations] Nov. vrem., v. 18, no. 37, Sept. 1960: 23.
Establishment of diplomatic relations with China.

1960. Nezakonnaia rezoliutsiia [An illegal resolution] Nov. vrem., v. 22, no. 31, July 1964: 1–2.
Relations with the countries of Latin America.

1961. Politika razuma i mira [A policy of reason and peace] Mir. ekon. i mezhdunar. otn., no. 11, Nov. 1962: 3–6.
Soviet policy during the 1962 Cuban crisis.

1962. SSSR i Kuba [The USSR and Cuba] Nov. vrem., v. 18, no. 21, May 1960: 9–10.
Relations with the USSR.

1963. Sorvalos' [They didn't succeed] Za rubezhom, no. 5, Feb. 1962: 1–2.
Relations with Latin American countries.

1964. Sovety Vashingtona otvergnuty [They didn't accept the advice of Washington] Za rubezhom, no. 12, Sept. 1960: 4–5.
Relations with Latin American countries.

1965. Sovremennik. Vashington i Kuba [Washington and Cuba] Nov. vrem., v. 22, no. 33, Aug. 1964: 4–5.
Relations with Latin American countries.

1966. Vashingtonskaia "amplituda" [The "amplitude" of the Washington government] Za rubezhom, no. 49, Dec. 1961: 2–3.
Relations with Latin American countries.

1967. Vizit pravitel'stvennoi delegatsii Kuby v MNR [Visit of the Cuban Government delegation to Mongolia] Sovr. Mong., v. 6, no. 1, Jan. 1961: 8.
Relations with Mongolia.

1968. Zakrepit' dostignutoe [Consolidating the gains] Nov. vrem., v. 20, no. 49, Dec. 1962: 2–3.
Relations with the USSR.

1969. Zilliacus, Konni. Angliia v dni kubinskogo krizisa [England during the Cuban crisis] Nov. vrem., v. 20, no. 50, Dec. 1962: 3–4.

See also entries no. 715, 2160, 2203, 2212, 2217, 2220, 4796, and 4806.

b. Cuba and the United States

1970. Merin, B. M. Amerikano-kubinskie otnosheniia, 1959–1961 gg. [U.S. relations with Cuba, 1959–1961] Moscow, 1963. 19 p.

Author's abstract of a dissertation for the degree of Candidate in Historical Sciences.

1971. Nikiforov, B. S. Bor'ba kubinskogo naroda protiv amerikanskogo imperializma i vnutrennei reaktsii v 1944–1948 gg. [How the Cuban people struggled against American imperialism and internal reaction, 1944–1948] Moscow, 1962. 19 p.
Author's abstract of a dissertation for the degree of Candidate in Historical Sciences.

1972. Tri Ameriki; sbornik [Three Americas; collected articles] Moscow, Pravda, 1964. 80 p.   DLC
Relations with the United States.

1973. Aleksandrova, N. Amerikanskii imperializm i Kubinskaia revoliutsiia [American imperialism and the Cuban Revolution] Mezhdunar. zhizn', v. 10, no. 11, Nov. 1963: 119–121.
A review of William Appleman Williams' The United States, Cuba, and Castro (New York, Monthly Review Press, 1962. 179 p.).

1974. Andrianov, V. K poezdke Kastro v SShA [Castro's visit to the United States] Mezhdunar. zhizn', v. 6, no. 6, June 1959: 139–140.

1975. Bako, G. Tretii postradavshii [The third "injured party"] Nov. vrem., v. 19, no. 19, May 1961: 14–15.
The invasion of 1961 and the U.S. press.

1976. Bezrassudnaia igra s ognem [A foolish game with fire] Nov. vrem., v. 20, no. 44, Oct. 1962: 1–2.
The quarantine of 1962.

1977. Bil'shak, Vasyl'. Reportazh iz N'iu-Iorka [News story from New York] Sov. Ukr., v. 13, no. 1, Jan. 1963: 160–168.

1978. Bochkarev, IU. Ruki proch' ot Kuby! [Hands off Cuba!] Nov. vrem., v. 20, no. 39, Sept. 1962: 3–5.

1979. ———. Zaboty mistera Raska [Mr. Rusk's troubles] Nov. vrem., v. 20, no. 41, Oct. 1962: 8–10.

1980. Borisov, IA. Neob"iavlennaia voina protiv Kuby [An undeclared war against Cuba] Za rubezhom, no. 28, July 1962: 24.
Activities of Cuban refugees.

1981. Borisov, V. Ruki proch' ot Kuby! [Hands off Cuba!] Mezhdunar. zhizn', v. 8, no. 2, Feb. 1961: 117–118.

1982. Borovik, Genrikh. Piraty v vozdukhe i na vode [Pirates in the air and on the water] Ogonek, v. 38, no. 12, Mar. 1960: 4–5.

1983. ———. Ty pobedish', Kuba! [You will triumph, Cuba!] Ogonek, v. 39, no. 17, Apr. 1961: 6–7.

1984. Borovskii, V. Proschitaiutsia! [That will be their error!] Za rubezhom, no. 37, Sept. 1962: 1–2.
The possibility of U.S. intervention.

1985. Buchanan, Thomas G. Uoll-strit protiv Kastro [Wall Street against Castro] V zashch. mira, no. 6, June 1961: 2–9.

1986. Burlak, A. Opasnyi put' [A dangerous path] Mezhdunar. zhizn', v. 9, no. 10, Oct. 1962: 110.

1987. ———. Provokatsii protiv Kuby [Provocations against Cuba] Mezhdunar. zhizn', v. 6, no. 12, Dec. 1959: 120–121.

1988. Carrillo, Santiago. O nekotorykh aktual'nykh mezhdunarodnykh problemakh [Some pressing international problems] Probl. mira i sots., v. 6, no. 5, May 1963: 3–10.
The quarantine of 1962.

1989. Castro, Fidel. Ne otstupim! [We shan't retreat!] Za rubezhom, no. 5, July 1960: 7.

1990. ———. S takim narodom nado schitat'sia! [Such people must be reckoned with!] Mezhdunar. zhizn', v. 7, no. 3, Mar. 1960: 104–115.
An abbreviated translation from the Spanish.

1991. Codovilla, Victorio. Dolg i zadacha kommunistov [The duty and mission of Communists] Za rubezhom, no. 29, July 1963: 12–13.
The possibility of U.S. intervention.

1992. Domarco, Andrés. Agressivnye deistviia SShA protiv Kuby [Aggressive U.S. actions against Cuba] Mezhdunar. zhizn', v. 7, no. 12, Dec. 1960: 61–65.

1993. Dubravin, IA. Avantiurizm i verolomstvo—atributy amerikanskoi politiki [Recklessness and perfidiousness are the characteristic features of American foreign policy] Komm. Bel., v. 35, no. 5, May 1961: 61–65.

1994. Dymov, V. Chernaia gvardiia Pentagona [The black guard of the Pentagon] Nov. vrem., v. 20, no. 42, Oct. 1962: 12–15; v. 20, no. 44, Oct. 1962: 7–11.
Cuban refugees in the United States.

1995. Galí Menéndez, E. Polozhit' konets ekonomicheskoi blokade ostrova svobody [Put an end to the economic blockade of the island of freedom] Vsem. prof. dvizh., no. 11, Nov. 1964: 20–22.

1996. Gavanskaia deklaratsiia [The Havana Declaration] Vop. mezhdunar. prava, no. 4, 1962: 189–195.

1997. Gel'bak, P. SSSR—nadezhda i oplot mira; k itogam krizisa v raione Karibskogo moria [The USSR is the hope and mainstay of peace; results of the crisis in the Caribbean area] Kommunist (Vilnius), no. 12, 1962: 65–69.
The quarantine of 1962.

1998. Gerasimov, G. Novaia kniga Bertrana Rassela [Bertrand Russell's new book] Nov. vrem., v. 20, no. 22, May 1963: 30–31.
The quarantine of 1962.
A review of Bertrand Russell's *Unarmed Victory* (London, Penguin Books, 1963).

1999. Glavnaia tsel' [The most important objective] Nov. vrem., v. 19, no. 5, Jan. 1961: 20.
Relations with the United States.

2000. God spustia [A year later] Nov. vrem., v. 21, no. 42, Oct. 1963: 1–2.
The 1962 missile crisis.

2001. Gurkov, G. Mir pomnit, kak eto bylo [The world remembers how it was] Ogonek, v. 40, no. 52, Dec. 1962: 4–5.
The quarantine of 1962.

2002. Gvozdarev, B. V chem prichina rezkogo obostreniia otnoshenii mezhdu SShA i Kubinskoi respublikoi [The reason for the marked aggravation of relations between the U.S. and the Cuban Republic] Otv. na vop. trud., no. 111, 1960: 41–47.

2003. Ikh chelovek v Gavane [Their man in Havana] Nov. vrem., v. 17, no. 47, Nov. 1959: 22.
Rumors about Russian guided missile bases.

2004. Izakov, B. "Kubinskii krizis" [The "Cuban crisis"] Nov. vrem., v. 20, no. 45, Nov. 1962: 18–20.
The quarantine of 1962.

2005. ———. Peregovory prodolzhaiutsia [The negotiations continue] Nov. vrem., v. 20, no. 46, Nov. 1962: 8 10.
The quarantine of 1962.

2006. Kartsev, A. Opasnaia pozitsiia [A dangerous position] Mezhdunar. zhizn', v. 11, no. 6, June 1964: 104–105.
U.S. aerial supervision of Cuban territory.

2007. Khrushchev, N. S. Pokonchit' s politikoi na grani voiny; iz rechi v Kubinskom posol'stve v Moskve 2 ianvaria 1961 goda [Let us do away with the "brink of war" policy; from a speech of January 2, 1961 in the Cuban Embassy in Moscow] Nov. vrem., v. 19, no. 2, Jan. 1961: 4–5.
Relations with the United States.

2008. Korionov, V. Mertvyi khvataet zhivogo [The dead hand of the past weighs heavily upon the present] Za rubezhom, no. 5, July 1960: 8.
The possibility of U.S. intervention.

2009. Kruglov, M. Neudachi Vashingtona v bor'be protiv Kuby [The failures of Washington in the struggle against Cuba] Nov. vrem., v. 19, no. 35, Aug. 1961: 11–13.

2010. Krymov, B. Kubinskoi revoliutsii— zhit'! [The Cuban Revolution will survive!] Rabotnitsa, v. 40, no. 2, Feb. 1962: 24.

2011. Kuba i Soedinennye Shtaty [Cuba and the United States] Nov. vrem., v. 18, no. 31, July 1960: 2–3.

2012. Kuba na strazhe [Cuba is alert] Za rubezhom, no. 4, Jan. 1961: 3–4.
The threat of U.S. intervention.

2013. Kubinskaia maniia Vashingtona [Washington's Cuban mania] Nov. vrem., v. 19, no. 47, Nov. 1961: 2–3.

2014. Kube ne zapugat'! [They cannot intimidate Cuba!] Za rubezhom, no. 21, Nov. 1960: 2–3.
The possibility of U.S. intervention.

2015. Kurdiumov, N. "Inertsiia bezumiia" [The "inertia of insanity"] Mezhdunar. zhizn', v. 11, no. 4, Apr. 1964: 122–123.

2016. Lemus, Germán. Esli oni napadaiut na nas . . . to eto potomu, chto my idem po puti progressa [If they attack us . . . it is because we follow the path of progress] Vsem. stud. nov., v. 14, no. 10, Oct. 1960: 22–23.

2017. ———. My khorosho usvoili nash urok [We have learned our lesson well] Vsem. stud. nov., v. 14, no. 6, June 1960: 5–7.

2018. Leont'ev, Boris. O politike razumnogo kompromissa [The policy of reasonable compromise] Nov. vrem., v. 20, no. 47, Nov. 1962: 2–4.
The quarantine of 1962.

2019. Levin, V. V karibskom more nespokoino [There is trouble in the Caribbean area] Nov. vrem., v. 20, no. 14, Apr. 1962: 13–14.
The possibility of U.S. intervention.

2020. The limit of power. World student news, v. 18, no. 5, 1964: 2–4.
U.S. reconnaissance flights over Cuba.

2021. Listov, V. Porazhenie amerikanskoi diplomatii v Punta-del'-Este [The defeat of American diplomacy at Punta del Este] Nov. vrem., v. 20, no. 7, Feb. 1962: 7–9.

2022. ———. Vokrug "operatsii Kondor" ["Operation Condor"] Nov. vrem., v. 19, no. 44, Oct. 1961: 20–21.
The possibility of U.S. intervention.

2023. Marinello, Juan. Zagovor protiv Kuby [The plot against Cuba] Nov. vrem., v. 17, no. 27, July 1959: 20–21.

2024. Matveev, V. Golos Bertrana Rassela [The voice of Bertrand Russell] Za rubezhom, no. 44, Nov. 1962: 7.
English philosopher's protest against the quarantine of 1962.

2025. Merin, B. M. K istorii razryva diplomaticheskikh otnoshenii mezhdu SShA i

Kuboi, 1959-ianvar' 1961 [On the history of the severance of diplomatic relations between the United States and Cuba, 1959–January 1961] Uch. zap. MOPI, v. 115, 1963: 221–253.

2026. Mir za nedeliu [The world events of this week] Za rubezhom, no. 40, Oct. 1962: 2.
U.S. preparations for a quarantine.

2027. Mykhal'chuk, M. Ruky het' vid Kuby! [Keep away from Cuba!] Ukraina, no. 19, Oct. 1962: 2.

2028. Naemniki TsRU [Mercenaries of the CIA] Za rubezhom, no. 39, Sept. 1964: 2.
Activities of Cuban refugees.

2029. Ne zaryvat'sia! [Don't go too far!] Nov. vrem., v. 20, no. 9, Feb. 1962: 3.

2030. Neobkhodimaia iasnost' [A timely clarification] Nov. vrem., v. 20, no. 10, Mar. 1963: 2–3.

2031. Nepomniashchii, K. Kto dal pravo? [Who gave you this right?] Ogonek, v. 40, no. 44, Oct. 1962: 2–3.
The quarantine of 1962.

2032. Nitoburg, E. L. Review. Nov. i noveish. ist., no. 3, 1962: 147–150.
A review of Robert F. Smith's *The United States and Cuba; Business and Diplomacy, 1917–1960* (New York, Bookman Associates [1961] 256 p.).

2033. No pasarán![They shall not pass!] Za rubezhom, no. 2, Jan. 1961: 4.
The possibility of U.S. intervention.

2034. Novyi afront [A new affront] Nov. vrem., v. 19, no. 3, Jan. 1961: 2–3.

2035. Novyi etap agressii [The new stage of aggression] Za rubezhom, no. 35, Sept. 1962: 3.
Activities of Cuban refugees.

2036. Obespechit' mir i bezopasnost' narodov! [We must preserve peace and ensure the security of nations] Agitator, no. 21, Nov. 1962: 3–5.

2037. Opasnye igry [Dangerous games] Za rubezhom, no. 39, Sept. 1963: 2.
Activities of Cuban refugees.

2038. Otravlennoe oruzhie [The poisoned weapons] Nov. vrem., v. 18, no. 19, May 1960: 24–25.
The Cuban Revolution and the U.S. press.

2039. Pakin, A. Kuba ne budet vtoroi Gvatemaloi [Cuba will not be another Guatemala] Agitator, no. 18, Sept. 1960: 22–23.

2040. Pakin, S. Proiski bankrotov [The machinations of political bankrupts] Mezhdunar. zhizn', v. 8, no. 11, Nov. 1961: 120–122.

2041. Paramonov, V. Bol'shaia lozh' "bol'shoi pressy"; o novoi provokatsionnoi kampanii protiv geroicheskoi Kuby v amerikanskoi pechati [The big lie of the "big press"; a new provocative campaign against heroic Cuba in the American press] Za rubezhom, no. 36, Sep. 1962: 5.

2042. ———. Pristup isterii [A hysterical fit] Za rubezhom, no. 38, Sept. 1962: 1–2.

2043. ———. Vashington i ten' "U-2" [Washington and the shadow of the "U-2"] Za rubezhom, no. 19, May 1964: 5.
The flights of U.S. reconnaissance planes.

2044. Pavlenko, A. Porazhenie amerikanskogo imperializma na Kube [The defeat of American imperialism in Cuba] Mezhdunar. zhizn', v. 6, no. 2, Feb. 1959: 122–123.

2045. Pidstupy imperialistiv proty Kuby [The intrigues of imperialists against Cuba] Blok. agit. [Ukr.] no. 7, Mar. 1960: 55–59.

2046. Piraty u beregov Kuby [Pirates off the shores of Cuba] Za rubezhom, no. 14, Apr. 1963: 10.
The raids of Cuban refugees.

2047. Piraty-atomshchiki [Pirates with atomic weapons] Za rubezhom, no. 43, Oct. 1962: 1–2.
The quarantine of 1962.

2048. Pis'mo amerikanskikh fermerov prezidentu Eizenkhaueru [A letter from American farmers to President Eisenhower] Nov. vrem., v. 18, no. 36, Sept. 1960: 24.

2049. Po staromu obraztsu [Old patterns] Nov. vrem., v. 18, no. 3, Jan. 1960: 22–23.
The possibility of U.S. intervention.

2050. Poliakov, V. Kubinskaia revoliutsiia i SShA [The Cuban Revolution and the

United States] Mezhdunar. zhizn', v. 10, no. 1, Jan. 1963: 154–157.

A review of Herbert L. Matthews' *The Cuban Story* (New York, George Braziller, 1961. 318 p.).

2051. Poliakovskii, V. Grozovye tuchi nad Kuboi [Storm clouds over Cuba] Za rubezhom, no. 2, Jan. 1961: 8–9.

The possibility of U.S. intervention.

2052. Pravoe delo Kuby [Cuba's just cause] Nov. vrem., v. 18, no. 46, Nov. 1960: 3–4.

2053. Prestupnaia blokada [An unlawful blockade] Za rubezhom, no. 41, Oct. 1962: 2.

2054. Profsoiuzy trebuiut sniat' blokadu protiv Kuby [Trade unions demand lifting the blockade against Cuba] Vsem. prof. dvizh., no. 2, Feb. 1964: 40.

2055. Proiski protiv Kuby [Intrigues against Cuba] Za rubezhom, no. 17, Oct. 1960: 4.

Possibility of U.S. intervention.

2056. Protiv ugrozy interventsii SShA na Kube [Against the menace of U.S. intervention in Cuba] Probl. mira i sots., v. 2, no. 1, 1959: 69–70.

2057. Rancaño, José María. Soobshchniki [Accomplices] Vsem. prof. dvizh., no. 12, Dec. 1962: 18–19.

The quarantine of 1962.

2058. Revoliutsiia idet vpered [The revolution is marching forward] Za rubezhom, no. 15, Apr. 1961: 4–5.

The possibility of U.S. intervention.

2059. Sartre, Jean Paul. Naemniki protiv Kuby [Mercenaries against Cuba] Inostr. lit., no. 8, Aug. 1961: 234–241.

Translated from the French.

2060. Sergeeva, N. Dni, kogda vse viselo na voloske [The days when everything was hanging by a thread] Nov. vrem., v. 20, no. 45, Nov. 1962: 14–17.

The quarantine of 1962.

2061. Snova agressiia? [Aggression again?] Za rubezhom, no. 48, Dec. 1961: 2.

Activities of Cuban refugees.

2062. Snova TsRU [The CIA again] Nov. vrem., v. 21, no. 25, July 1964: 21.

Military action of Cuban refugees.

2063. Sosnov, V. Uroki Kubinskogo krizisa [Lessons of the Cuban crisis] Komm. Sov. Latvii, v. 17, no. 12, Dec. 1962: 68–71.

The quarantine of 1962.

2064. Sotnikov, I. O prave na razboi; replika Uolteru Lippmanu [On the right to rob; an answer to Walter Lippman] Nov. vrem., v. 19, no. 30, July 1961: 22–23.

The possibility of U.S. intervention.

2065. Soto Díaz, Jesús. Kubintsy i Vashington [The Cubans and Washington] Nov. vrem., no. 50, Dec. 1961: 18–19.

2066. Sovremennik. Fidel' Kastro i Dzhon Kennedi [Fidel Castro and John Kennedy] Nov. vrem., v. 19, no. 18, May 1961: 12–14.

2067. Strel'nikov, Boris. Kogda mir visel na voloske; reportazh iz N'iu-Iorka [When peace hung by a thread; a news story from New York] Ogonek, v. 40, no. 47, Nov. 1962: 25–27.

The quarantine of 1962.

2068. Torzhestvo leninskoi politiki mirnogo sosushchestvovaniia [A triumph of the Leninist policy of peaceful coexistence] Kommunist, v. 39, no. 18, Dec. 1962: 12–19.

The quarantine of 1962.

2069. Toska po proshlomu [The good old days] Nov. vrem., v. 18, no. 36, Sept. 1960: 24.

2070. Ugroza ne minovala [The threat isn't removed] Za rubezhom, no. 18, May 1961: 4.

The possibility of U.S. intervention.

2071. Ugroza vozrastaet [A growing menace] Za rubezhom, no. 26, Dec. 1960: 4.

The possibility of U.S. intervention.

2072. V plenu otzhivshikh kontseptsii [Prisoners of obsolete conceptions] Nov.vrem., v. 18, no. 29, July 1960: 21.

2073. Vazhnaia vekha [A significant landmark] Nov. vrem., v. 20, no. 3, Jan. 1963: 1–2.

2074. Verevochka tianetsia v Vashington [The string leads to Washington] Za rubezhom, no. 37, Sept. 1963: 3.

Activities of Cuban refugees.

2075. Vmeste s Kuboi protiv amerikanskikh imperialistov [With Cuba against the American imperialists] Vsem. prof. dvizh., no. 12, Dec. 1962: 17–18.

2076. Voprosy bez otveta [The questions weren't answered] Za rubezhom, no. 7, Feb. 1962: 2.
The possibility of U.S. intervention.

2077. Vtoraia Gavanskaia deklaratsiia; narod Kuby—narodam Ameriki i vsego mira [The Second Havana Declaration; an appeal of the Cuban people to the nations of America and the whole world] Vop. mezhdunar. prava, no. 4, 1962: 196–227.

2078. Zagovor "beshenykh" [A plot of the "possessed"] Za rubezhom, no. 7, Feb. 1964: 2.
The possibility of U.S. intervention.

2079. Zagovor protiv narodov [A plot against the peoples] Ogonek, v. 40, no. 44, Oct. 1962: 2.
The quarantine of 1962.

2080. Zaslavskii, D. Pozhaluista, bez isteriki [Please, without hysterics] Nov. vrem., v. 18, no. 24, June 1960: 18–19.
The U.S. reaction to N.S. Khrushchev's plan to visit Cuba.

2081. Zbanats'kyi, IUrii. Khai zhyne chorna prymara! [Let this black shadow be dispelled!] Ukraina, no. 24, Dec. 1962: 4.
The quarantine of 1962.

See also entries no. 369, 370, 373, 378, 464, 468, and 2527.

c. *Reaction Abroad to the Cuban Revolution*

2082. Alvarez, Pedro Francisco. Batistu postigla sud'ba Khimenesa [Batista follows Pérez Jiménez] Vsem. stud. nov., v. 13, no. 3/4, Mar.-Apr. 1959: 3.

2083. Andrianov, V. Vmeste s Kuboi—milliony [Cuba has millions of friends] Agitator, no. 5, Mar. 1962: 21–22.

2084. Borisov, V. Dva podkhoda: "Kubinskii krizis" i zarubezhnaia pechat' [Two points of view; the "Cuban crisis" and the foreign press] Za rubezhom, no. 46, Nov. 1962: 15.

2085. Carrión, Benjamín. My ne stanem rabami [We shall never be slaves] Za rubezhom, no. 3, Jan. 1962: 5.

2086. Chudesnyi splav [A wonderful fusion] Nov. vrem., v. 20, no. 17, Apr. 1963: 3.

2087. Druz'ia i vragi Kuby [Cuba's friends and enemies] Za rubezhom, no. 13, Mar. 1963: 1.

2088. Ferrer, Raúl. Kuba—da! IAnki—net! [Cuba—yes! Yankee—no!] Ogonek, v. 38, no. 40, Oct. 1960: 9.

2089. Forum v Gavane [A forum in Havana] Za rubezhom, no. 4, Jan. 1962: 2.

2090. Gorbachev, B. My s toboi, Kuba! [We are with you, Cuba!] Agitator, no. 14, July 1964: 22–24.

2091. Gorev, I. Byt' na cheku! [Be on the alert!] Sov. profsoiuzy, v. 17, no. 9, May 1961: 43–44.

2092. Guevara, Ernesto. Kuba i "plan Kennedi" [Cuba and "The Kennedy Plan"] Probl. mira i sots., v. 5, no. 2, Feb. 1962: 27–33.

2093. Hands off Cuba! World student news, v. 16, no. 11/12, 1962: 6–10.

2094. Ignat'ev, Oleg. Golos kontinenta [Voice of a continent] Ogonek, v. 41, no. 15, Apr. 1963: 8.

2095. ———. Oni zashchishchaiut ostrov svobody [They defend the island of freedom] Nov. vrem., v. 20, no. 15, Apr. 1963: 11–12.

2096. Internatsional'nyi dolg [Our international duty] Nov. vrem., v. 18, no. 30, July 1960: 1–2.
Russian support of Cuba.

2097. Kak osushchestvliaetsia latinoamerikanskaia solidarnost' [Latin American solidarity takes effect] Vsem. prof. dvizh., no. 10, Oct. 1960: 20–21.

2098. "Kuba—da!"—govoriat narody Azii i Afriki ["Cuba—yes," the peoples of Asia and Africa say] Az. i Afr. seg., no. 5, May 1961: 35.

2099. "Kuba—da, ianki—net!" [Cuba—yes, Yankee—no!"] Mol. mira, no. 5, 1961: 23.

2100. Kuba—nadezhda Latinskoi Ameriki [Cuba is Latin America's hope] Inostr. lit., no. 3, Mar. 1962: 279–280.

2101. Kubinskaia revoliutsiia nepobedima [The Cuban Revolution is invincible] Vsem. prof. dvizh., no. 5, May 1961: 4–6.

2102. Latino-amerikantsy vmeste s Kuboi [The Latin Americans support Cuba] Za rubezhom, no. 22, Nov. 1960: 5.

2103. Latinskaia Amerika—za Kubu [Latin America supports Cuba] Nov. vrem., v. 20, no. 6, Feb. 1962: 2–3.

2104. Leont'ev, Boris. Chto dal'she? Mirovoe obshchestvennoe mnenie i kubinskii krizis [What next? World public opinion and the Cuban crisis] Nov. vrem., v. 20, no. 51, Dec. 1962: 11–13.

2105. Levin, V. Kongress solidarnosti s Kuboi [A congress of solidarity with Cuba] Mezhdunar. zhizn', v. 10, no. 5, May 1963: 110–111.

2106. Luk'ianov, IU. Narody s toboi, ostrov svobody! [The peoples are with you, island of freedom!] Sov. profsoiuzy, v. 18, no. 5, Mar. 1962: 42.

2107. Maldonado, Alberto. My pomnim slova Bolivara [We remember the words of Bolívar] Za rubezhom, no. 2, Jan. 1961: 20.

2108. Mezhdunarodnaia dobrovol'naia trudovaia brigada na Kube [An international volunteer work brigade in Cuba] Mol. mira, no. 12, 1960: 8–9.

2109. "My obiazany podderzhivat' Kubu" ["We must support Cuba"] Inostr. lit., no. 10, Oct. 1962: 285.
A group of Ecuadorian writers supports the Cuban Revolution.

2110. My riadom s Kuboi! [We are with Cuba!] Nov. vrem., v. 22, no. 43, Oct. 1964: 5–6.

2111. My s toboi, Kuba! [We are with you, Cuba!] Az. i Afr. seg., no. 10, Oct. 1962: 58.

2112. Nam pishet Lionel' Soto [Lionel Soto's letter to our editor] Vsem. stud. nov., v. 13, no. 6, June 1959: 24.

2113. Narody Kuby i Kongo, my podderzhivaem vas! [Peoples of Cuba and the Congo, we are behind you!] Kitai, no. 4, Feb. 1959: 4.
Support by Communist countries.

2114. Narody svitu z toboiu, Kubo! [The peoples of the world are with you, Cuba!] Ukraina, no. 9, May 1962: 16–17.

2115. Nepomniashchii, K. Kuba—da, da, da! [Cuba—yes, yes, and yes!] Ogonek, v. 40, no. 4, Jan. 1962: 4–5.

2116. "Net—agressii!" govorit Latinskaia Amerika ["There must be no aggression," Latin America says] Za rubezhom, no. 44, Nov. 1962: 6.

2117. Pearl, W. Bor'ba kanadskikh profsoiuzov v podderzhku naroda Kuby [Canadian trade unions fight to win support for the Cuban people] Vsem. prof. dvizh., no. 3, Mar. 1961: 31–32.

2118. Poliakovskii, Vadim. Kuba ne odinoka [Cuba isn't alone] Za rubezhom, no. 36, Sept. 1964: 5.

2119. Poslanie Benkhamina Karriona [A message from Benjamín Carrión] Inostr. lit., no. 11, Nov. 1961: 281.
Support of the Cuban Revolution in Ecuador.

2120. Poteriali samoobladanie [They couldn't control themselves] Nov. vrem., v. 19, no. 19, May 1961: 25.
Demonstrations against the United States in Colombia.

2121. Rabochie vsego mira privetstvuiut bol'shuiu pobedu kubinskogo naroda [Workers of the whole world greet the great victory of the Cuban people] Vsem. prof. dvizh., no. 2, Feb. 1959: 4–6.

2122. Ramírez, Angelo. Urugvaitsy na storone Kuby [The people of Uruguay are on Cuba's side] Nov. vrem., v. 19, no. 28, July 1961: 14.

2123. Rancaño, José María. Souchastniki agressii [Accomplices in the aggression] Vsem. prof. dvizh., no. 6, June 1961: 10–14.
The attitude of free trade unions to the Cuban Revolution.

2124. Rodrigo, José. Latinskaia Amerika podnimaetsia na zashchitu Kuby [Latin America comes to the defense of Cuba] Vsem. prof. dvizh., no. 4, Apr. 1962: 22–25.

2125. Solidarnost' s bor'boi Kuby i Venesuely [Solidarity with the struggle of Cuba and Venezuela] Vsem. prov. dvizh., no. 8/9, Aug.-Sept. 1960: 16–17.

2126. Solidarnost' s Kuboi [Solidarity with Cuba] Probl. mira i sots., v. 5, no. 11, Nov. 1962: 50.

2127. Solidarnost' s revoliutsionnoi Kuboi [Solidarity with revolutionary Cuba] Probl. mira i sots., v. 3, no. 11, Nov. 1960: 68–69.

2128. Solidarnost' so svobodnoi Kuboi [Solidarity with free Cuba] Probl. mira i sots., v. 2, no. 4, Apr. 1959: 79–80.
   U.S. Communist Party's support of Cuba.

2129. Tarasov, K. Kubinskaia revoliutsiia i latinoamerikantsy [The Cuban Revolution and Latin Americans] Nov. vrem., v. 19, no. 11, Mar. 1961: 3–5.

2130. V zashchitu kubinskogo naroda [In defense of the Cuban people] Inostr. lit., no. 12, Dec. 1960: 254.
   Bulgaria supports the Cuban people.

2131. V zashchitu Kubinskoi revoliutsii [In defense of the Cuban Revolution] Inostr. lit., no. 5, May 1961: 277–278.
   A group of Mexican intellectuals supports Cuba.

2132. V zashchitu Kubinskoi revoliutsii [In defense of the Cuban Revolution] Inostr. lit., no. 1, Jan. 1962: 273.
   Argentina's attitude toward the Cuban Revolution.

2133. Vpered, kubintsy! [Forward, Cubans!] Za rubezhom, no. 16, Apr. 1961: 3.

2134. Z Kuboiu—vse peredove liudstvo [All progressive mankind is with Cuba] Blok. agit. [Ukr.] v. 29, no. 7, Mar. 1962: 27.

2135. Zaiavlenie Pablo Nerudy [A statement by Pablo Neruda] Inostr. lit., no. 4, Apr. 1961: 281.
   See also entries no. 1482, 1637, 1649, and 2318.

8. Dominican Republic

2136. Dominikanskaia "iazva" [The Dominican "plague"] Nov. vrem., v. 18, no. 20, May 1960: 22.
   Relations with Latin American countries.

2137. Gerter i Trukhil'o [Herter and Trujillo] Nov. vrem., v. 18, no. 35, Aug. 1960: 22.

2138. Griaznaia igra [A dirty trick] Nov. vrem., v. 19, no. 1, Jan. 1961: 26.
   Relations with the United States.

2139. I na orla i na reshku [Betting on both sides of the coin] Za rubezhom, no. 51, Dec. 1962: 4.
   Political influence of the United States.

2140. Interventsiia na Gaiti [Intervention on "Haiti Island" (Hispaniola)] Nov. vrem., v. 18, no. 7, Feb. 1960: 22.
   The landing of U.S. marines.

2141. Levin, V. Snova "bol'shaia dubinka" [Once more the policy of a "big stick"] Mezhdunar. zhizn', v. 9, no. 1, Jan. 1962: 123–124.
   Relations with the United States.

2142. Morskaia pekhota i demokratiia [The Marines and democracy] Nov. vrem., v. 19, no. 48, Nov. 1961: 2–3.
   Relations with the United States.

2143. Osuzhdennye v San-Khose: Trukhil'o i SShA [Trujillo and the U.S.A. were denounced in San José] Za rubezhom, no. 11, Aug. 1960: 4.

   See also entry no. 911.

9. Ecuador

2144. V posol'stve zveniat stekla [The smashed windows of an embassy] Za rubezhom, no. 28, Dec. 1960: 5.
   Demonstrations against the United States.

10. Guatemala

2145. Spirin, V. G. Natsional'no-osvoboditel'naia bor'ba gvatemal'skogo naroda i agressiia SShA protiv Gvatemaly, 1951–1954 gg. [The national liberation struggle of the Guatemalan people and U.S. aggression against Guatemala, 1951–1954] [Moscow] 1962. (Institut mezhdunarodnykh otnoshenii)
   Abstract of a dissertation for the degree of Candidate in Historical Sciences.

11. The Guianas

2146. Poslanie Cheddi Dzhagana "Novomu vremeni" [A letter from Cheddi Jagan to "Novoe vremia"] Nov. vrem., v. 20, no. 3, Jan. 1963: 3.
   British Guiana.

12. Haiti

2147. Diktator perestaralsia [The dictator has overdone it this time] Nov. vrem., v. 20, no. 39, Sept. 1962: 22–23.
Relations with the United States.

2148. Grigor'ev, IA. G.   Narod Gaiti daet otpor kolonizatoram SShA [The Haitian people rebuff U.S. colonizers] Vop. ist., v. 38, no. 1, Jan. 1963: 172–173.
A review of an article by A. Martén in *Cuba socialista*, no. 9, 1962: 67–85.

2149. Koval'skaia, A. S.   Angliiskii zhurnal zashchishchaet kolonizatorov SShA [How an English periodical defends U.S. colonizers] Vop. ist., no. 12, Dec. 1962: 177–178.
Relations with the United States.

2150. Neozhidannyi vyvod [An unexpected conclusion] Nov. vrem., v. 20, no. 35, Aug. 1962: 26.
Relations with the United States.

2151. Operetka s posledstviiami [A comic opera with some consequences] Nov. vrem., v. 17, no. 35, Aug. 1959: 24.
Relations with Cuba.

13. Honduras

2152. Tuchi nad Gondurasom [Clouds over Honduras] Nov. vrem., v. 19, no. 8, Feb. 1961: 20.
Relations with Nicaragua.

14. Mexico

2153. Velasco Gil, Carlos M.   Nashi dobrye sosedi; amerikano-meksikanskie otno-sheniia [Our good neighbors; Mexican relations with the United States] Moscow, Izd-vo inostr. lit., 1959. 360 p.
Translated by M. N. Deev and G. K. Sergeev from the Spanish *Nuestros buenos vecinos*. Introductory article by A. F. Shul'govskii.
Reviewed by L. Slezkin in *Nov. vrem*, no. 51, Dec. 1959: 28–29.

2154. Afanas'eva, O.   Trevogi Vashingtona [Washington's anxieties] Mezhdunar. zhizn', v. 11, no. 5, May 1964: 113–114.
Relations with France.

2155. Argón Rebolledo, Eliseo.   Vneshniaia politika Meksiki [The foreign policy of Mexico] Nov. vrem., v. 20, no. 22, May 1963: 20–22.

2156. Dobrososedstvo po-amerikanski [The "good neighbor policy," American style] Nov. vrem., v. 19, no. 24, June 1961: 25–26.
Relations with the United States and Cuba.

2157. Dymov, V.   Kozni severnogo soseda [Intrigues of the northern neighbor] Mezhdunar. zhizn', v. 11, no. 10, Oct. 1964: 111–112.
Relations with the United States (the Colorado River problem).

2158. Gabriel' Lusio Arguel'es; biografiche-skaia spravka [Gabriel Lucio Argüelles; a biographical note] Nov. vrem., v. 19, no. 41, Oct. 1961: 30.

2159. Lapshev, E.   Vneshniaia politika Meksiki [The foreign policy of Mexico] Mezhdunar. zhizn', v. 11, no. 9, Sept. 1964: 64–70.

2160. Nazhim na Meksiku [Pressure upon Mexico] Za rubezhom, no. 23, June 1961: 4–5.
Relations with Cuba.

2161. Pavlenko, A.   Neudachnaia missiia [An unsuccessful mission] Mezhdunar. zhizn', v. 8, no. 3, Mar. 1961: 138–139.
Relations with Peru.

2162. Sizonenko, A.   Sovetskii Soiuz i Meksika; k 40-letiiu ustanovleniia diplo-maticheskikh otnoshenii [The Soviet Union and Mexico; on the 40th anniversary of the establishment of diplomatic relations] Nov. vrem., v. 22, no. 32, Aug. 1964: 6.

2163. Unzueta, Gerardo.   Sol' na poliakh Mekhikali [Salt covers the fields of the Mexicali Valley] Za rubezhom, no. 28, July 1962: 24.
The Colorado River problem.

2164. Vyzov Soedinennym Shtatam [A challenge to the United States] Za rubezhom, no. 12, Mar. 1964: 2–3.
Relations with France.

2165. Za slovami o "vzaimoponimanii" [Behind the assertions on a "mutual understanding"] Za rubezhom, no. 9, Feb. 1964: 3.
Foreign policy.

See also entry no. 2203.

15. Nicaragua

2166. Ikh chelovek v Managua [Their man in Managua] Nov. vrem., v. 19, no. 4, Jan. 1961: 20.
U.S. diplomats.

See also entry no. 2152.

16. Panama; the Panama Canal Problem

2167. Gonionskii, Semen Aleksandrovich. Panama—panamtsam [Panama for the Panamanians] Moscow, Gospolitizdat, 1963. 62 p.   DLC
The Panama Canal problem.

2168. Alba, Orso. Panama v bor'be za natsional'nyi suverenitet [Panama's struggle for national sovereignty] Probl. mira i sots., v. 7, no. 4, Apr. 1964: 14–15.

2169. Bel'skaia, A. Panama v ogne [Panama in flame] Rabotnitsa, no. 2, Feb. 1964: 25.

2170. Chichkov, V. Buntuiushchaia Panama [Rebellious Panama] Ogonek, v. 37, no. 52, Dec. 1959: 22–23.

2171. Dixon, Félix. Panama [Panama] Vsem. prof. dvizh., no. 8/9, Aug.-Sept. 1960: 11–12.

2172. Fuentes, Pedro. Solidarnost' s narodom Panamy [Solidarity with the Panamanian people] Probl. mira i sots., v. 7, no. 2, Feb. 1964: 78.

2173. Galin, S. Krovavye sobytiia v Paname [Bloodshed in Panama] Otv. na vop. trud., no. 2, Feb. 1964: 42–46.

2174. Gonionskii, S. Zatiazhnoi krizis vokrug Panamy [A lingering crisis in Panama] Nov. vrem., v. 22, no. 43, Oct. 1964: 21–23.

2175. Gvozdarev, B. Panama—dlia panamtsev [Panama for the Panamanians] Mezhdunar. zhizn', v. 7, no. 1, Jan. 1960: 122–123.

2176. Gvozdev, IU. IAnki, kanal i Panama [Yankees, the Canal, and Panama] Nov. vrem., v. 21, no. 3, Jan. 1964: 10–12.

2177. Hincker, Michel. Panama [Panama] V zashch. mira, no. 98/99, July-Aug. 1959: 81–87.

2178. Izakov, Boris. Smysl sobytii v Paname [The meaning of the events in Panama] Nov. vrem., v. 21, no. 4, Jan. 1964: 7–9.

2179. Kanal i natsional'nyi suverenitet [The Canal and national sovereignty] Vsem. stud. nov., v. 14, no. 2, Feb. 1960: 20.

2180. Karev, Nikolai. Vzryv v Paname [An explosion in Panama] Za rubezhom, no. 3, Jan. 1964: 3.

2181. Latinskaia Amerika segodnia: Panama [Latin America today: Panama] Mezhdunar. zhizn', v. 10, no. 3, Mar. 1963: 152–154.

2182. Okuneva, M. Khishchnik byl togda molodym [When the beast of prey was young] Mezhdunar. zhizn', v. 9, no. 10, Oct. 1962: 78–85.

2183. Orekhov, F. Krovavyi chetverg [Bloody Thursday] Mezhdunar. zhizn', v. 11, no. 2, Feb. 1964: 117.

2184. Panama: "IAnki, ubiraites' von!" [Panama: "Yankees, get out!"] Mol. mira, no. 3, 1960: 23.

2185. Panama and the canal. World student news, v. 18, no. 2, 1964: 2–4.

2186. Panama diary. World student news, v. 18, no. 2, 1964: 5–6.

2187. Panama protestuet [Panama protests] Nov. vrem., v. 17, no. 47, Nov. 1959: 24.

2188. Panama '64. World student news, v. 18, no. 4, 1964: 11–13.

2189. Panamskaia bomba [The Panamanian "bomb"] Nov. vrem., v. 18, no. 23, June 1960: 19–20.

2190. Panamskie "smut'iany" ["Troublemakers" in Panama] Nov. vrem., v. 18, no. 7, Feb. 1960: 24.

2191. Panamskii intsident [Panamanian incident] Nov. vrem., v. 17, no. 19, May 1959: 17–18.

2192. Panamskii kanal; spravka [The Panama Canal; an information note] Mezhdunar. zhizn', v. 11, no. 3, Mar. 1964: 144.

2193. Panamskoe "nedorazumenie" [Panamanian "misunderstanding"] Nov. vrem., v. 17, no. 49, Dec. 1959: 19.

2194. Pavlenko, A. Krizis prodolzhaetsia [The crisis continues] Mezhdunar. zhizn', v. 11, no. 3, Mar. 1964: 114–115.

2195. Po zakonu dzhunglei [Jungle law] Nov. vrem., v. 17, no. 46, Nov. 1959: 23–24.

2196. Poliakovskii, V. "IAnki, ubiraites' domoi!" ["Yankees, go home!"] Za rubezhom, no. 6, July 1960: 8.

2197. ———. Reportazh iz panamskoi "zony" [A news story from the Panama Canal "Zone"] Ogonek, v. 42, no. 6, Feb. 1964: 4.

2198. ———. Mezhdu stenoi i shpagoi [Between the wall and the sword] Za rubezhom, no. 5, Feb. 1964: 9.

2199. Rancaño, José María. Krovoprolitie v Paname [Bloodshed in Panama] Vsem. prof. dvizh., no. 2, Feb. 1964: 24.

2200. Sychev, M. K sobytiiam v Paname [Political events in Panama] Agitator, no. 3, Feb. 1964: 56.

2201. V bor'be za suverenitet [In the struggle for sovereignty] Probl. mira i sots., v. 3, no. 5, May 1960: 77.

2202. Zabyraites' dodomu, gringos! [Go home, gringos!] Ukraina, no. 12, June 1960: 3.

See also entries no. 469, 470, 1319, and 2947.

17. Peru

2203. Nelegkaia sluzhba [A difficult assignment] Nov. vrem., v. 19, no. 6, Feb. 1961: 23.
Relations with Mexico and Cuba.

2204. Skol'ko stoiat printsipy [How much they pay for principles] Nov. vrem., v. 19, no. 40, Sept. 1961: 21.
Relations with the United States.

2205. Tuchnin, R. Peruanskii virazh Vashingtona [A change in Washington's Peruvian policy] Nov. vrem., v. 20, no. 35, Aug. 1962: 21–23.
Relations with the United States.

2206. Viktor Andres Belaunde; biograficheskaia spravka [Victor Andrés Belaúnde; a biographical note] Nov. vrem., v. 17, no. 43, Oct. 1959: 31.

2207. Vizit s podoplekoi [A visit with a background] Za rubezhom, no. 39, Sept. 1961: 3.
Peruvian President's visit to the United States.

See also entry no. 2161.

18. Venezuela

2208. Logika prezidenta [The "logic" of the president] Za rubezhom, no. 51, Dec. 1961: 2–3.
President Kennedy's trip to Venezuela and Colombia.

2209. Nezvanyi gost' [A self-invited guest] Za rubezhom, no. 50, Dec. 1961: 3.
President Kennedy's trip to Venezuela and Colombia.

2210. Pavlenko, A. Podopleka odnogo vizita [Behind the scenes of a state visit] Mezhdunar. zhizn', v. 10, no. 4, Apr. 1963: 119–120.
Relations with the United States.

2211. Pikkvikskii smysl [A Pickwickian sense] Nov. vrem., v. 19, no. 52, Dec. 1961: 22.
President Kennedy's trip to Venezuela and Colombia.

2212. Pochemu toropitsia Betankur [Why Betancourt is in a hurry] Nov. vrem., v. 19, no. 48, Nov. 1961: 23.
Relations with Cuba.

2213. V Vashington za brandspoitami [A trip to Washington to ask for fire engines] Za rubezhom, no. 7, Feb. 1963: 4.
Relations with the United States.

C. LATIN AMERICA IN INTER-AMERICAN ORGANIZATIONS

2214. Antiasov, Marat Vasil'evich. Sovremennyi panamerikanizm; proiskhozhdenie i sushchnost' doktrin panamerikanskoi "solidarnosti" [Present-day Pan-Americanism; the origin and nature of the doctrines of Pan-American "solidarity"] Moscow, Izd-vo IMO, 1960. 326 p.   F1418.A65
Reviewed by V. Kropotov in *Vest. ist. mir. kul't.*, no. 4, July-Aug. 1961: 152–153.

2215. Gvozdarev, Boris Ivanovich. Organizatsiia amerikanskikh gosudarstv [The Organization of American States] Moscow, Izd-vo IMO, 1960. 322 p. F1402.G8

Reviewed by V. Viktorov in *Mir. ekon. i mezhdunar. otn.*, no. 12, Dec. 1960: 137–139; by IUr. Pavlov in *Nov. mir*, v. 37, no. 3, Mar. 1961: 277–279; by V. Kropotov in *Vest. ist. mir. kul't.*, no. 4, July-Aug. 1961: 153–154.

2216. Chizhov, Konstantin IAkovlevich. Mezhamerikanskii bank razvitiia—orudie neokolonializma SShA v strankakh Latinskoi Ameriki [The Inter-American Development Bank is a neocolonialist tool of the U.S.A. in the Latin American countries] *In his* Mezhdunarodnye valiutno-finansovye organizatsii kapitalizma. Moscow, Gosfinizdat, 1963. p. 174–192.
Entire book reviewed by I. Aizenberg and I. Zlobin in *Den. i kred.*, v. 22, no. 8, Aug. 1964: 81–86.

2217. "Dzhentl'meny"-naletchiki "Gentlemen"-robbers] Za rubezhom, no. 50, Dec. 1963: 2–3.
Cuba and the Organization of American States.

2218. Gramotov, A. G. OAG — orudie monopolii SShA [The Organization of American States is a tool of U.S. monopolies] Vop. mezhdunar. prava, no. 4, 1962: 59–87.

2219. Gvozdarev, B. I. Antikubinskie resheniia OAG protivorechat osnovnym printsipam mezhdunarodnogo prava [Anti-Cuban decisions of the Organization of American States violate the basic principles of international law] Vop. mezhdunar. prava, no. 4, 1962: 88–116.

2220. Manasov, M. Organizatsiia amerikanskikh gosudarstv [The Organization of American States] Otv. na vop. trud., no. 4, Apr. 1962: 32–37.

2221. Martillo, Trinidad. Evoliutsiia mezhamerikanskoi sistemy [The evolution of the inter-American system] Mezhdunar. zhizn', v. 7, no. 1, Jan. 1960: 78–86.

2222. Mezhamerikanskii bank razvitiia [The Inter-American Development Bank] Mezhdunar. zhizn', v. 8, no. 4, Apr. 1961: 151–152.

2223. Odin protiv dvadtsati [One against twenty] Nov. vrem., v. 17, no. 20, May 1964: 22.
Pan-American treaties and conventions.

2224. Organizatsiia amerikanskikh gosudarstv [The Organization of American States] Mezhdunar. zhizn', v. 7, no. 9, Sept. 1960: 153–154.

2225. Panamerikanizm i latinoamerikanizm [Pan-Americanism and Latin Americanism] Mezhdunar. zhizn', v. 10, no. 12, Dec. 1963: 148–149.

2226. Strelin, Al. Dlia chego sushchestvuet Organizatsiia amerikanskikh gosudarstv [The objectives of the Organization of American States] Nov. vrem., v. 21, no. 27, July 1964: 12-14.

2227. ———. OAG v tupike protivorechii [The Organization of American States is in a blind alley of contradictions] Nov. vrem., v. 22, no. 48, Nov. 1964: 16–17.

2228. Suárez, Luis. Panamerikanizm i latinoamerikanizm [Pan-Americanism and Latin Americanism] Za rubezhom, no. 1, Jan. 1961: 20.

2229. Tarasov, V. Zakat ery panamerikanizma [Decline of the era of Pan-Americanism] Mezhdunar. zhizn', v. 10, no. 12, Dec. 1963: 133–135.
A review of John C. Dreier's *The Organization of American States and the Hemisphere Crisis* (New York, Harper & Row, 1962. 147 p.).

See also entries no. 458, 1281, 1875, and 2686.

IX

INTERNATIONAL CULTURAL RELATIONS

❦

A. WRITINGS DEALING WITH THREE OR MORE COUNTRIES

1. Relations With the USSR

2230. Arismendi, Rodney. Nasha putevodnaia zvezda [Our lodestar] Agitator, no. 24, Dec. 1961: 33–36.
Latin America and the USSR.

2231. Gvozdev, IU. Triumf "Berezki" v Latinskoi Amerike ["Berezka's" triumph in Latin America] Muz. zhizn', v. 5, no. 23, Dec. 1962: 3–4.

2232. IAroshevskii, B. SSSR—Latinskaia America [The USSR and Latin America] Sov. Soiuz, no. 6, 1962: 18–20.

2233. Karieva, Bernara. Po stranam Latinskoi Ameriki [In the countries of Latin America] Zvezda Vost., v. 29, no. 3, Mar. 1961: 109–131.
Guest performances of a Russian ballet ensemble in Latin America.

2234. Khachaturian, Aram. Tak sblizhaiutsia kontinenty [This is how continents are drawn together] Kul't. i zhizn', v. 3, no. 11, 1959: 21–23.

2235. Khachaturian, Aram, and others. Zhelaem schast'ia i protsvetaniia [We wish you luck and prosperity] Kul't. i zhizn', v. 4, no. 8, 1960: 4–7.

2236. Khronika [Brief news] Kul't. i zhizn', v. 4, no. 8, 1960: 36–37.
Cultural relations with the USSR.

2237. Khrushchev, N. S. Poslanie meksikanskomu zhurnalu "S'empre" [A message to the Mexican magazine "Siempre"] Mezhdunar. zhizn', v. 10, no. 7, July 1963: 3–5.

2238. Kislova, L. D., and others. Assotsiatsiia druzhby [An association of friendship] Kul't. i zhizn', v. 4, no. 8, 1960: 31–35.

2239. Leonidov, B. Dalekaia i blizkaia Latinskaia Amerika [Close and distant Latin America] Kul't. i zhizn', v. 5, no. 12, 1961: 16–18.

2240. Mora, Juan Miguel de. Most mezhdu narodami [A bridge between peoples] Inostr. lit., no. 2, Feb. 1959: 230–233.

2241. Motina, E. Mezhdunarodnyi seminar prepodavatelei russkogo iazyka stran Azii, Afriki i Latinskoi Ameriki [An international conference of Russian language teachers in the countries of Asia, Africa, and Latin America] Rus. iaz. v nats. shkole, no. 5, 1962: 87–88.

2242. Na ekrane sovetskie fil'my [Soviet motion pictures on the screen] Inostr. lit., no. 8, Aug. 1960: 273.

2243. Nadezhdina, Nadezhda. Teplo chelovecheskikh serdets [The warmth of human hearts] Teatr. zhizn', no. 24, Dec. 1962: 2–3.
Performances of the "Berezka" ensemble.

2244. Nikulin, IU. 100 dnei v IUzhnoi Amerike [One hundred days in South America] Sov. tsirk, v. 4, no. 9, Sept. 1960: 14–15, 22–24; v. 4, no. 10, Oct. 1960: 23–26.
Guest performances of a Russian circus.

2245. Poezdka za okean [A trip abroad] Sov. muz., v. 24, no. 6, June 1960: 170–174.
Concerts by A. I. Khachaturian.

2246. Rogachev, IU. Po pros'be zapadnykh radioslushatelei [At the request of radio listeners in the West] Sov. radio i tel., v. 10, no. 1, 1961: 20–21.

2247. Tikhomirnova, Irina. Sem'desiat dnei v Latinskoi Amerike [Seventy days in Latin America] Muz. zhizn', v. 3, no. 14, July 1960: 13–15.
Guest performances of a Soviet dance ensemble.

2248. Trunina, L. Sovetskii balet v Latinskoi Amerike [Soviet ballet in Latin America] Teatr, v. 23, no. 1, Jan. 1962: 182.

See also entry no. 1817.

2. Relations With the United States

2249. Bestsennyi tovar [Priceless merchandise] Nov. vrem., v. 21, no. 28, July 1964: 25.
Education of Latin American trade-union workers in the United States.

2250. Mister Bolindzher zadumyvaetsia [Mister Dwight L. Bolinger has begun to wonder] Inostr. lit., no. 8, Aug. 1961: 247–249.
Cultural relations with the United States.

2251. Vaisbakh, R. Krepnut nashi sviazi s Latinskoi Amerikoi [Our ties with Latin America grow stronger] Mol. mira, no. 5, 1961: 20.
Contacts with "progressive" young people of the United States.

See also entry no. 4441.

B. INDIVIDUAL COUNTRIES

1. Relations With the USSR and Other Communist Countries.

a. *Argentina*

2252. Berezhnaia, N. Vstrechi s argentinskimi uchiteliami [Meetings with Argentine teachers] Nar. obr., no. 10, Oct. 1960: 123.

2253. Perel'shtein, Berta. Goriachii pobornik argentino-sovetskoi druzhby [An ardent advocate of friendship between the Soviet Union and Argentina] Kul't. i zhizn', v. 3, no. 7, 1959: 21–24.

2254. Sotrudnichat' vo imia mira [Let's co-operate in the name of peace] Kul't. i zhizn', v. 4, no. 8, 1960: 2–3.

b. *Brazil*

2255. Bol'shakov, I. Vystavka SSSR v Brazilii [USSR exhibition in Brazil] Vnesh. torg., v. 42, no. 8, 1962: 17–19.

2256. Budem druzhit' [Let's be friends] Ogonek, v. 39, no. 50, Dec. 1961: 4.

2257. Chuhunov, Vladyslav. Potsilunok Brazilii [The kiss of Brazil] Ukraina, no. 1, Jan. 1963: 11.

2258. Dorenskii, Sergei. V Brazilii; zametki pianista [In Brazil; notes of a pianist] Kul't. i zhizn', v. 4, no. 1, 1960: 52–55.

2259. Dubinina, IU. Sovetskii Soiuz v Rio-de-Zhaneiro [The Soviet Union in Rio de Janeiro] Ogonek, v. 40, no. 20, May 1962: 2.
Soviet exhibitions.

2260. Ersen, Sebastian de Oliveira. Khoroshie perspektivy [Good prospects] Kul't. i zhizn', v. 6, no. 2, 1962: 35.

2261. Khrushchev, Nikita Sergeevich. Poslanie k posetiteliam sovetskoi vystavki v Rio-de-Zhaneiro [A message to the visitors of the Soviet Exhibition in Rio de Janeiro] Vnesh. torg., v. 42, no. 6, June 1962: 3–5.

2262. Lushnikov, F. Braziliia rukopleshchet [Brazil applauds] Sov. voin, v. 45, no. 11, June 1963: 30–31.

2263. Sipovich, A., *and* G. Kalugin. Ego zvali Ze-do Burro [They called him "Zé-do-burro"] Teatr, v. 25, no. 7, July 1964: 91–92.
Performances of a Brazilian play in Vilnius.

2264. Vstrecha v Dome druzhby [A meeting in the Friendship House] Nar. obr., no. 2, Feb. 1960: 125.

See also entry no. 2270.

c. *Chile*

2265. Castro, Baltazar. Otkrylis' mnogie dveri [Many doors are open now] Kul't. i zhizn', v. 8, no. 1, Jan. 1964: 21.

2266. Zverev, M. S. Sovetskie astronomy v Chili [Soviet astronomers in Chile] Vest. AN SSSR, v. 33, no. 2, Feb. 1963: 88–91.

d. Cuba

2267. Bezrukov, E. Moskva—Gavana [Moscow to Havana] Sov. deput. trud., no. 6, June 1961: 106–108.

2268. Borovik, G. Pylaiushchii ostrov [An island in flames] Ogonek, v. 38, no. 7, 1960: 4–5.
    A Soviet industrial exhibition.

2269. Bugrimova, I. V dvukh Amerikakh [In two Americas] Sov. estrada i tsirk, no. 8, 1964: 31.
    Guest performances of the Soviet Circus in Cuba and Mexico.

2270. Denisov, N. Na orbite mira i druzhby [In the orbit of peace and friendship] Sov. pech., no. 10, Oct. 1961: 38–42.
    IU. Gagarin's visit to Cuba and Brazil.

2271. D'iakonov, N. N. "My—druz'ia Kuby" ["We are friends of Cuba"] Kul't. i zhizn', v. 5, no. 1, 1961: 32–33.

2272. Gal'tsev, V. Dlia nashikh kubinskikh druzei [For our Cuban friends] Vnesh. torg., v. 42, no. 4, 1962: 30–31.
    A Soviet industrial exhibition.

2273. Kamynin, L. Triumf sovetsko-kubinskoi druzhby [Triumph of Soviet-Cuban friendship] Mezhdunar. zhizn', v. 10, no. 7, July 1963: 105.

2274. Kotnitskii, G. Rastet v Tule Fidel' [There is a young Fidel in the city of Tula] Neva, no. 9, 1964: 219.

2275. Lenin i Kuba [Lenin and Cuba] Vop. arkh., v. 7, no. 2, Apr.-June 1962: 85.

2276. Makarova, Nina. Kuba moia dorogaia [My dear Cuba] Sov. zhen., v. 19, no. 7, 1963: 27.
    A visit of Russian musicians.

2277. Mashkin, V., and others. My riadom s toboiu, Kuba! [We are with you, Cuba!] Smena, v. 39, no. 2, Jan. 1962: 22–23.
    Friendly contacts between Soviet and Cuban youth.

2278. My s toboi, Kuba! [We are with you, Cuba!] Vozhatyi, v. 38, no. 12, Dec. 1962: 33.

2279. Pavlo Popovych sered kubyntsiv; fotoal'bom kosmonavta-4 [Pavel Popovich visits the people of Cuba; photographs of Cosmonaut no. 4] Ukraina, no. 7, Apr. 1963: 17–18.

2280. Perekhodin, A., and I. Nartsissov. Tezki ostrova svobody [Namesakes of the island of freedom] IUnost', v. 9, no. 7, July 1963: 101–104.
    Russian cities and settlements named "Kuba."

2281. Pis'mo chitatelia iz Kuby [Reader's letter from Cuba] Nov. vrem., v. 18, no. 16, Apr. 1960: 9.

2282. Poliakovskii, Vadim. Teplo bratskoi druzhby [The warmth of fraternal friendship] Za rubezhom, no. 43, Oct. 1964: 9.

2283. Prokopenko, V. Stroki ot serdtsa [Lines from the heart] Smena, v. 40, no. 14, July 1963: 14–15.

2284. SSSR—Kuba [The USSR and Cuba] Kul't. i zhizn', v. 7, no. 5, 1963: 27.

2285. Sierra, Gerardo. Izuchaiu russkii iazyk [I study Russian] Nov. vrem., v. 18, no. 15, Apr. 1960: 29.

2286. Slonim, O. M. Pis'mo kubinskogo krest'ianina [A letter from a Cuban peasant] Ist. arkh., v. 7, no. 3, May-June 1961: 276–277.

2287. Tulupov, N. Mesiats na Kube [A month in Cuba] Muz. zhizn', v. 7, no. 3, Feb. 1964: 14–15.
    Guest performances of a Soviet ensemble of amateur actors and musicians.

    See also entries no. 1923, 1928, 2778, 2779, and 3180.

e. Ecuador

2288. Maldonado, A. My uznaem novyi mir [We discover a new world] Za rubezhom, no. 44, Nov. 1963: 12.

f. El Salvador

2289. Nepomniashchii, K. Diskussii v Sal'vadore [Discussions in El Salvador] Za rubezhom, no. 48, Nov. 1964: 8.

g. Mexico

2290. Aleksandrov, Grigorii. Mexico. Kul't. i zhizn', v. 4, no. 8, 1960: 26–27.

2291. Andrianov, V. V gorode vechnoi vesny [In the city of eternal spring] Mezhdunar. zhizn', v. 7, no. 1, Jan. 1960: 117–118.
A Soviet exhibition in Mexico City.

2292. Beltrán, Alberto. Pis'mo meksikanskogo khudozhnika [Letter from a Mexican artist] Nov. vrem., v. 17, no. 51, Dec. 1959: 13.

2293. Borisov, S. A. Sovetskii Soiuz i Meksika [The Soviet Union and Mexico] Nov. vrem., v. 17, no. 50, Dec. 1959: 16–17.
Soviet exhibitions.

2294. Borovik, Genrikh. Dobroe utro, sovetsko-meksikanskaia druzhba! [Good morning, Soviet-Mexican friendship!] Ogon-ek, v. 37, no. 50, Dec. 1959: 6–7.
A. I. Mikoian's visit.

2295. ———. Meksikantsy: "Rusiia—khorosho!" ["Russia is good," the Mexicans say] Ogonek, v. 37, no. 49, Nov. 1959: 2–3.
Soviet exhibitions.

2296. Campos Ponce, Xavier. Nashei druzhbe krepnut' [Our friendship will grow stronger] Kul't. i zhizn', v. 8, no. 1, Jan. 1964: 20–21.

2297. Chto chitaiut v Meksike [What they read in Mexico] Inostr. lit., no. 9, Sept. 1959: 280.
Publication of Marxist literature and the works of Soviet writers.

2298. Interes k sovetskim knigam [They are interested in Soviet books] Inostr. lit., no. 3, Mar. 1959: 282.

2299. Khor'kov, N. Cheliabinsk—Mekhiko [From Chelyabinsk to Mexico City] Rabotnitsa, no. 8, Aug. 1964: 21.
Friendly contacts between Mexican and Soviet women.

2300. Koval', M. V SShA, Kanade, Meksike [In the U.S.A., Canada, and Mexico] Muz. zhizn', no. 24, Dec. 1959: 11–12.
Guest performances of a Russian choir.

2301. Kozyreva, V. V gostiakh u meksikantsev [Visiting with Mexicans] Prom. koop., v. 14, no. 4, Apr. 1960: 26.
Soviet exhibitions.

2302. Meshcheriakov, M. Sovetskaia vystavka v Meksike [Soviet exhibition in Mexico] Vnesh. torg., v. 30, no. 1, 1960: 5–7.
Summary in English.

2303. Mora, Juan Miguel de. Doroga k zvezdam—put' k bratstvu narodov [The route to the stars is the path to the brotherhood of peoples] Inostr. lit., no. 12, Dec. 1959: 229–231.

2304. Osmolovskii, IU. Vstrecha s Meksikoi [A meeting with Mexico] Tvorchestvo, no. 10, 1964: 12–14.
Mexico in a Russian painter's works.

2305. Ossovskii, Petr. Pamiat' o Meksike [Reminiscences on Mexico] Ogonek, v. 42, no. 40, Oct. 1964: 16 17.
Mexico in the paintings of a Russian artist.

2306. SSSR i Meksika [The USSR and Mexico] Nov. vrem., v. 17, no. 48, Nov. 1959: 2–3.
Soviet exhibitions.

2307. Sovetskie kompozitory v SShA i Meksike [A visit of Soviet composers to the U.S.A. and Mexico] Sov. muz., v. 24, no. 1, Jan. 1960: 180–181.

2308. Sovetskii Soiuz i Meksika [The Soviet Union and Mexico] Nov. vrem., v. 17, no. 51, Dec. 1959: 13.
Soviet exhibitions.

2309. Zakharov, V. "Boris Godunov" v Meksike ["Boris Godunov" in Mexico] Muz. zhizn', v. 4, no. 21, 1961: 7.

See also entry no. 2269.

h. Peru

2310. Castro Franco, Julio. Budem krepit' sviazi [We shall strengthen our relations] Sov. Soiuz, no. 2, Feb. 1959: 16.

i. Uruguay

2311. Bezbrezhnyi, V. Ot siurpriza k siurpriza [From surprise to surprise] Neva, no. 4, 1959: 222–223.

2312. Brekht v Montevideo [Brecht in Monte-video] Inostr. lit., no. 12, Dec. 1960: 261.
Cultural relations with East Germany.

2313. Kak Antoniia i Galina stali druz'iami [How Antonia and Galina have become friends] Sov. zhen., v. 18, no. 2, 1962: 13.
Uruguayan women's contacts with women in the USSR.

2314. Soriano, Alberto. Druzhba krepnet [Our friendly ties grow stronger] Kul't. i zhizn', v. 8, no. 8, 1964: 43.

2. Relations With the United States and Other Non-Communist Countries

a. Brazil

2315. Amerikanskii "kul'turtreger" i brazil'-skie uchenye [An American "Kulturträ-ger" and Brazilian scholars] Inostr. lit., no. 9, Sept. 1962: 275.

b. Colombia

2316. "IA videl noch'" ["I saw the night"] Inostr. lit., no. 9, Sept. 1962: 280.
A Colombian writer on the race problem in the United States.

c. Cuba

2317. Dodd, Martha. Ioho druha bat'kiv-shchyna [His second fatherland] Vsesvit, v. 6, no. 8, Aug. 1963: 23–25.
Ernest Hemingway and Cuba.
Translated from the English.

2318. Kheminguei za Kubinskuiu Revoliu-tsiiu [Hemingway supports the Cuban Revolution] Inostr. lit., no. 11, Nov. 1960: 266.

2319. Kul'turnye sviazi s Kuboi [Cultural contacts with Cuba] Inostr. lit., no. 12, Dec. 1960: 257–258.
Cultural contacts with Italy.

2320. Pamiat' o Kheminguee—v serdtse rybakov [Cuban fishermen won't forget Hemingway] Inostr. lit., no. 11, Nov. 1962: 280.

2321. Pleshakov, L. Don Ernesto ostaetsia na Kube [Don Ernesto will stay in Cuba] Don, v. 8, no. 8, Aug. 1964: 164–166.
Places associated with Ernest Hemingway.

2322. Raznyi obraz zhizni [A different way of life] Nov. vrem., v. 22, no. 36, Sept. 1964: 20.
Efforts to overcome the cultural influence of the United States.

d. Mexico

2323. Bonnskie "kul'turtregery" v Mekhiko [The Bonn "Kulturträgers" in Mexico City] Inostr. lit., no. 12, Dec. 1960: 256.
Cultural relations with West Germany.

X

ECONOMIC CONDITIONS AND POLICIES

ʚ

A. WRITINGS DEALING WITH THREE OR MORE COUNTRIES

2324. Avarin, Vladimir IAkovlevich, *and* M. V. Danilevich, *eds.* Ekonomicheskie problemy stran Latinskoi Ameriki [Economic problems facing the countries of Latin America] Moscow, Izd-vo Akad. nauk SSSR, 1963. 512 p.   HC165.A338

2325. Azamkulov, Kh. Minuia kapitalizm [Bypassing capitalism] Dushanbe, Tadzhikgosizdat, 1963. 48 p.
In Tajik.

2326. Baltra Cortés, Alberto. Ekonomicheskoe razvitie Latinskoi Ameriki; osnovnye problemy [Basic problems of the economic development of Latin America] Moscow, Izd-vo inostr. lit., 1963. 362 p.
Translated by A. Г. Rozhkov and M. P. Shelepin from the Spanish *Crecimiento económico de América Latina; problemas fundamentales.* Introductory article by IU. IA. Ol'sevich.

2327. Bobrov, V. IA., *ed.* Latinskaia Amerika; politiko-ekonomicheskii spravochnik [Latin America; a political and economic handbook] Kiev, Izd-vo Akad. nauk Ukr. SSR, 1963. 283. p.
                    HC163.L35

2328. Danilevich, M. V., *and others, eds.* Latinskaia Amerika; kratkii politiko-ekonomicheskii spravochnik [Latin America; a brief political and economic handbook] Moscow, Gospolitizdat, 1962. 310 p.   F1408.D26
Also published in Estonian.
Reviewed by S. Vorob'ev in *Nov. mir*, v. 38, no. 10, Oct. 1962: 277 p.

2329. Danilevich, M. V., *and* A. F. Shul'govskii, *eds.* Problemy sovremennoi Latinskoi Ameriki; sbornik statei [Present-day problems of Latin America; collected articles] Moscow, Izd-vo IMO, 1959. 430 p.   F1414.A45
Reviewed by A. Glinkin in *Mir. ekon. i mezhdunar. otn.*, no. 5, May 1961: 145–149.

2330. Goriunov, V. P., *ed.* Ekonomicheskoe polozhenie stran Azii, Afriki i Latinskoi Ameriki [The economic situation of the countries of Asia, Africa, and Latin America] Moscow, Vneshtorgizdat, 1959. 446 p.   HC59.A15M62

2331. Kelam, T. P. Strany TSentral'noi Ameriki [The countries of Central America] Tallinn, Estgosizdat, 1960. 43 p.
In Estonian.

2332. Klesmet, O. G. Osnovnye tendentsii promyshlennogo razvitiia Latinskoi Ameriki posle vtoroi mirovoi voiny [Basic trends in the industrial development of Latin America after the Second World War] Moscow, 1962. 19 p.
Author's abstract of a dissertation for the degree of Candidate in Economic Sciences.

2333. Kosarev, E. A., *and* V. V. Rogov, *eds.* Ekonomicheskoe polozhenie Latinskoi Ameriki [The economic situation of Latin America] Moscow, 1963. 131 p. (Biulleten' inostrannoi kommercheskoi informatsii; prilozhenie, no. 11)

2334. Loziuk, M. I. Borot'ba krain Latyns'koi Ameryky za ekonomichnu nezalezhnist' [The struggle of the Latin American countries for economic independence] Kiev, 1959. 48 p.

2335. Popov, K. M., *and others, eds.* Eko-nomiko-geograficheskie problemy stran Afriki, Azii i Latinskoi Ameriki; sbornik statei [Problems concerning the economic geography of the countries of Africa, Asia, and Latin America; collected articles] Moscow, Mysl', 1964. 192 p.

2336. Rymalov, Viktor Vladimirovich, *and* V. Tiagunenko. Slaborazvitye strany v mirovom kapitalisticheskom khoziaistve [The place of underdeveloped countries in the economy of the capitalist world] Moscow, Sotsekgiz, 1961. 494 p.
                                 HC59.R85

2337. Vol'f, Mark Borisovich, *and* Veniamin Solomonovich Klupt. Statisticheskii spravochnik po ekonomicheskoi geografii stran kapitalisticheskogo mira [Statistical reference book on the economic geography of the countries of the capitalist world] 4th rev. ed. Moscow, Sotsekgiz, 1959.   HC51.V6 1959
    Partial contents. —Argentina, p. 301–309. —Brazil, p. 317–329. —Chile, p. 524–526.

2338. Vol'skii, V. Latinskaia Amerika, neft' i nezavisimost' [Latin America, petro-leum, and independence] Moscow, Mysl', 1964. 364 p.
    Reviewed by S. Mikhailov in *Mezhdunar. zhizn'*, v. 11, no. 9, Sept. 1964: 133–134.

2339. Alvarez, C. The prospect for Latin America. World youth, no. 3, 1963: 15–16.

2340. Amerikanskaia deistvitel'nost' . . . v neskol'ko strok [American realities . . . in a few lines] Mol. mira, no. 1, 1960: 22.

2341. Arismendi, Rodney. Latinskaia Amerika vykhodit na avanstsenu [Latin America comes to the foreground] Kom-munist, v. 37, no. 5, Mar. 1961: 69–86.

2342. Castro, Josué de. Golod i nerazvitost' v Latinskoi Amerike [Hunger and under-development in Latin America] Vop. filos., v. 16, no. 10, 1962: 105–109.

2343. ———. Kolonializm, golod i progress [Colonialism, hunger, and progress] Probl. mira i sots., v. 4, no. 10, Oct. 1961: 67–70.

2344. Danilevich, M. V. Dvizhushchie sily osvoboditel'noi bor'by v Latinskoi

Amerike [The motive forces behind the liberation movement in Latin America] Mir. ekon. i mezhdunar. otn., no. 9, Sept. 1960: 90–98.

2345. Deistvuiushchii vulkan [An active vol-cano] Mezhdunar. zhizn', v. 8, no. 4, Apr. 1961: 148.

2346. Efimov, A. Perspektivy Latinskoi Ameriki [Prospects for Latin America] Nov. vrem., v. 20, no. 4, Jan. 1963: 9–10.

2347. Eliutin, IU. Kapital'nyi trud o Latin-skoi Amerike [A comprehensive study on Latin America] Mezhdunar. zhizn', v. 9, no. 6, June 1962: 118–122.
    A review of Rodney Arismendi's *Problemas de una revolución continental* (Montevideo, Ediciones Pueblos Unidos, 1962. 556 p.).

2348. Ermolaev, V. Ne na toi volne [On a different wave length] Mezhdunar. zhizn', v. 8, no. 12, Dec. 1961: 123–125.
    A review of *Social Change in Latin America Today; Its Implications for United States Policy*, by Richard N. Adams and others (New York, Harper, 1960. 353 p.).

2349. Faktor, G. Geografiia goloda [The geography of hunger] Mir. ekon. i mezhdunar. otn., no. 9, 1964: 132–136.

2350. González Alberdi, Paulino. Puti in-dustrializatsii ekonomicheski otstavshikh stran [The paths of industrialization of underdeveloped countries] Probl. mira i sots., v. 4, no. 8, Aug. 1961: 8–14.

2351. Grandissot, Jean. Na Antil'skikh ost-rovakh [On the Antilles] Nov. vrem., v. 19, no. 10, Mar. 1961: 23–24.

2352. Grechev, M. Nekotorye problemy ekonomicheskoi nezavisimosti stran Latinskoi Ameriki [Certain problems in the economic independence of the coun-tries of Latin America] Mir. ekon. i mezhdunar. otn., no. 10, Oct. 1960: 74–81.

2353. Gurov, A. Novye fakty ob ekonomi-cheskom polozhenii stran Latinskoi Ameriki [New data on the economic situ-ation of the Latin American countries] Mir. ekon. i mezhdunar. otn., no. 11, Nov. 1963: 131–136.

2354. Halperin, Maurice. Tempy razvitiia i krizis latinoamerikanskoi ekonomiki

[Rates of growth and the crisis of the Latin American economy] Mir. ekon. i mezhdunar. otn., no. 7, July 1961: 61–85.

2355. IAroshevskii, B. Gor'kii rai [Pitiful paradise] Za rubezhom, no. 28, July 1961: 23.
Caribbean area.

2356. Kalinin, A. Gosudarstvenno-kapitalisticheskii sektor v stranakh Latinskoi Ameriki [The state-capitalist sector in the countries of Latin America] Mir. ekon. i mezhdunar. otn., no. 2, Feb. 1959: 90–101.

2357. Kosarev, E. A., and others. Ekonomicheskoe polozhenie stran Latinskoi Ameriki v 1960 g. [Economic situation of the countries of Latin America in 1960] Biul. inostr. kommerch. inform. Prilozhenie, no. 13, Sept. 1961: 3–90.

2358. Latinskaia Amerika v tsifrakh [Latin America in figures] Mezhdunar. zhizn', v. 8, no. 8, Aug. 1961: 140.

2359. Loziuk, M. Zaria svobody zanimaetsia nad Latinskoi Amerikoi [The dawn of freedom rises over Latin America] Komm. Ukr., v. 37, no. 1, Jan. 1962: 72–81.

2360. Martillo, Trinidad. Polozhenie v Latinskoi Amerike [The situation in Latin America] Mezhdunar. zhizn', v. 6, no. 5, May 1959: 78–89.

2361. Mashbits, IA. G. Kuba ili Meksika? Amerikanskii sotsiolog o putiakh razvitiia stran Latinskoi Ameriki [Cuba or Mexico? Paths of the development of Latin American countries in the interpretation of an American sociologist] Vop. ist., no. 1, Jan. 1962: 183–185.
A review of Pedro C. M. Teichert's *Economic Policy and Industrialization in Latin America* (University, Miss., Bureau of Business Research, University of Mississippi, 1959. 282 p.).

2362. ———. Latinskaia Amerika v mezhdunarodnom kapitalisticheskom razdelenii truda [The place of Latin America in the international division of labor] Mir. ekon. i mezhdunar. otn., no. 11, Nov. 1964: 29–39.

2363. ———. Nadumannyi i podlinnyi put' k edinstvu Latinskoi Ameriki [The far-fetched and the true paths for the unity of Latin America] Vop. ist., v. 38, no. 11, Nov. 1963: 182–184.
A review of an article by F. Herrera in *Cuadernos Hispanoamericanos*, no. 157, 1963: 69–82.

2364. Mikhailov, S. Pylaiushchii kontinent [A continent in flame] Agitator, no. 9, May 1964: 24–25.

2365. Mikuson, I. Ekonomicheskoe bedstvie i politicheskaia neustoichivost' [Economic distress and political instability] Mezhdunar. zhizn', v. 9, no. 5, May 1962: 118–123.

2366. Nad Latinskoi Amerikoi zabrezzhala zaria [Dawn has broken over Latin America] Mol. mira, no. 1, 1960: 15.

2367. Nikiforov, B. S. Voprosy ekonomicheskoi nezavisimosti stran Latinskoi Ameriki; nauchnaia konferentsiia [A conference on problems concerning the economic independence of Latin American countries] Vest. AN SSSR, v. 34, no. 7, July 1964: 115–116.

2368. Paporova, G. Po stranitsam "Comercio Exterior de Mexico" [From the the pages of "Comercio exterior de México"] Vnesh. torg., v. 30, no. 9, 1960: 35–36.

2369. Poliakovskii, V. Latinoamerikanskii vulkan [The Latin American volcano] Krest'ianka, v. 40, no. 1, Jan. 1962: 9–10.

2370. Review. Mir. ekon. i mezhdunar. otn., no. 7, July 1964: 157.
A review of Gerald Clark's *The Coming Explosion in Latin America* (New York, McKay, 1963. 436 p.).

2371. Romanova, Z. Latinskaia Amerika; puti ekonomicheskogo razvitiia [Paths of the economic development of Latin America] Mir. ekon. i mezhdunar. otn., no. 11, Nov. 1963: 28–39.

2372. Rymalov, V. Ekonomicheski slaborazvitye strany v mirovom kapitalisticheskom khoziaistve [The role of underdeveloped countries in the economy of the capitalist world] Mir. ekon. i mezhdunar. otn., no. 3, Mar. 1962: 34–49.

2373. Shul'govskii, A. Krizis idei "zapadnoi tsivilizatsii" v Latinskoi Amerike [Crisis of the ideas of "western civilization" in Latin America] Mezhdunar. zhizn', v. 11, no. 4, Apr. 1964: 25–34.

2374. Sivolobov, A. Kooperatsiia v stranakh Latinskoi Ameriki [Cooperative societies in the countries of Latin America] Sov. potreb. koop., v. 6, no. 3, 1962: 52–55.

2375. Tarasov, K. Monopolisticheskie tendentsii v Latinskoi Amerike [Monopolistic trends in Latin America] Mezhdunar. zhizn', v. 11, no. 12, Dec. 1964: 51–59.

2376. Tarasov, V. Latinskaia Amerika; kapitalizm pod ugrozoi [Latin America; capitalism in jeopardy] Mir. ekon. i mezhdunar. otn., no. 7, 1963: 149–151.
     A review of Philip Alexander Ray's *South Wind Red; Our Hemispheric Crisis* (Chicago, Regnery, 1962. 242 p.).

2377. Tarasov, V. B. Revoliutsiia v kredit [A revolution on the installment plan] Vop. ist., v. 38, no. 12, Dec. 1963: 165–167.
     A review of Frank Tannenbaum's *Ten Keys to Latin America* (New York, A. Knopf, 1963. 237 p.).

2378. Velasco, Domingos. Tragediia "slaborazvitykh" stran [The tragedy of "underdeveloped" countries] V zashch. mira, no. 4, Apr. 1960: 18–24.

2379. Vieira, Gilberto. Put' k osvobozhdeniiu Latinskoi Ameriki [Latin America's path to freedom] Nov. vrem., v. 19, no. 46, Nov. 1961: 6–7.

2380. Vistinetskii, M. Golod vygoden kapitalu [Capitalists thrive on hunger] Agitator, no. 11, June 1959: 30–33.

2381. Zalamea, Jorge. V tiskakh nuzhdy [In the clutches of poverty] V zashch. mira, no. 6, June 1960: 75.

See also entry no. 295.

B. INDIVIDUAL COUNTRIES

1. Argentina

2382. Ekonomicheskoe polozhenie kapitalisticheskikh stran; kon"iukturnyi obzor za 1960 g. i nachalo 1961 g. [Economic situation of capitalist countries; a survey of business conditions in 1960 and early 1961] Moscow, Pravda, 1961.
                         HC10.E54, 1961

Partial contents. —Argentina, p. 81–84. —Brazil, p. 84–85.

2383. Ekonomicheskoe polozhenie kapitalisticheskikh stran; kon"iukturnyi obzor za 1961 g. i nachalo 1962 g. [Economic situation of capitalist countries; a survey of business conditions in 1961 and early 1962] Moscow, Pravda, 1962.
                         HC10.E54, 1962
Partial contents. —Argentina, p. 86–88. —Brazil, p. 88–89.

2384. Eliutin, IU. K sobytiiam v Argentine [Events in Argentina] Mezhdunar. zhizn', v. 6, no. 1, Jan. 1959: 163–165.

2385. ———. Polozhenie v Argentine [The situation in Argentina] Mezhdunar. zhizn', v. 6, no. 7, July 1959: 123–125.

2386. Fuchs, Jaime. Gosudarstvennyi kapitalizm v Argentine, sushchnost' i formy [The nature and forms of state capitalism in Argentina] Probl. mira i sots., v. 4, no. 6, June, 1961: 47–53.

2387. González Alberdi, Paulino. Puti razvitiia stran, zavoevavshikh natsional'nuiu nezavisimost'; Argentina [The paths of economic development in the countries which have won their national independence; Argentina] Probl. mira i sots., v. 5, no. 4, Apr. 1962: 80–82.

2388. Kosobchuk, S. Ekonomicheskie i finansovye problemy Argentiny [Argentina's economic and financial problems] Mir. ekon. i mezhdunar. otn., no. 7, July 1964: 99–102.

2389. ———. Gosudarstvennyi biudzhet Argentiny [The national budget of Argentina] Fin. SSSR, v. 24, no. 5, May 1963: 81–86.

2390. Levin, V. Postnye dni v Argentine [Lean days in Argentina] Za rubezhom, no. 34, Aug. 1964: 17.

2391. Operatsiia bez anestezii [Surgery without anesthetics] Za rubezhom, no. 16, Apr. 1962: 2–3.

2392. Protivorechivaia situatsiia [A contradictious situation] Za rubezhom, no. 27, July 1964: 10.

2393. Rogov, V. Plan ekonomii i zhertv [A plan of frugality and sacrifice] Mir. ekon. i mezhdunar. otn., no. 2, Feb. 1960: 93–95.

2394. Stroganov, A. I. Ekonomicheskoe razvitie Argentiny v 1929–1939 gg. [The economic development of Argentina in the years 1929–1939] *In* Moscow. Universitet. Istoricheskii fakul'tet. Sbornik nauchnykh rabot aspirantov. Moscow, 1963: p. 201–230.

2395. Tarasov, K. Argentina: porochnyi krug [Argentina's vicious circle] Nov. vrem., v. 17, no. 24, June 1959: 18–19.

2396. Ul'ianova, S. I. Ekonomicheskoe i sotsial'noe litso Argentiny [Economic and social conditions in Argentina] Vop. ist., v. 38, no. 9, Sept. 1963: 165–167.
A review of Marcelo Isacovich's *Argentina económica y social* (Buenos Aires, Editorial Quipo, 1961. 262 p.).

2397. Zholobov, V. Valiutno-finansovyi krizis v Argentine [Foreign-exchange and financial crisis in Argentina] Den. i kred., v. 21, no. 2, Feb. 1963: 84–90.

2. Bolivia

2398. Galin, IUrii Pavlovich. Boliviia [Bolivia] Moscow, Geografgiz, 1962. 61 p.
HC182.G3
Economic geography.

2399. Levin, V. Chto proiskhodit v Bolivii [What is happening in Bolivia] Agitator, no. 7, Apr. 1959: 57–59.

2400. Silva, José. Dva mesiatsa novoi vlasti [Two months of the new regime] Za rubezhom, no. 23, June 1964: 22.

3. Brazil

2401. Efimov, Aleksei Vladimirovich, *and others, eds.* Braziliia; ekonomika, politika, kul'tura [Brazil; its national economy, politics and culture] Moscow, Izd-vo Akad. nauk SSSR, 1963. 525 p.
HC187.A558
Reviewed by S. Semenov in *Nov. vrem.*, v. 21, no. 50, Dec. 1963: 30–31; by M. Artiushenkov in *Mezhdunar. zhizn'*, v. 11, no. 1, Jan. 1964: 125–127.

2402. Vladimirov, Boris, *and* Gennadii Dobrov. Strela letit v budushchee [The arrow flies into the future] Moscow, Mol. gvardiia, 1963. 128 p. DLC

2403. Aleksandrovskii, B. Golod v Brazilii [Famine in Brazil] Nov. vrem., v. 17, no. 7, Feb. 1959: 15–16.

2404. Brazil'skie kommunisty o polozhenii v strane [The Brazilian Communists review the situation in their country] Probl. mira i sots., v. 5, no. 11, Nov. 1962: 39–42.

2405. Domínguez, P. J. Golod v Brazilii [Famine in Brazil] V zashch. mira, no. 94, 1959: 8–15.

2406. Eliutin, IU. Braziliia segodnia [Brazil today] Mezhdunar. zhizn', v. 8, no. 9, Sept. 1961: 142–145.
A review of Rui Faco's *Brasil, século XX* (Rio de Janeiro, Vitória, 1960. 261 p.).

2407. Faco, Rui. Braziliia, XX vek [Brazil in the 20th century] Za rubezhom, no. 48, Dec. 1961: 20–21.
Translated from the Portuguese.

2408. Fainberg, L. A. Nekotorye cherty khoziaistva sovremennogo neindeiskogo naseleniia Amazonii [Some features of the economy of the present-day non-Indian population in the Amazon Valley] Sov. etn., no. 1, Jan.-Feb. 1964: 73–80.
Summary in English.

2409. Glin, A. Krupnaia krazha [Big theft] Nov. vrem., v. 17, no. 24, June 1959: 29–30.
Economic aspects of atomic energy.
A review of Dagoberto Salles' *Energia atomica, um inquérito que abalou o Brasil* (São Paulo, Editôra Fulgor, 1958. 191 p.).

2410. Glin, A., *and* O. Klesmet. Ob ekonomicheskom razvitii Brazilii [The economic development of Brazil] Mir. ekon. i mezhdunar. otn., no. 10, Oct. 1959: 117–128.

2411. Gorender, Jacob. Braziliia v tiskakh protivorechii [Brazil in the grip of contradictions] Probl. mira i sots., v. 6, no. 2, Feb. 1963: 25–32.

2412. IAroshevskii, B. V stranakh "velikikh vozmozhnostei" [In the lands of "great possibilities"] Krest'ianka, v. 37, no. 6, June 1959: 19.

2413. Ignat'ev, Oleg. Pervyi trekhletnii plan Brazilii [The first three-year plan of Brazil] Mir. ekon. i mezhdunar. otn., no. 4, 1963: 100–103.

2414. IUbilei Zhozue di Kastru [Josué de Castro's 50th birthday] Inostr. lit., no. 2, Feb. 1959: 273.

2415. Klusov, E. Braziliia [Brazil] Vsesvit, v. 3, no. 2, Feb. 1960: 146–152.

2416. Kosobchuk, S. Biudzhet Brazilii [The budget of Brazil] Fin. SSSR, v. 23, no. 4, Apr. 1962: 82–87.

2417. Lima, Pedro Motta. Puti razvitiia stran zavoevavskikh natsional'nuiu nezavisimost'; Braziliia [The paths of economic development in the countries which have won their national independence; Brazil] Probl. mira i sots., v. 5, no. 6, June 1962: 78–80.

2418. Pirrova pobeda [A Pyrrhic victory] Za rubezhom, no. 50, Dec. 1964: 3.

2419. Piruety na provoloke [Pirouettes on a tightrope] Za rubezhom, no. 30, July 1964: 3.

2420. Poliakovskii, V. Braziliia: slovo za narodom [It's the Brazilian people's turn to speak] Za rubezhom, no. 35, Sept. 1961: 16–17.

2421. ———. Braziliia govorit: "da" [Brazil says "yes"] Za rubezhom, no. 47, Nov. 1961: 29.

2422. ———. Trevozhnye budni [Restless workdays] Za rubezhom, no. 9, Feb. 1964: 7.

2423. Polishchuk, Ol. Gigant rozpravliaie plechi [A giant awakes] Ukraina, no. 5, Mar. 1963: 20–21.

2424. Prestes, Luis Carlos. Velichestvennye perspektivy stroitel'stva kommunizma i ukrepleniia mira [Great prospects for the building of communism and consolidating peace] Probl. mira i sots., v. 2, no. 1, Jan. 1959: 18–20.

2425. Rozhkov, A. "Plan stablizatsii valiuty" v Brazilii [A "plan for the stablization of Brazilian currency"] Mir. ekon. i mezhdunar. otn., no. 12, Dec. 1959: 103–104.

2426. Scheinvar, Leia. Istomlennaia zemlia na severo-vostoke Brazilii [Thirsty soil in northeastern Brazil] Zhen. mira, no. 12, 1962: 24–26.

2427. Seregin, IU. Tiazheloe nasledie [A grim legacy] Nov. vrem., v. 19, no. 10, Mar. 1961: 11–12.

2428. Stregulina, N. G. Gosudarstvennyi kapitalizm v Brazilii kak forma bor'by za ekonomicheskuiu nezavisimost' [Brazilian state capitalism as a form of the struggle for economic independence] Uch. zap. kaf. obshchestv. nauk vuz. g. Len.: Polit. ekon., no. 4, 1962: 212–223.

2429. ———. Nekotorye voprosy ekonomicheskogo razvitiia Brazilii na sovremennom etape [Some problems concerning the economic development of Brazil at the present stage] Uch. zap. kaf. obshchestv. nauk vuz. g. Len.: Polit. ekon., no. 6, 1963: 159–178.

2430. Tkachenko, V. Ognedyshushchii kontinent [A fire-spitting continent] Sov. voin, v. 44, no. 5, Mar. 1962: 44–45.

2431. Xavier, Silva. Ne zhdat' "manny nebesnoi" [We shouldn't wait for "manna from heaven"] Za rubezhom, no. 24, Nov. 1960: 14–15.

2432. Zdravyi podkhod [A sensible approach] Za rubezhom, no. 6, Feb. 1961: 1–2.

2433. Zholobov, V. Ekonomicheskoe polozhenie Brazilii [The economic situation of Brazil] Mir. ekon. i mezhdunar. otn., no. 2, Feb. 1962: 101–103.

2434. ———. Valiutno-finansovoe polozhenie Brazilii [The foreign-exchange and financial situation of Brazil] Den. i kred., v. 21, no. 9, Sept. 1963: 75–85.

See also entries no. 1619, 2382, and 2383.

4. Chile

2435. Araya, Bernardo. A mozhet byt' eto budet skoree: Chili [It could be sooner: Chile] Nov. vrem., v. 20, no. 1, Jan. 1962: 9–10.

2436. Bankovskaia sistema Chili [The banking system of Chile] Den. i kred., v. 18, no. 9, Sept. 1960: 85–86.

2437. Cademartori, José. Puti razvitiia stran zavoevavshikh natsional'nuiu nezavisimost'; Chili [The paths of economic development in the countries which have won their national independence; Chile] Probl. mira i sots., v. 5, no. 6, June 1962: 83–85.

2438. Fedorov, M. Chili [Chile] Otv. na vop. trud., no. 11, Nov. 1963: 38–46.

2439. M. Kh. Review. Mir. ekon. i mezhdunar. otn., no. 10, 1963: 156.

A review of Ricardo Lagos' *La concentración del poder económico* (Santiago de Chile, Editorial del Pacífico, 1961. 177 p.).

2440. Na povestke dnia: Chili [Chile is on the agenda] Zhen. mira, no. 9, 1960: 26.

2441. Santa Klaus i plan Klein-Saksa [Santa Claus and the Klein and Saks plan] Za rubezhom, no. 29, Dec. 1960: 5.

2442. Sepúlveda Hernández, Jorge. Kooperatsiia v Chili [Chilean cooperative societies] Sov. potreb. koop., v. 6, no. 1, 1962: 48–50.

See also entry no. 3048.

5. Colombia

2443. Bunegina, Irina Aleksandrovna. Kolumbiia; ekonomika i vneshniaia torgovlia [Colombia; its economy and foreign trade] Moscow, Vneshtorgizdat, 1959. 149 p.   HC197.B8

2444. Cardona Hoyos, José. Pravda o Kolumbii [The truth about Colombia] Probl. mira i sots., v. 7, no. 10, Nov. 1964: 94–95.

A review of Diego Montaña Cuéllar's *Colombia, país formal y país real* (Buenos Aires, Editorial Platina, 1963. 236 p.).

2445. Pakin, S. Ekonomicheskii zastoi i politicheskii krizis [Economic stagnation and political crisis] Mezhdunar. zhizn', v. 11, no. 5, May 1964: 114–115.

See also entry no. 4622.

6. Costa Rica

2446. Sierra Cantillo, Gonzalo. A mozhet byt' eto budet skoree: Kosta-Rika [It could be sooner: Costa Rica] Nov. vrem., v. 20, no. 1, Jan. 1962: 13–14.

7. Cuba

2447. Andrianov, Vasilii Vasil'evich. Nash drug Kuba [Our friend Cuba] Moscow, Izd-vo IMO, 1963. 102 p. HC157.C9A65

2448. Blasco Cobo, Juan. Drug nash Kuba [Our friend Cuba] Moscow, Znanie, 1963. 47 p.

Translated from the Spanish.

2449. Borovik, Genrikh. Pylaiushchii ostrov [An island in flame] Moscow, Mol. gvardiia, 1964. 143 p.

2450. Calderío, Francisco (Blas Roca, *pseud.*) Osnovy sotsializma na Kube [The foundations of socialism in Cuba] Moscow, Gospolitizdat, 1961. 243 p.

Translated from the Spanish *Los fundamentos del socialismo en Cuba*.

Reviewed by IU. Egorov in *Nov. i noveish. ist.*, no. 1, 1962: 164–165.

2451. Efimov, Anatolii Nikolaevich, *and* A. I. Anchishkin. Kuba planiruet natsional'nuiu ekonomiku [Cuba plans its national economy] Moscow, Ekonomizdat, 1963. 78 p.   HC157.C9E35

Reviewed by IA. Mashbits in *Vop. ekon.*, no. 9, Sept. 1963: 120–123.

2452. Fadeev, IU. A. Dva goda bor'by i pobed [Two years of struggle and achievements] Moscow, Znanie, 1961. 35 p.

2453. Gonionskii, S. A. Kuba idet vpered [Cuba is marching forward] Moscow, Znanie, 1962. 32 p.

2454. Khidaiatov, G. Kuba stroit novuiu zhizn' [Cuba builds a new life] Tashkent, Gosizdat UzSSR, 1962. 67 p.

In Uzbek.

2455. Klymko, Nat. Revoliutsionnye preobrazovaniia v ekonomike respubliki Kuba, ianvar' 1959 g.-oktiabr' 1963 g. [Revolutionary reforms in the economy of the Cuban Republic, January 1959– October 1963] Kiev, 1964. 20 p. (Kievskii institut narodnogo khoziaistva)

2456. ———. Sotsialistychni peretvorennia na Kubi [Socialist reforms in Cuba] Kiev, Politvydav Ukrainy, 1964. 102 p.

2457. Kokhreidze, P. G. Kuba—zaria pervogo ianvaria [Cuba at dawn on the first

of January] Tiflis, Sabchota Sakartvelo, 1963. 210 p.
In Georgian.

2458. Merin, B. M.   Svobodnaia Kuba [Free Cuba] Moscow, Prosveshchenie, 1964. 128 p.

2459. Podkolzin, Aleksandr Mikhailovich. Ekonomika Respubliki Kuba [The national economy of the Cuban Republic] Moscow, Un-t druzhby narodov im. Patrisa Lumumby, 1964. 64 p.
                              HC157.C9P63

2460. Ponizovskii, Vladimir Mironovich. Alaia zhemchuzhina Antil [The red pearl of the Antilles] Moscow, Mysl', 1964. 80 p.   DLC

2461. Popov, B. V.   Kuba stroit sotsializm [Cuba builds socialism] Moscow, Znanie, 1963. 47 p.   DLC

2462. Andrianov, V.   Kuba boretsia! [Cuba struggles!] Sov. profsoiuzy, v. 17, no. 15, Aug. 1961: 34–35.

2463. ———.   Kuba stroit novuiu zhizn' [Cuba builds a new life] Agitator, no. 23, Dec. 1964: 18–20.

2464. ———.   Uspekhi svobodnoi Kuby; k 5-letiiu pobedy revoliutsii [The achievements of free Cuba; on the fifth anniversary of the Cuban Revolution] Agitator, no. 24, Dec. 1963: 27–29.

2465. Arcocha, Juan.   Novogodniaia Gavana [New Year's Day in Havana] Za rubezhom, no. 52, Dec. 1961: 16–17.

2466. Borovik, G.   Litso druga [The face of a friend] Ogonek, v. 38, no. 47, Nov. 1960: 2–3.

2467. Borovskii, V.   Cherty kubinskoi revoliutsii [Features of the Cuban Revolution] Nov. vrem., v. 20, no. 48, Nov. 1962: 26–28.

2468. ———.   Za pobedu kubinskogo naroda [For the victory of the Cuban people] Za rubezhom, no. 29, Dec. 1960: 10.

2469. Calderío, Francisco (Blas Roca, pseud.) Kuba; revoliutsiia v deistvii [Cuba; the revolution in action] Probl. mira i sots., v. 2, no. 8, Aug. 1959: 17–23.

2470. ———.   Kuba stroit novuiu zhizn' [Cuba builds a new life] Agitator, no. 23, Dec. 1961: 39–41.

2471. ———.   Novyi etap revoliutsii na Kube [A new phase in the Cuban Revolution] Probl. mira i sots., v. 4, no. 10, Oct. 1961: 1–8.

2472. ———.   Puti razvitiia stran, zavoevavshikh natsional'nuiu nezavisimost'; Kuba [The paths of economic development in the countries which have won their national independence; Cuba] Probl. mira i sots., v. 5, no. 5, May 1962: 68–70.

2473. Castro, Fidel.   Glavnaia problema Kuby [Cuba's paramount problem] Nov. vrem., v. 18, no. 15, Apr. 1960: 14–16.

2474. ———.   O problemakh Kuby [Cuba's present-day problems] Nov. vrem., v. 19, no. 31, July 1961: 3–5.

2475. Chigir', N.   Nadezhdy nedrugov ne sbudutsia! [The hopes of the enemies will not come true] Mezhdunar. zhizn', v. 10, no. 11, Nov. 1963: 104–105.

2476. Chomón Mediavilla, Faure.   O politike Kuby [Cuba's policy] Nov. vrem., v. 18, no. 45, Nov. 1960: 14–15.

2477. Dolinin, A. A.   Perspektivy razvitiia Kuby [Prospects for the economic development of Cuba] Materialy po ekonomicheskoi geografii zarubezhnykh stran, no. 1, 1961: 16–47.

2478. Dubrovskii, A.   Ekonomika i finansy svobodnoi Kuby [The economy and finances of free Cuba] Fin. SSSR, v. 22, no. 7, July 1961: 39–42.

2479. Ernesto Gevara ob aktual'nykh problemakh kubinskoi ekonomiki [Ernesto Guevara describes the current problems of the Cuban national economy] Nov. vrem., v. 21, no. 39, Sept. 1963: 12–13.

2480. Farge, Germaine.   Fidel' i Raul' Kastro mne skazali . . . [Fidel and Raúl Castro told me . . .] V zashch. mira, no. 1, Jan. 1961: 19–26.

2481. Gabinskii, Nikolai.   Svobodnaia territoriia Ameriki [The free territory of America] Nov. mir, v. 38, no. 6, June 1962: 267–270.

2482. Gel'man, P. Ekonomicheskoie pre-obrazovaniia v Respublike Kuba [Economic changes in the Cuban Republic] Nauch. dokl. vys. shkoly; ekon. nauki, v. 6, no. 5, 1963: 3–15.

2483. Goitizolo, Juan. Narod v pokhode [The people on the march] Nov. mir, v. 40, no. 2, Feb. 1964: 102–139.
Translated from the Spanish.

2484. Govorit Fidel' Kastro [Fidel Castro speaks] Za rubezhom, no. 24, Nov. 1960: 3, 18–19.
Translated from the Spanish.

2485. Guevara, Ernesto. Interv'iu [An interview] Mir. ekon. i mezhdunar. otn., no. 5, 1964: 62–65.

2486. ———. Politicheskii suverenitet i ekonomicheskaia nezavisimost' [Political sovereignty and economic independence] Mir. ekon. i mezhdunar. otn., no. 6, June 1960: 59–67.

2487. Gvozdarev, B. I. Uspekhi narodnoi Kuby; nauchnaia konferentsiia v Moskve [A conference on the achievements of People's Cuba held in Moscow] Vest. AN SSSR, v. 34, no. 3, Mar. 1964: 130–132.

2488. Holda, Miroslav. Mnogoe izmenilos' pod solntsem [Many things under the sun have changed] Vsem. stud. nov., v. 14, no. 8, Aug. 1960: 6–7.

2489. Ivanov, V., and P. Ossovskii. Kuba segodnia [Cuba today] Kul't. i zhizn', v. 5, no. 8, 1961: 44.

2490. Juárez, Claudio. ¡Cuba Sí! ¡Yanqui No! V zashch. mira, no. 10, Oct. 1960: 8–19.

2491. Kalinin, A. Kharakter i dvizhushchie sily revoliutsii na Kube [The nature and motive power of the revolution in Cuba] Mir. ekon. i mezhdunar. otn., no. 10, Oct. 1960: 81–84.

2492. Kamynin, L. Gody pobed [The years of victories] Mezhdunar. zhizn', v. 11, no. 12, Dec. 1964: 109–110.

2493. ———. Postup' kubinskoi revoliutsii [The progress of the Cuban Revolution] Mezhdunar. zhizn', v. 10, no. 5, May 1963: 23–29.

2494. ———. Slavnoe piatiletie [Five glorious years] Mezhdunar. zhizn', v. 11, no. 1, Jan. 1964: 108.

2495. Klymko, Nat. Kuba stroit, Kuba pobezhdaet [Cuba is building, and Cuba is winning] Komm. Ukr., v. 38, no. 5, May 1963: 74–81.

2496. Kukharev, N. Svobodnaia Kuba idet vpered [Free Cuba marches forward] Vnesh. torg., v. 43, no. 11, 1963: 18–21.
Summary in English.

2497. L. S. Kubinskaia revoliutsiia razvivaetsia i uglubliaetsia [The Cuban Revolution is developing and deepening] Probl. mira i sots., v. 3, no. 6, June 1960: 68–70.

2498. Le Riverend, Julio. Istoriia razvitiia kubinskoi ekonomiki [History of the development of the Cuban national economy] Kuba, no. 4, Dec. 1964: 6–13.

2499. Levin, V. Kuba — da, ianki — net! [Cuba—yes, Yankee—no! [Mol. komm., no. 9, Sept. 1960: 90–94.

2500. Listov, V. Ernesto Gevara ob ekonomicheskikh perspektivakh Kuby [Ernesto Guevara on Cuba's economic prospects; (an interview)] Nov. vrem., v. 20, no. 27, July 1962: 12–14.

2501. ———. Zemlia nadezhdy [The land of hope] Nov. vrem., v. 17, no. 34, Aug. 1959: 26–28; v. 17, no. 35, Aug. 1959: 27–29.

2502. Loziuk, M. Narodnaia revoliutsiia na Kube; dva goda bor'by i pobed [The people's revolution in Cuba; two years of struggle and achievements] Komm. Ukr., v. 36, no. 1, Jan. 1961: 67–76.

2503. Marinello, Juan. Chto sdelano za dva goda na Kube [What has been done in Cuba in two years] Nov. vrem., v. 19, no. 4, Jan. 1961: 3–4.

2504. ———. Vtoraia godovshchina kubinskoi revoliutsii [The second anniversary of the Cuban Revolution] Kommunist, v. 37, no. 1, Jan. 1961: 96–103.

2505. Mashbits, IA. G. Novye cherty v geografii revoliutsionnoi Kuby [New features in the geography of revolutionary Cuba] Geog. v shkole, v. 25, no. 2, Mar.-Apr. 1962: 14–23.

2506. ———. Sdvigi v strukture i geografii khoziaistva i perspektivy razvitiia sotsialisticheskoi ekonomiki na Kube; k piatiletiiu Kubinskoi revoliutsii [Changes in the structure and geography of the national economy and prospects for developing the socialist economy of Cuba; on the fifth anniversary of the Cuban Revolution] Izv. AN SSSR. Ser. geog., no. 6, Nov.-Dec. 1963: 3–14.

2507. ———. Uverennaia postup' revoliutsionnoi Kuby [The confident steps of revolutionary Cuba] Vop. ist., no. 12, Dec. 1960: 196–198.

2508. Mashkin, V. Sila idei revoliutsii [The force of revolutionary ideas] Mezhdunar. zhizn', v. 10, no. 9, Sept. 1963: 107.

2509. Massovoe obsuzhdenie plana ekonomicheskogo razvitiia [A mass discussion of the economic development program] Probl. mira i sots., v. 4, no. 12, Dec. 1961: 59.

2510. Mikoian, A. I. O Kube; iz vystupleniia na press-konferentsii v Oslo 16 fevralia 1960 g. [On Cuba; from an interview at a press conference in Oslo, Feb. 16, 1960] Nov. vrem., v. 18, no. 9, Feb. 1960: 16–17.

2511. Mikoian, S. Kuba, zakalennaia v boiakh i trude [Cuba, a country hardened in battles and work] Za rubezhom, no. 48, Dec. 1962: 16–17.

2512. ———. Kubinskii narod boretsia za svetloe budushchee [The Cuban people struggle for their bright future] Polit. samoobr., v. 5, no. 5, May 1961: 10–21.

2513. Mokhnachev, M. I. Slavnyi iubilei ostrova svobody [Glorious anniversary of the island of freedom] Vop. ist. KPSS, v. 8, no. 1, Jan. 1964: 65–69.

2514. Muñoz, Honorio. Slavnaia godovshchina [A glorious anniversary] Sov. zhen., v. 20, no. 1, 1964: 12.

2515. Nachalo bol'shogo puti [The first steps of a long march] Za rubezhom, no. 29, Dec. 1960: 8.

2516. The new Cuba. World youth, no. 1, 1964: 28–29.

2517. Núñez Jiménez, Antonio. S Fidelem Kastro po Kube [Through Cuba with Fidel Castro] Neva, no. 5, 1961: 7–27.
    Translated from the Spanish.

2518. O sovremennom polozhenii na Kube [The present-day situation in Cuba] Probl. mira i sots., v. 2, no. 4, Apr. 1959: 69–71.

2519. Obolenskii, N. Finansy svobodnoi Kuby [The finances of free Cuba] Fin. SSSR, v. 23, no. 11, Nov. 1962: 41 49.

2520. Olteanu, O. Sozdanie gosudarstvennogo sektora v kubinskoi ekonomike [The creation of a state sector in the Cuban national economy] Mir. ekon. i mezhdunar. otn., no. 10, Oct. 1962: 119–123.

2521. Ostrov svobody [The island of freedom] Za rubezhom, no. 29, July 1961: 4–5.

2522. Pakin, S. Kuba planiruet svoiu ekonomiku [Cuba plans her economy] Mir. ekon. i mezhdunar. otn., no. 11, Nov. 1961: 91–93.

2523. ———. Kuba ukrepliaet natsional'nuiu ekonomiku [Cuba strengthens her national economy] Mir. ekon. i mezhdunar. otn., no. 4, Apr. 1961: 133–138.

2524. Perventsev, Vladimir. Kubinskaia nov' [New developments in Cuba] Sov. voin, no. 46, no. 8, Apr. 1964: 38–39.

2525. Piat' let novoi Kuby [The fifth anniversary of new Cuba] Nov. vrem., v. 21, no. 1, Jan. 1964: 6.

2526. Prazdnik Kuby [Festive meetings in Cuba] Nov. vrem., v. 19, no. 30, July 1961: 2.

2527. Proval blokady [Failure of the blockade] Za rubezhom, no. 6, Feb. 1964: 2–3.

2528. Respublika Kuba; k 6-i godovshchine pobedy narodnoi revoliutsii [The Republic of Cuba; the sixth anniversary of the victorious people's revolution] Kal. znam. i pam. dat, v. 9, no. 1, Jan. 1964: 4–6.

2529. Review. Nov. i noveish. ist., no. 4, 1964: 187.
    A review of V. Calo's *Cuba non é una eccezione* (Milan, 1963. 213 p.).

2530. Rodríguez, Carlos Rafael. Kuba na poroge 1962 goda [Cuba on the threshold of 1962] Nov. vrem., v. 20, no. 1, Jan. 1962: 18–19.

2531. Scheyven, Raymond. Ot Punta-del'-Este do Gavany; otryvki iz knigi [From Punta del Este to Havana; excerpts from a book] Za rubezhom, no. 39, Sept. 1962: 24–25.
Translated from the French.

2532. Serebrovskaia, M. A. O dvukh eta-pakh natsionalizatsii promyshlennosti na Kube [On the two stages of the nationalization of Cuban industry] Uch. zap. kaf. obshchestv. nauk vuz. g. Len.; Polit. ekon., no. 4, 1962: 146–158.

2533. Shustov, K. Kuba zhivet! [Cuba is alive!] Part. zhizn' Kazakh., v. 34, no. 12, Dec. 1964: 63–66.

2534. Sugiri. Trudiashchiesia Kuby sozdaiut budushchee svoei strany [The workers of Cuba build their country's future] Vsem. prof. dvizh., no. 2, Feb. 1962: 24–27, 31.

2535. Trutier, Teudis. Kubinskaia revoliutsiia i kooperatsiia [The Cuban Revolution and cooperative societies] Sov. potreb. koop., v. 6, no. 4, Apr. 1962: 60.

2536. TSvietkov, H. M. Kuba zhyve! [Cuba is alive!] Ukraina, no. 8, Apr. 1963: 9–11.

2537. V trude i v boiu [In work and in struggle] Ogonek, v. 39, no. 30, July 1961: 1.

2538. Vasil'kov, V. Kuba; dva goda bor'by i pobed [Cuba; two years of struggle and achievements] Mezhdunar. zhizn', v. 8, no. 1, Jan. 1961: 148–149.

2539. Zaikin, A. Pod znamenem svobody i sotsializma [Under the banner of freedom and socialism] Part. zhizn' Kazakh., v. 33, no. 7, July 1963: 78–80.

2540. Zaretskii, A., and G. Mesionzhnik. Kuba stroit sotsializm [Cuba builds socialism] Komm. Mold., v. 9, no. 12, Dec. 1964: 58–63.

2541. Zherdynivs'ka, M., and L. Olevs'kyi. Reportazh z Kuby [News stories from Cuba] Vsesvit, v. 7, no. 1, Jan. 1964: 158–159.

A review of Jesús Izcaray's *Reportaje en Cuba* (Havana, 1962).

2542. Zilliacus, Konni. Rabochie budni Kuby [Workdays in Cuba] Nov. vrem., v. 20, no. 9, Mar. 1963: 24–25.

See also entries no. 890, 1798, 2890, 3000, 4674, 4700, 4704, 4708, and 4713.

8. Ecuador

2543. Pakin, S. Skandal za skandalom [Recurrent scandals] Mezhdunar. zhizn', v. 11, no. 8, Aug. 1964: 111–112.

9. Guatemala

2544. Campos, C. Puti razvitiia stran, zavoevavshikh natsional'nuiu nezavisimost'; Gvatemala [The paths of development of countries which have won their national independence; Guatemala] Probl. mira i sots., v. 5, no. 7, July 1962: 78–79.

2545. Na povestke dnia: Gvatemala [On the agenda: Guatemala] Zhen. mira, no. 2, 1961: 22–23.

See also entry no. 413.

10. Haiti

2546. Rivière, Paul. Gaiti—gaitianam [Haiti for the Haitians] Vsem. prof. dvizh., no. 3, Mar. 1964: 8–10.

11. Honduras

2547. Korshuny nad plantatsiiami [Birds of prey over the plantations] Za rubezhom, no. 34, Aug. 1963: 20–21.

12. Jamaica

2548. Bartumian, E. IAmaika [Jamaica] Otv. na vop. trud., no. 6, June 1963: 56–59.

2549. Cox, Idris. IAmaika posle polucheniia nezavisimosti [Jamaica since it acquired independence] Probl. mira i sots., v. 7, no. 2, Feb. 1964: 82–84.

13. Mexico

2550. Mashbits, IAkov Grigor'evich. Meksika; ekonomichesko-geograficheskaia kharakteristika [Mexico; its geography

and economic conditions] Moscow, Geografgiz, 1961. 296 p.   HC135.M3
Reviewed by A. A. Dolinin in *Izv. Vses. geogr. o-va*, v. 95, no. 2, 1963: 188–189.

2551. Sheremet'ev, Igor' Konstantinovich. Gosudarstvennyi kapitalizm v Meksike [State capitalism in Mexico] Moscow, Izd-vo Akad. nauk SSSR, 1963. 135 p.
    HC135.S35

2552. ———. Razvitie gosudarstvenno-kapitalisticheskikh tendentsii v ekonomike Meksiki posle vtoroi mirovoi voiny [The development of trends to state capitalism in the national economy of Mexico after the Second World War] Moscow, 1961. 19 p.

2553. Tuchnin, Ruslan Aleksandrovich. Meksika bez ekzotiki [Mexico without the exotic] Moscow, Gospolitizdat, 1963. 125 p.   HC135.T8
Also published in Latvian.

2554. Dansos Palomino, Ramón. Kooperativnoe dvizhenie v Meksike [The cooperative movement in Mexico] Sov. potreb. koop., v. 5, no. 11, Nov. 1961: 57–59.

2555. Mashbits, IA. G. K voprosu o formirovanii ekonomicheskikh raionov v Meksike [The formation of economic regions in Mexico] Vop. geogr., no. 53, 1961: 101–103.

2556. ———. Osnovnye cherty razmeshcheniia proizvoditel'nykh sil v Meksike [Principal features of the distribution of productive forces in Mexico] *In* Geograficheskie soobshcheniia; materialy VI konferentsii molodykh uchenykh Instituta geografii AN SSSR. Moscow, Izd-vo Akad. nauk SSSR, 1959: p. 107–109.

2557. Sheremet'ev, I. Meksika v bor'be protiv inostrannogo imperializma [Mexico in the struggle against foreign imperialism] Mir. ekon. i mezhdunar. otn., no. 10, Oct. 1960: 87–89.

2558. Shul'govskii, A. F. Natsionalizatsiia neftianoi promyshlennosti v Meksike [The nationalization of the petroleum industry in Mexico] Nov. i noveish. ist., no. 1, 1960: 68–85.

2559. Vicentini, María Luisa. Prekrasnaia i stoikaia meksikanskaia zemlia [The beautiful and enduring Mexican land] Zhen. mira, no. 8, 1959: 23–25.

See also entry no. 2917.

14. Paraguay

2560. Nitoburg, E. L. Paragvai; ekonomiko-geograficheskii ocherk [Paraguay; an economic and geographical study] Moscow, Nauka, 1964. 94 p.

2561. Borisov, V. Paragvaiskaia drama [The Paraguayan drama] Mezhdunar. zhizn', v. 6, no. 11, Nov. 1959: 144–146.

2562. Eliutin, IU. K sobytiiam v Paragvae [Events in Paraguay] Mir ekon. i mezhdunar. otn., no. 3, Mar. 1960: 94–96.

15. Peru

2563. Dolinin, A. A., *and* L. I. Doroshkevich. Peru [Peru] Moscow, Mysl', 1964. 256 p.

2564. Castro Franco, Julio. Rodina moia, Peru [Peru, my native land] Nov. vrem., v. 17, no. 4, Jan. 1959: 30–31.

2565. Deiateli Peru o problemakh svoei strany [An interview with Peruvian public figures on the problems of their country] Nov. vrem., v. 18, no. 20, May 1960: 19.

2566. Kushcheev, L. Peru v tiskakh reaktsii [Peru in the grip of reaction] Nov. vrem., v. 19, no. 21, May 1961: 13–14.

2567. Prado, Jorge del. Trud, zovushchii k bor'be [A study which calls us to struggle] Probl. mira i sots., v. 3, no. 1, Jan. 1960: 87–89.
A review of José Carlos Mariátegui's *Siete ensayos de interpretación de la realidad peruana* (Lima, Editora Amauta, 1958. 307 p.).

16. Puerto Rico

2568. Bulavin, V. I. Puerto-Riko; ekonomiko-geograficheskii ocherk [Puerto Rico; an economic-geographic outline] Moscow, Geografgiz, 1962. 37 p.   DLC

17. Trinidad and Tobago

2569. Bartumian, E. Trinidad i Tobago [Trinidad and Tobago] Otv. na vop. trud., no. 3, Mar. 1963: 54–57.

18. Uruguay

2570. Romanova, Zinaida Ivanovna. Urugvai; ekonomika i vneshniaia torgovlia [Uruguay; its economy and foreign trade] Moscow, Vneshtorgizdat, 1962. 142 p.
HC232.R65

See also entry no. 1088.

19. Venezuela

2571. Andrianov, V. Uroki sobytii v Venesuele [The lesson of the events in Venezuela] Mezhdunar. zhizn', v. 7, no. 6, June 1960: 119–121.

2572. Mashbits, IA. G. Sub"ektivnaia otsenka roli srednikh sloev v ekonomicheskoi i politicheskoi zhizni Venesuely [A preconceived evaluation of the role of the middle classes in Venezuelan political life] Vop. ist., v. 39, no. 6, June 1964: 201–202.

2573. Shul'govskii, A. Patrioticheskie sily Venesuely v bor'be za ekonomicheskuiu nezavisimost' [The patriotic forces of Venezuela in the struggle for economic independence] Mir. ekon. i mezhdunar. otn., no. 10, Oct. 1960: 84–87.

See also entries no. 4782 and 4783.

20. West Indies

2574. Gunteaud, Walter. A mozhet byt' eto budet skoree: Martinika [It could be sooner: Martinique] Nov. vrem., v. 20, no. 1, Jan. 1962: 15.

2575. Kozel v ogorode [A wolf in charge of sheep] Nov. vrem., v. 19, no. 12, Mar. 1961: 23.
Virgin Islands.

2576. Martinika i Gvadelupa [Martinique and Guadeloupe] Mezhdunar. zhizn', v. 8, no. 10, Oct. 1961: 158–159.

2577. Pin, A. Marka Gvadelupy [A postage stamp from Guadeloupe] Vokrug sveta, no. 8, Aug. 1961: 10–11.

2578. Ponce, Maurice. Martinika, Gvadelupa [Martinique and Guadeloupe] Vsesvit, v. 4, no. 5, May 1961: 5–10.
Translated from the French.

XI

INTERNATIONAL ECONOMIC RELATIONS

℘

A. WRITINGS DEALING WITH THREE OR MORE COUNTRIES

2579. Bagirov, IU. A., *and others*. Zasilie monopolii SShA v stranakh Latinskoi Ameriki [The dominant position of U.S. monopolies in the countries of Latin America] Baku, 1962. 38 p.
In Azerbaijani.

2580. Bezrodnyi, IE. F. Anglo-amerikanskie protivorechiia v Latinskoi Amerike posle vtoroi mirovoi voiny, 1945–1955 gg. [Anglo-American rivalry in Latin America after the Second World War, 1945–1955] Kiev, 1964. 15 p. (Akademiia nauk Ukrainskoi SSR. Sektsiia obshchestvennykh nauk]
Abstract of a dissertation for the degree of Candidate in Historical Sciences.

2581. Eliutin, IU. P. Neokolonialistskaia politika SShA v Latinskoi Amerike i programma "Soiuza radi progressa" [The neocolonialist policy of the United States in Latin America and the program of the "Alliance for Progress"] Moscow, 1964. 18 p. (Institut Latinskoi Ameriki Akademii nauk SSSR)
Abstract of a dissertation for the degree of Candidate in Historical Sciences.

2582. Gvozdarev, Boris Ivanovich. "Soiuz radi progressa" i ego sushchnost' [The real nature of the "Alliance for Progress"] Moscow, Nauka, 1964. 183 p.

2583. Khokhlov, G. S. Eksport chastnogo amerikanskogo kapitala—orudie zakabaleniia Latinskoi Ameriki v period posle vtoroi mirovoi voiny [Postwar investments of American private capital are a tool for the enslavement of Latin America] Moscow, 1963. (Institut mirovoi ekonomiki i mezhdunarodnykh otnoshenii Akademii nauk SSSR]
Abstract of a dissertation for the degree of Candidate in Economic Sciences.

2584. Klusov, E. P. "Soiuz radi progressa"—orudie amerikanskoi ekonomicheskoi agressii [The "Alliance for Progress" is a weapon of American economic aggression] Moskva, Izd-vo Mosk. un-ta, 1963. 17 p.
Author's abstract of a dissertation for the degree of Candidate in Economic Sciences.

2585. ———. Znariaddia neokolonializmu SShA; pro neokolonialists'ku sut' "Soiuzu zarady progressu" [A tool of U.S. neocolonialism; the neocolonialist nature of the "Alliance for Progress"] Kiev, Politvydav, 1964. 41 p.

2586. Lavrichenko, M. V. Ekonomicheskoe sotrudnichestvo SSSR so stranami Azii, Afriki i Latinskoi Ameriki [The economic cooperation of the USSR with the countries of Asia, Africa, and Latin America] Moscow, Gospolitizdat, 1961. 144 p.
HF1558 1961.L3

2587. Levin, V. G. SShA i Latinskaia Amerika [The United States and Latin America] Moscow, Znanie, 1963. 31 p.

2588. Núñez Jiménez, Antonio. Imperiia ianki — vrag Latinskoi Ameriki [The Yankee empire is the enemy of Latin America] Moscow, Sotsekgiz, 1962. 109 p.
F1418.N83

Translated by E. L. Rovinskaia from the Spanish.
Reviewed by O. Olteanu in *Vop. ist.*, v. 38, no. 2, Feb. 1963: 179–180.

2589. Romanova, Zinaida Ivanovna. Ekonomicheskaia ekspansiia SShA v Latinskoi Amerike [The economic expansion of the United States in Latin America] Moscow, Sotsekgiz, 1963. 269 p.
HG5302.R58
Reviewed by S. Mikoian in *Vop. ist.*, v. 39, no. 4, Apr. 1964: 156–160; by I. Sheremet'ev in *Nov. mir*, v. 40, no. 4, Apr. 1964: 266–268.

2590. Skachkov, Semen Andreevich, *and others*. Pomoshch' i sotrudnichestvo vo imia mira; ekonomicheskoe sotrudnichestvo SSSR so stranami Azii, Afriki i Latinskoi Ameriki [Assistance and cooperation in the name of peace; Soviet economic cooperation with the countries of Asia, Africa, and Latin America] Moscow, Gospolitizdat, 1962. 54 p.
HF1558 1962.S55
Also published in Latvian and Moldavian.

2591. Tarasov, K. V interesakh monopolii; imperialisticheskaia "pomoshch'" SShA stranam Latinskoi Ameriki [In the interests of monopolies; the imperialist "assistance" of the United States to Latin American countries] Moscow, Mysl', 1964. 142 p.

2592. Aleksandrovskii, B. A. Evoliutsiia inostrannykh kapitalovlozhenii v Latinskoi Amerike [Evolution of foreign investments in Latin America] Trudy MIIZ, no. 13, 1961: 20–57.

2593. Andreasian, R. Strany Vostoka i Latinskoi Ameriki protiv neftianogo kartelia [The countries of the Near East and Latin America are against the oil cartel] Mir. ekon. i mezhdunar. otn., no. 3, Mar. 1962: 128–132.

2594. Andreev, G. Amerikanskii imperializm—ekspluatator Latinskoi Ameriki [American imperialism is an exploiter of Latin America] Mezhdunar. zhizn', v. 8, no. 1, 1961: 23–39.

2595. Andrianov, V. Etogo trebuet zhizn' [Life requires it] Mezhdunar. zhizn', v. 6, no. 10, Oct. 1959: 132–133.
Commercial contacts with the USSR.

2596. Andrianov, V. V. "Soiuz radi grabezha" [An "alliance for plunder"] Nov. i noveish. ist., no. 6, 1964: 146.
A review of Aríel H. Badano's *Autopsia del "caballo muerto"* (Montevideo, Ediciones "Estrella," 1964. 76 p.).

2597. Arkhipov, V. Ekspansiia IAponii v Latinskoi Amerike [Japanese economic expansion in Latin America] Mir. ekon. i mezhdunar. otn., no. 12, Dec. 1959: 107–109.

2598. Artiushenkov, M. Bunt protiv SShA [A revolt against the United States] Mezhdunar. zhizn', v. 11, no. 4, Apr. 1964: 127.
The Alliance for Progress.

2599. Badano, Aríel H. Anatomiia dokhloi loshadi; otryvki iz knigi [The anatomy of a dead horse; excerpts from a book] Za rubezhom, no. 11, Mar. 1964: 17–18.
The Alliance for Progress.
Translated from the Spanish.

2600. ———. Vozdushnye zamki neokolonializma; glavy iz knigi [The "pie in the sky" of neocolonialism; excerpts from a book] Mezhdunar. zhizn', v. 11, no. 6, June 1964: 115–125.
The Alliance for Progress.
Translated from the Spanish.

2601. Bakhtin, V. I. Vneshnie investitsii SShA—orudie ekspluatatsii narodov stran Latinskoi Ameriki [U.S. investments are a tool for the exploitation of the peoples of Latin America] Nauch. zap. Kiev. fin.-ekon. inst., no. 9, 1959: 313–326.

2602. Bezrodnyi, IE. Anglo-amerykans'ki superechnosti v Latyns'kii Amerytsi [Anglo-American competition in Latin America] Ekon. Rad. Ukr., no. 1, Jan.-Feb. 1962: 111–116.

2603. Bochkarev, IU. Politicheskii klimat k iugu ot Rio-Grande [The political climate south of the Rio Grande] Nov. vrem., v. 21, no. 52, Dec. 1963: 13–15.
The Alliance for Progress.

2604. Bogush, E. Osobennosti kolonial'noi politiki SShA na sovremennom etape [Special features of the present-day colonial policy of the United States] Mezhdunar. zhizn', v. 9, no. 5, May 1962: 35–44.

2605. Borisov, V. Zapadnogermanskie monopolii v Latinskoi Amerike [West German monopolies in Latin America] Mezhdunar. zhizn', v. 7, no. 12, Dec. 1960: 112–114.

2606. Chibisov, M. "Vtoroe osvobozhdenie" Latinskoi Ameriki ["The second liberation" of Latin America] Nov. vrem., v. 21, no. 49, Dec. 1963: 5–7.
Foreign investments.

2607. Chto skryvaetsia za shirmoi "Soiuza radi progressa"? [What is hidden behind the screen of the "Alliance for Progress?"] Komm. Vooruzh. Sil, v. 2, no. 10, May 1962: 88–90.

2608. Eliutin, IU. Ekonomicheskii nazhim [Economic pressure] Mezhdunar. zhizn', v. 11, no. 11, Nov. 1964: 108.
Exports of sugar and coffee to the United States.

2609. ———. Golos vstrevozhennykh kolonizatorov [The voice of alarmed colonizers] Mezhdunar. zhizn', v. 9, no. 4, Apr. 1962: 134–137.
A review of William Benton's *The Voice of Latin America* (New York, Harper, 1961. 204 p.).

2610. ———. "Novyi kurs" i starye antagonizmy ["The new deal" and old contradictions] Mir. ekon. i mezhdunar. otn., no. 3, Mar. 1964: 29–39.
Economic relations with the United States.

2611. ———. "Soiuz radi progressa"— novoe orudie imperialisticheskoi politiki SShA v Latinskoi Amerike ["Alliance for Progress" is a new instrument of U.S. imperialist policy in Latin America] Nov. i noveish. ist., no. 3, 1963: 36–48.
Summary in English, p. 180.

2612. Eliutin, IU., *and* B. IAroshevskii. Ni soiuza, ni progressa [Neither an alliance nor progress] Za rubezhom, no. 11, Mar. 1964: 20.
The Alliance for Progress.

2613. Galeano, Eduardo. Soiuz bez budushchego [A futureless alliance] Za rubezhom, no. 1, Jan. 1964: 5.
The Alliance for Progress.

2614. González Alberdi, Paulino. Imperialisticheskaia "integratsiia"—ugroza slaborazvitym stranam [Imperialist "integration" is a threat to underdeveloped countries] Probl. mira i sots., v. 6, no. 8, Aug. 1963: 17–22.

2615. ———. Latinskaia Amerika v tiskakh monopolii SShA [Latin America in the grip of U.S. monopolies] Probl. mira i sots., v. 2, no. 12, Dec. 1959: 22–27.

2616. Grigor'ian, IU. M. Amerikanskii professor v roli spasitelia "Soiuza radi progressa" [An American professor in the role of savior of the Alliance for Progress] Vop. ist., v. 39, no. 2, Feb. 1964: 198–199.

2617. ———. IUzhnoamerikanskii pryzhok Bonna [Bonn's South American jump] Mezhdunar. zhizn', v. 11, no. 2, Feb. 1964: 99–105.

2618. ———. Zapadnoevropeiskii "Obshchii rynok"—ugroza Latinskoi Amerike [The West European "Common Market" is a menace to Latin America] Vop. ist., v. 39, no. 7, July 1964: 193–194.

2619. ———. Zapadnogermanskii kapital v Latinskoi Amerike [West German capital in Latin America] Mir. ekon. i mezhdunar. otn., no. 4, 1963: 124–126.

2620. Gritsanov, A. Fal'shivaia emblema; "Soiuz radi progressa"—orudie amerikanskogo neokolonializma [A false emblem; the "Alliance for Progress" is a tool of American neocolonialism] Komm. Bel., v. 38, no. 8, 1964: 67–71.

2621. Guerra Borges, Alfredo, *and* Eduardo Mora Valverde. Problemy ekonomicheskoi integratsii TSentral'noi Ameriki [Some problems concerning the economic integration of Central America] Probl. mira i sots., v. 5, no. 6, June 1962: 40–47.

2622. Gvozdev, IU. "Dreifuiushchii" kontinent [A "drifting" continent] Nov. vrem., v. 20, no. 7, Feb. 1963: 11–13; v. 20, no. 8, Feb. 1963: 20–22.
Economic relations with the United States.

2623. ———. Sgovor v San-Khose [Agreement in San José] Za rubezhom, no. 11, Mar. 1963: 24.
Economic integration of Central America.

2624. IAroshevskii, B. Fakel, kotoryi chadit [A fuming torch] Za rubezhom, no. 5, Feb. 1962: 8.
U.S. economic assistance.

2625. IEremenko, V. Soiuz chy zashmorh? [Alliance or bondage?] Ukraina, no. 22, Nov. 1962: 28–29.
Alliance for Progress.

2626. IUdanov, N. S. Nekotorye aspekty otnoshenii stran Latinskoi Ameriki s zapadnoevropeiskim "obshchim rynkom" [Some aspects of Latin America's contacts with the West European "Common Market"] Uch. zap. IMO, no. 12, 1963: 253–262.

2627. ———. Treugol'nik protivorechii [A triangle of contradictions] Mezhdunar. zhizn', v. 11, no. 7, July 1964: 55–62.
Foreign economic contacts.

2628. Ivashchenko, P. Latinoamerikanskaia assotsiatsiia svobodnoi torgovli [The Latin American Free Trade Association] Mezhdunar. zhizn', v. 10, no. 9, Sept. 1963: 150–151.

2629. Kartsev, A. Ni soiuza, ni progressa [Neither an alliance nor progress] Mezhdunar. zhizn', v. 11, no. 1, Jan. 1964: 113–114.
Alliance for Progress.

2630. Khlopkovaia voina [The cotton war] Nov. vrem., v. 17, no. 19, May 1959: 19.
Cotton trade.

2631. Khokhlov, G. Latinskaia Amerika— sfera sopernichestva inostrannykh monopolii [Latin America, a rivalry sphere of foreign monopolies] Mir. ekon. i mezhdunar. otn., no. 12, Dec. 1962: 85–87.

2632. Klusov, E. Nesostoiatel'nost' "Soiuza radi progressa" [The failure of the "Alliance for Progress"] Nauch. dokl. vys. shkoly; ekon. nauki, v. 6, no. 6, 1963: 45–52.

2633. Kodachenko, A. Ekonomicheskoe sotrudnichestvo SSSR so slaborazvitymi stranami [Economic cooperation of the USSR with underdeveloped countries] Polit. samoobr., v. 6, no. 11, Nov. 1962: 112–117.

2634. ———. Vazhnaia forma ekonomicheskogo sotrudnichestva [An important form of economic cooperation] Mezhdunar. zhizn', v. 9, no. 2, Feb. 1962: 50–59.
Economic contacts with the USSR.

2635. Koliuchii kofe [The bitter coffee] Nov. vrem., v. 21, no. 8, Feb. 1964: 20.
Coffee exports.

2636. Kosarev, E. Istoriia odnogo dogovora [The history of an agreement] Mezhdunar. zhizn', v. 9, no. 11, Nov. 1962: 121–122.
Economic integration of Central America.

2637. ———. Latinskaia Amerika; nasushchnye zadachi, bol'shie nadezhdy [Latin America; its vital problems and great hopes] Mir. ekon. i mezhdunar. otn., no. 3, 1964: 107–110.

2638. ———. Latinskaia Amerika v poiskakh putei zashchity [Latin America in search of the best way to protect its interests] Vnesh. torg., v. 43, no. 12, 1963: 15–18.
Foreign economic relations.
Summary in English.

2639. ———. Problemy vneshnei torgovli stran Latinskoi Ameriki [Problems of the foreign trade of the Latin American countries] Vnesh. torg., v. 30, no. 3, 1960: 18–24.
Summary in English, p. 75.

2640. Larin, V. Imperializm IAnki i Latinskaia Amerika [Yankee imperialism and Latin America] Mir. ekon. i mezhdunar. otn., no. 9, 1963: 147–150.
A review of Arnold J. Toynbee's The Economy of the Western Hemisphere (London, Oxford University Press, 1962. 75 p.).

2641. Latinoamerikanskaia assotsiatsiia svobodnoi torgovli [The Latin American Free Trade Association] Mezhdunar. zhizn', v. 9, no. 2, Feb. 1962: 155–156.

2642. Latinskaia Amerika i amerikanskie monopolii [Latin America and American monopolies] Mezhdunar. zhizn', v. 7, no. 12, Dec. 1960: 145–147.

2643. Levin, V. Chto skryvaetsia za vyveskoi "Soiuz radi progressa" [What is concealed behind the name "Alliance for Progress"] Polit. samoobr., v. 7, no. 2, Feb. 1963: 83–87.

2644. ———. Lisa v kuriatnike [A fox in the chicken coop] Mezhdunar. zhizn', v. 10, no. 2, Feb. 1963: 115–116.
Economic integration of the countries of Central America.

2645. ———. Sovremennye konkistadory za Rio-Grande [Present-day conquistadors beyond the Rio Grande] Mezhdunar. zhizn', v. 10, no. 6, June 1963: 36–44.
Economic relations with the United States.

2646. Leyens, Germán. A mirage in the desert: The "Alliance for Progress." World student news, v. 17, no. 5, 1963: 16–20, 28; v. 17, no. 6, 1963: 14–16.

2647. Liudmilin, R. Sud'ba angliiskikh pozitsii na latinoamerikanskikh rynkakh [The fate of English positions in Latin American markets] Mir. ekon. i mezhdunar. otn., no. 11, Nov. 1960: 89–90.

2648. Loziuk, M. I. Deiaki pytannia ekonomichnykh vidnosyn mizh SShA i krainamy Latyns'koi Ameryky v roky druhoi svitovoi viiny [Some problems of economic contacts between the United States and the Latin American countries during the Second World War] Nauk. zap. Kyiv. un., v. 18, no. 4, 1960: 109–121.

2649. ———. Posylennia ekonomichnykh superechnostei mizh krainamy Latyns'koi Ameryky i SShA na suchasnomu etapi [Intensification of economic conflicts between the countries of Latin America and the United States during the current period] Ekon. Rad. Ukr., no. 4, July-Aug. 1961: 105–112.

2650. Manasov, M. Latinskaia Amerika i strany sotsializma [Latin America and the socialist countries] Otv. na vop. trud., no. 1, Jan. 1963: 20–27.

2651. Mashbits, IA. G. Kommentarii k "Soiuzu radi progressa" [Comments on the "Alliance for Progress"] Vop. ist., v. 38, no. 2, Feb. 1963: 191–193.
A review of an article by Frank Tannenbaum in Political Science Quarterly, no. 2, June 1962: 178–204.

2652. Mikhailov, S. Latinskaia Amerika; vremia bol'shikh peremen [Latin America; a time of great changes] Nov. vrem., v. 21, no. 12, Mar. 1964: 6–9.
The Alliance for Progress.

2653. Mikhailov, S., and B. Rudenko. "Soiuz radi progressa"—novaia forma imperialisticheskoi ekspansii [The "Alliance for Progress" is a new form of imperialist expansion] Kommunist, v. 40, no. 10, July 1963: 103–107.

2654. Mikhailov, S., and others. "Soiuz radi progressa"; biznes i ekspansiia SShA [The "Alliance for Progress"; business and U.S. expansion] Mezhdunar. zhizn', v. 10, no. 4, Apr. 1963: 70–93.

2655. Mikuson, I. Primechatel'naia otstavka [Noteworthy retirement] Mezhdunar. zhizn', v. 11, no. 7, July 1964: 111–112.
The Alliance for Progress.

2656. Na chto idet "pomoshch'" SShA v stranakh Latinskoi Ameriki [What American "aid" is spent for in the Latin American countries] Mezhdunar. zhizn', v. 9, no. 2, Feb. 1962: 147–149.

2657. Nikitin, M. Mezhdunarodnyi valiutnyi fond i Latinskaia Amerika [The International Monetary Fund and Latin America] Mir. ekon. i mezhdunar. otn., no. 5, May 1960: 113–114.

2658. Ornatskii, I. Latinskaia Amerika i SShA; protivorechiia obostriaiutsia [The contradictions between Latin America and the United States become more intense] Mir. ekon. i mezhdunar. otn., no. 3, Mar. 1959: 116–118.
Economic relations with the United States.

2659. Paparova, G. Problemy ekonomicheskoi integratsii v latino-amerikanskoi presse [Problems of economic integration in the Latin American press] Vnesh. torg., v. 42, no. 1, 1963: 35–37.

2660. ———. V poiskakh vykhoda iz trudnostei; obzor latinoamerikanskoi pechati [In search for a solution of difficulties; review of the Latin American press] Vnesh. torg., v. 42, no. 5, 1962: 39–41.
International commercial contacts.

2661. Paramonov, Vladimir. Otrechenie Vashingtona [The retreat of the Washington government] Za rubezhom, no. 13, Mar. 1964: 7.
Alliance for Progress.

2662. Pered Zhenevoi [On the eve of the Geneva Conference] Za rubezhom, no. 12, Mar. 1964: 2.
Economic relations with the United States.

2663. Poliakovskii, V. Zatrudneniia E. Stivensona [Adlai Stevenson's difficulties] Za rubezhom, no. 25, Dec. 1960: 13.
Economic relations with the United States

2664. Pomoshch' gosudarstv narodnoi demo-kratii stranam Azii, Afriki i Latinskoi Ameriki [How the people's democracies help the countries of Asia, Africa, and Latin America] Mezhdunar. zhizn', v. 8, no. 11, Nov. 1961: 149–153.

2665. Prazdnovat' nechego [There is no reason to be jubilant] Za rubezhom, no. 33, Aug. 1963: 2–3.
Alliance for Progress.

2666. Romanova, Z. Ekonomicheskoe so-trudnichestvo Latinskoi Ameriki s sotsialisticheskimi stranami [Economic cooperation between Latin America and the socialist countries] Mir. ekon. i mezhdunar. otn., no. 10, Oct. 1960: 92–94.

2667. Romanova, Z. I. Problema "obshchego rynka" v Latinskoi Amerike [The prob-lem of the "common market" in Latin America] Mir. ekon. i mezhdunar. otn., no. 1, Jan. 1960: 119–125.

2668. Rozhin, I. Chto skryvaetsia za "komi-tetom 21"? [What is the real face of the "Committee of 21"?] Otv. na vop. trud., no. 108, 1959: 53–57.
Economic relations with the United States.

2669. Schwarz, Nico. Stimul i kompas [A stimulus and a compass] Za rubezhom, no. 45, Nov. 1961: 8.
Economic relations with the United States and the USSR.

2670. Seleznev, G. "Soiuz radi progressa"—orudie imperialistov [The "Alliance for Progress" is a weapon of the imperialists] Otv. na vop. trud., no 6, June 1963: 47–55.

2671. Sergeeva, N. Kofe v aspektakh [Pros-pects for coffee exports] Nov. vrem., v. 18, no. 51, Dec. 1960: 17–18.
The exports of coffee.

2672. Sheremet'ev, I. Za kulisami "Soiuza radi progressa" [Behind the scenes of the "Alliance for Progress"] Mir. ekon. i mezhdunar. otn., no. 11, Nov. 1961: 87–91.

2673. Shul'govskii, A. Imperializm i ideo-logiia natsional-reformizma v Latinskoi Amerike [Imperialism and the ideology of national reformism in Latin America] Mir. ekon. i mezhdunar. otn., no. 8, Aug. 1961: 45–59.

2674. ———. Soiuz protiv progressa [The "Alliance against Progress"] Za rube-zhom, no. 24, June 1962: 19.

2675. Sidorov, V. "Nevidimaia imperiia" ianki ["The invisible Yankee empire"] Nov. vrem., v. 22, no. 34, Aug. 1964: 30–32.
A review of Lajpat Rai's Latin America; a Socio-Economic Study (New Delhi, Institute for Afro-Asian and World Affairs, 1963. 233 p.).

2676. Skorpiony izgotovilis' k skhvatke [The scorpions are ready to fight] Za rube-zhom, no. 14, Sept. 1960: 5.
Relations with West Germany.

2677. "Soiuz radi grabezha" [An "Alliance for Plundering"] Agitator, no. 8, Apr. 1962: 44–45.

2678. Sokol'nikov, G. Ekspansiia Bonna v Latinskoi Amerike [The expansion of Bonn in Latin America] Nov. vrem., v. 21, no. 22, May 1964: 22–23.

2679. Soveshchanie v Al'ta-Grasia [A con-ference in Alta Gracia] Nov. vrem., v. 21, no. 11, Mar. 1964: 2–3.
Foreign economic relations.

2680. Stevenson, Adlai E. Nashi zatrudne-niia v Latinskoi Amerike [Our difficulties in Latin America] Za rubezhom, no. 25, Dec. 1960: 12–14.
Economic relations with the United States. Translated from the English.

2681. Strelin, A. Soiuz radi nishchety [An alliance for poverty] Mezhdunar. zhizn', v. 9, no. 9, Sept. 1962: 85–90.
Alliance for Progress.

2682. Tarasov, K. Politika vysasyvaiushchego nasosa [The policy of the suction pump] Mezhdunar. zhizn', v. 7, no. 8, Aug. 1960: 68–78.
U.S. economic assistance.

2683. ———. Za kulisami tsentral'no-ameri-kanskoi integratsii [The Central American integration scheme] Nov. vrem., v. 21, no. 11, Mar. 1964: 9–11.

2684. Timofeev, N. Ital'ianskie monopolii i Latinskaia Amerika [The Italian monopolies and Latin America] Mir. ekon. i mezhdunar. otn., no. 9, Sept. 1961: 104–105.

2685. Tridtsat' serebrenikov [Thirty pieces of silver] Nov. vrem., v. 18, no. 32, Aug. 1960: 22.
U.S. economic assistance.

2686. Vasil'ev, IU. Latinskaia Amerika posle San-Khose [Latin America after San José] Nov. vrem., v. 18, no. 38, Sept. 1960: 18–20.
U.S. economic assistance.

2687. Vneshniaia torgovlia stran Latinskoi Ameriki [The foreign trade of the Latin American countries] Mezhdunar. zhizn', v. 9, no. 7, July 1962: 148–150.

2688. Volkova, A. P., and G. N. Veits. Pomoshch' Sovetskogo Soiuza stranam Azii, Afriki i Latinskoi Ameriki v razvitii gornoi promyshlennosti [Soviet assistance in the development of mining in the countries of Asia, Africa, and Latin America] Zap. Len. gor. inst., v. 45, no. 3, 1964: 107–112.

2689. Vosstanie protiv nishchety [A revolt against poverty] Za rubezhom, no. 14, Sept. 1960: 4–5.
U.S. economic assistance.

2690. Vynuzhdennaia shchedrost' [Generosity under pressure] Nov. vrem., v. 18, no. 37, Sept. 1960: 22–23.
U.S. economic assistance.

2691. Zakhmatov, M. "Soiuz radi progressa" v ego podlinnom vide [The true face of the Alliance for Progress] Vnesh. torg., v. 43, no. 11, 1963: 38–42.
Summary in English.

2692. "Zelenyi sprut" ["The green octopus"] Vsem. prof. dvizh., no. 3, Mar. 1962: 27–31, 40.
The role of the United Fruit Company in Latin America.

See also entries no. 304, 1817, 2362, 2372, 3089, 3091, and 3331.

B. INDIVIDUAL COUNTRIES

1. Argentina

2693. Fuchs, Jaime. Proniknovenie ameri-kanskikh trestov v Argentinu [The pene-tration of American trusts into Argen-tina] Moscow, Izd-vo inostr. lit., 1959. 566 p. HG5312.F817
Translated by S. A. Gonionskii from the Spanish *La penetración de los trusts yanquis en la Argentina.*

2694. Freire, Filippe F. "Drugogo puti net" ["There are no two ways about it"] Vnesh. torg., v. 41, no. 1, 1961: 30–31.
Commercial contacts with Communist countries.

2695. Gosudarstvo v gosudarstve [A state within a state] Nov. vrem., v. 18, no. 30, July 1960: 21–22.
U.S. investments.

2696. Nesterov, N. K 150-letiiu Argentiny [The 150th anniversary of Argentina] Mezhdunar. zhizn', v. 7, no. 6, June 1960: 112–114.
Foreign economic relations.

2697. Novaia stavka [Their new stake] Za rubezhom, no. 3, Jan. 1963: 4.
U.S. investments.

2698. Pavlenko, A. Patrioticheskii shag [A patriotic step] Mezhdunar. zhizn', v. 11, no. 1, Jan. 1964: 108–109.
Foreign investments.

2699. Rogov, V. V., and V. E. Ivashov. Organizatsiia vneshnei torgovli Argen-tiny [The organization of foreign trade in Argentina] Biul. inostr. kommerch. inform. Prilozhenie, no. 14, Dec. 1960: 1–21.

See also entries no. 2385, 2393, and 2857.

2. Bolivia

2700. "Gora dollarov" ["A mountain of dollars"] Nov. vrem., v. 17, no. 28, July 1964: 22–23.
U.S. economic assistance.

2701. Neozhidannaia reaktsiia [Unexpected reaction] Nov. vrem., v. 20, no. 37, Sept. 1962: 22.
U.S. economic assistance.

2702. Nikonov, V. Pochemu amerikanskie monopolii dushat ekonomiku Bolivii [Why American monopolies try to strangle the Bolivian national economy] Otv. na vop. trud., no. 104, 1959: 57–59.

2703. Oshelomlennyi Vashington [Bewildered Washington] Nov. vrem., v. 19, no. 40, Sept. 1961: 21.
Economic relations with the United States.

2704. Pavlenko, A. Ograblennaia Boliviia [Pillaged Bolivia] Mezhdunar. zhizn', v. 6, no. 4, Apr. 1959: 140–143.
U.S. influence in the petroleum industry.
A review of Sergio Almaraz' *Petróleo en Bolivia* (La Paz, Editorial Juventud, 1958. 292 p.).

2705. Ramírez, Humberto. Patrioty Bolivii protiv amerikanskoi ekspansii; pis'mo iz La-Pasa [Bolivian patriots take a stand against American expansion; a letter from La Paz] Mir. ekon. i mezhdunar. otn., no. 8, Aug. 1959: 131–133.
Economic relations with the United States.

2706. Rosso, Guillermo. Soobshchenie boliviiskogo inzhenera [A letter from a Bolivian engineer] Nov. vrem., v. 17, no. 1, Jan. 1959: 29.
U.S. influence in Bolivian industry.

3. Brazil.

2707. Alencastre, Amilcar. Braziliia i sotsialisticheskie strany; perspektivy razvitiia ekonomicheskikh sviazei [Brazil and the socialist countries; prospects for the development of their economic contacts] Moscow, Izd-vo inostr. lit., 1961. 134 p.
HF3408.C6A657
Translated by S. M. Starets from the Portuguese *O Brasil e as relações com o Lest ea U.R.S.S.*

2708. Moura, Aristoteles. Inostrannyi kapital v Brazilii [Foreign investments in Brazil] Moscow, Izd-vo inostr. lit., 1961. 433 p.
DLC
Translated by L. F. Kuz'mina and A. I. Filatova from the Portuguese *Capitais estrangeiros no Brasil*. Introductory article by O. G. Klesmet.

2709. Alencastre, Amilcar. Torgovlia s Vostokom? Otryvki iz knigi [Should we trade with the East? Excerpts from a book] Za rubezhom, no. 4, July 1960: 13–14.
Commercial contacts with the USSR.
Translated from the Portuguese.

2710. Besstydnyi shantazh [Shameless blackmail] Nov. vrem., v. 20, no. 9, Feb. 1962: 26.
U.S. investments.

2711. Brizola, Leonel. Pravda o "Soiuze radi progressa" [The truth about the "Alliance for Progress"] Za rubezhom, no. 15, Apr. 1962: 28.
Translated from the Portuguese.

2712. Bunegina, I. Braziliia razvivaet torgovliu s sotsialisticheskimi stranami [Brazil develops trade with socialist countries] Vnesh. torg., v. 42, no. 7, 1962: 16–20.
Summary in English in appendix.

2713. Chenchikovskii, S. Torgovye otnosheniia mezhdu SSSR i Braziliei uspeshno razvivaiutsia [Trade relations between the U.S.S.R. and Brazil are developing successfully] Vnesh. torg., v. 30, no. 7, 1960: 14–15.
Summary in English, p. 59.

2714. Dobroe nachalo [Good beginning] Nov. vrem., v. 18, no. 25, June 1960: 28–29.
Commercial contacts with the USSR.

2715. Eliutin, IU. Shag na puti k ekonomicheskoi nezavisimosti [A step toward economic independence] Mezhdunar. zhizn', v. 9, no. 10, Oct. 1962: 111–112.
Foreign investments.

2716. Ershov, I. Braziliia: monopolii SShA poluchaiut otpor [Brazil: U.S. monopolies meet with a rebuff] Mir. ekon. i mezhdunar. otn., no. 6, June 1962: 112–114.

2717. Gramotov, A. Khishchniku po rukam [Deserved punishment of a plunderer] Mezhdunar. zhizn', v. 9, no. 11, Nov. 1962: 117–118.
Monopoly on atomic materials.

2718. I zdes' ikh ne liubiat [They are not liked here either] Nov. vrem., v. 18, no. 39, Sept. 1960: 19–20.
U.S. economic assistance.

2719. Ignat'ev, Oleg. Lopnuvshii mif [A shattered myth] Mol. komm, no. 12, Dec. 1963: 109–115.
Alliance for Progress.

2720. ———. Razoblachennye "blagodeteli"; pis'mo iz Brazilii [Unmasked "benefactors"; a letter from Brazil] Mezhdunar. zhizn', v. 9, no. 12, Dec. 1962: 59–68.

2721. K sovetsko-brazil'skim torgovym otnosheniiam [Soviet-Brazilian trade relations] Vnesh. torg., v. 41, no. 7, July 1961, insert: 7.

2722. Kak zarabotat' million [How to make a million] Nov. vrem., v. 18, no. 32, Aug. 1960: 15.
U.S. economic assistance.

2723. Karavaev, A. Bor'ba protiv zasil'ia inostrannogo kapitala [The struggle against the dominant positions of foreign capital] Mir. ekon. i mezhdunar. otn., no. 1, 1963: 103–105.
Foreign investments.

2724. ———. Na povestke dnia—neotlozhnye problemy razvivaiushchikhsia stran [The urgent problems of developing countries are on the agenda] Vnesh. torg., v. 43, no. 7, 1963: 17–20.

2725. Kremnev, M. Braziliia smotrit na Vostok [Brazil looks toward the East] Nov. vrem., v. 17, no. 46, Nov. 1959: 16–17.
Economic contacts with the Soviet Union.

2726. Kuda devalos' brazil'skoe kofe? [What happened to the Brazilian coffee?] Teatr, v. 20, no. 1, Jan. 1959: 112–113.
Coffee trade.

2727. Kutuzov, V., and B. Karpov. Vneshnetorgovyi rezhim Brazilii [The regulation of the foreign trade of Brazil] Vnesh. torg., v. 44, no. 5, 1964: 58–60.

2728. Martins, Paolo Guilherme. A day in the life of Brasilino. World student news, v. 16, no. 9/10, 1962: 17–18.

2729. Ministr vneshnei torgovli N. S. Patolichev o sovetsko-brazil'skikh otnosheniiakh [Soviet-Brazilian relations; interview with N. S. Patolichev, USSR Minister of Foreign Trade] Nov. vrem., v. 20, no. 21, May 1962: 16–17.

2730. Perova, L. "Zhenites' na brazil'ianke!" ["You should marry a Brazilian woman!"] Za rubezhom, no. 45, Nov. 1962: 4.
Commercial contacts with Sweden.

2731. Petrov, A. Braziliia gotovitsia k konferentsii [Brazil prepares for a conference] Mir. ekon. i mezhdunar. otn., no. 11, Nov. 1963: 108–110.
Foreign economic relations.

2732. Poslednii zvonok "Ai-Ti-Ti" [The last call of the ITT] Za rubezhom, no. 10, Mar. 1962: 3.
Nationalization of the property of the U.S.-owned telephone company.

2733. Sa, Frederico. Inostrannyi kapital v Brazilii [Foreign investments in Brazil] Probl. mira i sots., v. 3, no. 3, Mar. 1960: 82–84.
A review of Aristoteles Moura's Capitais estrangeiros no Brasil (São Paulo, Editôra Brasiliense, 1959. 381 p.).

2734. Soglashenie o dogovorennosti, dostignutoe mezhdu Torgovoi delegatsiei SSSR i Torgovoi missiei Soedinennykh Shtatov Brazilii po voprosam torgovli i platezhei [Agreement on the understanding reached between the USSR trade delegation and the trade mission of the United States of Brazil on trade and payments questions] Vnesh. torg., v. 30, no. 2, 1960: 52–54.

2735. Sovmestnoe sovetsko-brazil'skoe kommiunike o prebyvanii v Brazilii ministra vneshnei torgovli SSSR N. S. Patolicheva [A joint communiqué on the visit to Brazil of N. S. Patolichev, Minister of Foreign Trade of the USSR] Vnesh. torg., v. 42, no. 6, 1962: 7–8.

2736. Tarasov, V. Trezvye dovody brazil'skogo ekonomista [Sober conclusions of a Brazilian economist] Mezhdunar. zhizn', v. 7, no. 3, Mar. 1960: 142–144.
Economic relations with the USSR.
A review of Amilcar Alencastre's O Brasil e as relações com o Lest ea U.R.S.S. (Rio de Janeiro, Gráfica Editora Nap S. A., 1959. 126 p.).

2737. Uolter Link i ego patrony [Walter Link and his protectors] Nov. vrem., v. 18, no. 50, Dec. 1960: 25.
Alleged U.S. efforts to impede the development of the Brazilian petroleum industry.

2738. Ustarelyi metod [An obsolete method] Nov. vrem., v. 17, no. 43, Oct. 1959: 23.
U.S. efforts to prevent the development of commercial contacts between Brazil and the Soviet Union.

2739. V chetyre raza vozrastet tovarooborot mezhdu SSSR i Braziliei [Commerce between the USSR and Brazil will increase fourfold] Sov. Soiuz, no. 6, 1963: 3.

2740. Vasil'ev, M. Braziliia nakhodit novye rynki [Brazil finds new markets] Nov. vrem., v. 18, no. 30, July 1960: 18–19.
Commercial contacts with the USSR.

2741. Vosstanovlenie sovetsko-brazil'skikh torgovykh otnoshenii [Restoration of Soviet-Brazilian commercial relations] Vnesh. torg., v. 29, no. 12, 1959: 26–27.

See also entries no. 428, 2861, 2866, 2870, and 4600.

4. British Honduras

2742. Listov, V. Anglo-amerikanskaia bor'ba v Britanskom Gondurase [The Anglo-American struggle in British Honduras] Mezhdunar. zhizn', v. 11, no. 5, May 1964: 98–101.

5. Chile

2743. Diko, N. S. Ekonomicheskaia ekspansiia SShA v Chili [The economic expansion of the United States in Chile] Moscow, 1964. 28 p. (Moskovskii gosudarstvennyi institut mezhdunarodnykh otnoshenii)
Abstract of a dissertation for the degree of Candidate in Economic Sciences.

2744. Ramírez Necochea, Hernán. Istoriia imperializma v Chili [The history of imperialism in Chile] Moscow, Progress, 1964. 254 p.
Translated by A. P. Malkov and G. P. Poporova from the Spanish *Historia del imperialismo en Chile.* Introductory article by S. A. Gonionskii.

2745. Artiushenkov, M. Vremia pokazhet [Time will tell] Mezhdunar. zhizn', v. 11, no. 12, Dec. 1964: 113–114.

2746. Cademartori, José. Chili i latinoamerikanskaia assotsiatsiia svobodnoi torgovli [Chile and the Latin American Free Trade Association] Probl. mira i sots., v. 6, no. 6, June 1963: 33–38.

2747. Gosti iz Chili [Guests from Chile] Vnesh. torg., v. 43, no. 8, 1963: 12.
Commercial contacts with the USSR.

2748. Millás, Orlando. Chto strashnee: zemletriasenie ili monopolii SShA? [Which is worse: earthquakes or the U.S. monopolies?] Za rubezhom, no. 22, June 1961: 26–27.

2749. Sovmestnoe kommiunike o prebyvanii v SSSR torgovo-promyshlennoi delegatsii Chili [Joint communiqué on the sojourn in the USSR of a commercial and industrial delegation from Chile] Vnesh. torg., v. 30, no. 2, 1960: 24.

2750. Vstrecha predstavitelei sovetskoi pechati i radio s glavoi chiliiskoi torgovo-promyshlennoi delegatsii Domingo Arteaga Infante [Interview of Domingo Arteaga Infante, head of the Chilean commercial and industrial delegation, by representatives of the Soviet press and radio] Vnesh. torg., v. 30, no. 2, 1960: 25–26.

6. Colombia

2751. "Blagodetelia" vstrechaiut v shtyki [They gave a hostile reception to their "benefactor"] Za rubezhom, no. 13, Sept. 1960: 5.
A visit of a U.S. economic delegation.

2752. Kartsev, A. Pokonchit' s kolonializmom! [Let's get rid of colonialism!] Mezhdunar. zhizn', v. 10, no. 6, June 1963: 109–110.

See also entries no. 1920 and 2443.

7. Costa Rica

2753. Kosarev, E. Kosta-Rika v usloviiakh integratsii [Costa Rica under the conditions of economic integration] Vnesh. torg., v. 44, no. 5, 1964: 35–38.
Summary in English, p. 80.

2754. Noskov, G. IAnki v Kosta-Rike [Yankees in Costa Rica] Nov. vrem., v. 20, no. 12, Mar. 1963: 12–13.

8. Cuba

2755. Adamovich, Andrei, *and* Vadim Chekhovich. V gorakh Or'ente [In the mountains of Oriente Province] Nov. vrem., v. 21, no. 24, June 1963: 23–25.

2756. Agafonova, T. My s toboi, Kuba! [We are with you, Cuba!] Rabotnitsa, v. 40, no. 10, Oct. 1962: 25.

2757. Arkhipov, I. Krepnet sovetsko-kubin-skoe ekonomicheskoe sotrudnichestvo [The consolidation of economic relations between Cuba and the Soviet Union] Mezhdunar. zhizn', v. 10, no. 12, Dec. 1963: 70–74.

2758. Avtobusy dlia Kuby [Motor buses for Cuba] Nov. vrem., v. 21, no. 6, Feb. 1964: 19.
Commercial contacts with Great Britain.

2759. Avtomobili dlia geroicheskoi Kuby [Motor vehicles for heroic Cuba] Avt. transp., v. 39, no. 3, Mar. 1961: 55.

2760. Babadzhanian, A. Ekonomicheskaia missiia Kuby v Moskve [The Cuban Economic Mission in Moscow] Vnesh. torg., v. 30, no. 7, 1960: 9–11.

2761. Beskorystnaia pomoshch' [Unselfish aid] Ryb. khoz., v. 38, no. 10, 1962: 88.

2762. Beznadezhnoe delo [Hopeless situation] Nov. vrem., v. 17, no. 37, Sept. 1959: 21.
Nationalization of American-owned property.

2763. Bochkarev, IU. Soglashenie s Kuboi [An agreement with Cuba] Nov. vrem., v. 18, no. 8, Feb. 1960: 10.

2764. Bondarev, V., and I. Shvartsshtein. Kuba—khoziain v svoem dome [Cuba is the master of its own house] Za rube-zhom, no. 6, July 1960: 9.
Economic relations with the United States.

2765. Borisov, B. Plodotvornyi vizit; k ito-gam poezdki tovarishcha A. I. Mikoiana na Kubu [A fruitful visit; on the results of the visit of Comrade A. I. Mikoian to Cuba] Vnesh. torg., v. 30, no. 3, 1960: 10–13.
Summary in English, p. 74.

2766. Brodskii, A. Leningrad—Gavana [Leningrad—Havana] Mor. flot, v. 23, no. 10, Oct. 1963: 6–7.
Commercial contacts with the USSR.

2767. Burlak, A. Kuba nacheku [Cuba on the alert] Mezhdunar. zhizn', v. 7, no. 8, Aug. 1960: 121–123.
Economic relations with the United States.

2768. Cherevkov, K. Eto vse dlia Kuby [This is all for Cuba] Ogonek, v. 40, no. 10, Mar. 1962: 2.

2769. Cherkashina, Larisa. Kuba—Donbass [Cuba—The Donets Basin] Donbass, no. 4, 1962: 110–121.

2770. David i Goliaf [David and Goliath] Nov. vrem., v. 18, no. 28, July 1960: 2–3.
Nationalization of U.S. property.

2771. Deshkov, S., and IU. Khoritskaia. God na Kube [A year in Cuba] Krest'-ianka, v. 41, no. 10, Oct. 1962: 12–13.
Soviet agriculturists in Cuba.

2772. Dorogami druzhby [Along the paths of friendship] Sov. Soiuz, no. 6, 1963: 4.
Economic contacts with the USSR.

2773. Eliutin, IU. Proiski reaktsii na Kube [The intrigues of reaction in Cuba] Mir. ekon. i mezhdunar. otn., no. 1, Jan. 1960: 106–108.
Opposition from U.S. sources to economic reforms.

2774. Fish, Gennadii. Norvegiia riadom [Norway is not far from us] Znamia, v. 31, no. 8, Aug. 1961: 139–158; v. 31, no. 9, Sept. 1961: 165–175: v. 31, no. 10, Oct. 1961: 172–182; v. 31, no. 11, Nov. 1961: 157–165; v. 31, no. 12, Dec. 1961: 183–193.
Economic relations with Norway.

2775. Grinevich, E. Kuba pered revoliutsiei [Cuba before the revolution] Mezhdunar. zhizn', v. 10, no. 7, July 1963: 87–96.
U.S. investments.

2776. Guevara, Ernesto. "Eto triumf druzhby nashikh narodov" ["This is a triumph of our peoples' friendship"] Vnesh. torg., v. 41, no. 1, 1961: 13.
Economic relations with the USSR.

2777. Gugushkin, V. My vsegda s toboi, Kuba! [Cuba, we are with you always!] Mol. komm., no. 12, Dec. 1962: 21–27.

2778. Gur'ianova, E. F. Sovetskie uchenye na Kube [Soviet scientists in Cuba] Vest. AN SSSR, v. 33, no. 8, Aug. 1963: 88–90.

2779. K sovetsko-kubinskim torgovo-eko-nomicheskim i kul'turnym otnosheniiam [Trade and cultural relations between the Soviet Union and Cuba] Vnesh. torg., v. 30, no. 7, 1960: 13.

2780. K torgovym otnosheniiam mezhdu SSSR i Respublikoi Kuba [Commercial contacts between the USSR and Cuba] Vnesh. torg., v. 42, no. 6, 1962: 7.

2781. Korostylev, Petr. S flazhkami Kuby [With the flags of Cuba] Vozhatyi, v. 38, no. 12, Dec. 1962: 34–35.

2782. Korshunov, N. Sakhar Kuby [Cuba's sugar] Nov. vrem., v. 18, no. 33, Aug. 1960: 27–28.
U.S. investments.

2783. Kosarev, E. Kuba reshaet vazhnuiu zadachu [Cuba tries to solve an important problem] Vnesh. torg., v. 44, no. 9, 1964: 12–15.
Sugar exports.
Summary in English, p. 64.

2784. ———. Vneshniaia torgovlia svobodnoi Kuby [Free Cuba's foreign trade] Vnesh. torg., v. 30, no. 12, Dec. 1960: 13–16.
Summary in English, p. 63.

2785. Kruchina, N., *and* V. Nizskii. Trista s "Korablia druzhby" [Three hundred from the "ship of friendship"] Smena, v. 39, no. 7, Apr. 1962: 18–20.

2786. Kuba: nas ne sognut' [They won't subdue us, the Cubans say] Za rubezhom, no. 20, Oct. 1960: 4.
Economic relations with the United States.

2787. Kuz'min, M. Dela i vstrechi s Kuboi [Business contacts and meetings with Cuba] Vnesh. torg., v. 42, no. 6, 1962: 17–20.
Commercial contacts with the USSR.

2788. Maldonado, R. "Kubinsko-sovetskie torgovye sviazi krepnut i razvivaiutsia" ["Trade ties between Cuba and the USSR are developing and becoming stronger"] Vnesh. torg., v. 42, no. 8, 1962: 24–25.

2789. Manevry "zelenogo spruta" [Maneuvers of the "green octopus"] Nov. vrem., v. 17, no. 40, Oct. 1959: 23.
Nationalization of American-owned plantations.

2790. Martillo, Trinidad. Porazhenie v Punta-del'-Este [Defeat in Punta del Este] Mezhdunar. zhizn', v. 8, no. 11, Nov. 1961: 94–105.
Foreign economic relations.

2791. Mel'nikov, F. Na ostrove svobody [On the island of freedom] Komm. Bel., v. 36, no. 5, May 1962: 62–66.

2792. My z toboiu, Kubo! [We are with you, Cuba!] Ukraina, no. 22, Nov. 1962: 7.

2793. Na prochnoi osnove [On a sound basis] Nov. vrem., v. 18, no. 26, June 1960: 3.
Economic relations with the USSR.

2794. Nauka ne po silam [Beyond their understanding] Nov. vrem., v. 17, no. 26, June 1959: 22.
Nationalization of U.S.-owned plantations.

2795. Negodnaia set' [Futile efforts] Nov. vrem., v. 17, no. 41, Oct. 1959: 22.
Commercial contacts with the Soviet Union.

2796. Negrin, A. Kuba—da, ianki—net! [Cuba yes, Yankees no!] Vsem. prof. dvizh., no. 1, Jan. 1961: 3–7.
Economic relations with the United States.

2797. Novaia glava? [A new chapter?] Nov. vrem., v. 17, no. 6, Feb. 1959: 23.
U.S. investments.

2798. Novyi nazhim na Kubu [New pressure on Cuba] Nov. vrem., v. 18, no. 27, July 1960: 22–23.
Sugar trade.

2799. Núñez Jiménez, Antonio. Kuba nachinaet nalazhivat' torgovliu so vsemi stranami mira [Cuba begins to establish trade with all countries of the world] Vnesh. torg., v. 30, no. 7, 1960: 12.

2800. Obmen ratifikatsionnymi gramotami sovetsko-kubinskikh soglashenii [Exchange of ratifications of the Soviet-Cuban agreements] Vnesh. torg., v. 30, no. 6, 1960: 20.

2801. Olteanu, O. Review. Vop. ist., no. 4, Apr. 1962: 176–177.
A review of Oscar Pino Santos' *El imperialismo norteamericano en la economía de Cuba* (Havana, Editorial Lex, 1960. 97 p.).

2802. Opasnyi virus [A dangerous virus] Nov. vrem., v. 18, no. 17, Apr. 1960: 28.
Sugar trade.

2803. Ostroverkhyi, I. I. Ukraina—Kubi [Ukrainian assistance to Cuba] Ukr. ist. zhur., v. 6, no. 6, Nov.-Dec. 1963: 94–97.

2804. Padilla, Heberto. Druzhba [Friendship] Vnesh. torg., v. 43, no. 8, 1963: 8–9.
Economic relations with the USSR.

2805. Plesovskikh, L. Ikh imia—amigos sovetiko [They call them "los amigos soviéticos"] Neva, no. 7, 1964: 216–217.
Soviet technicians.

2806. Proshli zolotye denechki [The golden days are over] Nov. vrem., v. 17, no. 24, June 1959: 23–24.
U.S. investments.

2807. SSSR—Kuba; primer bratskogo sotrudnichestva [The USSR and Cuba; an example of fraternal cooperation] Vnesh. torg., v. 43, no. 4, 1963: 5–13.
Summary in English.

2808. Saifulina, L. Kuba i strany-chleny SEV [Cuba and the member countries of the Council of Mutual Economic Assistance] Mezhdunar. zhizn', v. 11, no. 5, May 1964: 145–146.
Economic relations with Eastern Europe.

2809. Sakhar i politika [Sugar and politics] Nov. vrem., v. 18, no. 12, Mar. 1960: 13.
Sugar trade.

2810. Sheviakov, G. N. Sovetskii Soiuz—Kube [How the Soviet Union helps Cuba] Mezhdunar. zhizn', v. 9, no. 3, Mar. 1962: 97–98.

2811. Shvartsshtein, I. Sakhar i politika [Sugar and politics] Mir. ekon. i mezhdunar. otn., no. 3, 1963: 113–114.
Sugar trade.

2812. Sovremennik. Isterichnyi Vashington i spokoinaia Gavana [Hysterical Washington and calm Havana] Nov. vrem., v. 20, no. 37, Sept. 1962: 3–4.
Soviet economic assistance.

2813. Ugrozy i makhinatsii protiv Kuby [Threats and intrigues against Cuba] Nov. vrem., v. 17, no. 39, Sept. 1959: 19.
Nationalization of American-owned plantations.

2814. Vazhneishaia vekha v razvitii sovetsko-kubinskoi torgovli [The landmark of paramount importance in the development of Soviet-Cuban trade] Vnesh. torg., v. 41, no. 1, 1961: 11–13.

2815. Veto severnogo soseda [The veto of their northern neighbor] Za rubezhom, no. 36, Sept. 1962: 4.
Economic relations with Latin America.

2816. Wedekind, Kurt. Pochemu graf fon Shpreti uekhal iz Gavany [Why Count von Spreti left Havana] Nov. vrem., v. 20, no. 5, Feb. 1963: 21.
Establishment of commercial relations between Cuba and East Germany, and protest by West Germany.

2817. Zhuikov, G. Kapitalisticheskie strany torguiut s Kuboi [Cuba's trade with capitalist countries] Nov. vrem., v. 21, no. 15, Apr. 1964: 16–17.

See also entries no. 1923, 1928, 2009, 2473, 2475, 2969, and 4818.

9. Dominican Republic

2818. Nekotorye sekrety vashingtonskoi politiki [Some secrets of Washington policy] Nov. vrem., v. 20, no. 27, July 1962: 15.
U.S. economic assistance.

2819. Snova Trukhil'o [They trade with Trujillo again] Nov. vrem., v. 18, no. 41, Oct. 1960: 22.
Sugar trade with the United States.

10. Ecuador

2820. Bezdorozh'e [Bad roads] Nov. vrem., v. 22, no. 46, Nov. 1964: 25.
Alliance for Progress.

11. Guatemala

2821. Ivanov, K. K sotsial'no-ekonomicheskoi kharakteristike sovremennogo kolonializma [The socio-economic nature of present-day colonialism] Mezhdunar. zhizn', v. 8, no. 8, Aug. 1961: 9–24.
Economic relations with the United States.

2822. Kassis, Vadim. Bananovyi sprut [The banana octopus] Ogonek, v. 42, no. 29, July 1964: 30–31.
The role of the United Fruit Company.

2823. Spustia 60 let [Sixty years later] Nov. vrem., v. 21, no. 17, Apr. 1964: 25.
U.S.-owned railroads.

12. Mexico

2824. Cárdenas, V. Dlia vzaimovygodnoi torgovli imeetsia prochnaia osnova [There is a solid foundation for mutually advantageous trade] Vnesh. torg., v. 44, no. 10, 1964: 30.
Commercial contacts with the USSR.

2825. Il'inskii, M. Delovye liudi Meksiki v Moskve [Mexican businessmen in Moscow] Vnesh. torg., v. 44, no. 9, 1964: 35.

2826. Kolodkov, V. Nasha torgovlia s Meksikoi [Our trade with Mexico] Nov. vrem., v. 17, no. 31, July 1964: 20–21.

2827. Lilin, IU. M. "Soiuz protiv progressa" Meksiki [Mexico's "alliance against progress"] Vop. ist., v. 38, no. 11, Nov. 1963: 181–182.
A review of an article by Charlotte Baumgarten in *Deutsche Aussenpolitik*, no. 3, 1963: 120–127.

2828. Mikoian, A. I. Rech' na vstreche s predstaviteliami meksikanskikh delovykh krugov 26 noiabria 1959 goda [A speech at a meeting with representatives of Mexican business circles, November 26, 1959] Nov. vrem., v. 17, no. 50, Dec. 1959, supplement: 1–4.

2829. ———. Sovetskii Soiuz—strana mirnogo sozidatel'nogo truda. My za torgovliu, ravnopravnuiu i vzaimovygodnuiu [The Soviet Union is a country of peaceful and creative work. We shall promote commercial relations based on equality and mutual interest] Vnesh. torg., v. 29, no. 12, 1959, supplement: 3–7.

2830. Otvety pervogo zamestitelia Ministra vneshnei torgovli SSSR S. A. Borisova na voprosy korrespondenta zhurnala "Vneshniaia torgovlia" [S. A. Borisov, First Deputy Minister of Foreign Trade of the USSR, replies to the questions of the "Vneshniaia torgovlia" magazine correspondent] Vnesh. torg., v. 30, no. 1, 1960: 3–5.
Commercial contacts with the USSR.

2831. Paporova, G. P. Proizvodstvo i eksport meksikanskogo khlopka [The production and exports of Mexican cotton] Biul. inostr. kommerch. inform. Prilozhenie, no. 2, Feb. 1960: 13–24.

2832. Sheremet'ev, I. K. Ekonomika i vneshniaia torgovlia Meksiki, 1946–1958 gg. [The economy and foreign trade of Mexico, 1946–1958] Biul. inostr. kommerch. inform. Prilozhenie, no. 14, Dec. 1960: 72–133.

2833. Strelin, A. Neudobnyi sosed [Inconvenient neighbor] Nov. vrem., v. 20, no. 13, Mar. 1962: 28.
Economic relations with the United States.

See also entries no. 428, 2368, and 2914.

13. Panama

2834. Ortega, Gregorio. Panamskie vladeniia "IUnaited frut" [The Panamanian property of "United Fruit"] Ogonek, v. 38, no. 40, Oct. 1960: 12–13.

2835. Perlo, Victor. Dollar nad Panamoi [The dollar over Panama] Nov. vrem., v. 21, no. 8, Feb. 1964: 16–18.
U.S. investments.

See also entry no. 4777.

14. Paraguay

2836. Matveeva, N. R. Kolonial'naia ekspansiia Anglii v Paragvae [English colonial expansion in Paraguay] Uch. zap. Kalininsk. ped. inst., v. 26, 1962: 215–250.

15. Peru

2837. "Felipil'os" [The "felipillos"] Nov. vrem., v. 19, no. 12, Mar. 1961: 22.
U.S. investments.

2838. Listov, V. Vashington i Peru [Washington and Peru] Nov. vrem., v. 20, no. 6, Feb. 1963: 20–21.

See also entry no. 2921.

16. Puerto Rico

2839. Kobysh, V. IAnki v Puerto-Riko [The Yankees in Puerto Rico] Nov. vrem., v. 20, no. 47, Nov. 1962: 21–22.

2840. Mashbits, IA. G. Puerto-Riko—koloniia SShA [Puerto Rico is a U.S. colony] Vop. ist., no. 5, May 1961: 198–199.

17. Uruguay

2841. Otvergnutye missii [Rejected missions] Nov. vrem., v. 17, no. 32, Aug. 1959: 21.
A loan from the International Monetary Fund.

2842. Soiuz radi regressa? [Is it an "alliance for regress?] Nov. vrem., v. 22, no. 51, Dec. 1964: 22.
Alliance for Progress.

See also entry no. 2570.

18. Venezuela

2843. Bogdanov, I. I. Vneshniaia torgovlia Venesuely, 1946–1959 gg. [The foreign trade of Venezuela, 1946–1959] Biul. inostr. kommerch. inform. Prilozhenie, no. 14, Dec. 1960: 22–71.

2844. Chichkov, Vas. Neft' v savannakh [Oil in the savannas] Oktiabr', v. 38, no. 2, Feb. 1961: 190–204.
Economic relations with the United States.

2845. ———. Vysokoe napriazhenie v dzhungliakh [High tension in the jungle] Vokrug sveta, no. 3, Mar. 1961: 40–41.
American-owned oil fields.

2846. Eliutin, IU. Polozhenie v Venesuele [The situation in Venezuela] Mir. ekon. i mezhdunar. otn., no. 2, Feb. 1961: 106–108.
U.S. investments.

2847. Ne vyderzhali [They couldn't bear it any longer] Nov. vrem., v. 22, no. 36, Sept. 1964: 25.
Taxation of U.S.-owned enterprises.

2848. Yankee-exploited Venezuela. World youth, no. 2, 1963: 45–49.

XII

INDUSTRY, TECHNOLOGY, AND TRANSPORTATION

༄

A. INDUSTRY

1. Writings Dealing With Three or More Countries

2849. Banketov, A. K. Mednoporfirovye rudniki Severnoi i IUzhnoi Ameriki [Copper-porphyry mines in North and South America] Moscow, TSentr. in-t informatsii tsvetnoi metallurgii, 1961. 84 p.

2850. Bolotin, B. M. Truboprovody stran TSentral'noi i IUzhnoi Ameriki [Pipeline systems of Central and South America] Moscow, Vses. nauch.-issl. in-t po stroitel'stvu magistral'nykh truboprovodov, 1962. 35 p.

2851. Elanskii, A. N., *and* M. A. Ukrainskii, *eds*. Almozodobyvaiushchaia promyshlennost' kapitalisticheskikh stran [Diamond mining in capitalist countries] Moscow, TSentr. nauch.-issl. in-t informatsii i tekhn.-ekon. issledovanii tsvetnoi metallurgii, 1963. 209 p.

2852. Lisichkin, S. M. Neftianaia promyshlennost' Afriki, Avstralii, Latinskoi Ameriki i Kanady [The petroleum industry of Africa, Australia, Latin America, and Canada] Moscow, Nedra, 1964. 282 p.   HD9574.L3L5
      Reviewed by V. Shchelkachev in *Neft. khoz.*, v. 42, no. 8, Aug. 1964: 71–72.

2853. Kachevskii, V. Elektroenergetika stran Latinskoi Ameriki; sostoianie i perspektivy [Electric power in the countries of Latin America; the present state and the

outlook] Mir. ekon. i mezhdunar. otn., no. 12, Dec. 1961: 91–92.

2854. Leshchiner, R. Razvitie gazovoi promyshlennosti v stranakh IUzhnoi Ameriki [Development of the gas industry in the countries of South America] Gaz. prom., v. 5, no. 9, Sept. 1960: 54–56.

2855. Neftianaia promyshlennost' stran Latinskoi Ameriki [The petroleum industry of Latin American countries] *In* Koriagin, I. D., *ed*. Neftianaia promyshlennost' kapitalisticheskikh stran Zapadnoi Evropy, Blizhnego i Srednego Vostoka, Dal'nego Vostoka, Kanady i Latinskoi Ameriki; kratkii obzor statisticheskikh dannykh. Moscow, GOSINTI, 1959: p. 240–299.   HD9560.K6

2856. Solntsev, M. N. Razmeshchenie aliuminievoi promyshlennosti v stranakh Ameriki [Distribution of the aluminum industry in the countries of America] TSvet. met., v. 37, no. 7, July 1964: 86–90.

See also entries no. 2593 and 2688.

2. Individual Countries

a. Argentina

2857. Gorov, V. Bor'ba vokrug argentinskoi nefti [Struggle over Argentine oil] Mir. ekon. i mezhdunar. otn., no. 3, Mar. 1959: 119–121.

2858. Novyi koksokhimicheskii tsekh v Argentine [New coke plant in Argentina] Koks i khim., no. 5, 1961: 60–61.

2859. Ul'ianova, S. I. Review. Vop. ist., no. 8, Aug. 1964: 184–186.

A review of *Petróleo, soberania y la paz* by Alberto T. Casella and Alejandro Clara (Buenos Aires, Editorial Platina, 1963. 173 p.).

b. Bolivia

See entry no. 2704.

c. Brazil

2860. Almazy "zelenogo ada" [The diamonds of the "green hell"] Vokrug sveta, no. 10, Oct. 1961: 61.

2861. Araujo, Luzio. Borba za brazil'skuiu neft'; pis'mo iz Rio-de-Zhaneiro [Struggle for Brazilian oil; letter from Rio de Janeiro] Nov. vrem., v. 20, no. 11, Mar. 1962: 28–29.

2862. Bakirov, E. A., *and* E. I. Tagiev. Kak iskali neft' v Brazilii [How they prospected for oil in Brazil] Nov. vrem., v. 21, no. 46, Nov. 1963: 10–12.

2863. Chuprakova, R. N. Gidroelektrostantsiia Furnas v Brazilii [The Furnas Hydroelectric Power Station in Brazil] Energokhoz. za rub., no. 4, July-Aug. 1959: 32–35.

2864. Efremov, A., *and* A. Ol'shanyi. Bog "Monatsit" i ego zhretsy [God "monazite" and its priests] Vokrug sveta, no. 9, Sept. 1960: 59–61.

2865. "Garimpeiro" iz Diamantii [A "garimpéiro" from the city of Diamante] Vsesvit, v. 4, no. 4, Apr. 1961: 84–86.

Diamond industry.

2866. Gramotov, A. Neftianaia epopeia Brazilii [The oil saga of Brazil] Mezhdunar. zhizn', v. 10, no. 5, May 1963: 44–49.

2867. Kachevskii, V. Elektroenergetika Brazilii; sostoianie i perspektivy razvitiia [Brazil's electric power; condition and prospects] Mir. ekon. i mezhdunar. otn., no. 1, 1964: 120–126.

2868. Nikolaev, G. M. Sakharnaia promyshlennost' Brazilii [The sugar industry of Brazil] Sakh. prom., v. 38, no. 12, Dec. 1964: 61–62.

2869. Nosova, L. Bor'ba za razvitie neftianoi promyshlennosti Brazilii [Efforts to develop the Brazilian petroleum industry] Mir. ekon. i mezhdunar. otn., no. 12, 1963: 123–127.

2870. Spirin, V. Reviews. Mir. ekon. i mezhdunar. otn., no. 4, Apr. 1960: 153–155.

A review of Gondin da Fonseca's *Que sabe Voce sobre petróleo?* (Rio de Janeiro, Livraria São José, 1957. 273 p.), and of Epitacio Cao's *Eu vi o "trust" por dentro* (Rio de Janeiro, Edição de "Panfleto," 1957. 206 p.).

2871. Vol'fberg, D. B. Gidrouzel Tre Marias v Brazilii [The Tres Marias Hydroelectric Center in Brazil] Energokhoz. za rub., no. 5, Sept.-Oct. 1960: 39–42.

2872. Vol'skii, V. V. Ekonomiko-geograficheskie problemy razvitiia energetiki Brazilii [Economic and geographical problems concerning the development of electric power production in Brazil] Vop. geog., no. 64, 1964: 131–159.

2873. ———. Sovremennoe sostoianie i proekty ispol'zovaniia gidroenergoresursov iugo-vostoka Brazilii [Present-day status and projects for utilizing water power resources in southeastern Brazil] Vest. Mosk. un. Ser. 5: Geog., v. 17, no. 1, Jan.-Feb. 1962: 20–26.

2874. Zaglodin, L. S., *and* A. N. Nemirovskii. Proizvodstvo gorodskogo gaza iz brazil'skikh slantsev [Producing city gas from Brazilian shale] Gaz. prom., v. 8, no. 1, 1963: 18–21.

See also entry no. 2737.

d. Chile

2875. Kruglyi, I. U gorniakov Chili [On a visit to Chilean miners] Nov. vrem., v. 20, no. 19, May 1963: 26–28.

e. Colombia

2876. Alic, Antonio. Izumrudnaia likhoradka [Emerald fever] Vokrug sveta, no. 11, Nov. 1964: 18–21.

f. Cuba

2877. TSelliulozno-bumazhanaia i bumagopererabatyvaiushchaia promyshlennost' Kuby [The woodpulp and paper processing industry of Cuba] Moscow, TSentr. in-t tekhn. informatsii i ekonom. issl. po lesnoi i bumazhnoi i derevoobrabaty-vaiushchei promyshl., 1962. 52 p.

2878. Alinin, Ol. Industriia Kotorro [The industries of El Cotorro] Ukraina, no. 6, Mar. 1963: 2–3.
Steel industry.

2879. Bekarevich, A. D. Metallurgicheskaia promyshlennost' Kuby [The metallurgical industry of Cuba] TSvet. met., v. 37, no. 4, Apr. 1964: 95–96.

2880. ———. Metallurgiia ostrova svobody [The metallurgical industry of the island of freedom] Metallurg, v. 9, no. 4, Apr. 1964: 46–47.

2881. ———. Sakharnaia promyshlennost' Kuby [The sugar industry of Cuba] Sakh. prom., v. 38, no. 2, Feb. 1964: 63–67.

2882. ———. Tekstil'naia promyshlennost' Kuby [The textile industry of Cuba] Tekst. prom., v. 24, no. 3, Mar. 1964: 91–92.

2883. Borovskii, V. Kuba stroit [Cuba builds] Rabotnitsa, v. 39, no. 1, Jan. 1961: 24.
Residential construction.

2884. Castro, Fidel. Iz vystupleniia t. Fidelia Kastro Rus na torzhestvakh v Gavane 2 ianvaria 1964 g. [From the speech of Comrade Fidel Castro Ruz at a solemn meeting in Havana on January 2, 1964] Sakh. prom., v. 38, no. 2, Feb. 1964: 62–63.
Sugar industry.

2885. Chichkov, V. "Partagas" [The "Parta-gaz" Factory] Vokrug sveta, no. 1, 1964: 42–43.
Tobacco industry.

2886. Chuprakova, R. N. Nekotorye dannye ob energetike Kuby [Some data on Cuban power engineering] Energokhoz. za rub., no. 1, Jan.-Feb. 1959: 48.

2887. Danilin, A. Mel'nitsa v Sant'iago de Kuba [A flour mill in Santiago de Cuba] Muk.-elev. prom., v. 29, no. 1, Jan. 1963: 18–24.

2888. ———. Mukomol'no-elevatornaia promyshlennost' v Respublike Kuba [Flour mills and grain elevators in the Republic of Cuba] Muk.-elev. prom., v. 28, no. 11, Nov. 1962: 27–31.

2889. Domínguez, José A. Rabochie khimicheskoi i neftianoi promyshlennosti Kuby v bor'be za natsional'nuiu nezavisimost' i postroenie sotsializma [Cuban chemical and petroleum workers struggle for national independence and the construction of socialism] Neftianik, v. 8, no. 5, May 1963: 14–15.

2890. Guevara, Ernesto. O promyshlennom razvitii Kuby [The industrial development of Cuba] Nov. vrem., v. 22, no. 49, Dec. 1964: 16–17.

2891. Ivanov, E. M. Kubinskaia neft' [Cuban petroleum] Neft. khoz., v. 38, no. 12, Dec. 1960: 62–64.

2892. Kamenetskii, A. V. Proizvodstvo rafinirovannogo sakhara na Kube [Manufacture of refined sugar in Cuba] Sakh. prom., v. 37, no. 4, Apr. 1963: 63–66.

2893. ———. Proizvodstvo sakhara-syrtsa na Kube [Manufacture of unrefined sugar in Cuba] Sakh. prom., v. 37, no. 3, Mar. 1963: 68–74.

2894. Kornilov, IU. Nastoiashchaia "korona" [A genuine "La Corona"] Sov. profsoiuzy, v. 17, no. 21, Nov. 1961: 45–47.
Tobacco industry.

2895. Kozlov, A. V. Sakharnaia promyshlennost' Kuby [The Cuban sugar industry] Sakh. prom., v. 37, no. 1, Jan. 1963: 72–78.

2896. Krasil'nikova, K. Zhilishchnoe stroitel'stvo Kuby [Construction of residential buildings in Cuba] Arkhit. SSSR, no. 4, 1964: 55–63.

2897. Leonidov, K. Budni revoliutsionnoi stroiki [Ordinary days on the sites of revolutionary construction] Mezhdunar. zhizn', v. 10, no. 8, Aug. 1963: 147–148.
Construction of industrial enterprises.

2898. Listov, Vadim. Bitva za kubinskuiu neft' [The battle for Cuba's oil] Nov. vrem., v. 21, no. 9, Feb. 1964: 26–29.

2899. Mozhin, V. P., *and* N. L. Suslovich. Proizvodstvo sakhara na Kube [The production of sugar in Cuba] Pishch. promyshl., no. 1, 1960: 38–39.

2900. Naumov, S. I.   Moskva—Gavana [Moscow to Havana] Gor. khoz. Mosk., v. 35, no. 8, Aug. 1961: 42–44.
Construction industry.

2901. Neftianaia promyshlennost' Kuby [The petroleum industry of Cuba] Neft. khoz., v. 41, no. 6, June 1963: 66–67.

2902. Olteanu, O.   Novye narodnye imeniia na Kube [The new people's farms in Cuba] Mir. ekon. i mezhdunar. otn., no. 7, 1963: 110–111.
Sugar industry.

2903. Perekhrest, S. M. Vodokhoziaistvennoe stroitel'stvo v Respublike Kube [Water resources development in the Cuban Republic] Gidr. i mel., v. 12, no. 9, Sept. 1960: 93–97.

2904. Perventsev, Vl. Pal'my meniaiut adres [The palms change their address] Ogonek, v. 41, no. 48, Nov. 1963: 20–21.
Industrial efficiency.

2905. Rogachev, V. I. Konservnaia promyshlennost' Kuby [The canning industry of Cuba] Kons. i ov. prom., v. 18, no. 1, Jan. 1963: 31–38.

2906. Roselló Medina, Rafael.   Pis'mo kubinskogo mebel'shchika [A letter from a Cuban furniture maker] Mast. lesa, v. 5, no. 10, Oct. 1961: 25.

2907. Savchenko, V. V.   Zhilishchnoe stroitel'stvo Kuby [Construction of residential buildings in Cuba] *In* Kiev. Zonal'nyi nauchno-issledovatel'skii i proektnyi institut tipovogo i eksperimental'nogo proektirovaniia zhilykh i obshchestvennykh zdanii. Stroitel'stvo i arkhitektura; zhilye doma. no. 1. Kiev, 1964: p. 169–176.

2908. Shein, IA. Novoe nikelevoe predpriiatie [A new nickel enterprise] TSvet. met., v. 33, no. 9, Sept. 1960: 91–94.

2909. Shpeer, E. V.   Na poligraficheskikh predpriiatiakh Kuby [In Cuban printing plants] Poligrafiia, no. 7, July 1964: 36–37.

2910. Shul'gin, V. N., *and* V. I. Mudrik· TSelliulozno-bumazhnaia i bumagopererabatyvaiushchaia promyshlennost' Kuby [The woodpulp and paper industry and paper processing plants of Cuba] Bum. prom., v. 37, no. 3, Mar. 1962: 30–31; v. 37, no. 5, May 1962: 28–31.

2911. Tonner-Taylor, Lilian.   Nuevo vista alegre. Vsesvit, v. 4, no. 11, Nov. 1961: 81–83.
Construction of residential buildings.

2912. Vinogradov, N. V. Sakharnaia promyshlennost' Kuby [The sugar industry of Cuba] Sakh. prom., v. 33, no. 6, June 1959: 66.

See also entry no. 2782.

g. The Guianas

2913. Novyi spirto-romovyi zavod v Britanskoi Gviane [A new alcohol and rum distillery in British Guiana] Spir. prom., v. 25, no. 4, 1959: 45–46.

h. Mexico

2914. Kalinin, A.   Elektroenergetika Meksiki i monopolii SShA [Mexican electric power and U.S. monopolies] Mir. ekon. i mezhdunar. otn., no. 1, Jan. 1959: 111–113.

2915. Klusov, E.   Gazovaia promyshlennost' Meksiki [The gas industry of Mexico] Gaz. prom., v. 4, no. 6, June 1959: 52–54.

2916. Kokorev, B. V., *and* D. A. Gaisner. Neft' Meksiki [Petroleum in Mexico] Neft. khoz., v. 38, no. 5, May 1960: 63–68.

2917. Safronov, S.   Proizvodstvo i potreblenie produktov v Meksike [The production and consumption of goods in Mexico] Inform. biul. o zarubezh. khim. promyshl., no. 8, 1961: 10–14.

2918. Suvorov, A., *and* A. Platonov.   Na miasokombinatakh Meksiki [In the meat combines of Mexico] Mias. ind. SSSR, v. 33, no. 2, 1962: 58–63.

See also entry no. 2558.

i. Panama

2919. Neftepererabatyvaiushchii zavod v Paname [A petroleum refinery in Panama] Moscow, TSentr. nauch.-issl. in-t informatsii i tekhn.-ekon. issledovanii po neft. i gaz. prom., 1963. 6 p.

2920. Pervyi neftepererabatyvaiushchii zavod v Paname [The first petroleum refinery in Panama] Nefteper. i neftekhim., no. 3, 1963: 52–54.

j. Peru

2921. Kartsev, A. "Neblagodarnaia strana" ["The ungrateful country"] Mezhdunar. zhizn', v. 10, no. 12, Dec. 1963: 111–112.
Petroleum industry.

See also entry no. 2923.

k. Venezuela

2922. Faria, Jesús. Pravda o "novom" trudovom soglashenii neftianikov Venesuely [The truth about the "new" labor contract of Venezuelan petroleum workers] Probl. mira i sots., v. 6, no. 11, Nov. 1963: 45–48.

2923. Iz pisem chitatelei iz Limy i Karakasa [Readers' letters from Lima and Caracas] Nov. vrem., v. 18, no. 5, Jan. 1960: 31.
Petroleum industry.

2924. Osmanczyk, Edmund. Narod i neft' "malen'koi Venetsii" [People and oil of the "little Venice"] Ogonek, v. 41, no. 15, Apr. 1963: 4–5.
Petroleum industry.

2925. Relquimo, Giacomo, *pseud.* Nafta i krov Venesuely [Petroleum and blood of Venezuela] Vsesvit, v. 6, no. 9, Sept. 1963: 6–10.
Petroleum industry.

See also entry no. 2844.

B. TECHNOLOGY

1. Writings Dealing With Three or More Countries

2926. V. IA. Razvitie iadernoi energetiki v stranakh IUzhnoi i TSentral'noi Ameriki [The development of nuclear energy in Central and South American countries]
Atom. energ., v. 8, no. 5, May 1960: 467–470.

2. Individual Countries

a. Argentina

2927. Gershengorn, A. I. Proekt elektroperedachi 380 kv v Argentine [A project for 380 kv. power transmission in Argentina] Energokhoz. za rub., no. 2, Mar.-Apr. 1959: 44–45.

See also entry no. 2931.

b. Brazil

2928. Denisov, N. IA., *and* IU. G. Trofimenkov. Fundamento-stroenie v Brazilii [Foundation construction in Brazil] Osn. fund. i mekh. grun., no. 5, 1959: 26–28.

2929. Mitiaev, IU. Atomnaia energiia v Brazilii [Atomic energy in Brazil] Atom. energ., v. 16, no 4, Apr. 1964: 385–386.

2930. Umanskii, V. I. Kislorodnye konvertery v Brazilii [Converters with oxygen blow in Brazil] Biul. TSIICHM, no. 2, 1961: 52.

2931. V. IA. Ispol'zovanie atomnoi energii v Brazilii i Argentine [The use of atomic energy in Brazil and Argentina] Atom. energ., v. 8, no. 4, Apr. 1960: 381–382.

c. Chile

2932. Ershov, N. N. Transportirovka rudy avtomaticheskoi konveiernoi linici [Transporting ore on an automatic conveyor line] Gor. zhur., no. 4, Apr. 1963: 74–75.

2933. Pen'ko, A. Pererabotka khloridnykh mednykh rud v Mantos Blankos (Chili) [Processing copper chloride ores in the vicinity of Mantos Blancos, Chile] TSvet. met., v. 35, no. 8, Aug. 1962: 91–93.
Summary of an article that appeared originally in *Journal of Metals*, no. 1, 1962: 51–59.

2934. Primenenie gidrotsiklonov na fabrike Chukvakamata [The use of hydrocyclones at the Chuquicamata plant] TSvet. met., v. 32, no. 6, June 1959: 102–103.

2935. Shubov, L. IA. Obogatitel'naia fabrika El' Sal'vador [The El Salvador ore dressing plant] TSvet. met., v. 34, no. 11, Nov. 1961: 90–93.

2936. Zashikhin, N. V. Novaia medno-molibdenovaia obogatitel'naia fabrika El'-Sal'vador [The new El Salvador copper-molybdenum ore dressing plant] Obog. rud., v. 6, no. 5, 1961: 49–53.

d. Cuba

2937. Arkhipovich, N. A., *and* G. P. Voloshanenko. Bystryi metod opredeleniia redutsiruiushchikh veshchestv v kubinskom sakhare-syrtse [Rapid method for determining the reducing substances in unrefined Cuban sugar] Sakh. prom., v. 37, no. 3, Mar. 1963: 21–23.

2938. TSimbarg, I. E. Zhelezobetonnye mosty v Avstralii i Kube [Reinforced concrete bridges in Australia and Cuba] Bet. i zhel.-bet., no. 1, Jan. 1961: 41–45.

e. Mexico

2939. Banin, A. P. Perekhody meksikanskogo gazoprovoda [Crossings in the Mexican gas pipeline] Stroi. truboprov., v. 6, no. 11, Nov. 1961: 30.

2940. Karpman, M. A. Novyi stan dlia redutsirovaniia trub s natiazheniem [New mill for pipe reduction with elongation] Biul. TSIICHM, no. 1, 1961: 55–56.

2941. TSimbarg, I. E. Stroitel'stvo burovoi stantsii v otkrytom more [Constructing an offshore drilling station] Transp. stroi., v. 10, no. 8, Aug. 1960: 56–57.
    Sulfur mines and mining.

f. Peru

2942. Obogatitel'naia fabrika Tokepala (Peru) [The "Toqucpala" ore dressing plant in Peru] TSvet, met., v. 34, no. 6, June 1961: 91–95.

g. Venezuela

2943. Berlin, R. I., *and* IU. M. Matveev. Novyi truboprokatnyi tsekh v Venesuele [A new pipe rolling mill in Venezuela] Stal', v. 20, no. 9, Sept. 1960: 835–837.

2944. TSimbarg, I. E. Most iz predvaritel'no napriazhennogo zhelezobetona [A bridge made of prestressed concrete] Transp. stroi., v. 12, no. 5, May 1962: 55–56.

2945. ———. Sooruzhenie mosta bol'shoi protiazhennosti [Construction of a long-span bridge] Transp. stroi., v. 13, no. 5, May 1963: 72–73.

2946. Zaitsev, V. IU. Interesnyi proekt zhelezobetonnogo mosta [An interesting plan for a reinforced concrete bridge] Avt. dor., v. 22, no. 6, June 1959: 25.

C. TRANSPORTATION

1. Writings Dealing With Three or More Countries

2947. Sáenz, Vicente. Problemy mezhokeanskikh putei amerikanskogo kontinenta; vopros o Teuantepeke, Nikarague i Paname v sviazi s polozheniem Suetskogo kanala. S prilozheniem ofitsial'nykh tekstov dogovorov [Problems of transoceanic passages through the American continent; the question of Tehuantepec, Nicaragua, and Panama as related to the situation of the Suez Canal. Supplemented with the official texts of international treaties] Moscow, Izd-vo inostr. lit., 1959. 203 p.   JX4155.S317
    Translated by L. G. Mikhailov from the Spanish *Nuestras vías interoceánicas.* Introductory article by S. A. Gonionskii.

2948. Guberman, R. Problemy morskogo sudokhodstva razvivaiushchikhsia stran [Problems of maritime transportation in the developing countries] Mir. ekon. i mezhdunar. otn., no. 2, 1964: 111–114.

2949. Libman, M. R. Dispetcherskaia tsentralizatsiia v IUzhnoi Amerike [Centralized traffic control in South America] Avtom., telem. i sviaz', v. 7, no. 9, Sept. 1963: 46.

2950. Rybalkin, I. Ne letaite na samoletakh kompanii Braniff [Do not fly on airplanes of the Braniff Company] Nov. vrem., v. 20, no. 36, Sept. 1962: 15–16.
    Air travel.

2951. Simakov, V., *and others.* Sud'ba odnogo proekta [The fate of a project] Vokrug sveta, no. 1, Jan. 1963: 53–54.
    Canals.

2952. Vorokhobskii, A., *and* M. Maksimadzhi. Torgovyi flot stran IUzhnoi Ameriki [The merchant fleet of the South American countries] Mor. flot, v. 20, no. 1, Jan. 1960: 38–39.

2. Individual Countries

a. Argentina

2953. Elektrifikatsiia zheleznykh dorog Argentiny [Electrification of the Argentine railroads] Elek. i tepl. tiaga, v. 3, no. 10, Oct. 1959: 47.

b. Brazil

2954. Ivanov, N. N. Dorogi Brazilii [Highways in Brazil] Avt. dor., v. 25, no. 9, Sept. 1962: 28–29.

c. Cuba

2955. Alejandro. Na Kube [In Cuba] Av. i kosm., v. 45, no. 5, May 1963: 81–83; v. 46, no. 6, June 1963: 90–93.
Flight training.

2956. Armesto López, Juan. Bratskii privet ot avtotransportnikov Kuby [Fraternal greetings from the highway transport workers of Cuba] Avt. transp., v. 39, no. 6, June 1961: 3–4.

2957. Arutiunova, N. Hasta la vista! Rabotnitsa, no. 3, Mar. 1963: 24.
The Moscow-Cuba air line.

2958. Dennemark, A. Iz opyta plavaniia sudov na Kubu [From experience acquired in sailing ships to Cuba] Mor. flot, v. 21, no. 4, Apr. 1961: 25–26.

2959. Derbenev, P. Podvodnye tunneli Gavany [Underwater tunnels in Havana] Avt. transp., v. 42, no. 9, Sept. 1964: 58–59.

2960. Dolmatov, P., and V. Rozhkov. Opytnaia perevozka i peregruzka sakhara-syrtsa nasyp'iu [Experience in the transportation, loading, and unloading of raw sugar in bulk] Mor. flot, v. 20, no. 12, Dec. 1960: 5–8.

2961. Fidel' Kastro—pochetnyi moriak teplokhoda "Kura" [Fidel Castro is an honorary seaman of the motorship "Kura"] Mor. flot, v. 22, no. 7, July 1962: 47.

2962. IAkovlev, B. P. U kubinskikh zheleznodorozhnikov [Visiting Cuban railroad

workers] Put' i put. khoz., v. 7, no. 3, 1963: 31–33.

2963. Kamenetskii, A. V. Bestarnoe khranenie i perevozka sakhara-syrtsa v respublike Kuba [Bulk storage and transportation of unrefined sugar in the Cuban Republic] Sakh. prom., v. 36, no. 12, Dec. 1962: 11–14.

2964. Kapustin, S. K. Porty Kuby [The ports of Cuba] Biul. tekhn.-ekon. inform. Tekh. upr. Min. mor. flota, no. 12, 1960: 87–100.

2965. Más, Gustavo. Besudu vedut kubinskie aviatory [A conversation with Cuban pilots] Grazhd. av., v. 20, no. 6, June 1963: 21.

2966. Osipov, B. O vybore naivygodneishego puti plavaniia na Kubu [Selection of the most advantageous sailing route to Cuba] Mor. flot, v. 23, no. 12, Dec. 1963: 19–20.

2967. Perevozka sakhara-syrtsa navalom [Bulk transportation of unrefined sugar] Mor. flot, v. 22, no. 1, Jan. 1962: 48.
Cuban sugar shipments to Russia.

2968. Romanov, B. U avtotransportnikov geroicheskoi Kuby [Visiting the automobile transportation workers of heroic Cuba] Avt. transp., v. 41, no. 5, May 1963: 3–5.

2969. Sovetskie vertolety v Gavane [Soviet helicopters in Havana] Grazhd. av., v. 17, no. 5, May 1960: 16–17.

2970. Taratynov, V. Vybor putei pri plavanii mezhdu portami Kuby i Evropy [Choosing the course in navigation between the ports of Cuba and Europe] Mor. flot, v. 24, no. 6, June 1964: 18–21.

2971. TSkhovrebov, Kh. N. Na kryl'iakh druzhby [On the wings of friendship] Grazhd. av., v. 19, no. 12, Dec. 1962: 10–12.
Air travel.

2972. Valerius, IU. Kuba—liubov' moia [Cuba is my love] Grazhd. av., v. 20, no. 7, July 1963: 20–21.
Aeronautics.

See also entries no. 2766 and 4819.

d. Dominican Republic

2973. Kukibnyi, A. A. Bestarnoe khranenie i pogruzka sakhara v suda [Bulk storage and loading of sugar into ships] Sakh. prom., v. 34, no. 9, Sept. 1960: 75–76.

e. Ecuador

See entry no. 2820.

f. Guatemala

See entry no. 2823.

g. Mexico

2974. Morskoi flot Meksiki [Mexico's merchant marine] Mor. flot, v. 20, no. 8, Aug. 1960: 43.

2975. Tat'ianchenko, A. 56-ia General'naia konferentsiia FAI [The 56th General Conference of the International Aeronautical Federation] Kryl. rod., v. 15, no. 1, Jan. 1964: 20–21.

h. Panama; the Panama Canal

2976. Maksimadzhi, M. I. Lotsmanskaia sluzhba na Kil'skom, Suetskom i Panamskom kanalakh [Pilotage in the Kiel, Suez, and Panama Canals] Moscow, Morskoi transport, 1961. 42 p.

2977. Vyshnepol'skii, Semen Abramovich. Panamskii kanal [The Panama Canal] *In his* Mirovye morskie puti i sudokhodstvo; ocherki. 2d ed. Moscow, Morskoi transport, 1959. p. 231–251.

i. Uruguay

See entry no. 1505.

XIII

AGRICULTURE

༄

A. FARMING AND STOCK RAISING

1. Writings Dealing With Three or More Countries

2978. Chai v Iuzhnoi Amerike [Tea in South America] Subtrop. kul't., no. 3, 1959: 107–108.

2979. Landa, I. M. Ekonomicheskie osnovy geografii kofe, kakao i chaia v kapitalisticheskom mire [Basic economic aspects of the geography of coffee, cacao, and tea in the capitalist world] Uch. zap. Tirasp. ped. in-ta, no. 9, 1958 [publ. in 1960]: 99–109.
Coffee, cacao, and tea plantations.

2. Individual Countries

a. Argentina

2980. IUrlov, P. Polozhenie sel'skogo khoziaistva i krest'ianstva Argentiny v poslevoennyi period, 1945–1960 gg. [The postwar situation of Argentine agriculture and the peasantry, 1945–1960] Moscow, 1961. 16 p.
Author's abstract of a dissertation for the degree of Candidate in Economic Sciences.

2981. IUrlov, P. Zhivotnovodstvo Argentiny [Stockbreeding in Argentina] Ekon. sel'-khoz., v. 31, no. 4, Apr. 1960: 118–119.

2982. Novikova, L. Nekotorye sorta tovarnoi pshenitsy Argentiny [Certain varieties of commercial wheat from Argentina] Muk.-elev. prom., v. 28, no. 2, Feb. 1962: 31.

2983. Velkov, V. Plodovodstvo Argentiny [Fruit culture in Argentina] Sadovodstvo, v. 98, no. 10, Oct. 1960: 54–56.
Translated from Bulgarian.

b. Brazil

2984. Dyiavol z Amazonki [The devil from the Amazon Valley] Vsesvit, v. 5, no. 3, Mar. 1962: 151–153.
Rubber plantations.

2985. Shnitke, G. Chernyi, kak d'iavol, chistyi, kak angel . . . [Black as the devil and pure as an angel . . .] Nov. vrem., v. 20, no. 46, Nov. 1962: 29.
Coffee production and prices.

c. Colombia

2986. Lialikov, D. N. Nekotorye voprosy sel'skogo khoziaistva Kolumbii [Some problems in the agriculture of Colombia] Uch. zap. MGPI, v. 121, 1959: 56–86.

d. Costa Rica

See entry no. 1468.

e. Cuba

2987. Egorova, E. I. Sostoianie orosheniia v respublike Kuba [The state of irrigation in the Cuban Republic] Moscow, 1964. 37 p. (Goszemvodkhoz SSSR. Vsesoiuznyi gosudarstvennyi proektno-izyskatel'skii i NII "Giprovodkhoz")

2988. Sushchevskii, M. G. Sel'skoe khoziaistvo Kuby [Cuban agriculture] Moscow, Kolos, 1964. 80 p.

2989. Andrianov, V. Sakhar—osnovnoe bogatstvo naroda [Sugar as the basic wealth of the people] Mezhdunar. zhizn', v. 11, no. 3, Mar. 1964: 110.

2990. Aslanishvili, A. Budushchie mekhanizatory svobodnoi Kuby [Future machine

operators of free Cuba] Prof.-tekh. obr., v. 19, no. 3, Mar. 1962: 11.
Farm mechanization.

2991. Bekarevich. A. V kubinskoi derevne [In the rural areas of Cuba] Kolkh.-sovkh. proizv., no. 1, Jan. 1964: 55–56.

2992. Cordero Rodríguez, Mario. O pchelovodstve Kuby [Cuban apiculture] Pchelovodstvo, v. 39, no. 11, Nov. 1962: 36.

2993. Díaz, Félix. O pravovom polozhenii kooperativov po proizvodstvu sakhara na Kube [The legal status of Cuban cooperatives for the production of sugar] Vest. Mosk. un., Ser. 10: Pravo, v. 17, no. 3, July-Sept. 1962: 67–71.

2994. Dudar', IU. Fasol' na Kube [String beans in Cuba] Zernobobovye kul'tury, no. 4, 1964: 36.

2995. ———. Kukuruza na Kube [Corn in Cuba] Kukuruza, v. 8, no. 2, 1963: 52–53.

2996. ———. Sadovodstvo Kuby [Fruit culture in Cuba] Sadovodstvo, v. 102, no. 11, Nov. 1964: 41–42.

2997. ———. Sel'skoe khoziaistvo Kuby [Cuban agriculture] Vest. sel'khoz. nauki, v. 8, no. 1, Jan. 1964: 139–144.

2998. ———. TSvetovodstvo Kuby [Cuban floriculture] TSvetovodstvo, v. 6, no. 7, 1963: 33–34.

2999. Fedotov, A. Zhemchuzhina Antil'-skikh ostrovov [Pearl of the Antilles] IUn. nat., no. 6, June 1962: 24–25.
Sugar cane.

3000. Kalinin, A. Kuba; god osvobozhdeniia, god agrarnoi reformy [Cuba; the year of liberation and the year of agrarian reform] Mir. ekon. i mezhdunar. otn., no. 7, July 1960: 58–69.

3001. Osvoenie bolot na Kube [Reclamation of swamps in Cuba] Torf. prom., v. 40, no. 4, 1963: 36–37.

3002. Perekhrest, S. M. Bolota Kuby i vozmozhnosti ikh ispol'zovaniia [Swamps in Cuba and possibilities of their utilization] Gidr. i mel., v. 15, no. 8, Aug. 1963: 49–59.

3003. Pimenova, R. A. Strukturnye sdvigi v sel'skom khoziaistve Kuby [Structural changes in Cuban agriculture] Vop. geog., no. 64, 1964: 160–171.

3004. Shubin, F. F. Biologicheskii metod bor'by s vrediteliami sakharnogo trostnika Diatrae saccharalis [A biological method for controlling the Diatrae saccharalis, a sugarcane pest] Vest. sel'-khoz. nauki, v. 9, no. 12, Dec. 1964: 133–135.

3005. Sushchevskii, M. G. Sakharnyi trostnik na Kube [Sugarcane in Cuba] Sakh. svekla, v. 8, no. 9, Sept. 1963: 38–40.

3006. ———. Zemledelie Kuby [Agriculture in Cuba] Zemledelie, v. 25, no. 5, May 1963: 75–77.

3007. TSifry, fakty o sel'skom khoziaistve Respubliki Kuba [Facts and figures on agriculture in the Cuban Republic] Zhivotnovodstvo, v. 25, no. 6, June 1963: 91.

3008. TSymbal, I. Na ostrove svobody [On the island of freedom] Kon. i kon. sp., v. 32, no. 10, 1962: 35–37.
Stock farming.

3009. Vlasov, P. Skotovodstvo Kuby [Stock farming in Cuba] Moloch. i mias. skotovodstvo, v. 7, no. 10, Oct. 1962: 60–63.

3010. Vlasov, P. G. Zhivotnovodstvo v Respublike Kuba [Stock farming in the Cuban Republic] Zhivotnovodstvo, v. 24, no. 10, Oct. 1962: 89–93.

3011. Volkau, A. E. Vyroshchvanne slanechniku u respublitsy Kuba [Sunflower growing in the Republic of Cuba] Vestsi AN BSSR. Ser. sel'hosp. nav., no. 2, 1964: 133–137.

3012. Voronko, A. I. Kubinskii sakhar [Cuban sugar] Sakh. svekla, v. 5, no. 9, Sept. 1960: 46–47.

See also entries no. 2771 and 2902.

f. Mexico

3013. Firsov, B. P., and A. S. Sultankhodzhaev. Khlopkovodstvo v Meksike [Cotton growing in Mexico] Khlopkovodstvo, v. 10, no. 10, Oct. 1960: 51–58.

3014. Karapetian, S. K. XI Vsemirnyi nauchnyi kongress po ptitsevodstvu; zametki delegata [At the 11th World Poultry Congress; comments of a delegate] Agrobiologiia, no. 1, Jan.-Feb. 1959: 126–130.

3015. ———. Voprosy fiziologii i pitaniia na XI Vsemirnom kongresse po ptitsevodstvu [Physiological and nutritional problems discussed at the 11th International Congress on Poultry Farming] Izv. AN Arm. SSR, Biol. nauki, v. 12, no. 5, May 1959: 93–98.

3016. Kopanevich, P. P. Samoe krupnoe v mire pchelovodnoe khoziaistvo [The world's largest apiary] Pchelovodstvo, no. 9, Sept. 1963: 40–45.

3017. Kuvshinov, I. Ekonomika sel'skogo khoziaistva Meksiki [Economic aspects of Mexican agriculture] Ekon. sel'khoz., v. 33, no. 2, Feb. 1962: 120–123.

3018. Mashbits, IA. G. Oroshenie zemel' i ekonomika Meksiki [Land irrigation and the Mexican economy] Gidr. i mel., v. 11, no. 2, Feb. 1959: 50–53.

3019. Opisanie krupnogo pchelovodnogo khoziaistva Meksiki [Description of a large apicultural enterprise in Mexico] Pchelovodstvo, v. 38, no. 3, Mar. 1961: 42–43.

3020. Palacios, Oscar. Oroshenie v Meksike [Irrigation in Mexico] Gidr. i mel., v. 16, no. 11, Nov. 1964: 48–51.
Translated from the Spanish.

3021. Sushchevskii, M. G. Sel'skoe khoziaistvo Meksiki [The agriculture of Mexico] Zemledelie, v. 8, no. 9, Sept. 1960: 84–87.

3022. Topete, Jesús. Sbor urozhaia [Harvesting] Vokrug sveta, no. 9, Sept. 1960: 47–48.
Agricultural laborers.

3023. Volkov, V. A. Na ptitsevodcheskikh fermakh Meksiki [On the poultry farms of Mexico] Ptitsevodstvo, v. 9, no. 3, Mar. 1959: 34–37.

See also entry no. 2831.

g. Peru

3024. TSitrusy v Peru [Citrus fruits in Peru] Subtrop. kul't., no. 3, 1959: 107.

B. FISHING AND HUNTING

1. Argentina

3025. Darrell, John. Okhota na strausov [Hunting rheas] Vokrug sveta, no. 6, June 1963: 54–55.

2. Brazil

3026. Ignat'ev, Oleg. Zhangada ukhodit v more [The jangada weighs anchor] Ogonek, v. 41, no. 35, Aug. 1963: 17–18.
Fisheries.

3. Cuba

3027. Buesa, R. Kubinskii tsentr rybopromyslovykh issledovanii [Cuban center for fishery research] Okeanologiia, v. 4, no. 2, 1964: 357–359.

3028. Haubold, G. Ansel'mo z Kakhimara [Anselmo from Cojímar] Vsesvit, v. 6, no. 9, Sept. 1963: 88–89.
Fishermen.

3029. Lopatina, Ekaterina. V Atlantike [On the Atlantic] Znamia, v. 34, no. 1, Jan. 1964: 123–141.
Soviet fisheries.

3030. Marcel, Manuel. Okhotniki za langustami [Lobster catchers] Rybov. i rybolov., v. 6, no. 5, May 1963: 48 49.
Translated from the Spanish.

4. Jamaica

3031. Hedge, Mitchel. Moi soiuznik—opasnost'; glavy iz knigi [Danger is my ally; excerpts from a book] Vokrug sveta, no. 7, July 1961: 36–39.
Fishing.
Translated from the English.

5. Peru

3032. Kuz'michev, A. B. Rybnaia promyshlennost' Peru [The fishing industry of Peru] Ryb. khoz., v. 40, no. 3, 1964: 79–83.

XIV

SOCIETY AND SOCIAL CONDITIONS

❦

A. GENERAL WORKS

1. Writings Dealing With Three or More Countries

3033. Kornilov, IU. Na raznykh kontinentakh [On different continents] Sov. profsoiuzy, v. 18, no. 22, Nov. 1962: 31–33.

2. Individual Countries

a. Argentina

3034. Edelman, Fanny. Stakan moloka [A glass of milk] Sov. zhen., v. 18, no. 7, 1962: 19.

See also entry no. 4507.

b. Bolivia

3035. Pasynky Ameryky [The stepchildren of America] Vsesvit, v. 2, no. 11, Nov. 1959: 146–147.

See also entry no. 4587.

c. Brazil

3036. Aglin, Anatolii Nikolaevich. Budni i bitvy Brazilii [Everyday work and struggles in Brazil] Moscow, Gospolitizdat, 1963. 126 p.   HN283.5.A7
  Also published in Latvian.
  Reviewed by L. Novikova in *Nov. mir*, v. 39, no. 8, Aug. 1963: 278–280; in *V mire knig*, v. 3, no. 8, Aug. 1963: 4.

3037. Jesus, Carolina Maria de. Svalka [The city dump] Vilnius, Valst. grožinés lit-ros leidykla, 1962. 194 p.
  In Lithuanian. Translated by L. Valbasis from the Portuguese *Quarto de despejo*. Introductory article by A. Dant.

3038. Bor'ba protiv golodnoi smerti [The struggle against starvation] Vsem. prof. dvizh., no. 2, Feb. 1959: 47–48.

3039. Chumak, P. Kogda nebo zheltoe [When the skies are yellow] Ogonek, v. 41, no. 38, Sept. 1963: 18–19.
  A review of Carolina Maria de Jesus' *Quarto de despejo* (São Paulo, Livraria F. Alves, 1960. 182 p.).

3040. Izula. Bogataia strana, bednyi narod— takova Braziliia [A rich country and a poor people—this is Brazil] Zhen. mira, no. 2, 1960: 23–25.

3041. Jesus, Carolina Maria de. Dnevnik golodaiushchei zhenshchiny; otryvok iz knigi [The diary of a hungry woman; excerpt from a book] Nõukogude naine, no. 10, 1962: 19–20.
  In Estonian. Translated from the Portuguese.

3042. ———. Favela; shchodennyk [Favela; a diary] Vsesvit, v. 7, no. 12, Dec. 1964: 7–75.
  Translated from the Portuguese.

3043. ———. IA nachinaiu vozmushchat'sia [I have begun to feel indignant] Ogonek, v. 41, no. 38, Sept. 1963: 19.

3044. ———. "Kuarto de despekho"; dnevnik golodaiushchei zhenshchiny ["Quarto de despejo"; excerpts from the diary of a hungry woman] Zhen. mira, no. 6, 1962: 32–33.

3045. Moraes, Eneida de. Moia Braziliia [My Brazil] Nov. vrem., v. 17, no. 25, June 1959: 19.

See also entry no. 2415.

d. Chile

3046. Castro, Baltazar. Mezhdu morem i Andami [Between the sea and the Andes] Za rubezhom, no. 46, Nov. 1963: 21–22.

3047. Pechuro, E. E. Mozhno li dobit'sia "politicheskoi stabil'nosti" v Latinskoi Amerike? [Is it possible to achieve "political stability" in Latin America?] Vop. ist., v. 39, no. 1, Jan. 1964: 201–202.

3048. Vicentini, María Luisa. Chili; zemlia i liudi [Chile; the country and its people] Zhen. mira, no. 9, 1963: 9–12.

e. Colombia

3049. Kharytonov, Volodymyr. Den' svobody nastane! [The day of freedom will come!] Ukraina, no. 24, Dec. 1962: 10–11.

f. Cuba

3050. Espín de Castro, Vilma. Kuba—svobodnaia zemlia [Cuba—a free country] Zhen. mira, no. 6, 1960: 11–14.

3051. Krylova, N., *and* IU. Obraztsova. Pod zelenymi olivami [Under green olive trees] Ogonek, v. 40, no. 2, Jan. 1962: 7.

3052. Listov, V. Novoe v zhizni Kuby [New features in the life of Cuba] Nov. vrem., v. 20, no. 31, July 1962: 25–27.

3053. Rosenkranz, Heinz. Rodzher i Odalli; istoriia odniiei kubyns'koi rodyny [Roger and Odalli; the story of a Cuban family] Vsesvit, v. 5, no. 1, Jan. 1962: 67–79.
Disabled veterans.
Translated from the German.

See also entries no. 4655 and 4723.

g. Ecuador

3054. Borovskii, V. V doline vulkanov [In the volcano valley] Nov. vrem., v. 21, no. 40, Oct. 1963: 22–25; v. 21, no. 41, Oct. 1963: 26–29.
Social conditions.

h. Guatemala

3055. Echevarria, Carmen. V strane ketsalia [In the country of the quetzal] Zhen. mira, no. 8, 1964: 10–13.

3056. González, Sofia. V bor'be protiv ekspluatatsii i nishchety [In the struggle against exploitation and poverty] Sov. zhen., v. 18, no. 9, 1962: 38.

i. Jamaica

3057. IAmaika bez prykras [Jamaica in its true colors] Vsesvit, v. 6, no. 1, Jan. 1963: 60–61.

j. Mexico

3058. Ballester, Manuela. Meksika; strana kontrastov, iarkikh krasok, krasivykh kostiumov [Mexico; a land of contrasts, bright colors, and beautiful costumes] Zhen. mira, no. 2, 1961: 33–34.
Customs and social conditions.

3059. K. V. Review. Zhen. mira, no. 12, 1964: 34.
Family life of Mexican peasants.
A review of Oscar Lewis' *The Children of Sánchez; Autobiography of a Mexican Family* (New York, Random House, 1961. 499 p.).

3060. Koenigsberger, G. Blysk i zlydennist' Meksiky [The splendor and the misery of Mexico] Vsesvit, v. 6, no. 4, Apr. 1963: 135–141.
Translated from the English.

3061. Talyzin, F. F. Na zemle drevnikh atstekov [In the land of the ancient Aztecs] Zdorov'e, v. 6, no. 4, Apr. 1960: 25.

k. Paraguay

3062. Kremnev, M. Tragediia Paragvaia [The tragedy of Paraguay] Nov. vrem., v. 17, no. 52, Dec. 1959: 26–27.

3063. Rodríguez, Gregorio. Paragvai pod piatoi diktatury [Paraguay under the heel of the dictatorship] Vsem. prof. dvizh., no. 5, May 1962: 34–37.

l. Peru

3064. Review. Probl. mira i sots., v. 2, no. 3, 1959: 91.
A review of Carlos Núñez Anavitarte's *Mariátegui y el descentralismo* (Cuzco, Editorial Carciliaso, 1958. 76 p.).

m. Puerto Rico

3065. Delgado, Emilio. Obraztsy, ne popav-shie v vitrinu [Samples which the "show window" did not display] Za rubezhom, no. 1, Jan. 1963: 25.

3066. Iznanka ikh progressa [The seamy side of their progress] Nov. vrem., v. 21, no. 12, Mar. 1964: 27.

n. Uruguay

3067. Ramírez de Gadda, Velia. Bol'shikh vam uspekhov! [May you achieve the best results!] Rabotnitsa, v. 39, no. 11, Nov. 1961: 6–7.

3068. Villar de Grove, Antonia. IA zhivu v chelovecheskikh dzhungliakh [I live in a human jungle] Sov. zhen., v. 17, no. 2, 1961: 11.

3069. Weinberger, Luciano.   Stariki ne khotiat golodat' [Old people don't want to starve] Sots. obesp., v. 25, no. 7, July 1964: 60–63.
    Old-age pensions.

    See also entry no. 1083.

o. Venezuela

3070. García, Elena.   Venesuela boretsia [Venezuela struggles] Rabotnitsa, no. 10, Oct. 1963: 14.

3071. Gasparini, Pablo.   Prekrasnyi ostrov Margarity [Beautiful Margarita Island] Ogonek, v. 38, no. 40, Oct. 1960: 13.

p. West Indies

3072. Breton, Denise. Gvadelupa i Martinika; kartiny gor'koi deistvitel'nosti [Guadeloupe and Martinique; a bitter reality] Zhen. mira, no. 4, 1962: 23–25, 34.

B.   URBAN CONDITIONS

1. Writings Dealing With Three or More Countries

3073. Mashbits, IA. G. Nekotorye osoben-nosti urbanizatsii v Latinskoi Amerike [Some aspects of urbanization in Latin America] Moscow, Nauka, 1964. 8 p.

3074. Kolotilkin, B. Zhilishchnaia problema v razvivaiushchikhsia stranakh [The hous-

ing problem in the developing countries] Mir. ekon. i mezhdunar. otn., no. 3, 1964: 113–115.

3075. Mashbits, IA. G. Amerikanskii sotsio-log o roli gorodov v zhizni Latinskoi Ameriki [An American sociologist dis-cusses the role of cities in the life of Latin America] Vop. ist., v. 39, no. 3, Mar. 1964: 206–207.

3076. Zhilishchnyi krizis v stranakh Latinskoi Ameriki [The housing crisis in Latin America] Mol. komm., no. 2, Feb. 1961: 113.

2. Individual Countries

a. Brazil

3077. Koval', B. I.   Problema urbanizatsii v sovremennoi Brazilii [The problem of urbanization in present-day Brazil] Mos-cow, Nauka, 1964. 10 p.

3078. Pokshishevskii, V. V.   Noveishee razvitie gorodov Brazilii i ikh ekonomiko-geograficheskie tipy [Recent growth of Brazilian cities and their economic and geographical types] Vop. geog., no. 45, 1959: 150–177.

b. Chile

3079. Mertve misto [A ghost town] Vsesvit, v. 4, no. 2, Feb. 1961: 156.

3080. Vicentini, María Luisa. V bor'be za krov nad golovoi [Fighting for a roof over our heads] Zhen. mira, no. 6, 1962: 10, 33.

c. Cuba

3081. Novyi raion stolitsy Kuby [A new district in the Cuban capital] Stroi. i arkhit., v. 11, no. 10, Oct. 1963: 38–39.

    See also entries no. 2883, 2896, 2911, and 4179.

C.   RURAL CONDITIONS

1. Writings Dealing With Three or More Countries

3082. Rumiantsev, Aleksei Matveevich, *ed.* Agrarnyi vopros i natsional'no-osvobodi-tel'noe dvizhenie; materialy obmena

mneniiami marksistov-agrarnikov, so-
stoiavshegosia v iule-sentiabre 1960 g. v
Gavane i Bukhareste [The agrarian prob-
blem and the national liberation movement; materials from a conference of
Marxist specialists in the agrarian question in July-September 1960 in Havana
and Bucharest] Moscow, Sotsekgiz, 1963.
531 p.   HD156.R85
Reviewed by IU. Bochkarev in *Nov. mir*,
v. 39, no. 8, Aug. 1963: 270–273.

3083. Sivolobov, A. M. Ekonomicheskie
problemy soiuza rabochego klassa i
krest'ianstva v Latinskoi Amerike; k
agrarnomu voprosu na sovremennom
etape [Economic problems of the alliance
of Latin American workers and peasants;
present-day agrarian problems] Moscow,
1963. 133 p.

3084. Bernard, Guillermo. Zemlia bez liudei,
liudi bez zemli; agrarnyi vopros v Latinskoi Amerike [Land without people, and
people without land; the agrarian question in Latin America] Za rubezhom,
no. 7, Feb. 1963: 22–23.

3085. Eliutin, IU. Latinskaia Amerika:
krizis pomeshchich'ei oligarkhii [Latin
America: crisis of the landowning oli-
garchy] Mezhdunar. zhizn', v. 10, no. 2,
Feb. 1963: 52–61.

3086. Galkina, A. D. Agrarnyi vopros v
Latinskoi Amerike [The agrarian ques-
tion in Latin America] Vop. ist., v. 38,
no. 12, Dec. 1963: 178–179.
A review of an article by Max Zeiske in
*Wissenschaftliche Zeitschrift der Karl Marx
Universität*, Leipzig, no. 1, 1963: 11–12.

3087. ———. Zapadnogermanskii zhurnal
ob agrarnoi reforme v Latinskoi Amerike
[An article on agrarian reform in Latin
America published by a West German
magazine] Vop. ist., v. 39, no. 5, May
1964: 205.

3088. Kudy znyk kauchukovyi legion? [What
happened to the rubber legion?] Vsesvit,
v. 7, no. 2, Feb. 1964: 22–24.
Tragic fate of the workers hired to cultivate
rubber trees during the Second World War.

3089. Lytvynenko, O. Formy i metody
pidporiadkuvannia sil's'koho hospodar-
stva krain Latyns'koi Ameryky monopo-

liiamy SShA [Forms and methods em-
ployed by U.S. monopolies in dominating
Latin American agriculture] Ekon. Rad.
Ukr., no. 6, Nov.-Dec. 1962: 112–118.

3090. Saad, Pedro. Tragediia krest'ianstva v
Latinskoi Amerike [The tragedy of the
peasantry in Latin America] Nov. vrem.,
v. 20, no. 46, Nov. 1962: 20–22.

3091. Salazar, Marcos. Istoriia bananovoi
imperii [The history of a banana empire]
Mol. mira, no. 5, 1960: 10.

3092. Sivolobov, A. Krest'ianskoe dvizhenie
v Latinskoi Amerike [The peasant movement in Latin America] Kommunist,
v. 41, no. 12, Aug. 1964: 100–107.

2. Individual Countries

a. Argentina

3093. Bezzemel'nye krest'iane Argentiny [The
landless peasants of Argentina] Zhen.
mira, no. 9, 1960: 21–22.

3094. García, J. M. Agrarnyi vopros i
natsional'no-osvoboditel'noe dvizhenie;
Argentina [The agrarian problem and the
national liberation movement; Argen-
tina] Probl. mira i sots., v. 4, no. 3, Mar.
1961: 61–64.

3095. García, L. Agrarnyi vopros v Argentine
[The agrarian problem in Argentina]
Ekon. sel'khoz., v. 33, no. 1, Jan. 1962:
116–120.

3096. ———. Zemel'nye otnosheniia v
sovremennoi Argentine [Land relation-
ships in present-day Argentina] Nauch.
dokl. vys. shkoly; ekon. nauki, v. 4, no.
2, 1961: 115–126.

3097. IUrlov, P. Agrarnyi vopros v Argentine
[The agrarian problem in Argentina]
Mir. ekon. i mezhdunar. otn., no. 5, May
1961: 110–116.

3098. Jasovich, Rosa. Obrabatyvat' svoiu
sobstvennuiu zemliu—mechta argentinskoi krest'ianki [The dream of every
Argentine peasant woman is to till her
own land] Zhen. mira, no. 6, 1962: 18–19.

See also entry no. 2980.

b. Bolivia

3099. Gumución de Lima, Rosa.   Nishchie krest'iane . . . Latifundii, po ploshchadi ravnye Danii,—takova Boliviia [Destitute peasants . . . Latifundia equal to the area of Denmark; this is Bolivia] Zhen. mira, no. 8, 1960: 23–26.

3100. Lytvynenko, O. L.   Revoliutsiia 1952 r. i agrarna reforma v Bolivii [The revolution of 1952 and the agrarian reform in Bolivia] Ukr. ist. zhur., v. 7, no. 4, July-Aug. 1963: 90–94.

c. Brazil

3101. Sivolobov, Andrei Mikhailovich. Agrarnye otnosheniia v sovremennoi Brazilii [Agrarian relations in present-day Brazil] Moscow, Sotsekgiz, 1959. 209 p.
HD495.S5

3102. Artamonov, M.   Braziliia: perspektivy agrarnoi reformy [Prospects for an agrarian reform in Brazil] Nov. vrem., v. 21, no. 52, Dec. 1963: 22–23.

3103. Sivolobov, A. M.   Agrarnye otnosheniia v sovremennoi Brazilii [Agrarian relations in present-day Brazil] Uch. zap. kaf. polit. ekon., no. 1, 1959: 148–169.

3104. Souza, Ethel de.   Nad nashimi poliami veiut novye vetry [Fresh winds are blowing across our fields] Zhen. mira, no. 7, 1962: 29.

d. Chile

3105. Agrarnye programmy kommunisticheskikh partii Velikobritanii, Gretsii, Indii, Indonezii, Ispanii, Italii, Finliandii, Frantsii, Chili, IAponii [Agrarian programs of the Communist parties of Great Britain, Greece, India, Indonesia, Spain, Italy, Finland, France, Chile, and Japan] Moscow, Izd-vo VPSh, 1959. 15 p.

3106. Ahumada, Juan.   Agrarnyi vopros i natsional'no-osvoboditel'noe dvizhenie; Chili [The agrarian problem and the national liberation movement; Chile] Probl. mira i sots., v. 4, no. 2, Feb. 1961: 76–78.

3107. Carretín, Roberto.   Uaso—chiliiskii krest'ianin ["Huaso," the Chilean peasant] Vokrug sveta, no. 5, May 1959: 41–43.
Translated from the Spanish.

3108. Galkina, A. D.   Ob agrarnoi reforme v Chili [Agrarian reform in Chile] Vop. ist., v. 38, no. 9, Sept. 1963: 175–176.

3109. Millás, Orlando.   O bor'be chiliiskikh krest'ian [The struggle of Chilean peasants] Nov. vrem., v. 19, no. 22, May 1961: 20–21.

3110. Nikitin, M.   Bor'ba za agrarnuiu reformu v Chili [The struggle for agrarian reform in Chile] Ekon. sel'khoz., v. 35, no. 1, Jan. 1964: 109–112.

e. Colombia

3111. Sivolobov, A.   Agrarnyi vopros v Kolumbii [The agrarian problem in Colombia] Ekon. sel'khoz., v. 32, no. 7, July 1961: 121–124.

3112. Vieira, Gilberto.   Agrarnyi vopros i natsional'no-osvoboditel'noe dvizhenie; Kolumbiia [The agrarian problem and the national liberation movement; Colombia] Probl. mira i sots., v. 4, no. 1, Jan. 1961: 80–81.

f. Cuba

3113. Núñez Jiménez, Antonio.   Agrarnaia reforma na Kube; kratkii istoricheskii ocherk [Agrarian reform in Cuba; a brief historical study] Moscow, Izd-vo IMO, 1960. 39 p.   HD415.N818
Translated from the Spanish *Esquema de la historia de la reforma agraria cubana.*
Reviewed by M. Kremnev in *Nov. vrem.,* v. 18, no. 26, 1960: 29–30.

3114. Aguirre, Severo.   Agrarnyi vopros i natsional'no-osvoboditel'noe dvizhenie; Kuba [The agrarian problem and the national liberation movement; Cuba] Probl. mira i sots., v. 4, no. 1, Jan. 1961: 65–68.

3115. ———.   Uspekhi agrarnoi reformy; pis'mo iz Gavany [Achievements of agrarian reform; a letter from Havana] Probl. mira i sots., v. 3, no. 8, Aug. 1960: 90–93.

3116. Akulai, V. Agrarnye preobrazovaniia na Kube [Agrarian reforms in Cuba] Komm. Mold., v. 9, no. 11, Nov. 1964: 63–68.

3117. Aleksandrovskii, B. Primer Kuby [The example of Cuba] Nov. vrem., v. 18, no. 2, Jan. 1960: 11–13.
Land tenure.

3118. Chto dala kubintsam agrarnaia reforma [What the Cubans gained from the agrarian reform] Agitator, no. 2, Jan. 1962: 49.

3119. Churkin, M. Novoe v krest'ianskoi zhizni na Kube [New features in the life of Cuban peasants] Kolkh. proizv., v. 21, no. 11, 1961: 44.

3120. IAkovlev, V. Agrarnaia reforma na Kube [Agrarian reform in Cuba] Mezhdunar. zhizn', v. 6, no. 8, Aug. 1959: 116–117.

3121. Kooperativy v kubinskoi derevne [Co-operatives in Cuban villages] Mezhdunar. zhizn', v. 8, no. 8, Aug. 1961: 141–142.

3122. Kornin, A. Agrarnaia reforma na Kube [Agrarian reform in Cuba] Mir. ekon. i mezhdunar. otn., no. 9, Sept. 1959: 127–128.

3123. Lagunin, N. Na novom puti [On the new path] Ekon. sel'khoz., v. 34, no. 5, May 1963: 110–116.

3124. Listov, Vadim. V kubinskoi derevne [In a Cuban village] Nov. vrem., v. 20, no. 39, Sept. 1962: 26–28.

3125. Napalkov, S. Na zemliakh "Kuba libre" [On the soil of "Cuba Libre"] Neva, no. 12, 1960: 202–203.

3126. Olteanu, O. Agrarnye preobrazovaniia v revoliutsionnoi Kube [Agrarian reforms in revolutionary Cuba] Vest. Mosk. un. Ser. 10: Pravo, v. 16, no. 3, July-Sept. 1961: 47–55.

3127. ———. Korennye preobrazovaniia v sel'skom khoziaistve revoliutsionnoi Kuby [Radical agricultural reforms in revolutionary Cuba] Vest. Mosk. un. Ser. 10: Pravo, v. 19, no. 2, Apr.-June 1964: 57–61.

3128. Onufriev, IU. Agrarnaia reforma na Kube [Agrarian reform in Cuba] Ekon. sel'khoz., v. 31, no. 6, June 1960: 116–119.

3129. Poliakovskii, V. "Agrarnaia reforma idet!" ["Agrarian reform is going on!"] Za rubezhom, no. 1, June 1960: 16.

3130. Ponizovskii, V. Konets "t'empo muerte" [The end of the "tiempo muerte"] Vokrug sveta, no. 1, Jan. 1964: 39–41.

3131. Sel'skokhoziaistvennye kooperativy na Kube [Agricultural cooperatives in Cuba] Nov. vrem., v. 19, no. 15, Apr. 1961: 31.

3132. Serebrovskaia, M. A. Stanovlenie sotsialisticheskogo sposoba proizvodstva v sel'skom khoziaistve Kuby [The establishment of the socialist mode of production in Cuban agriculture] Uch. zap. kaf. obshchestv. nauk vuz. g. Len.: Polit. ekon., no. 6, 1963: 138–158.

3133. Sivolobov, A. Agrarnaia reforma na Kube [The agrarian reform in Cuba] Otv. na vop. trud., no. 2, 1961: 30–37.

3134. Usmanov, S. Agrarnye preobrazovaniia na Kube [Agrarian reforms in Cuba] Komm. Uz., v. 36, no. 1, Jan. 1964: 41–51.

See also entries no. 2902, 2990, 3003, and 4685.

g. Ecuador

3135. "Agrarnaia reforma—ne znamia vosstaniia, a osnova dlia polnogo i garmonichnogo razvitiia ekonomiki" ["Agrarian reform is not a standard of revolt but the foundation for the large-scale and harmonious development of the national economy"] Zhen. mira, no. 8, 1959: 8.

3136. Saad, Pedro Antonio. Agrarnyi vopros i natsional'no-osvoboditel'noe dvizhenie; Ekvador [The agrarian problem and the national liberation movement; Ecuador] Probl. mira i sots., v. 4, no. 3, Mar. 1961: 78–80.

3137. Zemliu—tem, kto ee obrabatyvaet [The land should belong to those who till it] Za rubezhom, no. 6, July 1960: 8.

h. Guatemala

3138. Rodríguez, José. Agrarnyi vopros i natsional'no-osvoboditel'noe dvizhenie; Gvatemala [The agrarian problem and the national liberátion movement; Guatemala] Probl. mira i sots., v. 4, no. 3, Mar. 1961: 67–69.

i. Mexico

3139. Pavlenko, A. Po sledam Vil'i i Sapaty; ocherk o bor'be meksikanskikh krest'ian za zemliu—polveka nazad i teper' [In the footsteps of Villa and Zapata; a study of the peasant struggle for land in Mexico, 50 years ago and now] Nov. vrem., v. 21, no. 38, Sept. 1963: 25–29.

3140. Shul'govskii, A. F. Review. Nov. i noveish. ist., no. 4, 1961: 155–157.
A review of Jesús Silva Herzog's *El agrarismo mexicano y la reforma agraria* (Mexico City, Fondo de Cultura Económica, 1959. 602 p.).

j. Paraguay

3141. Fernández, Elba. Paragvai; zemlia bez liudei, liudi bez zemli [Paraguay; land without people and people without land] Zhen. mira, no. 3, 1961: 9–10.

3142. Sakharov, V. Olimpiets Khoze; pis'mo iz Paragvaia [José, the Olympian; a letter from Paraguay] Don, v. 5, no. 7, July 1961: 132–141.
Peasantry.

k. Peru

3143. Egorova, N. Grozd'ia gneva [The grapes of wrath] Mezhdunar. zhizn', v. 11, no. 6, June 1964: 111.
Agrarian problem.

3144. Prado, Jorge del. Agrarnyi vopros i natsional'no-osvoboditel'noe dvizhenie; Peru [The agrarian problem and the national liberation movement; Peru] Probl. mira i sots., v. 4, no. 3, Mar. 1961: 76–78.

l. Uruguay

3145. Arismendi, Rodney. Agrarnyi vopros i natsional'no-osvoboditel'noe dvizhenie; Urugvai [The agrarian problem and the national liberation movement; Uruguay] Probl. mira i sots., v. 4, no. 3, Mar. 1961: 71–74.

m. Venezuela

3146. Ojeda, Alonso. Agrarnyi vopros i natsional'no-osvoboditel'noe dvizhenie; Venesuela [The agrarian problem and the national liberation movement; Venezuela] Probl. mira i sots., v. 4, no. 2, Feb. 1961: 68–72.

3147. Po primeru Kuby [Following the example of Cuba] Nov. vrem., v. 17, no. 32, Aug. 1959: 20–21.
Land tenure.

n. West Indies

3148. Put' resheniia agrarnogo voprosa [A path toward the solution of the agrarian problem] Probl. mira i sots., v. 4, no. 10, Oct. 1961: 57.
Guadeloupe.

D. LABOR

1. Writings Dealing With Three or More Countries

3149. Matlina, A. Review. Mir. ekon. i mezhdunar. otn., no. 9, 1963: 150–152.
A review of Robert J. Alexander's *Labor Relations in Argentina, Brazil, and Chile* (New York, McGraw-Hill, 1962. 411 p.).

3150. Rozhkov, A. Polozhenie trudiashchikhsia Latinskoi Ameriki [The situation of workers in Latin America] Sots. trud., v. 4, no. 5, May 1959: 38–47.

3151. Zhdanov, A. Sotsial'noe obespechenie v stranakh Latinskoi Ameriki [Social insurance in the countries of Latin America] Sots. obesp., v. 25, no. 4, Apr. 1964: 60–63.

2. Individual Countries

a. Argentina

3152. González Alberdi, Paulino. Kakie izmeneniia proiskhodiat v strukture rabochego klassa? [What changes are taking place in the structure of the working class?] Probl. mira i sots., v. 3, no. 12, Dec. 1960: 72–74.

3153. Kakie izmeneniia proiskhodiat v strukture rabochego klassa? Argentina [What
changes are taking place in the structure
of the working class? Argentina] Probl.
mira i sots., v. 4, no. 4, Apr. 1961: 63–67.

b. Brazil

3154. Cerequeira, Benedito. Za peresmotr
minimuma zarabotnoi platy [For a re-
vision of the minimum wage] Vsem. prof.
dvizh., no. 1, Jan. 1959: 33–35.

3155. Rozhkov, A. Struktura rabochego
klassa Brazilii [The structure of the
Brazilian working class] Mir. ekon. i
mezhdunar. otn., no. 10, Oct.1962: 26–28.

See also entry no. 2865.

c. Chile

3156. Ramírez Necochea, Hernán. Istoriia
rabochego dvizheniia v Chili, pervye
shagi, XIX vek [History of the Chilean
labor movement; the first steps, the 19th
century] Moscow, Izd-vo inostr. lit.,
1961. 290 p.
Translated by B. V. Kostritsyn from the
Spanish Historia del movimiento obrero en
Chile; antecedentes, siglo XIX. Introductory
article by V. Teitelboim.

3157. Figueroa, Luis. Kakie izmeneniia
proiskhodiat v strukture rabochego
klassa? Chili [What changes are taking
place in the structure of the working
class? Chile] Probl. mira i sots., v. 4, no.
4, Apr. 1961: 67–70.

3158. Nikitin, M. Pensionnoe obespechenie v
Chile [Social security benefits in Chile]
Sots. obesp., v. 24, no. 9, Sept. 1963:
62–63.

See also entry no. 2875.

d. Colombia

3159. El'shov, E. Korotkii vek shakhtera
Kolumbii [The short life of Colombian
coal miners] Mast. ugl., v. 9, no. 4, Apr.
1960: 29.

See also entry no. 2876.

e. Cuba

3160. Cardoza Arnaz, Santiago. Kaiukero
reki Toa [Cayuquero of the Toa River]
Vokrug sveta, no. 2, Feb. 1962: 30.
Abbreviated translation from the Spanish.

3161. Olteanu, O. Sotsial'noe obespechenie v
revoliutsionnoi Kube [Social insurance in
revolutionary Cuba] Sots. obesp., v. 25,
no. 2, Feb. 1964: 60–62.

See also entry no. 467.

f. Mexico

3162. Pavlenko, A. Sredi rabochikh Meksiki
[With the workers of Mexico] Nov. vrem.,
v. 21, no. 46, Nov. 1963: 22–24.

g. Peru

3163. Saavedra Fajardo, Teodoro. Strana,
raspiataia monopoliiami [A country
crucified by the monopolies] Za rubezhom, no. 22, June 1963: 15.

h. Venezuela

3164. Gorev, I. Raznye sud'by [Their dif-
ferent fates] Sov. profsoiuzy, v. 18, no. 9,
Sept. 1962: 40–41.
Laboring classes.

See also entries no. 2922 and 2925.

E. WOMEN

1. Writings Dealing With Three or More
Countries

See entry no. 3322.

2. Individual Countries

a. Argentina

3165. García, Rosita. Argentinskie domo-
khoziaiki protiv spekuliatsii i goloda
[Argentine housewives are against specu-
lation and hunger] Zhen. mira, no 4,
1964: 13–15.
Translated from the Spanish.

3166. Othar, Irma. Polozhenie i bor'ba
argentinskikh rabotnits [The situation
and struggle of Argentine working
women] Vsem. prof. dvizh., no. 6, June
1963: 31–33.

3167. Sarmiento, Domingo Faustino. Zhizn' moei materi [The life of my mother] Zhen. mira, no. 4, 1961: 30–31.
Translated from the Spanish.

3168. Zhenskaia pressa [The women's press] Zhen. mira, no. 1, 1961: 32.
A review of the periodical *Nuestras mujeres* (Buenos Aires, 1948–61).

b. Brazil

See entries no. 1444, 3037, 3039, 3041–3044, and 3104.

c. Chile

3169. Carrasco, Ana de. Pis'mo chiliiskoi zhenshchiny [A letter from a Chilean woman] Vsem. prof. dvizh., no. 11, Nov. 1964: 31–32.

3170. Vicentini, María Luisa. Pravo na trud sviashchenno [The sacred right to work] Zhen. mira, no. 9, 1959: 14–15.

d. Colombia

3171. Zhenskaia pressa [The women's press] Zhen. mira, no. 10, 1964: 34.
A review of the periodical *Emancipación* (Bogotá, 1961).

e. Costa Rica

3172. K. E. Zhenskaia pressa [The women's press] Zhen. mira, no. 12, 1964: 34.
A review of the periodical *Nuestra voz* (San José, 1961).

f. Cuba

3173. Borovskii, V. Materi Kuby [Cuban mothers] Rabotnitsa, no. 1, Jan. 1964: 8–9.

3174. Brodskii, A. Mat' Fidelia [Fidel's mother] Ogonek, v. 41, no. 20, May 1963: 4.

3175. Erdei, Edith. Poezdka na Kubu [A trip to Cuba] Zhen. mira, no. 3, 1963: 32–33.

3176. Espín de Castro, Vilma. Radostnye preobrazovaniia [Praiseworthy reforms] Sov. zhen., v. 16, no. 3, 1960: 34–35.

3177. Lebedeva, Z. "Vse budet khorosho," skazal nam Fidel' Kastro ["All will be well," said Fidel Castro] Zhen. mira, no. 8, 1961: 11–14, 34.

3178. O. A. Zhenskaia pressa [The women's press] Zhen. mira, no. 2, 1964: 34.
A review of the periodical *Romances* (Havana, 1961–64).

3179. Privalova, L. Sakhar teper' bez slez [There are no tears in their sugar now] Rabotnitsa, no. 6, June 1964: 20.
Rights and employment of women.

3180. Radchenko, Klavdiia. Kuba aploduie Kyianam [Cuba applauds the Kiev singers] Rad. zhin., v. 19, no. 1, Jan. 1964: 18–19.
Includes discussion of the position of women in Cuba.

3181. Review. Zhen. mira, no. 8, 1959: 10.
A review of the periodical *Unidad femenina* (Cuba, 1959).

3182. Santamaría, Haydee. Eto dala nam revoliutsiia [This was given to us by the revolution] Nov. vrem., v. 21, no. 26, June 1963: 12–13.

g. El Salvador

3183. J. V. Piat' kofeinykh derev'ev stoiat bol'she, chem chelovek [Five coffee trees are worth more than a human being] Zhen. mira, no. 7, 1959: 20–21.
Women's work on coffee plantations.

3184. Jiménez, Liliam. "Byt' privlekatel'noi i elegantnoi" ["You should be attractive and handsome"] Zhen. mira, no. 11, 1959: 26–27.
Employment of women.

h. Haiti

3185. Pis'mo rabotnitsy Gaiti [Letter from a Haitian woman worker] Vsem. prof. dvizh., no. 6, June 1963: 36–37.

i. Mexico.

See entry no. 2299.

j. Paraguay

3186. V Paragvae, nesmotria na repressii, oni otstoiali svoiu fabriku [In Paraguay, notwithstanding repressions, they safe-

guarded their factory] Zhen. mira, no. 7, 1964: 14.
Employment of women.

See also entry no. 3141.

k. Uruguay

See entry no. 2313.

l. Venezuela

3187. Clemente Travieso, Carmen. Gorek khleb zhenshchin-krest'ianok [The hard lot of peasant women] Zhen. mira, no. 10, 1960: 23–25.

3188. Zhenskaia pressa [The women's press] Zhen. mira, no. 8, 1961: 17.
A review of the periodical *Mujeres* (Caracas, 1961).

m. West Indies

3189. Archimede, Gerty. 15 tysiach sel'-skokhoziaistvennykh rabotnits v Gvade-lupe [Fifteen thousand women work in the agriculture of Guadeloupe] Zhen. mira, no. 4, 1964: 6–7.
Translated from the French.

3190. Lise, Rose-Marie. IAvliaetsia li zamu-zhestvo edinstvennym udelom? [Is marriage the only possible path?] Vsem. stud. nov., v. 13, no. 5, May 1959: 18–19.
Martinique.

3191. Rose-Marie. Na dalekom ostrove [On a distant island] Sov. zhen., v. 16, no. 7, 1960: 40.
Guadeloupe.

F. CHILDREN AND YOUTH

1. Writings Dealing With Three or More Countries

3192. Programme for working youth. World youth, no. 3, 1964: 20–23.

2. Individual Countries

a. Argentina

3193. Argentinskie komprachikosy [Argentine "comprachicos"] Nov. vrem., v. 19, no. 26, June 1961: 21.
The trafficking of newborn infants in Argentina.

3194. Canto, Estela. Terrasy nishchety [Terraces of poverty] Sov. zhen., v. 17, no. 6, 1961: 14–17.
Children.

3195. Falucho, F. Molodezh' Argentiny gotovitsia k VII Festivaliu [The young people of Argentina prepare for the Seventh Festival] Mol. mira, no. 3, 1959: 20.

3196. Jasovich, Rosa. Tarelka supa—eto tozhe pedagogika [A bowl of soup is also a means of education] Zhen. mira, no. 1, 1962: 28–29.

b. Bolivia

3197. Chichkov, Vas. Moi drug Armando [My friend Armando] Rabotnitsa, v. 22, no. 5, May 1960: 9–10.
Children.

c. Brazil

3198. Moschetti, Lydia. V Brazilii polmilliona detei zhivet v nishchete [In Brazil half a million children live in poverty] Zhen. mira, no. 6, 1959: 17.

d. Chile

3199. Gárdenas, Luis. Nashe puteshestvie po Evrope [Our travel in Europe] Vsem. stud. nov., v. 16, no. 1, Jan. 1962: 21–23.
Students.

3200. Namas, Martin. U molodykh shakhterov Chili [Visiting the young miners in Chile] Mol. mira, no. 7, 1961: 3.

3201. Valdés, Patricio. The Chilean youth in struggle for their rights. World youth, no. 3, 1964: 40–44.

e. Cuba

3202. Mashkin, V. V lagere pod Gavanoi [In a camp near Havana] Rabotnitsa, v. 39, no. 8, Aug. 1961: 23.
A camp for Cuban youth.

3203. Núñez Machín, Ana. Golos detei Kuby [Voice of Cuban children] Neva, no. 2, 1962: 215.

f. Mexico

3204. Frýd, Norbert. Golysh na samolete [A naked child on an airplane] Vokrug sveta, no. 9, Sept. 1960: 20–21.
Children.
Translated from the Czech.

3205. Meksike nuzhen kodeks o zashchite rebenka [Mexico needs a code of laws protecting the children] Zhen. mira, no. 2, 1962: 6–7, 32.

3206. Problemy molodykh meksikantsev [Problems of young Mexicans] Mol. mira, no. 1, 1959: 11.

3207. Rabel, Fanny. Deti Meksiki [Children of Mexico] Zhen. mira, no. 5, 1960: 20–22.

See also entry no. 4764.

g. Uruguay

3208. Kazhdyi piatyi rebenok zhivet v zhalkoi lachuge [One out of five children lives in a hovel] Zhen. mira, no. 8, 1959: 9.

G. ETHNIC GROUPS

1. Writings Dealing With Three or More Countries

3209. Lips, Eva. Kniga ob indeitsakh [A book on the Indians] Tallinn, Estgosizdat, 1963. 415 p.
In Estonian. Translated from the German *Das Indianerbuch.*

3210. Radzima i chuzhyna; zbornik artykulau [The homeland and foreign countries; a collection of articles] Minsk, Palats prafsaiuzau, 1959. 29 p.
Repatriation of White Russians from South America.

3211. Ulevičius, Pranas. Emigratsiia trudiashchikhsia Litvy v IUzhnuiu Ameriku, ekonomicheskie usloviia ikh zhizni, progressivnaia, obshchestvennaia i kul'turnaia deiatel'nost, 1909–1940 gg. [Emigration of Lithuanian workers to South America; their standard of living, progressive, social, and cultural activities, 1909–1940] Vilnius, 1962. (Vil'niusskii gosudarstvennyi universitet)
Author's abstract of a dissertation for the degree of Candidate in Historical Sciences.

3212. ———. Pietu Americos lietuviai [Lithuanians in South America] Vilnius, Valstybine politines ir mokslines literaturos liedykla, 1960. 251 p.
                    F2239.L7U4

3213. Horlach, Mykola. Vony povertaiut'sia na bat'kivshchynu [They are coming back to their fatherland] Prapor, no. 9, Sept. 1959: 107–112.
Repatriation of Ukrainians.

3214. Kravchuk, P. Ukraintsi v Latyns'kii Amerytsi [The Ukrainians in Latin America] Vsesvit, v. 4, no. 7, July 1961: 15–17.

3215. Mashbits, IA. G. Assimiliatsiia indeiskogo naseleniia v Latinskoi Amerike [The assimilation of the Indian population in Latin America] Vop. ist., v. 38, no. 6, June 1963: 195–197.

3216. Wasilewska, Wanda. Pod drugoi lunoi [Under a different moon] Ogonek, v. 41, no. 12, Mar. 1963: 6–7.
Russians in Latin America.
Translated from the Polish.

See also entry no. 3328.

2. Individual Countries

a. Argentina

3217. Hubarchuk, Panas. Za okeanom [Beyond the ocean] Lvov, Derzhvydav, 1960.
Ukrainians.
Reviewed by I. Brechak in *Vsesvit,* v. 4, no. 12, Dec. 1961: 126–128.

3218. Kunda, P. S. V poiskakh zaokeanskogo raia [In quest of an overseas paradise] Minsk, Gosizdat BSSR, 1963. 29 p.
                    DLC
White Russians.

3219. Altukhou, Mikola. Chalavek viarnusia damou [A woman has come home] Rab. i sial., v. 35, no. 9, Sept. 1959: 3–4.
Repatriation of White Russians.

3220. Datsii, IAkiv. Lysh borotys'— znachyt' zhyt' [Life means struggle] Zmina, no. 9, Sept. 1959: 7.
Repatriation of Ukrainians.

3221. Hordii, Oleksandr. Naidorozhche [The most valuable thing] Ukraina, no. 17, Sept. 1960: 9–10.
Repatriation of Ukrainians.

3222. Sterin, V. Izdaleka i vblizi [From far away and close by] Mol. komm., no. 6, June 1962: 91–96.
Ukrainians.

3223. Varela, Alfredo. Holub myru doletyt' do mety [The dove of peace will reach its destination] Vsesvit, v. 5, no. 11, Nov. 1962: 82.
Ukrainians.

3224. Vasilevich, Alena. "Liudzi i zviary" ["People and animals"] Rab. i sial., v. 38, no. 11, Nov. 1962: 18–19.
A motion picture showing the Russians in Argentina.

3225. Volkonskaia, Ol'ga. V chem ia ostaius' inostrankoi [In what respect I still remain a foreigner] Kul't. i zhizn', v. 6, no. 10, 1962: 39–41.
Repatriation of Russian immigrants.

3226. Vuiko, Ivan. "Chakerero" v poshukakh shchastia ["Chaquereros" in search of happiness] Vsesvit, v. 6, no. 11, Nov. 1963: 56–68.
Ukrainians.

b. Brazil

3227. Cowell, Adrian. V serdtse lesa [The heart of the forest] Moscow, Mysl', 1964. 229 p.
Indians.
Translated from the English.

3228. Jokubka, Jonas. Brazilijos plantacijose [Brazilian plantations] Vilnius, Valst. grožinės lit-ros leidykla, 1962. 254 p.
Lithuanians.

3229. Boglár, Lajo. IAguarnye liudi [Jaguar people] Nauka i zhizn', v. 28, no. 5, May 1961: 36–69.
Indians.
Translated from the Hungarian.

3230. Kerekesh, IUrii. Khlopchyk z Rio-de-Zhaneiro [A boy from Rio de Janeiro] Zhovten', v. 25, no. 8, Aug. 1964: 44–48.
Ukrainian political refugees.

3231. Khazanov, A. M. Vzaimovliianie Afriki i Brazilii [The reciprocal mutual influence of Africa and Brazil] Vop. ist., v. 38, no. 4, Apr. 1963: 169–180.
A review of an article by José Honorio Rodrigues in The Journal of African History, v. 3, no. 1, 1962: 49–67.
Negroes.

3232. V. K. Meshkantsi "zelenoho pekla" [The inhabitants of "Green Hell"] Ukraina, no. 19, Aug. 1963: 9.
Chavante Indians,

3233. Zahadka S'erra-Durados [Mystery of the Sierra Dorada] Vsesvit, v. 3, no. 3, March 1960: 153.
Indians.

See also entry no. 1535.

c. Cuba

3234. Alonso, Dora. Namuni; iz zhizni moei negritianskoi babushki ["Namuni"; the life of my Negro grandmother] Zhen. mira, no. 3, 1964: 32–33.
Pre-revolutionary racial relations.
Translated from the Spanish.

3235. IAroshenko, A. D. Z istorii ukrains'-ko-kubyns'kykh zv'iazkiv [History of Ukrainian contacts with Cuba] Ukr. ist. zhur., v. 6, no. 2, Mar.-Apr. 1963: 114–116.

3236. Koval', M. Ukraintsi na Kubi [Ukrainians in Cuba] Vsesvit, v. 6, no. 5, May 1963: 40–42.

d. Ecuador

3237. Mancheno, Edmundo L. Indeets—eto skorb' Ekvadora [The Indian, Ecuador's sorrow] Mol. mira, no. 4, 1959: 24.
Indians.

3238. Paredes, Leonardo. "My vse issykhaem!" ["We have all begun to wither!"] Mol. komm., no. 10, Oct. 1964: 116–119.
Indians.

See also entry no. 3374.

e. The Guianas

3239. Guppy, Nicholas. Poslednie iz maviianov [The last of the Mawayáns] Vokrug sveta, no. 6, June 1960: 36–41: no. 7, July 1960: 54–58.
Indians of British Guiana.
Translated from the English.

f. Mexico

3240. Chichkov, V.   Ugnetennoe plemia [Oppressed tribe] Vokrug sveta, no. 11, Nov. 1961: 42–43.
Indians.

3241. Gómez, Andrea.   Dobrye liudi Taraumary; iz indeiskikh zarisovok [The good people of the Taraumara Valley; sketches of Indians] Sov. zhen., v. 15, no. 5, 1959: 38–39.
An artist's sketches of Indians.

3242. Khoroshaeva, I. F.   Sovremennoe indeiskoe naselenie Meksiki [The present-day Indian population of Mexico] Trudy Inst. etn., v. 58, 1960: 156–202.

See also entry no. 3378.

g. Puerto Rico

3243. Rasovaia diskriminatsiia v Puerto-Riko [Race discrimination in Puerto Rico] Moscow, 1964. 21 p. (Molodezhnyi sekretariat dvizheniia za nezavisimost')
In Spanish.

H. PUBLIC HEALTH SERVICES

1. Writings Dealing With Three or More Countries

3244. Korovina, Z. A.   Nekotorye svedeniia o sanitarnom sostoianii stran Latinskoi Ameriki [Some information on sanitary conditions in the countries of Latin America] Zdrav. Ros. Feder., v. 7, no. 6, June 1963: 31–34.

2. Individual Countries

a. Brazil

3245. Uglov, F. G.   O poezdke v Braziliu [A trip to Brazil] Vest. khir., v. 91, no. 7, July 1963: 103–115.

b. Cuba

3246. Belova, Z. A.   Kuba stroit novoe zdravookhranenie [The new organization of public health services in Cuba] Zdrav. Bel., v. 10, no. 9, Sept. 1964: 84–85.

3247. Bremener, S. M.   V revoliutsionnoi Kube [In revolutionary Cuba] Kul't. i zhizn', v. 5, no. 7, 1961: 38–40.

3248. Furmenko, I. P.   Zdravookhranenie v Kubinskoi Respublike [Public health in the Cuban Republic] Sov. zdrav., v. 23, no. 1, 1964: 59–63.

3249. Grazhul', V. S.   Voprosy zdravookhraneniia v sotsialisticheskoi Kube [Public health problems in socialist Cuba] Zdrav. Ros. Feder., v. 6, no. 11, Nov. 1962: 27–31.

3250. Korovina, Z. A.   Narod Kuby v bor'be za zdorov'e [The people of Cuba in the fight for health] Sov. zdrav., v. 21, no. 6, 1962: 96.

3251. Mukhutdinov, I. Z.   Zdravookhranenie v Respublike Kuba [Public health protection in the Republic of Cuba] Zhur. mikrobiol., epid. i immun., v. 33, no. 10, Oct. 1962: 128–131.

c. West Indies

3252. Il'chev, V. S.   Demagogiia kolonizatorov v voprosakh zdravookhraneniia [Demogogy of the colonizers on problems of public health] Sov. zdrav., v. 20, no. 10, 1961: 63–67.

I. SPORTS AND HOBBIES

1. Writings Dealing With Three or More Countries

3253. Krasnitskii, Gennadii.   Ot Rio-de-Zhaneiro do Montevideo [From Rio de Janerio to Montevideo] Tashkent, Gosizdat UzSSR, 1964. 61 p.

3254. Mamedov, Alekper.   V chetyrekh chastiakh sveta; putevye zametki futbolista [In the four corners of the world; travel notes of a soccer player] Baku, Detiunizdat, 1961. 80 p.
In Azerbaijani.

3255. Gusarov, G.   Litsom k litsu s volshebnikami miacha [Face to face with soccer ball wizards] Sp. igry, v. 8, no. 1, Jan. 1962: 4–7.

3256. Iori, C.   1st Latin American University Sports Games and Seminar on Sports Development in Latin America. World youth, no. 1, 1963: 39–40.

3257. Lench, L. Vsemu vinoi virus [It was caused by a virus] Smena, v. 38, no. 3, Feb. 1961: 30–31.
Soccer.

3258. Leyens, Germán. First Latin American university games. World student news, v. 16, no. 11/12, 1962: 33–34.

3259. M. C. Latin American student sport off to good start. World student news, v. 16, no. 11/12, 1962: 35–36.

3260. Netto, Igor'. Viza—futbol'nyi miach [Their soccer ball was their visa] Ogonek, v. 38, no. 4, Jan. 1960: 30–31.
A Russian soccer team in South America.

3261. Spiridonov, V. Zaokeanskie pretendenty; kak v IUzhnoi Amerike gotoviatsia k chempionatu mira [Contenders from overseas; how the South Americans prepare for the world soccer tournament] Sp. igry, v. 6, no. 12, Dec. 1960: 26–28.

3262. ———. Vernetsia li boginia Nike v Evropu? Komandy IUzhnoi Ameriki gotoviatsia k chempionatu mira [Will the the goddess Nike return to Europe? Soccer teams of South America prepare for the world tournament] Sp. igry, v. 6, no. 11, Nov. 1960: 27–29.

3263. Vit, A., *and* V. Vladimirov. Ot svista do ovatsii; o futbol'nom chempionate IUzhnoi Ameriki [From the whistle to the ovation; the soccer championship of South Amcrica] Sp. igry, v. 5, no. 5, May 1959: 27–29.

3264. Vladimirov, V. Po tu storonu Atlantiki; futbol v strankah IUzhnoi Ameriki [On the other side of the Atlantic; soccer in South America] Sp. igry, v. 5, no. 2, Feb. 1959: 28–30.

2. Individual Countries

a. Argentina

3265. Brat'ia Tur, *pseud.* Futbol po-argentinski; rasskaz [Soccer Argentine style; a story] Ogonek, v. 38, no. 43, Oct. 1960: 18–20.

3266. Chempionat v Argentine [Championship in Argentina] Kryl. rod., v. 14, no. 6, June 1963: 22–23.
Aerial sports.

3267. Gonki ubiits [The races of murderers] Nov. vrem., v. 19, no. 5, Jan. 1961: 28–29.
Automobile races.

3268. Ignat'eva, M., *and* E. Rumiantseva. Igra v "pato" [The game of "pato"] Konevodstvo, v. 29, no. 7, July 1959: 45–47.
An equestrian sport.

3269. Taimanov, M. Turnir v Buenos-Airese [The tournament in Buenos Aires] Shakh. v. SSSR, v. 36, no. 11, Nov. 1960: 343–346; v. 36, no. 12, Dec. 1960: 378–380.
A chess tournament.

3270. Vit, A., *and* V. Vladimirov. Argentinskii zigzag [The Argentine zigzag] Sp. igry, v. 10, no. 10, Oct. 1964: 26–28.
Soccer.

See also entry no. 3271.

b. Brazil

3271. Kriukov, N. M., *and* M. IA. Nabatnikova. Tekhnika i trenirovka sil'neishikh zarubezhnykn plavtsov; IAponiia, SShA, Braziliia, Argentina [The technique and training methods of the best foreign swimmers; Japan, the United States, Brazil, Argentina] Moscow, Fizkul'tura i sport, 1962. 76 p.

3272. Andrade, Lauro. Sovetskii futbol glazami brazil'tsa [Soviet soccer as a Brazilian saw it] Fisk. i sport, v. 29, no. 5, May 1959: 20–21, 33.

3273. Bez sensatsii; Pele o svoem trenirovochnom rezhime [No sensational discoveries; Pelé tells us about the methods and ways of his training] Sp. igry, v. 7, no. 8, 1961: 7–8.
Soccer.

3274. Kachalin, G. Brazil'skii fint [Brazilian feint] Sp. igry, v. 6, no. 6, June 1960: 16–17.
Soccer.

3275. Nabokov, B. Kopirovat' li brazil'tsev? [Should we copy the play of Brazilians] Sp. igry, v. 5, no. 2, Feb. 1959: 23–24.
Soccer.

3276. Nascimento, Edson Arantes. IA—Pele [My name is Pelé] Mol. gvard., no. 2, Feb. 1963: 258–279.
Soccer.
Translated from the Portuguese.

3277. Ozerov, IUrii. Chto sluchilos' v Rio [What happened in Rio] Sp. igry, v. 9, no. 8, Aug. 1963: 6–8.
A basketball tournament.

3278. Pele—"chorna kobra" [Pelé, the "black cobra"] Vsesvit, v. 6, no. 10, Oct. 1963: 141–147.
Soccer.
Translated from the Portuguese.

3279. Rodos, L. Bez Didi i bez Garrinchi; sverdlovskie futbolisty osvaivaiut brazil'skii opyt [Without Dede and Garrinchi; Sverdlovsk soccer players try to master the methods of the Brazilians] Sp. igry, v. 5, no. 5, May 1959: 12–13; no. 6, June 1959: 11–13.

3280. Simonian, Nikita. Izliublennyi priem Pele [Pelé's favorite maneuver] Sp. igry, v. 9, no. 4, Apr. 1963: 24.
Soccer.

3281. Trifonov, IUrii. Odin vecher v Rime [An evening in Rome] Fisk. i sport, v. 30, no. 11, Nov. 1960: 10–12.
Basketball.

3282. "V odnii komandi z Pele" ["On the same team with Pelé"] Vsesvit, v. 6, no. 11, Nov. 1963: 147.
Soccer.

3283. Vit, A., and V. Vladimirov. Brazil'skii barometr [Brazilian barometer] Sp. igry, v. 7, no. 8, Aug. 1961: 26–28.
Soccer.

3284. ———. Proshchai "dubl'-ve!" Brazil'skie uroki i evropeiskii futbol [Goodbye, "W!" Brazilian lessons and European soccer] Sp. igry, v. 7, no. 3, Mar. 1961: 27–29.
Soccer.

c. Chile

3285. Beknazar-IUzbashev, B. Ukradennaia pobeda; chiliiskii dnevnik [Stolen victory; a Chilean diary] Moscow, Fizkul'tura i sport, 1960. 141 p.   GV885.B45
Basketball.

3286. Lartsuliani, Sh. K., and G. A. Metreveli. Chili, 1962 [Chile, 1962] Tbilisi, Nakaduli, 1962. 114 p.
Soccer.
In Georgian.

3287. Anderson, I. 1962, Chili [Chile, 1962] Mol. mira, no. 7, 1961: 15.
A soccer tournament.

3288. Chempionat pod mikroskopom; trener sbornoi Frantsii ob itogakh pervenstva mira po basketbolu [The championship tournament under a microscope; the French team's coach on the results of the world basketball championship] Sp. igry, v. 5, no. 3, Mar. 1959: 27–28.

3289. Flerovskii, A. Vperedi—Sant-IAgo [On the eve of the Santiago tournament] Moskva, v. 5, no. 2, 1961: 220–221.
Soccer.

3290. Gomel'skii, A. Zolotye nashi parni; sovetskie basketbolisty—istinnye chempiony mira [Our golden lads; Soviet basketball players are the real world's champions] Sp. igry, v. 5, no. 2, Feb. 1959: 3–8.

3291. IAkovlev, A., and V. Vladimirov. Futbol'noe zemletriasenie v Chili [An earthquake on the soccer field in Chile] Sp. igry, v. 8, no. 6, June 1962: 4–8, 28–29; v. 8, no. 7, July 1962: 11–15.
A soccer tournament.

3292. Kassil', Lev. "Sukhoi list" i lavry ["Dry leaf" and laurels] Ogonek, v. 40, no. 25, June 1962: 25.
Soccer.

3293. Korbut, E. Proigrannoe ochko [A lost point] Sp. igry, v. 9, no. 12, Dec. 1963: 24.
A match between Soviet and Chilean tennis players.

3294. Latyshev, N. G. Dvadtsat' tretii na pole [The twenty-third soccer player on the field] Ogonek, v. 40, no. 27, July 1962: 26–27.
Soccer.

3295. Parkhit'ko, V. Vokrug futbol'nogo miacha [Around the soccer ball] Sov. pechat', no. 8, Aug. 1962: 59.
A soccer tournament and the Chilean press.

3296. Privet pobediteliam! [Hail to the victors!] Fizk. i sport, v. 29, no. 3, Mar. 1959: [i]
A basketball tournament.

3297. Spandarian, S. Pobeda v Sant-IAgo [Our victory in Santiago] Ogonek, v. 37, no. 9, Feb. 1959: 28–29.
A basketball tournament.

3298. Van'iat, IUrii. Na gorizonte—Chili [Chile is on the horizon] Ogonek, v. 39, no. 41, Oct. 1961: 25.
A soccer tournament.

3299. ———. Put' v Sant-IAgo [The road to Santiago] Ogonek, v. 39, no. 14, Apr. 1961: 18–19.
A soccer tournament.

3300. ———. Rubikon pereiden! [The Rubicon is crossed!] Ogonek, v. 40, no. 20, May 1962: 26–27.
Soviet soccer players in Chile.

d. Cuba

3301. Simakov, IU. Sportivnaia iunost' ostrova svobody [Young sportsmen of the island of freedom] Moscow, Fizkul'tura i sport, 1964. 86 p.

3302. Bogoslovskii, V. P. Na Kube [In Cuba] Fiz. kul't. v shkole, no. 12, Dec. 1964: 47–49.
Sports.

3303. ¡Cuba sí! Fizk. i sport, v. 33, no. 7, July 1963: 6–8.
Physical education and sports.

3304. García Suárez, *and* Osvaldo Quintás. Chto takoe beisbol; pitcher po imeni Fidel' Kastro [What baseball is; a pitcher by the name of Fidel Castro] Kuba, no. 4, Dec. 1964: 2–5.

3305. Gavrilin, V. Saliut, Kuba! [Long live Cuba!] Fizk. i sport, v. 31, no. 1, 1961: 8–9.
Sports.

3306. IAkovenko, M. Marky revoliutsiinoi Kuby [Postage stamps of revolutionary Cuba] Ukraina, no. 23, Dec. 1962: 32.

3307. Isakov, B. Na rodine Kapablanki [In the homeland of Capablanca] Shakh. v SSSR, v. 39, no. 4, Apr. 1962: 122.
Chess.

3308. Klusov, E. Na ostrove Kuba [On the island of Cuba] Shakh. v SSSR, v. 36, no. 10, Oct. 1960: 316.
Chess.

3309. López Iguiscuza, Raúl. Sport na Kube [Sports in Cuba] Mol. mira, no. 4, 1961: 19.

3310. Marki revoliutsionnoi Kuby [Postage stamps of revolutionary Cuba] Sov. knizh. torg., v. 14, no. 5, 1962: 47–48.

3311. Oifebakh, Lev. Bezhit Enrike Figerola [Enrique Figuerola runs] Leg. atl., v. 10, no. 10, Oct. 1964: 17.
Field and track athletics.

3312. Prados, Raúl. Sport prikhodit v gory [Sports come to the mountains] Kuba, no. 3, Nov. 1964: 32–35.

3313. Simakov, IU. P. Fizicheskoe vospitanie i detskii sport v respublike Kuba [Physical education and children's sports in the Republic of Cuba] Teor. i prak. fiz. kul't., v. 27, no. 4, Apr. 1964: 65–68.

3314. ———. Organizatsiia fizicheskoi kul'tury i natsional'nyi sport Kuby [The organization of physical education and the national sports of Cuba] Teor. i prak. fiz. kul't, v. 27, no. 2, Feb. 1964: 67–70.

3315. Utekhina, Galina. Enrike Figerola, "El sputnik kubano" [Enrique Figuerola, "El sputnik cubano"] Leg. atl., v. 10, no. 6, June 1964: 26.
A Cuban runner.

e. Guatemala

3316. Horeniuk, IA. Ketsal'—ptakh svobody [The quetzal, a bird of freedom] Ukraina, no. 20, Oct. 1960: 32.
The postage stamps of Guatemala.

f. Mexico

3317. Chichkov, V. Skhvatka za krasnym zaborom [A fight behind the red fence] Vokrug sveta, no. 5, May 1962: 42–46.
Bullfights.

g. Peru

3318. Alekseeva, L. Dazhe simpatichnye; zametki o mirovom chempionate basketbolistok [They were rather likable; notes of the World Tournament of Women Basketball Players] Sp. igry, v. 10, no. 7, July 1964: 10–13.

3319. "My trebuem, chtoby vinovnye byli nakazany" ["We demand the punishment of the guilty"] Zhen. mira, no. 9, 1964: 8.
A disastrous accident in a soccer stadium.

h. West Indies

3320. Petrosian, Tigran. Vosem' nedel' v Kiurasao [Eight weeks in Curaçao] Lit. Armeniia, no. 12, Dec. 1962: 92–101.
A chess tournament.

See also entry no. 2577.

XV

CULTURAL AFFAIRS

A. EDUCATION

1. Writings Dealing With Three or More Countries

3321. Alambert, Zuleika. Za reformu obra-zovaniia [For the reform of education] Mol. mira, no. 9, 1960: 5.
Higher education.

3322. Alvarez, Justina. Pochemu by i im ne uchit'sia? [Why shouldn't they study?] Zhen. mira, no. 11, 1960: 15–16.
Education of women.

3323. Anan'ev, B. G. Vazhneishie pedago-gicheskie problemy latino-amerikanskikh stran [The most important educational problems of Latin America] Sov. pedag., v. 23, no. 1, Jan. 1959: 122–134.

3324. Belova, L. V stranakh Latinskoi Ameriki [In the countries of Latin America] Nar. obr., no. 12, Dec. 1963: 103–105.

3325. Carvalho, Milton de. Pervyi seminar latinoamerikanskikh stran po voprosam reformy i demokratizatsii vysshego obra-zovaniia [The first Conference of Latin American Countries on the Reform and Democratization of Higher Education] Vest. vys. shkoly, v. 19, no. 1, Jan. 1961: 84–86.

3326. ———. Pervyi seminar latinoameri-kanskikh stran po voprosam reformy i demokratizatsii vysshego obrazovaniia [The first Conference of Latin American Countries on the Reform and Democrati-zation of Higher Education] Vsem. stud. nov., v. 14, no. 9, Sept. 1960: 6–10.

3327. Estévez Boero, G. Chastnye univer-sitety i natsional'naia kul'tura [Private universities and national culture] Vsem. stud. nov., v. 14, no. 7, July 1960: 8–9.

3328. Indeitsy iz And: "My khotim byt' gramotnymi" ["We want to learn how to read and write," the Andean Indians say] Mol. mira, no. 8, 1960: 22.

3329. Khanykova, L. V. Bor'ba za demo-kratizatsiiu obrazovaniia v Latinskoi Amerike [The struggle for democratic education in Latin America] Vop. ist., v. 39, no. 3, Mar. 1964: 202–204.

3330. Leyens, Germán. Povorotnyi punkt v latinoamerikanskoi sisteme obrazovaniia [A turning point in the Latin American system of education] Vsem. stud. nov., v. 16, no. 1, Jan. 1962: 6–7.

3331. Marini, Salvador. Shkoly Kennedi i nasha geografiia negramotnosti [Ken-nedy's schools and our geography of illiteracy] Sov. zhen., v. 18, no. 11, 1962: 12–13.
Alliance for Progress.

2. Individual Countries

a. Argentina

3332. Godio, Julio. Another problem that needs tackling. World student news, v. 18, no. 1, 1964: 18.

3333. Pis'mo byvshemu lideru dvizheniia za reformu obrazovaniia [A letter to a former leader of the movement for edu-cational reform] Vsem. stud. nov., v. 13, no. 6, June 1959: 22.
Higher education.

b. Brazil

3334. Carneiro, R. R. Tekhnicheskoe obrazovanie v Brazilii [Technical education in Brazil] Mir. nauki, no. 4, 1962: 18–20.

3335. Denisov, N. IA. Podgotovka inzhenerov v Brazilii [Training of engineers in Brazil] Vest. vys. shkoly, v. 17, no. 2, Feb. 1959: 89–91.

3336. Lima, Pedro Motta. Brazil'skie kommunisty—zastrel'shchiki likvidatsii negramotnosti [The Brazilian Communists initiate the struggle against illiteracy] Probl. mira i sots., v. 7, no. 4, Apr. 1964: 54–55.

c. Chile

3337. K. S. Problema detskikh sadov v Chili [The problem of Chilean kindergartens] Zhen. mira, no. 5, 1964: 32–33.

d. Cuba

3338. Davydov, I. Universitetskaia reforma v revoliutsionnoi Kube [University reform in revolutionary Cuba] Vest. vys. shkoly, v. 19, no. 1, Jan. 1961: 78–83.

3339. Deklaratsiia naroda Kuby [Declaration of the people of Cuba] Nar. obr., no. 6, June 1962: 99.
Education.

3340. Efremov, G. P., *and* A. A. Bogdanov. Zametki ob obrazovanii v Respublike Kuba [Notes on education in the Republic of Cuba] Sred. spets. obr., v. 11, no. 7, July 1964: 56–58.

3341. Fedorov, V. Prosveshchenie v Respublike Kuba [Education in the Republic of Cuba] Nar. obr., no. 1, Jan. 1961: 92–96.

3342. Fidel' Kastro beseduet s det'mi v den' peredachi voennoi kreposti pod shkolu [Fidel Castro's talk with children when the buildings of a military fortress were converted into a school] Sov. zhen., v. 17, no. 6, 1961: 14–15.
Elementary education.

3343. Fuentes, Norberto. Minas-de-Frio [Minas de Frío] Kuba, no. 3, Nov. 1964: 18–25.
The training of teachers.

3344. Gallo, G., *and* S. Zakhir. Vysshee obrazovanie vo vnov' razvivaiushchikhsia stranakh [Higher education in the newly developing countries] Vest. vys. shkoly, v. 20, no. 10, Oct. 1962: 26–30.

3345. Grigulevich, I. R. Dostizheniia kul'turnoi revoliutsii na Kube [The achievements of the cultural revolution in Cuba] Vop. ist., v. 38, no. 12, Dec. 1963: 86–102.
Summary in English, p. 221–222.

3346. ———. Kul'turnaia revoliutsiia na Kube [The cultural revolution in Cuba] Nov. vrem., v. 21, no. 35, Aug. 1963: 19–20.

3347. Guerra, Reinaldo F. Rabochii fakul'tet Gavanskogo universiteta [The Workers' Faculty of Havana University] Kuba, no. 3, Nov. 1964: 36–37.

3348. Hart Dávalos, Armando. Natsional'naia kampaniia po bor'be s negramotnost'iu na Kube [The national campaign against illiteracy in Cuba] Vsem. stud. nov., v. 16, no. 4, Apr. 1962: 4–6.

3349. Hryshchenko, O. Imeni Makarenka [The A. S. Makarenko Pedagogical Institute] Vsesvit, v. 7, no. 8, Aug. 1964: 101.

3350. Kharytonov, V. S. Shkola revoliutsiinoi Kuby [Schools in revolutionary Cuba] Rad. shk., v. 40, no. 7, July 1961: 84–88.

3351. Klein, Lena. Kuba uchitsia [Cuba studies] Krest'ianka, v. 40, no. 3, Mar. 1962: 20.
Adult education.
An abbreviated translation from the German.

3352. Kovalenko, I. Itogi goda obrazovaniia na Kube [Results of the year of education in Cuba] Nar. obr., no. 6, June 1962: 100–101.

3353. ———. Na tret'em kongresse rabotnikov narodnogo obrazovaniia Kuby [At the Third Congress of the Public Education Personnel of Cuba] Nar. obr., no. 5, May 1963: 98–100.

3354. ———. Narodnoe obrazovanie v revoliutsionnoi Kube [Public education in revolutionary Cuba] Sov. pedag., v. 26, no. 1, Jan. 1962: 114–118.

3355. ———. V professional'nykh shkolakh Kuby [The vocational schools of Cuba] Prof.-tekh. obr., v. 18, no. 8, Aug. 1961: 30–31.

3356. ———. V Respublike Kube [In the Republic of Cuba] Nar. obr., no. 10, Oct. 1961: 103–106.
Education.

3357. Kuba; god prosveshcheniia [Cuba; the year of education] Inostr. lit., no. 12, Dec. 1961: 201–212.

3358. Lemus, Germán. Byt' obrazovannymi —znachit byt' svobodnymi [To be educated means to be free] Vsem. stud. nov., v. 15, no. 3/4, Mar.-Apr. 1961: 14–15.
Adult education.

3359. ———. Neugasimyi ogon' [Inextinguishable flame] Vsem. stud. nov., v. 15, no. 3/4, Mar.-Apr. 1961: 16–17.
Adult education.

3360. Marinello, Juan. O kul'turnoi revoliutsii na Kube [On the cultural revolution in Cuba] Nov. vrem., v. 20, no. 24, June 1962: 20–21.

3361. Mochalina, S. God na Kube [A year in Cuba] Nar. obr., no. 1, Jan. 1964: 103–106.
Russian language studies.

3362. Nas privetstvuiut: Khuan Marinel'o, rektor Gavanskogo universiteta [Greetings from Juan Marinello, the rector of Havana University] Zhen. mira, no. 3, 1964: 2.

3363. Nazarov, N. I. Reforma v deistvii [A reform in action] Vest. vys. shkoly, v. 20, no. 6, June 1962: 73–76.
Education.

3364. ———. Revoliutsionnyi entuziazm, razum, muzhestvo [Revolutionary enthusiasm, intelligence, and courage] Vest. vys. shkoly, v. 19, no. 12, Dec. 1961: 60–63.
Higher education.

3365. Núñez Machín, Ana. Eshche odna pobeda Kuby [Still another triumph for Cuba] Neva, no. 6, 1962: 214–215.
Adult education.

3366. Periu de los Angeles, María. Kuba— territoriia, svobodnaia ot negramotnosti [Cuba, a territory free of illiteracy] Zhen. mira, no. 6, 1962: 11–14.

3367. Poll, Irene. Na ostrovke Megano [On the isle of Megano] Inostr. lit., no. 11, Nov. 1961: 246–250.
Education.

3368. Pylila, IA. Kuba vuchytstsa [Universal education in Cuba] Nar. asv., no. 12, Dec. 1962: 86–87.

3369. Rodríguez, Félix. Revoliutsiia i universitetskaia reforma [Revolution and university reform] Vsem. stud. nov., v. 13, no. 8, Aug. 1959: 20–21.

3370. Rostovtseva, O. Kuba uchitsia [Cuba studies] Sov. pedag., v. 26, no. 5, May 1962: 158–160.

3371. S oruzhiem i knigoi v rukakh [Armed with weapons and books] Vech. sred. shkola, v. 4, no. 3, May-June 1961: 92–93.

3372. Sommer, Georg. Bor'ba s negramotnost'iu—zadacha vsego naroda i studentov [The struggle against illiteracy is a problem facing the whole Cuban people as well as university students] Vsem. stud. nov., v. 15, no. 7, July 1961: 5–6.

3373. Zandin, K. Podgotovka rabochikh kadrov na Kube [Training of worker cadres in Cuba] Prof.-tekh. obr., v. 19, no. 9, Sept. 1962: 30–31.

e. Ecuador

3374. Blomberg, Rolf. Svezhii veter u podnozh'ia Kaiambe [Fresh wind in the foothills of Cayambe] Vokrug sveta, no. 4, Apr. 1959: 57–58.
The education of Indians.
Translated from the Swedish.

f. Haiti

3375. Greenfield, C. Gaiti pod piatoi tiranii [Haiti under the heel of tyranny] Vsem. stud. nov., v. 16, no. 2, Feb. 1962: 11.
Education.

3376. Guedou, Castel. Vysshee obrazovanie na Gaiti [Higher education in Haiti] Vsem. stud. nov., v. 13, no. 8, Aug. 1959: 6–7.

g. Mexico

3377. Literatory v bor'be s negramotnost'iu [Writers in the struggle against illiteracy] Inostr. lit., no. 12, Dec. 1960: 259.
   Mexican writers and adult education.

3378. Tat'ianichev, V. Schastlivchik iz plemeni Otomi [A lucky boy from the Otomi tribe] Vokrug sveta, no. 7, July 1962: 30–31.
   Higher education.

h. Panama

3379. Rivera, Pedro. A policy for the university; democratisation of education. World student news, v. 18, no. 3, 1964: 13–14.

i. Venezuela

3380. González, Asdrúbal. Universitety na sluzhbu narodu! [Universities should serve the people!] Vsem. stud. nov., v. 14, no. 7, July 1960: 17.
   Adult education.

3381. Urbina Ortiz, Ivan. Novyi universitetskii zakon nedostatochno nov [The new university law is not new enough] Vsem. stud. nov., v. 13, no. 7, July 1959: 6–7.
   Higher education.

j. West Indies

3382. Na ostrove Martinika ot 20 do 40 protsentov negramotnykh [On the island of Martinique, from 20% to 40% are illiterate] Zhen. mira, no. 5, 1959: 17.
   Education of children.

B. LIBRARIES

1. Writings Dealing With Three or More Countries

3383. Ambartsumian, V. A. Pokazatel'nye biblioteki IUNESKO v stranakh Azii, Afriki i Latinskoi Ameriki [Model libraries of UNESCO in Asia, Africa, and Latin America] Bibliotekoved. i bibl. za rub., no. 12, 1963: 48–64.

2. Cuba

3384. Chitaiushchaia Kuba [The Cuba that reads] Kul't.-pros. rab., v. 22, no. 8, Aug. 1961: 32–33.

3385. Kirik, O. K. Natsional'naia biblioteka Kuby [The National Library of Cuba] Sov. bibl., no. 4, 1960: 117–119.

3386. ———. Razvitie bibliotechnogo dela na Kube i Natsional'naia biblioteka im. Khoze Marti [The development of library work in Cuba and the José Martí National Library] Sov. bibl., no. 4, 1963: 139–148.

3387. Os'kina, V. M. Biblioteki Kuby i perspektivy razvitiia bibliotechnogo dela v strane [Libraries and prospects for the development of library work in Cuba] Bibliotekoved. i bibl. za rub., no. 12, 1963: 3–18.

3388. Topalova, T. Bibliotechnoe delo na Kube [Library work in Cuba] Bibliotekar', no. 12, Dec. 1963: 45–47.

C. MISCELLANEOUS CULTURAL ACTIVITIES

1. Argentina

3389. Kirik, O. Komitet zashchity knigi [A committee for the defense of books] Sov. knizh. torg., no. 10, Oct. 1959: 42.
   Booksellers and bookselling.

3390. Rudaia, E. M. Problemy kul'turnoi politiki [Problems of cultural policy] Vest. ist. mir. kul't., no. 2, Mar.-Apr. 1959: 164–167.
   A review of Héctor Pablo Agosti's *Para una política de la cultura* (Buenos Aires, Ediciones Procyon, 1956. 158 p.).

2. Bolivia

3391. Reyes Mérida, Jaime. First national student work camp in Bolivia. World student news, v. 16, no. 7/8, 1962: 26–28.

3. Cuba

3392. Cardoso, Onelio Jorge, *and* Manuel Samuel Reguero. Zavtrashnii den' Kuby prekrasnyi [Cuba's tomorrow will be beautiful] Vsesvit, v. 4, no. 7, July 1961: 65.
   Cultural life.

3393. Isbakh, Aleksandr. V Gavane [In Havana] V mire knig, v. 4, no. 9, 1964: 42–43.
   Bookstores.

3394. Kirik, O. Na Kube [In Cuba] Sov. knizh. torg., no. 8, Aug. 1959: 57–58.
Booksellers and bookselling.

3395. Kongress deiatelei kul'tury [A Congress of Workers in Education and Culture] Inostr. lit., no. 11, Nov. 1961: 280–281.

3396. Kuba za mesiats [Cuba in October] Kuba, no. 3, Nov. 1964: 38–40.
Cultural events.

3397. Kuba za mesiats [Kuba in November] Kuba, no. 4, Dec. 1964: 14, 32–33.
Cultural events.

3398. Narodnaia entsiklopediia [A popular encyclopedia] Inostr. lit., no. 4, Apr. 1961: 281.
A Cuban encyclopedia for people of little education.

3399. Natsional'nyi sovet kul'tury [The National Council of Culture] Inostr. lit., no. 5, May 1961: 277.
The administration of cultural work.

3400. Pugachev, V. Kluby ostrova svobody [Community centers of the island of freedom] Kul't.-pros. rab., v. 24, no. 2, Feb. 1963: 51–52.

See also entries no. 384 and 3574.

XVI

LANGUAGES, LITERATURES, AND FOLKLORE

A. LANGUAGES

1. Aboriginal Languages

3401. IAzyki amerikanskikh indeitsev [The languages of the American Indians] Nov. inostr. lit. po iaz., no. 6, 1964: 38–39.
Bibliography of Indian languages.

3402. Shprintsin, N. G. Iz arkhivnykh materialov po iazykam indeitsev Brazilii [From archival materials concerning the languages of the Brazilian Indians] Sov. etn., no. 3, May-June 1964: 139–140.

3403. ————. Iz materialov po iazyku botokudov [From materials relating to the language of the Botocudo Indians] Vop. iaz., v. 10, no. 6, Nov.-Dec. 1961: 101–107.

2. Non-aboriginal Languages

3404. Stepanov, G. V. Ispanskii iazyk v stranakh Latinskoi Ameriki [The Spanish language in Latin American countries] Moscow, Izd-vo lit-ry na inostr. iazykakh, 1963. 201 p.

3405. Vasil'eva-Shvede, Ol'ga Konstantinovna, and Anatolii Mikhailovich Gakh. Antologiia portugal'skoi i brazil'skoi literatur, XIX–XX vv.; Antologia da literatura portuguesa e brasileira . . . , dos séculos XIX–XX [Anthology of Portuguese and Brazilian literatures of 19th and 20th centuries] Leningrad, Izd-zo Leningr. un-ta, 1964. 290 p.
Text in Portuguese. Introductory article by the compilers in Russian.

3406. Bylinkina, M. I. Obshchie cherty semanticheskogo razvitiia ispanskogo iazyka v Latinskoi Amerike [General trends in the semantic development of the Spanish language in Latin America] Nauch. dokl. vys. shkoly; filol. nauki, v. 4, no. 2, 1961: 3–14.

3407. Popov, V. P. Ob orfoepicheskoi norme portugal'skogo iazyka sovremennoi Brazilii [The orthoepic rule of the Portuguese language in present-day Brazil] Uch. zap. IMO, no. 11, 1963: 112–129.

3408. Stepanov, G. V. Ispanoamerikanskaia rech' i substrat [The Spanish-American spoken language and its substratum] Uch. zap. LGU, no. 301, 1961: 211–217.

3409. ————. O natsional'nom iazyke v stranakh Latinskoi Ameriki [The national language in the countries of Latin America] Trudy Inst. iaz., v. 10, 1960: 143–157.

3410. ————. Ob indeiskikh zaimstvovaniiakh v ispanskom iazyke [Indian words in the Spanish language] Uch. zap. LGU, no. 299, 1961: 205–212.

3411. ————. Ob ispano-amerikanskom slovoobrazovanii [Word formation in the Spanish-American language] Vop. iaz., v. 9, no. 1, Jan.-Feb. 1960: 68–73.

B. LITERARY CRITICISM; HISTORY OF LITERATURE

1. Writings Dealing With Three or More Countries

3412. Kuteishchikova, V. N. Roman Latinskoi Ameriki v XX veke [The Latin American novel in the 20th century] Moscow, Nauka, 1964. 334 p.
PQ7082.N7K8

3413. Ospovat, L. S. Govorit Latinskaia Amerika; o sovremennom latinoamerikanskom romane [Latin America tells its story; the present-day Latin American novel] Moscow, Znanie, 1961. 47 p.

3414. Plavskin, Zakhar Isaakovich. Progressivnaia poeziia Latinskoi Ameriki [Progressive poetry of Latin America] Leningrad, Ob-vo po rasprostr. polit. i nauch. znanii, 1959. 47 p.

PQ7082.P7P6

3415. Carpentier, Alejo. Znachenie L'va Tolstogo dlia Latinskoi Ameriki [The significance of Lev Tolstoi's literary work for Latin America] Inostr. lit., no. 11, Nov. 1960: 226–229.

3416. Cherez okeany [Across the oceans] Inostr. lit., no. 12, Dec. 1960: 258.
Chinese translations of Latin American literary works.

3417. Gal'perina, E. Buri i shtili Karibskogo moria [Tempest and calm in the Caribbean Sea] Vop. lit., v. 7, no. 10, Oct. 1963: 80–108.

3418. Gravina, Alfredo. Zhizn' i sud'by romana [Life and the fate of the novel] Inostr. lit., no. 12, Dec. 1960: 218–222.
Latin American literature.

3419. Gutiérrez, Joaquín. Nakanune bol'shogo rastsveta [On the eve of a great upswing] Inostr. lit., no. 10, Oct. 1964: 233–237.

3420. Kandel', Boris L'vovich. Latinoamerikanskie literatury [Latin American literatures] In his Putevoditel' po inostrannym bibliografiiam i spravochnikam po literaturovedeniiu i khudozhestvennoi literature. Leningrad, Gos. publichnaia biblioteka im. Saltykova-Shchedrina, 1959: p. 388–401.   Z6511.K3
Bibliography of Latin American literatures.

3421. ———. Literatura Latinskoi Ameriki [The literature of Latin America] In his Bibliografiia russkikh bibliografii po zarubezhnoi khudozhestvennoi literature i literaturovedeniiu. Leningrad, Gos. publichnaia biblioteka im. Saltykova-Shchedrina, 1962: p. 128–130.
Z6511.K28
Bibliography of Latin American literatures.

3422. Knigi pisatelei Latinskoi Ameriki v SSSR; tsifry i fakty [The books of Latin American authors published in the USSR; facts and figures] Kul't. i zhizn', v. 4, no. 8, 1960: 21–23.

3423. Korotko ob avtorakh [Brief notes on authors] Inostr. lit., no. 12, Dec. 1960: 263–264.
Latin American authors.

3424. Kuteishchikova, V. Bor'ba za vtoroe osvobozhdenie [Struggle for a second liberation] Vop. lit., v. 5, no. 10, Oct. 1961: 173–184.
Latin American literature.

3425. ———. Tvorchestvo L. N. Tolstogo i obshchestvenno-literaturnaia zhizn' Latinskoi Ameriki kontsa XIX-nachala XX veka [L. N. Tolstoi's works and the social and literary life of Latin America in the late 19th and the early 20th century] In Akademiia nauk SSSR. Institut mirovoi literatury. Iz istorii literaturnykh sviazei XIX veka. Moscow, Izd-vo Akad. nauk SSSR, 1962: p. 227–247.

PN863.A55

3426. ———. Voprosy istorii literatur Latinskoi Ameriki [Problems in the history of Latin American literatures] Vest. AN SSSR, v. 30, no. 12, Dec. 1960: 117–118.

3427. Kuteishchikova, V., and others. V bor'be za realizm i narodnost' [The struggle for realism and national character] Inostr. lit., no. 12, Dec. 1960: 210–217.
Latin American literature.

3428. Literaturnaia zhizn' Latinskoi Ameriki [The literary life of Latin America] Inostr. lit., no. 3, Mar. 1962: 241–243.

3429. Nesbyvshiesia nadezhdy [Vain expectations] Inostr. lit., no. 2, Feb. 1962: 274.
West Indian writers.

3430. Ospovat, L. Golosa dalekikh druzei; poeziia Latinskoi Ameriki v Sovetskom Soiuze [The voices of distant friends; Latin American poetry in the Soviet Union] Kul't. i zhizn', v. 4, no. 8, 1960: 20–24.

3431. ———. Literatura vulkanicheskogo kontinenta [Literature of a volcanic continent] V mire knig, v. 4, no. 8, 1964: 40–41.

Bibliography of Russian translations of Latin American literature.

3432. ――――. Slovo bere P'iatnytsia; pro antykolonialists'kyi roman Latyns'koi Ameryky [Man Friday tells his story; anticolonial Latin American novels] Vsesvit, v. 2, no. 9, Sept. 1959: 121–125.

3433. ――――. Traditsii narodnogo tvorchestva v latinoamerikanskoi poezii epokhi bor'by za nezavisimost' [Folklore traditions in Latin American poetry during the struggle for independence] Izv. AN SSSR. Otd. lit. i iaz., v. 20, no. 2, Mar.- Apr. 1961: 161–165.

3434. Ot Rio Grande do Ognennoi Zemli; govoriat pisateli Latinskoi Ameriki [From the Rio Grande to Tierra del Fuego; Latin American writers speak] Inostr. lit., no. 12, Dec. 1960: 223–228.

3435. Pogosov, IU. Slovo pisatelia-bortsa [Voice of a militant writer] Inostr. lit., no. 12, Dec. 1960: 250–251.

A review of Juan Marinello's *Meditación americana* (Buenos Aires, Ediciones Procyón, 1959. 219 p.).

3436. Shur, L. A. Ob osnovnykh periodakh istorii russko-latinoamerikanskikh literaturnykh sviazei; problema rasprostraneniia i vospriiatiia latinoamerikanskikh literatur v Rossii v XVII–XIX vv. [Principal periods in the history of Russian and Latin American literary ties; dissemination and perception of Latin American literatures in Russia in the 18th and 19th centuries] Izv. AN SSSR. Otd. lit. i iaz., v. 20, no. 4, July-Aug. 1961: 332–335.

3437. Teitelboim, Volodia. Literatura, narod, sotsializm; pis'mo iz Chili [Literature, the people, and socialism; a letter from Chile] Probl. mira i sots., v. 3, no. 3, Mar. 1960: 48–53.

Latin American literatures.

3438. Zherdynivs'ka, M. Veter predveshchaet buriu [A breeze precedes a storm] Sov. Ukr., v. 13, no. 2, Feb. 1963: 165–170.

Latin American literature.

See also entries no. 6 and 12.

2. Individual Countries

a. Argentina

3439. Arconada, César. "Na reke Parana"; neskol'ko slov o poete ["On the Parana"; a few words about its author] Inostr. lit., no. 12, Dec. 1962: 68–69.

Rafael Alberti, a Spanish poet who lives and works in Argentina.

3440. Beseda s dramaturgom [A talk with a playwright] Inostr. lit., no. 4, Apr. 1962: 267–268.

Argentine drama.

3441. Beseda s Osval'do Dragunom [A talk with Osvaldo Dragún] Inostr. lit., no. 9, Sept. 1962: 274.

Argentine drama.

3442. Dashkevich, IU. Vybor Anibala Ponse [Aníbal Ponce's choice] Inostr. lit., no. 5, May 1963: 260–261.

Argentine literature.

3443. Echegaray, Aristóbulo. Zametki ob argentinskoi literature [Notes on Argentine literature] Zvezda, no. 3, Mar. 1959: 138–140.

Translated from the Spanish.

3444. IAsnyi, V. Poet-voin [Poet and fighter] Inostr. lit., no. 2, Feb. 1960: 266–267.

A review of Elvio Romero's *Miguel Hernández, destino y poesía* (Buenos Aires, Editorial Losanda, 1958. 165 p.)

3445. "Istoriia argentinskoi literatury" ["The history of Argentine literature"] Inostr. lit., no. 12, Dec. 1960: 253–254.

A review of *Historia de la literatura argentina* (Buenos Aires, Ediciones Peuser, 1958–60. 5 v.).

3446. IUbilei Al'varo IUnke [The 70th birthday of Alvaro Yunque] Inostr. lit., no. 10, Oct. 1959: 270.

3447. K stoletiiu so dnia rozhdeniia Frai Mocho [On the centenary of Fray Mocho's birth] Inostr. lit., no. 1, Jan. 1959: 270.

José Sixto Alvarez, an Argentine writer.

3448. K. V. Chuzhaia svad'ba [Another girl's wedding] Zhen. mira, no. 2, 1964: 34.

A review of Sara Gallardo's *Enero* (Buenos Aires, Editorial Suramericana, 1958. 150 p.).

3449. Lystopad, M. Na styku tr'okh derzhav [Where three states meet] Vsesvit, v. 3, no. 6, June 1960: 141–142.
A review of Raúl Larra's *Gran Chaco* (Kiev, Molod', 1958).

3450. Nad chem rabotaiut pisateli [The themes that Argentine writers work on] Inostr. lit., no. 5, May 1960: 274–275.

3451. Neruda, Pablo. Sobaka, podarennaia Rafaeliu Al'berti [The dog given to Rafael Alberti] Ogonek, v. 41, no. 1, Jan. 1963: 5.

3452. Olevs'kyi, L. Dvi knyhy pys'mennyka-komunista [Two books of a Communist author] Vsesvit, v. 2, no. 12, Dec. 1959: 126–127.
A review of Amaro Villanueva's *La mano y otros cuentos* (Buenos Aires, Editorial Cartago, 1957. 119 p.), and his *Garibaldi en Entre Ríos* (Buenos Aires, Editorial Cartago, 1957. 156 p.).

3453. Oliver, María Rosa. My zashchishchaem argentinskuiu kul'turu [We defend Argentine culture] Inostr. lit., no. 6, June 1959: 244–246.

3454. Paporova, G. IUnym o druzhbe i blagorodstve [Friendship and generosity; stories for the young] Inostr. lit., no. 12, Dec. 1960: 252.
A review of Alvaro Yunque's *La barra de siete Ombues* (Buenos Aires, Editorial Futuro, 1959. 126 p.).

3455. Pevtsov, IU. V bor'be za svet [The struggle for light] Inostr. lit., no. 3, Mar. 1961: 264.
A review of Rubén Benítez' *Ladrones de luz* (Buenos Aires, Emecé Editores, 1959. 209 p.).

3456. Razgovor o poezii [A discussion of poetry] Inostr. lit., no. 4, 1961: 222–224.

3457. Satiricheskaia p'esa Solli [A satirical play by Solli] Inostr. lit., no. 2, Feb. 1959: 272.

3458. Shur, L. Sud'ba romana "Amaliia" v Rossii [The fate of "Amalia," an Argentine novel, in Russia] Kul't. i zhizn', v. 4, no. 8, 1960: 55.

3459. Smert' Manuelia Gal'vesa [Manuel Gálvez' death] Inostr. lit., no. 4, Apr. 1963: 277.

3460. Stikhi Raulia Gonsalesa Tun'ona [Raúl González Tuñón's poems] Inostr. lit., no. 3, Mar. 1963: 270.

3461. Tragichnyi grotesk Agustina Kussani [A tragic sketch by Agustín Cuzzani] Prapor, no. 5, May 1959: 121–122.

See also entries no. 342 and 4446.

b. Bolivia

3462. Stikhi Khesusa Lary [Jesús Lara's poems] Inostr. lit., no. 4, Apr. 1962: 270.
A review of Jesús Lara's *Flor de loto; mensaje de amor a la mujer china* (Cochabamba, Editorial América, 1960. 60 p.).

c. Brazil

3463. Amado, Jorge. Kastro Alves [Castro Alves] Moscow, Mol. gvardiia, 1963. 251 p.
Translated by IU. Kalugin and A. Sipovich from the Portuguese. Introductory article by I. Terterian.

3464. Terterian, I. A. Brazil'skii "severo-vostochnyi roman" i nekotorye problemy razvitiia realizma v literature Brazilii [The Brazilian "northeastern novel" and some problems concerning the development of realism in Brazilian literature] Moscow, 1964. 20 p. (Akademiia nauk SSSR. Institut mirovoi literatury imeni M. Gor'kogo)
Author's abstract of a dissertation for the degree of Candidate in Philological Sciences.

3465. Amado, Jorge. Zhizn', bor'ba i nadezhda naroda [The life, struggle, and hope of our people] Za rubezhom, no. 37, Sept. 1962: 31.
Brazilian literature.

3466. Bazarian, Zh. A. K 40-letiiu so dnia smerti Limy Barreto [The 40th anniversary of Lima Barreto's death] Vop. ist., no. 11, Nov. 1962: 214–217.

3467. Braga, P. Reportazh [A news story] Svyturys, no. 7, 1962: 22–23.
An article on Brazilian literature.
In Lithuanian.

3468. Dashkevich, IUrii. Brazil'skie strofy [Brazilian stanzas] Inostr. lit., no. 10, Oct. 1963: 112–113.
An article on Brazilian poetry.

3469. Festival' pisatelei [A festival of writers] Inostr. lit., no. 1, Jan. 1962: 275.

3470. Galins, H.　Pevets svoego naroda, velikii borets za mir [A bard of his people and a great fighter for peace] Karogs, no. 8, 1962: 150–151.
Jorge Amado, the Brazilian writer.
In Latvian.

3471. IUbilei Zhorzhi Amadu [The 30th anniversary of Jorge Amado's creative work] Inostr. lit., no. 9, Sept. 1961: 272.

3472. Ivanov, Vl.　Pust' bol'she ne budet korablekrushenii! [There should be no more shipwrecks!] Inostr. lit., no. 12, Dec. 1960: 248–249.
A review of Moacir C. Lopes' *Maria de cada porto* (Rio de Janeiro, Edição Princeps, 1959. 236 p.).

3473. Kalugin, IU.　Mulatka Gabriela iz kraia kakao [Gabriela, a mulatto girl from the land of cacao] Inostr. lit., no. 12, Dec. 1960: 251–252.
A review of Jorge Amado's *Gabriela, cravo e canela* (São Paulo, Martins, 1958. 453 p.).

3474. Klassiki na prokrustovom lozhe [Great authors in a procrustes bed] Inostr. lit., no. 4, Apr. 1960: 271–272.

3475. Kuteishchikova, V.　Nash drug Zhorzhi Amadu [Our friend Jorge Amado] Inostr. lit., no. 9, Sept. 1962: 198–199.

3476. Lima, Pedro Motta.　Marksizm-leninizm i kul'turnaia zhizn' Brazilii [Marxism-Leninism and the cultural life of Brazil] Probl. mira i sots., v. 5, no. 10, Oct. 1962: 21–26.

3477. Novyi literaturnyi zhurnal [A new literary periodical] Inostr. lit., no. 4, Apr. 1963: 278.
A review of the periodical *Tempo brasileiro* (Rio de Janeiro).

3478. Roman Dalsidiu Zhurandira [A novel by Dalcidio Jurandir] Inostr. lit., no. 8, Aug. 1959: 271–272.

3479. Roman "1935 god" ["The Year 1935," a novel] Inostr. lit., no. 5, May 1961: 270.

3480. Shur, L.　Brazil'skaia literatura v Rossii; k istorii russko-brazil'skikh literaturnykh otnoshenii [Brazilian literature in Russia; history of Russo-Brazilian literary contacts] Kul't. i zhizn', v. 3, no. 6, 1959: 60–61.

3481. Smert' Sesilii Meirelis [The death of Cecilia Meireles] Inostr. lit., no. 12, Dec. 1964: 271.

3482. Terterian, I. A.　Antikolonial'naia satira Tomasa Antonio Gonzagi i ee rol' v razvitii realizma v Brazilii [Thomaz Antonio Gonzaga's anticolonial satirical works and their role in the development of Brazilian realism] Izv. AN SSSR. Otd. lit. i iaz., v. 20, no. 4, July-Aug. 1961: 336–338.

3483. ———.　"Brazil'skoe vremia" ["Brazilian time"] Vop. lit., v. 7, no. 7, July 1963: 188–190.
A review of the periodical *Tempo brasileiro* (Rio de Janeiro).

3484. ———.　Zhorzhi Amadu, kotorogo my znaem [Jorge Amado as we know him] Inostr. lit., no. 5, May 1963: 198–201.

3485. Tynianova, Inna.　"Serdtse moe neob"iatnee mira"; k 220-letiiu so dnia rozhdeniia Tomasa Antoniu Gonzagi ["My heart is bigger than the whole world"; on the 220th anniversary of Thomaz Antonio Gonzaga's birth] Inostr. lit., no. 8, Aug. 1964: 251–252.

3486. Uspekh romana Zhorzhi Amadu [The success of Jorge Amado's novel] Inostr. lit., no. 7, July 1959: 273–274.

3487. "Zdes' ne rai dlia pisatelei" ["This country isn't a paradise for writers"] Inostr. lit., no. 3, Mar. 1960: 275.

3488. Zhorzhi Amadu o dolge literatora [Jorge Amado on the duty of writers] Inostr. lit., no. 12, Dec. 1960: 255.

See also entry no. 3045.

d. Chile

3489. Ospovat, L.　Pablo Neruda; ocherk tvorchestva [Pablo Neruda; a study of his creative works] Moscow, Sov. pisatel', 1960. 358 p.
Reviewed by V. Ognev in *Vop. lit.*, v. 6, no. 1, Jan. 1962: 223–228: by T. Motyleva in *Inostr. lit.*, no. 6, 1962: 222–227.

3490. Shur, Leonid Avel'evich, *comp.* Pablo Neruda; bio-bibliografcheskii ukazatel' [Pablo Neruda; a biobibliographical index] Moscow, Izd-vo Vses. knizhn. palaty, 1960. 74 p.　　Z8619.3.M6

3491. Antologiia realisticheskogo rasskaza [An anthology of realistic stories] Inostr. lit., no. 1, Jan. 1963: 286.

3492. Beseda s Pablo Nerudoi [A talk with Pablo Neruda] Inostr. lit., no. 12, Dec. 1959: 280.

3493. Beseda s Pablo Nerudoi [A talk with Pablo Neruda] Inostr. lit., no. 12, Dec. 1960: 260–261.

3494. Borovskii, V. U Pablo Nerudy [Visiting Pablo Neruda] Ogonek, v. 42, no. 30, July 1964: 17–18.

3495. Dashkevich, IUrii. Pablo Neruda [Pablo Neruda] Inostr. lit., no. 9, Sept. 1960: 257–259.

3496. Délano, Luis Enrique. Chiliiskaia literatura [Chilean literature] Inostr. lit., no. 6, June 1960: 204–209.

3497. ———. Spory v kafc imeni Lopesa Velardo; pis'mo iz Sant'iago-de-Chili [Discussions at the López Velardo Coffeehouse; a letter from Santiago de Chile] Inostr. lit., no. 1, Jan. 1964: 205–207.

3498. Duarte, María Cristina. Pervaia v Chile kriticheskaia stat'ia o romane L. N. Tolstogo "Voina i mir" [The first Chilean critical article on L. N. Tolstoi's novel "War and Peace"] Nauch. dokl. vys. shkoly; filol. nauki, v. 7, no. 4, 1964: 161–163.

3499. Ehrenburg, Il'ia. Pablo Neruda; k 60-letiiu so dnia rozhdeniia [Pablo Neruda; on his 60th birthday] Inostr. lit., no. 7, July 1964: 238–246.

3500. Geroi p'esy—indeitsy [Indians as the heroes of a play] Inostr. lit., no. 11, Nov. 1964: 286.

3501. Kedrov, A. O zhizni, o liubvi, o bor'be [On life, love, and struggle] Inostr. lit., no. 2, Feb. 1960: 259–262.
A review of Pablo Neruda's *Izbrannye proizvedeniia v dvukh tomakh* (Moscow, Gos. izd-vo khudozh. lit., 1958. 2 v.).

3502. Kolosovskaia, T. Novyi roman Manuelia Rokhasa [Manuel Rojas' new novel] Inostr. lit., no. 2, Feb. 1960: 268–269.
A review of Manuel Rojas' *Mejor que el vino; novela* (Santiago de Chile, Empresa Editora Zig-Zag, 1958. 264 p.).

3503. Kuteishchikova, V. Pablo Neruda; k 60-letiiu so dnia rozhdeniia [Pablo Neruda; on his 60th birthday] Kul't. i zhizn', v 8, no. 7, 1964: 45.

3504. Mal'tsev, Orest. Nash druh iz Sant-IAgo [Our friend from Santiago] Ukraina, no. 13, July 1959: 20–21.
Francisco A. Coloane, a Chilean writer.

3505. Mesto khudozhnika v obshchestve [The artist's place in society] Inostr. lit., no. 5, May 1964: 286.
Chilean dramaturgy.

3506. Morozov, B. Nochi i dni Pisagua [The nights and days of Pisagua] Vsesvit, v. 2, no. 1, Jan. 1959: 138–139.
A review of Volodia Teitelboim's *La semilla en la arena* (Santiago, Editora Austral, 1957. 564 p.).

3507. Neruda, Pablo. Zhizn' poeta [A poet's life] Inostr. lit., no. 12, Dec. 1963: 185–208.

3508. Novye knigi Pablo Nerudy [Pablo Neruda's new books] Inostr. lit., no. 4, Apr. 1960: 285.

3509. Ospovat, L. Mir, otkryvaemyi zanovo [A newly discovered world] Vop. lit., no. 9, 1959: 60–81.
A review of Pablo Neruda's *Odas elementales* (Buenos Aires, Editorial Losada, 1954. 235 p.).

3510. Otvet Pablo Nerudy prezidentu Venesuely [Pablo Neruda's answer to the Venezuelan President] Inostr. lit., no. 7, July 1961: 286.

3511. Pablo Neruda; k 60-letiiu so dnia rozhdeniia [Pablo Neruda; on his 60th birthday] Kal. znam. i pam. dat, v. 9, no. 6, July 1964: 10–12.
Bibliography of Neruda's literary works.

3512. "Pokolenie 50-kh godov" v poiskakh puti ["The generation of the 1950's" in search of a way] Inostr. lit., no. 7, July 1959: 216–218.

3513. Poslanie Pablo Nerudy Markosu Ane [Pablo Neruda's message to Marcos Ana] Inostr. lit., no. 7, July 1962: 261–262.

3514. Roman Margarity Agirre [A novel by Margarita Aguirre] Inostr. lit., no. 11, Nov. 1959: 286.

3515. V Soiuze pisatelei [The Union of Chilean Writers] Inostr. lit., no. 8, Aug. 1961: 285.

3516. Vicentini, María Luisa. Gabriela—doch' vsei Ameriki [Gabriela, the daughter of all America] Zhen. mira, no. 11, 1963: 16–17.
　　Gabriela Mistral, the Chilean poetess.

e. Colombia

3517. Ibánez, Jaime. Chelovek i zemlia v kolumbiiskom romane [Man and the land in the Colombian novel] Inostr. lit., no. 2, Feb. 1961: 210–214.

3518. Manuel' Sapata Olivel'ia rasskazyvaet [An interview with Manuel Zapata Olivella] Inostr. lit., no. 8, Aug. 1959: 279–280.

3519. Zherdynivs'ka, M. Pedro Khose znaide shliakh do maibutn'oho [Pedro José will find his path toward the future] Vsesvit, v. 3, no. 1, Jan. 1960: 137–138.
　　A review of Arnoldo Palacios' La selva y la lluvia; novela (Moscow, Ediciones en lenguas extranjeras, 1958).

f. Costa Rica

3520. Fal'ias: Kak ia stal pisatelem ["How I became a writer"; Fallas tells us his story] Inostr. lit., no. 5, May 1960: 281.

3521. Ospovat, L. Budem znakomy: Markos Ramires [Let's get acquainted: Marcos Ramírez] Nov. mir, v. 35, no. 6, June 1959: 258–260.
　　A review of Carlos Luis Fallas' Markos Ramires; prikliucheniia kostarikanskogo mal'chishki (Moscow, Detgiz, 1958. 222 p.).

3522. Pevtsov, IU. Ne tol'ko dlia detei [Not only for children] Inostr. lit., no. 6, June 1959: 266–267.
　　A review of Carlos Luis Fallas' Markos Ramires; prikliucheniia kostarikanskogo mal'chishki (Moscow, Detgiz, 1958. 222 p.).

3523. Smert' Khoakina Garsia-Monkhe [The death of Joaquín García Monje] Inostr. lit., no. 1, Jan. 1959: 279.

3524. Za svobodu pechati [For freedom of the press] Inostr. lit., no. 5, May 1963: 280–281.
　　Censorship of literary works.

g. Cuba

3525. Kuz'minskaia, I. Tvorchestvo Nikolasa Gil'ena [The works of Nicolás Guillén] Leningrad, Vyssh. profsoiuznaia shkola, 1963. 35 p.

3526. Marinello, Juan. Khose Marti—ispanoamerikanskii pisatel'; Marti i modernizm [José Martí, the Spanish-American writer; Martí and modernism] Moscow, Progress, 1964. 336 p.
　　Translated from the Spanish José Martí, escritor americano; Martí y el modernismo.

3527. Portuondo, José Antonio. Istoricheskii ocherk kubinskoi literatury [Outline history of Cuban literature] Moscow, Izd-vo inostr. lit., 1961. 155 p.
　　Translated from the Spanish Bosquejo histórico de las letras cubanas.
　　Reviewed by L. Ospovat in Vop. lit., v. 6, no. 4, Apr. 1962: 218–222; by I. Kuz'minskaia in Zvezda, no. 7, July 1962: 214–215.

3528. Roig de Leuchsenring, Emilio. Khose Marti—antiimperialist [José Martí as anti-imperialist] Moscow, Izd-vo inostr. lit., 1962. 143 p.
　　Translated from the Spanish Martí, antiimperialista.
　　Reviewed by S. Emel'iannikov in Inostr. lit., no. 5, May 1964: 264–266.

3529. Shur, Leonid Avel'evich, comp. Nikolas Gil'en; biobibliograficheskii ukazatel' [Nicolás Guillén; a biobibliographical index] Moscow, Kniga, 1964. 99 p.
　　　　　　　　　　　Z8374.65.M6
　　Introductory article by Z. I. Plavskin, with summary in Spanish.

3530. Vizen, L. Khose Marti; khronika zhizni povstantsa [José Martí; the life story of a guerrilla fighter] Moscow, Mol. gvardiia, 1964. 304 p.

3531. Alekho Karpent'er o sebe [Alejo Carpentier tells his story] Inostr. lit., no. 11, Nov. 1963: 282–283.

3532. Beilinson, IA. Proizvedeniia kubinskikh pisatelei [The works of Cuban writers] Nov. knigi, v. 9, no. 1, Jan. 1964: 57–60.

3533. Beseda s avtorom "Gimna 26 iiulia" [A talk with the author of the "Hymn of July 26"] Inostr. lit., no. 9, Sept. 1963: 280.

3534. Beseda s Gil'ermo Kabreroi Infante [A talk with Guillermo Cabrera Infante] Inostr. lit., no. 3, Mar. 1963: 279–280.

3535. Beseduia s Alekho Karpent'erom [A talk with Alejo Carpentier] Inostr. lit., no. 1, Jan. 1963: 278–279.

3536. Beseduia s laureatami [A talk with the winners of a literary contest] Inostr. lit., no. 7, July 1962: 263.

3537. Beseduia s Nikolasom Gil'enom [A talk with Nicolás Guillén] Inostr. lit., no. 5, May 1963: 281.

3538. Bulia, P. Kubinskii poet Nikolas Gil'en [The Cuban poet Nicolás Guillén] Mnatobi, no. 5, 1964: 131–135.
In Georgian.

3539. Castro, Fidel. My—semena griadushchego [We are the seeds of the future] Inostr. lit., no. 12, Dec. 1961: 198–199.
The tasks of Cuban writers and authors.

3540. Dashkevich, IUrii. Beseduia s N. Gil'enom [Talking with Nicolás Guillén] Inostr. lit., no. 11, Nov. 1964: 262–264.

3541. ———. Iz okopov, gde zashchishchaiut kul'turu [From the trenches where culture is defended] Inostr. lit., no. 7, July July: 251–256.

3542. ———. Pevets Kuby [The bard of Cuba] Inostr. lit., no. 1, Jan. 1960: 223–225.
Nicolás Guillén.

3543. ———. Poet kubinskoi revoliutsii [Poet of the Cuban Revolution] Inostr. lit., no. 4, Apr. 1962: 257–259.
A review of Manuel Navarro Luna's Odas mambisas (Havana, Impr. Nacional de Cuba, 1961. 77 p.).

3544. ———. Put' kubinskoi literatury [The path of Cuban literature] Inostr. lit., no. 3, Mar. 1961: 259–261.
A review of José Antonio Portuondo's Bosquejo histórico de las letras cubanas (Havana, Ministerio de Educación, Dirección General de Cultura, 1960. 79 p.).

3545. ———. Slovo Khose Marti [The word of José Martí] Inostr. lit., no. 1, Jan. 1963: 259–261.

3546. Dorticós Torrado, Osvaldo. Revoliutsiia trebuet vashikh usilii [The revolution needs your help] Inostr. lit., no. 12, Dec. 1961: 196–197.
The problems facing Cuban writers and artists.

3547. "Estetika i revoliutsiia" ["Aesthetics and the revolution"] Inostr. lit., no. 11, Nov. 1963: 283.

3548. Faktorovich, D. Golos Kuby [The voice of Cuba] Neman, v. 12, no. 2, Mar.-Apr. 1963: 144–148.

3549. Govorit Nikolas Gil'en [An interview with Nicolás Guillén] Inostr. lit., no. 7, July 1959: 282.

3550. Guillén, Nicolás. Massam—luchshie plody nashego tvorchestva [We should give to the masses the best fruits of our creative work] Inostr. lit., no. 12, Dec. 1961: 199–201.

3551. IUbilei Alekho Karpent'era [Alejo Carpentier's 60th birthday] Inostr. lit., no. 12, Dec. 1964: 277.

3552. Khose Marti [José Martí] Rev.-ist. kalendar'-spravochnik, 1963: 28–30.

3553. Kongress rabotnikov kul'tury [A congress of workers in culture] Karogs, no. 1, 1962: 157.
A congress of Cuban writers and artists.
In Latvian.

3554. Kuteishchikova, V. N. K rastsvetu revoliutsionnogo iskusstva; I Kongress pisatelei i khudozhnikov Kuby [The flowering of revolutionary art; the First Congress of Cuban Writers and Artists] Vop. lit., v. 6, no. 2, Feb. 1962: 170–175.

3555. Kuz'minskaia, Irina. Kuba—liubov' moia! [Cuba—my love!] Neva, no. 7, 1962: 185–186.
Nicolás Guillén's poems.

3556. ———. Review. Zvezda, no. 7, July 1962: 214–215.
A review of José Antonio Portuondo's Bosquejo histórico de las letras cubanas (Havana, Ministerio de Relaciones Exteriores, Departamento de Asuntos Culturales, División de Publicaciones, 1960. 79 p.).

3557. ———. V nogu s istoriei; poeziia revoliutsionnoi Kuby [In step with history; the poetry of revolutionary Cuba] Neva, no. 4, 1964: 167–171.

3558. Lirika Eberto Padil'i [Heberto Padilla's lyric verse] Inostr. lit., no. 1, Jan. 1963: 278.

3559. Literaturnyi konkurs v Gavane [A literary contest in Havana] Inostr. lit., no. 7, July 1964: 282.

3560. "Nasha poeziia—revoliutsiia" ["The revolution is our poetry"] Inostr. lit., no. 5, May 1964: 280.
    Fidel Castro on present-day Cuban poetry.

3561. Novye issledovaniia o Khose Marti [New studies devoted to José Martí] Inostr. lit., no. 6, June 1960: 280.

3562. Novymi putiami [Along new paths] Inostr. lit., no. 1, Jan. 1961: 223–224.

3563. O tvorchestve Nikolasa Gil'ena [Nicolás Guillén's creative work] Inostr. lit., no. 9, Sept. 1963: 280.

3564. Ospovat, L. Nikolas Gil'en i narodnaia pesnia [Nicolás Guillén and folk songs] Vop. lit., v. 4, no. 12, 1960: 166–184.

3565. Padilla, Heberto. Serdtse s Kuboi [His heart belongs to Cuba] Inostr. lit., no. 11, Nov. 1963: 264–265.
    A review of Manuel Navarro Luna's Obra poética (Havana, Ediciones Unión, 1963).

3566. Pisateli v revoliutsii [Writers and the revolution] Inostr. lit., no. 5, May 1960: 282.

3567. "Poet, kotoryi vsegda ostanetsia molodym" [A poet who will always be young"] Inostr. lit., no. 11, Nov. 1964: 281.
    The 70th birthday of Manuel Navarro Luna.

3568. Pogosov, IU. Rozhdennye revoliutsiei [Born of the revolution] Inostr. lit., no. 11, Nov. 1962: 227–229.
    A review of César Leante's Con las milicias (Havana, Unión de Escritores, 1962. 97 p.) and Edmundo Desnoes' No hay problema (Havana, Ediciones Revolución, 1961. 225 p.).

3569. Polevoi, B. Pevets Kuby; k 60-letiiu so dnia rozhdeniia N. Gil'ena [The bard of Cuba; on Nicolás Guillén's 60th birthday] Inostr. lit., no. 7, July 1962: 228–229.

3570. Premiia Faiadu Khamisu [A prize awarded to Fayad Jamis] Inostr. lit., no. 6, June 1962: 297.

3571. Savich, O. Urok istorii [A lesson of history] Inostr. lit. no. 3, Mar. 1963: 260–261.
    Cuba in Spanish poetry.
    A review of España canta a Cuba (Paris, Ruedo libérico, 1962).

3572. Somov, V. Pesni Gil'ena [Guillén's songs] Neva, no. 5, 1961: 212–214.

3573. Stikhi—oruzhie [Poems are a weapon] Inostr. lit., no. 6, July 1960: 280.

3574. Tvorit' dlia naroda; Kongress deiatelei kul'tury revoliutsionnoi Kuby [Let us work for our people; a congress of the cultural workers of revolutionary Cuba] Inostr. lit., no. 12, Dec. 1961: 194–196.

3575. Vizen, L. Plot' ot ploti naroda Kuby [The flesh of Cuban people's flesh] Mol. komm., no. 5, May 1961: 92–95.
    José Martí.

3576. Vorob'ev, S. Issledovanie o Khose Marti [A study on José Martí] Inostr. lit., no. 1, Jan. 1960: 250–251.
    A review of Juan Marinello's José Martí, escritor americano (Mexico City, Editorial Grijalbo, 1958. 333 p.).

3577. Zherdynivs'ka, M. Holosy Pivdenno-Amerykans'koho kontinentu [Voice of the South American continent] Vsesvit, v. 7, no. 6, June 1964: 156–157.
    A review of Emilio Carballido's Un pequeño día de ira (Havana, Casa de las Américas, 1962. 69 p.) and Fayad Jamis' Por esta libertad (Havana, Casa de las Américas, 1962. 68 p.).

h. Ecuador

3578. Khalems'kyi, N. Pid kryk gual'gury [When the gualgura cried] Vsesvit, v. 2, no. 10, Oct. 1959: 133–134.
    A review of Adalberto Ortiz' Juyungo (Buenos Aires, Editorial América Lee, 1943. 268 p.).

3579. Pisateli i bor'ba naroda [Writers and the struggle of the people] Inostr. lit., no. 2, Feb. 1959: 286.

3580. "Sovremennyi ekvadorskii roman" ["The present-day Ecuadorian novel"] Inostr. lit., no. 12, Dec. 1960: 262.

A review of Edmondo Ribadeneira's *La moderna novela ecuatoriana* (Quito, Editorial Casa de la Cultura Ecuatoriana, 1958. 271 p.).

i. El Salvador

3581. Slovo Liliam Khimenes [Liliam Jiménez' poems] Inostr. lit., no. 4, Apr. 1960: 281–282.

A review of Liliam Jiménez' *Sinfonía popular* (Mexico City, Ediciones Revista de Guatemala, 1959. 63 p.).

j. Guatemala

3582. Pevtsov, IU. A.   Migel' Ankhel' Asturias; biobibliograficheskii ukazatel' [Miguel Angel Asturias; a biobibliographical index] Moscow, Vses. kn. palata, 1960. 28 p.

Z8045.8.M6

3583. Dashkevich, IUrii.   Migel' Ankhel' Asturias [Miguel Angel Asturias] Inostr. lit., no. 12, Dec. 1962: 252–254.

3584. Kuteishchikova, V.   Glazami indeitsev Gvatemaly [Through the eyes of the Guatemalan Indians] Vop. lit., v. 7, no. 9, Sept. 1963: 233–236.

A review of Atilio Jorge Castalpoggi's *Miguel Angel Asturias* (Buenos Aires, La Mandrágora, 1961. 222 p.).

3585. O novom romane Asturiasa [Asturias' new novel] Inostr. lit., no. 12, Dec. 1960: 256.

A review of Miguel Angel Asturias' *Los ojos de los enterrados* (Buenos Aires, Editorial Losada, 1960. 482 p.).

3586. Pevtsov, IU.   Dokumenty epokhy [Documents of our epoch] Vsesvit, v. 4, no. 7, July 1960: 99–102.

The works of Miguel Angel Asturias.

3587. Zherdynivs'ka, M.   "Ochi pokhovanykh" ["Eyes of the buried"] Vsesvit, v. 5, no. 3, Mar. 1962: 92.

A review of Miguel Angel Asturias' *Los ojos de los enterrados; novella* (Buenos Aires, Editorial Losada, 1960. 482 p.).

k. The Guianas

3588. Carew, Jan.   My pishem dlia naroda [We write for the people] Inostr. lit., no. 10, Oct. 1964: 227–233.

The literature of British Guiana and the West Indies.

3589. Gal'perina, E.   Put' IAna Ker'iu [Jan Carew's path of life] Inostr. lit., no. 2, Feb. 1963: 207–215.

3590. Gor'kie stranitsy [Bitter pages] Inostr. lit., no. 2, Feb. 1962: 273.

The literature of British Guiana.

l. Haiti

3591. Alexis, Jacques Stephen.   Dorogoi zhivykh traditsii [Along the road of living traditions] Inostr. lit., no. 2, Feb. 1961: 219–224.

3592. ———.   Sovremennye problemy gaitianskoi literatury [Present-day problems in Haitian literature] Inostr. lit., no. 2, Feb. 1960: 203–205.

3593. Dépestre, René.   Dolg literatorov [The duty of writers] Inostr. lit., no. 2, Feb. 1961: 193–196.

3594. Gal'perina, E.   Poety Antil'skikh ostrovov [Poets of the Antilles] Vop. lit., v. 5, no. 1, Jan. 1961: 39–62.

3595. ———.   Poety Gaiti [Poets of Haiti] Inostr. lit., no. 1, Jan. 1960: 131–132.

3596. ———.   Poeziia i pravda gaitianskogo naroda [The poetry and truth of the Haitian people] Inostr. lit., no. 2, Feb. 1961: 273–274.

A review of Jacques Stephen Alexis' *L'espace d'un cillement* (Paris, Gallimard, 1959. 346 p.) and his *Romancero aux étoiles* (Paris, Gallimard, 1960. 271 p.).

3597. ———.   Problemy realizma i modernizma v sovremennoi literature Afriki [The problems of realism and modernism in present-day African literature] Vop. lit., no. 12, 1959: 67–96.

Includes the literatures of Haiti and the French West Indies.

3598. ———.   Zhak Rumen [Jacques Roumain] Inostr. lit., no. 5, May 1964: 189–199.

3599. Gnevnoe slovo poetov [The fiery message of poets] Inostr. lit., no. 3, Mar. 1960: 276.

3600. Kakova sud'ba Aleksisa? [What happened to Alexis?] Inostr. lit., no. 9, Sept. 1961: 273–274.

3601. Svobodu Zhaku-Stefenu Aleksisu! [They must free Jacques Stephen Alexis!] Inostr. lit., no. 4, Apr. 1963: 279.

3602. Syn Gaiti [Son of the Haitian people] Nov. vrem., v. 20, no. 19, May 1962: 13. Jacques Stephen Alexis.

3603. Vspominaia Zhaka Rumena [Reminiscences about Jacques Roumain] Inostr. lit., no. 3, Mar. 1962: 274.

m. Mexico

3604. Kuteishchikova, V. N., *ed.* Meksikanskii realisticheskii roman XX veka; sbornik statei [The Mexican realistic novel of the 20th century; collected articles] Moscow, Izd-vo Akad. nauk SSSR, 1960. 166 p. PQ7203.A4
Reviewed by Z. Plavskin in *Vop. lit.*, v. 5, no. 9, Sept. 1961: 227–231; by IU. Uvarov in *Inostr. lit.*, no. 12, Dec. 1960: 246–247.

3605. Biblioteka Al'fonso Reiesa [Alfonso Reyes' library] Inostr. lit., no. 9, Sept. 1960: 281.

3606. Dashkevich, IUrii. Karlos Fuentes [Carlos Fuentes] Inostr. lit., no. 12, Dec. 1963: 251–253.

3607. Gabriel' Martines vernulsia na rodinu [Gabriel Martínez has returned to his country] Inostr. lit., no. 5, May 1961: 278.
A review of Agustín Yáñez' *La tierra pródiga* (Mexico City, Fondo de Cultura Económica, 1960. 315 p.).

3608. Kremnev, M. Na toi storone [On the other side] Nov. vrem., v. 18, no. 22, May 1960: 30–31.
A review of Luis Spota's *Murieron a mitad del río* (Mexico City, Libro Mex, 1959. 261 p.).

3609. Kuteishchikova, Vera Nikolaevna. Osnovopolozhnik meksikanskoi literatury Fernandes Lisardi [Fernández Lizardi, the founder of Mexican literature] Izv. AN SSSR. Otd. lit. i iaz., v. 20, no. 2, Mar.-Apr. 1961: 154–160.

3610. Mora, Juan Miguel de. Poety uzhe ne pishut dlia korolei; zametki meksikanskogo pisatelia [Poets do not write for kings any more; notes of a Mexican writer] Druzh. nar., no. 3, Mar. 1959: 211–214.

3611. Neizvestnaia povest' Khose Mansisidora [An unpublished tale by José Mancisidor] Inostr. lit., no. 6, June 1959: 280.

3612. Pisateli i revoliutsiia [Writers and the revolution] Inostr. lit., no. 12, Dec. 1960: 258–259.
Mexican literary works describing the Mexican Revolution.

3613. Pisateli o Meksikanskoi Revoliutsii [Writers describe the Mexican Revolution] Inostr. lit., no. 9, Sept. 1960: 280.

3614. Pobedit svet [The light will win] Inostr. lit., no. 6, June 1961: 280.
A review of Carlos Fuentes' *La region más transparente* (Mexico City, Fondo de Cultura Económica, 1958. 460 p.).

3615. Proizvedeniia prozaikov [The works of prose writers] Inostr. lit., no. 6, June 1963: 282.

3616. Rasskazy Bassol'sa-Batal'i [Bassols Batalla's stories] Inostr. lit., no. 12, Dec. 1960: 259.
A review of Angel Bassols Batalla's *Mi teniente Ambrosio y otros relatos* (Mexico City, Ediciones De Andrea, 1960. 77 p.).

3617. Rasskazy Emilio Karbal'ido [Emilio Carballido's stories] Inostr. lit., no. 7, July 1963: 282.

3618. Rasskazy o revoliutsii [Stories about the revolution] Inostr. lit., no. 7, July 1961: 279.
A review of Rafael Muñoz' *Fuego en el Norte; cuentos de la Revolución* (Mexico City, Libro Mex, 1960. 175 p.).

3619. Sbornik po istorii literatury [Collected articles on the history of literature] Inostr. lit., no. 1, Jan. 1960: 279.
Articles of literary criticism (Spain, Latin America, and Mexico).

3620. Shlagbaum pered Karlosom Fuentesom [A barrier before Carlos Fuentes] Inostr. lit., no. 7, July 1962: 264.

3621. Smert' Al'fonso Reiesa [The death of Alfonso Reyes] Inostr. lit., no. 2, Feb. 1960: 280.

3622. Zhitomirskaia, Z. "Novyi" Traven [The "new" Traven] Inostr. lit., no. 8, Aug. 1961: 193–196.
B. Traven, a writer who lives in Mexico.

See also entry no. 3577.

n. Nicaragua

3623. Ospovat, L. Ruben Dario na russkom iazyke [Rubén Darío in Russian] Inostr. lit., no. 1, Jan. 1959: 249–251.
A review of Rubén Darío's *Stikhi* (Moscow, Goslitizdat, 1958. 138 p.).

o. Panama

3624. Rogachevskii, Leonid. Changmarin— poet Panamy [Chang Marín, a Panamanian poet] Ogonek, v. 42, no. 13, Mar. 1964: 16.

p. Paraguay

3625. Ospovat, L. Partizanskaia gitara [A guerrilla guitar] Inostr. lit., no. 11, Nov. 1962: 225–226.
A review of Elvio Romero's *Esta guitarra dura; libro de guerrilleros, Paraguay, 1960* (Havana, Impr. Nacional de Cuba, 1961. 77 p.).

q. Peru

3626. Grodzenskaia, E. R. Poeziia bor'by, poeziia mira [The poetry of struggle is the poetry of peace] Smena, v. 40, no. 4, Feb. 1963: 16.
A review of *En alas de la paz* (Lima).

3627. Rasskazy o krest'ianskoi zhizni [Stories describing the life of peasants] Inostr. lit., no. 4, Apr. 1961: 283.
A review of Rubén Sueldo Guevara's *Los agrarios; cuentos* (Lima, Editorial Peruanas, 1960. 125 p.).

3628. Zubritskii, IU. Poeziia starodavn'oho mista [Poetry of an old city] Vsesvit, v. 2, no. 11, Nov. 1959: 125–126.
A review of *Exposición de la poesía cuzqueña contemporánea*, v. 1–2 (Cuzco, Festival del Libro Cuzqueño, 1958).

r. Puerto Rico

3629. Antologiia rasskaza [An anthology of Puerto Rican stories] Inostr. lit., no. 9, Sept. 1960: 282.

3630. Enamorado-Cuesta, José. Vozrodit' natsional'nuiu kul'turu Puerto-Riko [Let us revive the national culture of Puerto Rico] Inostr. lit., no. 12, Dec. 1959: 222–223.

s. Trinidad and Tobago

3631. Lennart-Presto, U. Zagadki Robinzona Kruzo [Problems of Robinson Crusoe] Vokrug sveta, no. 8, Aug. 1963: 50–51.
Tobago Island in literature.
Translated from the Swedish.

t. Uruguay

3632. Al'fredo Gravina o literature [Alfredo Gravina on literature] Inostr. lit., no. 4, Apr. 1962: 282.

3633. Burkatov, B. Krai, de panuie holod [A region of hungry people] Vsesvit, v. 2, no. 2, Feb. 1959: 130–132.
A review of Enrique Amorim's *Korral' ab'ierto* (Kiev, Rad. pys'mennyk, 1958. 231 p.).

3634. Chestvovanie Enrike Amorima [A meeting in Enrique Amorim's honor] Inostr. lit., no. 1, Jan. 1959: 283.

3635. Kel'in, F. Put' ot strakha k gordosti [The path from fear to pride] Inostr. lit., no. 12, Dec. 1960: 246–247.
A review of Alfredo Dante Gravina's *Del miedo al orgullo* (Montevideo, Ediciones Pueblos Unidos, 1959. 307 p.).

3636. Mamontov, S. Florensio Sanches [Florencio Sánchez] Kul't. i zhizn', v. 4, no. 8, 1960: 59.

3637. Parkhomovs'ka, Olena. "Drovoruby tilom i dusheiu" ["The true lumberjacks"] Vitchyzna, v. 28, no. 1, Jan. 1960: 212–213.
A review of Enrique Amorim's *Korral' ab'ierto* (Kiev, Rad. pys'mennyk, 1958. 231 p.).

3638. Zherdynivs'ka, M. Oda bat'kivshchyni [An ode to the fatherland] Vsesvit, v. 4, no. 10, Oct. 1961: 143–144.
A review of Enrique Amorim's *Mi patria; poemas* (Montevideo, Ediciones Papel de Poesía, 1960. 108 p.).

3639. Zherdynivs'ka, M., *and* L. Olevs'kyi. Lisoruby [Loggers] Vsesvit, v. 2, no. 4, Apr. 1959: 109–110.
A review of Enrique Amorim's *Los montaraces* (Buenos Aires, Editorial Goyanarte, 1957. 181 p.).

u. Venezuela

3640. Carrera, Gustavo Luis. Tam, gde idet bitva [Where the battle is being fought] Inostr. lit., no. 10, Oct. 1964: 238–240.

3641. Efremov, A. Ektor Mukhika [Héctor Mujica] Sov. pech., no. 10, Oct. 1962: 56–57.

3642. Liudi Meksikanskoi revoliutsii v romane Gal'egosa [The people of the Mexican Revolution in a novel by Gallegos] Inostr. lit., no. 12, Dec. 1960: 255–256.

3643. Novyi roman Migelia Otero Sil'vy [Miguel Otero Silva's new novel] Inostr. lit., no. 3, Mar. 1962: 273–274.
 A review of Miguel Otero Silva's *Oficina no. 1* (Buenos Aires, Editorial Losada, 1961. 246 p.).

3644. Romulo Gal'egos—kandidat na nobelevskuiu premiiu [Rómulo Gallegos is a candidate for the Nobel Prize] Inostr. lit., no. 9, Sept. 1960: 274.

3645. Spustia tridtsat' let [Thirty years later] Inostr. lit., no. 7, July 1960: 274.
 Rómulo Gallegos.

3646. Stikhi Andresa Eloia Blanko [Andrés Eloy Blanco's poems] Inostr. lit., no. 4, Apr. 1961: 275.
 A review of Andrés Eloy Blanco's *Obras* (Caracas, Editorial Cordillera, 1960. 10 v.).

3647. V dzhungliakh Verkhnego Orinoko [In the jungle of the upper Orinoco Valley] Inostr. lit., no. 2, Feb. 1960: 274.
 History and criticism of Venezuelan literature.

3648. 2 [Vtorogo] avgusta ispolniaetsia 75 let vydaiushchemusia venesuel'skomu pisateliu i vidnomu demokraticheskomu deiateliu Latinskoi Ameriki—Romulo Gal'egosu [Rómulo Gallegos, a prominent Venezuelan author and an outstanding democratic leader of Latin America, will be 75 years old on August 2 (1959)] Inostr. lit., no. 7, July 1959: 275.

v. West Indies

3649. Remizov, B. Kolir ridnoi zemli [The color of his native land] Vsesvit, v. 4, no. 6, June 1961: 150–151.
 A review of Edouard Glissant's *La lézarde; roman* (Paris, Editions du Seuil, 1958. 250 p.).
 See also entries no. 3588, 3594, and 3597.

C. TRANSLATIONS OF LATIN AMERICAN AUTHORS

1. Writings by Authors From Various Countries

3650. Fal'shivye monety; sbornik rasskazov [Counterfeit coins; collected stories] Moscow, Profizdat, 1959. 66 p.
        PQ7300.R8F3

3651. Lalu; latinoamerikanskie rasskazy [Lalu; Latin American stories] Moscow, Mol. gvardiia, 1962. 254 p.
 Translated from the Spanish and the Portuguese.

3652. Morov, A., *comp.* Skromnye dorogi; rasskazy pisatelei stran Latinskoi Ameriki [Modest paths; stories by Latin American authors] Moscow, Iskusstvo, 1959. 125 p.
        PQ6269.R8M6
 Translated from the Spanish and the Portuguese.

3653. Pesni svobody i mira; golosa latinoamerikanskikh i afrikanskikh poetov [Songs of freedom and peace; the voice of Latin American and African poets] Kiev, Goslitizdat Ukrainy, 1962. 202 p.
 In Ukrainian. Latin American poems are translated from the Spanish by E. Narubina.

3654. Pis'mo Bogu; rasskazy pisatelei Latinskoi Ameriki [A letter to God; stories by Latin American authors] Moscow, Pravda, 1963. 46 p.
 Translated from the Spanish and Portuguese.

3655. Soldaty svobody; sbornik stikhov [Soldiers of freedom; collected poems] Moscow, Goslitizdat, 1963. 207 p.
 Translated from the Spanish. Introductory article by L. Ospovat.

3656. Slushaite! Stikhi molodykh poetov Latinskoi Ameriki [Listen! Verse of the young poets of Latin America] Moscow, Mol. gvardiia, 1961. 239 p.
 Translated from the Spanish, the Portuguese, and the French. Introductory article by L. Ospovat.

3657. Vremia plameneiushchikh derev'ev; poety Antil'skikh ostrovov [The time of flaming trees; poets of the Antilles] Moscow, Izd-vo vost. lit., 1961. 244 p.
 Translated from various languages.

2. Works of Individual Authors (listed by country of origin)

a. Argentina

3658. Alberti, Rafael. Noch' voiny v muzee Prado; odnoaktnyi ofort s prologom [A night in the Prado Museum during the war; a sketch in one act and a prologue] Moscow, Izd-vo inostr. lit., 1961. 74 p.
  Translated by P. Grushko from the Spanish. Introductory article by F. Kel'in.

3659. ———. Stikhi [Poems] Leningrad, Izd-vo khud. lit., 1963. 349 p.
  Translated from the Spanish. Introductory article by R. Zernova.

3660. Argentinskie rasskazy [Argentine stories] Moscow, Izd-vo inostr. lit., 1962. 152 p.
  Translated from the Spanish. Introductory article by IU. Dashkevich.

3661. Argentinskie rasskazy [Argentine stories] Yerevan, Aipetrat, 1961. 134 p.
  In Armenian. Translated by L. Khudoian from the Russian.

3662. Canto, Estela. Noch' i griaz'; roman [The night and mud; a novel] Moscow, Progress, 1964. 176 p.
  Translated by R. Sashina from the Spanish La noche y el barro.

3663. Castro, Ernesto L. Ostrovitiane; roman [The islanders; a novel] Moscow, Goslitizdat, 1961. 291 p.
  Translated by S. Alenikova and V. Vinogradov from the Spanish Los isleros. Introductory article by G. V. Stepanov.

3664. ———. Vspakhannoe pole; roman (Plowed field; a novel) Moscow, Izd-vo inostr. lit., 1960. 255 p.
  Translated by K. Naumov from the Spanish Campo arado.
  Reviewed by N. Gabinskii in Inostr. lit., no. 9, Sept. 1961: 256–257.

3665. Cuzzani, Agustín. Funt miasa; predstavlenie v odnom akte [A pound of meat; a one-act play] Moscow, Iskusstvo, 1959. 75 p.
  Translated from the Spanish Una libra de carne.

3666. Gandolfi Herrero, Arístides (Alvaro Yunque, pseud.) Bumazhnye korabliki; rasskazy [Paper ships; stories] Kiev, Ditvydav, 1960. 145 p.

In Ukrainian. Translated from the Spanish. Introductory article by V. Pashchenko.

3667. ———. Futbol'nyi klub "Parni iuga"; povest' ["The boys from the South" soccer team; a tale] Moscow, Detgiz, 1960. 224 p.
  Translated from the Spanish Muchachos del sur. Also published in Lithuanian.

3668. ———. Khrustal'nyi sharik; rasskazy [A crystal ball; stories] Kiev, Ditvydav, 1962. 64 p.
  In Ukrainian. Translated from the Spanish.

3669. ———. Malen'kie muzhchiny; rasskazy [Little men; stories] Riga, Latgosizdat, 1959. 159 p.
  In Latvian. Translated by M. Kempe from the Spanish.

3670. ———. Martin nichego ne ukral; rasskazy [Martin didn't steal a thing; stories] Ashkhabad, Turkmengosizdat, 1959. 48 p.
  In Turkmen. Translated by T. Kurbanov from the Russian.

3671. ———. Muzhchiny dvenadtsati let; povest' [The twelve-year-old men; a tale] Kishinev, Kartia moldoveniaske, 1960. 197 p.
  In Moldavian. Translated by E. Busuiok from the Russian. Also published in Lithuanian.

3672. González Tuñón, Raúl. Rozy v brone; stikhi [Armorclad roses; verse] Moscow, Goslitizdat, 1962. 191 p.
  Translated from the Spanish La rosa blindada.
  Reviewed by M. Aliger in Inostr. lit., no. 8, Aug. 1963: 262–265.

3673. Güiraldes, Ricardo. Don Segundo Sombra; roman [Don Segundo Sombra; a novel] Moscow, Goslitizdat, 1960. 207 p.
  Translated by V. Krylova from the Spanish. Introductory article by F. Kel'in. Also published in Estonian.
  Reviewed by S. Marini in Inostr. lit., no. 12, 1960: 245.

3674. Larra, Raúl. Bez perepochynku; roman [Without respite; a novel] Kiev, Rad. pys'mennyk, 1959. 284 p.
  Translated by A. Kretova and I. Vorona from the Spanish Sin tregua.

3675. ———. Ioho zvaly chubatyi; povist' [They called him "shaggy"; a tale] Kiev, Derzhvydav, 1961. 63 p.

Translated by L. V. Dobrians'ka from the Spanish.

Reviewed by S. Volyns'kyi in *Vsesvit*, v. 4, no. 7, July 1961: 156.

3676. Larreta, Enrique Rodríguez. Slava dona Ramiro; istoricheskii roman [The glory of Don Ramiro; a historical novel] Moscow, Goslitizdat, 1961. 279 p.

Translated by K. Zhikhareva from the Spanish *La gloria de don Ramiro*. Introductory article by F. Kel'in.

3677. Lynch, Benito. Sterviatniki "Floridy"; roman [The vultures of "Florida"; a novel] Moscow, Goslitizdat, 1963. 172 p.

Translated by A. Starostin from the Spanish *Los caranchos de La Florida*. Introductory article by M. Bylinkina.

3678. Mármol, José. Amalia; istoricheskii roman [Amalia; a historical novel] Moscow, Goslitizdat, 1961. 647 p.

Translated by M. Abezgauz and M. Deev from the Spanish. Introductory article by Z. Plavskin and L. Shur.

3679. Payró, Roberto Jorge. Zhenit'ba Lauchi; povest' [Laucha's marriage; a tale] Moscow, Goslitizdat, 1961. 48 p.

Translated by R. Lintser from the Spanish *El casamiento de Laucha*. Introductory article by A. Berezova.

3680. Rodríguez Alvarez, Alejandro (Alejandro Casona, *pseud.*) Derev'ia umiraiut stoia; komediia v trekh deistviiakh [The trees are dying standing upright; a comedy in three acts] Leningrad, Iskusstvo, 1959. 66 p.

Translated by N. L. Trauberg from the Spanish *Los árboles mueren de pie*.

3681. Ruiz Daudet, Carlos. Khuan nakhodit svoi put'; roman [Juan finds his way; a novel] Moscow, Izd-vo inostr. lit., 1961. 252 p.

Translated by R. Pokhlebkin from the Spanish *Juan se encuentra*. Introductory article by V. Kuz'mishchev.

3682. Valera y Alcalá Galiano, Juan. Pepita Khimenes; povest' [Pepita Jiménez; a tale] Moscow, Goslitizdat, 1959. 159 p.

Translated by A. Starostin from the Spanish. Introductory article by Z. Plavskin.

3683. Cambas, Alberto N. Batikum; rasskaz [Drumbeating; a story] Svyturys, no. 4, 1961: 23.

In Lithuanian. Translated from the Spanish.

3684. Constantini, Humberto. Skazhite chtonibud', doktor; rasskaz [Tell us something, doctor; a story] Zvezda, no. 3, Mar. 1959: 118–122.

Translated from the Spanish.

3685. Erbshtein, Pedro. Neobyknovennoe chudo; rasskaz [An unusual miracle; a story] V zashch. mira, no. 4, Apr. 1960: 72–75.

Translated from the Spanish.

3686. Floriani, Juan Armando. Obmanchivaia nadezhda. V polden'; rasskazy [Illusory hope. At noon; stories] Sov. profsoiuzy, v. 18, no. 24, Oct. 1962: 36–38.

Translated from the Spanish.

3687. ———. Ozarennye nadezhdoi; roman [Inspired with hope; a novel] Neva, no. 9, 1960: 95–148.

Translated from the Spanish.

3688. ———. Pervaia poluchka. Velosiped; rasskazy [First payday. A bicycle; stories] Smena, v. 37, no. 2, Jan. 1960: 22–23.

Translated from the Spanish.

3689. ———. Pervaia poluchka; rasskaz [The first payday; a story] Liesma, no. 3, 1960: 30–31.

In Latvian.

3690. Gandolfi Herrero, Aristides (Alvaro Yunque, *pseud.*) Bul'bul' nakhodit pokrovitelia. Deti nishchety; rasskazy ["Bulbul" finds a protector. The children of poverty; stories] Zvezda, no. 3, Mar. 1959: 122–129.

Translated from the Spanish *Bulbul encuentra un protector* and *Muchachos pobres*.

3691. ———. Butylka moloka; rasskaz [A bottle of milk; a story] Sabchota kali, no. 6, 1959: 5–7.

In Georgian. Translated from the Spanish.

3692. ———. Trilli nakhodit pokrovitelia; rasskaz [Trilli has found a protector; a story] Skola un gimene, no. 7, 1964: 36–38.

In Latvian. Translated from the Spanish *Bulbul encuentra un protector*.

3693. Gelman, Juan. Rech' v zashchitu Kuby; stikhi [A speech in defense of Cuba; verse] Inostr. lit., no. 9, Sept. 1961: 77–78.
Translated from the Spanish.

3694. ———. Vozzvanie protiv podgotovki atomnoi voiny. Oziabshie ruki—v karmanakh. Molitva bezrabotnogo; stikhi [An appeal against preparations for atomic war. Cold hand in pockets. The prayer of an unemployed worker; verse] Zvezda Vost., v. 27, no. 7, July 1959: 92–94.
Translated from the Spanish.

3695. González Tuñón, Raúl. Dobryi den' sen'ora Luna! Stikhi [Hello, Señora Luna! Verse] Inostr. lit., no. 1, Jan. 1960: 3–4.
Translated from the Spanish.

3696. ———. Iz "Pesni o Lenine"; stikhi [From the "Song about Lenin"; verse] Sib. ogni, no. 1, Jan. 1963: 7–8.
Translated from the Spanish.

3697. ———. Moe serdtse. Gitaristy iz Katuny [My heart. Guitarists from Catuna; verse] Inostr. lit., no. 12, 1960: 155–156.
Translated from the Spanish.

3698. ———. Moe serdtse. Gitaristy iz Katuny; stikhi [My heart. Guitarists from Catuna; verse] Agidel', no. 8, 1961: 75.
In Bashkir. Translated from the Spanish.

3699. ———. Pesn' o Lenine; stikhi [A song about Lenin; verse] Ogonek, v. 38, no. 16, Apr. 1960: 16.
Translated from the Spanish.

3700. ———. Stroki Uzbekistanu; stikhi [A letter to Uzbekistan; verse] Zvezda Vost., v. 32, no. 10, Oct. 1964: 93.
Translated from the Spanish.

3701. Hernández, Juan José. Igrai, Inesita; rasskaz [You must play, Inecita! A story] V zashch. mira, no. 12, Dec. 1961: 89–94.

3702. Huasi, Julio. Syn naroda. Poet snova na lone prirody; stikhi [Son of the people. A poet has returned to the country; verse] Inostr. lit., no. 9, Sept. 1961: 80–81.
Translated from the Spanish.

3703. Larra, Raúl. Bez perepochynku; roman [Without respite; a novel] Vsesvit, v. 2, no. 2, Feb. 1959: 29–115.
Translated from the Spanish.

3704. Palant, Pablo. Otets; rasskaz [Father; a story] Svyturys, no. 5, 1959: 24–25.
In Lithuanian. Translated from the Spanish.

3705. Pedroni, José B. Dereviannaia tachka; stikhi [A wooden wheelbarrow; verse] Agidel', no. 8, 1961: 76.
In Bashkir. Translated from the Spanish.

3706. ———. Masterok kamenshchika. Dereviannaia tachka; stikhi [A mason's trowel. A wooden wheelbarrow; verse] Inostr. lit., no. 12, 1960: 156–157.
Translated from the Spanish.

3707. Pisarello, Gerardo. Starik Poli; rasskaz [Old Poli; a story] Zvezda, no. 3, Mar. 1959: 129–133.
Translated from the Spanish.

3708. Ruiz Daudet, Carlos. Brat'ia; rasskaz [Brothers; a story] Ogonek, v. 38, no. 40, Oct. 1960: 10–11.
Translated from the Spanish.

3709. Silvain, Julio César. Segodniashnii den'; stikhi [This day; verse] Inostr. lit., no. 9, Sept. 1961: 78–80.
Translated from the Spanish.

3710. Tavosnanska, Gregorio. Otets; rasskaz [Father; a story] Zvezda, no. 3, Mar. 1959: 134–137.
Translated from the Spanish.

3711. Tejada Gómez, Armando. Devushka; stikhi [A girl; verse] Nov. mir., v. 37, no. 1, 1961: 16–17.
Translated from the Spanish.

b. Bolivia

3712. Lara, Jesús. Nasha krov'; roman [Our blood; a novel] Moscow, Izd-vo inostr. lit., 1962. 264 p.
Translated by T. Kumar'ian and I. Nikolaeva from the Spanish. Introductory article by IU. Dashkevich.

3713. Ramírez Velarde, Fernando. Shakhty skorbi; roman [The mines of gloom; a novel] Moscow, Goslitizdat, 1962. 199 p.
Translated by IU. Paporov from the Spanish Socavones de angustia. Introductory article by S. Mamontov.

3714. González Martínez de Ruiz, Guillermina. Zhenshchina; stikhi [A woman; verse] Sib. ogni, no. 1, Jan. 1963: 6–7.
Translated from the Spanish.

3715. Rus, Juan, *pseud.* Boliviie, krov'iu tvoieiu pyshu; virsh [Bolivia, I am writing with your blood; verse] Vsesvit, v. 6, no. 11, Nov. 1963: 3–8.
Translated from the Spanish.

c. Brazil

3716. Almeida, Manuel Antonio de. Zhizn' Leonardo, serzhanta politsii; roman [Reminiscences of Leonardo, a police sergeant; a novel] Moscow, Khudozh. lit., 1964. 255 p.
Translated by B. Nikonov from the Portuguese *Memórias de um sargento de milícias.* Introductory article by I. Terterian.

3717. Amado, Jorge. Gabriela; khronika odnogo provintsial'nogo goroda. Roman [Gabriela; chronicle of a provincial town. A novel] Moscow, Izd-vo inostr. lit. 1961. 500 p.   PQ9697.A647G34
Translated by G. Kalugin and A. Sipovich from the Portuguese *Gabriela, cravo e canela; crônica de uma citade do interior.* Introductory article by IU. Dashkevich. Also published in Estonian.
Reviewed by I. Terterian in *Inostr. lit.,* no. 5, 1963: 198–201.

3718. ———. Gorod Il'eus; roman [The city of Ilhéus; a novel] Moscow, Goslitizdat, 1963. 390 p.
Translated by I. Tynianova from the Portuguese *São Jorge dos Ilhéus.* Also published in Turkmen.

3719. ———. Krasnye vskhody; roman [Red shoots; a novel] Vologda, Knizhn. izd-vo, 1961. 311 p.
Translated from the Portuguese *Seara vermelha.* Also published in Ukrainian.

3720. ———. Neobychainaia konchina Kinkasa Sgin' Voda; satiricheskaia povest' [The strange death of Quincas Berro Dágua; a satirical tale] Baku, Azerneshr., 1964. 52 p.
In Azerbaijani. Translated by F. Eivazly from the Portuguese *A morte e a morte de Quincas Berro Dágua.*

3721. ———. Podpol'e svobody; roman [The underground of freedom; a novel] Riga, Latgosizdat, 1959. 811 p.
In Latvian. Translated by P. Vilip from the Portuguese *Os subterrâneos da liberdade.* Introductory article by F. Kel'in.
Reviewed by A. Tirzmala in *Padomju Latvijas sieviete,* no. 3, 1960: 26–27.

3722. ———. Starye moriaki; dve istorii porta Baiia [Old seamen; two stories of the port of Bahia] Moscow, Izd-vo inostr. lit., 1963. 278 p.
Translated by IU. Kalugin from the Portuguese *Os velhos marinheiros; duas histórias do cais Bahia.* Introductory article by Pedro Motta Lima.
Reviewed by I. Terterian in *Inostr. lit.,* no. 5, May 1963: 198–201; by V. Kuteishchikova in *Nov. mir,* v. 40, no. 7, July 1964: 242–244.

3723. ———. Starye moriaki; dve istorii porta Baiia [Old seamen; two stories of the port of Bahia] Moscow, Progress, 1964. 287 p.
Translated by IU. Kalugin from the Portuguese *Os velhos marinheiros; duas histórias do cais Bahia.* Introductory article by Pedro Motta Lima.

3724. Azevedo, Aluizio. Trushchoby; roman [Slums; a novel] Moscow, Goslitizdat, 1960. 256 p.
Translated by N. IA. Voinova from the Portuguese *O cortiço.* Introductory article by N. Voinova and Z. Plavskin.

3725. Barroso, Maria Alice. V doline Serra-Alta; roman [In the Serra Alta Valley; a novel] Moscow, Mol. gvardiia, 1960. 416 p.
Translated by V. Zhitkov and N. Tul'chinskaia from the Portuguese.

3726. Brazil'skie rasskazy [Brazilian stories] Moscow, Goslitizdat, 1959. 111 p.
Translated from the Portuguese. Introductory article by I. Terterian.
Reviewed by VI. Ivanov in *Inostr. lit.,* no. 5, May 1960: 260–261.

3727. Dias da Costa. Rabota; povest' [Work; a tale] Kiev, Derzhlitvydav, 1963. 38 p.
In Ukrainian. Translated from the Portuguese.

3728. Figueiredo, Guilherme de. Lisa i vinograd. Smeshnaia tragediia; pes'y [The fox and the grapes. Humorous tragedy; plays] Moscow, Iskusstvo, 1960. 169 p.
Translated by S. Liminik and P. Liminik from the Portuguese. Introductory article by Jorge Amado.

3729. Gomes, Alfredo Dias. Obet; p'esa v 3-kh deistviiakh [A vow; a play in three acts] Moscow, Iskusstvo, 1963. 104 p.
Translated by IU. Kalugin from the Portuguese.

3730. Gonzaga, Thomaz Antônio. Liry. Chiliiskie pis'ma; stikhi [Lyres. Chilean letters; verse] Moscow, Khudozh. lit., 1964. 175 p.
Translated by I. Tynianova from the Portuguese.

3731. Jurandir, Dalcidio. Parkovaia liniia; roman [The park line; a novel] Moscow, Izd-vo inostr. lit., 1962. 574 p.
Translated by G. Kalugin from the Portuguese Linha do parque. Introductory article by Jorge Amado.

3732. Lobato, José Bento Morteiro. Orden Zheltogo Diatla; povest' [The Order of the Yellow Woodpecker; a tale] Moscow, Detgiz, 1961. 288 p.
Translated by I. Tynianova from the Portuguese. Also published in Latvian, Ukrainian. and Estonian.

3733. Machado de Assis, Joaquim Maria. Don Kasmurro; roman [Don Casmurro; a novel] Moscow, Goslitizdat, 1961. 319 p.
Translated by T. Ivanova from the Portuguese. Introductory article by I. Terterian.

3734. Magno, Paschoal Carlos. Zavtra budet inym; p'esa v trekh deistviiakh [Tomorrow will be different; a play in three acts] Leningrad, Iskusstvo, 1963. 99 p.
Translated by P. V. Melkova from the Portuguese.

3735. Pedrosa, Milton. Noch' i nadezhda; rasskazy [Night and hope; stories] Moscow, Izd-vo inostr. lit., 1963. 83 p.
Translated by I. Nikolaeva from the Portuguese Noite e esperança.
Reviewed by Pedro Motta Lima in Inostr. lit., no. 5, May 1964: 262–263.

3736. Ramos, Graciliano. Issushennye zhizni; roman [Wasted lives; a novel] Moscow, Goslitizdat, 1961. 87 p.
Translated by S. Brandão and Z. Chernova from the Portuguese Vidas seccas. Introductory article by I. Terterian.

3737. Rego, José Lins do. Kangaseiro; roman [Cangaceiro; a novel] Moscow, Izd-vo inostr. lit., 1960. 293 p.

Translated by N. Tul'chinskaia from the Portuguese. Introductory article by V. Ermolaev.

3738. Santos, Marcelino dos. Pesnia istinnoi liubvi; stikhi [The song of true love; verse] Moscow, Goslitizdat, 1962. 101 p.
Translated by L. Nekrasova from the Portuguese. Introductory article by Nazim Hikmet.
Reviewed by L. Feigina in Inostr. lit., no. 12, 1963: 260.

3739. Schmidt, Afonso. Tainy San-Paulo; roman [Secrets of São Paulo; a novel] Vilnius, Goslitizdat, 1963. 311 p.
In Lithuanian. Translated from the Russian.

3740. Soromenho, Fernando Monteiro de Castro. Mertvaia zemlia; roman [Dead land; a novel] Moscow, Goslitizdat, 1962.
Translated by A. Dolgopol'skii and L. Nekrasova from the Portuguese Terra morta.

3741. Amado, Jorge. Neobychainaia konchina Kinkasa Sgin' Voda; satiricheskaia povest' [The strange death of Quincas Berro Dágua; a satirical tale] Inostr. lit., no. 5, May 1963: 87–114.
Translated from the Portuguese.

3742. Dias de Costa. Chemodan; opovidannia [A valise; a story] Vsesvit, v. 7, no. 11, Nov. 1964: 152–154.
Translated from the Portuguese.

3743. Figueiredo, Guilherme de. Lisa i vinograd; p'esa [The fox and the grapes; a play] Sovetakan grakanutiun, no. 12, 1962: 96–127.
In Armenian. Translated from the Portuguese.

3744. Freitas, R. de. Liudy—syl'ni. Novyi budynok; opovidannia [The people are strong. The new house; stories] Vsesvit, v. 3, no. 2, Feb. 1960: 94–100.
Translated from the Portuguese.

3745. Lima Barreto, Afonso Henrique de. Chelovek, kotoryi znal iavanskii iazyk; rasskaz [A man who spoke Javanese; a story] Svyturys, no. 23, 1959: 21–23.
In Lithuanian. Translated from the Portuguese.

3746. Lobato, José Bento Monteiro. Donna Ekspedita; rasskaz [Dona Expedita; a story] Svyturys, no. 16, 1960: 21–22.

In Lithuanian. Translated from the Portuguese.

3747. Medeiros, Selene de. Alma-Atinskie gory; stikhi [The mountains of Alma-Ata; verse] Zhuldyz, no. 11, 1962: 91.
In Kazakh. Translated from the Portuguese.

3748. Osorno, L. Mir; stikhi [Peace; verse] Liesma, no. 7, 1961: 10.
In Latvian. Translated from the Portuguese.

3749. Souza, Ethel de. Gordost' materi; novella [A mother's pride; a story] Kazakstan aielderi, no. 7, 1960: 25.
In Kazakh. Translated from the Portuguese.

3750. ———. Materinskaia gordost'; brazil'skaia novella [A mother's pride; a Brazilian story] Zhen. mira, no. 8, 1959: 32–33.
Translated from the Portuguese.

d. Chile

3751. Alvarado, Edesio. Beglets; povest' [The fugitive; a tale] Tallinn, Gas.-zhurn. izd-vo, 1964. 63 p.
In Estonian. Translated by O. Ojamaa from the Spanish.

3752. Blest Gana, Alberto. Martin Rivas; roman [Martín Rivas; a novel] Moscow, Goslitizdat, 1963. 416 p.
Translated by E. Braginskaia and IA. Lesiuk from the Spanish. Introductory article by IA. Lesiuk.

3753. Castro, Baltazar. Moi tovarishch otets; roman [My comrade father; a novel] Moscow, Izd-vo inostr. lit., 1960. 200 p.
Translated by N. Zagorskaia and IU. Paporov from the Spanish Mi camarada padre.

3754. Chiliiskie rasskazy [Chilean stories] Moscow, Goslitizdat, 1961. 191 p.
Translated from the Spanish. Introductory article by N. Lozinskaia.

3755. Coloane, Francisco A. Ognennaia Zemlia; rasskazy [Tierra del Fuego; stories] Moscow, Izd-vo khud. lit., 1963. 223 p.
Translated from the Spanish. Introductory article by I. Vinnichenko.
Reviewed by G. Kornilova in Vokrug sveta, no. 9, Sept. 1964: 62–63.

3756. Délano, Luis Enrique. Ol'ga; roman [Olga; a novel] Moscow, Izd-vo inostr. lit., 1962. 112 p.
Translated by IU. Dashkevich from the Spanish.

3757. Gutiérrez, Joaquín. Kokori; povist'-kazka [Cocori; a fairy tale] Kiev, Ditvydav, 1960. 63 p.
Translated by L. Olevs'kyi and M. Sydorenko from the Spanish.

3758. Lillo, Baldomero. Post no. 12; rasskazy [Post no. 12; stories] Moscow, Goslitizdat, 1962. 160 p.
Translated from the Spanish.

3759. Mistral, Gabriela. Lirika [Lyric poems] Moscow, Goslitizdat, 1963. 207 p.
Translated from the Spanish. Introductory article by O. Savich.

3760. ———. Stikhi [Poems] Moscow, Goslitizdat, 1959. 247 p.
Translated from the Spanish. Introductory article by O. Savich.
Reviewed by A. Martynova in Inostr. lit., no. 3, Mar. 1961: 255; by L. Ospovat in Nov. mir, v. 36, no. 3, Mar. 1960: 244–246.

3761. Negro, Juan. Mal'chik s poberezh'ia; povest' [A boy from the seashore; a tale] Moscow, Detgiz, 1962. 63 p.
Translated by I. Cherevataia from the Spanish.

3762. Neruda, Pablo. "Gimny Kube" i drugie poemy ["Hymns to Cuba" and other poems] Moscow, Pravda, 1961. 32 p.
Translated by P. Grushko from the Spanish.

3763. ———. Plavan'ia i vozvrashcheniia; izbrannoe [Voyages and homecomings; selected verse] Moscow, Progress, 1964. 399 p.
Translated by M. Aliger and O. Savich from the Spanish Navigaciones y regresos. Introductory article by I. Ehrenburg.

3764. ———. Vseobshchaia pesnia; izbrannye stikhi i poemy [Universal song; selected verse and poems] Tiflis, Nakaduli, 1963. 118 p.
In Georgian. Translated from the Spanish Canto general.
Reviewed by K. Koberidze in Georgian in Tsiskari, no. 11, 1963: 149–151.

3765. Parra, Nicanor. Iz raznykh knig; stikhi [From different books; verse] Moscow, Progress, 1964. 94 p.
Translated by M. Aliger from the Spanish.

3766. Teitelboim, Volodia. Semia v peske; roman [Seed in the sand; a novel] Moscow, Izd-vo inostr. lit., 1959. 415 p.
Translated by B. Kostritsyn from the Spanish *La semilla en la arena.*
Reviewed by B. Morozov in *Vsesvit*, v. 2, no. 1, 1959: 138–139; by V. Kuteishchikova in *Inostr. lit.*, no. 7, July 1960: 262–264.

3767. Aguirre, Margarita. Karolina Freire; rasskaz [Carolina Freire; a story] Kobieta radziecka, no. 7, 1961: 4–5.
In Polish. Translated from the Spanish.

3768. ———. Karolina Freire; rasskaz [Carolina Freire; a story] Tarybine moteris, no. 7, 1961: 4–5.
In Lithuanian. Translated from the Spanish.

3769. Délano, Luis Enrique. Ol'ga; glavy iz romana [Olga; excerpts from a novel] Inostr. lit., no. 12, Dec. 1960: 126–150.
Translated from the Spanish.

3770. ———. Pesn' o Sovetskom Soiuze; stikhi [A song about the Soviet Union; verse] Druzh. nar., no. 1. Jan. 1959: 107.

3771. Espinoza, Leonardo. Port obmana; roman [The port of deceit; a novel] Sov. Ukr., v. 10, no. 2, Feb. 1960: 92–125; v. 10, no. 3, Mar. 1960: 100–134.
Translated from the Spanish.

3772. Franzani, Victor. Ozarennaia Kuba; stikhi [Radiant Cuba; verse] Don, v. 5, no. 1, Jan. 1961: 59.
Translated from the Spanish.

3773. Lillo, Baldomero. "Serebrianaia udochka"; rasskaz [The silver fishing rod; a story] Smena, v. 37, no. 24, Dec. 1960: 19–21.
Translated from the Spanish.

3774. Mistral, Gabriela. Iz tsikla "Privideniia"; stikhi [From the cycle "Ghosts"; verse] Tsiskari, no. 6, 1964: 44–48.
In Georgian. Translated from the Spanish.

3775. ———. Poemy materei [Poems of mothers] Nõukogude naine, no. 5, 1960: 14.
In Estonian. Translated from the Spanish.

3776. ———. Poemy materei. Poemy skorbiashchei materi [Poems of mothers. Poems of a grieving mother] Sabchota kali, no. 2, 1960: 21.
In Georgian. Translated from the Spanish.

3777. Moncada, J. Lenin; stikhi [Lenin; verse] Edebi Bashkortostan, no. 4, 1960: 47.
In Bashkir. Translated from the Spanish.

3778. Neruda, Pablo. Chto oni ostavili v kosmose; stikhi [What they left in outer space; verse] Inostr. lit., no. 9, Sept. 1962: 3–4.

3779. ———. Gimny Kube; stikhi [Hymns to Cuba; verse] Druzh. nar., no. 1, Jan. 1961: 9–11.
Translated from the Spanish.

3780. ———. Golos poeta; stikhi [A poet's voice; verse] Ogonek, v. 42, no. 30, July 1964: 17–18.
Translated from the Spanish.

3781. ———. Griadushchee rozhdaetsia seichas; stikhi [The future is being born now; verse] Sov. zhen., v. 16, no. 3, 1960: 35.

3782. ———. Heraichnae dzeianne; versh [A heroic deed; verse] Belarus', v. 21, no. 7, July 1964: 10.
Translated from the Spanish.

3783. ———. I vosprianula gordaia Kuba; stikhi [Proud Cuba is alive again; verse] Drosha, no. 1, 1962: 18.
In Georgian. Translated from the Spanish.

3784. ———. Kamni Chili; stikhi [The stones of Chile; verse] Inostr. lit., no. 3' Mar. 1963: 57–60.
Translated from the Spanish.

3785. ———. Lenin; otryvok iz stikhotvoreniia [Lenin; excerpt from a poem] Sovetakan grakanutiun, no. 4, 1959: 9–11.
In Armenian. Translated from the Spanish.

3786. ———. Lenin; stikhi [Lenin; verse] Padomju Latvijas sieviete, no. 4, 1960: insert.
In Latvian. Translated from the Spanish.

3787. ———. Leninu; stikhi [To Lenin; verse] Looming, no. 4, 1960: 536–539.
In Estonian. Translated from the Spanish.

3788. ———. Mat' i Zemlia; rasskaz [Mother and the Earth; a story] Zhen. mira, no. 3, 1964: 34.
Translated from the Spanish.

3789. ———. Molodezhi Karibskogo moria. No vse-taki skol'ko? Stikhi [To the youth of the Caribbean region. How much it is, after all? Verse] Tsiskari, no. 12, 1961: 70–71.
In Georgian. Translated from the Spanish.

3790. ———. Novye stikhi [New poems] Ogonek, v. 40, no. 36, Sept. 1962: 12–13.
Translated from the Spanish.

3791. ———. Oda zvezdam [An ode to the stars] Nistrul, no. 7, 1960: 90–91.
In Moldavian. Translated from the Spanish.

3792. ———. Pesn' o podvige; glavy iz poemy [Song about a heroic deed; excerpts from a poem] Inostr. lit., no. 12, 1960: 2–21.
Translated from the Spanish.

3793. ———. Pesnia mira; stikhi [The song of peace; verse] Zhuldyz, no. 3, 1962: 92–93.
In Kazakh. Translated from the Spanish.

3794. ———. Pesnia mira; stikhi [The song of peace; verse] Zhuldyz, no. 7, 1964: 107.
In Kazakh. Translated from the Spanish.

3795. ———. Privet dushistomu khlebu i kamniu; novye stikhi [Greetings to the fragrant bread and stone; new poems] Ogonek, v. 38, no. 40, Oct. 1960: 17.
Translated from the Spanish.

3796. ———. Stikhi etogo goda [Poems of this year] Inostr. lit., no. 7, July 1964: 3–5.
Translated from the Spanish.

3797. Quevedo, Franklin. I u nas poiavitsia rumianets; rasskaz [Our cheeks will be rosy too; a story] Inostr. lit., no. 8, Aug. 1964: 88–92.
Translated from the Spanish.

3798. Rokha, Winétt de. Lenin; stikhi [Lenin; verse] Sovetakan grakanutiun, no. 4, 1960: 41.
In Armenian. Translated from the Spanish.

3799. Urrutia, Praccedes. Shchob ty synku, z myrom spav; virsh [So that you, my son,

may sleep quietly; verse] Vsesvit, v. 2, no. 1, Jan. 1959: 67.

3800. Vicentini, María Luisa. Odnazhdy vecherom; rasskas [One evening; a story] Sov. profsoiuzy, v. 16, no. 4, Feb. 1960: 58–59.
Translated from the Spanish.

e. Colombia

3801. Caballero Calderón, Eduardo. S'ervo bezzemel'nyi; roman [Landless Siervo; a novel] Moscow, Goslitizdat, 1963. 208 p.
Translated by S. Alenikova and N. Farfel' from the Spanish Siervo sin tierra. Introductory article by Z. Plavskin.

3802. López, Luis Carlos. Griby na kochke; satiricheskie stikhi [Mushrooms on a mound; satirical poems] Moscow, Goslitizdat, 1961. 222 p.
Translated by O. Savich from the Spanish. Reviewed by E. Levontin in Inostr. lit., no. 7, July 1962: 244–245.

3803. Arias Suárez, Eduardo. Guardian i ia; rasskaz [Guardian and I; a story] Nov. mir, v. 37, no. 5, May 1961: 123–216.
Translated from the Spanish.

3804. López, Luis Carlos. Izbrannye stikhi [Selected poems] Inostr. lit., no. 1, Jan. 1959: 138–143.

3805. Novás Calvo, Lino. Plokhoi chelovek; rasskaz [The bad man; a story] Nov. mir, v. 37, no. 5, May 1961: 108–119.
Translated from the Spanish.

3806. Truque, Carlos Arturo. Da zdravstvuiut tovarishchi! Rasskaz [Long live comrades! A story] Don, v. 6, no. 1, Jan. 1962: 114–119.
Translated from the Spanish.

3807. Zalamea, Jorge. Vykradennia sabinianok; romantychnyi fars na 3 dii [The rape of the Sabine women; a romantic farce in three acts] Vsesvit, v. 4, no. 7, July 1960: 80–98.
Translated from the Spanish.

f. Costa Rica

3808. Fallas, Carlos Luis. Zelenyi ad; roman [Green hell; a novel] Tallinn, Estogsizdat, 1961. 199 p.

In Estonian. Translated by I. Apanaskii and V. Villandi from the Spanish *Mamita Yunai*. Introductory article by I. Palchenkov and I. Apanaskii.

3809. Fallas, Carlos Luis. Vybory v legendarnom Tizingali; otryvok iz romana [Elections in legendary Tisingal; excerpt from a novel] Noorus, no. 2, 1959: 23–26.
In Estonian. Translated from the Spanish.

g. Cuba

3810. Alonso, Dora. Bezzashchitnaia zemlia; roman [Defenseless land; a novel] Moscow, Izd-vo inostr. lit., 1963. 167 p.
Translated by S. Vaf and T. Kumar'ian from the Spanish *Tierra inerme*. Introductory article by L. Ospovat. Also published in Ukrainian.

3811. Cardoso, Onelio Jorge. Korallovyi kon'; rasskazy [The coral horse; stories] Moscow, Goslitizdat, 1962. 159 p.
Translated from the Spanish. Introductory article by O. Savich. Also published in Estonian.
Reviewed by V. Kuteishchikova in *Inostr. lit.*, no. 1, Jan. 1964: 267–268.

3812. Carpentier, Alejo. Poteriannye sledy; roman [Lost tracks; a novel] Moscow, Khudozh. lit., 1964.
Translated from the Spanish *Los pasos perdidos*.

3813. ———. TSarstvo zemnoe; povest' [The kingdom of this world; a tale] Moscow, Izd-vo inostr. lit., 1962. 112 p.
Translated by R. Pokhlebkin from the Spanish *El reino de este mundo*. Introductory article by IU. Dashkevich.

3814. ———. TSarstvo zemnoe; povest' [The kingdom of this world; a tale] 2d ed. Moscow, Izd-vo inostr. lit., 1963. 112 p.
Translated by R. Pokhlebkin from the Spanish *El reino de este mundo*. Introductory article by IU. Dashkevich.

3815. Crespo López, Margarita. Gory stanoviatsia krasnymi; p'esa v 3-kh deistviiakh [The mountains are turning red; a play in three acts] Moscow, Izd-vo inostr. lit., 1962. 75 p.
Translated by IU. Paporov from the Spanish.

3816. Desnoes, Edmundo. Vozvrashchenie; roman [Homecoming; a novel] Moscow, Progress, 1964. 159 p.
Translated by IU. Pogosov from the Spanish *No hay problema*. Introductory article by B. Polevoi.

3817. Gaviria, Rafael Humberto. Luna i vintovka; roman [The moon and a rifle; a novel] Moscow, Izd-vo inostr. lit., 1963. 205 p.
Translated by M. Abezgauz from the Spanish. Introductory article by V. Kuteishchikova.
Reviewed by Ezra Levontin in *Inostr. lit.*, no. 11, Nov. 1964: 266–267.

3818. González de Cascorro, Raúl. Oni ne proshli; rasskazy [They did not pass through; stories] Moscow, Voenizdat, 1963. 102 p.
Translated by IU. Pevtsov and others from the Spanish *Gente de Playa Girón*. Introductory article by S. Avdeev.

3819. Guillén, Nicolás. Stikhi [Poems] Tbilisi, Sabchota Sokartvelo, 1961. 87 p.
In Georgian. Translated by G. Gogiashvili from the Spanish.
Reviewed by N. Mshvildadze in *Mnatobl*, no. 1, 1963: 190–191.

3820. ———. Stikhi [Poems] Frunze, Kyrgyzstan, 1964. 140 p.
In Kirghiz. Translated by A. Toktomushev from the Spanish.

3821. Hernández Catá, Alfonso. Zhemchuzhina; rasskazy [The pearl; stories] Moscow, Gos. izd-vo khudozh. lit., 1962. 165 p.   PQ7389.H33Z27
Translated from the Spanish *El huevo de cristal*. Also published in Lithuanian.
Reviewed by V. Kuteishchikova in *Inostr. lit.*, no. 1, Jan. 1964: 267–268.

3822. Jamís, Fayad. Za etu svobodu; stikhi [For this freedom; verse] Kiev, Molod', 1964. 100 p.
In Ukrainian. Translated by A. Dovhonos and T. IUkova from the Spanish *Por esta libertad*. Introductory article by T. IUkova.

3823. Kubinskie rasskazy [Cuban stories] Yerevan, Aipetrat, 1961. 129 p.
In Armenian. Translated by M. Maksapetian from the Russian. Introductory article by S. Mamontov. Also pubished in Turkmen and Tatar.

3824. Martí, José. Severoamerikanskie stseny [North American scenes] Moscow, Goslitizdat, 1963. 363 p.

Translated from the Spanish *Escenas norteamericanas.* Introductory article by V. Stolbov. Also published in an edition for the blind.

Reviewed by N. Tomashevskii in *V mire knig*, v. 3, no. 9, Sept. 1963: 38; by S. Emel'iannikov in *Inostr. lit.*, no. 5, May 1964: 264–266.

3825. Mcza y Suárez Inclán, Ramón. Moi diadia chinovnik; roman [My uncle, the government employee; a novel] Moscow, Khudozh. lit., 1964. 294 p.

Translated by V. Vinogradov from the Spanish *Mi tío el empleado.* Introductory article by V. S. Stolbov.

3826. Obyden, K., *and* V. Stolbov, *comps.* Kubinskaia poeziia [Cuban poetry] Moscow, Goslitizdat, 1959. 183 p.

Translated by V. Stolbov from the Spanish. Introductory article by V. Stolbov.

Reviewed by F. Matveev in *V mire knig*, v. 1, no. 2, Feb. 1961: 33.

3827. Olema García, Daura. Volontery revoliutsii; povest' [Volunteers of the revolution; a tale] Moscow, Mol. gvardiia, 1963. 142 p.

Translated by IU. Pogosov from the Spanish *Maestra voluntaria.*

3828. Paporov, IU. N., *comp.* Zaria nad Kuboi; stikhi [Dawn over Cuba; verse] Moscow, Goslitizdat, 1962. 255 p.

Translated from the Spanish. Introductory article by Juan Marinello.

Reviewed by S. Emel'iannikov in *V mire knig*, v. 3, no. 4, Apr. 1963: 40.

3829. Perera Soto, Hilda. Negritenok Apolo; rasskaz [Apolo, a little Negro; a story] Moscow, Detgiz, 1962. 64 p.

Translated by E. Vol'f from the Spanish *Cuentos de Apolo.* Also published in Ukrainian and Estonian.

3830. Pesni trostnika; obraztsy kubinskoi poezii [Songs of sugar cane; samples of Cuban poetry] Dushanbe, Tadzhikgosizdat, 1962. 66 p.

In Tajik. Translated by A. Adkhamov from the Russian.

3831. Samoilov, D., *ed.* Molodye poety Kuby; sbornik [Young poets of Cuba; a collection] Moscow, Mol. gvardiia, 1963. 104 p.

Translated from the Spanish. Introductory article by Heberto Padilla.

3832. Soler Puig, José. Bertil'on 166; roman [Bertillon 166; a novel] Moscow, Goslitizdat, 1961. 45 p.

Translated by A. Makarov from the Spanish.

3833. ————. Bertil'on 166; roman [Bertillon 166; a novel] Moscow, Mol. gvardiia, 1961. 140 p.

Translated by A. Makarov from the Spanish. Also published in Ukrainian, Moldavian, Estonian, Latvian, Turkmen, and Azerbaijani.

Reviewed by I. Gubanov in *Mol. gvardiia*, no. 4, Apr. 1963: 311–312; by IU. Korzov in *Vsesvit*, v. 5, no. 10, Oct. 1962: 119–120; by B. Riabinin in *Ural*, no. 9, 1961: 171–172.

3834. Vesna Kuby; virshi ta opovidannia kubyns'kykh pys'mennykiv [Cuban spring; poems and stories by Cuban authors] Kiev, Molod', 1962. 253 p.

Translated from the Spanish. Introductory article by D. Pavlychko.

3835. Villaverde, Cirilo. Sesiliia Val'des ili Kholm Angela; roman [Cecilia Valdés or Angel's Hill; a novel] Moscow, Goslitizdat, 1963. 582 p.

Translated by P. Glazova and L. Pokrovskaia from the Spanish *Cecilia Valdés, o La Loma del Angel.* Introductory article by G. Stepanov and IU. Khokhlov.

3836. Alonso, Dora. Staryi Chano; opovidannia [Grandfather Chano; a story] Vsesvit, v. 4, no. 4, Apr. 1961: 10–13.

Translated from the Spanish.

3837. Arenal, Humberto. Svyntseve sontse; povist' [The sun beats down; a tale] Vsesvit, v. 6, no. 1, Jan. 1963: 75–102.

Translated from the Spanish.

3838. Badia, Nora. Negr Senen; rasskaz [Senen, the Negro; a story] Znamia, v. 33, no. 1, Jan. 1963: 145–149.

Translated from the Spanish.

3839. ————. Negr Senen; rasskaz [Senen, the Negro; a story] Sadoi Shark, no. 7, 1964: 87–92.

In Tajik. Translated from the Russian.

3840. Ballagas, Emilio. Kolybel'naia; stikhi [The lullaby; verse] Zanoni Tochikiston, no. 4, 1962: 16.
In Tajik. Translated from the Spanish.

3841. Barnet, Enrique. Kali na belym svetse; versh [When in this good world; verse] Belarus', v. 20, no. 5, 1963: 1.
Translated from the Spanish.

3842. Barsino i ego druz'ia; skazka [Barzino and his friends; a tale] Sem'ia i shkola, v. 18, no. 8, Aug. 1963: 28–29.
Translated from the Spanish,

3843. Bayo, Alberto. Kommunistom budesh' nazvan ty; stikhi [They will call you "the Communist"; verse] Don, v. 7, no. 10, Oct. 1963: 122–123.
Translated from the Spanish.

3844. Boti y Barreiro, Regino Eladio. Dozhd' v gorakh; stikhi [Rain in the mountains; verse] Mnatobi, no. 12, 1963: 67.
In Georgian. Translated from the Spanish.

3845. Capote, María Elena. Aloima; rasskaz [Aloima; a story] Zhen. mira, no. 10, 1964: 29.
Translated from the Spanish.

3846. Cardoso, Onelio Jorge. Moia sestra Visiia; rasskaz [My sister Vicia; a story] Literaturuli Adzhara, no. 3, 1964: 36–39.
In Georgian. Translated from the Spanish.

3847. ———. Nino. U gornoi dorogi; rasskazy [Nino. At the site of a mountain road; stories] Pergale, no. 1, 1964: 108–114.
In Lithuanian. Translated from the Russian.

3848. ———. O khrabrykh okhotnikakh, natianutykh lasso i krovozhadnykh zhiteliakh Kasimbu; rasskaz [Brave hunters, taut lassos, and the bloodthirsty inhabitants of Casimba; a story] Musu girios, no. 12, 1963: 26–27.
In Lithuanian. Translated from the Spanish.

3849. ———. Stare zalizo; opovidannia [Old iron; a story] Vsesvit, v. 5, no. 2, Feb. 1962: 108–110.
Translated from the Spanish.

3850. ———. Ugol'shchiki; rasskaz [Charcoal burners; a story] Vokrug sveta, no. 6, June 1962: 9–12.
Translated from the Spanish.

3851. Carrión, Miguel de. Sfinks; roman [The sphinx; a novel] Vsesvit, v. 7, no. 9, Sept. 1964: 11–55.
Translated from the Spanish.

3852. Castellanos, Julio. Znamia; rasskaz [The banner; a story] Sadoi Shark, no. 7, 1964: 92–95.
In Tajik. Translated from the Russian.

3853. ———. Znamia; rasskaz [The banner; a story] Jaunimo gretos, no. 10, 1960: 19–20.
In Lithuanian. Translated from the Spanish.

3854. ———. Znamia; rasskaz [The banner; a story] Svyturys, no. 20, 1960: 25.
In Lithuanian. Translated from the Spanish.

3855. Desnoes, Edmundo. Vozvrashchenie; roman [Homecoming; a novel] Inostr. lit., no. 7, July 1963: 4–100.
Translated from the Spanish.

3856. Díaz Martínez, Manuel. Khleb. IA zdes'; stikhi [Bread. I am here; verse] Inostr. lit. no. 4, Apr. 1964: 163–164.
Translated from the Spanish.

3857. Fernández, P. A. Kantata gorodu Sant-IAgo; otryvok iz poemy [A cantata to the city of Santiago; excerpt from a poem] Sovet edebiiaty, no. 2, 1961: 8–9.
In Tatar. Translated from the Spanish.

3858. Fernández Retamar, Roberto. Polehlym; virsh [To those who died for their country; verse] Vsesvit, v. 4, no. 4, Apr. 1961: 5.
Translated from the Spanish.

3859. ———. Smena; stikhi [A new generation; verse] Inostr. lit., no. 12, Dec. 1960: 125.
Translated from the Spanish.

3860. ———. Smena; stikhi [A new generation; verse] Sovet edebiiaty, no. 2, 1961: 9.
In Tatar. Translated from the Spanish.

3861. Francia, Sergio. Otvazhnye narody; stikhi [Brave peoples; verse] Sib. ogni, no. 1, Jan. 1963: 4.
Translated from the Spanish.

3862. González de Cascorro, Raúl. Kubinskie rasskazy [Cuban stories] Inostr. lit., no. 11, Nov. 1962: 10–19.
Translated from the Spanish.

3863. ———. S chuzhogo plecha; rasskaz [A secondhand dress; a story] Musu žodis, no. 4, 1963: 5–8.
In Lithuanian. Translated from the Spanish.

3864. ———. Shostyi trup; opovidannia [The sixth corpse; a story] Vsesvit, v. 4, no. 4, Apr. 1961: 14–18.
Translated from the Spanish.

3865. ———. Vot pochemu ia rasskazyvaiu vam; rasskaz [That is why I am telling you; a story] Pergale, no. 1, 1964: 114–120.
In Lithuanian. Translated from the Russian.

3866. Guerra, Jorge. Reforma; rasskaz [The reform; a story] Sov. zhen., v. 17, no. 3, 1961: 29–30.

3867. Guillén, Nicolás. Chetyre stikhotvoreniia [Four poems] Inostr. lit., no. 7, July 1962: 173–177.
Translated from the Spanish.

3868. ———. Chto znaiu o shakhmatakh ia? Stikhi [What do I know about chess? Verse] Shakh. v SSSR, v. 36, no. 1, Jan. 1960: 6.
Translated from the Spanish.

3869. ———. Devochka, stavshaia vzrosloi; stikhi [The girl who grew up; verse] Sib. ogni, no. 1, Jan. 1963: 3–4.
Translated from the Spanish.

3870. ———. Dobryi den' Fidel'! Stikhi [Hello, Fidel! Verse] Inostr. lit., no. 12, 12, 1960: 122–123.
Translated from the Spanish.

3871. ———. Dobryi den', Fidel'! Stikhi [Hello, Fidel! Verse] Agidel', no. 8, 1961: 70.
In Bashkir. Translated from the Spanish.

3872. ———. Dobryi den', Fidel'! Stikhi [Hello, Fidel! Verse] Svyturys, no. 3, 1961: 3.
In Lithuanian. Translated from the Spanish.

3873. ———. Dobryi den' Fidel'! Stikhi [Hello, Fidel! Verse] IAlkyn, no. 7, 1963: 6.
In Tatar. Translated from the Spanish.

3874. ———. Dobryi den', Fidel'! Stikhi [Hello, Fidel! Verse] Sovet edebiiaty, no. 2, 1961: 4–5.
In Tatar. Translated from the Spanish.

3875. ———. Dva mal'chonka. Kolybel'naia chtoby razbudit' malen'kogo negra; stikhi [Two boys. A lullaby to wake up a little Negro boy; verse] Skynteia leniniste, no. 9, 1960: 6–7.
In Moldavian. Translated from the Spanish.

3876. ———. Elegiia; stikhi [Elegy; verse] Nistrul, no. 7, 1960: 94–96.
In Moldavian. Translated from the Spanish.

3877. ———. Gimn rodnoi stranc; stikhi [A hymn to my country; verse] Sovet edebiiaty, no. 2, 1961: 5–6.
In Tatar. Translated from the Spanish.

3878. ———. Gliadia na "Oksford." Anna-Mariia. Otvechai! Stikhi [When I see the "Oxford." Ana-María. Answer! Verse] Sov. zhen., v. 20, no. 10, 1964: 27.
Translated from the Spanish.

3879. ———. Khose Ramon poet v bare; stikhi [José Ramón sings in a barroom; verse] Nistrul, no. 11, 1960: 11.
In Moldavian. Translated from the Spanish.

3880. ———. Kogda solovei poet na vershine Turkino; stikhi [When a nightingale sings atop Turquino Hill; verse] Karogs, no. 1, 1961: 3–4.
In Latvian. Translated from the Spanish.

3881. ———. Kolumbiia; stikhi [Colombia; verse] Isk. kino, no. 11, 1962: 15.
Translated from the Spanish.

3882. ———. Kubinskaia pesnia; stikhi [Cuban song; verse] Ogonek, v. 38, no. 8, Feb. 1960: 5.
Translated from the Spanish.

3883. ———. Lenin; stikhi [Lenin; verse] Smcna, v. 37, no. 13, July 1960: 10.
Translated from the Spanish.

3884. ———. Lenin. Zemlia na gorakh i na ravnine. Ty mozhesh'? Stikhi [Lenin. The land of our mountains and valleys. Can you? Verse] Nov. mir, v. 36, no. 1, Jan. 1960: 73–76.
Translated from the Spanish.

3885. ———. Moia liubimaia; stikhi [My beloved; verse] Tavan Atal, no. 3, 1964: 82.
In Chuvash. Translated from the Spanish.

3886. ———. Novoe; stikhi [New poems] Inostr. lit., no. 11, Nov. 1964: 3–6.
Translated from the Spanish.

3887. ——. Pesnia dvukh soldat; stikhi [The song of two soldiers; verse] Nov. mir, v. 37, no. 1, Jan. 1961: 15. Translated from the Spanish.

3888. ——. Pisni [Songs] Vsesvit, v. 7, no. 1, Jan. 1964: 3–5. Translated from the Spanish.

3889. ——. Po doroge. Moia devchonka. Malen'kaia plovdivskaia ballada. Venetsuela; stikhi [On the road. My girl. A brief Plovdiv ballad. Venezuela; verse] Nõukogude naine, no. 3, 1962: 2. In Estonian. Translated from the Spanish.

3890. ——. Puerto-rikans'ka pisnia; virsh [Puerto Rican song; verse] Vsesvit, v. 4, no. 4, Apr. 1961: 7. Translated from the Spanish.

3891. ——. Ruka Lenina; stikhi [Lenin's hand; verse] Sovetakan grakanutiun, no. 4, 1960: 39. In Armenian. Translated from the Spanish.

3892. ——. Svershilos'! Stikhi [It happened! Verse] Don, v. 5, no. 1, Jan. 1961: 57–58. Translated from the Spanish.

3893. ——. Vizhu tvoiu krasotu; stikhi [I see your beauty; verse] Zanoni Tochikiston, no. 4, 1962: 16. In Tajik. Translated from the Spanish.

3894. Heredia, José María. Gimn izgnannika; stikhi [An exile's hymn; verse] Mnatobi, no. 12, 1963: 67–68. In Georgian. Translated from the Spanish.

3895. Hernández Catá, Alfonso. Malen'kaia galisiika; rasskaz [The little Galician girl; a story] IAlov, no. 5, 1963: 20–22. In Chuvash. Translated from the Russian.

3896. Indio Nabori, *pseud.* Boiahuzy; virsh [Cowards; verse] Dnipro, v. 38, no. 1, Jan. 1964: 63. Translated from the Spanish.

3897. Jamís, Fayad. Korabli; virsh [Ships; verse] Dnipro, v. 38, no. 1, Jan. 1964: 64. Translated from the Spanish.

3898. ——. Milisiana; virsh [A "miliciana"; verse] Rad. zhin., v. 19, no. 1, Jan. 1964: 19. Translated from the Spanish.

3899. ——. Pisnia [A song] Zmina, no. 2, Feb. 1964: 7.

3900. ——. Slushaite! Stikhi [Listen! Verse] Inostr. lit., no. 12, 1960: 123–125. Translated from the Spanish.

3901. ——. Slushaite! Stikhi [Listen! Verse] Agidel', no. 8, 1961: 73. In Bashkir. Translated from the Spanish.

3902. ——. Sredi liudei. Korabli v portu Gavany; stikhi [Among people. Ships in the port of Havana; verse] Inostr. lit., no. 4, Apr. 1964: 162–163. Translated from the Spanish.

3903. ——. Vam poiu; stikhi [I sing for you; verse] Sovet edebiiaty, no. 2, 1961: 6–8. In Tatar. Translated from the Spanish.

3904. López-Charcález, Luis M. A ion zha byu dzitsem; apaviadanne [He was a child after all; a story] Belarus', v. 21, no. 1, Jan. 1964: 18. Translated from the Spanish.

3905. Lorenzo Fuentes, José. Goio ide v kooperatyv; opovidannia [Goyo joins an agricultural cooperative; a story] Vsesvit, v. 4, no. 4, Apr. 1961: 19–20. Translated from the Spanish.

3906. ——. Golos sovesti; rasskaz [The voice of conscience; a story] Zvaigzne, no. 23, 1960: 18. In Latvian. Translated from the Spanish.

3907. ——. Sim realiv; opovidannia [Seven reales; a story] Vsesvit, v. 4, no. 4, Apr. 1961: 8–9. Translated from the Spanish.

3908. Manzano, Juan Francisco. Mne tridtsat' let; stikhi [I am 30 years old; verse] Mnatobi, no. 12, 1963: 66. In Georgian. Translated from the Spanish.

3909. ——. Mne tridtsat' let; stikhi [I am 30 years old; verse] Drosha, no. 1, 1963: 8. In Georgian. Translated from the Spanish.

3910. Martí, José. Khochu kak tsvetok umeret' na lugu. Moi khram; stikhi [I wish to die like a meadow flower. My temple; verse] Mnatobi, no. 12, 1963: 65–66. In Georgian. Translated from the Spanish.

3911. ——. Moe sviatilishche; stikhi [My sanctuary; verse] Drosha, no. 1, 1963: 8. In Georgian. Translated from the Spanish.

3912. Navarrete, Diego. Chervonyi prapor. Mii radians'kyi brat; virshi [The red banner. My Soviet brother; verse] Vsesvit, v. 7, no. 11, Nov. 1964: 5–6.
Translated from the Spanish.

3913. Navarro Luna, Manuel. Fidel'; stikhi [Fidel; verse] Ogonek, v. 41, no. 19, Apr. 1963: 2.
Translated from the Spanish.

3914. ———. Kolokol. Mat'. Gimn S'erry; stikhi [The bell. Mother. The hymn of the Sierra; verse] Mol. gvard., no. 9, Sept. 1962: 81–84.
Translated from the Spanish.

3915. ———. My pobedim; stikhi [We shall win; verse] Ogonek, v. 41, no. 18, Apr. 1963: 17.
Translated from the Spanish.

3916. ———. Pesn' zvezdy na kubinskom flage. Trud, ucheba, vintovka; stikhi [A song of the star from the Cuban flag. Work, study, and a rifle; verse] Inostr. lit., no. 4, Apr. 1964: 161–162.
Translated from the Spanish.

3917. ———. Sant'iago-de-Kuba. Predatel'; stikhi [Santiago de Cuba. A traitor; verse] Mol. gvard., no. 9, Sept. 1964: 95–97.
Translated from the Spanish.

3918. ———. Vpered! Stikhi [Forward! Verse] Ogonek, v. 38, no. 22, May 1960: 9.
Translated from the Spanish.

3919. Núñez Machín, Ana. Privet Sovetskomu Soiuzu; stikhi [My greetings to the Soviet Union; verse] Neva, no. 12, 1961: 131–132.
Translated from the Spanish.

3920. ———. Svoboda; stikhi [Freedom; verse] Ogonek, v. 39, no. 3, Jan. 1961: 2.
Translated from the Spanish.

3921. Olema García, Daura. Volontery revoliutsii; povest' [Volunteers of the revolution; a tale] Mol. gvard., no. 8, Aug. 1963: 143–207.
Translated from the Spanish.

3922. Orta Ruiz, Jesús. Poklyk narodu do soldata armii Batysty. Narodnyi polkovodets'; virshi [Our people appeal to a soldier of the Batista army. A people's

commander; verse] Vsesvit, v. 4, no. 4, Apr. 1961: 6.
Translated from the Spanish.

3923. Ortega, M. Vchera i segodnia—vragi; stikhi [Enemies yesterday and enemies today; verse] Sovet edebiiaty, no. 2, 1961: 9.
In Tatar. Translated from the Spanish.

3924. Otero, José Manuel. Povernennia; opovidannia [Homecoming; a story] Vsesvit, v. 4, no. 4, Apr. 1961: 21–23.
Translated from the Spanish.

3925. Parra, Nicanor. Na prostom iazyke nashikh dnei; stikhi [In the plain language of our time; poems] Inostr. lit., no. 2, Feb. 1964: 42–52.

3926. Pérez, Rafael Alcides. Korin' sontsia; virsh [The root of the sun; verse] Dnipro, v. 38, no. 1, Jan. 1964: 64.
Translated from the Spanish.

3927. Pita Rodríguez, Félix. Vintovka No. 5764; stikhi [Rifle No. 5764; verse] Inostr. lit., no. 6, June 1961: 163.
Translated from the Spanish.

3928. Plácido. Kliatva; stikhi [The oath; verse] Mnatobi, no. 12, 1963: 66.
In Georgian. Translated from the Spanish.

3929. Riverón Hernández, Francisco. Prysiaha; virsh [The oath; verse] Vsesvit, v. 4, no. 10, Oct. 1961: 30.
Translated from the Spanish.

3930. Ruiz Nabori, Jesús Orta. Oda kubinskoi revoliutsii; stikhi [Ode to the Cuban Revolution; verse] Sib. ogni, v. 40, no. 2, Feb. 1961: 5–17.
Translated from the Spanish.

3931. Salinas y López, Marcelo. Deti serzhanta Belafonte; rasskaz [Sergeant Belafonte's children; a story] Smena, v. 37, no. 9, May 1960: 22–23.
Translated from the Spanish.

3932. ———. Deti serzhanta Belafonte; rasskaz [Sergeant Belafonte's children; story] Punalippu, no. 6, 1961: 77–80.
In Finnish. Translated from the Spanish.

3933. ———. Deti serzhanta Belafonte; rasskaz [Sergeant Belafonte's children; a story] Sovet edebiiaty, no. 2, 1961: 10–13.
In Tatar. Translated from the Spanish.

3934. Soler Puig, José. "Bertil'on, 166"; roman [Bertillon 166; a novel] Druzh. nar., no. 2, Feb. 1961: 114–179.
Translated from the Spanish.

3935. Suárez, Romualdo. Sen'or posol; stikhi [Señor ambassador; verse] Sib. ogni, v. 39, no. 10, Oct. 1960: 3–4.
Translated from the Spanish.

3936. Tejera, Nivaria. Khoziain pekarni; virsh [The bakery owner; verse] Vsesvit, v. 4, no. 4, Apr. 1961: 7.
Translated from the Spanish.

3937. Torriente-Brau, Pablo de la. Aposhni akt; apaviadanne [His last action; a story] Belarus', v. 21, no. 1, Jan. 1964: 18–19.
Translated from the Spanish.

3938. Viceso, Abelardo. Iz pesni o Kube; stikhi [From a song about Cuba; verse] Sib. ogni, v. 39, no. 10, Oct. 1960: 5.
Translated from the Spanish.

3939. Vol'naia gramota; kubinskaia skazka [An emancipation certificate; a Cuban fairy tale] Vokrug sveta, no. 1, Jan. 1962: 37.
Translated from the Spanish.

h. Dominican Republic

3940. Galván, Manuel de Jesús. Enrikil'o; roman [Enriquillo; a novel] Moscow, Goslitizdat, 1963. 479 p.
Translated by I. Leitner and R. Lintser from the Spanish. Introductory article by IA. Svet.

i. Ecuador

3941. Cuadra, José de la. Morskaia rakovina; rasskazy [A seashell; stories] Moscow, Izd-vo khudozh. lit., 1963. 167 p.
Translated from the Spanish. Introductory article by E. Braginskaia.

3942. Ekvadorskie rasskazy [Ecuadorian stories] Moscow, Izd-vo inostr. lit., 1962. 166 p.
Translated from the Spanish.

3943. Gil Gilbert, Enrique. Nash khleb; roman [Our bread; a novel] Moscow, Khudozh. lit., 1964. 336 p.
Translated from the Spanish *Nuestro pan.* Introductory article by V. Goncharov.

3944. Icaza, Jorge. Na ulitsakh; roman [In the streets; a novel] Moscow, Izd-vo inostr. lit., 1963. 208 p.
Translated by N. Zagorskaia from the Spanish *En las calles.* Introductory article by F. Kel'in.

3945. Ortiz, Adalberto. Zhuingo; istoriia odnoho negra, odnoho ostrova i inshykh negriv; roman [Juyngo; history of a Negro, an island, and other Negroes; a novel] Kiev, Rad. pys'mennyk, 1959. 296 p.
Translated from the Spanish *Juyngo; historia de un negro, una isla y otros negros.*

3946. Rivadeneyra A., Jorge. Uzhe rassvetaet; roman [The dawn is breaking; a novel] Moscow, Mol. gvardiia, 1962. 206 p.
Translated by V. Krylova from the Spanish *Ya está amaneciendo.*

3947. Vera, Pedro Jorge. "Vechnyi traur" i drugie rasskazy ["Eternal mourning" and other stories] Moscow, Izd-vo inostr. lit., 1962. 135 p.
Translated from the Spanish *Luto eterno y otros relatos.*

3948. Aguilera Malta, Demetrio. Cholo, kotoryi nenavidel zoloto; rasskaz [A Cholo who hated gold; a story] V zashch. mira, no. 11, Nov. 1960: 80–82.
Translated from the Spanish.

3949. Cuadra, José de la. Fal'shivye monety; rasskaz [Counterfeit coins; a story] Zvaigzne, no. 15, 1963: 29.
In Latvian. Translated from the Spanish.

3950. ———. Fal'shivye monety; novella [Counterfeit coins; a novella] Karogs, no. 4, 1964: 97–99.
In Latvian. Translated from the Spanish.

3951. Vera, Pedro Jorge. Durak; rasskaz [A fool; a story] Literaturuli Adzhara, no.1, 1964: 57–61.
In Georgian. Translated from the Spanish.

3952. ———. Ostrov v serdtse; stikhi [An island in the heart; verse] Sib. ogni, no. 1, Jan. 1963: 5.
Translated from the Spanish.

3953. Viteri, Eugenia. Kol'tso; rasskaz [The ring; a story] Zvaigzne, no. 15, 1963: 28.
In Latvian. Translated from the Spanish.

j. El Salvador

3954. Herrera Velado, Francisco. Kokosovoe moloko; rasskazy [Coconut milk; stories] Moscow, Izd-vo inostr. lit., 1962. 136 p.
Translated from the Spanish *Agua de coco.*

3955. Peralta Lagos, José María. Smert' golubki ili zlokliucheniia korrespondenta [The death of a dove, or the misfortunes of a reporter] Moscow, Goslitizdat, 1962. 207 p.
Translated by A. Kozlov from the Spanish *La muerte de la tórtola; o, Malandangas de un corresponsal.* Introductory article by E. Braginskaia. Also published in Lithuanian.

k. Guatemala

3956. Asturias, Miguel Angel. Sen'or Prezident; roman [Mister President; a novel] Moscow, Goslitizdat, 1959. 255 p.
Translated by M. Bylinkina and N. Trauberg from the Spanish *El Señor presidente.* Introductory article by L. Ospovat.

3957. ———. Uik-end v Gvatemale; rasskazy [Week end in Guatemala; stories] Moscow, Izd. inostr. lit., 1961. 238 p.
Translated from the Spanish. Introductory article by IU. Pevtsov. Also published in Estonian.

3958. ———. Zelenyi papa; roman [The green pope; a novel] Moscow, Izd-vo khud. lit., 1964. 340 p.
Translated by M. Bylinkina from the Spanish *El papa verde.* Introductory article by IU. Pevtsov.

3959. Asturias, Miguel Angel. Dlia hramads'koi dumky; opovidannia [For public opinion; a story] Vsesvit, v. 2, no. 10, Oct. 1959: 93–102.
Translated from the Spanish.

3960. ———. Ego Zelenoe Sviateishestvo; roman [The green pope; a novel] Inostr. lit., no. 12, Dec. 1960: 26–121.
Translated from the Spanish.

3961. Cruz, Roberto. Germanu Titovu; stikhi [To German Titov; verse] Inostr. lit., no. 9, Sept. 1961: 13–14.
Translated from the Spanish.

3962. Morales Obregón, Roberto. Kolokol. Smotri! Stikhi [The bell. Look! Verse] Mol. gvard., no. 7, July 1964: 125.
Translated from the Spanish.

3963. Pellicar, Carlos Manuel. Khoncho; rasskaz [Honcho; a story] Vokrug sveta, no. 5, May 1963: 41–43.
Translated from the Spanish.

3964. Villacorta de Vidaurre, L. Uvolennaia; rasskaz [A dismissed woman; a story] Zvaigzne, no. 1, 1960: 27.
In Latvian. Translated from the Spanish.

l. The Guianas

3965. Carew, Jan. Prikosnovenie Midasa; roman [The Midas touch; a novel] Moscow, Goslitizdat, 1963. 271 p.
Translated by N. Vysotskaia from the English. Introductory article by E. Gal'perina.

3966. Carew, Jan. Prikosnovenie Midasa; roman [The Midas touch; a novel] Inostr. lit., no. 1, Jan. 1963: 141–175; no. 2, Feb. 1963: 8–127.
Translated from the English.

3967. Carter, Martin. Smert' raba; stikhi [The death of a slave; verse] Zvezda, no. 7, July 1960; 146–147.
Translated from the English.

m. Haiti

3968. Alexis, Jacques Stephen. Derev'ia-muzykanty; roman [The musical trees; a novel] Moscow, Khudozh. lit., 1964. 312 p.
Translated by M. Vaksmakher and O. Moiseenko from the French *Les arbres musiciens.* Introductory article by S. Emel'iannikov.

3969. ———. Dobryi general Solntse; roman [Good General Sun; a novel] Moscow, Izd-vo inostr. lit., 1960. 357 p.
Translated by O. Volkov from the French *Compère Général Soleil.* Introductory article by E. Gal'perina. Also published in Lithuanian and Latvian.
Reviewed by I. Nikiforova in *Inostr. lit.,* no. 1, 1961: 253–254; by E. Pranckus in *Pergale,* no. 12, 1962: 167–168.

3970. ———. General Solntse; roman [General Sun; a novel] Moscow, Goslitizdat, 1961. 71, 62 p. (Roman-gazeta, nos. 4, 5)
Translated by O. Volkov from the French *Compère Général Soleil.*

3971. ———. Romansero pri svete zvezd; rasskazy [Romancero in the light of the stars; stories] Tallinn, Gas.-zhurn. izd-vo, 1961. 51 p.

In Estonian. Translated by O. Ojamaa and H. Rajandi from the French *Romancero aux étoiles*.

3972. Dépestre, René. Chernaia ruda; stikhi [Black ore; verse] Moscow, Izd-vo inostr. lit., 1961. 67 p.

Translated by P. Antokol'skii from the French *Minerai noir*.

Reviewed by S. Severtsev in *Inostr. lit.*, no. 3, 1962: 248–250.

3973. Roumain, Jacques. Khoziaeva rosy; roman [The masters of the dew; a novel] Vilnius, Goslitizdat, 1959. 240 p.

In Lithuanian. Translated by J. Naujokaitis from the French *Gouverneurs de la rosée*.

3974. Alexis, Jacques Stephen. Derev'iamuzykanty; roman [The musical trees; a novel] Inostr. lit., no. 1, Jan. 1962: 6–67; no. 2, Feb. 1962: 57–100; no. 3, Mar. 1962: 87–141.

Translated from the French.

3975. Brierre, Jean Fernand. "Chernaia dusha." IA s toboi, Garlem; stikhi ["Black soul." I am with you, Harlem; verse] Inostr. lit., no. 1, Jan. 1960: 136–141.

Translated from the French.

3976. Dépestre, René. Pust' solntse snova ulitsy zal'et; stikhi [May our streets be sunlit again; verse] Inostr. lit., no. 8, Aug. 1964: 178–179.

Translated from the French.

3977. ———. Skreshchenie dorog; stikhi [The crossroads; verse] Inostr. lit., no. 4, Apr. 1960: 6–8.

Translated from the French.

3978. ———. Svoboda rasskazyvaet. Pavshie na pole pravdy. Oruzhie krovi moei; stikhi [Freedom tells us its story. Those who died for the truth. A weapon of my blood; verse] Druzh. nar., no. 6, June 1960: 166–169.

Translated from the French.

3979. ———. Vstan' negritianskoe serdtse! Ogonechek v otkrytom more; stikhi [Wake up, Negro heart! Offshore light; verse] Druzh. nar., no. 4, Apr. 1961: 138–141.

Translated from the French.

3980. Laforest, Jean-Richard. Solntse nashei liubvi; stikhi [The sun of our love; verse] Znamia, v. 34, no. 7, July 1964: 132–133.

Translated from the French.

3981. Roumain, Jacques. "Griaznye negry." Gvineia. Groza; stikhi ["The dirty Negroes." Guinea. A thunderstorm; verse] Inostr. lit., no. 1, Jan. 1960: 132–136.

Translated from the French.

3982. ———. "Griaznye negry." Groza; stikhi ["The dirty Negroes." A thunderstorm; verse] Karogs, no. 10, 1961: 62–65.

In Latvian. Translated from the French.

3983. Vzorvannoe molchanie; stikhi molodykh poetov Gaiti [Shattered silence; the poems of young Haitian poets] Inostr. lit., no. 3, Mar. 1963: 179–186.

n. Jamaica

3984. Reid, Victor Stafford. Leopard; povest' [The leopard; a tale] Moscow, Izd-vo vost. lit., 1961. 149 p.

Translated by A. Sergeev from the English. Introductory article by E. Gal'perina. Also published in Estonian, Georgian, and Armenian.

Georgian edition reviewed by I. Kenchoshvili in *Mnatobi*, no. 3, 1963: 185–186.

3985. Carberry, D. H. IA budu pomnit'; stikhi [I shall remember; verse] Zvezda, no. 7, July 1960: 148–149.

Translated from the English.

3986. Ingram, Kenneth E. IAshcheritsa; stikhi [The lizard; verse] Zvezda, no. 7, July 1960: 148.

Translated from the English.

3987. Reid, Victor Stafford. Leopard; povest' [The leopard; a tale] Inostr. lit., no. 10, Oct. 1960: 196–256.

Translated from the English.

3988. ———. Leopard; povest' [The leopard; a tale] Tsiskari, no. 6, 1961: 62–97.

In Georgian. Translated from the English.

3989. Roberts, Walter A. Pamiatnik Khose Marti. Metiska; stikhi [A monument to José Martí. A mestizo woman; verse] Druzh. nar., no. 11, Nov. 1960: 162.
Translated from the English.

o. Mexico

3990. Algarra, María Luisa. Vozrast ispytanii; p'esa v trekh deistviiakh [The age of trials; a play in three acts] Moscow, Otd. raspr. dram. proizvedenii VUOAP, 1960. 90 p.
Translated from the Spanish.

3991. Azuela, Mariano. Prokliattia; roman [The curse; a novel] Kiev, Rad. pys'mennyk, 1959. 246 p.
Translated by B. Morozov from the Spanish La maldición.
Reviewed by Dmytro Hryn'ko in Vsesvit, v. 2, no. 7, July 1959: 131–132.

3992. ———. Te kto vnizu; roman o meksikanskoi revoliutsii [The underdogs; a novel of the Mexican Revolution] Moscow, Goslitizdat, 1960. 126 p.
Translated by V. Gerasimova and A. Kostiukovskaia from the Spanish Los de abajo. Introductory article by I. Grigulevich.

3993. ———. Te kto vnizu; roman o meksikanskoi revoliutsii [The underdogs; a novel of the Mexican Revolution] 2d ed. Moscow, Goslitizdat, 1961. 127 p.
Translated by V. Gerasimova and A. Kostiukovskaia from the Spanish Los de abajo. Introductory article by I. Grigulevich.

3994. Benítez, Fernando. Staryi korol'; roman [The old king; a novel] Kiev, Derzhlitvydav, 1962. 175 p.
Translated by P. Sokolovs'kyi from the Spanish El rey viejo.
Reviewed by IU. Korzov in Vsesvit, v. 6, no. 7, July 1963: 146–147.

3995. Fernández de Lizardi, José Joaquín. Perikil'o Sarn'ento; roman [Periquillo Sarniento; a novel] Moscow, Khudozh. lit., 1964. 791 p.
Translated from the Spanish El Periquillo Sarniento. Introductory article by V. Shor.

3996. Guitérrez Nájera, Manuel. Stikhi [Poems] Moscow, Goslitizdat, 1960. 87 p.
Translated from the Spanish.

3997. Guzmán, Martín Luis. Ten' kaudil'o; roman [The shadow of the caudillo; a novel] Moscow, Khudozh. lit., 1964. 207 p.
Translated by S. Mamontov and I. Trist from the Spanish La sombra del caudillo. Introductory article by I. Vinnichenko and S. Semenov.

3998. Mancisidor, José. Ee zvali Katalina [She was called Catalina] Moscow, Izd-vo khudozh. lit., 1963. 135 p.
Translated by M. Filippova from the Spanish Se llamaba Catalina. Introductory article by V. Vinogradov.

3999. Meksikanskie rasskazy [Mexican stories] Moscow, Goslitizdat, 1960. 182 p.
Translated from the Spanish. Introductory article by R. Lintser.

4000. Rodríguez, Antonio. Besplodnoe oblako; roman [The barren cloud; a novel] Moscow, Mol. gvardiia,1961. 208 p.
Translated from the Spanish La nube estéril. Introductory article by V. Aleksandrova.

4001. Traven, B. Pokhod v stranu Kaoba; povest' [The march to Caobaland; a tale] Moscow, Detgiz, 1959. 255 p.
Translated from the German Marsch ins Reich der Caoba.

4002. ———. Sborshchiki khlopka; roman [Cotton pickers; a novel] Tallinn, Estgosizdat, 1964. 188 p.
In Estonian. Translated by A. Tulik from the German.

4003. Zoloto, kon' i chelovek; rasskazy meksikanskikh pisatelei [Gold, the horse and man; stories by Mexican writers] Moscow, Izd-vo inostr. lit., 1961. 357 p.
Translated from the Spanish. Introductory article by I. Grigulevich.

4004. Carballido, Emilio. Poldiuzhiny prostyn'; rasskaz [Six sheets; a story] Padomju Latvijas sieviete, no. 3, 1964: 13–15.
In Latvian. Translated from the Spanish.

4005. Chacón Nardi, Rafaela. Elegiia na smert' Khesusa Menendersa; stikhi [Elegy on Jesús Menénderes' death; verse] Mnatobi, no. 12, 1963: 66–67.
In Georgian. Translated from the Spanish.

4006. González Martínez, Enrique. Lirika [Lyric verse] Inostr. lit., no. 3, Mar. 1964: 162–167.
Translated from the Spanish.

4007. Mancisidor, José. Teo; opovidannia [Teo; a story] Vsesvit, v. 2, no. 3, Mar. 1959: 17–20.
Translated from the Spanish.

4008. Mir, Pedro. Klych Zhovtnia; virsh [The call of the October Revolution; verse] Vsesvit, v. 5, no. 11, Nov. 1962: 3.

4009. Montero, José Antonio. Etot mir budet nashim! Stikhi [This world will belong to us! Verse] Agidel', no. 8, 1961: 76.
In Bashkir. Translated from the Spanish.

4010. ———. Etot mir stanet nashim; stikhi [This world will belong to us; verse] Inostr. lit., no. 12, 1960: 168.
Translated from the Spanish.

4011. Rejano, Juan. Mir slavit Lenina; stikhi [The whole world praises Lenin; verse] Don, v. 4, no. 4, Apr. 1960: 44–45.
Translated from the Spanish.

4012. ———. Pesni mira; stikhi [Songs of peace; verse] Nov. mir, v. 36, no. 9, Sept. 1960: 188–190.
Translated from the Spanish.

4013. Reyes, Alfonso. Detstvo; stikhi [Childhood; verse] Inostr. lit., no. 12, 1960: 166–168.
Translated from the Spanish.

4014. Rodríguez, Antonio. Besplodnoe oblako; otryvok iz romana [A barren cloud; excerpts from a novel] Vokrug sveta, no. 11, Nov. 1961: 42–47.
Translated from the Spanish.

4015. Rojas González, Franciso. Khlopchyk liakaie ptakhiv; opovidannia [A boy frightens the birds; a story] Rad. zhin., v. 14, no. 6, June 1959: 24.
Translated from the Spanish.

4016. Rubín, Ramón. Razboiniki; rasskaz [Brigands; a story] Nov. mir, v. 37, no. 5, May 1961: 119–123.
Translated from the Spanish.

4017. ———. Razboiniki; rasskaz [The brigands; a story] Juanimo gretos, no. 11, 1961: 22–23.
In Lithuanian. Translated from the Spanish.

4018. Vasconcelos, José. Boevoi petukh; rasskaz [A fighting cock; a story] Sov. Ukr., v. 9, no. 3, Mar. 1959: 88–90.
Translated from the Spanish.

p. Panama

4019. Chang Marín, Carlos Francisco. Mest' Tauro; rasskazy [Tauro's vengeance; stories] Moscow, Progress, 1964. 126 p.
Translated from the Spanish. Introductory article by V. Vinogradov.

4020. ———. Pesni Panamy [The songs of Panama] Moscow, Izd-vo inostr. lit., 1963. 111 p.
Translated by B. Okudzhava from the Spanish *Socabón, décimas populares para cantar*.

4021. ———. Zhizn' vo mrake; rasskazy o Paname [A life in darkness; stories about Panama] Moscow, Mol. gvardiia, 1964. 86 p.
Translated by A. F. Kozlov from the Spanish *Mansión de la bruma*. Introductory article by S. A. Gonionskii.

4022. Chang Marín, Carlos Francisco. Khotel by ia schastlivym byt'. Proshchai, proshchai, zemlia moia! Stikhi [I wish to be happy. Good-by my homeland! Verse] Ogonek, no. 42, no. 13, Mar. 1964: 16.
Translated from the Spanish.

4023. Sánchez, José María. Lalu; rasskaz [Lalu; a story] Vokrug sveta, no. 9, Sept. 1960: 33–35.
Translated from the Spanish.

q. Paraguay

4024. Romero, Elvio. Stikhi [Poems] Moscow, Izd-vo inostr. lit., 1961. 63 p.
Translated by P. Grushko from the Spanish. Introductory article by L. Ospovat.
Reviewed by A. Belkin in *Nov. mir*, v. 38, no. 6, June 1962: 284–285.

4025. Garcete, Carlos. Oplachennyi dolg; rasskaz [A debt paid off; a story] Ogonek, v. 37, no. 12, Mar. 1959: 22–23.
Translated from the Spanish.

4026. ———. Oplachennyi dolg; rasskaz [A debt paid off; a story] Sov. Ukr., v. 9, no. 3, Mar. 1959: 84–87.
Translated from the Spanish.

4027. ———. Oplachennyi dolg; rasskaz [A debt paid off; a story] Noorus, no. 11, 1961: 37–39.
In Estonian. Translated from the Spanish.

4028. ———. Oplachennyi dolg; rasskaz [A debt paid off; a story] Tsiskari, no. 2, 1960: 68–72.
In Georgian. Translated from the Spanish.

4029. ———. Oplachennyi dolg; rasskaz [A debt paid off; a story] Amudar'ia, no. 6, 1961: 73–76.
In Kara-Kalpak. Translated from the Spanish.

4030. ———. Oplachennyi dolg; rasskaz [A debt paid off; a story] Kazakstan aielderi, no. 1, 1959: 17–18.
In Kazakh. Translated from the Spanish.

4031. Romero, Elvio. Eto iug! Po storonam zheleznodorozhnoi nasypi. Ei paren'! TSveta zari; stikhi [This is the South! On both sides of the railroad embankment. Hello, boy! The color of dawn; verse] Ogonek, v. 38, no. 26, June 1960: 20.
Translated from the Spanish.

r. Peru

4032. Calvo, César. Pis'mo na Kubu; stikhi [A letter to Cuba; verse] Sib. ogni, v. 39, no. 10, Oct. 1960: 6.
Translated from the Spanish.

4033. Carcuero, A. Poiu zelenoe olivkovoe derevo; stikhi [I praise the green olive tree; verse] Don, v. 5, no. 1, Jan. 1961: 58–59.

4034. Vallejo, César Abraham. Chelovech'i stikhi [Human poems] Inostr. lit., no. 4, Apr. 1963: 57–64.
Translated from the Spanish.

s. Puerto Rico

4035. González, José Luis. Na etoi storone; rasskazy [On this side; stories] Moscow, Izd-vo inostr. lit., 1962. 93 p.
Translated by IU. Paporov from the Spanish *En este lado.*

4036. González, José Luis. Santa Klaus prikhodit k Pichirilo Sanchesu; rasskaz [Santa Claus pays a visit to Pichirilo Sánchez; a story] Zhen. mira, no. 12, 1960: 28–30.
Translated from the Spanish.

4037. Palés Matos, Luis. Uveseleniia; stikhi [Amusements; verse] Nov. mir, v. 37, no. 1, Jan. 1961: 20.
Translated from the Spanish.

t. Uruguay

4038. Amorim, Enrique. Korral'-ab'erto; roman [Open corral; a novel] Moscow, Goslitizdat, 1961. 199 p.
Translated by A. M. Gnilits and R. A. Zauber from the Spanish *Corral abierto.* Introductory article by G. V. Stepanov.

4039. ———. Lisoruby; roman [Loggers; a novel] Kiev, Molod', 1962. 246 p.
Translated by T. IUkova and L. Olevs'kyi from the Spanish *Los montaraces.*

4040. Gravina, Alfredo Dante. Granitsy vetram; roman [Frontiers to the wind; a novel] Kiev, Derzhvydav Ukrainy, 1960. 311 p.
In Ukranian. Translated by E. Drobiazko and L. Olevs'kyi from the Spanish *Fronteras al viento.*

4041. ———. Ostrov liubvi; p'esa v chetyrekh deistviiakh [The island of love; a play in four acts] Moscow, Izd-vo inostr. lit., 1960. 118 p.
Translated by E. Kolchina from the Spanish.

4042. ———. Ot strakha k gordosti; roman [From fear to pride; a novel] Moscow, Izd-vo inostr. lit., 1962. 256 p.
Translated by N. Tul'chinskaia from the Spanish *Del miedo al orgullo.* Introductory article by F. Kel'in.

4043. Patrón, Juan Carlos. Podsudimyi 1040; p'esa v 2-kh deistviiakh [Prisoner no. 1040; a play in two acts] Moscow, Izd-vo inostr. lit., 1961. 95 p.
Translated by P. Nikolaev from the Spanish *Procesado 1040.*

4044. Quiroga, Horacio. Anakonda; rasskazy [The anaconda; stories] Moscow, Goslitizdat, 1960. 343 p.
Translated from the Spanish *Anaconda.* Introductory article by S. Mamontov.

4045. ———. Skazki sel'vy [Tales of the jungle] Yerevan, Aipetrat, 1963. 72 p.
In Armenian. Translated by R. K. Avetisian from the Russian.

4046. Urugvaiskie rasskazy [Uruguayan stories] Tbilisi, Sabchota Sakartvelo, 1962. 86 p.
In Georgian. Also published in Armenian.

4047. Abad, Américo. Khoziaika doma; stikhi [The lady of the house; verse] Inostr. lit., no. 9, Sept. 1961: 83–84.
Translated from the Spanish.

4048. ———. Moi kvartal; stikhi [My residential block; verse] Nov. mir, v. 37, no. 1, Jan. 1961: 17–18.
Translated from the Spanish.

4049. Gravina, Alfredo Dante. Padenie; rasskaz [The fall; a story] Zhen. mira, no. 1, 1964: 30–31.
Translated from the Spanish.

4050. Massoni, F. Malen'kaia; rasskaz [The little one; a story] Zanoni Tochikiston, no. 2, 1959: 20.
In Tajik. Translated from the Spanish.

4051. Medeiros, María Paulina. V sirotskom dome; otryvok iz romana [In an orphanage; excerpt from a novel] Zhen. mira, no. 4, 1964: 32–33.
Translated from the Spanish.

4052. Pedemonte, Hugo Emilio. Budushchii muzhchina; rasskaz [One who will be a man; a story] Inostr. lit., no. 4, Apr. 1964: 64–69.
Translated from the Spanish.

4053. Pérez, Saúl. Chelovek—gorod; stikhi [Man is a city; verse] Inostr. lit., no. 9, Sept. 1961: 81–83.
Translated from the Spanish.

u. Venezuela

4054. Arráiz, Antonio. Diadiushka IAguar i diadiushka Krolik; satiricheskie skazki [Uncle Jaguar and Uncle Rabbit; satirical fairy tales] Moscow, Goslitizdat, 1962. 175 p.
Translated from the Spanish Tío Tigre y Tío Conejo. Introductory article by V. Krylova.

4055. Dozhd' nad morem; venesuel'skie rasskazy [Rainfall over the sea; Venezuelan stories] Tallinn, Gas.-zhurn. izd-vo, 1961. 56 p.
In Estonian. Translated by T. Hallap from the Spanish.

4056. Gallegos, Rómulo. Bednyi negr; roman [A poor Negro; a novel] Moscow, Khudozh. lit., 1964. 311 p.
Translated by R. Pokhlebkin from the Spanish Pobre negro. Introductory article by I. Vinnichenko.

4057. ———. Don'ia Barbara; roman [Doña Barbara; a novel] Moscow, Goslitizdat, 1959. 301 p.   PQ8549.G24D627
Translated by V. Krylova from the Spanish. Introductory article by V. Kuteishchikova. Also published in Lithuanian and Estonian.

4058. ———. Kanaima; roman [Canaima; a novel] Moscow, Mol. gvardiia, 1959. 262 p.
Translated by V. Krylova. Introductory article by V. Kuteishchikova.

4059. León, Carlos Augusto. Izbrannoe [Selected works] Moscow, Izd-vo inostr. lit., 1959. 204 p.
Translated from the Spanish. Introductory article by E. Kolchina.

4060. Otero Silva, Miguel. Likhoradka; roman [Fever; a novel] Moscow, Khudozh. lit., 1964. 183 p.
Translated by A. Minin and L. IAkovlev from the Spanish Fiebre; novela de la revolución venezolana. Introductory article by V. Krylova.

4061. ———. Mertvye doma; roman [Dead houses; a novel] Moscow, Izd-vo inostr. lit., 1961. 105 p.
Translated by E. Liuberetskaia and A. Morov from the Spanish Casas muertas.

4062. Venesuel'skie rasskazy [Venezuelan stories] Moscow, Goslitizdat, 1962. 199 p.
Translated from the Spanish. Introductory article by I. Vinnichenko.

4063. Bencomo, Carmen Delia. Tret'e padenie; rasskaz [The third downfall; a story] Smena, v. 41, no. 12, June 1964: 26–27.
Translated from the Spanish.

4064. Eloy Blanco, Andrés. Rifmy gneva; stikhi [The rhymes of wrath; verse] Inostr. lit., no. 5, May 1964: 108–113.
Translated from the Spanish.

4065. Gallegos, Rómulo. Ogon' v kliuve vorona; glavy iz romana [Fire in the beak of a raven; excerpts from a novel] Inostr. lit., no. 12, Dec. 1960: 158–165.
Translated from the Spanish.

4066. Laya, Pedro. Inoskazanie o spiashchikh detiakh; stikhi [The legend of sleeping children; verse] Nov. mir., v. 37, no. 1, Jan. 1961: 19.
Translated from the Spanish.

4067. León, Carlos Augusto.   Bezdomnye deti; stikhi [Homeless children; verse] Sib. ogni, no. 1, Jan. 1963: 5–6.
Translated from the Spanish.

4068. ———. Chelovek i zvezda. Vecher, ne osypaisia. Daite mne staryi voennyi rozhok! Esli b stikhi moi byli derev'iami lesa. Idoly v trave; stikhi [A man and a star. The leaves shouldn't fall this evening. Give me an old bugle! I wish my poems were the trees in a forest. Idols in the grass; verse] Inostr. lit., no. 11, Nov. 1964: 143–148.
Translated from the Spanish.

4069. ———. Pisnia pro Lenina; fragmenty z poemy [A song about Lenin; excerpts from a poem] Vsesvit, v. 5, no. 4, Apr. 1962: 4–5.
Translated from the Spanish.

4070. Mujica, Héctor.   Belyi korall; rasskaz [The white coral; a story] Svyturys, no. 24, 1962: 12–13.
In Lithuanian. Translated from the Spanish.

v. West Indies

4071. Collymore, Frank A.   Ikh pamiati; stikhi [In memory of them; verse] Zvezda, no. 7, July 1960: 147.
Translated from the English.

4072. Glissant, Edouard.   Chernaia sol'. Afrika; otryvok iz poemy [Black salt. Africa; excerpts from a poem] Inostr. lit., no. 6, June 1960: 104–106.
Translated from the French.

4073. Julia, Lucie.   Dve podlinnye istorii [Two true stories] Zhen. mira, no. 4, 1961: 29.
Translated from the French.

4074. ———.   "Moi rebenok umret, esli vy ne dadite mne eto lekarstvo"; rasskaz ["My child will die if you do not give me this medicine"; a story] Zhen. mira, no. 10, 1959: 24–25.
Translated from the French.

4075. ———.   Nikita; rasskaz [Nikita; a story] Sov. zhen., v. 19, no. 9, 1963: 24.
Translated from the French.

D. FOLKLORE

1. Writings Dealing With Three or More Countries

4076. Zibert, E., *ed.*   Legendy i skazki indeitsev Latinskoi Ameriki [Legends and tales of the Indians of Latin America] Moscow, Gos. izd-vo khudozh. lit., 1962. 301 p.
Reviewed by L. Ospovat in *Inostr. lit.*, no. 7, July 1963: 267–269.

2. Individual Countries

a. Argentina

4077. Poeziia gaucho [The poetry of gauchos] Moscow, Khudozh. lit., 1964. 238 p.
Translated from the Spanish. Introductory article by Z. Plavskin.

————

4078. Raduga i ptitsy; argentinskaia legenda [A rainbow and birds; an Argentine legend] Vokrug sveta, no. 9, Sept. 1960: 58.
Translated from the Spanish.

4079. Ustnoe   tvorchestvo   argentinskogo naroda [Oral literature of the Argentine people] Inostr. lit., no. 4, Apr. 1961: 273–274.

b. Brazil

4080. Brazil'skie skazki i legendy [Brazilian fairy tales and legends] Moscow, Goslitizdat, 1962. 239 p.
Translated from the Portuguese. Introductory article by I. Terterian.
Reviewed by A. Trubnikov in *Nov. mir*, v. 38, no. 10, Oct 1962: 279.

————

4081. Entsiklopediia fol'klora [An encyclopedia of Brazilian folklore] Inostr. lit., no. 7, July 1961: 272.

c. Cuba

4082. Chelovek i zemlia; kubinskaia skazka [Man and the earth; a Cuban fairy tale] Vokrug sveta, no. 1., Jan. 1962: 58.
Translated from the Spanish.

d. The Guianas

4083. Skazki indeitsev taulipang i arekuna iz IUzhnoi Gviany: Maisovaia lepeshka.

Liana timbo [Fairy tales of the Taulipang and Arecuna Indians in southern Guiana: A corn pancake. A timbo tree] Prostor, v. 30, no. 3, Mar. 1963: 105.

e. Haiti

4084. Haitians'ki prysliv'ia, prykazky ta zahadky [Haitian proverbs, sayings, and puzzles] Vsesvit, v. 6, no. 1, Jan. 1963: 59.

f. Mexico

4085. Narodnaia meksikanskaia poeziia [Mexican folk poetry] Moscow, Goslitizdat, 1962. 191 p.
Translated by G. Stepanov from the Spanish.
Reviewed by L. Ospovat in *Nov. mir*, v. 38, no. 9, Sept. 1962: 286; by M. Aliger in *Inostr. lit.*, no. 8, Aug. 1963: 262–265.

4086. Trejo, Blanca Lydia. Marimba; skazka meksikanskikh indeitsev [Marimba; a fairy tale of the Mexican Indians] Moscow, Detgiz, 1961. 21 p.
Translated by E. Kedrova and I. Cherevataia from the Spanish.

g. Panama

4087. Santiso, Felicia. Negritianskii fol'klor v Paname [Negro folklore in Panama] Zhen. mira, no. 4, 1962: 28–29.

E. LATIN AMERICA IN SOVIET AND OTHER LITERARY WORKS

1. Writings Dealing With Three or More Countries

4088. Koenne, Manfred. Okhotniki za kauchukom; roman ob odnom vide syr'ia [Rubber hunters; a novel about one kind of raw material] Moscow, Izd-vo inostr. lit., 1962. 438 p.
Latin America in German literature.
Translated by E. Mikhelevich and A. Raikhstein from the German. Introductory article by V. Berezhkov.
Reviewed by F. I. IAshunskaia in *Kauch. i rez.*, v. 21, no. 8, Aug. 1962: 64.

4089. Valle-Inclán, Ramón del. Tiran Banderas; roman [Banderas, the tyrant; a novel] Moscow, Goslitizdat, 1959. 215 p.
Latin America in Spanish literature.
Translated by T. A. Glikman from the Spanish *Tirano Banderas, novela de Tierra*

caliente. Introductory article by G. V. Stepanov.

2. Individual Countries

a. Argentina

4090. Slepukhin, IU. G. U cherty zakata; roman [The edge of the sunset; a novel] Leningrad, Sov. pisatel', 1961. 588 p.
A Russian novel on Argentina.

b. Brazil

4091. Braziliia v stikhakh arabskogo poeta [Brazil in the poems of an Arab poet] Inostr. lit., no. 12, Dec. 1960: 258.

c. Chile

4092. Annenkov, IUlii Lazarevich. Shakhterskii senator; roman [A miners' senator; a novel] Moscow, Detgiz, 1962. 238 p.
PG3476.A537S5
A Russian novel on the life and work of Pablo Neruda, the Chilean poet.

d. Cuba

4093. Antsiferov, Nikolai Stepanovich, *and* Sergei Polikarpov, *comps.* Tebe, Kuba! Stikhi [To you, Cuba! Collected poems] Moscow, Sov. pisatel', 1961. 95 p.
PG3235.C8T4

4094. Borovik, Genrikh. Povest' o zelenoi iashcheritse [The story of a green lizard] Moscow, Mol. gvardiia, 1962. 223 p.
PG3479.4.O68P6
A Russian novel on Cuban history.
Reviewed by L. Kostina in *Vokrug sveta*, no. 11, Nov. 1962: 61–62.

4095. Chichkov, V. Mal'chishki iz Gavany; p'esa v 3-kh deistviiakh [The boys from Havana; a play in three acts] Moscow, Mol. gvardiia, 1963. 96 p.
Cuba in a Russian play.
Reviewed by Georgii Mdivani in *Teatr. zhizn'*, no. 2, Jan. 1963: 14–15.

4096. ———. Pepe—malen'kii kubinets; povest' [Pepe, a little Cuban; a tale] Moscow, Detgiz, 1963. 112 p.

4097. Mdivani, G. Den' rozhdeniia Terezy [Teresa's birthday] Moscow, Iskusstvo, 1962. 78 p.
The Cuban Revolution in a Russian play.
Reviewed by IU. Nekhoroshev in *Teatr*, v. 23, no. 1, Jan. 1962: 115–117.

4098. Pavlychko, Dmytro Vasyl'ovych. Pal'-
mova vit' [A palm leaf] Kiev, Derzhlitvy-
dav, 1962. 110 p.   PG3949.26.A9P3
   A volume of Ukrainian poems devoted to
Cuba.
   Reviewed by I. Zub in *Sov. Ukraina*, no. 2,
Feb. 1963: 175–179; by O. Buzynnyk in
Ukraina, no. 22, Nov. 1962: 19.

4099. Shervashidze, Amiran.   Devushka iz
Sant'iago (viva Kuba!); p'esa v 3-kh
deistviiakh [A girl from Santiago (viva
Cuba!); a play in three acts] Moscow,
Sov. Rossiia, 1963. 63 p.
   A Soviet play on Cuba.
   Translated from the Georgian.

4100. Viva Kuba! Poety Kuby i progressivnye
poety Latinskoi Ameriki o Kube [Long
live Cuba! Cuban and progressive Latin
American poets describe Cuba] Moscow,
Iskusstvo, 1963. 31 p.
   Translated from the Spanish.

4101. Bikchentaev, A.   Ad"iutanty ne umiraiut; povest' [Aides-de-camp do not die;
a tale] Oktiabr', v. 39, no. 5, May 1962:
7–34.
   Cuban revolutionary events in a Russian
tale.

4102. ———. Trudno cheloveku bez borody;
rasskaz [It is better to grow a beard; a
story] Druzh. nar., no. 5, May 1960:
105–108.
   A story on the Cuban Revolution.

4103. Bozhilov, Bozhidar. Dimitrov na Kube;
stikhi [Dimitrov in Cuba; verse] Znamia,
v. 34, no. 7, July 1964: 105–106.
   Translated from the Bulgarian.

4104. Chichkov, V. M.   Mal'chishki iz
Gavany; p'esa. Sokrashchennyi variant
dlia pionerskogo teatra [The boys from
Havana; an abridged version of a play
for the Pioneer theater] Vozhatyi, v. 38,
no. 12, Dec. 1962: 36–46.

4105. Davydychev, L.   Doch' revoliutsii;
rasskaz [Daughter of the revolution; a
story] Ural, no. 2, 1961: 66–67.
   The Cuban Revolution in a Russian story.

4106. Evtushenko, Evgenii Aleksandrovich.
IA—Kuba; poema v proze [This is
Cuba; a poem in prose] Znamia, v. 33,
no. 3, Mar. 1963: 3–89.

4107. IAkovleva, N. "Plamia Puerto-Sorido"
["The flame of Puerto Sorido"] Smena,
v. 41, no. 1, Jan. 1964: 28–29.
   Performances of a Soviet play on the
subject of the Cuban Revolution.

4108. Kogda poliaki sprazhalis' za svobodu
Kuby [When the Poles fought for the
freedom of Cuba] Inostr. lit., no. 12, Dec.
1960: 260.
   History of the Cuban Revolution of 1898
as described in a Polish novel.

4109. "Kuba, ia privetstvuiu tebia!" ["I
greet you, Cuba"] Inostr. lit., no. 12,
Dec. 1960: 258.
   Cuba in Chinese poetry.

4110. Leontovskaia, T. "Kubinskaia novella"
["Cuban novella"] Muz. zhizn', v. 6, no.
20, Oct. 1963: 8–9.
   Cuba in a Russian musical comedy.

4111. ———.   Poet Karibskoe more [The
songs of the Caribbean Sea] Muz. zhizn',
v. 7, no. 7, Apr. 1964: 8–9.
   Performance of "Cuba, My Love," a Soviet
musical comedy.

4112. Makarenko, Mykola. Viter revoliutsii,
viter svobody [The wind of revolution
and the wind of freedom] Ukraina, no. 11,
June 1962: 12–13.
   Cuban Revolution in a Russian play.

4113. Mdivani, G. Den' rozhdeniia Terezy;
geroicheskaia drama v 3 d. [Teresa's
birthday; a heroic play in three acts]
Sovr. dram., no. 3(25), 1961: 3–52.
   A play on the Cuban Revolution.

4114. Pichugin, P.   "Kuba—liubov' moia"
["Cuba, my love"] Sov. muz., v. 28, no. 4,
Apr. 1964: 36–41.
   A Russian musical comedy on the subject
of the Cuban Revolution.

4115. Poety Ispanii—Kube; stikhi [Spanish
poets praise Cuba; verse] Inostr. lit., no.
1, Jan. 1964: 3–7.
   Translated from the Spanish.

4116. Tel'pugov, V. No pasaran! Rasskaz
[No pasarán! A story] Estrada, no. 3,
1961: 35–39.

4117. Vanslav, V. "Patria o muerte." Teatr.
zhizn', no. 21, Nov. 1962: 11.
   A note on a Russian opera on the Cuban
Revolution.

4118. Zahorul'ko, Borys. Chotyry kubyns'-kykh balady [Four Cuban ballads] Prapor, no. 9, 1963: 37–45.

Ukrainian ballads devoted to Cuba.

4119. Zhdanova, K. P'ese o Kube—sto let [A play about Cuba is one hundred years old] Teatr, v. 22, no. 5, May 1961: 166.

Cuba in a Russian play of the 19th century.

e. Guatemala

4120. Slepukhin, IU. G. Dzhoanna Alarika; povest' [Juana Alarica; a tale] Moscow, Mol. gvardiia, 1962. 310 p.

Guatemala in a Russian novel.

f. Venezuela

4121. Ignat'ev, O. Skripka barabanshchika; rasskaz [The drummer's fiddle; a story] Vokrug sveta, no. 9, Sept. 1960: 13–16.

Venezuela in a Russian story.

4122. Maciejwski, Rafał. V peshchere Gua-charo; povest' [In the Guácharo cavern; a tale] Vokrug sveta, no. 6, June 1964: 21–29; no. 7, July 1964: 42–47; no. 8, Aug. 1964: 33–37.

A Polish tale on Venezuela. Translated from the Polish.

g. West Indies

4123. Seghers, Anna, pseud. Karibskie rasskazy [Caribbean stories] Moscow, Izd-vo inostr. lit., 1963. 222 p.

Translated from the German. Introductory article by T. Motyleva.

XVII

FINE ARTS

❧

A. GENERAL WORKS

1. Writings Dealing With Three or More Countries

4124. Chlenova, E. V., *and* R. A. Glukhov-skaia. "Aziia, Afrika, Latinskaia Amerika"; katalog vystavki rabot moskovskikh khudozhnikov, Moskva, 1961 ["Asia, Africa, and Latin America"; catalog of the paintings exhibited by Moscow painters, Moscow, 1961] Moscow, Soiuz khudozhnikov RSFSR, 1961. 48 p.   DLC

4125. Golomshtok, I. N., *and* I. A. Karetnikova. Iskusstvo stran Latinskoi Ameriki [The art of Latin America] Moscow, Iskusstvo, 1959. 51 p.   N6502.G6

2. Individual Countries

a. Argentina

4126. Guerrero, Lila. Iskusstvo Argentiny [The art of Argentina] Iskusstvo, v. 26, no. 2, 1963: 51–57.

4127. ———. Khuan Kastan'ino [Juan Castagnino] Iskusstvo, v. 26, no. 8, 1963: 51–54.

b. Brazil

4128. Chabukiani, V., *and* D. Mchedidze. Brazil'skii skul'ptor Irina Sakheishvili [Irina Sakheishvili, a Brazilian sculptor] Sabchota khelovneba, no. 3, 1960: 84–85. In Georgian.

4129. Klusov, E. Narodnaia keramika Brazilii [Folk ceramics of Brazil] Dekorat. isk. SSSR, no. 8, Aug. 1959: 16.

4130. Vystavka latinoamerikanskoi kul'tury [An exhibition of Latin American culture] Inostr. lit., no. 5, May 1961: 270.
An exhibition of Latin American culture in Brazil.

c. Chile

4131. Venturelli, José. V bor'be za natsional'nuiu nezavisimost' [Struggle for national independence] Tvorchestvo, no. 6, 1959: 22–23.

d. Cuba

4132. Aguilar, Onelia. Kubinskie narodnye umel'tsy [Skilled artisans of Cuba] Zhen. mira, no. 8, 1963: 9–12.

4133. Borovskii, V. Iskusstvo ostrova svobody [The art of the island of freedom] Ogonek, v. 40, no. 44, Oct. 1962: 8.

4134. García, Mario. Monument pobedy v Plaiia Khiron [A monument commemorating the victory at Playa Girón] Arkhit. SSSR, no. 5, 1964: 55–62.

4135. Karetnikova, I. Iskusstvo ostrova svobody [The art of the island of freedom] Maksla, no. 4, 1962: 24.
In Latvian.

4136. Skul'ptor—soldat revoliutsii [The sculptor is a soldier of the revolution] Inostr. lit., no. 4, Apr. 1960: 279–280.

See also entries no. 3553, 3554, and 4742.

e. Mexico

4137. Iskusstvo Meksiki ot drevneishikh vremen do nashikh dnei, Moskva-Lenin-

grad, 1960–1961; katalog [Catalog of the exhibition "Mexican art from the ancient period to our time," Moscow-Leningrad, 1960–1961] Leningrad, Izd-vo Gos. Ermitazha, 1961. 125 p.
Translated from the Spanish.

4138. Iskusstvo Meksiki ot drevneishikh vremen do nashikh dnei, Moskva, 1960; katalog [Catalog of the exhibition "Mexican art from the ancient period to our time," Moscow, 1960] Moscow, Gos. muzei izobrazit. iskusstv, 1960. 132 p.
N6550.M62

4139. Karetnikova, I. Iskusstvo sovremennoi Meksiki [Present-day Mexican art] Moscow, Znanie, 1962. 32 p.

4140. Alpatov, M. Na Vystavke meksikanskogo iskusstva [At the Exhibition of Mexican Art] Tvorchestvo, no. 1, 1961: 3–7.

4141. Chlenov, A. Otkrytie Meksiki [Discovery of Mexico] Nov. vrem., v. 18, no. 48, Nov. 1960: 28–29.
A Mexican exhibition in Moscow.

4142. Gotoviashchiesia vystavki [Forthcoming exhibitions] Iskusstvo, v. 22, no. 11, 1959: 71.
Mexican exhibitions in Moscow.

4143. Kazarnovskii, M., and S. Shamsonov. Sokrovishcha iskusstva Meksiki [Treasures of Mexican art] Neva, no. 6, 1961: 204–211.

4144. Khoroshaeva, I. F. Meksikanskaia vystavka v Moskve [Mexican Exhibition in Moscow] Sov. etn., no. 2, Mar.-Apr. 1961: 124–131.

4145. Klusov, E. V bor'be za svobodu [In the struggle for freedom] Khudozhnik, v. 6, no. 5, May 1963: 51–54.
Mexican art.

4146. Lebedev, IU. Skul'ptura Zapadnoi Meksiki [The sculpture of western Mexico] Iskusstvo, v. 24, no. 3, 1961: 51–53.

4147. Levitin, E. Iskusstvo Meksiki [The art of Mexico] Kul't. i zhizn', v. 5, no. 1, 1961: 41–43.
A Mexican exhibition in Moscow.

4148. Nikitiuk, O. Iskusstvo Meksiki [Mexican art] Khudozhnik, no. 2, Feb. 1961: 48–49.

4149. Polevoi, V. Khudozhestvennaia zhizn' Meksiki [Artistic life of Mexico] Tvorchestvo, no. 7, 1960: 20–23.

4150. Predlozhenie Sikeirosa [Siqueiros' suggestion] Inostr. lit., no. 3, Mar. 1963: 280–281.

4151. Put' skul'ptora [A sculptor's creative path] Inostr. lit., no. 6, June 1960: 280–281.

4152. Raam, V. Tri s polovinoi tysiachi let meksikanskogo iskusstva [Thirty-five hundred years of Mexican art] Kunst, no. 3, 1961: 23–32, 50–51.
Exhibitions of Mexican art in the USSR.
In Estonian. Summary in Russian.

4153. Staroe i novoe [The old and the new] Noorus, no. 4, 1961: 20–21.
Exhibitions of Mexican art in the USSR.
In Estonian.

4154. Tikhonov, IA. Meksikanskoe iskusstvo [Mexican art] Zvaigzne, no. 24, 1960: 26–27.
In Latvian.

4155. Trudy po teorii meksikanskogo iskusstva [New theoretical works on Mexican art] Inostr. lit., no. 7, July 1960: 280.

4156. V chest' Diego Rivery [In Diego Rivera's memory] Inostr. lit., no. 5, May 1959: 281.
An art exhibition in Mexico.

f. Puerto Rico

4157. Chlcnov, A. Grafika "Bogatoi Gavani" [Graphics of the "Rich Harbor"] Nov. vrem., v. 19, no. 8, Feb. 1961: 24–26.
An exhibition of Puerto Rican art in Moscow.

g. Uruguay

4158. Merzhanov, M. V gostiakh u Armando Gonsalesa [Visiting Armando González] Inostr. lit., no. 8, Aug. 1964: 246–250.
Armando González, a Uruguayan sculptor.

B. ARCHITECTURE

1. Brazil

4159. Khait, Vladimir L'vovich, and O. N. IAnitskii. Oskar Nimeier [Oscar Niemeyer] Moscow, Gosstroiizdat, 1963. 156 p.
DLC
Reviewed by D. Borisov in *V mire knig*, v. 4, no. 4, 1964: 34.

4160. Niemeyer Soares, Oscar. Moi opyt stroitel'stva Brazilia [My experience in building the city of Brasilia] Moscow, Izd-vo inostr. lit., 1963. 63 p.
Translated from the Portuguese *Minna experiencia em Brasilia*. Introductory article by A. Adzhubei.
Reviewed by D. Borisov in *V mire knig*, v. 4, no. 4, 1964: 34.

4161. Bako, G. Novaia stolitsa Brazilii [The new capital of Brazil] Nov. vrem., v. 19, no. 4, Jan. 1961: 27–28.

4162. Brodskii, B. V Brazilia [In Brasilia] Dekorat. isk. SSSR, no. 5, May 1963: 43–48.

4163. Fainberg, L. Novaia stolitsa Brazilii [The new capital of Brazil] Sov. etn., no. 4, July-Aug., 1960: 188.

4164. IAnitskii, O. Zodchii goroda Brazilia [The architect who designed the city of Brasilia] Znan.-sila, no. 10, Oct. 1963: 53–55.

4165. Khait, V., *and* O. IAnitskii. Braziliia stroit novuiu stolitsu [Brazil builds its new capital] Sov. arkhit., no. 13, 1961: 135–152.

4166. ———. Novaia stolitsa Brazilii [The new capital of Brazil] Zhil. stroi, no. 8, 1960: 27–31.

4167. ———. Oskar Nimeier [Oscar Niemeyer] Arkhit. SSSR, no. 7, 1963: 9–13.

4168. Kolomiets, N. Oskar Nimeier [Oscar Niemeyer] Stroi. i arkhit., v. 11, no. 7, July 1963: 37–38.

4169. Maiorescu, G. V prostranstve Nimeiera [In Niemeyer's space] Tekh. mol., v. 32, no. 12, 1964: 14–17.
Translated from the Rumanian.

4170. Niemeyer Soares, Oscar. Ob arkhitekture Brazilii; otryvki iz stat'i [Brazilian architecture; excerpts from an article] Maksla, no. 3, 1963: 52–53.
In Latvian. Translated from the Portuguese.

4171. Nurmukhammedov, N. Goroda i liudi Brazilii [The cities and people of Brazil] Tvorchestvo, no. 11, 1963: 16–17.

4172. Pokshishevskii, V. V. Braziliia—novaia stolitsa v IUzhnoi Amerike [Brasilia—a new capital city in South America] Izv. AN SSSR. Ser. geog., no. 6, Nov.-Dec. 1959: 118–121.

4173. Stolitsa pereekhala [The capital has moved] Vokrug sveta, no. 4, Apr. 1960: 55.

4174. Taremiae, A. Novaia stolitsa Brazilii [The new capital city of Brazil] Stroi. i arkhit., v. 8, no. 5, May 1960: 56–69.

2. Cuba

4175. Filipovskaia, N. Arkhitektura revoliutsionnoi Kuby [The architecture of revolutionary Cuba] Arkhit. SSSR, no. 6, 1963: 49–59.

4176. Ikonnikov, A. V. Arkhitektura revoliutsionnoi Kuby [The architecture of revolutionary Cuba] Stroi. i arkhit. Len., v. 26, no. 5, May 1964: 28–32.

4177. ———. Novaia arkhitektura Kuby [New Cuban architecture] Dekorat. isk. SSSR, no. 6, June 1964: 37–40.

4178. Krasnopol'skii, V. Beseda s kubinskimi arkhitektorami [A talk with Cuban architects] Nov. vrem., v. 19, no. 38, Sept. 1961: 14–16.

4179. Zhadova, L. Kuba stroit [Cuba builds] Dekorat. isk. SSSR, no. 7, July 1962: 41–45.

See also entry no. 4817.

3. Mexico

4180. Evsina, N. A. Universitetskii gorodok v Meksike [The University City in Mexico City] Vop. sovr. arkhit., no. 2, 1963: 193–220.

4181. Zhadova, L. V gorode monumental'nogo iskusstva [In a city of monumental art] Dekorat. isk. SSSR, no. 6, June 1960: 41–43.

4. Peru

4182. Otero, Roberto. Gorod v oblakakh [A city in the clouds] Vokrug sveta, no. 2, Feb. 1959: 23–25.
The city of La Paz.
Translated from the Spanish.

C. PAINTING

1. Writings Dealing With Three or More Countries

4183. Levitin, E. V Muzee imeni A. S. Pushkina [In the A. S. Pushkin Museum] Kul't. i zhizn', v. 4, no. 8, 1960: 24–25.
A collection of Latin American paintings in the USSR.

4184. Skorb', gnev, nadezhda [Sorrow, anger, and hope] Ogonek, v. 38, no. 40, Oct. 1960: 15.
Latin American art.

2. Individual Countries

a. Argentina

4185. Abstraktsionisty pod ofitsial'nym pokrovitel'stvom [Official patronage of the works of abstractionists] Inostr. lit., no. 5, May 1959: 270–271.

4186. Araújo, O. F. de. Novyi "Don Kikhot" [A new "Don Quixote"] Isk. knigi, no. 3, 1962: 323–329.
Painting.

4187. Merzhanov, Martyn. V gostiakh u argentinskikh khudozhnikov [Visiting with Argentine painters] Ogonek, v. 41, no. 43, Oct. 1963: 27.

b. Brazil

4188. Golomshtok, I. Brazil'skii zhivopisets Kandido Portinari [Candido Portinari, a Brazilian painter] Kunst, no. 1, 1961: 52–57, 81.
In Estonian. Summary in Russian.

4189. Gorokhova, R. Protest khudozhnika [The protest of a painter] Smena, v. 37, no. 3, Feb. 1960: 16.

4190. Karetnikova, I. Brazil'skii khudozhnik Kandido Portinari [Candido Portinari, a Brazilian painter] Tvorchestvo, no. 10, 1959: 22–24.

4191. Prazhane smotriat raboty Kandidu Portinari [The people of Prague view Candido Portinari's works] Inostr. lit., no. 12, Dec. 1960: 262.

4192. Smert' Kandido Portinari [The death of Candido Portinari] Inostr. lit., no. 6, June 1962: 290.

4193. Vystavka sovremennogo brazil'skogo iskusstva [An exhibition of present-day Brazilian art] Inostr. lit., no. 12, Dec. 1960: 261.
An exhibition of Brazilian art in France.

c. Chile

4194. Dubin, Kh. Iskusstvo, govoriashchee na iazyke vulkanov [An art which speaks the language of volcanoes] Maksla, no. 3, 1962: 48.
José Venturelli, a Chilean painter.
In Latvian.

4195. Krol', Anatolii. Venturelli—chiliis'kyi khudozhnyk [Venturelli, a Chilean painter] Vsesvit, v. 2, no. 4, Apr. 1959: 126–128.

4196. Marinello, Juan. Kubinskaia revoliutsiia v tvorchestve Khoze Venturelli [The Cuban Revolution in José Venturelli's works] Inostr. lit., no. 11, Nov. 1963: 253–257.

4197. Prokof'eva, M. Obrazy stradaiushchego i boriushchegosia naroda [Images of a suffering and struggling people] Iskusstvo, v. 23, no. 4, 1960: 50–53.

d. Cuba

4198. "Grafika Kuby"; katalog vystavki ["Cuban painting"; catalog of an exhibition] Moscow, Soiuz khudozhnikov SSSR, 1960. 9 p.

4199. Marinello, Juan. Beseda s nashimi khudozhnikami-abstraktsionistami [A talk with our abstract painters] Moscow, Sov. khudozhnik, 1961. 83 p.
Translated by A. M. Chlenov from the Spanish *Conversación con nuestros pintores abstractos.*
Reviewed by I. Golomshtok in *Tvorchestvo*, no. 6, 1961: 23; by V. Polevoi in *Khudozhnik*, no. 8, 1961: 63.

4200. ———. Beseda s nashimi khudozhnikami-abstraktsionistami [A talk with our abstract painters] 2d ed. Moscow, Sov. khudozhnik, 1963. 60 p.
Translated by A. M. Chlenov from the Spanish *Conversación con nuestros pintores abstractos.* Also published in Latvian.
Reviewed by V. Shleev in *V mire knig*, v. 3, no. 10, Oct. 1963: 40; by N. Zhukov in *Inostr. lit.*, no. 4, Apr. 1963: 246–248.

4201. Zhivopis' Kuby, Moskva, 1962: katalog vystavki [Catalog of the exhibition "Cuban Painting," Moscow, 1962] Moscow, Soiuz khudozhnikov SSSR, 1962. 12 p.

4202. Dokuchaeva, V. Vystavka kubinskoi grafiki v Moskve [An exhibition of Cuban paintings in Moscow] Maksla, no. 3, 1960: 54.
In Latvian.

4203. Golomshtok, I. N. Zhivopis' Kuby [Cuban painting] Tvorchestvo, no. 11, 1962: 18–20.

4204. Khudozhnik i revoliutsiia [Artists and the revolution] Inostr. lit., no. 3, Mar. 1962: 280.

4205. Khudozhnik naroda [A painter of the Cuban people] Inostr. lit., no. 9, Sept. 1962: 281.

4206. Krivich, E. Kuba boretsia [Cuba struggles] Khudozhnik, no. 1, Jan. 1961: 26–27.
An exhibition of Cuban paintings in Moscow.

4207. Kuz'mishchev, V. Shagi revoliutsii [Strides of the revolution] Khudozhnik, no. 8, Aug. 1961: 29–36.
The Cuban Revolution in the paintings of Soviet artists.

4208. Ol'shevskii, V. Grafika revoliutsionnoi Kuby [The painting of revolutionary Cuba] Iskusstvo, v. 24, no. 1, 1961: 42–44.

4209. Pavlova, L. Grafika Kuby [Cuban painting] Nar. obr., no. 1, Jan. 1961: 116–117.

4210. Prokof'eva, N. Grafika Kuby [Cuban painting] Tvorchestvo, no. 12, 1960: 14–16.

4211. Ryps'ka, N. Grafika Kuby [Cuban painting] Mystetstvo, v. 9, no. 1, Jan.-Feb. 1962: 36.

4212. Shkoliarenko, O. V nohu z zhyttiam [In step with life] Vsesvit, v. 5, no. 7, July 1962: 116–119.

4213. Sushchenko, Ivan. Patria o muerte! Ogonek, v. 40, no. 47, Nov. 1962: 14–15.
Cuba in Russian art.

4214. Turova, V. Na vystavke zhivopisi Kuby [At the Exhibition of Cuban Painting] Iskusstvo, v. 25, no. 12, 1962: 52–55.

4215. Uloza, V. Grafika revoliutsionnoi Kuby v Vil'niuse [The paintings of revolutionary Cuba in Vilnius] Pergale, no. 8, 1962: 185–186.
In Lithuanian.

4216. Vladimirov, V., and L. Shur. Vereshchagin; Kuba, 1902 [The Cuba of 1902 in V. V. Vereshchagin's paintings] Ogonek, v. 40, no. 21, May 1962: 25–27.
Cuba in Russian art.

4217. Vystavka rabot khudozhnikov-milisianos [An exhibition of militiamen's paintings] Inostr. lit., no. 4, Apr. 1962: 278–279.

4218. Weisberger, Helga. Rospis' v Gavane [A mural painting in Havana] Tvorchestvo, no. 6, 1963: 22–24.

4219. Zhivopis'—tozhe boevoe oruzhie [Painting is a weapon too] Inostr. lit., no. 2, Feb. 1963: 282–283.

e. Ecuador

4220. Oskorblenie iskusstva [An offense to the arts] Inostr. lit., no. 8, Aug. 1964: 286.
An exhibition of Ecuadorian paintings.

f. Mexico

4221. Frýd, Norbert. Grafika Meksiki [Mexican painting] Moscow, Iskusstvo, 1960. 236 p.
Translated from the Czech *Mexická grafika.*
Reviewed by I. Golomshtok in *Tvochestvo*, no. 9, 1961: 23.

4222. Arutiunian, Sh. Vystavka Raulia Angiano [An exhibition of Raúl Anguiano's works] Sovetakan arvest, no. 1, 1963: 26.
An exhibition of Mexican paintings in the USSR.
In Armenian.

4223. Beseda s Davidom Al'faro Sikeirosom [A talk with David Alfaro Siqueiros] Inostr. lit., no. 1, Jan. 1962: 280.

4224. Bol'botenko, T. Peresliduvannia vydatnoho khudozhnyka Meksiky [Persecution of an outstanding Mexican painter] Rad. pravo, no. 3, May-June 1962: 135–136.

4225. Cohen, R. Sikeiros dolzhen tvorit'! [Siqueiros must be returned to creative work!] Iskusstvo, v. 25, no. 8, 1962: 35–36.

4226. David Al'faro Sikeiros [David Alfaro Siqueiros] Noorus, no. 10, 1962: 32–33.
In Estonian.

4227. David Al'faro Sikeiros chitateliam zhurnala "Inostrannaia literatura" [David Alfaro Siqueiros' letter to the readers of "Inostrannaia literatura"] Inostr. lit., no. 11, Nov. 1964: 248.

4228. Dereviannyi zanaves nad freskami Sikeirosa [A wooden screen covering frescoes by Siqueiros] Inostr. lit., no. 8, Aug. 1959: 280–281.

4229. Diego Rivera v vospominaniiakh [Reminiscences about Diego Rivera] Inostr. lit., no. 7, July 1961: 279.

4230. Dolinskii, M., and S. Chertok. Poslednee pis'mo Diego Rivery [Diego Rivera's last letter] Smena, v. 36, no. 10, May 1959: 22–23.

4231. Efimov, V. David Al'faro Sikeiros [David Alfaro Siqueiros] Neva, no. 5, 1961: 214–215.

4232. ———. Vstrecha s Sikeirosom [A meeting with Siqueiros] Kul't. i zhizn', v. 6, no. 2, 1962: 36.

4233. ———. David Sikeiros [David Siqueiros] Neva, no. 2, 1964: 203–208.

4234. Ehrenburg, Il'ia. Diego Rivera; otryvok iz knigi vospominanii [Diego Rivera; an excerpt from a book of reminiscences] Ogonek, v. 38, no. 40, Oct. 1960: 14–15.

4235. Geronskii, G. David Sikeiros [David Siqueiros] Iskusstvo, v. 23, no. 3, 1960: 45–48.

4236. Golomshtok, I. Meksikanskaia khudozhestvennaia vystavka v Moskve [An exhibition of Mexican art in Moscow] Maksla, no. 4, 1960: 50–51.
In Latvian.

4237. ———. Traditsii i sovremennost' [Traditions and our times] Iskusstvo, v. 24, no. 3, 1961: 42–50.
An exhibition of Mexican art in Moscow.

4238. IUtkevich, S. Zhivopis', nachinennaia piroksilinom [Paintings filled with pyroxylin] Inostr. lit., no. 12, Dec. 1960: 229–242.

4239. Kalnina, D., and K. Fridrichson. David Al'faro Sikeiros [David Alfaro Siqueiros] Maksla, no. 2, 1962: 12–13.
In Latvian.

4240. Karetnikova, I. Meksikanskii khudozhnik [A Mexican painter] Tvorchestvo, no. 12, 1962: 22.
R. Anguiano, a Mexican painter.

4241. ———. Po Meksike [In Mexico] Tvorchestvo, no. 10, 1960: 17.
Mexico in Soviet paintings.

4242. Kazarnovskii, M. Glazami meksikanki [As a Mexican woman saw it] Neva, no. 10, 1959: 180–182.
Mexican paintings devoted to Communist China.

4243. Kniga o Diego Rivera [A book about Diego Rivera] Inostr. lit., no. 9, Sept. 1959: 280–281.
A review of Samuel Ramos' Diego Rivera (Mexico City, Universidad, 1958. 200 p.).

4244. Koik, R. O sovremennoi grafike Meksiki [Present-day Mexican painting] Kunst, no. 2, 1959: 50–54, 95–96.
In Estonian. Summary in Russian.

4245. Loginov, V. Sinteticheskie materialy v monumental'noi zhivopisi Meksiki [Synthetic materials used in Mexican monument painting] Iskusstvo, v. 23, no. 3, 1960: 49–51.

4246. ———. Tekhnika meksikanskikh monumentalistov [The technique of Mexican "monumentalists"] Dekorat. isk. SSSR, no. 5, May 1961: 36–39.

4247. Meksikanskie khudozhniki v bor'be za prava naroda [How Mexican artists try to protect the rights of the people] Khudozhnik, no. 3, Mar. 1959: 49.

4248. Memuary Diego Rivery [Diego Rivera's memoirs] Inostr. lit., no. 5, May 1960: 282–283.

4249. Na vystavke rabot Raulia Angiano [An exhibition of Raúl Anguiano's works] Inostr. lit., no. 3, Mar. 1960: 281.

4250. Neokonchennaia freska Davida Al'faro Sikeirosa [David Alfaro Siqueiros' unfinished mural] Vsem. stud. nov., v. 15, no. 2, Feb. 1961: 16–17.

4251. Novikova, L. Eto sozdano v tiuremnoi kamere [This was created in a prison cell] Inostr. lit., no. 11, Nov. 1964: 249–254.
David Alfaro Siqueiros' paintings.

4252. Obrashchenie Ankheliki Sikeiros [An appeal of Angélica Siqueiros] Nov. vrem., v. 19, no. 4, Jan. 1961: 22–23.
Imprisonment of the Mexican painter David Alfaro Siqueiros.

4253. Pavlenko, A. Meksikanskie freski [Mexican frescoes] Nov. vrem., v. 22, no. 32, Aug. 1964: 25–27.

4254. ———. Uznik tiur'my "Lekumberri" [The prisoner of Lecumberri] Nov. vrem., v. 21, no. 20, May 1964: 22–25.
David Siqueiros.

4255. Petukhova, K. I. Meditsina v proizvedeniiakh sovremenhykh khudozhnikov Meksiki [Medical subjects in the paintings of present-day Mexican painters] Iz ist. med., no. 4, 1962: 205–207.

4256. Protest protiv aresta Sikeirosa [A protest against the detention of Siqueiros] Inostr. lit., no. 12, Dec. 1960: 259.

4257. Renau Montoro, José. Khudozhnik i ego "sol'dadera" [A painter and his "soldadera"] Zhen. mira, no. 2, 1964: 9–12.
Translated from the Spanish.

4258. Sikeiros na svobode! [Siqueiros is free!] Zhen. mira, no. 9, 1964: 35.

4259. Sikeiros na vystavke v Parizhe [Siqueiros' paintings at an exhibition in Paris] Inostr. lit., no. 9, Sept. 1962: 282.

4260. Sikeiros shlet privet [Greetings from Siqueiros] Neva, no. 4, 1962: 217.

4261. Simonov, Konstantin. O velikom meksikantse [The great Mexican] Vop. lit., v. 8, no. 4, Apr. 1964: 136–138.
David Alfaro Siqueiros, the Mexican painter.

4262. Siqueiros, David Alfaro. Khudozhnik i revoliutsiia [The artist and the revolution] Vop. lit., v. 8, no. 4, Apr. 1964: 138–160.

4263. Siqueiros speaks from behind bars. World student news, v. 17, no. 2/3, 1963: 26–28.

4264. Svobodu Sikeirosu! [They must free Siqueiros!] Inostr. lit., no. 11, Nov. 1961: 276.

4265. TSyrlin, I. Meksikanskaia grafika [Mexican painting] In Khudozhestvennye napravleniia v sovremennom zarubezhnom iskusstve; sbornik statei. Moscow, Sov. khudozhnik, 1959: 103–122.

4266. Unzueta, Gerardo. Svobodu D. A. Sikeirosu! [Freedom for D. A. Siqueiros!] Probl. mira i sots., v. 5, no. 1, Jan. 1962: 93–94.

4267. V zashchitu Sikeirosa [In David Alfaro Siqueiros' defense] Nov. vrem., v. 19, no. 38, Sept. 1961: 18.

4268. Vydatnyi khudozhnyk za hratamy [An outstanding artist in prison] Vsesvit, v. 4, no. 1, Jan. 1961: 11.
David Alfaro Siqueiros.

4269. Zhadova, L. Iskusstvo Kh. K. Orosko [The art of José Clemente Orozco] Iskusstvo, v. 23, no. 10, 1960: 37–45.

4270. ———. Iskusstvo nel'zia zakliuchit' v tiur'mu [They cannot imprison the arts] Tvorchestvo, no. 4, 1962: 21–24.
The imprisonment of David Alfaro Siqueiros.

4271. ———. Khudozhnik novogo tipa [A painter of a new type] Dekorat. isk. SSSR, no. 10, Oct. 1962: 36–39.
José Chávez Morado, a Mexican painter.

4272. ———. Uchytel' natsii [A teacher of his nation] Vsesvit, v. 4, no. 11, Nov. 1961: 143–148.
Diego Rivera.

4273. ———. V Meksike [In Mexico] Kul't. i zhizn', v. 6, no. 7, 1962: 40–41.

4274. ———. Vstrecha s Sikeirosom [A meeting with Siqueiros] Dekorat. isk. SSSR, no. 10, Oct. 1960: 33–36.

g. Puerto Rico

4275. Grafika Puerto-Riko; katalog vystavki. Moskva, 1960 g. [Puerto Rican painting; a catalog of an exhibition. Moscow, 1960] Moscow, 1960. 15 p.

4276. Golomshtok, I. Grafika Puerto-Riko [Puerto Rican painting] Iskusstvo, v. 24, no. 5, 1961: 46–48.

4277. Karetnikova. I. Puertorikanskaia grafika v Moskve [Puerto Rican paintings in Moscow] Tvorchestvo, no. 6, 1961: 21–22.

4278. Uloza, V. Grafika Puerto-Riko [Puerto Rican painting] Pergale, no. 11, 1962: 183–184.
An exhibition of Puerto Rican paintings in the USSR.
In Lithuanian.

h. Uruguay

4279. Armando Gonsales, khudozhnik i skul'ptor [Armando González, painter and sculptor] Inostr. lit., no. 2, Feb. 1959: 285.

4280. Hernández, Angelo. Abstraktsionizm teriaet svoikh zritelei [Abstractionism is losing its viewers] Tvorchestvo, no. 12, 1960: 22–23.

4281. ———. Iz istorii zhivopisi Urugvaia [From the history of Uruguayan painting] Iskusstvo, v. 23, no. 10, 1960: 46–50.

4282. Vystavka urugvais'koi grafiky [An exhibition of Uruguayan paintings] Vsesvit, v. 7, no. 9, Sept. 1964: 118.
An exhibition of Uruguayan paintings in Bulgaria.

i. Venezuela

4283. Venesuel'skii khudozhnik Luis Gevara Moreno [Luis Guevara Moreno, a Venezuelan artist] Mol. mira, no. 1, 1959: 22.

XVIII

THEATRICAL AND PERFORMING ARTS

❧

A. THEATER

1. Writings Dealing With Three or More Countries

4284. Latinoamerikanskii teatral'nyi festival' [A Latin American theatrical festival] Inostr. lit., no. 4, Apr. 1962: 279.
A theatrical festival in Cuba.

2. Individual Countries

a. Argentina

4285. Barletta, Leonidas. Dvadtsat' sed'mogo oktiabria v Argentine [October 27, 1961 in Argentina] Teatr, v. 23, no. 3, Mar. 1962: 95–96.
Argentine theater.

4286. Itogi sezona [Results of the theatrical season] Inostr. lit., no. 6, June 1959: 272.

4287. Krizis teatra [The crisis of the Argentine theater] Inostr. lit., no. 4, Apr. 1959: 271–272.

4288. Maska i litso teatra [The mask and the real face of the Argentine theater] Inostr. lit., no. 6, June 1962: 289.

4289. Serdiukova, N. Argentinskii estradnyi ansambl' [An Argentine variety show] Sov. muz., v. 23, no. 11, Nov. 1959: 146.
Guest performances of an Argentine variety theater in the USSR.

b. Brazil

4290. A. A. Brazil'skii teatr i ego spektakl' "Dzhimba" [The Brazilian theater and its performances of "Jimba"] Teatr, v. 21, no. 8, Aug. 1960: 186–187.

4291. Braziliia . . . v bol'shom zale [Brazil . . . in our large music hall] Sovetakan arvest, no. 9, 1962: 57.
A Brazilian variety show in the USSR.
In Armenian.

4292. Brazil'skii vodevil' [Brazilian vaudeville] Inostr. lit., no. 12, Dec. 1960: 260.
A Brazilian vaudeville performance in Warsaw.

4293. E. Sh. Figeiredo o brazil'skom teatre [Figueiredo on the Brazilian theater] Teatr, v. 22, no. 11, Nov. 1961: 191–192.

4294. Leonov, N. Rasskaz o spektakle [Story of a theatrical performance] Teatr, v. 20, no. 9, Sept. 1959: 100.
Performance of a play by Guilherme de Figueiredo in the Samarkand Theater.

4295. Sobolevskii, Anatolii. Akter i obraz; B. Platonov v roli Ezopa [An actor and his role; B. Platonov in the role of Aesop] Sov. otchizna, v. 8, no. 5, Sept.-Oct. 1959: 152–156.
Performance of a Brazilian play by Guilherme de Figueiredo in the Minsk Theater.

4296. Terterian, I. Brazil'skii teatr smotrit v budushchee [The Brazilian theater looks toward the future] Teatr, v. 24, no. 5, May 1963: 153–157, 160.

c. Chile

4297. Malinarich, Humberto. U kolybeli teatra Chiliiskogo universiteta [The birth of the theater of the Chilean University] Vsem. stud. nov., v. 16, no. 3, Mar. 1962: 16–17.

4298. Núñez, Guillermo. Eksperimental'nyi teatr v Chili [An experimental theater in Chile] Vsem. stud. nov., v. 13, no. 12, Dec. 1959: 7–8.

d. Colombia

4299. Guzmán Celis, Gilberto. Festival' eksperimental'nogo teatra [A festival of the experimental theater] Mol. mira, no. 1, 1959: 23.

e. Cuba

4300. Druz'ia iz Kuby [Friends from Cuba] Teatr, v. 23, no. 3, Mar. 1962: 21.
Cuban visitors discuss a Russian play about the Cuban Revolution.

4301. E. S. Rozhdaetsia kubinskii teatr [The birth of the Cuban theater] Teatr, v. 21, no. 5, May 1960: 184.

4302. González Freire, Natividad. Dvadtsat' sed'mogo oktiabria na Kube [October 27, 1961 in Cuba] Teatr, v. 23, no. 3, Mar. 1962: 123–126.

4303. Montes Huidobro, Matías. Sistema Stanislavskogo i kubinskii teatr; k 100-letiiu so dnia rozhdeniia K. S. Stanislavskogo [Stanislavskii's system and the Cuban theater; on the centenary of K. S. Stanislavskii's birth] Teatr. zhizn', no. 13, July 1962: 23.
Translated from the Spanish.

4304. Nusinova, IU. Teatr Kuby izuchaet svoe proshloe [The Cuban theater studies its history] Teatr, v. 24, no. 1, Jan. 1963: 68–69.
A review of *Historia del teatro en La Habana*, v. 1, by Edwin T. Tolón and Jorge Antonio González (Santa Clara, Universidad de Las Villas, 1961).

4305. Shvedov, IU. Teatr revoliutsionnoi Kuby [The theater of revolutionary Cuba] Teatr, v. 22, no. 2, Feb. 1961: 174–178.

4306. Tamaev, A. Nash novyi drug s Kuby [Our new friend from Cuba] Muz. zhizn', v. 5, no. 1, Jan. 1962: 9.
Guest performances of Cuban actors in Russia.

4307. Teatr Kuby so svoim narodom [The theater in Cuba stands with its people] Teatr, v. 22, no. 7, July 1961: 171–175.

4308. V. K. Gor'kovskaia Nilovna v Gavane [Gor'kii's "Nilovna" in Havana] Teatr, v. 24, no. 5, May 1963: 163.

4309. Zherdynivs'ka, Marharyta. Teatr heroichnoi Kuby [The theater of heroic Cuba] Mystetstvo, v. 8, no. 1, Jan.-Feb. 1961: 34–35.

f. The Guianas

4310. Teatral'noe iskusstvo—narodu [Theatrical art should serve the people] Inostr. lit., no. 11, Nov. 1963: 277.
British Guiana.

g. Mexico

4311. Novikova, L. Za kulisami "zolotogo sezona" [Behind the scenes of a "golden season"] Teatr, v. 24, no. 5, May 1964: 147–151.

4312. V. Ch. Trudnosti i iskaniia meksikanskogo teatra [The difficulties and creative quests of the Mexican theater] Teatr, v. 21, no. 7, July 1960: 191–192.

4313. V. K. Proshloe i budushchee meksikanskogo teatra [The past and future of the Mexican theater] Teatr, v. 20, no. 6, June 1959: 189.

4314. ———. Puti meksikanskogo teatra [Paths of the Mexican theater] Teatr, v. 24, no. 4, Apr. 1963: 160.

h. Uruguay

4315. S. B. "Nezavisimye" v Urugvae [The "Independents" in Uruguay] Teatr, v. 20, no. 8, Aug. 1959: 182.

4316. "Vishnevyi sad" v Montevideo ["The Cherry Orchard" in Montevideo] Inostr. lit., no. 3, Mar. 1959: 285.

i. Venezuela

4317. Studenty staviat p'esu Brekhta [Performance of a Brecht play by university students] Inostr. lit., no. 3, Mar. 1959: 272–273.

B. OPERA

4318. Listov, Konstantin. Ankhela [Angela] Sov. zhen., v. 19, no. 3, 1963: 15.
A Russian opera about the Cuban Revolution.

4319. Vershinina, I. Ankhela Alonso—geroinia opery [Angela Alonso, the heroine of an opera] Ogonek, v. 40, no. 15, Apr. 1962: 28.

A Russian opera about the Cuban Revolution.

C. BALLET AND DANCE

1. Argentina

4320. Pichugin, P. Tango i ego istoriia [The tango and its history] Sov. muz., v. 26, no. 5, May 1962: 18–19.

2. Brazil

4321. The Bossa Nova knows where it's going. World student news, v. 17, no. 4, 1963: 28ff.

A Brazilian dance.

4322. Zoin, A. "Brazil'skaia samba" u Minsku ["Brazilian samba" in Minsk] Belarus', v. 17, no. 10, Oct. 1960: 24.

Guest performances of a Brazilian ensemble in White Russia.

3. Cuba

4323. Alonso, Fernando, *and* Alicia Alonso. "My vstrechaem liudei veselykh, dobrykh, krasivykh" ["We see joyful, warmhearted, and beautiful people"] Teatr. zhizn', no. 22, Nov. 1964: 2–3.

Guest performances of a Cuban ballet group in the USSR.

4324. Asarkan, A. Mariia-Antoniia, kotoraia ne tantsovala [María Antonia, who did not dance] Teatr, v. 20, no. 11, Nov. 1959: 187–191.

Guest performances of a Cuban ensemble in the USSR.

4325. Balet svobodnoi Kuby [The ballet of free Cuba] Sov. zhen., v. 17, no. 3, 1961: 40.

Guest performances of a group of Cuban dancers in the USSR.

4326. Čanga, J. Prekrasnyi balet tsvetushchei strany [An excellent ballet ensemble of a flourishing country] Maksla, no. 4, 1960: 43–46.

Guest performances of a Cuban ballet ensemble.

In Latvian.

4327. El'iash, N. Spektakli kubinskogo baleta [Performances of the Cuban ballet] Sov. muz., v. 25, no. 2, Feb. 1961: 104–107.

Cuban ballet dancers in Moscow.

4328. Gabovich, M. Balet svobodnoi Kuby [The ballet of free Cuba] Teatr, v. 22, no. 3, Mar. 1961: 167–171.

4329. Gol'derness, E. Balet Respubliki Kuby [The ballet ensemble of the Cuban Republic] Sabchota khelovneba, no. 10, 1961: 49–55.

Guest performances of a Cuban ballet company in the USSR.

In Georgian.

4330. ———. Narodnaia Kuba v Tbilisi [People's Cuba in Tiflis] Sabchota khelovneba, no. 11, 1962: 74–75.

Guest performances of Cuban dancers in the USSR.

In Georgian.

4331. Kalmykov, Vl. U Alisii Alonso [Visiting Alicia Alonso] Teatr. zhizn', no. 18, Sept. 1963: 7.

4332. Kaupužs, V. Ballet de Cuba. Zvaigzne, no. 22, 1960: 18.

In Latvian.

4333. Kubinskii natsional'nyi ansambl' tantsa v Moskve [Guest performances of the National Ensemble of Cuban Dancers in Moscow] Teatr, v. 22, no. 8, Aug. 1961: 186–187.

4334. Malen'kii ostrov—bol'shoi balet [A great ballet ensemble from a small island] Vsem. stud. nov., v. 15, no. 6, June 1961: 12–13.

Guest performances of a Cuban dancing ensemble in the USSR.

4335. Okuneva, V., *and* V. Svetinskaia. Kubinskii tanets [The Cuban dance] Vozhatyi, v. 38, no. 12, Dec. 1962: 47–48.

4336. Roslavleva, N. Balet svobodnoi Kuby [The ballet of free Cuba] Muz. zhizn', no. 24, Dec. 1960: 11–12.

4337. ———. Novaia vstrecha s kubinskim baletom [We see the Cuban ballet again] Muz. zhizn', v. 7, no. 21, Nov. 1964: 7–8.

Guest performances of a Cuban ballet ensemble in the USSR.

4338. Smirnova, I. Viva, Cuba! Sov. muz., v. 25, no. 7, July 1961: 92–93.
Guest performances of a Cuban dancing ensemble in the USSR.

4339. Verina, N. "Pliashet Gavana" ["Havana dances"] Ogonek, v. 37, no. 15, Apr. 1959: 25.
A Cuban ballerina in the USSR.

D. MOTION PICTURES

1. Writings Dealing With Three or More Countries

4340. Sadoul, Georges. U kinematografistov Latinskoi Ameriki [With the movie-makers of Latin America] Isk. kino, no. 7, July 1961: 126–131.

4341. Tur, Petr. S kameroi po Latinskoi Amerike [Through Latin America with a motion-picture camera] Isk. kino, no. 11, 1962: 16–19.

2. Individual Countries

a. Argentina

4342. Fil'm po rasskazam Al'varo IUnke [A motion picture based on Alvaro Yunque's stories] Inostr. lit., no. 11, Nov. 1962: 273.

4343. Goldovskaia, M. Review. Isk. kino, v. 33, no. 6, 1963: 146–147.
A review of the periodical *Tiempo de cine* (Argentina).

4344. Kholendro, Dm. Glaza dobrogo cheloveka [The eyes of a kind man] Ogonek, v. 38, no. 48, Nov. 1960: 18–19.
Documentary motion pictures.

4345. Novyi fil'm Ugo del' Karrilia [Hugo del Carill's new motion picture] Inostr. lit., no. 5, May 1960: 275.

4346. Oliver, María Rosa. Argentinskoe kino v poru "novoi volny" [Argentine motion pictures during the "new wave"] V zashch. mira, no. 12, Dec. 1961: 82–88.

4347. Politseiskie dekrety protiv iskusstva [Police decrees tend to circumscribe the arts] Inostr. lit., no. 11, Nov. 1962: 273.
Censorship of motion pictures.

4348. "Poslednii etazh" ["The upper floor"] Inostr. lit., no. 4, Apr. 1962: 268–269.

4349. Protest Al'varo IUnke [Alvaro Yunque's protest] Inostr. lit., no. 12, Dec. 1960: 254.

4350. Suárez, Martínez. Novye fil'my— novye imena [New films and new names] Isk. kino, v. 33, no. 7, 1963: 131–133.

4351. V pogone za deshevym effektom [In search of cheap effect] Inostr. lit., no. 8, Aug. 1960: 273.

b. Brazil

4352. Ekranizatsiia p'esy Garsia Lorki [The filming of a García Lorca play] Inostr. lit., no. 8, Aug. 1962: 274–275.

4353. IUtkevich, Sergei. O brazil'skom kino [Brazilian motion pictures] Nov. vrem., v. 20, no. 42, Oct. 1962: 26–28.

4354. "Krasnye vskhody" v kaatinge ["Red Shoots" in the drought-stricken area] Inostr. lit., no. 5, May 1964: 275.

4355. Zasokhshie zhizni [Withered lives] Zhen. mira, no. 9, 1964: 32–33.

c. Chile

4356. Pod gnetom tsenzury [In the clutches of censorship] Inostr. lit., no. 3, Mar. 1963: 286.
Censorship of motion pictures.

d. Colombia

4357. Kinofil'm "Istochniki kamnei" (?) [The motion picture "Sources of Stones"] Mol. mira, no. 6, 1961: 16.

e. Cuba

4358. Gaevskii, V. "Kuba-da," "Prekrasnyi mai" ["Cuba-sí" and "Beautiful May"] Isk. kino, v. 33, no. 10, 1963: 134–135.
French motion pictures on Cuba.

4359. Goldovskaia, M. Review. Isk. kino, v. 33, no. 8, 1963: 143.
A review of the periodical *Cine cubano*.

4360. Guevara, Alfredo. O kubinskoi kine-matografii [Cuban motion pictures] Nov. vrem., v. 19, no. 30, July 1961: 16–17.

4361. "IA—Kuba" ["This is Cuba"] Kuba, no. 4, Dec. 1964: 34–37.

4362. Karmen, R. S"emki na pylaiushchem ostrove; iz dnevnika [Making a motion picture on an island in flame; from a diary] Isk. kino, no. 6, 1962: 123–131; no. 7, 1962: 125–132.

4363. Khulio Garsia Espinoza [Julio García Espinosa] Vsesvit, v. 6, no. 3, Mar. 1963: 126–127.
A motion-picture producer.

4364. Pavlova, N. Otkrytoe dlia liubvi [Open for love] Ogonek, v. 39, no. 23, June 1961: 21.
A Soviet documentary motion picture on Cuba.

4365. Pineda Barnet, Enrique. Eto budet sovetsko-kubinskii fil'm [It will be a Soviet-Cuban motion picture] Nov. vrem., v. 20, no. 10, Mar. 1962: 16–18.

4366. Pomnite Plaiia-Khiron! [Remember Playa Girón!] Inostr. lit., no. 4, Apr. 1962: 279.
A documentary motion picture.

4367. Rozhdenie novogo [Birth of the new] Isk. kino, no. 7, July 1961: 21–22.
Translated from the Spanish.

4368. Segodnia i zavtra kubinskogo kino [Today and tomorrow of the motion-picture industry of Cuba] Vsem. stud. nov., v. 14, no. 11/12, Nov.-Dec. 1960: 19–21.

4369. Shagi kubinskogo kino [The progress of Cuban motion pictures] Inostr. lit., no. 7, July 1963: 281.

4370. Smirnov, S. S. Kuba na ekrane [Cuba on the motion-picture screen] Isk. kino, no. 6, June 1961: 102–105.
A documentary film on Cuba.

See also entry no. 4749.

f. Jamaica

4371. Pervaia kinostudiia [The first motion-picture studio] Inostr. lit., no. 8, Aug. 1963: 286.

g. Mexico

4372. Alvarado, César Alonso. "Korni"—novoe v kinoiskusstve ["The Roots" is a new development in cinema art] Vsem. stud. nov., v. 13, no. 6, June 1959: 12–13.

4373. Cota Ramos, Elsie. Moe mnenie o fil'me "Korni" [My opinion about the motion picture "The Roots"] Vsem. stud. nov., v. 14, no. 2, Feb. 1960: 24.

4374. Fil'm o meksikanskoi revoliutsii [A motion picture on the Mexican Revolution] Inostr. lit., no. 10, Oct. 1959: 280–281.

4375. Kryzhanivs'kyi, B. "Zolotyi vik" ne skinchyvsia [The "golden age" isn't over] Vsesvit, v. 6, no. 8, Aug. 1963: 93–96.

4376. Mariia Feliks o Gollivude [María Félix on Hollywood] Inostr. lit., no. 7, July 1960: 280–281.

4377. Ospovat, L. Svidanie ne sostoialos' [The meeting did not take place] Isk. kino, no. 2, Feb. 1959: 104–105.

4378. Pod nebom Meksiki; meksikanskii fil'm [Under the skies of Mexico; a Mexican film] Zhen. mira, no. 5, 1959: 34.

4379. Pyr'ev, I. Mekhiko, 1958 [Mexico City, 1958] Isk. kino, no. 3, Mar. 1959: 131–139.
A motion-picture festival.

4380. "Schast'e" na ekrane ["Happiness" on the motion-picture screen] Inostr. lit., no. 2, Feb. 1960: 279–280.

4381. Sergeeva, L. Meksikanskoe kinoiskusstvo vchera i segodnia [The Mexican motion picture yesterday and today] Isk. kino, no. 1, Jan. 1961: 139–146.

4382. V zashchitu khudozhestvennoi pravdy [In defense of artistic truth] Inostr. lit., no. 9, Sept. 1960: 280–281.

h. Venezuela

4383. Araia; venesuel'skii dokumental'nyi fil'm v postanovke Margo Benaserraf [Arayá; a Venezuelan documentary motion picture produced by Margot Benacerraf] Zhen. mira, no. 7, 1963: 22–23.

E. MISCELLANEOUS

1. Argentina

4384. Villafañe, Javier. My—kukol'niki iz Argentiny [We are the puppeteers from Argentina] Teatr, v. 20, no. 1, Jan. 1959: 184–186.

2. Cuba

4385. Mikhailova, N. Spektakl' o geroicheskom ostrove [A pantomime about the
heroic island] Sov. tsirk, v. 6, no. 8,
Aug. 1962: 1–3.
   A pantomime about events in Cuba.

3. Mexico

4386. Voloshin, A.   Trio Kodona [The
Codona trio] Sov. tsirk, v. 3, no. 1, Jan.
1959: 27–28.
   Mexican acrobats.

XIX

MUSIC

A. WRITINGS DEALING WITH THREE OR MORE COUNTRIES

4387. Pichugin, P.   Pesni Meksiki, Brazilii, Kuby [The songs of Mexico, Brazil, and Cuba] Sov. muz., v. 27, no. 12, Dec. 1963: 91–94.

B. INDIVIDUAL COUNTRIES

1. Argentina

4388. Il'in, V.   Gost'ia iz Argentiny [Our guest from Argentina] Sov. muz., v. 25, no. 12, Dec. 1961: 108.
   Guest performances of an Argentine pianist in the USSR.

4389. Pichugin, P.   Narodnye pesni Argentiny [The folk songs of Argentina] Sov. muz., v. 27, no. 9, Sept. 1963: 113–118.

4390. Zargarian, IA.   Odin iz luchshikh ispolnitelei Shopena [One of the best interpreters of Chopin] Sovetakan arvest, no. 7, 1963: 62.
   Guest performances of an Argentine pianist in the USSR.
   In Armenian.

2. Brazil

4391. Almeida, Renato.   Melodii moho narodu [Melodies of my people] Vsesvit, v. 2, no. 2, Feb. 1959: 138.

4392. Pichugin, P.   Eitor Villa-Lobos [Heitor Villa-Lobos] Sov. muz., v. 26, no. 5, May 1962: 39–45.

4393. Shneerson, G.   Pamiati Villa-Lobosa [In memory of Villa-Lobos] Sov. muz., v. 24, no. 3, Mar. 1960: 184–185.

4394. Sveshnikova, A.   Eitor Villa-Lobos [Heitor Villa-Lobos] Muz. zhizn', v. 5, no. 5, Mar. 1962: 17–18.

4395. Tamaev, A.   S solntsem v krovi [Sunshine in the blood] Muz. zhizn', v. 3, no. 18, Sept. 1960: 14–15.
   Guest performances of a Brazilian musical ensemble in the USSR.

3. Chile

4396. Allende Blín, Juan Adolfo.   Muzyka Chili [The music of Chile] Sov. muz., v. 23, no. 5, May 1959: 182–185.

4397. Pichugin, P.   Vystupaiut chiliiskie artisty [Chilean singers and dancers perform] Muz. zhizn', v. 4, no. 18, Sept. 1961: 14–15.

4398. Vicentini, María Luisa.   Violeta Parra; ritm, pesnia, kraski [Violeta Parra; rhythms, songs, and colors] Zhen. mira, no. 1, 1963: 21–24.
   Chilean folk singers.

4. Cuba

4399. Carpentier, Alejo.   Muzyka Kuby [The music of Cuba] Moscow, Muzgiz, 1962. 162 p.   ML207.C8C37 1962
   Translated by N. N. Serdiukova from the Spanish *La música en Cuba*.
   Reviewed by A. Sveshnikova in *Muz. zhizn'*, v. 6, no. 8, Apr. 1963: 18; by P. Pichugin in *Sov. muz.*, v. 27, no. 6, June 1963: 132–135.

4400. Dirizher i boets [Conductor and fighter] Sovetakan arvest, no. 2, 1963: 60.
   Guest performances of Cuban musicians in the USSR.
   In Armenian.

4401. Fere, Vladimir. Gody bor'by i pobed [The years of struggle and achievements] Muz. zhizn', v. 7, no. 1, 1964: 4–5.
Cuban music.

4402. G. E. Muzyka na ostrove svobody [Music on the island of freedom] Sov. muz., v. 26, no. 11, Nov. 1962: 118–122.

4403. Gavrilin, V. Sovetskaia pesnia na Kube [Soviet songs in Cuba] Sov. muz., v. 25, no. 10, Oct. 1961: 135–136.

4404. I. Ch. Artisty Kuby [Cuban singers and dancers] Sov. muz., v. 23, no. 11, Nov. 1959: 145–146.
Guest performances of a Cuban musical ensemble in the USSR.

4405. León, Argeliers. Rasskazyvaet kubinskii muzykant [A Cuban musician tells us his story] Muz. zhizn', v. 7, no. 20, Oct. 1964: 16–17.

4406. Mar, N. Iz roda tabachnikov Borkha [From the Borja type of tobacco workers] Teatr. zhizn', no. 5, Mar. 1962: 12–13.
Cuban singers.

4407. Mironenko, I. Poet svobodnaia Kuba [Free Cuba sings] Teatr. zhizn', no. 20, Oct. 1963: 2.

4408. Pichugin, P. Dirizhiruet Enrike Mantichi [Enrique Manticci conducts] Muz. zhizn', v. 6, no. 6, Mar. 1963: 6–7.
A concert by Cuban musicians in Moscow.

4409. ———. Muzyka, vozvrashchennaia narodu [Music was returned to the people] Sov. muz., v. 28, no. 1, Jan. 1964: 122–123.

4410. ———. Pesni i tantsy Kuby [Cuban songs and dances] Muz. zhizn', v. 5, no. 23, Dec. 1962: 5 6.

4411. Pichugin, P., and A. Sveshnikova. Tvortsy kubinskoi muzyki [Creators of Cuban music] Muz. zhizn', v. 5, no. 11, June 1962: 11–13.

4412. Saldívar, Rudel. Gimn revoliutsionnoi Kuby [The national anthem of revolutionary Cuba] Muz. zhizn', v. 6, no. 10, May 1963: 4.

4413. ———. Pevets svobodnoi Kuby [The bard of free Cuba] Muz. zhizn', v. 6, no. 14, July 1963: 11–12.
Translated from the Spanish.

4414. Timokhin, V. Novoe znakomstvo [A new friend] Muz. zhizn', v. 5, no. 10, May 1962: 5.
Guest performances of a Cuban singer in the USSR.

4415. Vasilevskii, L. Pesni revoliutsionnogo naroda [The songs of a revolutionary people] Sov. muz., v. 28, no. 11, Nov. 1964: 120–123.

4416. Zvuchit pesnia nad Karibskim morem [This song resounds over the Caribbean Sea] Smena, v. 38, no. 23, Dec. 1961: 5–6.
"Cuba libre," a Russian song on the Cuban Revolution.

See also entries no. 4664–4666.

5. Mexico

4417. Koval', Marian. Pevtsy iz Meksiki [Singers from Mexico] Sov. muz., v. 25, no. 11, Nov. 1961: 117.
Guest performances of Mexican singers in the USSR.

4418. Muzyka Raulia Lavisty [Raúl Lavista's music] Inostr. lit., no. 1, Jan. 1959: 279–280.

4419. Oratoriia—prizyv k miru [An oratorio which calls for peace] Inostr. lit., no. 4, Apr. 1961: 282.
Performance of Pablo Casals' new oratorio in Mexico.

4420. Pichugin, P. Kogda iz pesni vykidyvaiut slovo [When the words of a song are changed] Muz. zhizn', v. 5, no. 19, Oct. 1962: 14–15.

4421. ———. Muzyka Meksiki [Mexican music] Muz. zhizn', v. 4, no. 14, July 1961: 13.

4422. ———. Pesni meksikanskoi revoliutsii [Songs of the Mexican Revolution] Sov. muz., v. 27, no. 11, Nov. 1963: 131–137.

4423. ———. Sil'vestre Revuel'tas i meksikanskii fol'klor [Silvestre Revueltas and Mexican folklore] Sov. muz., v. 25, no. 5, 1961: 170–176.

4424. Sabinina, M. Gost' iz Meksiki [A visitor from Mexico] Muz. zhizn', v. 4, no. 23, Dec. 1961: 9–10.
A Mexican violinist in Moscow.

4425. Schering, G. Dusha muzyki [The spirit of music] Sov. muz., v. 26, no. 7, July 1962: 128–129.

4426. Sveshnikova, A. Pesni Meksiki [Mexican songs] Muz. zhizn', v. 6, no. 15, Aug. 1963: 17.
Guest performances of an ensemble of Mexican singers in Moscow.

4427. Zabotin, L. Poet Elia Kasanovas [Ella Casanovas sings] Muz. zhizn', v. 3, no. 16, Aug. 1960: 13.
Guest performances of a Mexican singer in Moscow.

6. Paraguay

4428. "Los Paragvaios" ["Los paraguayos"] Sovetakan arvest, no. 5, 1964: 62.
Guest performances of a Paraguayan musical ensemble in the USSR.
In Armenian.

4429. Pichugin, P. Ansambl' iz Paragvaia [An ensemble from Paraguay] Muz. zhizn', v. 7, no. 12, June 1964: 23.

7. Peru

4430. Biriukov, Vadim. Doch' solntsa [A daughter of the sun] Ogonek, v. 38, no. 47, Nov. 1960: 29.
Guest performances of Yma Sumac in the USSR.

4431. Golovin, Vitalii. Tak poet Ima Sumak [Such is Yma Sumac's manner of singing] Teatr. zhizn', no. 1, 1961: 19.

4432. Guevara Ochoa, Armando. Zametki o peruanskoi muzyke [Notes on Peruvian music] Sov. muz., v. 24, no. 11, Nov. 1960: 181–184.

4433. Kavtaradze, N. Pesnia And [The song of the Andes] Sabchota khelovneba, no. 10, 1961: 72.
Guest performances of Yma Sumac in the USSR.
In Georgian.

4434. Medvedev, A. Poet Ima Sumak [Yma Sumac sings] Muz. zhizn', v. 4, no. 2, Jan. 1961: 12.

4435. Polinin, D. Poet Ima Sumak [Yma Sumac sings] Uzbekiston, no. 3, 1961: 23.
In Uzbek.

4436. Rudakov, E. Zagadki neobychnykh golosov [Unsolved problems of the unusual range of voice] Znan.-sila, v. 36, no. 1, Jan. 1961: 32–33.
Yma Sumac.

4437. S. V. Otzvuk And [The echo of the Andes] Zvaigzne, no. 1, 1961: 30.
Guest performances of Yma Sumac.
In Latvian.

4438. Timokhin, V. Ima Sumak [Yma Sumac] Muz. zhizn', v. 3, no. 20, Oct. 1960: 17.

8. Uruguay

4439. Pichugin, P. Za pul'tom—Khuan Protassi [Juan Protassi at the podium] Muz. zhizn', v. 5, no. 12, June 1962: 5.
An orchestra conductor from Uruguay.

XX

PHILOSOPHY

❧

A. WRITINGS DEALING WITH THREE OR MORE COUNTRIES

4440. Anan'ev, B. G. O razvitii psikhologi-cheskoi nauki v nekotorykh stranakh IUzhnoi Ameriki [The development of psychology in some countries of South America] Vop. psikhol., v. 5, no. 1, Jan.-Feb. 1959: 157–165.

4441. Antiasov, M. Problemy kul'turnogo edinstva stran Latinskoi Ameriki i SShA [Problems of cultural unity between Latin American countries and the United States] Vest. ist. mir. kul't., no. 3, May-June 1959: 99–112.

4442. Portuondo, José Antonio. Osnovnoe protivorechie nashei epokhi i budushchee latinoamerikanskikh narodov [The funda-mental contradiction of our times and the future of the Latin American peoples] Vop. filos., v. 18, no. 3, 1964: 11–16.

4443. Shul'govskii, A. F. Romantizm i pozitivizm v Latinskoi Amerike; otvet na stat'iu L. Sea [Romanticism and posi-tivism in Latin America; a reply to an article by Leopoldo Zea] Vest. ist. mir. kul't., no. 4, July-Aug. 1960: 3–21.
Summary in English.

4444. Zea, Leopoldo. Ot romantizma k pozitivizmu v Latinskoi Amerike [The turn from romanticism to positivism in Latin America] Vest. ist. mir. kul't., no. 3, May-June 1960: 12–26.

4445. Zubritskii, IU. A. Latinidad i ego sushchnost' ["La Latinidad" and its real nature] Vest. ist. mir. kul't., no. 1, Jan.-Feb. 1961: 112–117.

B. INDIVIDUAL COUNTRIES

1. Argentina

4446. Agosti, Héctor Pablo. Natsiia i kul'-tura [The nation and its culture] Moscow, Izd-vo inostr. lit., 1963. 262 p.
Translated by R. Burguete and A. Deriugina from the Spanish Nación y cultura. Introductory article by N. V. Pukhovskii.

4447. Agosti, Héctor Pablo. Ideologicheskie problemy v sovremennoi Argentine [Ideological problems in present-day Argentina] Probl. mira i sots., v. 3, no. 6, June 1960: 38–41.

4448. Burguete A., R. Filosofskie vzgliady Florentino Amegino [Florentino Ame-ghino's philosophical views] Vest. ist. mir. kul't., no. 3, May-June 1959: 154–161.

2. Brazil

4449. Cruz Costa, João. Obzor istorii filo-sofii v Brazilii [A historical survey of Brazilian philosophy] Moscow, Izd-vo inostr. lit., 1962. 146 p.
Translated from the Portuguese Panorama da história da filosofia no Brasil. Introductory article by Zh. A. Bazarian.

4450. Terterian, I. Euklides da Kunia—natsional'nyi geroi Brazilii [Euclydes da Cunha, the national hero of Brazil] Moscow, Znanie, 1959. 24 p.

4451. Bazarian, Zh. Brazil'skii progressivnyi myslitel' Evklides da Kun'ia, 1866–1909 [Euclydes da Cunha, a progressive Brazilian thinker, 1866–1909] Vest. ist. mir. kul't., no. 5, Sept.-Oct. 1961: 97–106.

4452. ———. Pisatel' i myslitel' [Writer and philosopher] Inostr. lit., no. 12, Dec. 1959: 239–241.
Euclydes da Cunha.

4453. ———. Vydaiushchiisia brazil'skii myslitel' 19 veka Tobias Barreto [Tobias Barreto, an outstanding Brazilian philosopher of the 19th century] Vest. ist. mir. kul't., no. 6, Nov.-Dec. 1959: 111–121.

4454. Gabinskii, N. Euklides da Kun'ia; k 50-letiiu so dnia smerti [Euclydes da Cunha; on the 50th anniversary of his death] Sov. Soiuz, no. 8, 1959: 56.

4455. Terterian, Inna. Syn Brazilii [A son of Brazil] Ogonek, v. 37, no. 40, Oct. 1959: 29.
Euclydes da Cunha.

3. Cuba

4456. Ternovoi, O. S. Obshchestvenno-politicheskie i filosofskie vzgliady Khose Marti [José Martí's sociopolitical and philosophical views] Minsk, 1962. 15 p.
Author's abstract of a dissertation.

4457. Ratan, S. Pratsa pra Kubinskaha revaliutsyianera [A study of a Cuban revolutionary] Belarus', v. 19, no. 12, Dec. 1962: 30.
Review of a dissertation on José Martí by O. S. Ternovoi.

4458. Ternovoi, O. S. Vydaiushchiisia kubinskii myslitel' Khose Marti [José Martí, an outstanding Cuban thinker] Vop. filos., v. 13, no. 2, 1959: 129–136.

4. Mexico

4459. Gortari, Eli de. Vvedenie v dialekticheskuiu logiku [Introduction to dialectical logic] Moscow, Izd-vo inostr. lit., 1959. 356 p.   B809.8.G587
Translated by A. V. Deriugina and I. E. Shokina from the Spanish *Introducción a la lógica dialéctica.*

4460. León Portilla, Miguel. Filosofiia nagua [Philosophy of the Nahuas] Moscow, Izd-vo inostr. lit., 1961.
Translated by R. Burguete from the Spanish *La filosofía náhuatl estudiada en sus fuentes.*
Reviewed by A. Makarov in *Kul't. i zhizn'*, v. 6, no. 12, 1962: 38–39.

4461. Fedoseev, P. Torzhestvo materializma i upadok burzhuaznoi filosofii [The triumph of materialism and the decline of bourgeois philosophy] Kommunist, v. 40, no. 16, Nov. 1963: 37–47.
A philosophical congress in Mexico City.

4462. Mitin, M. B. Filosofskii kongress v Meksike [The Philosophical Congress in Mexico] Vest. AN SSSR, v. 34, no. 1, Jan. 1964: 74–78.

4463. Rutkevich, M. Filosofskie spory v Meksike [Philosophical discussions in Mexico] Ural, no. 2, 1964: 126–134.

4464. ———. Na filosofskom kongresse v Meksike [At the Philosophical Congress in Mexico] Nauch. dokl. vys. shkoly; filos. nauki, v. 7, no. 1, 1964: 37–48.

4465. Sánchez Vásquez, Adolfo. Nasha sviaz' s epokhoi [Our contacts with our epoch] Vop. filos., v. 18, no. 1, 1964: 45–54.
Mexican philosophy.

4466. Shteinberg, V. Vokrug chego sporili v Meksiko [Problems which were discussed in Mexico] Komm. Sov. Latvii, v. 18, no. 12, Dec. 1963: 36–42.

5. Peru

4467. Kuteishchikova, V. Rol' Khose Karlosa Mariategi v razvitii natsional'noi kul'tury Peru [José Carlos Mariátegui's role in the development of Peruvian national culture] Vest. ist. mir. kul't., no. 6, Nov.-Dec. 1960: 3–19.

XXI

MEDIA OF COMMUNICATION

꿩

A. THE PRESS

1. Writings Dealing With Three or More Countries

4468. Pechat' zarubezhnykh stran; Zapadnaia Evropa, Amerika, Avstraliia [The press of foreign countries; Western Europe, America, and Australia] Moscow, Gospolitizdat, 1962.   Z6941.P4

Partial contents. —Argentina, p. 219–223. —Bahama Islands, p. 224. —Barbados, p. 225. —Bermuda, p. 226. —Bolivia, p. 227–228. —Brazil, p. 229–237. —British Guiana, p. 250. —British Honduras, p. 254. —Chile, p. 384–387. —Colombia, p. 277–280. —Costa Rica, p. 281–283. —Cuba, p. 284–290. Curaçao, p. 291. —Dominican Republic, p. 255–256. —Ecuador, p. 388–390. —El Salvador, p. 319–320. —French Guiana, p. 251. —Guadeloupe, p. 245–246. —Guatemala, p. 247–249. —Haiti, p. 243–244. —Honduras, p. 252–253. —Jamaica, p. 391. —Leeward Islands, p. 316. —Martinique, p. 292. —Mexico, p. 293–302. —Nicaragua, p. 304–305. —Panama, p. 306–308. —Paraguay, p. 309–311. —Peru, p. 312–315. —Puerto Rico, p. 317–318. —Surinam, p. 374. —Trinidad and Tobago, p. 375. —Uruguay, p. 376–383. —Venezuela, p. 238–241. —Virgin Islands, p. 242. —Windward Islands, p. 303.

4469. Silveira, Paulo da. Istoriia odnogo press-sindikata [History of a press syndicate] Za rubezhom, no. 51, Dec. 1961: 24.

2. Individual Countries

a. Argentina

See entry no. 1181.

b. Brazil

4470. Pokhvalin, V. I. Kratkii obzor brazil'skoi pechati [Brief review of the Brazilian press] Vest. Mosk. un. Ser. 7: Filol., zhur., v. 18, no. 3, May-June 1963: 66–72.

c. Chile

4471. Gutiérrez, Joaquín. "El Siglo"; orudie bol'shogo kalibra ["El Siglo", a large-caliber weapon] Za rubezhom, no. 18, May 1963: 14–15.

A large-circulation Communist newspaper.

See also entry no. 1224.

d. Colombia

4472. Il'inskii, V. Eto lish fiktsiia [It is only fiction] Sov. pech., no. 8, Aug. 1961: 59.

Journalism.

e. Cuba

4473. Gladkii, Viktor Borisovich. Pechat' kubinskoi revoliutsii, 1958–1961 gg. [The press of the Cuban Revolution, 1958–1961] Moscow, 1964. 20 p. (Moskovskii gosudarstvennyi universitet imeni M. V. Lomonosova. Fakul'tet zhurnalistiki. Kafedra zarubezhnoi pechati i literatury)

Abstract of a dissertation for the degree of Candidate in Historical Sciences.

4474. ———. Pechat' Kuby; 1959–1962 gg. [The Cuban press; 1959–1962] Moscow, Izd-vo Mosk. un-ta, 1964. 58 p.

PN4934.G55

4475. Davydov, I. Gazeta boriushchegosia kubinskogo naroda [A newspaper of the fighting Cuban people] Sov. pech., no. 6, June 1960: 53–54.

4476. Gazeta Kubinskoi revoliutsii [The newspaper of the Cuban Revolution] Sov. pech., no. 6, June 1963: 53.

4477. Gladkii, V. B. Organizatsiia sistemy pechati na Kube [Organization of the press in Cuba] Vest. Mosk. un. Ser. 7: Filol., zhur., v. 17, no. 6, Nov.-Dec. 1962: 84–92.

4478. ———. Po stranitsam "La Kal'e" [Through the pages of "La Calle"] Vest. Mosk. un. Ser. 7: Filol., zhur., v. 16, no. 3, May-June 1961: 73–75.

4479. ———. Pod sen'iu S'erra-Maestry [In the shadow of the Sierra Maestra] Sov. pech., no. 8, Aug. 1960: 56–60.

4480. ———. Poslantsy geroicheskoi Kuby [The envoys from heroic Cuba] Sov. pech., no. 11, Nov. 1960: 58.

4481. Gnilye plody [Rotten fruit] Nov. vrem., v. 18, no. 21, May 1960: 23–24.
Cuban anti-Castro newspapers.

4482. Na perednem krae [At the forefront] Za rubezhom, no. 19, May 1961: 25.

4483. Okuneva, Maiia. "My rabotaem dlia revoliutsii" ["We work for the revolution"] Sov. pech., no. 4, Apr. 1962: 53–55.
Cuban journalists.

4484. Parkhit'ko, V. V dome pod krasnoi zvezdoi [In the building under the red star] Sov. pech., no. 2, Feb. 1963: 61.

4485. Premiia gazete "Revolius'on" [A prize awarded to the newspaper "Revolución"] Sov. pech., no. 4, Apr. 1961: 56.

4486. "Revolius'on" na strazhe revoliutsii ["Revolución," a guardian of the revolution] Sov. pech., no. 5, May 1961: 55–56.

f. Mexico

4487. Suárez, Luis. Renato Leduk [Renato Leduc] Sov. pech., no. 5, May 1959: 56–57.
A Mexican journalist.
Translated from the Spanish.

g. Panama

See entry no. 1318.

h. Uruguay

See entry no. 1353.

i. Venezuela

4488. Natsional'naia konferentsiia venesuel'skikh zhurnalistov [The National Conference of Venezuelan Journalists] Sov. pech., no. 9, Sept. 1964: 58.

B. PERIODICALS

1. Writings Dealing With Three or More Countries

See entry no. 320.

2. Individual Countries

a. Argentina

4489. 10 [Desiat'] let "Kuadernos de kul'tura" [The tenth anniversary of the periodical "Cuadernos de cultura"] Inostr. lit., no. 12, Dec. 1960: 253.

4490. Zhurnal dlia intelligentsii [A periodical for the intelligentsia] Probl. mira i sots., v. 3, no. 11, Nov. 1960: 81–82.

See also entries no. 343, 1191, 3168, and 4343.

b. Brazil

4491. I. R. Vykhod novogo zhurnala v Brazilii [Publication of a new periodical in Brazil] Nov. i noveish. ist., no. 3, 1959: 181–182.
A review of the periodical *Estudios sociais* (Rio de Janeiro, 1958–1959).

See also entries no. 1618, 3477, and 3483.

c. Colombia

See entry no. 3171.

d. Costa Rica

See entry no. 3172.

e. Cuba

4492. Kalinin, A., *and* M. Mokhnachev. Golos revoliutsionnoi Kuby [The voice of revolutionary Cuba] Kommunist, v. 39, no. 8, May 1962: 113–115.
A review of the periodical *Cuba socialista* (Havana, 1961–1962).

4493. Mashbits, IA. G. Teoreticheskii organ kubinskoi revoliutsii [The theoretical organ of the Cuban Revolution] Vop. ist., no. 11, Nov. 1962: 184–190.

A review of the periodical *Cuba socialista* (Havana).

4494. Olevs'kyi, L., *and* L. Shul'chuk. Review. Vsesvit, v. 6, no. 3, Mar. 1963: 156.

A review of the periodical *Unión* (Havana).

4495. Review. Za rubezhom, no. 45, Nov. 1961: 25.

A review of the periodical *Cuba socialista* (Havana, 1961).

4496. Zykova, A. B. Review. Vop. filos., v. 16, no. 8, 1962: 178–180.

A review of the periodical *Cuba socialista* (Havana).

See also entries no. 3178, 3181, 4359, 4513, 4517, 4522, and 4537.

f. Mexico

See entries no. 305, 425, and 1314.

g. Uruguay

See entry no. 1337.

h. Venezuela

See entries no. 201, 453, 634, and 3188.

C. RADIO AND TELEVISION

1. Writings Dealing With Three or More Countries

See entry no. 2246.

2. Individual Countries

a. Brazil

See entry no. 1441.

b. Cuba

4497. Chichkov, V. Govorit svobodnaia territoriia Ameriki [This is the free country of America] Sov. pech., no. 12, Dec. 1963: 50–52.

Radio and television broadcasting in Cuba.

4498. Quiroga Puerta, Ramiro. Govorit i pokazyvaet Kuba [Cuban radio and television broadcasting] Sov. pech., no. 1, Jan. 1963: 58–59.

4499. ———. Radio svobodnoi Kuby [Radio of free Cuba] Radio, no. 2, Feb. 1963: 15–16.

4500. V gostiakh u sviazistov Kuby [On a visit to Cuban communication workers] Vest. sviazi, v. 22, no. 9, Sept. 1962: 1 of cover.

See also entry no. 1938.

c. Uruguay

See entry no. 1344.

XXII

SCIENCE AND MEDICINE

A. SCIENCE

1. Writings Dealing With Three or More Countries

4501. Nikol'skii, S. I. Mezhamerikanskii seminar po kosmicheskim lucham [Inter-American Conference on Cosmic Rays] Vest. AN SSSR, v. 33, no. 3, Mar. 1963: 101–104.

2. Individual Countries

a. Argentina

4502. Rapoport, E. Sovremennoe sostoianie nauki v Argentine (?) [Present status of science in Argentina] Mir nauki, no. 5, 1959: 37–38.

b. Chile

4503. Sostoianie nauchno-issledovatel'skoi raboty v Chili [Present-day status of research work in Chile] Mir nauki, no. 2, 1963: 10–12.

c. Cuba

4504. Kiiaev, E. V. Organizatsiia sluzhby nauchno-tekhnicheskoi informatsii v Respublike Kuba; po lichnym vpechatleniiam [Organization of science and technology information services in Cuba; personal impressions] NTI, no. 7, 1964: 47–49.

d. Mexico

4505. Narikashvili, S. P., and P. G. Kostiuk. Konferentsiia fiziologov v Meksike [A conference of physiologists in Mexico] Vest. AN SSSR, v. 33, no. 9, Sept. 1963: 71–72.

See also entry no. 430.

B. MEDICINE

1. Argentina

4506. Haas, Emilio. O maliarii v Argentine [Malaria in Argentina] Med. paraz. i paraz. bol., no. 2, 1962: 170–171.
Summary in English.

4507. Palermo, Epifanio. Tuberkulez, pitanie i usloviia zhizni v Argentine [Tuberculosis, nutrition, and living conditions in Argentina] Usl. zhiz. i zdorov., v. 1, no.5, 1959: 30–34.

2. Brazil

4508. Aquino, Ilses Motta de. Frambeziia v Brazilii [Frambesia in Brazil] Vest. derm. i ven., v. 34, no. 9, 1960: 32–37.
Translated from the Portuguese.

4509. Aziatskii gripp [Asian flu] Vop. virus., v. 5, no. 4, July-Aug. 1960: 501.
A review of M. Bruno-Lobo's *Gripe asiatica* (Rio de Janeiro, 1959).

3. Cuba

4510. Bogoiavlenskii, N. A., and IU. P. Lisitsyn. O russko-kubinskikh meditsinskikh sviaziakh [Russo-Cuban medical contacts] Moscow, Medgiz, 1963. 86 p.
DLC

4511. Chogovadze, A. V., and A. IA. Nemenov. Razvitie vrachebnogo kontrolia i lechebnoi fizkul'tury na Kube [Development of medical control and therapeutic physical training in Cuba] Teor. i prak. fiz. kul't., v. 26, no. 2, Feb. 1963: 60–61.

4512. Kassirskii, I. A. Desiatyi Natsional'nyi meditsinskii kongress v Gavane [The

Tenth National Medical Congress in Havana] Klin. med., v. 41, no. 10, Oct. 1963: 150–155.

4513. Khronika [Brief news] Lab. delo, v. 7, no. 5, May 1961: 62.
A review of the journal *Revista cubana de laboratorio clínico* (Havana).

4514. Rakov, A. I. O sostoianii onkologicheskoi pomoshchi v Kubinskoi Respublike [Oncologic aid in the Cuban Republic] Vop. onk., v. 8, no. 8, 1962: 114–115.

4515. Rybakov, A. I. Uchastie sovetskikh stomatologov v X natsional'nom Kongresse vrachei Kuby [The participation of Soviet stomatologists in the Tenth Congress of Cuban Physicians] Stomatologiia, v. 42, no. 5, Sept.-Oct. 1963: 78–82.

4516. Suárez, Genaro. Sudebnaia meditsina revoliutsionnoi Kuby [Forensic medicine in revolutionary Cuba] Sud.-med. ekspert., v. 7, no. 3, 1964: 31–32.

4517. Zabludovskii, P. E. Istoriko-meditsinskie zhurnaly revoliutsionnoi Kuby [Periodicals devoted to the history of medicine in revolutionary Cuba] Sov. zdrav., v. 22, no. 11, 1963: 92–94.

See also entry no. 4799.

4. Mexico

4518. Mamamtavrishvili, D. G. V gostiakh u meksikanskikh khirurgov [On a visit to Mexican surgeons] Tbilisi, Sabchota Sakartvelo, 1960. 82 p.

4519. Agaronov, M. A. Nekotorye itogi XVII Internatsional'nogo kongressa khirurgov [Some results of the 17th International Congress of Surgeons] Akush. i gin., v. 35, no. 1, Jan.-Feb. 1959: 121–122.

See also entry no. 4255.

XXIII

LATIN AMERICAN STUDIES

❧

A. IN THE SOVIET UNION

4520. Al'perovich, M. S. Sovetskaia latino-amerikanistika v osveshchenii "Ispano-amerikanskogo istoricheskogo zhurnala" [How the "Hispanic American Historical Review" presents Soviet studies on Latin America] Vop. ist., no. 3, Mar. 1962: 186–187.

4521. Dabagian, E. S. Problemy izucheniia Latinskoi Ameriki [Problems in the study of Latin America] Nov. i noveish. ist., no. 5, 1962: 177–178.

4522. Dal'nev, Oleg. "Kuba"—novyi zhurnal [Cuba, a new periodical] Sov. pech., no. 9, Sept. 1964: 56.
A Russian periodical devoted to Cuba.

4523. Diko, N. S. Rastet interes sovetskogo studenchestva k Latinskoi Amerike [Soviet university students are more and more interested in the problems of Latin America] Vest. vys. shkoly, v. 21, no. 7, July 1963: 76–78.

4524. Gvozdarev, B. I. Piatiletie Respubliki Kuby; nauchnaia konferentsiia [A conference devoted to the fifth anniversary of the Cuban Republic] Nov. i noveish. ist., no. 2, 1964: 187–188.

4525. IUdanov, N. S. Nauchnaia konferentsiia po problemam natsional'no-osvoboditel'nogo dvizheniia Latinskoi Ameriki [A conference on the national liberation movement in Latin America] Nov. i noveish. ist., no. 2, 1963: 179–180.

4526. Klusov, E. P. III konferentsiia po problemam Latinskoi Ameriki [The Third Conference on the Problems of Latin America] Vest. vys. shkoly, v. 22, no. 8, Aug. 1964: 89.

4527. ———. Vtoraia Vsesoiuznaia nauchnaia konferentsiia [The Second All-Union Conference] Vest. vys. shkoly, v. 21, no. 7, July 1963: 76–78.
A conference on Latin America.

4528. Koval', B. I. Problemy natsional'no-osvoboditel'nogo dvizheniia v program-mnykh dokumentakh kompartii stran Latinskoi Ameriki [The problems of the national liberation movement in the programs of Latin American Communist parties] Nov. i noveish. ist., no. 2, 1964: 95–107.
Soviet studies on Latin America.
Summary in English, p. 195.

4529. Kropotov, V. Latin America and the United States; Soviet studies. Vest. ist. mir. kul't., no. 4, July-Aug. 1961: 150–155.
Soviet studies on Latin America's relations with the United States.
In English.

4530. Mal'kov, V. L. Problemy istorii mezhdunarodnogo rabochego i natsional'-no-osvoboditel'nogo dvizheniia [Problems concerning the history of the international labor and national liberation movement] Vest. AN SSSR, v. 32, no. 10, Oct. 1962: 101–105.
Latin American studies in the USSR.

4531. ———. V Prezidiume Akademii nauk SSSR [In the Presidium of the Academy of Sciences of the USSR] Nov. i noveish. ist., no. 1, 1963: 184–185.
Latin American studies.

4532. Mashbits, IA. G. Argumentirovannaia kritika ili bezdokazatel'nye napadki? [Well-founded criticism or groundless faultfinding?] Vop. ist., no. 12, Dec. 1962: 160–165.

A review of Juan Antonio Ortega y Medina's *Historiografía soviética iberoamericanista; 1945–1960* (Mexico City, Universidad Nacional Autónoma de México, 1961. 194 p.).

4533. Mikhailov, S. S. Izuchenie Latinskoi Ameriki v Sovetskom Soiuze [Latin American studies in the Soviet Union] Vop. ist., no. 4, Apr. 1962: 98–106.
Summary in English, p. 221–222.

4534. ———. Izuchenie problem Latinskoi Ameriki [Studying the problems of Latin America] Vest. AN SSSR, v. 32, no. 5, May 1962: 54–59.

4535. ———. Nekotorye voprosy izucheniia Latinskoi Ameriki [Some problems of Latin American studies] Nov. i noveish. ist., no. 2, 1964: 29–36.
Summary in English, p. 195.

4536. Noemi Grigor'evna Shprintsin; nekrolog [Noemi Grigor'evna Shprintsin; obituary] Sov. etn., no. 3, May-June 1964: 145.
A Soviet student of Latin America.

4537. Novyi zhurnal "Kuba" ["Kuba," a new periodical] Nov. vrem., v. 22, no. 36, Sept. 1964: 30.

4538. Pogosov, IU. Znakomias' s Latinskoi Amerikoi [Studying Latin America] Vokrug sveta, no. 9, Sept. 1960: 62–63.

4539. Slezkin, L. IU. Neobosnovannyi vypad protiv sovetskoi latinoamerikanistiki [An unfounded criticism of Soviet studies on Latin America] Nov. i noveish. ist., no. 1, 1964: 177–178.
Mexico in Soviet historiography.

4540. Sozdan Institut Latinskoi Ameriki [Establishment of the Institute of Latin America] Nov. i noveish. ist., no. 2, 1962: 177.

4541. Stroganov, A. I. Vsesoiuznye nauchnye studencheskie konferentsii po problemam Latinskoi Ameriki [All-Union conferences of university students on the problems of Latin America] Vop. ist., v. 38, no. 11, Nov. 1963: 112.

4542. Volkov, Valerii. Studencheskii latinoamerikanskii [A study group on Latin America] Kul't. i zhizn', v. 7, no. 12, Dec. 1963: 18–21.

See also entries no. 296 and 321.

B. IN ARAB COUNTRIES

4543. Araby i Latinskaia Amerika [Arabs and Latin America] Inostr. lit., no. 12, Dec. 1960: 258.
Latin American studies in Arab countries.

C. IN EAST GERMANY

4544. Grigor'ian, IU. M. Novye raboty uchenykh GDR o Latinskoi Amerike, 1960–1963 [New studies on Latin America in the German Democratic Republic, 1960–1963] Vop. ist., v. 38, no. 11, Nov. 1963: 196–199.

4545. ———. Sovremennye problemy Latinskoi Ameriki v osveshchenii istorikov GDR [Present-day problems of Latin America in the interpretation of East German historians] Vop. ist., no. 5, May 1962: 178–179.

4546. M. A. Aktual'nye problemy razvitiia Latinskoi Ameriki [Current problems in the development of Latin America] Nov. i noveish. ist., no. 3, 1962: 174.
Latin American studies in East Germany.

See also entry no. 339.

D. IN THE UNITED STATES

4547. Koval', B. I. Zadachi izucheniia Latinskoi Ameriki v interpretatsii amerikanskogo professora [How an American professor describes the objectives of Latin American studies] Vop. ist., no. 6, June 1962: 195–197.

4548. Lavretskii, I. R. Replika professoru Dzh. Gregori Osval'du [An answer to Professor J. Gregory Oswald] Vop. ist., no. 2, Feb. 1961: 206–208.
Latin American studies in the United States.

See also entries nos. 338 and 394.

XXIV

TRAVEL

❦

A. FOREIGN VISITORS IN LATIN AMERICA

1. Writings Dealing With Three or More Countries

4549. Adzhubei, Aleksei Ivanovich. Kueka i modern-meshchane [Cueca and the modern petty bourgeoisie] Moscow, Pravda, 1959. 63 p.
Reviewed by M. Vilenskii in *Mol. gvard.*, no. 9, Sept. 1959: 208–210.

4550. ———. Na raznykh shirotakh [At various latitudes] Moscow, Pravda, 1959. 109 p.   PG3476.A26N3
Includes three sketches describing the countries of Latin America.

4551. Chichkov, Vasilii Mikhailovich. Buntuiushchaia zemlia; puteshestviia i vstrechi [Rebellious land; travels and meetings] Moscow, Detgiz, 1961. 158 p.
F1409.2.C5

4552. Gribachev, Nikolai Matveevich. Dym nad vulkanom; ocherki o stranakh Latinskoi Ameriki [Smoke over the volcano; sketches of the countries of Latin America] Moscow, Mol. gvardiia, 1959. 110 p.   F2224.G73

4553. Grigorian, Bersabe. Iz putevykh zametok [From my travel notes] Yerevan, Aipetrat, 1960. 110 p.
In Armenian.

4554. Hanzelka, Jiří, *and* Miroslav Zikmund. Cherez Kordil'ery [Crossing the Cordilleras] Moscow, Mol. gvardiia, 1960. 348 p.   F2224.H317
Translated by S. Babin and R. Nazarov from the Czech *Přes Kordillery*.

4555. ———. Mezh dvukh okeanov [Between two oceans] Moscow, Mol. gvardiia, 1961. 391 p.

Translated by S. Babin and R. Nazarov from the Czech *Mezi dvěma oceány*.
Reviewed by G. Malinina in *Vokrug sveta*, no. 3, Mar. 1961: 61–62; by Sergei L'vov in *Nov. mir*, v. 38, no. 6, June 1962: 270–273.

4556. ———. Ot Argentiny do Meksiki [From Argentina to Mexico] Leningrad, Detgiz, 1960–61. 2 v.
Translated by S. Babin and R. Nazarov from the Czech.

4557. Helbig, Karl Martin. V strane u Karibskogo moria; puteshestviia po TSentral'noi Amerike [A country by the Caribbean Sea; travels in Central America] Moscow, Geografgiz, 1963. 302 p.
Translated from the German. Introductory article by M. Okuneva.

4558. Ignat'ev, Oleg Konstantinovich. Ot Argentiny do Venesuely [From Argentina to Venezuela] Moscow, Znanie, 1961. 93 p.   F1409.2.I4

4559. IUdovich, A. B. Pod parusami v XX veke; plavanie shkhuny "Zaria" [Sailing in the 20th century; a voyage of the schooner "Zaria"] Moscow, Geografgiz, 1960. 174 p.   QC825.I9
Introductory article by M. Ivanov.

4560. Krasnitskii, Gennadii. Ot Rio-de-Zhaneiro do Montevideo [From Rio de Janeiro to Montevideo] Tashkent, Gosizdat UzSSR, 1964. 64 p.
In Uzbek.

4561. Lundkvist, Artur. Vulkanicheskii kontinent; puteshestvie po IUzhnoi Amerike [A volcanic continent; a journey in South America] Moscow, Geografgiz, 1961. 367 p.
Translated from the Swedish *Vulkanisk*

kontinent. Introductory article by Il'ia Ehrenburg. Also published in Estonian.
Reviewed by B. IAroshevskii in *Za rubezhom*, no. 35, Sept. 1961: 24.

4562. Polevoi, Boris Nikolaevich. Blizko i daleko; novye dnevniki [Near and faraway places; new diaries] Moscow, Sov. pisatel', 1960. 333 p.   G464.P57

4563. Sofronov, Anatolii. Puteshestvie, kotoroe khochetsia povtorit' [A trip which I would like to repeat] Moscow, Sov. pisatel', 1964. 349 p.
Reviewed by VI. Drobyshev in *Znamia*, v. 34, no. 8, Aug. 1964: 244–246; by V. Poliakovskii in *Za rubezhom*, no. 40, Oct. 1964: 31.

4564. Grebnev, A., *and* K. Khachaturov. Vstrechi na dalekikh meridianakh [Meetings in the regions of faraway meridians] Sov. pech., no. 12, Dec. 1963: 55–57.

4565. Gribachev, Nikolai Matveevich. Dym nad vulkanom [Smoke over the volcano] *In his* Puteshestviia. 2d ed. Moscow, Mol. gvardiia, 1960: p. 352–437.
Reviewed by G. Borisova in *Za rubezhom*, no. 6, July 1960: 29.

4566. Hanzelka, Jiří, *and* Miroslav Zikmund. Iz Kosta-Riki v Kosta-Riku [From Costa Rica to Costa Rica] Don, v. 4, no. 7, July 1960: 149–163; v. 4, no. 8, Aug. 1960: 168–172.
Translated from the Czech.

4567. IUdovich, Aleksandr. Pod parusami v XX veke [Under sail, in the 20th century] Vokrug sveta, no. 9, 1959: 26–32; no. 10, 1959: 36–41; no. 11, 1959: 55–60; no. 12, 1959: 52–58.

4568. Lundkvist, Artur. Vulkanicheskii kontinent [Volcanic continent] Vokrug sveta, no. 1, Jan. 1960: 18–23; no. 2, Feb. 1960: 18–23: no. 3, Mar. 1960: 54–59; no. 4, Apr. 1960: 56–60; no. 5, May 1960: 36–39; no. 6, June 1960: 54–58.
Translated from the Swedish.

4569. Ot Meksiki do Chili [From Mexico to Chile] Vokrug sveta, no. 9, Sept. 1960: 32a–32d.

4570. Stal'skii, N. Knigi o velikoi sem'e liudei; o putevykh ocherkakh I. Ganzelki i M. Zikmunda [Books on the great family of man; on the travel sketches by J. Hanzelka and M. Zikmund] Inostr. lit., no. 4, Apr. 1960: 257–260.

4571. Wasilewska, Wanda. Vo imia vsekh liudei [In the name of all people] Druzh. nar., no. 7, July 1962: 3–8.

See also entries no. 3253, 3254, and 4341.

2. Individual Countries

a. Argentina

4572. Arletti, Antonio. Trampeador ["El trampeador"] Moscow, Mysl', 1964. 144 p.
Translated from the Italian.

4573. Hanzelka, Jiří, *and* Miroslav Zikmund. Tam za rekoiu—Argentina [There, beyond the river, is Argentina] Moscow, Mol. gvardiia, 1959. 428 p.   F2815.H257
Translated by S. Babin and R. Nazarov from the Czech.

4574. Zenkovich, B. A. Puteshestvie v IUzhnyi okean i vokrug sveta [A voyage to the South Atlantic Ocean and around the world] Moscow, Geografgiz, 1960. 327 p.   G464.Z4

4575. Arletti, Antonio. Trampeador ["El trampeador"] Vokrug sveta, no. 7, July 1964: 17–23; no. 8, Aug. 1964: 50–54; no. 10, Oct. 1964: 20–23; no. 11, Nov. 1964: 42–45.
Translated from the Italian.

4576. Galin, IU. Stolitsa serebrianoi strany [The capital city of a silver land] Vokrug sveta, no. 9, Sept. 1960: 22–24.

4577. Mashbits, IA. G. Review. Geog. v shkole, v. 22, no. 2, Mar.-Apr. 1959: 92.
A review of O. K. Ignat'ev's *Argentina i argentintsy* (Moscow, Mol. gvardiia, 1958. 94 p.).

4578. Sytin, A. Argentinskie zapiski [Argentine travel notes] Nash sovrem., no. 1, Jan. 1964: 70–85.

b. Bolivia

4579. Hanzelka, Jiří, *and* Miroslav Zikmund. Cherez Kordil'ery; glavy iz knigi [Cross-

ing the Cordilleras; chapters from a book] Moscow, Pravda, 1959. 64 p.
Translated by S. Babin and R. Nazarov from the Czech *Přes Kordillery*.

4580. Rodionov, N. V. V strane inkov; putevye ocherki [In the land of the Incas; travel notes] Alma-Ata, Kazgoslitizdat, 1963. 71 p.

4581. Sobolev, Leonid Sergeevich. Nishchii na zolotom trone; boliviiskii dnevnik [A beggar on a golden throne; a Bolivian diary] Moscow, Mol. gvardiia, 1962. 107 p.
DLC

4582. Chichkov, V. V serdtse IUzhnoi Ameriki [In the heart of South America] Vokrug sveta, no. 9, Sept. 1960: 1–6.

4583. ———. V vysokikh Andakh [In the high Andes] Ogonek, v. 37, no. 24, June 1959: 14–16.

4584. Kraminov, D. La-Pas—znachit mir [La Paz means peace] Za rubezhom, no. 43, Oct. 1963: 16–18.

4585. Rodionov, N. Za moriami, za dolami [Beyond the seas and faraway valleys] Zvezda, no. 4, Apr. 1962: 172–177.

4586. Rybalkin, I. V Bolivii; putevye zametki [In Bolivia; travel notes] Nov. vrem., v. 20, no. 47, Nov. 1962: 26–28.

4587. Sergeev, V. Strana mogla by protsvetat'; 10 dnei v Bolivii [The country could have flourished; ten days in Bolivia] Sov. profsoiuzy, v. 18, no. 18, Sept. 1962: 43–44.

4588. Shumov, IU., *and* V. Grigor'ev. Na Boliviiskom ploskogor'e [On the Bolivian plateau] Nov. vrem., v. 19, no. 20, May 1961: 27–29.

4589. Sobolev, Leonid. Rukopozhatie v Andakh [Handshake in the Andes] Ogonek, v. 39, no. 16, Apr. 1961: 12–15; v. 39, no. 17, Apr. 1961: 22–25.

4590. ———. V Bolivii [In Bolivia] Znamia, v. 31, no. 5, May 1961: 137–187.

4591. Spadshchyna Bolivara [The heritage of Bolivar] Vsesvit, v. 4, no. 7, July 1961: 76–78.

See also entry no. 1617.

c. Brazil

4592. Arushanian, Sh. M. V Brazilii i Urugvae [In Brazil and Uruguay] Yerevan, Aipetrat, 1959. 151 p.

4593. Beekman, Vladimir. Dalekaia strana—Braziliia [Brazil, a faraway country] Tallinn, Estgosizdat, 1963. 130 p.
In Estonian.

4594. Blomberg, Rolf. Shavanti; rasskaz o shvedskoi kinoekspeditsii v Braziliiu [Chavante; the story of a Swedish motion-picture expedition to Brazil] Riga, Latvijas valsts izdevnieciba, 1962. 119 p.
In Latvian. Translated from the Swedish *Xavante; historien om en svensk filmexpedition i Brasilien.*

4595. ———. V poiskakh anakondy [In search of the anaconda] Moscow, Detgiz, 1959. 159 p.
Translated by L. Zhdanov from the Swedish.
Reviewed by B. Kartashev in *Znan.-sila*, v. 34, no. 8, Aug. 1959: 25.

4596. Ignat'ev, Oleg Konstantinovich. Braziliia—gigant tropicheskii; zapiski korrespondenta [Brazil, a tropical giant; the notes of a reporter] Moscow, Mol. gvardiia, 1963. 158 p. F2516.I5

4597. Beauvoir, Simone de. Razbuzhennaia Braziliia [Awakened Brazil] Za rubezhom, no. 28, Dec. 1960: 20–21.
Translated from the French.

4598. Garuba, Caio. Braziliia v budni i prazdniki [Brazil on workdays and on holidays] Vokrug sveta, no. 8, Aug. 1961: 39–42.

4599. Gvozdev, IU. Goroda i liudi Brazilii; putevye zametki [The cities and people of Brazil; travel notes] Nov. vrem., v. 21, no. 32, Aug. 1963: 25–27.

4600. Karaganov, A. Idei i bomby; zametki uchastnika torgovo-promyshlennoi vystavki v Rio-de-Zhaneiro [Ideas and bombs; notes of a guide at the Soviet Commercial and Industrial Exhibition in Rio de Janeiro] Sib. ogni, no. 12, Dec. 1962: 130–144.

4601. Karnaval v Rio [Carnival in Rio] Zhen. mira, no. 6, 1961: 23–25.

4602. Kostritsyn, B. Na brazil'skikh pere-krestkakh [At the Brazilian crossroads] Ogonek, v. 39, no. 38, Sept. 1961: 30–31.

4603. Mikoian, S. Po obe storony tropika Kozeroga [On both sides of the Tropic of Capricorn] Ogonek, v. 42, no. 7, Feb. 1964: 23–24.

4604. Nachbar, Herbert. Brazil'skii reis [A trip to Brazil] Druzh. nar., no. 8, 1962: 223–252.
Translated from the German *Brasilienfahrt*.

4605. Plotnov, A. Mol'bert na solntse [An easel in the sun] Ogonek, v. 41, no. 37, Sept. 1963: 24.
Russian painters on a visit to Brazil.

4606. Poliakovskii, V. Odin den' Brazilii [One day in the life of Brazil] Za rube-zhom, no. 42, Oct. 1962: 24–25.

4607. Rondière, Pierre. Brazil'skie paradoksy [Brazilian paradoxes] Ogonek, v. 42, no. 33, Aug. 1964: 18–21.

4608. Rossi, Vincenzo. Sem' dnei nadezhdy [Seven days of hope] Smena, v. 37, no. 1, Jan. 1960: 22–23.

4609. Rusinek, Michal. Rio de Zhaneiro—San Paulu [From Rio de Janeiro to São Paulo] Vsesvit, v. 5, no. 3, Mar. 1962: 99–105.
Translated from the Polish.

4610. Shprintsin, N. G. Review. Izv. Vses. geog. ob-va, v. 91, no. 4, July-Aug. 1959: 371–372.
A review of S. V. Kalesnik's *Po Brazilii; putevye ocherki* (Moscow, Geografgiz, 1958. 176 p.).

See also entries no. 1439, 3245, 4171, and 4573.

d. Chile (*including Easter Island*)

4611. Listov, V. V. Na kraiu sveta; putevye ocherki [At the end of the world; travel notes] Moscow, Profizdat, 1963. 126 p.
DLC
Reviewed by L. Novikova in *Nov. mir*, v. 39, no. 8, Aug. 1963: 278–280.

4612. Ezov, Eduard. Na ostrove Paskhi; zapiski kinooperatora [On Easter Island; notes of a cameraman] Nov. vrem., v. 17, no. 22, May 1959: 27–28.

4613. Gerasimov, M. A. Osen' . . . v marte [Autumn . . . in March] IUn. nat., no. 8, Aug. 1960: 20–22.

4614. Listov, V. Poezd idet v Konseps'on [The train goes to Concepción] Ogonek, v. 40, no. 38, Sept. 1962: 14–15.

4615. ———. U podnozh'ia Kordil'er [At the foothills of the Cordilleras] Nov. vrem., v. 19, no. 11, Mar. 1961: 26–29; v. 19, no. 12, Mar. 1961: 25–26.

4616. Markov, K. K. Den' na ostrove Paskhi [A day on Easter Island] Izv. Vses. geog. ob-va, v. 91, no. 6, Nov.-Dec. 1959: 529–535.

4617. Podzerko, V. A. V strane postoiannogo solntsa [In the land of constant sunshine] Metallurg, v. 6, no. 4, Apr. 1961: 37–38.

4618. Sofronov, Anatolii. Dobro pozhalovat' v Chili! [Welcome to Chile!] Moskva, v. 7, no. 5, 1963: 196–204.

e. Colombia

4619. Blomberg, Rolf. Zoloto i anakonda [Gold and the anaconda] Kiev, Molod', 1961. 136 p.
In Ukrainian. Translated by O. D. Seniuk from the Swedish.

4620. Cuéllar Gacharna, Miguel. Po obe storony And [On both sides of the Andes] Vokrug sveta, no. 1, Jan. 1959: 40–43.

4621. Gvozdev, IU. Gor'kii kofe Kolumbii [The bitter coffee of Colombia] Ogonek, v. 40, no. 51, Dec. 1962: 28–29.

4622. ———. Na zemle El'dorado [The land of Eldorado] Nov. vrem., v. 21, no. 43, Oct. 1963: 26–28.

4623. ———. V strane zolotoi legendy [In the country of a golden legend] Nauka i rel., v. 5, no. 10, Oct. 1964: 83–87.

f. Cuba

4624. Drda, Jan. Pod zvezdoi novoi i smeloi; nemnogo o Kube [Under a new and bold star; brief notes on Cuba] Moscow, Pravda, 1963. 46 p.
Translated by G. IUnakov from the Czech. Reviewed by A. Klitko in *Vokrug sveta*, no. 9, Sept. 1963: 62–63.

4625. Francos, Ania. Na Kube prazdnik; ocherki [Cuban holiday; sketches] Moscow, Izd-vo inostr. lit., 1963. 280 p.
Translated from the French *La fête cubaine*. Introductory article by A. M. Zorina.

4626. Gaidaenko, Ivan. Gavana, Beirut [Havana, Beirut] Odessa, Knizhn. izd-vo, 1963. 138 p. G469.G3

4627. Gavrilin, V. Kontinenty, strany, liudi; putevye zametki [Continents, countries, and people; travel notes] Moscow, Kr. zvezda, 1963. 31 p.

4628. Geroicheskii ostrov; zametki zhurnalistov o poezdke na Kubu, ianvar'—iiun' 1961 g. [A heroic island; the notes of newspapermen on their journey to Cuba, January-June, 1961] Moscow, Pravda, 1961. 112 p. DLC
Reviewed by L. Prokhorova in *Vokrug sveta*, no. 11, Nov. 1961: 63–64.

4629. Goriunov, D. P. Zdravstvui, Kuba! [Hello, Cuba!] Moscow, Pravda, 1961. 51 p.
Reviewed by Mykola Kostcnko in *Zhovten'*, v. 13, no. 1, Jan. 1963: 158–159; by IU. Trushin in *Za rubezhom*, no. 13, Mar. 1962: 18.

4630. Granin, Daniil Aleksandrovich. Neozhidannoe utro [Unexpected morning] Moscow, Sov. pisatel', 1962. 129 p. DLC
Reviewed by N. Bazhin in *Neva*, no. 1, 1964: 191–192.

4631. ———. Ostrov molodykh; rasskazy o Kube [Island of the young; stories on Cuba] Leningrad, Lenizdat, 1962. 100 p. F1765.G75

4632. Guliam, Khamid. Rasskazy o Kube [Stories about Cuba] Tashkent, Gos. izd-vo khudozh. lit., 1961. 56 p.
Translated by A. Kakhimi from the Uzbek.

4633. IAnkoshvili, Natela. Na geroicheskom ostrove [On a heroic island] Tbilisi, Nakaduli, 1963. 39 p.
In Georgian.

4634. Ivanov, IUrii. Kurs na Gavanu [Destination Havana] Kaliningrad, Knizhn. izd-vo, 1964. 75 p.

4635. Ivanov, V. I., *and* P. Ossovskii. Kuba; al'bom [Cuba; an album] Moscow, Sov. khudozhnik, 1961. 68 p.

4636. Kovalkin, V. 13 mesiatsev na Kube [Thirteen months in Cuba] Minsk, Belarus', 1964. 70 p.

4637. Kuz'mishchev, Vladimir Aleksandrovich. Kuba; al'bom [Cuba; an album] Moscow, Sov. khudozhnik, 1961. 67 p. F1765.K9

4638. Leonov, I. D. Zdravstvui, Kuba! Dve nedeli na ostrove svobody [Hello, Cuba! Two weeks on the island of freedom] Leningrad, Lenizdat, 1963. 86 p. DLC

4639. Listov, Vadim Vadimovich. Po dorogam novoi Kuby [Along the roads of the new Cuba] Moscow, Profizdat, 1960. 152 p. F1758.L7
Reviewed by A. Sergeev in *Sov. profsoiuzy*, v. 17, no. 1, Jan. 1961: 57.

4640. Mashkin, Valentin Konstantinovich. V strane "dlinnoborodykh"; kubinskii reportazh [In the country of the "long beards"; a news story on Cuba] Moscow, Mol. gvardiia, 1960. 93 p. F1788.M3
Reviewed in *Dnestr*, v. 14, no. 1, 1961: 153–155.

4641. Napalkov, Sergei Nikolaevich. Solntse nad Kuboi; ocherki o Kube i kubintsakh [Sunlit Cuba; sketches of Cuba and the Cubans] Riga, Latgosizdat, 1964. 230 p.
In Latvian.

4642. ———. Vstrechi na Kube; reportazh [Meetings in Cuba; news stories] Leningrad, Lenizdat, 1960. 182 p. F1765.N3

4643. Pod solntsem druzhby; putevye zametki [Under the sunshine of friendship; travel notes] Moscow, Kr. zvezda, 1962. 31 p.

4644. Smirnov, Sergei Sergeevich. Poezdka na Kubu [A trip to Cuba] Moscow, Sov. pisatcl', 1962. 246 p. F1765.S6
Also published in Estonian.

4645. TSvietkov, H. M. Na ostrove svobody [On the island of freedom] Kiev, 1963. 40 p.
In Ukrainian.

4646. Volodkin, Vladimir Ivanovich, *and* Sergei Sergeevich Smirnov. Kuba, 1961; reportazh [Cuba in 1961; news stories] Moscow, Mol. gvardiia, 1961. 75 p. F1765.V65
Reviewed by L. Prokhorova in *Vokrug sveta*, no. 11, Nov. 1961: 63–64.

4647. Wasilewska, Wanda. Desiat' dniv na Kubi [Ten days in Cuba] Kiev, Rad. pys'mennyk, 1962. 137 p.
Translated from the Polish.
Reviewed by Mykola TSivyna in *Ukraina*, no. 2, Jan. 1963: 19.

4648. Agafonova, T. Kurs na Kubu [Destination Cuba] Vokrug sveta, no. 2, Feb. 1962: 26–29.

4649. Alleg, Henri. Pobedonosnaia Kuba [Victorious Cuba] Ogonek, v. 41, no. 30, July 1963: 10–11.
Translated from the French.

4650. Arkhipova, Liudmila. Dom v Mar'ianao [A house in Marianao] IUnost', v. 10, no. 8, Aug. 1964: 54–64.

4651. Artsyshevskaia, G. Dalekaia, no blizkaia [Distant but near] Smena, v. 38, no. 8, Apr. 1961: 28–30.

4652. Bahmut, Ivan. Notatky pro Kubu [Notes about Cuba] Prapor, no. 12, 1963: 66–73.

4653. Beauvoir, Simone de. S veroi v budushchee [With faith in the future] Inostr. lit., no. 7, July 1960: 241–244.
Translated from the French.

4654. Beneslavskii, D. Liudi geroicheskogo ostrova [The people of a heroic island] V mire knig, v. 3, no. 5, 1963: 35.
A review of Bodo Uhse's *Im Rhytmus der Conga; ein kubanisher Sommer* (Berlin, Aufbau-Verlag, 1962. 197 p.).

4655. Borovskii, V. Veter revoliutsii; kubinskie zarisovki [Wind of the revolution; Cuban sketches] Nov. vrem., v. 20, no. 1, Jan. 1963: 23–26.

4656. Breza, Tadeusz. Lysty z Havany [Letters from Havana] Vsesvit, v. 6, no. 1, Jan. 1963: 3–11.
Translated from the Polish.

4657. Brutents, K. Kuba—svobodnaia territoriia Ameriki; zametki korrespondenta [Cuba, a free American country; a reporter's notes] Probl. mira i sots., v. 4, no. 2, Feb. 1961: 37–42.

4658. Burlak, Boris. IUnaia Amerika [Young America] Ural, no. 6, 1964: 62–83.

4659. Chernega, P. Do vstrechi, Al'berto [See you again, Alberto] Sov. tsirk, v. 7, no. 3, Mar. 1963: 8–9.

4660. Denisov, N. Poka "TU-114" stoial na aerodrome Khose Marti [While the "TU-114" was at the José Martí Airport] Sov. pech., no. 2, Feb. 1963: 52–55.

4661. Dodd, Martha. Dvi zustrichi z Kuboui [Two encounters with Cuba] Ukraina, no. 18, Aug. 1963: 8.
Translated from the English.

4662. Drda, Jan. Govorit Fidel' [This is Fidel] Inostr. lit., no. 2, Feb. 1963: 242–244.
Translated from the Czech.

4663. Drozdenko, Vasyl'. Sontse nad Kuboiu [Sunlit Cuba] Ukraina, no. 13, July 1960: 20–22.

4664. Fere, Vladimir. Deti ostrova svobody [Children of the island of freedom] Muz. zhizn', v. 6, no. 13, July 1963: 16–17.

4665. ———. Kubinskii dnevnik [A Cuban diary] Sov. muz., v. 27, no. 6, June 1963: 114–119.

4666. ———. "Patria o muerte!" Sov. muz., v. 27, no. 1, Jan. 1963: 117–119; v. 27, no. 2, Feb. 1963: 121–128.

4667. Francos, Ania. Cuban symphony. World student news, v. 17, no. 6, 1963: 6–9.
Translated from the French.

4668. Gaganova, Valentina. Chto ia videla na Kube [What I saw in Cuba] Znamia, v. 32, no. 6, June 1962: 196–200.

4669. ———. Vkusivshie radost' svobody [They tasted the joy of freedom] Sov. zhen., v. 18, no. 5, 1962: 34.

4670. Gaidaenko, Ivan. Polum'iane sertse Kuby [The passionate heart of Cuba] Ukraina, no. 3, Feb. 1963: 23–24.

4671. Gaidar, Timur. Kubinskii Ded-Moroz [The Cuban "Grandfather Frost"] Ogonek, v. 42, no. 1, Jan. 1964: 25.

4672. Gaudio, Attilio. Kuba smotrit v budushchee [Cuba looks toward its future] V zashch. mira, no. 7/8, July-Aug. 1961: 17–26.

4673. Gavrilov, IU. Ostrov svobody—ostrov druzei [The island of freedom is an island of friends] Kul't. i zhizn', v. 7, no. 1, 1963: 30–33.

4674. Gómez, J. Schast'e prishlo na Kubu [Happiness has come to Cuba] Vsem. prof. dvizh., no. 8, Aug. 1961: 32–33.

4675. Goriunov, Dmitrii. Zdravstvui, Kuba! [Hello, Cuba!] Ogonek, v. 39, no. 13, Mar. 1961: 12–14; v. 39, no. 14, Apr. 1961: 6–9; v. 39, no. 15, Apr. 1961: 4–8.

4676. Granin, Daniil. Eto—Kuba [This is Cuba] Nov. vrem., v. 19, no. 45, Nov. 1961: 25–27.

4677. ———. Ostrov molodykh [Island of the young] Nov. mir, v. 38, no. 6, June 1962: 190–215.

4678. Guliam, Khamid. Kasimiro Kalero [Casimiro Calero] Uzbekiston, v. 20, no. 6, June 1961: 10–11.

4679. Isbakh, Aleksandr. Na linii ognia [On the battlefront] Inostr. lit., no. 9, Sept. 1964: 266–268.
A review of Henri Alleg's *Victorieuse Cuba* ([n.p.] Les Editions de Minuit et "Alger Républicain," 1963).

4680. Ivanov, V. Na revoliutsionnoi Kube [In revolutionary Cuba] Iskusstvo, v. 24, no. 8, 1961: 42–49.
Travel notes and drawings.

4681. Ivanov, V., *and* P. Ossovskii. Ostrov svobody [The island of freedom] Vokrug sveta, no. 7, July 1961: 12–15.

4682. Jacob, Charles. Kuba glazami ochevidtsa [Cuba as I saw it] Vsem. stud. nov., v. 15, no. 10/11, Oct.-Nov. 1961: 30–31.

4683. Kacharava, A., *and* A. Piriutko. Kubinskii reis [The Cuban run] Neva, no. 7, 1961: 221–222.

4684. Kafanova, L. Dve vstrechi [Two encounters] Ogonek, v. 41, no. 20, May 1963: 5.

4685. Kalinin, A. Rozhdennye revoliutsiei [Born of the revolution] Nov. vrem., no. 18, May 1963: 25–27.

4686. Kalmykov, V. Svet respubliki [The light of a republic] Smena, v. 41, no. 1, Jan. 1964: 10–11.

4687. Kamynin, L. Geroicheskaia Kuba; fotovystavka v Sovetskom Soiuze [Heroic Cuba; a photographic exhibition in the Soviet Union] Sov. foto, v. 23, no. 3, Mar. 1963: 4–10.

4688. ———. Vid Havany do Barakoa; z kubyns'koho shchodennyka [From Havana to Baracoa; from a Cuban diary] Vsesvit, v. 6, no. 2, Oct. 1963: 78–81.

4689. Karmen, Roman Lazarevich. "Pylaiushchii ostrov" ["An island in flame"] *In his* Po stranam trekh kontinentov. Moscow, Mol. gvardiia, 1962: p. 108–143.
                                          DP269.17.K3

4690. ———. Pylaiushchii ostrov; reportazh iz Kuby [An island in flame; news stories from Cuba] Baikal, v. 9, no. 1, Jan.-Feb. 1963: 78–129.

4691. ———. Tret'ia vstrecha s Kuboi [Third meeting with Cuba] Ogonek, v. 41, no. 1, Jan. 1963: 8.

4692. Kochubei, Vadim. My idem v Gavanu [We sail to Havana] Don, v. 5, no. 6, June 1961: 141–148.

4693. Korbach, Ivan. Kuba blyz'ko! [Cuba is nearby!] Ukraina, v. 23, no. 30, Nov. 1963: 10–11.

4694. ———. Kubinskie byli [News stories from Cuba] Raduga, v. 14, no. 6, 1964: 152–165.

4695. Kornilov, IU. Nastoiashchee delo; ocherki kubinskoi zhizni [The real thing; sketches of Cuban life] Nov. vrem., v. 19, no. 47, Nov. 1961: 24–25.

4696. Korotkov, Vl. Vstrechi na ostrove svobody [Meetings on the island of freedom] Don, v. 7, no. 8, Aug. 1963: 150–156.

4697. Korzhevskii, B. Dusha i kraski Kuby [The soul and colors of Cuba] Ogonek, v. 41, no. 34, Aug. 1963: 8–9.

4698. ———. Na ostrove svobody [On the island of freedom] Sov. zhen., v. 20, no. 7, 1964: 28.

4699. ———. Tri mesiatsa na ostrove svobody [Three months on the island of freedom] Iskusstvo, v. 26, no. 7, 1963: 54–57.

4700. Kosarev, E. Eto vse ia videl na Kube [I have seen all this in Cuba] Vnesh. torg., v. 41, no. 1, 1961: 21–23.

4701. Kovalenko, I. My s toboi, Kuba! [We are with you, Cuba!] Znan.-sila, v. 36, no. 5, May 1961: 36.

4702. Kuz'mishchev, V. Na kubinskoi zemle [On Cuban soil] Nov. vrem., v. 19, no. 18, May 1961: 23–27.

4703. Lebedeva, Valentina. Svidanie s Kuboi [My meeting with Cuba] Zvezda, no. 11, Nov. 1962: 169–174.

4704. Listov, V. Iz kubinskikh vpechatlenii [Cuban impressions] Nov. vrem., v. 18, no. 10, Mar. 1960: 23–25; v. 18, no. 13, Mar. 1960: 25–28.

4705. ———. Kubinskaia iav' [Present-day Cuba] Vokrug sveta, no. 12, Dec. 1959: 42–45.

4706. ———. Kubinskaia zima [Cuban winter] Nov. vrem., v. 21, no. 1, Jan. 1964: 26–28.

4707. ———. Morskie vorota Kuby [The Cuban gateway to the seas] Nov. vrem., v. 21, no. 3, Jan. 1964: 25–28.
The city of Havana.

4708. ———. Sakhar stanovitsia sladkim [Sugar has become sweet] Nov. vrem., v. 21, no. 6, Feb. 1964: 8–11.

4709. ———. V boio prishel svet [The "bohíos" are supplied with light] Ogonek, v. 37, no. 39, Sept. 1959: 12–14.

4710. Logvin, I. Takoiu ia bachyv Kubu [Cuba as I saw it] Nauka i zhyttia, no. 11, Nov. 1961: 54–56.

4711. Lukovets, A. Kubinskie vstrechi [Meetings in Cuba] Za rubezhom, no. 30, July 1963: 16–18.

4712. Malaviya, Harsh Dev. Narod s chistoi dushoi i shchedrym serdtsem [The people of pure souls and warm hearts] Za rubezhom, no. 34, Aug. 1964: 9–10.
Translated from the English.

4713. Manasov, M. Kuba glazami turista [Cuba as seen by a tourist] Otv. na vop. trud., no. 6, June 1963: 31–38.

4714. Markos Ana na Kube [Marcos Ana in Cuba] Zhen. mira, no. 7, 1963: 8.
A Spanish poet.

4715. Mashkin, V. Vozdukh, kotorym dyshit Gavana [The air one breathes in Havana] Za rubezhom, no. 52, Dec. 1963: 3.

4716. Maslennikov, V. Kuba—da! Stranichki iz dnevnika [Cuba—yes! Pages from a diary] Enisei, no. 2, 1963: 85–91.

4717. Mikoian, Sergo. Saliut, Kuba! [Salute to Cuba!] Moskva, v. 4, no. 5, 1960: 146–171.

4718. Mishakov, Oleksandr. Ostriv svobody [The island of freedom] Ukraina, no. 15, Aug. 1961: 21–22.

4719. "My byli v Kube ["We were in Cuba"] Zhen. mira, no. 6, 1961: 10.

4720. Napalkov, S. Narod—voin, narod—sozdatel'! [These people are warriors and builders!] Neva, no. 9, 1960: 181–186.

4721. North, Joseph. IA videl novuiu Kubu [I saw the new Cuba] Druzh. nar., no. 9, Sept. 1960: 209–221.
Translated from the English.

4722. ———. Svoboda, zemlia i khleb [Freedom, land, and bread] Za rubezhom, no. 4, July 1960: 3, 24–25.
Translated from the English.

4723. Okuneva, M. A. Poezdka na Kubu v ianvare 1962 goda [A trip to Cuba in January 1962] Sov. etn., no. 6, Nov.-Dec. 1962: 140–149.

4724. Orel, V. Cuba is not alone. World youth, no. 2, 1963: 28–33.

4725. Ossovskii, P. Po Kube [In Cuba] Tvorchestvo, no. 7, 1961: 2–3.

4726. Ostrovinskaia, IU. Stroki, zapisannye na Kube [Brief notes jotted down in Cuba] Sov. tsirk, v. 7, no. 3, Mar. 1963: 6–7.

4727. Pavlova, Liudmila. Lainer idet k Kube [A liner sails for Cuba] Sov. zhen., v. 17, no. 7, 1961: 5–6.

4728. Piriutko, Al'bert. Vstrechi v Mansanil'o [Meetings in Manzanillo] Neva, no. 5, 1961: 211–212.

4729. Podel'shchikov, G. V strane druzei [In a land of friends] Sov. profsoiuzy, v. 17, no. 7, Apr. 1961: 43–45.

4730. Pogosov, IU. Kogda tantsuet vsia Gavana [When all Havana dances] Vokrug sveta, no. 5, May 1963: 14–16.
Carnival in Cuba.

4731. Poliakovskii, V. Kuba—da! [Cuba— yes!] Za rubezhom, no. 13, Apr. 1961: 16–18.

4732. ———. Zemlia kubinskaia [The Cuban land] Nauka i zhizn', v. 28, no. 5, May 1961: 49–54.

4733. Ponizovskii, Vladimir. 24 chasa Gavany [24 hours in Havana] Vokrug sveta, no. 8, Aug. 1963: 30–33, 59.

4734. Popov, G. Vsiudu u nas druz'ia [We have friends everywhere] Sel'khoz. Povol., v. 8, no. 11, Nov. 1962: 92–94.

4735. Popova, N. V. Vstrechi na Kube [Meetings in Cuba] Nov. vrem., v. 20, no. 36, Sept. 1962: 12–13.

4736. Popovich, Pavel. Na zemnykh orbitakh [In terrestrial orbits] Vsesvit, v. 7, no. 11, Nov. 1964: 7–14.

4737. Posysaev, N. Pamiat' o dalekoi Kube [Remembrance of faraway Cuba] Grazhd. av., v. 17, no. 11, Nov. 1960: 24.

4738. Rozhe Garodi: Zdes' nadezhdy stano-viatsia deistvitel'nost'iu [Here I see the realization of hopes, Roger Garaudy says] Inostr. lit., no. 6, June 1962: 297.

4739. Schumacher, Guenther. Kuba, rik druhyi [Cuba, the second year] Vsesvit, v. 4, no. 11, Nov. 1960: 70–73.
Translated from the German.

4740. Shliapnikov, R. Iz zhizni Kuby [Life in Cuba] Nov. vrem., v. 19, no. 13, Mar. 1961: 24–25.

4741. Smirnov, S. S. Poezdka na Kubu [A trip to Cuba] Znamia, v. 31, no. 6, June 1961: 135–178: v. 31, no. 7, July 1961: 132–177.

4742. Sushchenko, Ivan. Kuba—gordaia strana svobodnykh liudei; zapiski khu-dozhnika [Cuba, a proud country of free people; a painter's notes] Mol. gvard., no. 1, Jan. 1963: 266–282.

4743. Timonen, Antti. Dvenadtsat' dnei na Kube [Twelve days in Cuba] Na rub., v. 25, no. 1, Jan. 1964: 68–75.
Translated from the Finnish.

4744. V gostiakh na Kube [Guests in Cuba] Sov. pech., no. 2, Feb. 1961: 58–59.

4745. Vakhov, Anatolii. Asta lavista! O poezdke na Kubu [Hasta la vista! Cuban travel notes] Dal'nii Vostok, no. 2, 1964: 33–35.

4746. Varela, Alfredo. "Kuba—da!"; glavy iz knigi ["Cuba—yes!"; chapters from a book] Inostr. lit., no. 12, Dec. 1960: 173–209.
Translated from the Spanish.

4747. Volodkin, V. ¡Cuba si! IUn. tekh., v. 5, no. 7, July 1961: 62–64.

4748. Zandin, Konstantin. Trista dnei na ostrove svobody; pis'ma s Kuby [Three hundred days on the island of freedom; letters from Cuba] Sib. ogni, no. 7, July 1963: 157–169; no. 8, Aug. 1963: 138–154.

4749. Zavattini, Cesare. Kubinskii dnevnik [Cuban diary] Inostr. lit., no. 8, Aug. 1960: 227–236.
Translated from the Italian.

4750. Zhimbiev, TSyden-Zhap. Kuba— liubov' moia! [You are my love, Cuba!] Baikal, v. 10, no. 3, May-June 1964: 56–66; v. 10, no. 4, July-Aug. 1964: 42–50.

See also entries no. 1474, 2771, 2791, 3175, 3361, 3367, 4362, and 4500.

g. *Ecuador*

4751. Hanzelka, Jiří, *and* Miroslav Zikmund. K okhotnikam za cherepami [On a visit to head-hunters] Moscow, Mol. gvardiia, 1960. 288 p.
Translated by S. Babin and R. Nazarov from the Czech.

4752. ———. K okhotnikam za cherepami; glavy iz knigi [On a visit to head-hunters;

chapters from a book] Moscow, Pravda, 1963. 46 p.

Translated by S. Babin and R. Nazarov from the Czech.

4753. Gvozdev, IU. V ust'e reki Guaias [In the estuary of the Guayas River] Nov. vrem., v. 20, no. 11, Mar. 1963: 24–25.

4754. Hanzelka, Jiří, *and* Miroslav Zikmund. K okhotnikam za cherepami [On a visit to head-hunters] Don, v. 3, no. 1, Jan. 1959: 130–142; v. 3, no. 2, Feb. 1959: 141–155; v. 3, no. 3, Mar. 1959: 147–166; v. 3, no. 4, Apr. 1959: 154–167; v. 3, no. 5, May 1959: 141–154.

Translated from the Czech.

4755. ———. Myslyvtsi za cherepamy [Head-hunters] Znan. ta pratsia, no. 8, Aug. 1959: 18–21.

Translated from the Czech.

4756. Ignat'ev, Oleg. Liudi, gory i banany [People, mountains, and bananas] Za rubezhom, no. 41, Oct. 1961: 16–17.

4757. Mostovets, N. My s vami, tovarishchi [We are with you, comrades] Agitator, no. 9, May 1964: 25–26.

4758. ———. Vstrecha s Ekvadorom [A visit to Ecuador] Nov. vrem., v. 20, no. 23, June 1962: 25–27.

4759. Rodker, Joan. Oni zhivut v korolevstve Kito [They live in the Quito kingdom] Ogonek, v. 38, no. 40, Oct. 1960: 12–13.

4760. Strana na ekvatore [A country on the equator] Mol. mira, no. 1/2, 1962: 19–20.

h. El Salvador

See entry no. 4776.

i. Guatemala

4761. IUr'ev, V. Na rodine ketsalia [In the quetzal's native land] Vokrug sveta, no. 9, Sept. 1960: 44–46.

j. Mexico

4762. Paleckis, Justas. V Meksike; putevye zametki [In Mexico; travel notes] Vilnius, Vaga, 1964. 198 p.

In Lithuanian.

4763. Borovik, Genrikh. Schast'ia vam, meksikantsy! [Good luck to you, Mexicans!] Ogonek, v. 38, no. 3, Jan. 1960: 16–16d.

4764. Chichkov, V. U meksikanskoi molodezhi [With Mexican youth] IUnost', v. 5, no. 6, June 1959: 97–103.

4765. Kamynin, L. Meksikanskie zametki [Mexican notes] Sov. pech., no. 1, Jan. 1960: 56–59.

4766. L'vov, Sergei. Puteshestvie v Meksiku [Travels in Mexico] Nov. vrem., v. 19, no. 16, Apr. 1961: 25–27; v. 19, no. 17, Apr. 1961: 22–25.

4767. Mikhailov, Sergei. Po Meksike [In Mexico] Sov. foto, v. 20, no. 7, July 1960: 40–43.

4768. Paleckis, Justas. Solntse Meksiki ne pogasnet [The Mexican sun will shine forever] Nov. vrem., v. 21, no. 8, Feb. 1964: 23–25.

4769. Perventsev, Vl. Tampiko; fotoocherk [Tampico; a photo-sketch] Vokrug sveta, no. 10, Oct. 1964: 10–12.

4770. Sergei Bondarchuk v SShA, Meksike, Italii [Sergei Bondarchuk in the United States, Mexico, and Italy] Kul't. i zhizn', v. 5, no. 2, 1961: 22–23.

Travels of the Soviet motion-picture actor.

4771. Steinbeck, John, *and* Edward F. Ricketts. More Kortesa [Sea of Cortez] Zvezda, no. 7, July 1964: 120–135; no. 8, Aug. 1964: 112–136.

Translated from the English.

4772. Tankina, Marharyta. México es bonito. Vitchyzna, v. 31, no. 1, Jan. 1963: 190–199.

4773. Tkachenko, V. Takoiu my pobachyly Meksyku [Mexico as we saw it] Vsesvit, v. 5, no. 6, June 1962: 118–122.

4774. Wasilewska, Wanda. Esli uvidish' ee khot' raz [Even if you saw it just once] Sov. zhen., v. 17, no. 12, 1961: 24–26.

See also entry no. 4518.

k. Panama

4775. Borovskii, V. Nasledniki konkistadorov [The heirs of conquistadors] Za rubezhom, no. 7, Feb. 1964: 17–18.

4776. Hanzelka, Jiří, *and* Miroslav Zikmund. Panama, Sal'vador [Panama and El Salvador] Vsesvit, v. 2, no. 5, May 1959: 130–137, 154–155.

4777. ———. Vo vlasti "IUnaited Frut" [Under the rule of the "United Fruit Company"] Don, v. 4, no. 5, May 1960: 144–153; v. 4, no. 6, June 1960: 164–170. Translated from the Czech.

l. Peru

4778. Weaver, Kenneth. "Kraina chotyr'okh chvertei" ["The country of four quarters"] Vsesvit, v. 7, no. 8, Aug. 1964: 102–107. Translated from the English.

See also entry no. 4751.

m. Uruguay

4779. Khachaturov, K. Za rekoi pestrykh ptits [Beyond the river of multicolored birds] Vokrug sveta, no. 9, Sept. 1962: 27–31.

4780. Ramírez, Velia. Matreshka edet v IUzhnuiu Ameriku [Matreshka goes to South America] Sov. zhen., v. 17, no. 9, 1961: 42. Imaginary voyage to Uruguay of a Russian doll.

4781. Rodionov, P. Narod boretsia, narod pobedit! [The people are struggling and they will win!] Agitator, no. 23, Dec. 1963: 23–28.

See also entries no. 1617 and 4592.

n. Venezuela

4782. Chichkov, Vas. Neft' i liudi [Oil and people] Ogonek, v. 37, no. 42, Oct. 1959: 24–25.

4783. Saakov, R. Karibe i chernoe zoloto [The caribe and black gold] Ogonek, v. 39, no. 19, May 1961: 19–21.

o. West Indies

4784. Averbakh, IU. Na ostrove Kiurasao [On Curaçao Island] Znan.-sila, v. 37, no. 12, Dec. 1962: 49–51.

4785. Klingel, Gilbert C. Nochnoe shestvie [A night march] Vokrug sveta, no. 12, Dec. 1962: 40–41. Bahama Islands. Translated from the English.

4786. L'vov, Sergei. Den' na ostrove Kiurasao; putevye vpechatleniia [A day on Curaçao Island; travel notes] Nov. vrem., v. 19, no. 29, July 1961: 23–24.

B. LATIN AMERICANS ABROAD

1. In the Soviet Union

a. Travelers From More Than One Country

4787. Kondratov, V., *and* B. Khvostov. Forum druzhby; o seminare kooperatorov Azii, Afriki i Latinskoi Ameriki [A meeting of friends; a conference of the personnel of Asian, African, and Latin American cooperative societies] Sov. potreb. koop., v. 5, no. 10, Oct. 1961: 48–52.

4788. Rumiantsev, S. V. Universitet druzhby narodov v Moskve—molodezhi stran Azii, Afriki, Latinskoi Ameriki [The Moscow University of Friendship among Peoples for the youth of Asia, Africa, and Latin America] Vsem. stud. nov., v. 16, no. 5/6, May-June 1962: 26–27, 35–36.

b. Travelers From Individual Countries

(1) Brazil

4789. Estrella, Arnoldo. IA priobrel mnogo druzei [I acquired many friends] Kul't. i zhizn', v. 4, no. 8, 1960: 51–53. A Brazilian pianist on his visit to the USSR.

4790. Jean, Yvonne. Pshenitsy aromat i solntse na voskhode [The smell of wheat and the rising sun] Sov. zhen., v. 19, no. 9, 1963: 33.

4791. Martins, Justino. Spil'na peremoha [Our joint victory] Ukraina, no. 24, Dec. 1961: 3.

4792. Massera, Mercedes. Serdtsu dorogie dni [These days are dear to my heart] Sov. zhen., v. 20, no. 2, 1964: 36–37. A Brazilian painter's visit to the USSR.

See also entry no. 4845.

(2) Chile

4793. Lipschutz, Alexander. Chto ia videl svoimi glazami [This I saw with my own eyes] Kul't. i zhizn', v. 7, no. 2, 1963: 31–32.

4794. Nashi hosti; Fransisko Koloane [Our guests; Francisco Coloane] Lit. Odesa, no. 23, 1959: 102–103.
A Chilean writer on his visit to the USSR.

See also entry no. 2747.

(3) Cuba

4795. Ríos Pérez, Esteban. IA poliubil tebia Zolotonosha; dnevnik kubintsa [I love you, dear city of Zolotonosha; diary of a Cuban student] Cherkassy, Obl. kn.-gaz. izd-vo, 1963. 78 p.

4796. Viva Kuba! Vizit Fidelia Kastro Ruz v Sovetskii Soiuz [Long live Cuba! The visit of Fidel Castro Ruz to the Soviet Union] Moscow, Pravda, 1963. 196 p.
                                    DLC
Also published in Spanish.
Reviewed by S. L'vov in *Nov. mir*, v. 39, no. 8, Aug. 1963: 272–275.

4797. Arcocha, Juan. Liudi budushchego [People of the future] Moskva, v. 5, no. 10, 1961: 188–189.
Cuban visitors in the USSR.

4798. Bal'termants, Dm. Pis'mo v Sant'iago-de-Kuba [A letter to Santiago de Cuba] Ogonek, v. 42, no. 52, Dec. 1964: 18–19.
Training of Cuban workers in the USSR.

4799. Barsana, T. Segodnia gost' zhurnala— Krasnyi Krest Kuby [Cuban Red Cross is a guest of the periodical today] Sov. kras. krest, v. 11, no. 1, Jan.-Feb. 1961: 16–17.

4800. Borovik, Genrikh. Pervye shagi po Sovetskoi zemle [First steps on Soviet land] Ogonek, v. 41, no. 19, May 1963: 28–29.
Fidel Castro's visit to the USSR.

4801. Cabrera, Luis Rolando. Nashi serdtsa ostaiutsia s vami! [Our hearts remain with you!] Sov. pech., no. 7, July 1963: 55–57.
Cuban visitors.

4802. Castro, Fidel. "Narod gigantov" ["A nation of giants"] Agitator, no. 11, June 1963: 15–16.
Fidel Castro on the USSR.

4803. Cherevkov, K., *and* M. IAkhontova. Rebiata s ostrova borodachei [Children from the island of bearded men] Ogonek, v. 39, no. 41, Oct. 1961: 30.
A visit of Cuban Pioneers to the USSR.

4804. Cherkasov, B., *and* L. Splendor. Zdravstvui, molodaia Kuba! [Welcome, young Cuba!] Smena, v. 38, no. 7, Apr. 1961: 12–14.
Young Cuban guerrillas on a visit to the USSR.

4805. Dolgopiatov, G. Gosti iz Kuby [Our guests from Cuba] Leg. atl., no. 2, Feb. 1961: 20–21.
Cuban sportsmen in the USSR.

4806. Eto i est' internatsionalizm [This is true internationalism] Nov. vrem., v. 20, no. 22, May 1963: 1–3.
Fidel Castro's visit to the USSR.

4807. "Eto prevzoshlo vse nashi ozhidaniia . . . " ["This exceeds all our expectations . . ."] Sov. pech., no. 11, Nov. 1960: 11–12.
Cuban journalists on a visit to the USSR.

4808. Gosti s ostrova svobody (?) [Visitors from the island of freedom] Zashch. rast. ot vred. i bol., v. 9, no. 9, 1964: 57–58.

4809. Guevara, Ernesto. IA voskhishchen trudovymi podvigami sovetskoi molodezhi [I admire the labor achievements of Soviet youth] Smena, v. 37, no. 24, Dec. 1960: 24.

4810. Gurkov, Genrikh. Soldaty revoliutsii [Soldiers of the revolution] Ogonek, v. 40, no. 23, June 1962: 4–5.
Cuban students in the USSR.

4811. Karmen, R. S Fidelem Kastro po SSSR [Through the USSR with Fidel Castro] Oktiabr', v. 40, no. 7, July 1963: 173–175.

4812. Khai shchastyt' tobi, sestro Kuba! [May you flourish, our sister Cuba!] Ukraina, no. 19, Oct. 1961: 6.
Cuban visitors in Kiev.

4813. Khorol'skii, V. Kubinskie rabotniki prosveshcheniia v SSSR [Cuban educators in the USSR] Nar. obr., no. 8, Aug. 1961: 109.

4814. Klusov, E. Gosti s dalekoi Kuby [Our guests from faraway Cuba] Ogonek, v. 37, no. 40, Sept. 1959: 31.

4815. Kossakovskaia, E. Gosti iz Kuby [Our Cuban visitors] Doshk. vosp., v. 35, no. 1, Jan. 1962: 109–113.
A visit of Cuban teachers.

4816. Kuba—da! [Cuba, yes!] Ogonek, v. 39, no. 39, Sept. 1961: 1.
Cuban visitors.

4817. Kubinskie arkhitektory v Erevane [Cuban architects in Yerevan] Sovetakan Aiastan, no. 6, 1962: 38.
In Armenian.

4818. Kubinskie kooperatory v SSSR [Cuban cooperators in the USSR] Sov. potreb. koop., v. 5, no. 7, July 1961: 1–2.

4819. Kubyns'ki zaliznychnyky v IAsynu-vatii [Cuban railroad employees came to study in Yasunovataya] Ukraina, no. 14, July 1962: 7.

4820. Kurganov, V. Poslanets Kuby [An envoy of Cuba] Ogonek, v. 41, no. 16, Apr. 1963: 25.

4821. Levit, L., and S. Mariuts. Kubyntsi na Ukraini [Cubans in the Ukraine] Ukraina, no. 4, Feb. 1962: 26–27.

4822. Mariuts, S. Kubyns'ki moriaky v Khersoni [Cuban sailors in Kherson] Ukraina, no. 12, June 1961: 12.

4823. Molodye kubintsy privetstvuiut Uni-versitet druzhby narodov [Young Cubans greet the University of Friendship among the Peoples] Inostr. lit., no. 7, July 1960: 280.
Cuban students in the USSR.

4824. Mykhal'chuk, M. Nash dim—tse tvii dim, Fidel'! [Our house belongs to you, Fidel!] Ukraina, no. 10, May 1963: 1.

4825. Nartsissov, Igor'. Pervaia borozda [Their first furrow] Sov. zhen., v. 19, no. 8, 1963: 29.
Cuban students in the USSR.

4826. Nidze, Mykhailo. Na dobru zhadku [A keepsake] Ukraina, no. 16, July 1963: 8.
Cuban visitors.

4827. Nidze, Mykhailo, and Oleh Vasil'iev. Viva Cuba! Viva Fidel! Ukraina, no. 11, June 1963: 1–3.

4828. Pilar sa Leal, María del. Kuba, tsudounaia Kuba [Cuba, the beautiful Cuba] Rab. i sial., v. 38, no. 4, Apr. 1962: 11.
Cuban students in the Soviet Union.

4829. Podkliuchnikov, M. Fidel' Castro v "Pravde" [Fidel Castro visiting "Pravda"] Sov. pech., no. 6, June 1963: 12–13.

4830. Popov, I. Poslantsy geroicheskogo ostrova [Envoys of the heroic island] Krest'ianka, v. 40, no. 6, June 1962: 8–9.

4831. Privetstvuem tebia, molodaia Kuba! [Greetings, young Cuba!] Ogonek, v. 39, no. 29, July 1961: 1.

4832. Rakhmaninov, G. I. Kubinskie uchenye v Sovetskom Soiuze [Cuban scientists in the Soviet Union] Vest. AN SSSR, v. 33, no. 8, Aug. 1963: 84–88.

4833. Ratan, S. Dreva Fidelia Kastra [Fidel Castro's three] Belarus', v. 20, no. 6, June 1963: 4.
Cuban students in Minsk.

4834. Rubiera, Alberto. Nashi serdtsa b'iutsia vmeste [Our hearts beat in unison] Sov. profsoiuzy, v. 19, no. 12, June 1963: 26–27.
Cuban visitors.

4835. Sagal, G. "Iz Moskvy, ot Khuana Arkochi" [Juan Arcocha reports from Moscow] Sov. pech., no. 6, June 1962: 60–61.
Cuban reporters in Russia.

4836. Stanin, V. Poslantsy Kuby na uchebe [The messengers from Cuba at study] Prof.-tekh. obr., v. 18, no. 11, Nov. 1961: 19.

4837. TSepulin, G. Idet teplokhod na Kubu; dokumental'naia povest' [A motorship sails to Cuba; a documentary tale]

Vokrug sveta, no. 9, Sept. 1964: 7–10; no. 10, Oct. 1964: 13–15.
Cuban peasants who studied the Soviet methods of cooperative agriculture.

4838. ———. Parni s ostrova svobody [Lads from the island of freedom] Vokrug sveta, no. 12, Dec. 1961: 21.

4839. Vernemsia na Kubu mekhanizatorami! [We shall return to Cuba as agriculture mechanizers!] IUn. tekh., v. 6, no. 3, Mar. 1962: 18–19.

4840. Viva Kuba! [Viva Cuba!] Ogonek, v. 42, no. 5, Jan. 1964: 2–3.
Fidel Castro's visit to the Soviet Union.

4841. Z ostrova svobody—na bat'kivshchynu svobody! [From the island of freedom to the fatherland of freedom!] Ukraina, no. 3, Jan. 1964: 3.
Fidel Castro's visit to the USSR.

4842. Zolototrubov, A. Fidel' Kastro u severomortsev [Fidel Castro with the sailors of the Northern Fleet] Sov. voin, v. 45, no. 13, July 1963: 7.

See also entries no. 4323 and 4480.

(4) Guatemala

4843. Méndez, Francisco. Svidetel'stvo zapadnogo zhurnalista [Impressions of a western journalist] Sov. zhen., v. 17, no. 11, 1961: 25.
Guatemalan visitors.

(5) Mexico

4844. Ivanov, E. "Vashi serdtsa otkryty dlia gostei" ["Your hearts are open to guests"] Sov. kras. krest, v. 12, no. 5, Sept.-Oct. 1962: 17–18.
Mexican visitors.

4845. Martins, Justino. "Mir! IA slyshal eto prekrasnoe slovo" ["Peace! I heard this beautiful word"] Sov. pech., no. 12, Dec. 1961: 56–57.
The visits of Mexican and Brazilian newspapermen to the USSR.

See also entry no. 2825.

(6) Peru

4846. Gvozdev, IU. Reportazh iz griadushchego [A news story about the future] Nov. vrem., v. 21, no. 49, Dec. 1963: 30–31.
Peruvian visitors to the USSR.
A review of Gustavo Valcárcel's *Reportaje al futuro* (Lima, Editora Perú Nuevo, 1963. 383 p.).

4847. Valcárcel, Gustavo. U Lenina [At the Lenin tomb] Inostr. lit., no. 11, Nov. 1964: 246–247.
A Peruvian writer's visit to the USSR.

(7) Uruguay

4848. Etchepare, Alberto. SSSR—strana iunykh [The USSR, a land of the young] Kul't. i zhizn', v. 3, no. 4, 1959: 16–18.
Uruguayan visitors.

4849. Goberna, Paulino, *and others.* Nashi vpechatleniia o prebyvanii v SSSR [Impressions from our trip to the USSR] Avt. transp., v. 38, no. 11, Nov. 1960: 8–9.
Uruguayan visitors.

2. In the United States

4850. Freeman, Harry. Splava ne poluchilos' [There is no melting pot] Nov. vrem., v. 21, no. 52, Dec. 1963: 34–35.
A review of *Beyond the Melting Pot; the Negroes, Puerto Ricans, Jews, and Irish in New York City* by Nathan Glazer and Daniel Patric Moynihan (Cambridge, Mass., M.I.T. Press, 1963. 360 p.).

4851. Lialin, V. Po tu storonu Rio-Grande [Across the Rio Grande] Vokrug sveta, no. 9, Sept. 1960: 47–49.
Mexican agricultural workers in the United States.

4852. Po stranitsam zarubezhnykh gazet [A review of foreign newspapers] Sots. zakon., v. 37, no. 8, Aug. 1960: 126–127.
Puerto Ricans in the United States.

4853. "Rabota, zhil'e, zemlia"—basni "Soiuza radi progressa" ["Work, housing, land," these are the fables spread by the Alliance for Progress] Vsem. prof. dvizh., no. 5, May 1963: 22–23.
Mexicans in the United States.

XXV

MISCELLANY

❧

4854. Belen'kii, M. Zhertvy ostrova sokro-vishch [Victims of "treasure island"] Vokrug sveta, no. 7, July 1963: 36–37.
Treasure hunting in the Carribbean area.

4855. Robinson, Fernando, Khuan-Khose, Otto i Mario [Robinson, Fernando, Juan José, Otto, and Mario] Vsesvit, v. 7, no. 11, Nov. 1964: 135.
Venezuelan quintuplets.

4856. Rodríguez, Armesino. Vladimir Il'ich Rodriges [Vladimir Ilich Rodríguez] Nov. vrem., v. 20, no. 30, July 1962: 22.
A name given to his son by a sympathizer of the USSR.

4857. Sakhnin, Arkadii. Ego znaiut po imeni [They know his name] Moskva, v. 8, no. 1, 1964: 5–9.
The name "Lenin" was given to his son by a Cuban friend of the USSR.

APPENDIXES

APPENDIX I

List of Abbreviated Names of Publishing Houses With Expansions*

Derzhlitvydav—Derzhavne vydavnytstvo khudozhn'oi literatury

Derzhpolitvydav—Derzhavne vydavnytstvo politychnoi literatury

Derzhvydav—Derzhavne vydavnytstvo

Det. lit.—Detskaia literatura

Detgiz—Gosudarstvennoe izdatel'stvo detskoi literatury

Detiunizdat—Gosudarstvennoe izdatel'stvo detskoi i iunosheskoi literatury

Dytvydav—Vydavnytstvo dytiachoi literatury

Ekonomizdat—Izdatel'stvo ekonomicheskoi literatury

Estgosizdat—Estonskoe gosudarstvennoe izdatel'stvo

Geografgiz—Gosudarstvennoe izdatel'stvo geograficheskoi literatury

Gidrometeoizdat—Gosudarstvennoe nauchno-tekhnicheskoe gidrometeorologicheskoe izdatel'stvo

Gos. biblioteka SSSR im. Lenina—Gosudarstvennaia biblioteka SSSR imeni Lenina

Gos. izd-vo khudozh. lit.—Gosudarstvennoe izdatel'stvo khudozhestvennoi literatury

Gos. muzei izobrazit. iskusstv—Gosudarstvennyi muzei izobrazitel'nykh iskusstv

Gos. nauch.-issled. in-t nauch. i tekhn. informatsii—Gosudarstvennyi nauchno-issledovatel'skii institut nauchnoi i tekhnicheskoi informatsii

Gos. publichnaia biblioteka im. Saltykova-Shchedrina—Gosudarstvennaia publichnaia biblioteka imeni Saltykova-Shchedrina

GOSINTI—Gosudarstvennyi nauchno-issledovatel'skii institut nauchnoi i tekhnicheskoi informatsii

Gosiurizdat—Gosudarstvennoe izdatel'stvo iuridicheskoi literatury

Gosizdat BSSR—Gosudarstvennoe izdatel'stvo Belorusskoi SSR

Gosizdat UzSSR—Gosudarstvennoe izdatel'stvo Uzbekskoi SSR

Goslitizdat—Gosudarstvennoe izdatel'stvo khudozhestvennoi literatury

Gospolitizdat—Gosudarstvennoe izdatel'stvo politicheskoi literatury

Gospolitnauchizdat—Gosudarstvennoe izdatel'stvo politicheskoi i nauchnoi literatury

Gostoptekhizdat—Gosudarstvennoe nauchno-tekhnicheskoe izdatel'stvo neftianoi i gorno-toplivnoi literatury

In-t mir. ekon. i mezhdun. otn. AN SSSR—Institut mirovoi ekonomiki i mezhdunarodnykh otnoshenii Akademii nauk SSSR

Izd-vo Akad. nauk SSSR—Izdatel'stvo Akademii Nauk SSSR

Izd-vo. Akad. nauk Ukr. SSR—Izdatel'stvo Akademii nauk Ukrainskoi SSR

Izd-vo Gos. Ermitazha—Izdatel'stvo Gosudarstvennogo Ermitazha

Izd-vo IMO—Izdatel'stvo Instituta mezhdunarodnykh otnoshenii

Izd-vo inostr. lit.—Izdatel'stvo inostrannoi literatury

Izd-vo khud. lit.—Izdatel'stvo khudozhestvennoi literatury

Izd-vo Leningr. un-ta—Izdatel'stvo Leningradskogo universiteta

Izd-vo lit-ry na inostr. iazykakh—Izdatel'stvo literatury na inostrannykh iazykakh

Izd-vo Mosk. un-ta—Izdatel'stvo Moskovskogo universiteta

Izd-vo vost. lit.—Izdatel'stvo vostochnoi literatury

---

*Includes only the names of those publishing houses which are abbreviated in the bibliographical citations.

Izd-vo VPSh i AON—Izdatel'stvo Vysshei partiinoi shkoly i Akademii obshchestvennykh nauk

Izd-vo Vses. knizhn. palaty—Izdatel'stvo Vsesoiuznoi knizhnoi palaty

Izogiz—Gosudarstvennoe izdatel'stvo izobrazitel'nogo iskusstva

Kazakh. gos. un-t im. S. M. Kirova—Kazakhskii gosudarstvennyi universitet imeni S. M. Kirova

Kazgoslitizdat—Kazakhskoe gosudarstvennoe izdatel'stvo khudozhestvennoi literatury

Kazuchpedgiz—Kazakhskoe gosudarstvennoe uchebno-pedagogicheskoe izdatel'stvo

Khudozh. lit.—Khudozhestvennaia literatura

Kirgizgosizdat—Kirgizskoe gosudarstvennoe izdatel'stvo

Knizhn. izd-vo—Knizhnoe izdatel'stvo

Kr. zvezda—Krasnaia zvezda

Latgosizdat—Gosudarstvennoe izdatel'stvo Latviiskoi SSR

Lenizdat—Izdatel'stvo Leningradskogo obkoma i gorkoma KPSS

Medgiz—Gosudarstvennoe izdatel'stvo meditsinskoi literatury

Mol. gvardiia—Molodaia gvardiia

Mosk. zaochn. ped. institut—Moskovskii zaochnyi pedagogicheskii institut

Muzgiz—Gosudarstvennoe muzykal'noe izdatel'stvo

Obl. kn. izd-vo—Oblastnoe knizhnoe izdatel'stvo

Obl. otd. O-va po rasprostr. polit. i nauch. znanii—Oblastnoe otdelenie Obshchestva po rasprostraneniiu politicheskikh i nauchnykh znanii

Ob-vo po rasprostr. polit. i nauch. znanii—Obshchestvo po rasprostraneniiu politicheskikh i nauchnykh znanii

Otd. nauch.-tekh. informatsii VIMS—Otdel nauchno-tekhnicheskoi informatsii VIMS

Otd. raspr. dram. proizvedenii VUOAP—Otdel rasprostraneniia dramaticheskikh proizvedenii Vsesoiuznogo upravleniia po okhrane avtorskikh prav

Pedagog. in-t im. V. P. Potemkina—Pedagogicheskii institut imeni V. P. Potemkina

Pedagogich. in-t im. V. P. Chkalova—Pedagogicheskii institut imeni V. P. Chkalova

Profizdat—Izdatel'stvo Vsesoiuznogo tsentral'nogo soveta professional'nykh soiuzov

Rad. pys'mennyk—Radians'kyi pys'mennyk

Rad. shkola—Radians'ka shkola

Sotsekgiz—Izdatel'stvo sotsial'no-ekonomicheskoi literatury

Sov. khudozhnik—Sovetskii khudozhnik

Sov. pisatel'—Sovetskii pisatel'

Sov. Rossiia—Sovetskaia Rossiia

Tadzhikgosizdat—Tadzhikskoe gosudarstvennoe izdatel'stvo

TSentr. in-t informatsii tsvetnoi metallurgii—TSentral'nyi institut informatsii tsvetnoi metallurgii

TSentr. in-t tekhn. informatsii i ekonom. issl. po lesnoi i bumazhnoi i derevoobrabatyvaiushchei promyshl. — TSentral'nyi institut tekhnicheskoi informatsii i ekonomicheskikh issledovanii po lesnoi i bumazhnoi i derevoobrabatyvaiushchei promyshlennosti

TSentr. nauch.-issl. in-t informatsii i tekhn.-ekon. issledovanii po neft. i gaz. prom.—TSentral'nyi nauchno-issledovatel'skii institut informatsii i tekhniko-ekonomicheskikh issledovanii po neftianoi i gazovoi promyshlennosti

TSentr. nauch.-issl. in-t informatsii i tekhn.-ekon. issledovanii tsvetnoi metallurgii—TSentral'nyi nauchno-issledovatel'skii institut informatsii i tekhnichesko-ekonomicheskikh issledovanii tsvetnoi metallurgii

T-vo "Znannia" URSR—Tovarystvo "Znannia" Ukrains'koi RSR

Uchpedgiz—Gosudarstvennoe uchebno-pedagogicheskoe izdatel'stvo

Valst. grožinés lit-ros leidykla—Valstybine grožinés literaturos leidykla

Vneshtorgizdat—Gosudarstvennoe izdatel'stvo Vneshtorgizdat

Voenizdat—Voennoe izdatel'stvo Ministerstva oborony SSSR

Vses. biblioteka inostr. lit.—Vsesoiuznaia biblioteka inostrannoi literatury

Vses. nauch.-issl. in-t miner. syr'ia—Vsesoiuznyi nauchno-issledovatel'skii institut mineral'nogo syr'ia

Vses. nauch.-issl. in-t po stroitel'stvu magistral'nykh truboprovodov—Vsesoiuznyi nauchno-issledovatel'skii institut po stroitel'stvu magistral'nyikh truboprovodov

Vyssh. shkola—Vysshaia shkola

APPENDIX II

List of Periodicals Cited

Includes expansions of abbreviations used, Library of Congress form of entry and call number where applicable, and National Union Catalog symbols for libraries holding materials not received or not cataloged by LC. Items without either LC call number or National Union Catalog symbol are not known to be held by any major research library in the United States or Canada. Titles marked with asterisks are also published in English language editions. See p. 277 for a list of English language titles.

Agidel'
Agitator   DK266.A2A35
Agrobiologiia   SB13.A53
Akush. i gin.—Akusherstvo i ginekologiia
       DNLM
Amudar'ia
Arkhit. SSSR—Arkhitektura SSSR
       NA6.A74
Atom. energ.—Atomnaia energiia
       QC770.A83
Av. i kosm.—Aviatsiia i kosmonavtika
       TL504.V45
Avt. dor.—Avtomobil'nye dorogi
       TE4.S73
Avt. transp.—Avtomobil'nyi transport
       TL4.A87
Avtom., telem. i sviaz'—Avtomatika, tele-
   mekhanika i sviaz'   TF615.A85
Az. i Afr. seg.—Aziia i Afrika segodnia
       DS1.S7
Baikal   AP50.S786
Belarus'   AP58.W5B4
Bet. i zhel.-bet.—Beton i zhelezobeton
       TA680.B38
Bibliotekar'   Z671.B5804
Bibliotekoved. i bibl. za rub.—Biblioteko-
   vedenie i bibliografiia za rubezhom
       Z671.B5813
Biul. inostr. kommerch. inform. Prilozhenie—
   Biulleten' inostrannoi kommercheskoi
   informatsii. Prilozhenie   HF25.B5
Biul. MOIP Otd. geol.—Moskovskoe obshche-
   stvo ispytatelei prirody. Biulleten'. Otdel
   geologicheskii   Q60.M8

Biul. Ob-va po rasprostr. polit. i nauchn.
   znanii RSFSR—Biulleten' Obshchestva
   po rasprostraneniiu politicheskikh i nauchnykh znanii RSFSR
Biul. tekh.-ekon. inform. Tekh. upr. Min. mor.
   flota—Russia (*1923–U.S.S.R.*) *Minister-*
   stvo morskogo flota. Tekhnicheskoe
   upravlenie. Biulleten' tekhniko-ekonomi-
   cheskoi informatsii   DLC
Biul. TSIICHM—Moscow. TSentral'nyi in-
   stitut informatsii chernoi metallurgii.
   Biulleten'   TS300.M6A15
Blok. agit. [Bel.]—Bloknot agitatora (Minsk)
       JN6598.K86B6
Blok. agit. [Len.]—Bloknot agitatora (Lenin-
   grad)   JN6598.K4B59
Blok. agit. [Sov. Armii]—Russia (*1923–*
   U.S.S.R.) *Glavnoe politicheskoe uprav-*
   lenie Sovetskoi Armii i Voenno-Morskogo
   Flota. Bloknot agitatora   U717.R9A32
Blok. agit. [Ukr.]—Bloknot agitatora (Kiev)
       HD1992.B55
Bot. mat. Gerb.—Akademiia nauk SSSR.
   Botanicheskii institut. Gerbarii. Botani-
   cheskie materialy   QK73.A55A65
Bot. zhur.—Botanicheskii zhurnal
       QK1.V713
Bum. prom.—Bumazhnaia promyshlennost'
       TS1080.B8
Chto chitat'   Z1007.C62
Dal'nii Vostok   AP50.D27
Dekorat. isk. SSSR—Dekorativnoe iskusstvo
   SSSR   NK7.D4

Den. i kred.—Den'gi i kredit   HG25.D4
Dnipro   AP58.U5D6
Don   PG3504.R6D6
Donbass   AP50.D67
Doshk. vosp.—Doshkol'noe vospitanie
        L51.D6
Drosha   DLC
Druzh. nar.—Druzhba narodov
        PN6065.R9D7
Edebi Bashkortostan   DLC
Ekon. Rad. Ukr.—Ekonomika Radians'koi
    Ukrainy   HC337.U5A13
Ekon. sel'khoz.—Ekonomika sel'skogo
    khoziaistva   S13.S874
Elek. i tepl. tiaga—Elektricheskaia i teplo-
    voznaia tiaga   TF4.E45
Energokhoz. za rub.—Energokhoziaistvo za
    rubezhom   TK4.E7765
Enisei   PG3505.K7E6
Estrada   PG3228.A72E8
Ezhegodnik Muzeia istorii religii i ateizma—
    Akademiia nauk SSSR. *Muzei istorii
    religii i ateizma.* Ezhegodnik
        BL2710.A55
Fin. SSSR—Finansy SSSR   HJ109.R8F5
Fiz. kul't. v shkole—Fizicheskaia kul'tura v
    shkole   GV201.F47
Fizk. i sport—Fizkul'tura i sport
        GV201.F55
Gaz. prom.—Gazovaia promyshlennost'
        TP700.G35
Geod. i kart.—Geodeziia i kartografiia
        QB275.G45
Geog. v shkole—Geografiia v shkole
        G1.G313
Gidr. i mel.—Gidrotekhnika i melioratsiia
        TC1.G53
Gor. khoz. Mosk.—Gorodskoe khoziaistvo
    Moskvy   HD4677.M6G6
Gor. zhur.—Gornyi zhurnal   TN4.G8
Grazhd. av.—Grazhdanskaia aviatsiia
        TL504.G7
IAlav   DLC
IAlkyn
Inform. biul. o zarubezh. khim. promyshl.—
    Informatsionnyi biulleten' o zarubezhnoi
    khimicheskoi promyshlennosti
Inostr. lit.—Inostrannaia literatura
        AP50.I53
Isk. kino—Iskusstvo kino   PN1993.I7

Isk. knigi—Iskusstvo knigi   NC985.I8
Iskusstvo   N6.I85
Ist. arkh.—Istoricheskii arkhiv
        DK1.A3274
IUn. nat.—IUnyi naturalist   QH7.I86
IUn. tekh.—IUnyi tekhnik   T4.I89
IUnost'   AP50.I93
Iz ist. med.—Iz istorii meditsiny
        R131.I9
Izv. AN Arm. SSR. Biol. nauki—Akademiia
    nauk Armianskoi SSR, *Erivan.* Izvestiia.
    Biologicheskie nauki   SB13.A56
Izv. AN SSSR. Otd. lit. i iaz.—Akademiia
    nauk SSSR. Izvestiia. Seriia literatury i
    iazyka   PG6.A553
Izv. AN SSSR. Ser. geog.—Akademiia nauk
    SSSR. Izvestiia. Seriia geograficheskaia
        G23.A35
Izv. Vor. gos. ped. inst.—Voronezh, Russia
    (City) Gosudarstvennyi pedagogicheskii
    institut. Izvestiia   AS262.V48A2
Izv. Vses. geog. ob-va—Geograficheskoe ob-
    shchestvo SSSR. Izvestiia   G23.G16
Izv. vys. ucheb. zav.; prav.—Russia (*1923–
    U.S.S.R.*) *Ministerstvo vysshego i srednego
    spetsial'nogo obrazovaniia.* Izvestiia
    vysshikh uchebnykh zavedenii; pravove-
    denie   DLC-LL
Jaunimo gretos   DLC
Kal. znam. i pam. dat—Kalendar' znamena-
    tel'nykh i pamiatnykh dat   D11.5.K3
Karogs   AP95.L4K37
Kazakstan aielderi   DLC
Khlopkovodstvo   SB245.K5
Khudozhnik   N6.K53
*Kitai   DS701.K5
Klin. med.—Klinicheskaia meditsina
        DNLM
Kobieta radziecka   DLC
Koks i khim.—Koks i khimiia   TP1.K6
Kolkh. proizv.—Kolkhoznoe proizvodstvo
        S13.K7
Kolkh.-sovkh. proizv.—Kolkhozno-sovkhoz-
    noe proizvodstvo   DLC
Komm. Bel.—Kommunist Belorussii
        HX8.K566
Komm. Mold.—Kommunist Moldavii
        HX8.K567
Komm. Sov. Latvii—Kommunist Sovetskoi
    Latvii   HX8.K568

Komm. Ukr.—Kommunist Ukrainy
HX8.K575
Komm. Uz.—Kommunist Uzbekistana
HX8.K577
Komm. Vooruzh. Sil—Kommunist Vooru-
zhennykh Sil   U717.R9A27
Kommunist   HX8.K56
Kommunist (Vilnius)   HX8.K565
Kon. i kon. sp.—Konevodstvo i konnyi sport
DNAL
Konevodstvo   SF277.K6 (–1959)
DNAL (1960–)
Kons. i ov. prom.—Konservnaia i ovo-
shchesushil'naia promyshlennost'
TX599.K58
Kora vyvetr.—Kora vyvetrivaniia
QE571.K6
Kosm. issl.—Kosmicheskie issledovaniia
DLC
Krat. soob. Inst. etn.—Akademiia nauk SSSR.
Institut etnografii. Kratkie soobshcheniia
GN2.A2144
Krest'ianka   AP50.K74
Kryl. rod.—Kryl'ia rodiny   TL504.V683
Kuba   DLC
Kukuruza   DNAL
*Kul't. i zhizn'—Kul'tura i zhizn'
AP50.K8
Kul't.-pros. rab.—Kul'turno-prosvetitel'naia
rabota   DK1.K8
Kunst   N8.K87
Lab. delo—Laboratornoe delo
RB1.L3 (–1959)
DNLM (1960–)
Latvijas sieviete
Leg. atl.—Legkaia atletika   GV1060.5.L42
Les.khoz.—Lesnoe khoziaistvo
SD1.L397
Liesma   DLC
Lit. Armeniia—Literaturnaia Armeniia
AP50.L46
Lit. Odesa—Literaturna Odesa
PG3957.O2L5
Literaturuli Adzhara
Looming   AP95.E4L6
Maksla   DLC
Mast. lesa—Master lesa   SD430.M3
Mast. ugl.—Master uglia, *see* Sov. shakht.
Mat. po ekon. geog. zarub. stran—Materialy

po ekonomicheskoi geografii zarubezh-
nykh stran   HC10.M34
Med. paraz. i paraz. bol.—Meditsinskaia
parazitologiia i parazitarnye bolezni
DNLM
Metallurg   TS300.M4
Mezhdunar. ezhegodnik; politika i ekono-
mika—Mezhdunarodnyi ezhegodnik; po-
litika i ekonomika   D839.M46
Mezhdunar. polit.-ekon. ezhegodnik, *see*
Mezhdunar. ezhegodnik; politika i
ekonomika
*Mezhdunar. zhizn'—Mezhdunarodnaia
zhizn'   D839.M45
Mias. ind. SSSR—Miasnaia industriia SSSR
TS1950.M5
Mir. ekon. i mezhdunar. otn.—Mirovaia eko-
nomika i mezhdunarodnye otnosheniia
HC10.M5357
*Mir nauki
Mnatobi   DLC
Mol. gvard.—Molodaia gvardiia
AP50.M62
Mol. kolkh.—Molodoi kolkhoznik
HQ799.R9S36
Mol. komm.—Molodoi kommunist
HQ799.R9M6
*Mol. mira—Molodezh' mira
HQ796.W633
Moloch. i mias. skotovodstvo—Molochnoe i
miasnoe skotovodstvo   DNAL
Mor. flot—Morskoi flot   VM4.M6
Mosk. prop.—Moskovskii propagandist
JN6598.V7A185
Moskva   AP50.M667
Muk.-elev. prom.—Mukomol'no-elevatornaia
promyshlennost'   TS2120.M9
Muso girios
Musu zodis
Muz. zhizn'—Muzykal'naia zhizn'
ML5.M9947
Mystetstvo   N6.M63
NTI—Moscow. Vsesoiuznyi institut nauchnoi
i tekhnicheskoi informatsii. Nauchno-
tekhnicheskaia informatsiia   DLC
Na rub.—Na rubezhe   AP50.N315
Nar. asv.—Narodnaia asveta   L51.N283
Nar. Azii i Afr.—Narody Azii i Afriki
DS1.P7

Nar. obr.—Narodnoe obrazovanie
L51.N295
Nash sovrem.—Nash sovremennik
AP50.N34
Nauch. dokl. vys. shkoly; ekon. nauki—
Russia (*1923–U.S.S.R.*) *Ministerstvo
vysshego i srednego spetsial'nogo obra-
zovaniia.* Nauchnye doklady vysshei
shkoly. Ekonomicheskie nauki
HC10.R8
Nauch. dokl. vys. shkoly; filol. nauki—
Russia (*1923–U.S.S.R.*) *Ministerstvo
vysshego i srednego spetsial'nogo obra-
zovaniia.* Nauchnye doklady vysshei
shkoly. Filologicheskie nauki   P19.R8
Nauch. dokl. vys. shkoly; filos. nauki—
Russia (*1923–U.S.S.R.*) *Ministerstvo
vysshego i srednego spetsial'nogo obra-
zovaniia.* Nauchnye doklady vysshei
shkoly. Filosofskie nauki   B6.R8
Nauch. zap. Kiev. fin.-ekon. inst.—Kiev.
Finansovo-ekonomichnyi instytut. Na-
uchnye zapiski   DLC
Nauk. zap. Kyiv. un.—Kiev. Universytet.
Naukovi zapysky   Q4.K5
Nauka i chelovechestvo; ezhegodnik
Q9.N3
Nauka i rel.—Nauka i religiia
BL2700.N35
Nauka i zhizn'   Q4.N43
Nauka i zhyttia   AS261.N286
Neft. khoz.—Neftianoe khoziaistvo
TN860.N465
Nefteper. i neftekhim.—Neftepererabotka i
neftekhimiia   DLC
Neftianik   TN860.N46
Neman   AP50.S596
Neva   AP50.N43
Nistrul   DLC
Noorus   AP95.E4N6
Nõukogude naine   HQ1104.N6
Nov. i noveish. ist.—Novaia i noveishaia
istoriia   D1.A3525
Nov. inostr. lit. po iaz.—Novaia inostrannaia
literatura po iazykoznaniiu
Z7003.N59
Nov. knigi—Novye inigi   Z2495.N6
Nov. mir—Novyi mir   AP50.N683
*Nov. vrem.—Novoe vremia   D410.N653

Obog. rud.—Obogashchenie rud
TN500.O25
Ogonek   AP50.O42
Okeanologiia   GC1.A47A23
Oktiabr'   AP50.O45
Osn., fund. i mekh. grun.—Osnovaniia,
fundamenty i mekhanika gruntov
TA710.A108
Otv. na vop. trud.—Otvety na voprosy
trudiashchikhsia   HD4811.O83
Padomju Latvijas sieviete   AP95.L4P3
Part. zhizn'—Partiinaia zhizn'
JN6598.V7P28
Part. zhizn' Kazakh.—Partiinaia zhizn'
Kazakhstana   HX8.P25
Pchelovodstvo   SF521.P3
Pergale   PG8501.P4
Pirveli skhivi
Pishch. promyshl.—Pishchevaia promysh-
lennost'   TX341.P53
Poligrafiia   Z119.P76
Polit. samoobr.—Politicheskoe samoobrazo-
vanie   HX8.V22
Prapor   AP58.U5P64
Prep. ist. v shkole—Prepodavanie istorii v
shkole   D16.2.P7
Priroda   Q4.P8
*Probl. mira i sots.—Problemy mira i
sotsializma   HX8.P72
Prof.-tekhn. obr.—Professional'no-tekhni-
cheskoe obrazovanie   T61.P7
Prom. koop.—Promyslovaia kooperatsiia
HD3514.P7
Prop. i agit.—Propagandist i agitator
U717.R9R7
Prostor   AP50.P76
Ptitsevodstvo   SF488.R8P8 (–1959)
DNAL (1960–)
Punalippu   PH344.P8
Put' i put. khoz.—Put' i putevoe khoziaistvo
TF4.P86
Rab. i sial.—Rabotnitsa i sialianka
AP58.W5R3
Rabotnitsa   AP50.R33
Rad. pravo—Radians'ke pravo   DLC-LL
Rad. shk.—Radians'ka shkola   L51.R33
Rad. zhin.—Radians'ka zhinka   HQ1661.R3
Radio   TK6540.R155
Raduga   DLC

Razved. i okh. nedr.—Razvedka i okhrana
nedr   TN4.R23
Rech. transp.—Rechnoi transport
                                  TC601.R4
Rev.-ist.   kalendar'-spravochnik—Revoliu-
tsionno-istoricheskii kalendar'-spravoch-
nik   D11.5.R4
Rus. iaz. v nats. shkole—Russkii iazyk v
natsional'noi shkole   PG2065.R8
Ryb. khoz.—Rybnoe khoziaistvo   SH1.R8
Rybov. i rybolov.—Rybovodstvo i rybolov-
stvo   SH401.R9
Sabchota kali
Sabchota khelovneba   DLC
Sadoi Shark   DLC
Sadovodstvo   DNAL
Sakh. prom.—Sakharnaia promyshlennost'
                                  HD9115.R9S6
Sakh. svekla—Sakharnaia svekla   DNAL
Sbor. Muz. ant. i etn.—Akademiia nauk
SSSR. *Muzei antropologii i etnografii.*
Sbornik   GN2.A215
Sel'khoz.   Povol.—Sel'skoe   khoziaistvo
Povolzh'ia   S13.S434
Sem'ia i shkola   L51.S38
Shakh. v. SSSR—Shakhmaty v SSSR
                                  GV1313.S48
Sib. ogni—Sibirskie ogni   AP50.S53
Skola un gimene   DLC
Skynteia leniniste   DLC
Smena   AP215.R9S6
Soob. Gos. Erm.—Leningrad. Ermitazh.
Soobshcheniia   N3350.A6535
Sots. obesp.—Sotsial'noe obespechenie
                                  HN521.S6
Sots. trud—Sotsialisticheskii trud
                                  HD4811.S65
Sots. zakon.—Sotsialisticheskaia zakonnost'
                                  DLC-LL
Sov. arkheol.—Sovetskaia arkheologiia
                                  DK30.A1733
Sov. arkhit.—Sovetskaia arkhitektura
                                  NA1188.S64
Sov. bibl.—Sovetskaia bibliografiia
                                  Z1007.S67
Sov. deput. trud.—Sovety deputatov trudia-
shchikhsia   JS6058.S68
Sov. etn.—Sovetskaia etnografiia
                                  GN1.S65
Sov. foto—Sovetskoe foto   TR1.S82

Sov. gos. i pravo—Sovetskoe gosudarstvo i
pravo   DLC-LL
Sov. iust.—Sovetskaia iustitsiia   DLC-LL
Sov. knizh. torg.—Sovetskaia knizhnaia tor-
govlia   Z372.S6
Sov. kras. krest—Sovetskii krasnyi krest
                                  HV580.R78A35
Sov. muz.—Sovetskaia muzyka   ML5.S675
Sov. otchizna—Sovetskaia otchizna
                                  AP50.S596
Sov. pech.—Sovetskaia pechat'   PN5274.S63
Sov. pedag.—Sovetskaia pedagogika
                                  L51.S64
Sov. potreb. koop.—Sovetskaia potrebitel'-
skaia kooperatsiia   HD3514.S65
Sov. profsoiuzy—Sovetskie profsoiuzy
                                  HD8522.V8744
Sov. radio i tel.—Sovetskoe radio i televidenie
                                  PN1991.3.R8S6
Sov. shakht.—Sovetskii shakhter
                                  TN808.R9M28
*Sov. Soiuz—Sovetskii Soiuz
                                  DK266.A2S57
Sov. tsirk—Sovetskii tsirk   GV1800.S6
Sov. Ukr.—Sovetskaia Ukraina   AP58.U5S6
Sov. voin—Sovetskii voin   U4.S645
Sov. zdrav.—Sovetskoe zdravookhranenie
                                  RA727.S6
*Sov. zhen.—Sovetskaia zhenshchina
                                  AP50.S6
Sovet edebiiaty   DLC
Sovetakan Aiastan
Sovetakan arvest   DLC
Sovetakan grakanutiun   DLC
Sovr. dram.—Sovremennaia dramaturgiia
                                  PG3242.S65
Sovr. Mong.—Sovremennaia Mongoliia
                                  DS798.S6
Sp. igry—Sportivnye igry   GV561.S722
Spir. prom.—Spirtovaia promyshlennost'
                                  TP500.S58
Sred. spets. obr.—Srednee spetsial'noe
obrazovanie   LC1047.R9S7
Sred. veka—Akademiia nauk SSSR. *Institut
istorii.* Srednie veka   D111.A452
Stal'   TS300.S72
Starsh.-serzh.—Starshina-serzhant   U4.S69
Stavropol'e   PG3505.S842S8
Stomatologiia   RK1.S75 (–1959)
                                  DNLM (1960–)

Strany i nar. Vost.—Strany i narody Vostoka
DS1.S78
Stroi. i arkhit.—Stroitel'stvo i arkhitektura
NA6.B76
Stroi. i arkhit. Len.—Stroitel'stvo i arkhitektura Leningrada NA6.A7274
Stroi. truboprov.—Stroitel'stvo truboprovodov TN879.5.S75
Subtrop. kul't.—Subtropicheskie kul'tury
SB111.A2S9
Sudebnomed. ekspertiza—Sudebno-meditsinskaia ekspertiza DLC-LL
Svyturys AP95.L5S95
Tarybinė moteris DLC
Távan Atál DLC
Teatr PN2007.T37
Teatr. zhizn'—Teatral'naia zhizn'
PN2007.T378
Tekh. mol.—Tekhnika molodezhi
T4.T2285
Tekst. prom.—Tekstil'naia promyshlennost'
TS1300.T122
Teor. i prak. fiz. kul't.—Teoriia i praktika fizicheskoi kul'tury GV201.T4
Torf. prom.—Torfianaia promyshlennost'
TN840.R9T6
Transp. stroi.—Transportnoe stroitel'stvo
TF4.T66
Trudy GGO—Leningrad. Glavnaia geoficheskaia observatoriia. Trudy
QC801.L46
Trudy Inst. etn.—Akademiia nauk SSSR. *Institut etnografii. Trudy* GN2.A214
Trudy Inst. iaz.—Akademiia nauk SSSR. *Institut iazykoznaniia.* Trudy
P381.R8A7
Trudy Inst. okean.—Akademiia nauk SSSR. *Institut okeanologii.* Trudy GC1.A4
Trudy LOII AN SSSR—Akademiia nauk SSSR. *Institut istorii. Leningradskoe otdelenie.* Trudy DLC
Trudy MIIZ—Moscow. Institut inzhenerov zemleustroistva. Trudy TA715.M57
Tsiskari DLC
TSvet. met.—TSvetnye metally TN4.T8
TSvetovodstvo SB403.T8 (–1959)
DNAL (1960–)
Tvorchestvo N6.T8
Uch. zap. IMO—Moscow. Institut mezhduna-

rodnykh otnoshenii. Uchenye zapiski
AS262.M5743
Uch. zap. Ivan. gos. ped. inst.—Ivanovo, Russia (City) Gosudarstvennyi pedagogicheskii institut. Uchenye zapiski
AS262.I8A2
Uch. zap. kaf. obshchestv. nauk vuz. g. Len.; Polit. ekon.—Uchenye zapiski kafedr obshchestvennykh nauk vuzov g. Leningrada; Politicheskaia ekonomiia
H8.U3
Uch. zap. kaf. polit. ekon.—Uchenye zapiski kafedr politicheskoi ekonomii vysshykh partiinykh shkol HC331.A1U35
Uch. zap. Tirasp. ped. in-ta—Tiraspol', Russia (City) Gosudarstvennyi pedagogicheskii institut. Uchenye zapiski
AS262.T475A2
Ukr. ist. zhur.—Ukrains'kyi istorychnyi zhurnal DK508.A2U68
Ukraina AP58.U5U5
Ural AP50.U7
Usl. zhiz. i zdorov.—Usloviia zhizni i zdorov'ia DLC
Uzb. geol. zhur.—Uzbekskii geologicheskii zhurnal QE1.A374A2
Uzbekistan DK941.U9
Uzbekiston, *see* Uzbekistan
V mire knig Z2495.V5
*V zashch. mira—V zashchitu mira
JX1903.V2
Vech. sred. shkola—Vecherniaia sredniaia shkola LC5201.V57
Vest. AN SSSR—Akademiia nauk SSSR. Vestnik AS262.A627
Vest. derm. i ven.—Vestnik dermatologii i venerologii RC201.A1V4 (–1959)
DNLM (1960–)
Vest. ist. mir. kul't.—Vestnik istorii mirovoi kul'tury CB3.V45
Vest. khir.—Vestnik khirurgii
RD1.K43 (–1959)
DNLM (1960–)
Vest. LGU—Leningrad. Universitet. Vestnik
AS262.L463
Vest. Mosk. un. Ser. 5: Geog.—Moscow. Universitet. Vestnik. Seriia 5: Geografiia
G1.M68
Vest. Mosk. un. Ser. 7: Filol.,zhur.—Moscow.

Universitet. Vestnik. Seriia 7: Filologiia, zhurnalistika   P19.M622

Vest. Mosk. un. Ser. 10: Pravo—Moscow. Universitet. Vestnik. Seriia 10: Pravo   DLC-LL

Vest. sel'khoz. nauki—Vestnik sel'skokhoziaistvennoi nauki   DNAL

Vest. sviazi—Vestnik sviazi   TK4.V45

Vest. vys. shkoly—Vestnik vysshei shkoly   L51.V42

Vestsi AN BSSR—Akademiia navuk BSSR, *Minsk*. Vestsi   AS262.A75A3

Vitchyzna   AP58.U5V56

Vnesh. torg.—Vneshniaia torgovlia   HF25.V6

Voen.-ist. zhur.—Voenno-istoricheskii zhurnal   DK50.A3

Voen. znan.—Voennye znaniia   U4.V874

Voiov. ateist—Voiovnychyi ateist   BL2700.V6

Vokrug sveta   G1.V6

Vop. antr.—Voprosy antropologii   GN1.V63

Vop. arkh.—Voprosy arkhivovedeniia   CD15.R9V6

Vop. filos.—Voprosy filosofii   B8.R9V6

Vop. geog.—Voprosy geografii   G23.V6

Vop. iaz.—Voprosy iazykoznaniia   P9.V6

Vop. ist.—Voprosy istorii   D1.V6

Vop. ist. KPSS—Voprosy istorii KPSS   JN6598.K4V6

Vop. ist. rel. i ateiz.—Voprosy istorii religii i ateizma   BL80.A522

Vop. lit.—Voprosy literatury   PN9.V6

Vop. mezhdunar. prava—Voprosy mezhdunarodnogo prava   DLC-LL

Vop. onk.—Voprosy onkologii   DNLM

Vop. psikhol.—Voprosy psikhologii   BF8.R8V6

Vop. sovr. arkhit.—Voprosy sovremennoi arkhitektury   DLC

Vop. virus.—Voprosy virusologii   QR360.V6

Vozhatyi   HS3325.R8D43

*Vsem. prof. dvizh.—Vsemirnoe profsoiuznoe dvizhenie   HD6475.A2W468

*Vsem. stud. nov.—Vsemirnye studencheskie novosti   LB3602.I64533

Vsesvit   AP58.U5V8

World student news   LB3602.I6453

World youth   HQ793.W7

Za rubezhom   D839.Z2

Zanoni Tochikiston   DLC

Zap. Len. gor. inst.—Leningrad. Gornyi institut. Zapiski   QE1.L4

Zashch. rast. ot vred. i bol.—Zashchita rastenii ot vreditelei i boleznei   DNAL

Zdorov'e   R421.Z28

Zdrav. Bel.—Zdravookhranenie Belorussii   R91.Z3

Zdrav. Ros. Feder.—Zdravookhranenie Rossiiskoi Federatsii   RA412.5.R9Z3

Zemledelie   S13.Z48

Zernobobovye kul'tury   DNAL

*Zhen. mira—Zhenshchiny mira

Zhil. stroi—Zhilishchnyi stroi   TN4820.Z5

Zhivotnovodstvo   SF1.Z45 (–1959)   DNAL (1960–)

Zhovten'   AP58.U5Z45

Zhuldyz   DLC

Zhur. mikrobiol., epid. i immun.—Zhurnal mikrobiologii, epidemiologii i immunobiologii   QR1.Z5

Zhur. Mosk. Patr.—Orthodox Eastern Church, Russian. *Patriarch*. Zhurnal Moskovskoi Patriarkhii   BX460.O7

Zmina   AP58.U5Z5

Znamia   AP50.Z5

Znan.-sila—Znanie-sila   T4.Z5

Znan. ta pratsia—Znannia ta pratsia   Q4.Z7

Zvaigzne   AP95.L439

Zvezda   AP50.Z93

Zvezda Vost.—Zvesda Vostoka   AP50.Z94

APPENDIX III

Periodicals Available in English

Kitai. English edition: China pictorial
    DS777.5.C447

Kul't. i zhizn'—Kul'tura i zhizn'. English
    edition: Culture and life   DK1.C8

Mezhdunar. zhizn'—Mezhdunarodnaia zhizn'.
    English edition: International affairs
    D839.I465

Mir nauki. English edition: Scientific world
    Q1.S8415

Mol. mira—Molodezh' mira. English edition:
    World youth   HQ793.W7

Nov. vrem.—Novoe vremia. English edition:
    New times   D839.N483

Probl. mira i sots.—Problemy mira i
    sotsializma. English edition: World Marx-
    ist review   HX8.P723

Sov. Soiuz—Sovetskii Soiuz. English edition:
    Soviet Union   DK266.A2S574

Sov. zhen.—Sovetskaia zhenshchina. English
    edition: Soviet woman   HQ1661.S69

V zashch. mira—V zashchitu mira. English
    edition: Peace review

Vsem. prof. dvizh.—Vsemirnoe profsoiuznoe
    dvizhenie. English edition: World trade
    union movement   HD6475.A2W47

Vsem. stud. nov.—Vsemirnye studencheskie
    novosti. English edition: World student
    news   LB3602.I6453

Zhen. mira—Zhenshchiny mira. English edi-
    tion: Women of the whole world
    HQ1101.W755

AUTHOR INDEX

Includes also names of editors, compilers, and translators. Numbers refer to entries, not pages.

SUBJECT INDEX

Includes major subject categories with subdivision by geographic area, and geographic areas with subdivision by subject category. Numbers refer to entries, not pages.

A

Aboriginal languages, 3401–3403. *See also* Archaeology
Agrarian problems, *see* Rural conditions
Agrarian reform, *see* Rural conditions
Agriculture, *see* Farming and stock raising, *and* Fishing and hunting. *See also* Rural conditions
Aid, foreign, *see* International economic relations
Air forces, *see* Military affairs
Alliance for Progress, *see* International economic relations *and* Foreign relations
Animal life, *see* Flora and fauna
Anthropology, *see* Anthropology—general, Archaeology, Ethnohistory, *and* Ethnology
Anthropology—general:
  The area, 197
  Brazil, 198
  Chile, 199
  Cuba, 200
  Easter Island, *see above* under Chile
  Venezuela, 201
Archaeology:
  The area, 202–213
  Argentina, 214
  Brazil, 215
  Chile, 216–224
  Cuba, 225, 226
  Easter Island, *see above* under Chile
  Ecuador, 227
  Jamaica, 228, 229
  Mexico, 230–240
  Peru, 241
Architecture:
  Brazil, 4159–4174
  Cuba, 4175–4179, 4817
  Mexico, 4180, 4181
  Peru, 4182
Area studies, *see* Latin American studies
ARGENTINA:
  Archaeology, 214
  Ballet and dance, 4320
  Children and youth, 3193–3196
  Church, 1717, 1718
  Cultural activities—miscellaneous, 3389, 3390
  Economic conditions and policies, 2382–2397
  Education, 3332, 3333
  Ethnic groups, 3217–3226

Ethnology, 246
Farming and stock raising, 2980–2983
Fine arts—general, 4126, 4127
Fishing and hunting, 3025
Flora and fauna, 172
Folklore, 4077–4079
Foreign relations, 1897–1900, 1957
General works, bibliographies, and reference aids, 22, 23, 460, 2391, 2696, 3094
Geography and geology—general, 85–88
History, 340–347
Industry, 2857–2859
International cultural relations, 2252–2254
International economic relations, 2385, 2393, 2693–2699, 2857
Labor, 3152, 3153
Law, 459
Literary criticism; history of literature, 342, 3439–3461, 4446
Literary works about, 4090
Literature of, 3658–3711
Medicine, 4506, 4507
Military affairs, 1753
Motion pictures, 4342–4351
Music, 4388–4390
Painting, 4185–4187
Periodicals, 343, 1191, 3168, 4343, 4489, 4490
Philosophy, 4446–4448
Political activity of Communist Party, 1168–1196, 1615
Political activity of labor and trade unions, 1412–1431
Political activity of women, 1525–1532, 3166
Political activity of youth, 1607–1616
Politics and government—general, 459, 556–595, 2391, 2396
Press, 1181
Rural conditions, 2980, 3093–3098
Science, 4502
Social conditions—general, 3034, 4507
Sports and hobbies, 3265–3270, 3271
Technology, 2927, 2931
Theater, 4285–4289
Theatrical and performing arts—miscellaneous, 4384
Transportation, 2953
Travel in, 4572–4578
Women, 3165–3168
Army, *see* Military affairs

COSTA RICA (cont.)
Politics and government—general, 703–706, 2446
Women, 3172
CUBA:
Anthropology—general, 200
Archaeology, 225, 226
Architecture, 4175–4179, 4817
Ballet and dance, 4323–4339
Children and youth, 3202, 3203
Church, 1722–1728
Cultural activities—miscellaneous, 384, 3392–3400, 3574
Economic conditions and policies, 890, 1798, 2447–2542, 2890, 3000, 4674, 4700, 4704, 4708, 4713
Education, 3338–3373
Ethnic groups, 3234–3236
Ethnology, 251
Farming and stock raising, 2771, 2902, 2987–3012
Fine arts—general, 3553, 3554, 4132–4136, 4742
Fishing and hunting, 3027–3030
Flora and fauna, 178–181
Folklore, 4082
Foreign relations, 369, 370, 373, 378, 464, 468, 715, 1482, 1637, 1649, 1923–2135, 2160, 2203, 2212, 2217, 2220, 2318, 2527, 4796, 4806
General works, bibliographies, and reference aids, 35–50
Geographical expeditions, 151
Geography and geology—general, 102–121, 2505, 2506
History, 367–409, 1478, 3235, 3528, 3530
Industry, 2782, 2877–2912
International cultural relations, 1923, 1928, 2267–2287, 2317–2322, 2778, 2779, 3180
International economic relations, 1923, 1928, 2009, 2473, 2475, 2755–2817, 2969, 4818
Labor, 467, 3160, 3161
Law, 463–468, 1996, 2219, 2993, 4516
Libraries, 3384–3388
Literary criticism; history of literature, 3525–3577
Literary works about, 4093–4119
Literature of, 3810–3939
Medicine, 4510–4517
Military affairs, 465, 721, 1757–1801, 2020, 2043, 2046
Miscellany, 4856, 4857
Motion pictures, 4358–4370, 4749
Music, 4399–4416, 4664–4666
Opera, 4318, 4319
Painting, 4198–4219
Periodicals, 3178, 3181, 4359, 4492–4496, 4513, 4517, 4522, 4537
Philosophy, 4456–4458
Political activity of Communist Party, 1263–1271
Political activity of labor and trade unions, 1471–1483, 4834

Political activity of women, 1550–1573
Political activity of youth, 1641–1665
Politics and government—general, 707–891, 2449, 2452, 2456, 2458, 2462, 2463, 2465–2469, 2483, 2484, 2488, 2490, 2497, 2499, 2501–2504, 2507, 2508, 2510, 2514, 2517, 2518, 2525, 2526, 2528, 2529, 2533, 2536, 2538, 3052, 3114, 3396, 3397, 4649, 4653, 4661, 4691, 4717, 4719, 4721, 4741
Press, 4473–4486
Public health services, 3246–3251
Radio and television, 1938, 4497–4500
Rural conditions, 2902, 2990, 3003, 3113–3134, 4685
Science, 4504
Social conditions—general, 3050–3053, 4655, 4723
Sports and hobbies, 3301–3315
Technology, 2937, 2938
Theater, 4300–4309
Theatrical and performing media—miscellaneous, 4385
Transportation, 2766, 2955–2972, 4819
Travel from, 4323, 4480, 4795–4842
Travel in, 1474, 2771, 2791, 3175, 3361, 3367, 4362, 4624–4750
Urban conditions, 2883, 2896, 2911, 3081, 4179
Women, 3173–3182
Cultural affairs, see Cultural affairs—miscellaneous cultural activities, Education, and Libraries. See also International cultural relations.
Cultural affairs—miscellaneous cultural activities:
Argentina, 3389, 3390
Bolivia, 3391
Cuba, 384, 3392–3400, 3574
Cultural exchange, see International cultural relations
Curaçao, see West Indies

D

Dance, see Ballet and dance
Demography, see Ethnology
Description and travel, see Travel and Geographical expeditions
Diplomatic relations, see Foreign relations
DOMINICAN REPUBLIC:
Foreign relations, 911, 2136–2143
History, 410
International economic relations, 2818, 2819
Literature, 3940
Political activity of Communist Party, 1272–1274
Political activity of youth, 1666
Politics and government—general, 892–923
Transportation, 2973
Dutch Guiana, see The Guianas
Dutch West Indies, see West Indies

HONDURAS:
Economic conditions and policies, 2547
Foreign relations, 2152
Political activity of Communist Party, 1297–1299
Political activity of women, 1578
Political activity of youth, 1678, 1679
Politics and government—general, 1017–1024, 2547
Housing, *see* Urban conditions
Hunting, *see* Fishing and hunting
Hurricanes, *see* Earthquakes, hurricanes, and floods

I

Indian writings, *see* Archaeology
Indians, *see* Ethnic groups, Ethnohistory, *and* Ethnology
Industry:
The area, 2593, 2688, 2849–2856
Argentina, 2857–2859
Bolivia, 2704
Brazil, 2737, 2860–2874
Chile, 2875
Colombia, 2876
Cuba, 2782, 2877–2912
The Guianas, 2913
Mexico, 2558, 2914–2918
Panama, 2919–2920
Peru, 2921, 2923
Venezuela, 2844, 2922–2925
Inter-American organizations, 458, 1281, 1519, 1875, 2214–2229, 2686
International cultural relations:
The area, 1817, 2230–2251, 4441
Argentina, 2252–2254
Brazil, 2255–2264, 2270, 2315
Chile, 2265, 2266
Colombia, 2316
Cuba, 1923, 1928, 2267–2287, 2317–2322, 2778, 2779, 3180,
Ecuador, 2288
El Salvador, 2289
Mexico, 2269, 2290–2309, 2323
Peru, 2310
Uruguay, 2311–2314
International economic relations:
The area, 304, 1817, 2362, 2372, 2579–2692, 3089, 3091, 3331
Argentina, 2385, 2393, 2693–2699, 2857
Bolivia, 2700–2706
Brazil, 428, 2707–2741, 2861, 2866, 2870, 4600
British Honduras, 2742
Chile, 2743–2750
Colombia, 1920, 2443, 2751, 2752
Costa Rica, 2753, 2754
Cuba, 1923, 1928, 2009, 2473, 2475, 2755–2817, 2969, 4818
Dominican Republic, 2818, 2819

Ecuador, 2820
Guatemala, 2821–2823
Mexico, 428, 2368, 2824–2833, 2914
Panama, 2834, 2835, 4777
Paraguay, 2836
Peru, 2837, 2838, 2921
Puerto Rico, 2839, 2840
Uruguay, 2570, 2841, 2842
Venezuela, 2843–2848
International relations, *see* Foreign relations. *See also* International cultural relations *and* International economic relations

J

JAMAICA:
Archaeology, 228, 229
Economic conditions and policies, 2548, 2549
Ethnology, 253
Fishing and hunting, 3031
Literature of, 3984–3989
Motion pictures, 4371
Politics and government—general, 1025–1027, 2549
Social conditions—general, 3057

L

Labor:
The area, 3149–3151
Argentina, 3152, 3153
Brazil, 2865, 3154, 3155
Chile, 2875, 3156–3158
Colombia, 2876, 3159
Cuba, 467, 3160, 3161
Mexico, 3162
Peru, 3163
Venezuela, 2922, 2925, 3164
See also Political activity of labor and trade unions
Labor unions, *see* Political activity of labor and trade unions *and* Labor
Land tenure, *see* Rural conditions
Languages:
Aboriginal languages, 3401–3403
Non-aboriginal languages, 3404–3411
Languages, literatures, and folklore, *see* Folklore, Languages, Latin America in Soviet and other literary works, Literary criticism; history of literature, *and* Translations of Latin American authors
LATIN AMERICA:
Anthropology—general, 197
Archaeology, 202–213
Children and youth, 3192
Church, 318, 1383, 1713–1716
Earthquakes, hurricanes, and floods, 187
Economic conditions and policies, 295, 2324–2381

308 SUBJECT INDEX

LATIN AMERICA IN SOVIET WRITINGS

A Bibliography—Volume II: 1959–1964

Compiled by Leo Okinshevich
Edited by Robert G. Carlton

designers:	Edward King and Cecilie Smith
typesetter:	Baltimore Type and Composition Corporation
typefaces:	Times Roman (text) and Perpetua (display)
printer:	Universal Lithographers, Inc.
paper:	Perkins & Squier Smooth White Offset
binder:	Moore & Co., Inc.
cover material:	Columbia Riverside Linen